JEAN TOOMER

A Critical Evaluation

JEAN TOOMER

A Critical Evaluation

Edited by

Therman B. O'Daniel

for the College Language Association

HOWARD UNIVERSITY PRESS
Washington, D.C.
1988

Printed in the United States of America

Library of Congress Cataloging-in-Publication Data

Jean Toomer : a critical evaluation.

Bibliography: p.
Includes index.
1. Toomer, Jean, 1894–1967—Criticism and interpretation. I. O'Daniel, Therman B., 1908–
PS3539.0478Z68 1988 813'.52 88-27390
ISBN 0-88258-111-2

The following publishers have generously given permission to use extended quotations from copyrighted works: From "The Blue Meridian," by Jean Toomer, Yale Collection of American Literature, Beinecke Rare Book and Manuscript Library, Yale University. From *Cane*, by Jean Toomer, Liveright Publishing Corporation. Copyright 1923 by Boni & Liveright. Copyright 1951 by Jean Toomer.

Elegy for Therman B. O'Daniel

I remember his voice, rich and golden;
And his urbane manner, majestic as a king;
And how, once meeting, a smile leaped for us,
And he thundered beliefs about journals and
words
And how they last.
We sang, too, his melodies
And dreamed,
Our leafs turning to poems and stories;
Our songs tremble their criticism now.

He kindled an eternal flame
That burns hearts, young and old,
And sacrificed twilight years for stars,
And enjoyed the sunrise and sunsets.

If only we could assure him now
That his work reaped harvests for all seasons,
The fruits of his labors save the world.

Leonard A. Slade, Jr.

Contents

Jean Toomer: Aspects of His Life and Art

Jean Toomer, Waldo Frank, Sherwood Anderson, and Hart Crane

The Toomer-Ouspensky-Gurdjieff Connection

Selected Interpretations of *Cane*

Jean Toomer as the *Cane* Short-Story Writer

Jean Toomer as Playwright

Women and Male-Female Relationships in *Cane*

Celebration and Biblical Myth; Surrealism and the Blues in *Cane*

Foreword

At the time of his death, in 1986, Therman B. O'Daniel was completing the work on this collection of essays on Jean Toomer for the College Language Association. To continue the project, the association named me as director of special publications and selected Cason L. Hill, editor of the *CLA Journal*, as editor of special publications. As always, the association knew to count on the support of our respective institutions, Morgan State University in Baltimore and Morehouse College in Atlanta. My participation on the Toomer project was supported by the Morgan State University Faculty Research Committee in the form of released time during the 1988 spring term. Cason Hill's work on this book continued to be liberally assisted by Morehouse College with special staff and facilities arrangements.

In addition, our efforts were generously facilitated by Ms. Renée Mayfield, managing editor of the Howard University Press, whose familiarity and long association with the project and commitment to it proved to be absolutely indispensable to its successful realization.

I am also grateful to the staff of the Soper Library at Morgan State University and especially to Ms. Maggie Wanza, its associate director for technical services, for their enormously valuable assistance in locating essential files and materials.

I extend my special thanks to Leonard A. Slade, Jr., professor of English at the State University of New York, Albany, for allowing us to include his "Elegy to Therman B. O'Daniel" in this volume.

Just as it was a privilege to know Therman B. O'Daniel as a colleague at Morgan State University and as a fellow officer of the College Language Association, it has been singularly rewarding to collaborate with Cason L. Hill and the Howard University Press in the publication of Professor O'Daniel's *Jean Toomer: A Critical Evaluation*.

Ann Venture Young
Morgan State University

Preface

Jean Toomer: A Critical Evaluation is the third in a series of comprehensive studies of major twentieth-century Afro-American authors, prepared by this editor, and issued under the auspices of the College Language Association. In general format it follows the plan of the previous books on Langston Hughes and James Baldwin, and its purpose is the same—to present an in-depth and as broad a critical treatment of the author and his works as possible. The volume contains forty-six essays of varying lengths, contributed by thirty-nine authors, plus an extensive bibliography.

Since 1967, the *CLA Journal*, official quarterly publication of the College Language Association, has published a considerable amount of scholarly research on Jean Toomer, including one Special Number (June 1974) devoted entirely to the author of *Cane*. Likewise, since 1967, the year of Toomer's death, *Black American Literature Forum* has published a dozen or more critical essays on the same author. Hence, the bulk of the material included in this collection comes from these two journals that have played a leadership role in Toomer research, but we are fortunate also to be able to include several fine Toomer articles from *Phylon: The Atlanta University Review of Race and Culture* and *The Markham Review*, published by the Horrmann Library of

Wagner College, plus eight additional articles and the bibliography prepared especially for this collection.

One of the contributors to this volume, Darwin T. Turner, who has published three books and a number of scholarly articles on Toomer's work, has rapidly become recognized as a Toomer expert. Eight other contributors, between 1967 and 1978, have written doctoral dissertations on Toomer and his works and have continued their interests and investigations to the present time. Because of this and the many other contributions covering a wide spectrum of facts and ideas, and also because of the eight additional especially prepared essays, it is hoped that this collection will not only be comprehensive in scope and intensively penetrating in its revelations but also representative of the best recent and up-to-date Toomer scholarship available.

As editor, I wish again to thank the College Language Association, publisher of the *CLA Journal*, and the publishers of *Black American Literature Forum*, *Phylon*, and *The Markham Review* for granting me permission to use the copyrighted material herein reprinted.

For their contributions, prepared especially for this collection, I am indebted to Professors Nellie Yvonne McKay, for three essays, including the introduction and the afterword; William L. Dutch; Burney J. Hollis; Sue R. Goodwin; and Harry L. Jones.

I wish to thank Mr. George C. Grant, former Director of Soper Library, Morgan State University, and his staff, for regular assistance provided in a prompt and courteous manner. I am especially indebted to the staffs of the Reference, Special Collections, Micromedia, and Periodicals departments for their assistance, and to Mr. Lawrence Padgett for locating and ordering important materials from libraries outside the immediate Baltimore area, including Brown University, the University of Maryland-College Park, and North Carolina State University. I also wish to thank the librarians at The Johns Hopkins University and at the Enoch Pratt Free Library of Baltimore for their help—the reference librarians, at the latter, for supplying some information, in an emergency, by telephone.

I wish to thank Mrs. Ann Allen Shockley, Editor of *BANC!* and Head of the Special Collections, Fisk University Library, for a copy of the Special Jean Toomer Number of *BANC!*, and, on behalf of all Toomer students and researchers, I wish to express my thanks and theirs to the Fisk University Library and its staff, and particularly to Mrs. Marjorie Content Toomer.

My special thanks must go to Mrs. Mae Wright Peck for granting me permission to interview her; and to artist and sculptor James E. Lewis, for his pen and ink drawing of Jean Toomer.

Finally, I thank my wife, Lillian, the editor behind the editor, who really made it all possible.

Therman B. O'Daniel

Acknowledgments

Grateful acknowledgments are made to:

Black American Literature Forum, *BALF*, and *Negro American Literature Forum*, *NALF* (its former name), for permission to reprint the following articles:

"And Another Passing," by Darwin T. Turner. *NALF* 1 (Fall 1967): 3–4;

"*Cane* as Blues," by Benjamin F. McKeever. *NALF* 4 (July 1970): 61–63;

"Male and Female Interrelationship in Toomer's *Cane*," by Rafael A. Cancel. *NALF* 5 (Spring 1971): 25–31;

"Images of Celebration in *Cane*," by Sister Mary Kathryn Grant. *NALF* 5 (Spring 1971): 32–34, 36;

"Design in Jean Toomer's *Balo*," by Michael J. Krasny. *NALF* 7 (Fall 1973): 103–4;

"Sherwood Anderson and Jean Toomer," by Mark Helbling. *NALF* 9 (Summer 1975): 35–39;

"Jean Toomer's Life Prior to *Cane*: A Brief Sketch of the Emergence of a Black Writer," by Michael J. Krasny. *NALF* 9 (Summer 1975): 40–41;

"Jean Toomer's 'Bona and Paul': The Innocence and Artifice of Words," by Jack M. Christ. *NALF* 9 (Summer 1975): 44–46;

"Jean Toomer's 'Box Seat': The Possibility for 'Constructive Crisises'," by Elizabeth Schultz. *BALF* 13 (Spring 1979): 7–12; and

"Jean Toomer's 'Blue Meridian': The Poet as Prophet of a New Order of Man," by Bernard W. Bell. *BALF* 14 (Summer 1980): 77–80.

The College Language Association for permission to reprint the following articles from its official publication, the *CLA Journal:*

"The Failure of a Playwright," by Darwin T. Turner. *CLA Journal* 10 (June 1967): 308–18;

"Design and Movement in *Cane,*" by Todd Lieber. *CLA Journal* 13 (September 1969): 35–50;

"A Key to the Poems in *Cane,*" by Bernard W. Bell. *CLA Journal* 14 (March 1971): 251–58;

"The Women in *Cane,*" by Patricia Chase. *CLA Journal* 14 (March 1971): 259–73;

"Jean Toomer's 'Fern': A Mythical Dimension," by Hargis Westerfield. *CLA Journal* 14 (March 1971): 274–76;

"The Search for Identity in Jean Toomer's 'Esther'," by Edward E. Waldron. *CLA Journal* 14 (March 1971): 277–80;

"Jean Toomer's *Cane* Again," by W. Edward Farrison. *CLA Journal* 15 (March 1972): 295–302;

"The Unity of Jean Toomer's *Cane,*" by Catherine L. Innes. *CLA Journal* 15 (March 1972): 306–22;

"Jean Toomer's *Cane:* A Modern Black Oracle," by Bowie Duncan. *CLA Journal* 15 (March 1972): 323–33;

"An Intersection of Paths: Correspondence Between Jean Toomer and Sherwood Anderson," by Darwin T. Turner. *CLA Journal* 17 (June 1974): 455–67;

"Jean Toomer—The Veil Replaced," by Mabel M. Dillard. *CLA Journal* 17 (June 1974): 468–73;

"'Just Americans': A Note on Jean Toomer's Marriage to Margery Latimer," by Daniel P. McCarthy. *CLA Journal* 17 (June 1974): 474–79;

"The 'Mid-Kingdom' of Crane's 'Black Tambourine' and Toomer's *Cane,*" by Victor A. Kramer. *CLA Journal* 17 (June 1974): 486–97;

"The Tensions in Jean Toomer's 'Theater'," by George Kopf. *CLA Journal* 17 (June 1974): 498–503;

"The Influence of Ouspensky's *Tertium Organum* upon Jean Toomer's *Cane,*" by Alice Poindexter Fisher. *CLA Journal* 17 (June 1974): 504–15;

"The Spectatorial Artist and the Structure of *Cane*," by Susan L. Blake. *CLA Journal* 17 (June 1974): 516–34;

"Jean Toomer's *Cane* and Biblical Myth," by Louise Blackwell. *CLA Journal* 17 (June 1974): 535–42;

"Toomer's *Cane*: The Artist and His World," by George C. Matthews. *CLA Journal* 17 (June 1974): 543–59;

"Another Note on Toomer's Marriage to Margery Latimer" [from "Letters to the Editor"], by Merle A. Richmond. *CLA Journal* 18 (December 1974): 300;

"'Spirit-Torsos of Exquisite Strength': The Theme of Individual Weakness vs. Collective Strength in Two of Toomer's Poems," by Udo O. H. Jung. *CLA Journal* 19 (December 1975): 261–67;

"Jean Toomer's Contributions to *The New Mexico Sentinel*," by Tom Quirk and Robert E. Fleming. *CLA Journal* 19 (June 1976): 524–32;

"'Nora' is 'Calling Jesus': A Nineteenth Century European Dilemma in an Afro-American Garb," by Udo O. H. Jung. *CLA Journal* 21 (December 1977): 251–55;

"The Unifying Images in Part One of Jean Toomer's *Cane*," by Richard Eldridge. *CLA Journal* 22 (March 1979): 187–214; and

"Frustrated Redemption: Jean Toomer's Women in *Cane*, Part One," by J. Michael Clark. *CLA Journal* 22 (June 1979): 319–34.

The Markham Review for permission to reprint the following article:

"Jean Toomer's *Cane*," by James Kraft. *The Markham Review* 2 (October 1970): 61–63.

PHYLON: The Atlanta University Review of Race and Culture for permission to reprint the following articles:

"Jean Toomer: Lost Generation, or Negro Renaissance?" by S. P. Fullinwider. *Phylon* 27 (Fourth Quarter, December 1966): 396–403;

"Jean Toomer's Ralph Kabnis: Portrait of the Negro Artist as a Young Man," by William J. Goede. *Phylon* 30 (First Quarter, March 1969): 73–85; and

"Jean Toomer and Waldo Frank: A Creative Friendship," by Mark Helbling. *Phylon* 41 (Second Quarter, Summer 1980): 167–78.

An original pen and ink drawing of Jean Toomer, author of Cane *(1923), by James E. Lewis, artist and sculptor.*

JEAN TOOMER

A Critical Evaluation

Jean Toomer in His Time: An Introduction

NELLIE MC KAY

"When America was in winter I was born the day after Christmas 1894,"[1] begins Jean Toomer's "Outline of an Autobiography." Although no record of the event exists, there is no reason to doubt the accuracy of this date. Named Nathan Eugene, he was the son of Nathan Toomer and the former Nina Pinchback. They were married in March 1894 in Washington, D.C., where their son was born. But Nathan Toomer deserted his family some months after Jean's birth. Having no independent means of support, Nina Pinchback Toomer was forced to return to her father's house. In 1896 she secured a divorce from Toomer, after which she resumed use of her maiden name. Jean Toomer was called Eugene Pinchback for several years.

Toomer's seventeen years in Washington were largely influenced by the dominant personality of his grandfather, P. B. S. Pinchback, and his own sensitive awareness of the world around him. Pinchback, a charismatic figure sufficiently light-skinned to have been taken for a white man, chose to claim African heritage, and as a black man, he gained political eminence in Louisiana during Reconstruction. In the aftermath of the Democratic rise to power in the South during the latter part of the nineteenth century, he moved his family to Washington in the early 1890s, and from his grandson's account, ruled his household in the manner of a benevolent despot.

Toomer wrote of Bacon Street in Washington as a "glorious playground." The neighborhood was almost rural, with fields of weeds, wildflowers, and insects all around, and a farm nearby. It was a delightful blend of city and country, of the urban and rural, of civilization and nature. He loved all the natural things, and although he was acutely aware of the buildings going up around him, he felt no hostility toward the changing landscape. The buildings were paralleling his own growth. "While I myself [was] growing," he later wrote, "I had pictures of constructive activity, the symbol of building, impressed upon me."[2]

The families living in this area were predominantly white middle- and upper-class, and in his words, he was surrounded by "a tone of fineness and refinement." Against this background, Pinchback, a hearty and outgoing man of wide and varied contacts and who enjoyed having people around him, entertained and associated with men of all colors. He insisted, however, that his young grandson attend a Negro school, although this meant Toomer would be away from his neighborhood friends for several hours each day. It was important to Pinchback that even at that age Toomer should have personal, direct, and concrete links to the black community, while at home he experienced an atmosphere of racial tolerance. Later, when Pinchback suffered financial losses, they moved into other, less affluent areas of the city where more black people lived.

In 1907 Nina Pinchback remarried and moved with her husband and son, first to Brooklyn, New York, and then to New Rochelle, New York. Toomer was acutely aware of the differences between his new and old environments. In Brooklyn he had his first contact with the indifference and hostility of the city, with commercial development and industry, with apartment living in contrast to living in a house, and with "tough boys." He did not like the city, but he made friends and found it stimulating. In New Rochelle he had only a few friends but enjoyed bicycling, swimming, fishing, and sailing his own boat along Long Island Sound. He discovered the public library and read intensively while in New Rochelle; earlier, in Washington, an uncle had introduced him to literature. This reading stimulated his imagination, and he began to create an inner life for himself.

In 1909 Toomer's mother died, and in 1910 he returned to his grandparents' home. The death of his mother, the financial decline of his grandparents, and the direct consequences of these events on his living arrangements contributed to insecurities and emotional problems that plagued Toomer for many years.

Between 1914 and 1919 Toomer attended a half dozen colleges and universities but remained in no place long enough to earn a degree. After many ponderings in philosophy, history, sociology, and literature, in a time of conflicts with his grandfather over money, and after an intensive internal struggle to determine what his life's work should be, in 1919 he decided to become a writer. Once the decision was made, he settled down, as he had not done before, to learn the writer's craft.

The years of his apprenticeship were difficult. He read a great deal of Shakespeare, Shaw, Dickens, Flaubert, Goethe, Dostoyevsky, the Bible, and Eastern philosophy, particularly Buddhist writings, to name a few. American writers who inspired him included Waldo Frank, who became his mentor, Walt Whitman, and Sherwood Anderson, with whom Toomer shared a warm friendship between 1922 and 1923. Although Toomer claims that he also read some literature by or about blacks in America, all of which he dismissed as nonsense, no record of what these were exists. In like manner, although by his own account, before *Cane* was conceived, he had a trunkful of manuscripts, none of his earliest writings are extant. In the beginning writing was difficult for him, and he was dissatisfied with his efforts. The excellence to which he aspired eluded him. Furthermore, he was convinced that he would be able to write successfully only if he were able to achieve a state of personal harmony between the physical, emotional, and intellectual parts of himself.

This was not a new idea for Toomer. As early as 1912, while he was still in high school and enduring in solitude the physical and mental strains of early manhood, he was concerned with the problems of harmony between his body and his mind. At one point in this period he thought he had found a suitable system by which he could achieve it in the works of Bernarr MacFadden, one that would help him to gain control over himself.[3] But the achievement of internal harmony eluded him. Despite many years of body building and attempts to control his mind and emotions, the problem remained, and between 1919 and 1921 he felt that it was an ever-present hindrance to his ability to learn to write. Nor was this his only concern. In the middle of 1920 he moved from New York City, where he had been living for almost two years, back to his grandparents' home in Washington. The move was prompted by his need for money and because the Pinchbacks, who were growing feeble, needed care and attention. He agreed to stay with them and to take over the household duties in return for a weekly allowance of five dollars.

This arrangement had obvious drawbacks. However, Toomer had decided on it not only for the security of a place to live and the small monetary reward but more so because of his love for his grandparents. They had been more parental to him than his parents, and their needy condition touched him deeply. But the duties he undertook seriously curtailed the time needed to explore ideas which suggested new approaches to literary materials and personal development. He felt that he had a great deal to say and that he was full of it and under pressure to get it out, but that his life experiences exceeded his ability to write them down. Furthermore, he felt disorganized, and he despaired of achieving organization. Nevertheless, he remained in Washington from the middle of 1920 until the fall of 1921. In September 1921 he received an offer to teach in a rural Georgia school for a short time. He accepted it without hesitation and with feelings of having been rescued from a quagmire. In October of that year he arrived in Sparta, Georgia, for his first experience among rural, poor black people.

Subsequent events in Toomer's life have led to a great deal of interest in, and many speculations about, his feelings about race. The meaning of race in America was an issue that he encountered early in his life. At age six he was sent to a Negro school outside of his almost all-white neighborhood, and even then he was aware of the racial differences in the two communities. As he grew up, he heard many conversations at home about the race problem in America. When he returned to Washington from New Rochelle in 1910, the Pinchbacks were living in a predominantly black area of the city, and he attended a high school for young black people. On the other hand, his grandfather, no matter what his claims of African blood, looked like a white man, his grandmother like a white woman, and for most of their lives they had lived in a manner characteristic of the white American middle class. As a result of this combination of factors, he had gained an awareness of the implications of race while he was still a child, even though his early years had not been assaulted by racial discrimination or limited by the economic deprivation that a large number of black Americans experience. As a teenager, he lived in both worlds and saw their problems from the inside. In New Rochelle he lived in an all-white world; in Washington he lived first in a mostly white world and later in an almost all-black world.

Toomer's awareness of racial differences was heightened in 1914, as he contemplated the choice of a college to attend. At this time the matter of his racial identity seemed to him a problem. He feared the reception he would receive in an all-white college when it became known that he had attended a Negro high school. He felt vulnerable on this account and decided to adopt a nonracial identity. Later, he insisted that in repudiating racial designation at that time, he was making an effort to encompass and conduct his life as close as possible to the truth of his biological heritage. He noted that many bloodlines ran in his veins (French, English, Dutch, African, Jewish, and Indian, it was said), that he wanted to deny none of them, and that he was, above all, an American. His contention was that most people in America were of mixed racial strain. The only reasonable alternative, he argued, was to adopt the notion of an American race. He also felt that in time this idea would become socially acceptable to all Americans.

Although the question of Toomer's race surfaced at least once while he was at the University of Wisconsin, there is no reason to believe it was ever a critical issue during his college years. His failure to settle down for more than a semester in any one place was a result of his ambivalence toward his personal goals and his inability to tolerate the idea of failure or defeat in anything he did. As a result, he flirted for brief periods with a variety of career ideas but gave each one up in turn at the merest suggestion of a difficulty. His determination to be a writer was the one idea of his young life in which he persisted, in spite of the frustrations he experienced from 1919 to 1921.

The impact of the 1921 Georgia experience on Jean Toomer was enormous. From "Outline of an Autobiography" we know that the folk culture affected him as nothing else had done before and that he immediately set out to record the feelings that were awakened in his soul.

> No plot of ground had been like this or so moved me. Here the earth seemed part of the people, and the people part of the earth, and they worked upon each other and upon me, so that my earth-life was liberated from the rest of myself. The roots of my earth-life went down and found hold in this red soil and the soil became a shining ground.

> I had seen and met people of all kinds. I had never before met with a folk. I had never before lived in the midst of a people gathered together by a group spirit. Here they were. They worked and lived close to the earth, close to each other. They worked and sang as part of living. They worked and loved and hated and got into trouble and felt a great weight on them. . . . And what I saw and felt and shared entered me, so that my people-life was uncased from the rest of myself. The roots of my people-life went out to those folk, and found purchase in them, and the people became people of beauty and sorrow.

And further, he wrote:

> My seed was planted in the cane-and-cotton fields in the souls of the black and white people in the small southern town. My seed was planted in myself down there.[4]

In addition to the positive rhythms of black life, he also observed and was touched by the tensions that surrounded that life—the bitterness, strain, and violence of the southern racial situation.

Toomer spent two months in Georgia and returned to Washington in November of 1921. But before he left the South he sent a poem, "Georgia Dusk," to *The Liberator*, and on the train north he began to write the sketches that appeared in the first section of *Cane*. By the end of the year, they were completed. The southern experience had inspired him to a lyrical interpretation of the harshness, cruelty, strength, and beauty of black American reality. *Cane* was *his* song of celebration to the elements of the Afro-American experience, but it was not the only result of his cultural exposure. During the winter of 1921 to 1922 he wrote two plays as well: *Balo*, a folk play which was presented by the Howard University Repertory Company during its 1923 to 1924 season, and *Natalie Mann*, an expressionistic drama that satirizes middle-class black people in Washington. His discovery of poetic elements within the black experience in America provided him with the source of his first full-blown literary expression.

Nineteen twenty-two was the year of Jean Toomer's high watermark. Early in that year he returned to New York, where he renewed old friendships and made new ones within the circle of the city's literati. His social group included Kenneth Burke, Hart Crane, Van Wyck Brooks and Waldo Frank—men who perceived themselves as being in the vanguard of American letters and who respected him as a new writer. During this year he wrote with enthusiasm, and his work began to appear in literary journals and received favorable criticism. He was sought out by Sherwood Anderson, and both men corresponded for a while. After years of ambivalence and abortive attempts to find his place in the world, he was coming into his own.

Although there is only very little to link Toomer with the literary and artistic stirrings that were beginning to take place in Harlem in 1921 and 1922, there is evidence to show that during that period of his life he was not antagonistic toward blackness. His friends were white, but on the street where he lived in New York most of the families were black.[5] He made no secret of his relationship to Pinchback and discussed his racial background with a number of people. In a letter to Waldo Frank, in March 1922, Toomer noted that there were six bloodlines in his family, that the culture, history, and traditions of five of them were fairly well known and discussed with an "approximation of the truth," but that the "Negro" line had been subject to perversion for "purposes of propaganda." He was determined, he said, that in his life and work he would symbolize "a synthesis in the matters of the mind and spirit analogous, perhaps, to the actual fact of . . . the blood minglings."[6] In another letter to Frank in which he discussed some of his ideas in *Cane*, in his reference to "Kabnis" he states: "And Kabnis is Me."[7]

Waldo Frank was not the only person with whom Toomer shared the facts of his racial heritage. In letters to Sherwood Anderson he acknowledged his mixed ancestry and pointed out that he hoped his art would help to "give the Negro back to himself." He even championed the cause of black writers as a means of "building . . . Negro consciousness."[8] In addition, during this period, he was in love with Mae Wright, a young black woman from Baltimore, Maryland, who had close relatives in Washington, D.C. She was several years younger than he, but he felt deeply about her and discussed his ideas on race very freely with her. It was with her that he noted the "tyranny of the Anglo-Saxon Ideal," an ideal which expressed only the beauty of white people. He insisted that black people needed to be awakened to the significance of their lives and the sensitivity of their beauty. The goals to which he aspired in writing were to educate white people about black people and to inspire black people to the value of their lives.[9]

However, it is doubtful that Toomer saw himself as a black man at this or at any other time in his life, even if he never considered himself to be a white man either. His emphasis on blackness was on its artistic qualities. Yet, in his concentration on the aesthetic merits of black culture, he made no efforts to connect himself to a black tradition in letters, and his interactions with contemporary black artists were, at best, minimal and individualized. He acknowledged no black writers as having had an impact on him, and no one black read, criticized, or made suggestions about *Cane* while it was in progress. Nevertheless, Toomer admitted to Frank that his "need for artistic expression [had] pulled [him] deeper . . . into the Negro group . . . and as [his] powers of receptivity increased, [he] found [himself] loving [it] in a way [he] could never love the other."[10] He noted that after he heard the folk songs from the "lips of Negro peasants" and had seen their "rich, dusk beauty," all of his previous skepticism, which was based on what he had heard of the folk culture, vanished, and a "deep part of [his] nature, a part that [he] had long repressed sprang suddenly into life and responded to them."[11] But these feelings were never superimposed on his idea of his Americanness or, by extension, his separateness from blackness. In time, Jean Toomer would assert that the Negro blood in his veins was no more than a fiction created by Pinchback for his own political ambitions.

Toomer saw *Cane* as the beginning of his life as a creative writer. Confident that the South would be the center for the new American literary renaissance, he joined the Poetry Society of South Carolina as a nonresident member, an action that proved embarrassing for the society, which had never anticipated that nonwhite persons would seek membership. He was excited in his expectations of the fulfillments of the literary life. *Cane* was only the beginning, he thought. Still maintaining close associations with his white friends, he had some contacts with black writers. He knew and admired Alain Locke and Charles Johnson, and he had warm correspondence with Countee Cullen and Claude McKay. He even agreed to submit his work to Claude Barnett of the Associated Negro Press for publication in black newspapers and went as far as to suggest to Sherwood Anderson the need for a black arts journal.[12]

In 1922 Toomer was happy. *Cane* was completed and had been accepted for publication by Boni and Liveright, which had taken an option on his next two books. Frank was writing the introduction to this first work. Toomer wrote, in wonder, "My words had become a book . . . I had actually finished something."[13] He was exhilarated and felt he was part of a living world of promise. He felt united to others and wrote: "I lived in life, in love . . . I found new life . . . in a deep rich being."[14]

But before the book was published in 1923, Toomer's hopeful anticipation of pursuing a literary career collapsed. The story is well known. He was distressed that Frank, in his introduction to the book, and the publisher, in promoting it, had made an issue of his racial background. He was particularly upset with Frank, to whom he had explained his racial vision in great detail, with the assumption that Frank had understood how he felt and would respect those feelings. Thus, he turned away from Frank and withdrew from the literary world. The reasons for his rejection of a racial label may never be fully known, but to dismiss them as only the manifestation of his deep racial trauma is to do injustice to the complications of the human mind. Toomer went on to spend his life asking the most fundamental questions about human existence and to reach outward in his search for answers. He was never indifferent to the concerns of racial groups, as later papers in his collection prove, but he thought of racial issues as detrimental to the development of the human race as a whole. To be labeled a Negro writer imposed restrictions on him that he could not tolerate; thus, he ceased to create literary art.

Toomer's break with the world that he had pursued for almost four years was on one level a break with Frank, the man who had been his mentor and his model. At the same time, Frank's inability to understand his friend's sensitivity to racial designations was more than an individual's failing; it was the failure of a system, and Toomer turned away from it also. Shortly after, he met Georges Gurdjieff and became a disciple of the Eastern mystic for a number of years.

While Toomer struggled with the problems of his development and the ramifications of societal limitations on the writer, *Cane* took on a life of its own. Although the sales were low, the book was hailed as a masterpiece by black and white writers: Allen Tate, Lola Ridge, Sherwood Anderson, Countee Cullen, W. E. B. Du Bois, William Stanley Braithwaite, and Langston Hughes were among those who paid tribute to the writer and his work.

In 1966 Arna Bontemps, writing of the impact of *Cane* in its time in "The Negro Renaissance and the Writers of the 1920's," noted that black writers of the early part of that decade who were aware of the book "went quietly mad." Contemporary reviews of *Cane* reveal that these writers were enormously affected by the work. Among other things it opened up new possibilities in writing for them. For the first time in America there was a black writer in the forefront of the literary movement, participating on equal terms with white writers in the creation of new forms and trends. The most persistent emphasis in the analyses of *Cane* during the 1920s, on the part of black writers at least, is on the inherent "self-revelation" in the work. Toomer had faced the black experience in America without shame or abasement and had spun, from what others might have seen only as broken threads, a magnificent tapestry of words. He had avoided propaganda and polemic and given a moving description, through words that held color and mood, of what it meant to be black in America. He had, more than any other black writer until then, liberated black creative writing from narrow and parochial boundaries and set it on its journey toward genuine art and self-affirmation through exploration of the past. Later critics, black and white, have acknowledged Toomer's achievement and have unanimously accorded him a place of honor in the annals of the Harlem Renaissance and black creative writing.

After his disappearance from the literary horizon, for black writers Toomer represented the sphinx of their age. Nevertheless, they understood that his problem was also their own and that the black artist is vulnerable to the constant buffetings of negative social focus. Until *Cane* was published, Afro-American literature and black writers were always a step behind their white contemporaries; now, for the first time, there was a black writer whose work had placed him in the forefront of the literary movement. But more important, Toomer had looked at the folk culture and had seen in it beauty, strength, and value, as well as pain, suffering, and emptiness. He had not hesitated to examine the persistent despair and sterility of black urban life, but he had not omitted its dynamic energy. He had liberated the would-be black artist through his own journey toward genuine art and through his search into the past for an affirming self. And although no school of writers bearing his name sprang up after *Cane* was published, the later writings of the renaissance reveal a greater concern for the past, a more complete acceptance of the self, and a greater willingness to experiment with style and form than had ever before been seen in black writing.

But while Toomer no longer paid homage to the muse of artistic literature after 1923, he never gave up the idea of writing as a vocation. After *Cane* he continued to explore themes that had interested him even before he decided to become a writer. The form and manner of his writings changed after 1923, but his philosophic concern with the human condition never altered. His rejection of art as a goal in writing led to changes in his style that raised questions regarding the literary merits of his work. However, the wide neglect of his post-1923 writings, which lasted until the 1960s, inhibited the flow of information that was vital to determining his rightful place in the world of letters.

When Toomer rejected the label of "Negro writer," one of his motives was to transcend the limits of that identity, but the attitudes of the world would not allow him to so do in a graceful fashion. He wanted to accomplish what James Weldon Johnson once defined as the responsibility of the black artist: "to fashion something that rises above race and reaches out to the universal in truth and beauty."[15] When he felt compelled to turn aside from art, it was a great loss for American literature, and the decision altered the course of his life. In his time Jean Toomer was a powerful symbol: a rising star that fell in its ascendancy because he refused to accept the status quo.

Jean Toomer: Aspects of His Life and Art

Jean Toomer: Lost Generation, or Negro Renaissance?

S. P. FULLINWIDER

Now that the Jean Toomer papers have found a home at the Fisk University library, it is no longer necessary to speculate as to why Toomer ceased to write after he published *Cane* in 1923. In fact, he did not cease to write. He continued to write and write voluminously, but to no avail—he could find no publisher. The story of Toomer's literary effort after 1923 is a story of frustration, despair, and failure—this after what was surely one of the most promising beginnings in the history of American literature. Toomer's story is one of a young man caught up in the tangled skein of race relations in America. But it goes beyond even that. For a time, at least, it was the story of modern man, the story of a search for identity—for an absolute in a world that had dissolved into flux. It is a story of success. At the age of thirty-one his search for an identity-giving absolute was over. It is a story of tragedy. As long as he was searching, he was a fine creative artist. When the search ended, so did his creative powers. So long as he was searching, his work was the cry of one caught in the modern human condition; it expressed modern man's lostness, his isolation. Once Toomer found an identity-giving absolute, his voice ceased to be the cry of modern man and became the voice of the schoolmaster complacently pointing out the way—his way. It now seems possible to take a few hesitant steps toward a closer understanding of the Negro American literary tradition by asking the question: "Who was Jean Toomer?"

Toomer's overriding concern for the human condition grew out of an early lack of self-esteem, a concomitant tendency toward introspection and soul-searching, and a loss of his childhood absolutes. His problem with self-esteem was a product of his early family life, particularly his relationship with an imperious grandfather, P. B. S. Pinchback. The former Reconstruction lieutenant governor of Louisiana had suffered political and financial reverses when the Republicans lost power in the South and had removed to an imposing house on Washington's Bacon Street, an all-white neighborhood. There, Pinchback lived a high life—the life of a social lion—while his prestige lasted. But a politician out of office quickly loses status and influence. As his fortunes declined, Pinchback became increasingly autocratic toward his daughter, Nina, and his sons. The beautiful Nina married twice, first to a young southern planter who disappeared after a year, and then to a ne'er-do-well who misrepresented his wealth. The second marriage, with its drudgery and lack of love, killed her. So Jean, a product of the first match, led a troubled young life with his grandfather.[1]

As Toomer grew in childhood he turned in upon himself, away from the tyrannical grandfather, away from his unhappy mother. Slowly, he created a rich inner life, but it was a life almost totally disassociated from the outside world.[2] Pinchback's fortunes continued to decline. One day he moved the family from Bacon Street and its white neighborhood to a house on Florida Avenue, the heart of the Negro upper-class world. Looking back, Toomer wrote, "With this world—an aristocracy—such as never existed before and perhaps will never exist again in America—mid-way between the white and Negro worlds. For the first time I lived in a colored world." Toomer liked his new life. He felt that he found here "more emotion, more rhythm, more color, more gaiety"[3] than he had met in the chilling atmosphere of white society. But this was a time, too, of morbid introspection. Now fourteen, he became a nuisance in the classroom, an inveterate troublemaker. He became the victim of overpowering sex impulses and seems to have concluded that these impulses were destroying his health. He turned to barbells and special diets. By then the Pinchbacks were on the verge of poverty, and family relations were deteriorating. A three-year period of revolt and wandering began for the boy. His revolt first took him to the University of Wisconsin to study agriculture (this lasted a semester), then back to Washington, to endure hard looks of reproach. He was assailed by self-doubt. He tried the Massachusetts College of Agriculture for almost a week, then a physical training college in Chicago. There he paid more attention to lectures at the Loop than to physical education. Men like Clarence Darrow held forth there on exciting subjects like Darwinism and the ideas of Haeckel—and atheism. Toomer felt his intellectual world collapse. His belief in God, he thought, evaporated. He felt "condemned and betrayed." "In truth," he later wrote, "I did not want to live."[4] His old absolutes were gone; he began a desperate search for new ones. For a time, socialism seemed to serve the need.

> I had been, I suppose, unconsciously seeking—as man must ever seek—an intelligible scheme of things, a sort of whole into which everything fit . . . it was the *body*, the *scheme*, the order and inclusion. These evoked and promised to satisfy all in me that had been groping for order from amid the disorder and chaos of my personal experiences.[5]

After Chicago there were further wanderings, further soul-searchings. A reading of Lester F. Ward's *Dynamic Sociology* led to a short fraternization with that subject at New York University. But he found a history course at City College more attractive. Then history became a bore, and psychology took its place. World War I came to America, and he was rejected by the draft. He tried odd jobs for a year: he sold Fords in Chicago, taught physical education in Milwaukee, and did a ten-day stint as a shipfitter in a New Jersey shipyard. His contact with the construction workers there caused him to lose interest in socialism. In 1920 Toomer returned, defeated, to his grandfather in Washington, D. C. It was not a cheerful reunion. In a mood of bitterness and an atmosphere of rejection he turned to reading literature—Robert Frost, Sherwood Anderson, the imagists. He wrote incessantly, hour upon hour for month after month, tearing up what he wrote. He learned to handle words, learned their symbolic potential. He became an artist.[6]

Toomer learned as he handled words that they had no meaning beyond what he gave them arbitrarily. He began to see that words are mere symbols of things and not the things themselves.[7] He was traveling the road to nominalism, and as he traveled that road he felt the concrete world begin to dissolve about him. He was entering the world of modern alienated man. Apparently, it was during this period that he began to experience the severing of his intellect from his emotions—the seemingly peculiar phenomenon of the modern mind that has been described as the "frigidization of the self." The phenomenon has been described as an overwhelming sense of self-consciousness—a standing outside oneself, as it were; an objectification of the self. The intellect seems to overpower the emotions, making it impossible to have effective emotional relations with other people. One finds an impenetrable wall standing between oneself and those one would love.[8] Toomer made the solution of this problem—this frigidization of the self—his major intellectual theme. Again and again in his later writings he reverted to his argument that the intellect must somehow be fused with the emotions: "Themosense (thought *and* emotion *and* sensing) is the inner synthesis of functions, which represents the entire individual and gives rise to complete action."[9] Of course, in Toomer's case, much of this frigidization of the self can be traced to his deliberate retreat from an outside world (his family life) that was too threatening—a retreat into the isolation of subjectivity. In one place he tells of wrongs being inflicted upon him in such profusion that "finally we reached the stage where we vowed to suffer no more. Of people, of life, of the world we said, 'Don't touch me.' We resolved that no one ever would."[10] It was while in this mood that he accepted an offer in 1921 to act as temporary superintendent of a small, Negro industrial school in rural Georgia.

Georgia was for Toomer a small shack in the hills. It was the whispering pines. It was the folksinging that drifted over in the evenings from the Negro dwellings. Most of all, it was the southern Negro spirit—a spirit with which he developed a deep feeling of kinship. *Cane* was at once the joy of discovering this folk spirit and the sadness of the realization that it was a passing thing.

He wrote of the spirituals:

> But I learned that the Negroes of the town objected to them. They called them "shouting." They had victrolas and player-pianos. So, I realized with deep regret, that the spirituals, meeting ridicule, would be certain to die out. With Negroes also the trend was towards the small town and towards the city—and industry and commerce and the machines. The folk-spirit was walking in to die on the modern desert. That spirit was so beautiful. Its death was so tragic.[11]

Toomer, suffering intensely from frigidization of the self, appears to have entertained the idea that in the southern Negro folk-spirit he might find emotional release—that in this spirit he might find not only his own salvation but salvation for the modern industrial world. This, at least, is the message of "Box Seat," one of the more substantial of *Cane*'s prose-pictures. In it appears Dan, a southern Negro with a redemptive mission. The setting of "Box Seat" is Washington, D. C., or, in other words, the large city. There one is crushed and shorn of spirit by the heavy hand of civilization.

> Houses are shy girls whose eyes shine reticently upon the dusk body of the street. Upon the gleaming limbs and asphalt torso of a dreaming nigger. Shake your curled wool-blossoms, nigger. Open your liver lips to the lean white spring. Stir the root-life of a withered people. Call them from their houses, teach them to dream.[12]

Dan, hot-blooded and virile, is up from the primitive regions of the South to restore vigor and passion to a jaded, overcivilized people—people conquered by "zoo-restrictions and keeper-taboos." "I am Dan Moore," he says, "I was born in a cane-field. The hands of Jesus touched me. I am come to a sick world to heal it."[13]

To Toomer's mind the plight of modern man is that industrial civilization has shorn him of emotional spontaneity—has made him the passive mechanical pawn of social forces. While living in the hills of Georgia, Toomer could almost believe the answer lay with Dan. During those months Toomer must have felt a closer identification with the Negro race than he had ever felt before, or was to feel thereafter. A year later, in mid-1922, he wrote of his feelings to the editor of *The Liberator*: "Within the last two or three years, however, my growing need for artistic expression has pulled me deeper and deeper into the Negro group. . . . I found myself loving it in a way that I could never love the other."[14] There is every reason to believe that this was a sincere statement; Toomer, after all, had been searching for an identity throughout most of his life. But there is good evidence that Toomer was not secure in his newfound faith, even while in the midst of composing *Cane*. In "Kabnis," the final and most compelling sketch of the book, he put on record his doubts concerning the Negro race in America. Kabnis, a product of white men's Christianity, a slave religion, is portrayed as a weak and groveling character who projects his self-hatred outward against an ex-slave, blind and deaf from years of toil. In Kabnis's eyes the old man is a servile product of the Christian religion—an Uncle Tom. A much stronger character in the sketch, Lewis, saw in the old man something much different. He saw strength growing out of hardship and pain. Thus, Toomer had two points of view toward Negroes: one expressing his doubts, one expressing his hope; one repelling him, the other attracting him. The significant point is that neither point of view gained the ascendancy in "Kabnis."

Thus, for a period of perhaps a year or two, the period during which he composed *Cane*, Toomer found a new identity-giving absolute in the Negro folk-spirit. But the absolute had, at best, a tenuous hold on the poet. It proved no more enduring than those that had gone before. Shortly after the publication of *Cane*, Toomer again felt himself immersed in chaos and doubt: "Everything was in chaos. I saw this chaos clearly, I could and did describe and analyze its factors so well that I got a reputation for being a sort of genius of chaos."[15]

What happened to Toomer in the years between 1923 and 1925 is described by Gorham Munson, who knew him well at the time. Toomer continued his quest for what Munson calls "unity," or "personal wholeness," first by training his "conscious control of the body," and then by spending the summer of 1924 at the Gurdjieff Institute, Fontainebleau, France.[16] Toomer found what he was looking for in Gurdjieff's philosophy—an interesting blend of Freudian categories and religion—became a disciple, and spent many of his summers in Fontainebleau, returning each fall to organize psychological experiments in the United States. But the crucial moment for Toomer came one summer evening in 1926. It happened at the end of one of those humdrum days of no special significance. Toomer was waiting on an El platform in New York City, when suddenly, as he says, he transcended himself: "I was born above the body into a world of psychological reality. . . . In my private language I shall call this experience the Second Conception."[17]

That was it for Toomer; he had his absolute; his search was over. From that time he began to proselytize in the age-old tradition of missionaries. He wrote novels, he wrote philosophic works, he wrote descriptions of psychological experiments,[18] and he wrote volumes of material that is unclassifiable—all with the purpose of persuasion. The publishers were not buying; his literary life after 1926 became a dreary round of rejection slips. The fault was not his or his publishers'. He had come up with an answer to the troubles that plagued the age. He had an answer for Van Wyck Brooks's cry of "externalization," for Waldo Frank's plight of being "objectified." He had found an answer for modern man's agonizing sense of incompleteness. His answer was couched disconcertingly in half-psychological, half-mystical language

("Our center of gravity is displaced. Our essence is passive; and we lack essential self-activating energies. . . . We have no being-aims and purposes."),[19] but what he was doing, in essence, was putting into his own symbols the age-old experience of religious conversion. Following willy-nilly behind Gurdjieff, he had got himself completely at cross-purposes with the whole thrust of American intelligence of the 1920s. Van Wyck Brooks, Charles S. Johnson, Alain Locke—all were asking that man, through his creative art, turn to experience. The answer found by these modern critics lay in creating beauty and meaning out of the living contact with the world of reality. Toomer was saying just the opposite: turn for beauty and meaning to your inner essence. "An artist," he wrote, "is able, by effort to contact his own essence, wherein exist common universal symbols."[20] Toomer was asking his age to adopt another absolute. The age was not buying.

Toomer's artistic expression lost something once he had found his answer—it became didactic, it became unconvincing. His unpublished novel "Eight-Day World" (c. 1932) is a case in point. It pictures a group of people aboard a transatlantic liner escaping from their unsatisfactory lives in America. The critique of life in America was the one expressed by a hundred writers in the 1920s. Life had become materialistic, commercial, and unfulfilling. The group escaping from this life aboard the liner was no sooner at sea than infighting and backbiting began. The people felt inadequate to themselves, and yet strove for independence from others. It was Toomer's early experience being retold. Hugh was the one man of the story who understood something of what was going on, but he was in the same predicament as the others, trying to break down the barriers his own inadequacy built up between him and them, trying, without success, to find fulfillment. Finally, Hugh found his fulfillment in the beautiful Vera and, at the same time, crystallized a philosophy of it all. He had come to understand that each person must attain a satisfactory independence and yet give of self. That is the goal. But in order to achieve it, one must transcend oneself: "This means," said Hugh, "that we must recapture our full *being. Being* is the base of everything."[21]

"Eight-Day World" ended as Toomer had ended, with all problems solved, with everyone satisfied. The artist could no longer express modern man's restlessness and lostness. His work had become smug—and dead. Toomer had been modern in *Cane*. There the author had confronted his readers with the pain of reality unmitigated by the pleasant knowledge of having in hand The Answer. After writing *Cane*, Toomer fled from reality, found his absolute, and clung to it. He talked about finding "being," but he would have been horrified at the modern definition of *being*—the *being* of Heidegger or of Sartre. He turned from experience of outward reality to an inner thing he called "essence" or "being," thinking that the thing he was camouflaging with the symbols of psychology was newly discovered. By 1940 he realized it was not new. He requested admittance to the Society of Friends, saying: "For some time we have shared the fundamental faith of the Friends. . . ."[22] His "essence" had been none other than the Quakers' "inner light"; in his 1926 experience of "Second Conception" had been the experience of religious conversion. Toomer had gone full cycle, from his childhood faith in God, through total rejection in *Cane*, and then back again to God.

What, then, shall we say about Jean Toomer? Does he stand within the Negro American literary tradition? The question is not an easy one, and the answer must be a much more arbitrary one than has always been assumed. In none of his literary efforts subsequent to *Cane* did he make race a central or even important issue. Beyond that, he made some positive efforts to disassociate his name from Negro literature. When, for example, James Weldon Johnson, in 1930, asked his permission to use some of his poetry from *Cane* in the revised edition of *The Book of American Negro Poetry*, Toomer replied in the negative, saying:

> My poems are not Negro poems, nor are they Anglo-Saxon or white or English poems. My prose likewise. They are, first, mine. And, second, in so far as general race or stock is concerned, they spring from the result of racial blending here in America which has produced a new race or stock. We may call this stock the American stock or race. . . . [23]

Evidently the division of mankind into categories of race was not one of Toomer's preoccupations after his 1926 conversion experience—he had found his identity in religion and not race. Before 1926 he had made one serious attempt to find the answer to his emotional needs through an identification with the Negro race. The result had been *Cane*. I suspect that *Cane* should be seen as the point at which the broad current represented by the aspirations and needs of the Lost Generation touched the current of Negro social protest, leaving a minor monument to both.

Jean Toomer and Mae Wright: An Interview with Mae Wright Peck

THERMAN B. O'DANIEL

It was purely by chance that I learned that my good friend Mae Wright Peck of Baltimore, Maryland, was the same beautiful May[1] Wright with whom Jean Toomer was romantically involved during the early 1920s. At a 1979 Christmas party, given by Mae for her Washington cousins, our lively conversation on many topics eventually became centered on a discussion of early Negro writers, to whom some of those present were related; and, from this, we proceeded to talk about some of the younger writers of the Harlem Renaissance—Langston Hughes, Arna Bontemps, Countee Cullen, and others—whom some of us had known personally, when Mae informed us that she had also known Jean Toomer.

This announcement was particularly interesting to me because, at the moment, I was working on a collection of critical studies on Toomer, and, at various times, I had run across brief references to Mae Wright in the Toomer literature. Naturally, I wished immediately to pursue this topic further but thought that I should wait for a more opportune time. Just before my wife and I left the Christmas party, and as we were thanking Mae for her hospitality, I told her about the Toomer book which I had in progress and asked her if she would be willing, at some time soon, to talk with me about Toomer. Without hesitation, she said that she would.[2]

Several weeks later, after the busy Christmas and New Year holiday season had passed, we invited Mae to our home for dinner and for the promised discussion of Toomer. Mae came and brought with her three books that had been gifts from Toomer. Two of them bore inscriptions, and one book, of course, was a first edition of *Cane:*

To
May
with love
Jean

Another was *New Hampshire: A Poem with Notes and Grace Notes,* by Robert Frost, with woodcuts by J. J. Lankes, published by Henry Holt and Company (New York, 1923). It was identically inscribed, but with an added date—*Christmas: 1923.* The third book was an unautographed copy of Waldo Frank's *Holiday.*

Mae said she thought I might be interested in seeing these books, and, indeed, I was; and, as we engaged in some general conversation, I gave them a brief examination. However, the time came to talk specifically about Toomer, and, without further ado, we began.

INTERVIEWER: Was it in Washington, D.C., that you first met Jean Toomer?

MAE: No, he and I met for the first time at Harpers Ferry, West Virginia.[3]

INTERVIEWER: Oh, I knew that Washington was Toomer's home, and thought perhaps that you had once lived there too, or had met Toomer there while visiting that city.

MAE: No. Baltimore is my home; I was born here and finished high school here.

INTERVIEWER: Douglass High School?

MAE: It was named Frederick Douglass High School a little later, but it was just called the Baltimore Colored High School when I graduated.

INTERVIEWER: Then you have spent most of your life in this city.

MAE: In a way, you might say so. However, I have traveled, of course, to many parts of the world. Also, I attended preparatory school and college away from Baltimore; then lived and taught elsewhere for a few years before returning here to teach in the public school system, and later, to work for the State of Maryland in instructional television.

INTERVIEWER: That is very interesting, but somehow, I had associated you with Washington to some extent, as well as with Baltimore.

MAE: Well, that is true to the extent that I always had relatives in Washington. Before my mother and father were married, she lived there with her parents. It was her home at that time. She was a graduate of the Miner Normal School and taught for one year in one of the elementary schools. She met my father there. He was a graduate of the Yale Medical School and had gone to Washington to serve his internship at Freedmen's Hospital. After this, he moved to the nearby city of Baltimore to begin the practice of medicine, and in five years he had purchased and furnished a home and an office. Thus, when he married my mother in 1905, it was to Baltimore that he brought his bride, and later it was here that I was born. In a way, Washington was a second home for me during my childhood. I was very fond of my grandparents and other relatives there and was a frequent visitor to their homes.

INTERVIEWER: Now tell me about Harpers Ferry and how it happened that you met Jean Toomer there?

MAE: It was in the month of June, during the summer of 1922, and I had gone to Harpers Ferry on vacation with my family. The YMCA, that year, had taken over Storer College for its summer conferences, and it had invited some Baltimore and Washington families and, perhaps, some persons from other places to spend their vacations there. As a matter of fact, the YMCA needed the participation of these families in order to keep the facilities of the college open during the summer and provide funds to support the conferences. Because of its elevation, Harpers Ferry was very pleasant in the summer, and it was reasonably close to Baltimore and Washington. Therefore, it was convenient for professional men, who had to attend to business during the week, to commute and spend their weekends with their families.

INTERVIEWER: Were there many families there?

MAE: Yes, a goodly number, I should say, including Attorney and Mrs. Perry Howard of Washington and their two young sons; Attorney and Mrs. William C. McCard from Baltimore; Mr.

Clyde McDuffy, a Latin teacher at Washington's Dunbar High School; Mr. and Mrs. John Nalle of Washington, and their daughter, Blanche, who later became Mrs. Clyde McDuffy, and others. Then there were many who seemed to come for a few days or a week at a time, rather than for the entire summer. I remember Mordecai Johnson being there for about a week on one vacation. This was before he became president of Howard University.

INTERVIEWER: And Jean Toomer?

MAE: Yes, and Jean Toomer, of course, was there. A Mr. Hamlin and a Mr. McGrew were the YMCA officials in charge of the conferences and were the persons who managed the entire operation. They assigned the families to rooms in the dormitories and to tables in the dining hall where we all ate our meals. The girls in our group were assigned a table together, and, there being no vacancy at the tables for the older persons, Toomer was assigned to our table. I remember that we young girls gave him a hard time, at first, trying to get enough to eat. He was playing the gentleman's role and held back until all of us were served. This amused us very much.

INTERVIEWER: What kind of person was Toomer? What did he look like?

MAE: Physically, Jean was a man over six feet tall, slender with a light olive complexion and a full head of black or very dark-brown hair. He had an athletic build, but he was not heavy—more the physique of a runner, I would say.

INTERVIEWER: By looking at him, could one identify him as a Negro?

MAE: No. If one had not been told that he had Negro blood in him, one never would have known it. He would have had no trouble whatever passing for white.

INTERVIEWER: What about his personality?

MAE: He was an excellent conversationalist and was very sociable and charming when he wanted to be, but at times he was withdrawn and stayed to himself.

INTERVIEWER: Did he ever discuss color with you?

MAE: No, he never did.

INTERVIEWER: What was the program at Harpers Ferry?

MAE: The YMCA had a program for its conferences, but the vacationers had nothing to do unless they made their own entertainment.

INTERVIEWER: How did Toomer fit in with this?

MAE: At first, I suppose that it was difficult for him, especially when one considers his age.

INTERVIEWER: What do you mean?

MAE: Well, I have mentioned the fact that Harpers Ferry, that summer, was somewhat of an improvised summer resort for the families in our group. The grown-up people were much older than Jean, and their children were many years younger. Except for its beautiful scenery and delightful climate—the cool, pleasant nights for sleeping, in contrast to the extremely hot and humid weather of Baltimore and Washington—Harpers Ferry had absolutely nothing else to offer the vacationers in our group. For company for me, since I was an only child, my mother had invited my younger cousin, Catherine Baker, from Washington, and a friend from Wilmington, Delaware, Alice Banton, daughter of Dr. and Mrs. Conwell Banton. Also, there was another friend, Elizabeth "Chita" McCard, of Baltimore, who was there for the summer with her uncle and aunt, Attorney and Mrs. William C. McCard. Her father, Dr. Harry S. McCard, was the attorney's brother. The three of us—Alice, "Chita," and I—often spent our vacations together, as we were the only children of families that had been friendly for years.

INTERVIEWER: Were you about the same age?

MAE: Yes, just about; Alice was a year older, and "Chita," about two years younger than I.

INTERVIEWER: Toomer must have been twenty-seven years old, going on twenty-eight.

MAE: Yes, he was twenty-seven at the time, and I was sixteen. I had just finished high school in three and a half years and was looking forward to entering college in the fall, or a preparatory school, for one year, before going on to college.

INTERVIEWER: How did the older people spend their time at Harpers Ferry?

MAE: Mostly resting and relaxing, and taking short walks to enjoy the beautiful scenery and the mountain air. Also, card playing, reading, and needlework were other forms of entertainment in which they engaged. Often, having much to talk about, they just sat on the campus and conversed with each other. At other times, after dinner, they arranged their chairs in a big circle and sang many of their favorite and well-known songs. Also, there were tennis courts, and some of them played and enjoyed the game of tennis. On the weekends there were plenty of good players on hand, and sometimes the spectators saw some good matches.

INTERVIEWER: What happened on rainy days?

MAE: In inclement weather, all of us used a large recreation room in the main dormitory, which also housed the dining hall. There, such games as whist, checkers, and dominoes were engaged in, along with the group singing.

INTERVIEWER: It is said that Toomer was fond of music; did he join in?

MAE: No, he never did.

INTERVIEWER: How did he spend his time? Had he come to Harpers Ferry to write?

MAE: If so, he did not, at first, discuss his writing with me, and after we got to know each other, we spent most of each day together. He could have been doing some writing when he was alone in his room, but in the beginning, he was not always talking about it to me or to my mother. As far as I could tell, he had just come to Harpers Ferry for a vacation.

INTERVIEWER: In other words, he did not seem to have a writing schedule while he was there?

MAE: No. But, as I have said, if so, he was very private about it, when we first met. Later on, however, my mother and I did come to know that Jean had written a few pieces and that he did aspire to become a professional writer. At this time, of course, he had done very little and was saying little or nothing about it. As a matter of fact, he did more talking about my writing than he did about his own.

INTERVIEWER: Had you written something?

MAE: Not really. I had just won a city-wide essay contest while in school, and Jean read the piece and favorably commented on it. He told me that he thought I had literary promise, if I would apply myself. At a later time, he sent me a list of authors to read and said that he would discuss them with me after I had read them. Also later, he sent me Waldo Frank's *Holiday* and some other books to read.

INTERVIEWER: Did you ever meet Waldo Frank?

MAE: Yes, and I saw him briefly on one or two occasions with Jean. Once he accompanied Jean when he visited my home in Baltimore. Also, because of his friendship with Jean, when I was applying for admittance to a preparatory school, Frank wrote a letter of recommendation in my behalf to Cushing Academy. However, going back to your earlier question, I do recall Jean having quoted a line or phrase from a poem that he could have been writing at the time: "Ephemerally immolating hills,"[4] but, other than this, he was not one to talk about what he was writing, if anything, at that time—at least, not to me when we were together. I suppose that the reason I remember this line is because I had to look up the words to understand it.

INTERVIEWER: How did Toomer get along with your cousin and your girlfriends?

MAE: Quite often we were all together, and he got along fine with them and they with him, when he felt like being sociable. When he wished to be alone with me, he was very good at planning things for them to do. He organized them into, what he called, his squad, like an army unit, and whenever he wished to do so, he assigned them well-conceived tasks to execute and told them to return in an hour or so and report to him.

INTERVIEWER: How did they react?

MAE: It is surprising how cooperative they were and how faithfully they carried out his orders. Regarding my young cousin, Catherine, Jean told me that since her father was dead and my parents kept Catherine with them so much, I had the responsibility to help her mature into a lovely woman.

INTERVIEWER: Did Toomer ever discuss his college experiences with you, or his teaching experiences in Sparta, Georgia?

MAE: No, he never did. The only thing that he mentioned about a past experience that might have been remotely connected with one of these, was that one time when he was out West, there was a forest fire and he had helped to fight it. And the only reason, perhaps, that he mentioned this was that he was wearing a sweater that was partly burned, and when my mother asked him about it, that is what he told her.

INTERVIEWER: Did you and Toomer take hikes together?

MAE: Not hikes as such, but we did take long walks together, almost daily. Two of the spots frequented by us on these walks are famous and dear to the hearts of most visitors to Harpers Ferry: the legendary projecting rock, high above and overlooking the rivers, called "Lover's Leap";[5] and the place where one can stand and look into three states—Maryland, Virginia, and West Virginia. Jean was a lover of nature and was very observant of the natural wonders in the beautiful Harpers Ferry environment. After he had been at Harpers Ferry for approximately a month, I guess, he returned to Washington for a week's visit. When he came back, Catherine, "Chita" McCard, Alice Banton, and I met him at the station, and he offered to engage the only taxicab there to take us up the hill to the college. I was in favor of that idea, but "Chita" and Alice took me aside and reminded me of the cost of such an expedition; so we all walked back to Storer College together. After returning from the Washington trip, he alluded, on one occasion, to the fact that he had had something published but said nothing that was specific, nor did he elaborate.

INTERVIEWER: Other than this brief trip to Washington, did Toomer spend the whole summer at Harpers Ferry?

MAE: Yes, I think so, at least most of it. He was still there when my family and I returned to Baltimore in August, but he must have left very soon afterwards because the YMCA program was coming to an end. Later on he told my mother that when our car left, it was like the empire leaving the czar.

INTERVIEWER: Did you see him anymore before you left for school?

MAE: Yes, he visited our home in Baltimore, from time to time, until I left for Cushing Academy. Having finished high school in three and a half years, I discovered that, although I had the required units for graduation, I was minus certain specific units needed for entrance to one of the New England colleges. Therefore, I spent one year in Cushing Academy, a preparatory school. After I went away, I did not see Jean anymore until Thanksgiving, but we wrote letters frequently to each other. In one of his letters, he told me that Miss Burrell, an outstanding teacher of English and dramatics at Washington's Dunbar High School, had told him that she had heard that he had fallen in love with a Baltimore girl.

Interviewer: What was Toomer's reaction to this?

Mae: He said that, "being the diplomat that I am," he evaded the subject and gave her no satisfaction; just passed over it and continued talking to her on another topic

Interviewer: But it was true, was it not?

Mae: I suppose so. I think, at the time, we both thought that we were very much in love. When I came home for the Thanksgiving vacation, we saw each other frequently, and he took me to the Howard-Lincoln football game in Washington. After the game, we went dancing at the Lincoln-Colonnade. Jean was a marvelous dancer, and we had great fun.

Interviewer: Yes, but the vacation period was short.

Mae: That is true, but the Christmas vacation period was longer, and we saw a great deal of each other at that time, and again during the Easter vacation. My friend Anne DeBerry of Springfield, Massachusetts, visited me during the Christmas holidays, and at times, my home was full of girlfriends of our own ages. On one such occasion, Jean told my mother that he felt like a grandfather among such a youthful group. He never, however, expressed such sentiments to me.

Interviewer: Were you two ever engaged?

Mae: Yes, in an informal manner. What I mean by this is that my mother knew about it, but it had not reached the point where my father was informed and his consent was requested.

Interviewer: But your father knew him, of course?

Mae: Certainly; he met Jean and knew him quite well at Harpers Ferry and saw him on many occasions when he visited me and had dinner with the family in Baltimore. But my father was busy with his profession, while my mother was always around when Jean came and got to know him very well. As a matter of fact, he sometimes wrote to my mother about our romance and about his hopes to become a writer of fame and fortune. In other words, they were very fond of each other, and she seemed to encourage our courtship, or at least did not oppose it. Thus, as Jean and I talked of marriage, we shared this hope with my mother. However, all three of us realized that marriage, in that day, required that the man have money or an income, and Jean had neither. He did have confidence in the success of the book he was writing[6] and expected that its sale would launch him as a serious member of the writing profession. Also, he expected money from the book's sale, as well as from the sale of other writings later. Then, and only then, would he be in a position to approach my father and ask for a formal engagement. Unfortunately, you and I both know that he did not get the merited acceptance that he expected; that recognition did not come until many years later; and that he never did realize substantive money from his writings.

INTERVIEWER: So, with fated circumstances working against it, the engagement really got bogged down, did it not?

MAE: It certainly did. I should state here, however, that although my father was a very loving and indulgent parent in other ways, he was adamant in regard to my finishing college. For this reason, the subject of an engagement was never discussed with him, and from what he had always emphatically told me—even before I met Jean—I knew there was no use talking to him at that time. Uppermost in my father's mind was a good education for his daughter at one of the better New England colleges, and he had always stressed the fact that he would support me as long as I stayed in school, but should I decide to leave school, all support would be withdrawn immediately. I knew that he meant this. As for Jean, at that time, as has already been stated, he had no visible means nor any very promising prospects of being able to support the two of us.

INTERVIEWER: And yet, he still remained hopeful?

MAE: At that time, yes. I have spoken to you of Jean's letters to my mother. In them, he constantly reassured her of his love and respect for me, and his hopes for our happy future together. Indeed, there had to have been some sort of *understanding* if he were to continue to see me after the summer of 1922. My mother and her family came from a culture in which it was customary for a young man to *state his intentions* after he had come calling on a girl enough times to indicate a serious interest. Yet, because of my youth, Jean's impecunious circumstances, and my parents' desire that I get an education, a formal engagement was not encouraged.

INTERVIEWER: Let me ask you a few questions about Toomer's family. Did he have much to say about his family?

MAE: No, it was not his practice to talk about the members of his family when we were together. I know that he was very fond of his grandmother, and occasionally she would be mentioned by him as he talked, but he never began a conversation specifically about her or any other family member.

INTERVIEWER: He dedicated the first two parts of *Cane* to his grandmother, which might indicate his deep affection for her.[7] His grandfather, however, died in December of 1921, some six months before you met Toomer. Did your family know his family?

MAE: My mother and her family, having lived in Washington, knew of the Pinchbacks, of course, but they were not personal friends of theirs.

INTERVIEWER: What about Toomer's Uncle Bismarck? Did you ever meet him?

MAE: No, nor did Jean ever discuss him with me, but I did hear the name somewhere without any particulars. I guess the reason that I remember this at all is that, at the time, I thought *Bismarck* to be a rather odd name for an uncle.

INTERVIEWER: Did Toomer ever discuss his theories about physical exercise and body building with you?

MAE: No, but he was a great believer in taking long walks, and there could have been a connection between this and whatever he might have believed on the subject.

INTERVIEWER: What, if anything, did Toomer have to say about the moral and social codes of behavior? Did he consider these codes repressive and damaging to one's effort to find fulfillment and self-realization?

MAE: No, he did not discuss any of this with me. If he had such ideas in mind, perhaps he thought he should discuss more interesting topics when we were together.

INTERVIEWER: You will pardon me for mentioning this, but I think that it should be discussed to some extent, to prevent false conclusions from being drawn about it.

MAE: What is it that you have in mind?

INTERVIEWER: I am thinking about the story "Avey," in which a very important scene is laid at Harpers Ferry. Since it is known that you met Toomer in Harpers Ferry, that he spent the summer there while you and your family were vacationing there, and that your romance began there, it is very likely that some interpreters of this story, not having all of the facts, might conclude that Toomer was thinking of you when he drew his portrait of the character Avey. If this were to occur what would be your comment on it?

MAE: I would say, first of all, that such an interpretation would certainly be a false one. The narrator of the story had met Avey the year before. She was a grown woman and already a teacher. He saw her the next year in Harpers Ferry, and five years later, he met her in Washington, and they went to the grounds of Soldiers' Home at night. The only similarity to my life with Jean is the description of Harpers Ferry, which is a good and accurate description: Lover's Leap . . . the river and a railroad track beneath . . . other vivid details presented with an economy of words—certainly a beautiful description which makes the setting real and the character Avey realistic, but who, in no way, resembles me. Talented writers of fiction frequently use a snatch of a situation here and another snatch there to create a background for a scene or an incident; or they may create a character that is a composite of many persons. There is no telling what the creative mind will do. For instance, regarding a poem that Jean sent to me, he said that he was dedicating the poem to me and to our meeting at Harpers Ferry but that the poem itself had nothing to do with Harpers Ferry. At the time that I knew Jean, I had never even heard of Soldiers' Home, and to this day I have never been on the grounds of the place. Also, there is no way that I could have been out past nine o'clock at night—that was my curfew time at home. When I went to Cushing Academy and during my first year at Tufts University, the school rule deadline, imposed by the student government, was eight o'clock at night for all at the academy and for freshmen at college. Thus, I was never out at night with a boy or man past eight or nine o'clock unless there was a chaperone. I attended my first dance in June of 1922—my high school commencement dance—and went with my escort, Charlie Drew, a friend since childhood, and my father, who came in and sat with the other fathers who had accompanied their daughters and escorts. It is difficult, perhaps, with today's relaxed standards, to understand the world in which I grew up more than a half century ago. In "Avey" there is an incident on a pleasure steamer, the *Jane Mosely*, that "puffed up the Potomac." I never went with Jean on any steamer either on the Potomac River or the Chesapeake Bay. In my younger days I went to Brown's Grove just about every Sunday. Captain Brown, a black man who owned *The Starlight*, and my maternal grandfather were very close friends, and my grandfather came to Baltimore every Sunday, in the summer, when we were not out of the city, and took us on the cruise at Captain Brown's invitation. It was a delightful cruise on *The Starlight*, but Jean and I never went on that boat (if the excursions were still running in 1922) nor on any other excursion boat. The male character in the story is supposed to have tried to teach Avey to swim. Jean never tried to teach me to swim. I was an expert swimmer. Having spent several of my summers at Highland Beach right on the Chesapeake Bay, I was soon thrown into the water by some of the older kids and learned what a sink-or-swim experience was like. Also, though I am not sure of the year, we went to Colton one summer, where, there being no beach, the guests were taken out into deep water in a yacht. We jumped off into deep water and swam near the boat until time to return to the hotel. Jean and I never went to the seashore together, but had we gone, he would not have needed to teach me to swim. Finally, Avey is described as being lazy, too lazy to write, sloppy, and indolent. I was certainly not lazy. I was a good swimmer, a fair basketball player, and played guard on the freshman team at college. I was extremely studious, having lopped off two and a half years of the normal twelve-year public education stint by "skipping" grades in elementary school and finishing high school a half year early. While at Harpers Ferry, I studied advanced Latin for one hour daily with Mr. McDuffy, whom I mentioned earlier. I had already read Caesar, Cicero, and Vergil in high school. My grades in college remained high, and I was elected to Phi Beta Kappa. These are not the hallmarks of a lazy person.

INTERVIEWER: I should say not; and likewise, there is no way possible, realistically or imaginatively, that Avey could have been a portrayal of Mae Wright.

MAE: After reading some of Jean's stories, my mother asked him why he always wrote about the sordid, seamy side of life.

INTERVIEWER: How did he respond to this?

MAE: I am very sorry that I cannot remember what she said his reply was, but I seem to remember that his answer did not satisfy her.

INTERVIEWER: By the way, I have seen several photographs of Toomer; do you have a picture of him?

MAE: No, not a picture of Jean himself, except of him in group snapshots taken at Harpers Ferry, but I do have a photograph of a bust of him.

INTERVIEWER: Are you speaking of a photograph of a sculptured likeness of Toomer?

MAE: I am not surprised that this amazes you, but that is exactly what I am talking about, and you might find the story of my connection with this picture both interesting and amusing.

INTERVIEWER: I am sure that I would.

MAE: Well, when I went away to school, I found it customary for the girls to display pictures of their boyfriends in their dormitory rooms. Naturally, I wished to be in vogue, so I wrote to Jean and asked him to send me a picture. He replied that he did not have a regular picture but he did have this photograph of his bust, which he would get to me.

INTERVIEWER: And that is what he sent?

MAE: Well, he did not send it, for it must have been near a holiday period, and I got it while I was home on vacation. He and Waldo Frank were leaving on a trip, so he sent me the following undated letter:

Saturday Evening

Dear Mae—

Waldo is just in. He wants to push ahead, so we're leaving on the 10:25 train.

I haven't a picture. I'm leaving this one of my bust for you.

I'll write as soon as we reach Spartanburg.

Love —

Jean.

If you don't come to the house Sunday, I'll have Ken mail this to you.

I learned that the bust of Jean, of which the photograph was taken, was executed by May Howard Johnson, a sculptor who was born and educated in Philadelphia. Later, she moved to Washington, where she taught at Howard University but also had her own studio. When I got back to school and the students saw my picture of Jean's bust, they said it looked like a bust of Milton.

INTERVIEWER: I must agree, that is certainly an interesting and humorous story. Now tell me what happened during the year of 1923.

MAE: That was a very busy year for me and for Jean. After a year at Cushing Academy, I entered Tufts University, in September, as a college freshman. Jean was busy getting his book published and was moving about a good bit in a new environment, associating with new friends who were writers and creative artists of various types.

INTERVIEWER: Did you keep in touch with each other?

MAE: Yes, to some extent, but we did not see each other often, nor did we correspond as regularly as in the past. However, he sent me a poem that was mainly descriptive of the natural beauties of Harpers Ferry and which he said was reminiscent of our summer there, and when *Cane* was published, he sent me a copy of it immediately. Later, when I saw him, he wondered why I had not written to him about the book.

INTERVIEWER: Do you have the letters that he wrote to you?

MAE: Sometimes now, I wish that I had saved them, but I did not. You know how it is in early life, such things as letters are kept only for a short time. I do remember keeping one more of them, in addition to the one about the photographed bust, and finally putting it away somewhere—the one in which he sent the poem. I was really looking for it, when the other one turned up.

INTERVIEWER: What did you think of *Cane*?

MAE: Well, that was my problem. I thoroughly enjoyed parts of the book, and yet I found it rather confusing. I had not written to him about it because, really, I had been groping for something to say. You see, I had been accustomed to reading literary works that were more structured, or let me say, structured in a more conventional manner, and *Cane* was in a new vein unfamiliar to me at that time.

INTERVIEWER: What happened then?

MAE: Well, nothing really that had anything seriously to do with *Cane*. It was natural that he should be curious to know my opinion of his book, even though he was not expecting any weighty appraisal from me, and he was a bit disappointed when I failed to respond. However, no major issue occurred because of this incident. It was just coincidental that about this time our correspondence became less frequent, and we gradually began to drift apart. Both of us suddenly were facing new and exciting experiences. All at once our horizons were widening on separate frontiers, and all of our associates were new and different. I was in college with students and new friends of my own age, enjoying each and every challenging new experience and looking forward to my life ahead. The highly intellectual and talented Jean Toomer, as we know him today, was among his more mature peers, an energetic avant-garde group of creative artists and thinkers of new ideas and theories, and our paths were destined not to meet again.

Jean Toomer's Life Prior to *Cane*: A Brief Sketch of the Emergence of a Black Writer

MICHAEL J. KRASNY

In 1914 Jean Toomer was graduated from Washington's M Street High School (later renamed Dunbar High after Negro poet Paul Laurence Dunbar), where the black poet Angelina Grimké taught for a number of years, including those of Toomer's enrollment.[1] From M Street High Toomer went on in 1914 to enroll in a two-year agricultural degree program at the University of Wisconsin, perhaps, as Darwin Turner has suggested, because of a desire to settle, eventually, in the South as a gentleman planter.[2] In an autobiographical note to "Eight-Day World" Toomer states in third person:

> When college time arrived he turned away from cities and went to the University of Wisconsin with an urge toward the soil to study agriculture. However, he soon found he was not suited to be a farmer, scientific or otherwise.[3]

Toomer's constantly fluctuating interests, his love of working with his hands, and his intense love of nature can account for his having enrolled in an agricultural program. He took courses in animal husbandry, agronomy, chemistry, and English, then dropped out for a semester and returned that summer to take courses in French, mathematics, and English. He was a "generally average" student.[4] Later, he would claim the pursuit of a love affair as the reason for his decision to leave the University of Wisconsin after the summer of 1915.[5]

From Wisconsin Toomer went to the Massachusetts College of Agriculture for a week and then to a physical training center at the University of Chicago.[6] He attended a host of the lectures given in the Loop on subjects such as dietetics and the work of men like Ernst Haeckel and Charles Darwin. It was during this time that he became convinced of the "irrefutable logic of atheism." In the Loop lectures he also listened raptly to talks given on such literary figures as George Bernard Shaw, Victor Hugo, and Walt Whitman. Toomer's fascination with literature, philosophy, and art continued to increase, and he turned into a voracious reader.

Toomer became especially interested in yoga and psychoanalysis, and after becoming excited by Lester Ward's *Dynamic Sociology*, he decided to take courses in sociology at New York University. He soon lost interest, however, and subsequently enrolled in 1918 in a City College of New York pre-law social science program, after having been turned down by the military because of a hernia. He managed to get an *A* in history and a *B* in political science, but his grades generally suffered at City College because of absences and difficulty with a mathematics course. Though he made some important initial contacts with members of the black literary circles, at twenty-four he was still obviously trying to pass as a white man—on the admission blank to City College he had entered "French Cosmopolitan" as his heritage.[7]

Near the end of the term at CCNY, Toomer decided to abandon formal education. He resolved instead to be a writer. In the autobiographical note which he wrote as a preface to "Eight-Day World," there is further substantiation that 1918 was the year in which he made the fateful decision to create literature:

> In time the field narrowed down to a choice between music and literature. Ever since boyhood, he had loved music, displaying some facility composing. All along, too, he had shown spasmodic talent for speaking and writing. The final decision was against music and for literature. This was in 1918. The three following years were devoted entirely to learning by practice the craft and art of writing.[8]

The next few years for Toomer were ones of soul-searching and wandering. The decision to become a writer was particularly difficult for him. By deciding to be a writer he was compelled to defy his grandfather's wish that he become either a professional man or a musician. Furthermore, Toomer believed literary creation to be predicated upon self-discovery and experience, even what he judged to be painful. Instead of furthering his education as his grandfather would have had him do, Toomer felt the need to travel a great deal and seek work where he could find it.[9] He decided to leave New York and CCNY and return to Chicago with art as his religion.

In Chicago Toomer sold Fords, then went to Milwaukee, where he taught physical education in the city school system. His wanderings even took him back East to a shipyard in New Jersey,[10] where he worked for ten days as a shipfitter and in the process lost an ephemeral infatuation for socialism. He finally returned to Washington in 1920, where he found his family in rapid decline. Because of his grandfather's near insolvency, Toomer found it necessary to help out by working. He took jobs as a grocery clerk, library assistant, and theater manager, the latter probably providing the background for "Theater" and "Box Seat" in *Cane*.

Toomer was forced into a kind of monastic life, dutifully working long hours to help eke out a living. He devoted the rest of his time to the decision he had made two years earlier—to become a writer. Despite all his wanderings after leaving CCNY, he accomplished an extraordinary amount of studying and reading on his own. In 1920, socially isolated and filled with despair at watching his once powerful grandfather deteriorate both physically and mentally, he directed his studies even more to understanding the craft of writing. As Fullinwider notes about Toomer's return in 1920:

> In a mood of bitterness and an atmosphere of rejection he turned to reading literature—Robert Frost, Sherwood Anderson, the imagists. He wrote incessantly, hour upon hour for month after month, tearing up what he wrote. He learned to handle words, learned their symbolic potential.[11]

Toomer's reading during this period was not limited solely to literature. He read books on social philosophy, yoga, and psychoanalysis, continuing to cultivate previous interests. But the fact that his primary interests were literary becomes evident in his recollections of major literary influences in "Outline of an Autobiography." Besides mentioning Frost, Anderson, and the imagists, he includes a number of other contemporary American poets that he fervently read during his period of isolation in 1920: Edgar Lee Masters, Carl Sandburg,

Vachel Lindsay, and Edwin Arlington Robinson. Other literary figures frequently appear in his autobiographical manuscript, including a host of novelists: Dostoyevsky, Tolstoy, Flaubert, Joyce, Sinclair Lewis, and Theodore Dreiser. Toomer also speaks frequently of George Bernard Shaw, who, he says, inspired his drama prior to *Cane*. He also notes the importance for him of Blake, Coleridge, Pater, Baudelaire, and Jules Romains. Clearly, however, Toomer felt most inspired in his early work by Walt Whitman and Waldo Frank, the two writers he most conspicuously admired. But it is also feasible to assume, as Mabel Dillard has done,[12] that he was familiar with Negro writers such as Paul Laurence Dunbar, Phillis Wheatley, James Weldon Johnson, and Charles Waddell Chesnutt. Toomer may indeed owe a great deal to Chesnutt's use of folk materials, as well as the sermons in Johnson's *God's Trombones*[13] and the lyricism and thematic unity which characterize Johnson's *The Autobiography of an Ex-Coloured Man*.

Toomer's eventual decision to write of the black experience was prompted by his relationship with Waldo Frank. The two met soon after Toomer left Washington in 1920 and returned to New York. The following year they went to Georgia together to gather indigenous materials for their art from the still existing black folk culture. Toomer's work was also concerned with blacks, however, because he came to equate them symbolically with his own identity. Yet, it is necessary to consider briefly the other forces that were at work hastening him toward the decision to live and write as a black man.

One could easily conclude from his autobiographical writings and the associations he was to have in the early twenties with authors such as Sherwood Anderson, Waldo Frank, and Kenneth Burke that his predilections would have been toward aesthetics and an American art form. In point of fact they were. But as much as Toomer was immersed in the world of white American letters, he was also probably drawn to the emerging concepts that became associated with the writers of the Negro Renaissance. It is understandable that his early work would have a profound effect upon many of the writers linked to that movement. There was a great deal of similarity between the precepts of Negro literary giants such as Alain Locke and Charles S. Johnson and those of Toomer's mentors, Waldo Frank and Sherwood Anderson. Locke and Johnson were also urging writers to find meaning and beauty in their own experience and to create native art forms of universal significance. Toomer, in effect, began to consider art in terms of both his own experience, his own quest for consciousness and identity, and materials of the folk culture. He fixed upon the idea of an amalgam of his white and black responses to life, the Caucasian and Negro blend in his own consciousness, in order to create a distinctly new "essence" and art form. The Negro side of experience and consciousness, however, increasingly became a medium with which he was captivated; he was moved more toward exploring and understanding it.

Jean Toomer in Wisconsin

NELLIE MC KAY

It has scarcely been noted that Jean Toomer's post-high school career began at the University of Wisconsin in Madison in 1914. "Far from the beaten tracks" of his southern forebears, Wisconsin was the area of the country that Toomer sought out to give shape to his identity when he was most impressionable. Some of the important events of his life occurred in the state.

Toomer spent most of his early life in Washington, D.C., except for the period between 1907 to 1910, when he lived in Brooklyn, New York, then in New Rochelle, New York, with his mother, Nina Pinchback, and her new husband. Nina Pinchback died unexpectedly in 1909, and Jean Toomer returned to Washington to the home of his aging maternal grandparents in 1910.

Until a few years prior to this time, the Pinchbacks had been relatively affluent, living in a veritable mansion on Bacon Street, one of the most exclusive white residential sections of Washington. But by the middle of the first decade of the twentieth century, bad investments and a penchant for the races had taken a toll on P. B. S. Pinchback's financial resources. By 1910 he was in a swift decline into poverty, no longer able to afford to maintain his home in the more prosperous area of the city. The family made moves to poorer neighborhoods, areas where larger numbers of black people lived.

Toomer graduated from the M Street High School, which was later renamed the Paul Laurence Dunbar High School, now illustrious for its register of the many well-known artistic and civic-minded American blacks who have attended it during the course of this century. He had several months to wait before he could go on to college. During this time he tried to decide on a profession and on the school that he would attend. He was not attracted to any of the occupations of which he had some knowledge. Later, he wrote, "They all seemed dull: office jobs, teaching, law, medicine. They were routines that appeared deadly and most people seemed folded up."[1]

In spite of his reduced financial circumstances, Pinchback, a man of haughty and aristocratic mien, wanted the best for his grandson. He wanted the young man to attend one of the country's prestigious colleges or universities and to enter one of the well-established professions, though Pinchback was partial to law. As a means of financing Toomer's education, Pinchback accepted a position in the Department of Internal Revenue in New York, the last of a series of minor government jobs he was appointed to between 1890 and 1910. He hoped to send young Toomer to a prep school like Andover and, from there, to Harvard University, and perhaps to the Harvard Law School. Pinchback's three sons had all received training at schools with outstanding reputations like Andover and Yale. However, their lives did not fulfill the hopes of their ambitious father. Pinckney, the eldest, did tolerably well as a pharmacist after graduating from the Philadelphia School of Pharmacy, but Bismarck, Toomer's favorite uncle, and Walter, the youngest son of the family, who had studied law, were not successful in their professions. Bismarck entered the medical field but ended up in a nonrelated civil service appointment and spent much of his early manhood under the paternal roof of the Bacon Street mansion. As Toomer later recalled, prior to their marriages, both Bismarck and Walter lived with his grandparents and had jobs with the government, courtesy of their father's political influence. Some years later, after the death of his wife, Walter moved to New York and took a job with Macy's. Pinchback was disappointed in his sons' failure to achieve with the aggressiveness that had characterized his own youth and manhood. His ambitions for Toomer may have been a final effort to transfer his sturdy spirit to one of his generations. However, his plans for his grandson were never to be realized, and the first disappointment was with Pinchback himself. Ill health forced him to resign the New York position and return to Washington not long after he had accepted it.

In the end Toomer decided to go to the University of Wisconsin in Madison, mainly because it was far away from the people he knew. He planned to study scientific agriculture, and as he saw it, the combination of Wisconsin and agriculture would make a "clean break" with his life up to that time.[2]

The decision to go to a white institution, however, raised problems for Toomer. In the house in which he had grown up and matured, where only Pinchback's claims of African heritage marked its members as other than white, the atmosphere was always one of tolerance toward all groups of people. The racial background of the family, its economic and social status, and the temperament and political views of the patriarch accounted for the tolerance that Toomer observed even when he was very young. As he got older, he gained firsthand knowledge of the lives of blacks and whites. He knew that in American life and society black people were continually and unjustly discriminated against and that their humanity was violated and denied on the basis of their race. Although he was certain that his fair complexion and Caucasian features would protect the details of his ancestry from easy detection, he worried about the repercussions when it became known, in the white university, that he had attended a Negro high school. He knew that it would be assumed that he was a Negro, and he expected to be harassed. These prospects created serious anxieties for him.

He resolved that he would deny no part of his ancestry, that he would stake his claim as a member of the American race. He decided to live his life on the basis of the facts. This was a course that he insisted on pursuing for a great deal of his life after that. During this period he wrote a poem, "The First American," in which he explored his newly formed philosophy. It was the first draft of the second most important work in the Toomer canon. "The First American" went through many revisions before it was published in the *New Caravan* in 1936 under the title "Blue Meridian." In the meantime Toomer decided to go to Madison, to volunteer no information about his racial background, and if queried about it, to declare himself the first conscious member of the American race.

Toomer arrived in Madison for the summer session of May 1914. This was his first solo adventure away from home. Initial homesickness gave way to the gaiety of his surroundings, and he became, in a very short time, the center of an admiring group of students. He took courses in English, French, and mathematics, all of which went well, especially English. A warm, vivacious, outgoing person, a good athlete and conversationalist, he made a number of friends, and with one in particular, Rose Hahn, he went sailing and swimming, played tennis, and danced a great deal. In the fall he entered the freshman class and continued to be extremely popular. He was invited to parties and was often seen with a woman who was a senior. He enjoyed this social success immensely, for Toomer had often been lonely during those early years in his grandfather's home. His mother had been very unhappy and unable to give him the amount of attention that he craved, partly because of her father's autocratic disposition. After the move to New York, Nina Pinchback continued to be unhappy. Toomer was unsympathetic toward her because he blamed her for having made what he called an unsatisfactory marriage. Among other things, he felt that her new husband was below the social status of the Pinchback family. In addition to the lack of closeness to his mother, he also had difficulty making friends among his peers, and when he returned to Washington in 1910, he found it impossible to develop a close relationship with his grandparents. Although he was sympathetic to his grandmother, he blamed his grandfather for his mother's death. He felt that the old man's dominating ways had driven his mother into her second marriage and that her death was at least indirectly connected to that marriage.

In the wake of his social success in Madison over the summer, Toomer decided to run for class president in the fall of 1914. Never one to contemplate new directions in his life without assessing the possible negative repercussions connected to them, and always assuming that the worst would occur, he then decided, almost immediately, that he lacked the political connections to succeed in such a competition because he did not belong to a fraternity. Faced with the fear of an imagined defeat, he withdrew his candidacy. In doing this it seemed to him that his popularity began to diminish, even though he later wrote that his room continued to be a gathering place for beer parties and a meeting place for a group of friends. The joy of the college experience went out of his life. He began to feel lonely and critical of the people around him:

> I was convinced that the majority of people were uncritical and fickle, attracted to glitter, never examining the worth of their idols, merely following the shifting winds of popularity.[3]

Madison appeared to him to lack both love and warmth, and he longed for these qualities as he thought he had experienced them in Washington.

In a short time he lost interest in his studies, which included a course in agronomy and another in animal husbandry. He summarily decided that he was unsuited for a career in farming, scientific or otherwise. However, the semester was not a complete loss. A new world had opened for him. Through the interest of an English teacher, he became acquainted with *The Nation*, *The New Republic*, and *The Manchester Guardian*, and he was awakened to the possibilities of a literary career. At the time he had no intention of following it, for in spite of his disaffection with campus life as a whole, he was still mainly enraptured by the social life of the university. Yet, because Toomer had been intrigued by literature earlier in his life—by the stories Uncle Bismarck read to him when he was very young and by books he read during his excursions into the public library while living in New York—the discovery of a living literature in contemporary journals was meaningful to him at this time.

Toomer's withdrawal from the race for class president set the pattern for the series of propitious beginnings and disappointing endings that continued for much of his life. Among other things, this pattern dominated the way in which he selected and rejected career choices. He explored many fields, and he always entered with high hopes but retreated when he suspected problems that he might not surmount.

Toomer returned to Madison after the Christmas vacation of 1914 but remained for only a few weeks. Then he withdrew from the university. During the next four years he would make equally brief sojourns into a number of other schools: Massachusetts College of Agriculture, American College of Physical Training in Chicago, the University of Chicago, New York University, and City College of New York. He remained at none long enough to develop any disciplinary interest beyond its earliest stages.

In his own assessment of this pattern in his behavior, Toomer wrote that he spent his life seeking "an intelligible scheme . . . a sort of whole into which everything fits . . . a body of ideas which holds a consistent view of life and . . . enables one to understand as one does when he sees a map."[4] For a short time he thought he found it in socialism, then in Western literature and art, followed by the Gurdjieff philosophy, the words of the Holy Men of India, the Society of Friends, and dianetics, all in their turn. His search rewarded him with only brief moments of illumination and always ended in disappointment, for he never found the scheme he sought.

In 1919 creative literature held forth career possibilities for Jean Toomer, and he decided to become a writer. Surprisingly, he endured two years of frustrations in this pursuit. The breakthrough came in 1921 during a brief trip to the South. Two years later, as a direct result of this trip, he was able to publish *Cane*. In "Avey," one of the narratives of *Cane*, Toomer goes back six years and draws on his University of Wisconsin experience. Avey is the woman whom the narrator of the piece knew in his youth in Washington, D.C. He and his friends of that time tried, without success, to engage her affections while she was a young girl. Her indifference to the boys on the edge of manhood frustrated the narrator, so that when he went away to college, he made up his mind to forget her. He reasoned that since she was too "lazy" to further her education, such action toward her on his part was justified, and he later compared her "slovenly" behavior to that of a cow's: "Hell! she was no better than a cow," he wrote, and went on to say: "I was certain that she was a cow when I felt an udder in a Wisconsin stock-judging class."[5] But he was not able to forget her, even though her attitude toward him continued to fill him with chagrin. Finally, he admitted to himself that he cared deeply for her and that she meant more to him than the "ambitious" women whom he met at the university. "The girls up that way, at least the ones I knew, havent got the stuff: they dont know how to love. Giving themselves completely was tame beside just the holding of Avey's hand."[6]

Although "Avey" is not an analysis of Jean Toomer's experiences in Madison, and the references to the place are slight, the commentary is noteworthy. In the first instance Toomer recalls his intentions to study scientific agriculture at the University of Wisconsin; in the second he confirms that sexual attractions and activities were among the important concerns of college-age young people during the early part of this century. For purposes of evaluating Jean Toomer's career, it is also possible to say that the interest of an English teacher at the university in 1914 probably played an important role in fanning the flames that eventually burst forth in the splendid blaze of *Cane* and established him as a man of literature.

Although *Cane* was a success, by the time it was published, Toomer was no longer involved with literary art. The work had brought him applause and recognition, but it had also characterized him as a "Negro" writer, and this was extremely painful to him. This turn of events, which he seemed not to have anticipated, must have reactivated all the reservations that motivated "The First American" in 1914. He felt that literature, as a profession, had fallen short of fulfilling his expectations of it as a source of unity and harmony in the world for the individual and for all people in general. Consequently, he turned aside from that path, and in 1924 he became intensely involved with Georges Gurdjieff, an Eastern mystic, whose program promised internal harmony to all who followed its precepts. Toomer was not only a disciple of Gurdjieff; for many years he organized and directed Gurdjieff groups in different parts of the country, including Chicago's Gold Coast area.

Jean Toomer returned to Wisconsin in the summer of 1931, this time to a cottage outside of Portage. He spent his time conducting an intensive teaching session in the Gurdjieff philosophy. For two months a group of six people lived together in a farmhouse called Witt Cottage, which was owned by a woman by the name of Marion Kilbourn. Toomer later wrote about the experience, referring to it as the Cottage Experiment. The experiment was a miniature representation of those conducted at the Gurdjieff Institute in Fontainebleau, France. In their search for internal harmony, Gurdjieff disciples followed specific rules and performed specific activities. Toomer directed these activities in Portage.

During the session at Witt Cottage, the participants did all of the work that was necessary to living and to attaining spiritual growth. The cottage was near a lake and surrounded by woods, which gave the group the isolation it desired. They spent most of their time out-of-doors in order to get the full benefit of the air and sunlight. During the daytime they walked, swam, sunned, and played tennis and croquet. In the evenings they held serious discussions during and after supper. As Toomer and others involved in it described it later, it was a clean, healthy life—a combination of psychological effort and outdoor exercise. He wrote about it in "Portage Potential," one of his unpublished manuscripts.

> I threw myself vigorously into things and gave literally of my energies . . . I was building a world. I was creating a form. It was to be my

> own; and I was putting into it a quantity and quality of functional energy greater and finer than I had ever before experienced. I saw the cottage life as an entity, as a single living organism—at least as a potential one. Each of us was of its parts—and I aimed that we be functioning parts. Like an individual being it had a body and a psyche. But I was determined . . . that I would eliminate appearances, break up and reduce properties, correct mal-functions, energize functions and coordinate them for a doing which would produce results.[7]

One of the main ideas behind this kind of Gurdjieffian group experience was that each person should become fully aware of his or her self within the general situation. Each was responsible for helping others gain this awareness. The purpose was for each to eliminate the negative in the self and to build up whatever was good in the self. For instance, it was not possible in such a living situation for the participants to avoid irritating each other. Each person was responsible for trying to understand the cause and nature of the irritants and to work to eliminate them as much as possible. In time the tensions were supposed to relax so that people could understand and control their intolerance of others. "The experiences of the summer," wrote Toomer, "convinced me that the sharing of a common existence for purposes of self-development and group development was not only possible but fruitful."[8] A few years later, when he moved to Pennsylvania, he conducted another experiment, with the same goals, which lasted for several years. This was the "Mill House Experiment," but in this one the participants did not live together.

Among the people involved in the Witt Cottage experiment was Margery Latimer, a native Wisconsin writer who had roots that went back to New England and Anne Bradstreet. Toomer and Latimer first met in 1925, but a deep friendship did not develop between them until the summer of 1931. When the experiment was over, on October 30, 1931, they were married. Shortly after, they embarked on a trip which took them to New Mexico and California. In California Toomer worked on "Portage Potential" while he and his wife awaited the birth of their first child. For a long time before, Margery Latimer Toomer had imagined that giving birth was one of the most fulfilling experiences that a woman could have. During her pregnancy she wrote to her friend Meridel Le Seur that "the mystery of [this] new birth, the mystery of love [was] a new fusion." She noted that under ordinary life circumstances, one contained "all the deadly suffering . . . the being of the body . . . the reiterative dying . . . [and that] the new life [was]—a physical absolution—a baptism."[9]

Jean and Margery Toomer returned to Wisconsin for the birth of their child. They wanted the event to be the fullest experience and decided on a home birth. But complications developed, and when medical attention reached her it was too late. On August 16, 1932, Margery Toomer died while giving birth to a baby girl. The child was named Margery for her mother, and she remained in Wisconsin in the care of her maternal grandparents until Jean Toomer remarried in 1934.

In the story of Jean Toomer's life, Wisconsin holds a prominent and positive place. In 1914 the University of Wisconsin represented wide horizons to him. He was perhaps correct when he decided he did not want to be a farmer. Later events proved he had the talent and ability to be a great writer, and toward that end he received his encouragement at that university. Although he did not choose to make a permanent home in the state, he appears to have had one of the happiest personal periods of his life during the year he spent with Margery Latimer, and the daughter who survived her greatly enriched his life in the years that followed.

"Just Americans": A Note on Jean Toomer's Marriage to Margery Latimer

DANIEL P. MC CARTHY

Little is known and almost nothing has been written about Jean Toomer's abortive marriage to Margery Latimer in 1931. However, before the union ended with Margery's death in childbirth barely ten months later, it had raised a tremendous hue and cry against miscegenation that reverberated through a national magazine and produced a devastating effect on Toomer's already sagging literary career.

Much has been made of Toomer's vacillation between a white and a black identity,[1] and to many it seems incredible that the same man who wrote *Cane* in 1923 could have refused in 1930 to have his work included in an anthology of black poetry.[2] One critic, commenting on Toomer's contribution to the Harlem Renaissance, has described him as "a writer who passed briefly through Harlem on his way downtown and back permanently into the white world he had just left."[3] Toomer's rejection of his black identity, however, was much more than a simple denial of an unwanted heritage or a fervent attempt to "pass." Largely through the influence of the Gurdjieffian philosophy he came to embrace in the late 1920s, Toomer became an advocate of the "raceless" society. This became part of his vision for a "new" America, as he wrote in "Brown River, Smile":

> Thou, great fields, waving thy growth across the world,
> Couldst thou find the seed which started thee?
> Can you remember the first great hand to sow?
> Have you memory of His intention?
> . . . .
>
> It is a New America,
> To be spiritualized by each new American.[4]

The seed that was to fertilize the "new America" was, for Toomer, a race of citizens of mixed blood—European, Oriental, Negro, and Indian. It was this philosophy that was to lead Toomer, indirectly, into an interracial marriage and directly into a confrontation with an outraged white America.

Toomer first encountered the Gurdjieffian philosophy in 1924 while he was in Europe.[5] During the next few years he periodically attempted to expose various groups of friends and interested students to these new ideas. It was during one of these "sensitivity sessions," as they would no doubt be called today, that he met Margery Latimer. Darwin T. Turner gives the following account:

> In the summer of 1931 Toomer established a cottage in Portage, Wisconsin, where for two months he conducted an experiment in spiritual growth among a group of male and female followers of Gurdjieff. Toomer believed that he succeeded in helping his followers "realize" themselves. He was especially pleased with the assistance he gave to Margery Latimer, a talented writer who, Toomer felt, used her literary ability to shield herself from a world which she could not accept. . . . In 1931, he fell in love, and on October 20 married her.[6]

Margery Latimer has always been something of a nonentity in discussions of the marriage, and a closer look at her is overdue. Forgotten today, she was at that time a successful novelist whose reputation was rising swiftly. By 1930, though only thirty-one, she had published three well-received books. A contemporary critic had this appreciation to offer:

> Among the younger writers of Wisconsin none give greater promise of an eminent career in letters than Margery B. Latimer. And Miss Latimer's work is not wholly prospective. She had already secured a position among literary folk and recognition has come from far distant sections of the country. . . . Of her story called "The Family," included in her *Nellie Bloom and Other Stories*, the *New York Times*

> *Book Review* said: "It is one of the most important stories published in America in 25 years."[7]

Margery formed the nucleus of a literary circle at the University of Wisconsin that included such well-known figures as novelists Mark Schorer and August Derleth. Having achieved her own success, she acted as a patron for lesser-known writers, sending letters of introduction and support to publishers and magazine editors. That she enjoyed a certain modicum of national fame is demonstrated by her obituary in the *New York Times*, which described her as "a young novelist of note."[8] That she was a strong-willed, though overly romantic, young woman will be seen below.

The marriage began happily and uneventfully, and the couple left Portage for Carmel, California. It is unknown as to whether or not the wedding was held secretly, but it did not become public knowledge for four months, and then only as the result of another scandal. The Gurdjieffian session in Portage had included some activities that were then unacceptable to American morality. *Time* magazine later described the occasion: "All [of Toomer's party] slept in two rooms on cots, following the Gurdjieff method, made themselves uncomfortable to break down thought and body habits, and sat around nights discussing their reactions."[9] One man apparently took part in the experiment without his wife's knowledge or consent, and she consequently sued him for divorce, claiming adultery. The publicity ensuing from the court case brought both the experiment and the Toomers's marriage to local and, subsequently, national attention. Although no laws had been broken, a backlash of race-oriented reactions set in.

Toomer did little to calm the troubled waters. When questioned about his marriage, he responded with arguments spun from his Gurdjieffian views. *Time* quoted one of his most inflammatory statements:

> Americans probably do not realize it, but there are no racial barriers any more, because there are so many Americans with strains of Negro, Indian and Oriental blood. As I see America, it is like a great stomach into which are thrown the elements which make up the life blood. From this source is coming a distinct race of people. They will achieve tremendous works of art, literature and music. They will not be white, black or yellow—just Americans.

This was, of course, a red rag to the bull. Toomer was quite right in supposing that Americans did not "realize" that all "racial barriers" had magically disappeared, and instead of quelling the uproar, he intensified it. Life must have become sheer hell for the Toomers by this time. Margery wrote to Richard Johns, the editor of the short-lived but distinguished literary journal *Pagany*, and her anguish fairly leaps from the page:

> Since reading, on top of everything, the vulgar article in *Time* about us, I feel more than ever before that I must try to do something. Would you care to use the enclosed essay or review in *Pagany?* I have been so misquoted and we have both been so vulgarized that to have this positive appreciation printed, even if the mass of people does not see it, would mean much—much—to me.[10]

The above-mentioned essay, intended to offset the diatribe that was run in *Time*, was not published and, unfortunately, is not extant. But it is easy to see why she felt a reply was needed. The article, sneeringly entitled "Just Americans," was indeed "vulgar." The opening lines of the piece establish a tone that was sustained throughout: "No Negro can legally marry a white woman in any Southern State. But Wisconsin does not mind, nor California." The article went on to describe, in lurid detail, Toomer's Gurdjieffian session in Portage (3), and to quote Toomer's view of American race relations (3). Through innuendo and self-serving quotations, *Time* was able to present the marriage as little more than a sordid and immoral adventure.

If Margery was hurt, Toomer was bewildered. He attempted to explain his position in "Caromb," a short novel which Turner describes as full of "the artistic defects which might be expected in a hastily written apologia written by a man who did not fully understand why there was any scandal."[11] "Caromb" stayed in manuscript, rejected by Toomer's publisher as "interesting" but "formless." It is not surprising, in light of Toomer's conception of race, that he saw nothing extraordinary about his marriage and did not know what to apologize for, or to whom. His worldview put him, as Fullinwider has commented, "completely at cross-purposes with the whole thrust of American intelligence of the 1920s."[12] He took the opportunity that his notoriety gave him to proselytize, and his beliefs were unpopular, as well as misunderstood. America was not in the market for what many, then and now, would call "mongrelization."

The Toomers's marriage, and the scandal, came to an abrupt end with Margery's death, an event which has been but briefly mentioned elsewhere. A recent letter from one of her old friends, Mark Schorer, to another, Richard Johns, gives this detailed account, which also serves to shed more light on Mrs. Toomer's character:

> But you are right about Margery Latimer. I had just come east from Wisconsin in the autumn of 1929, and she was my friend, the first writer I had known. She encouraged me, and wisely, saying "Specify, Specify!" (Which she didn't always do herself, as I now remember.) You ask about her death. It was in childbirth. She had a real country notion that a child should be born in its house, not in a hospital. She insisted on this in her little town, Portage, Wisconsin. She died of hemorrhages because adequate and immediate medical assistance was not at hand. The child was a daughter, and I'm ashamed that I can't tell you what happened to her. The father was Jean Toomer, a negro [*sic*] poet, and I can't remember if he was her husband or lover. I can check on these details if they are of importance to you. I do remember going to her funeral. She was buried on the top of a hill outside that town, a hill covered with wild flowers and weeds, and it was very windy.[13]

So ended the brief but stormy marriage of Jean Toomer and Margery Latimer. Toomer, gone from the public eye, drifted into the obscurity from which he has been but recently rescued. His continual inability to publish his works is too well known to need discussion here, but critics agree that it was the unpopularity of his ideas, not the quality of his writing, that kept him out of print. The notoriety of his first marriage, I suggest, also did much to hurt his career by branding him a radical and a miscegenist, in the eyes of both publishers and the reading public. He was labeled pariah and remained so to the end of his life. It is unfortunate that no one, in the twenties or in later years, listened to Margery Latimer's plea to the interviewer from *Time* magazine: "You do not protest against a person's religion . . . why should you judge people by their color? I and hundreds of others have taken my husband for what he is—a brilliant man."

Another Note on Toomer's Marriage to Margery Latimer

MERLE A. RICHMOND

Mr. Daniel P. McCarthy's "Note on Jean Toomer's Marriage to Margery Latimer" (*CLA Journal*, XVII, 4 [June, 1974], 474–79) is too interesting a comment to permit a factual error* to pass unnoticed, lest future interest in the subject should perpetuate it.

He states: "It is unknown as to whether or not the wedding was held secretly, but it did not become public knowledge for four months . . ." (476). The point would be of small importance in itself except that the subsequent furor about miscegenation might invite unfortunate inferences from any ambiguity about the public nature of the wedding.

It certainly was no secret in Portage, Wisconsin, where the wedding took place. The *Wisconsin State Register* (Portage) for October 30, 1931, announces the date, time, and place of the ceremony, by whom

*Editor's Note: "Another Note on Toomer's Marriage to Margery Latimer" first appeared in the *CLA Journal*, 18 (December 1974): 300, as "Jean Toomer and Margery Latimer" in the LETTERS TO THE EDITOR section. After reading Mr. Daniel P. McCarthy's article in the June 1974 issue of the *CLA Journal*, Miss Richmond wrote to correct "a factual error" and to add a few more interesting details pertaining to the marriage.

the rites are to be performed, the reception to follow, and the couple's plans following the wedding. The November 6, 1931, issue of the same newspaper, subsequent to the ceremony, has a detailed description of the occasion. An example: "For the ceremony Miss Latimer wore a black velvet gown and black galyak hat. Her bouquet was of yellow roses. She had as matron of honor Mrs. Samuel Rodgers of Madison, who appeared in green velvet gown and hat and carried a bouquet of pale lavender chrysanthemums." The story contains, as well, the names of the best man, the ushers, and those assisting at the reception, and a long list of guests, local and out-of-town, and concludes: "Many friends of the bridal couple attended the ceremony and reception to wish them 'bon voyage.' A large group also showered them with farewells at the train last evening as they left for Chicago."

Jean Toomer's Contributions to *The New Mexico Sentinel*

TOM QUIRK AND
ROBERT E. FLEMING

The 1930s were as cruel to Jean Toomer as the 1920s had been kind. During the earlier of the two decades, Toomer had found his niche in American literature after years of drifting about in search of a purpose in life. In the early twenties, besides publishing poems and short stories in such varied journals as *Broom*, *The Crisis*, *The Double Dealer*, *The Liberator*, *The Little Review*, and *Opportunity*, Toomer assured himself of a lasting reputation with the publication of *Cane* (1923). The final half of the decade continued auspiciously as editors accepted several poems and stories, as well as a play.

But as Darwin Turner has observed, there were weaknesses even in *Cane* which made Toomer's future uncertain.[1] By the end of the 1920s, Toomer's career had run down—partly because of his new fascination with Gurdjieff—and the author was unable to interest publishers in his literary and philosophical projects. The thirties brought forth little of significance besides the privately published *Essentials* (1931) and one major poem: "The Blue Meridian."[2]

One receptive outlet for Toomer's writings during the late 1930s was a feature entitled, "New Mexico Writers" in the *New Mexico Senti-*

nel, a weekly newspaper published in Albuquerque, New Mexico. Such distinguished New Mexicans as Witter Bynner, Erna Fergusson, Paul Horgan, and Frieda Lawrence served as associate editors of the page. Toomer had visited New Mexico as early as 1925, when a Taos patron, Mabel Dodge Luhan, had invited him to the state to lecture on Gurdjieff.[3] He married his second wife, Marjorie Content Toomer, in Taos in 1934, and the Toomers revisited the state in 1940.[4] Toomer apparently maintained a correspondence with some New Mexico writers, for from July 1937 to July 1938, six contributions by Toomer were printed in the *Sentinel*, ranging from a brief letter of encouragement to the editors to a poem hitherto unlisted in bibliographies of Toomer's works. Darwin Turner lists three contributions to the *New Mexico Sentinel*, two under 1937 and one under 1941, giving no specific dates.[5] The *Sentinel* files, however, yield four contributions from 1937 and two from 1938.[6] The "New Mexico Writers" page was dropped by the *Sentinal* after publication of the January 1, 1939, issue.

Toomer's 1937 contributions take the form of an occasional column in the *Sentinel* under the boxed heading "Meditations," which he signs, "Nathan Jean Toomer," a compromise between the familiar name under which his literary work had been published and the name with which he had been christened—Nathan Eugene Toomer. The first column is devoted mainly to a dialogue between J. T. and P. B. The former is obviously Toomer, while the latter may well be the spirit of Toomer's grandfather, P. B. S. Pinchback, with whom the author had conflicts aplenty (if not exactly dialogues of this sort) during his formative years.

J. T. and P. B.

By Nathan Jean Toomer

Now, my dear P. B., it is time for the worm to turn ever so slightly. For years I have listened to you as you told me of my duty to the world of my time. The gist of your harangue was this—Get into it, take off your coat, roll up your sleeves, and get into the fight. I have listened attentively. I have done so because, in the first place, I too feel and even realize that I have a responsibility to the world I live in, and because in the second place your view reflects the view that is just contrary to my own understandings. Each time you talked I felt new incentive to do my job in my terms—terms you would neither understand nor approve of. Moreover, through you as a particularized expression of it, I gained insight into the workings of the type you represent. So far, so good. Now, however, I feel called upon to ask you a simple question. It is this.

Suppose you happened to be outside of an insane asylum. As you walked past, the inmates caught a glimpse of you and clamored that you must come in and do just as they were doing. What would your position be?

"I'd feel it was my duty to help them."

No, that is not the answer to my question. I did not say they asked you to help them. I said they clamored for you to come in and do just as they were doing.

"I'd refuse."

Exactly. Now suppose that, finding that you would not come in and do as they were doing, one of the more sane of them bethought himself to ask your help.

"I'd respond."

Even though you realized that in going in, you ran the risk of being swamped by their insanity and yourself becoming one of them, one no longer in a position to help, but now simply an added one in need of help?

"I would."

Very well. Suppose, now, that in you went, retained your senses, but soon realized that the help they asked of you was not at all in terms of what should be done if they were to become sane and free, but only in terms of the very illnesses which had reduced them to their wretched condition. What then would you do?

"Dissuade them from their obsession. Persuade them to the truth."

The truth, you say. Now at last we agree. Let this henceforth be our common ground. But what of your shirt sleeves and getting into the fight? Would you consider it necessary to get into the fight with them in order to persuade them to the truth?

"It depends upon what fight. If I fought with them, I'd simply become a brother in insanity. No, I'd fight for them."

Against whom?

"Against whoever and whatever tried to keep them insane and prevent them from regaining sanity."

And would you try to do it in your way, the way for which you were qualified, or would you imitate some one else, try to take on some other way at which you were not specially qualified?

"My own, of course."

P. B., you are exceptionally sensible today.[7]

Appended to the dialogue in this same column are two shorter pieces, "Make Good" and "Lines." The former is particularly interesting, since it seems to suggest that Toomer was then working on a book and had projected a series of additional books.

Make Good

Will I then devote this book and the next books to giving due content and meaning to this popular American precept? It seems that I will. For it seems that this phrase covers all that I would do and have men do—make good.

It must be useful to be good for the body and the being. It must be beautiful to be good for the emotions and the spirit. It must be true to be good for the mind and the soul. Thus to make good is to eliminate waste, to cleanse of impurity, to purify, and perfect. It is to make ourselves of use, it is to perceive and create Beauty, it is to grasp and reveal Truth. To make good is to make a good man, to develop unto completion the whole human being as human being. So I will dedicate my life to making good.

Make good. Make good use. Make effort to make good use. Make effort to make good use in order to Be of Use to one's own being and to beings of every kind wherever in the universe.

Lines

Minor artists but decorate the pit with pictures of the pit.

Major artists place in the pit pictures of the free world which they have glimpsed and would have others see, as testaments of what is possible.[8]

In his meditations for August, Toomer dwelt on two prejudices which had affected his own life—prejudice against his race and that against his apparent purposelessness. These two brief essays (the second echoing some of the imagery of "Blue Meridian," lines 52–55) offer a meaningful glimpse into Toomer's thought during the thirties.

FROM A FARM

Two mares have colts at about the same time. The "families" are kept separate. One mare and her offspring are in one wing of the barn, the other mare and her offspring in another wing. The colts grow up and soon are old enough to be let out. They are taken to pasture and each sees the other for the first time. They are startled. They keep their distance and stand looking, each curious, each frightened. Neither has ever seen a colt before!

* * *

A horse has a sore leg. A child refers to it as "the sore horse." So the children of the world refer to a man who has a black skin as a "black man," to a man who lives in China as a "Chinaman," to a person who has committed some felony as a ["]criminal," to a man who writes as a "writer," etc. These labels which should refer to fractions but which we assume to cover wholes! True enough, we need a reform of language. But the first truth is that we who misuse language must ourselves be reformed.

One leg of the world is sore. Do we call it the "sore world"? One lung of a man is disintegrating. Do we not call him a "consumptive"? What more proof be needed that we, the parents and grandparents, are still children in our minds? There is indeed a child in our minds. Adult is only in our words.

Peas About to Pod

Below a certain level of development, the social career uses the essence. Above this level, the essence uses the social career. Those human beings who have outgrown the first stage but have not yet developed into the second stage, give signs of their inner condition by not wanting ready-made careers, yet not being able to make their own essential careers. Dissatisfied with what the world is doing, they are also dissatisfied with what they try to do. They are restless, therefore. They try this, they try that. Their potentialities are uneasy. Into their restlessness come particles of divine discontent. Of course they give the impression of being unstable. People sometimes form the opinion of them that they'll never amount to anything. Within themselves they often are baffled, sometimes in despair; but underlying all moods and states is an unshakable certainty which they cannot explain to themselves. They know something, yet cannot tell precisely what it is. They know they are right, yet often feel they are wrong. They have values which seem strange to the ordinary world. They quit what others would continue. They start what others would never attempt. Until they find their place and function they are "bad bets" from the usual point of view. Employers who "hire" them will lose them, unless the employment be essential. Once placed all they seem to lack shows itself more splendidly than in other men. Steady, responsible, firmly centered, they move with accelerated integration and direction straight towards the essential and complete development of themselves and corresponding contributions to mankind.[9]

Toomer's philosophical vein surfaces in his brief column published a week later.

"Evil"

The root of all evil is not money but scarcity. This revision of an old saying is accepted by the contemporary mind. We of today know that money itself is not evil. It is but an instrument, good, bad or indifferent according to how it is used or misused. Accurately speaking, nothing "out there" is evil. If evil exists at all it exists in us, the living human beings of this planet; and our "evil" is obviously not religious or metaphysical, it is psychological, it is simply wrong functioning. Through wrong functioning we misuse science, religion and art as well as finance and politics, and by this misuse of our higher instruments we make them as harmful as misused money. I would, as you see, locate "evil" where it actually exists, namely, in me and you, in so far as we function wrongly.[10]

Prejudice is again the focus of "Meditations" for November, as Toomer repeats his injunctions against condemning a person on the basis of one unfavorable property. Obviously his intention here is not to condemn racial prejudice alone, but any prejudice.

A Skunk Used as an Example

Do you dislike the skunk? Or do you dislike something in him when it comes out of him? The answer is obvious. No one dislikes the entire skunk. Some people are even fond of skunks, having them for pets. What we dislike is a certain property in him, put there by Nature as a means of protection, when this property manifests in our vicinity.

So then. Do you dislike the man? Or do you dislike something in him when it comes out of him? Again the answer is obvious. No one dislikes the entire man, be this man a second person or oneself. Most of us, in point of fact, like people. We hate a man only when some one image of something believed to be in him, arouses our negative emotions and obsesses us.

What we dislike—and we will say that in this case we have real cause for disliking it—is a certain property in him—falseness, or conceit, or dishonesty, etc. Once having seen this property, we dislike it even when it is not manifesting, because we know it is there. When it becomes active and comes out, we actively dislike it all the more.

But what? How do we act with respect to our dislikes of the property in the skunk? Sometimes we hold our nose and run away. In order to get away from the smell we have to get away from the entire skunk. We identify the entire animal with the ordor [*sic*], we identify (and reduce) the whole to the part. Thus blind, we may even kill the creature in order to get rid of the stench. Our dislike of the property spreads to a consuming hatred of a living creature, and we kill it to rid ourselves of an odor, not disagreeable to it, natural to it, disagreeable only to ourselves at the time because we happen to be in the skunk's vicinity. Is this sane or insane?

Be it skunk or man, we cannot guarantee sane and decent behavior towards him unless we effectively discriminate between the whole and the parts, between the living creature and the properties in him, between our likes and dislikes and his reality, and realize through and through that the property is not the man, that the smell is not skunk, that our opinions and emotions are not the reality of that skunk, of that man, of that woman, of that race, of that religion, of that being.

Not the most vicious property in a man warrants our becoming insane. Each and every property, existing or manifesting in ourselves or in others, should be regarded as an opportunity for making use of it in our effort to discriminate between the property and the man, and to make ourselves act in accordance with the total reality. Just this effort alone, if made by all of us on every occasion, would insure the recreation of inner and outer relationships by breaking down the chief disjective mechanisms and preparing men for contacts with each other on the basis of feeling-subjects to feeling-subjects.[11]

Toomer began 1938 with a poem, apparently his first since "Blue Meridian," which had been published two years before, although it had been composed much earlier. As in certain lines of that earlier poem, where he invokes Indian dancers, priests, the Shalako (masked dancers representing deities), and the Koshare (sacred clowns), Toomer uses Pueblo dancers as symbols of a people more closely attuned to the universe than their fellow men, and he goes on to suggest that the landscape and architecture of rural New Mexico contribute to his feeling of unity with the universe.

Imprint for Rio Grande

The Indians beat drums, sing and dance to assert themselves as
human beings (or to surrender themselves?) in the vast universe
that comes to earth in New Mexico.
Perhaps, too, they have quiet rituals which swing the body-mind to
acquiescence, that the faculties the outer world knows nothing

of, may gain the wakefulness which relates a man to higher worlds.

When I leave places that men call great and return to the State of which I am curiously native, I beat thoughts against the drum of mind, sing music that never leaves my instruments, and dance without gestures to assert myself (or to surrender myself?) in that same universe that comes to the same earth.

There are some things so basic that they are seldom mentioned between men. Yet they come out now and again, and it is one of these I honestly inscribe upon that ether, the memory of earth, above the Rio Grande, from Taos and above Taos, to Santa Fe and below Santa Fe.

There is an Exile in me, and sometimes I am him, and whem I am, the mountains of the Southwest, each cliff and peak, all ridges and even the flat lands arise from an ancient deluge that I may be engulfed again, or crushed, or driven out.

You there who have seen me but did not realize the Exile, who have seen this body of a man and a human mask walking plazas in Taos and Santa Fe and the main street of Espanola, how could you know my feeling that the earth and all her Nature, that heaven and all its gods were gunning for cosmic outlaws, you and I being of the driven band?

Adobe walls are friendly to the touch because hands put them there, but I recall times when I was my exile in New Mexico, when even within these walls, and friends around, and pinon burning in the fireplace, the walls exposed me to at-one-ment or extinction.

And there is a Being in me. Sometimes, though more rarely, I am him, and when I am, there is such marvel in the Rio Grande, such ecstacy [*sic*] of inner sun to outer sun, or inner breath to the blazing winds, that I and everyone seem re-born upon that ark which still rides high, straight above the mesas of all sunken lands.

I remember one twilight I walked into Santa Fe, and you were walking with me, but did not know it—or did you? You, the beings of many people who have no names to distinguish you as on plazas. We moved together, descending as from a hill, yet ascending in spiral, and came upon the essence of pinon as it arose [my reading] from the houses into an air so marvelous that even Being took it in and was enhanced.

So I know that the struggle of Being and Exile, the central contest which no man resolves until he gives utter allegiance to the radiant, can be won and celebrated by mended instruments, as that

> of us which belongs to it rises, and blends with the vast universe that comes to earth in New Mexico.[12]

Following the publication of "Imprint for Rio Grande," his most ambitious project for the *Sentinel*, Toomer contributed no further literary or philosophical pieces, although he did praise the literary page in a letter printed in a later issue, saying that the page had "encouraged things that might not otherwise have been written" and "made possible the reading of things that might not otherwise have been read. . . ."[13] These remarks suggest that Toomer might have found the *Sentinel* both a market for items already written and a spur to cause him to write new pieces. "Imprint for Rio Grande" in particular, because of its many local references, seems to have been tailored for publication in the *Sentinel*.

Without exaggerating the importance of the material found in the *Sentinel*, it is obvious that it can be significant in leading scholars to a better understanding of Toomer during a period when he was publishing little. Not only are there biographical insights to be gained from the philosophical columns, but perhaps from smaller clues as well: Does his resumption of the name Nathan (his father's first name) indicate that Toomer had come to terms with the memory of the father who had deserted him and his mother when Toomer was only a baby? Does his use of P. B. in the dialogue suggest a mellowing of his memories of his autocratic grandfather? Certainly the fact that Toomer published "Imprint for Rio Grande" proves that he had not entirely forsaken art for philosophy, and while the poem is not as ambitious as "Blue Meridian," it does stand on its own merits as a work of art.

Jean Toomer—
The Veil Replaced

MABEL M. DILLARD

With the publication of *Cane* in 1923, Jean Toomer was recognized as a very promising young author; among Negro authors, he was considered one of the best. By 1928, however, Toomer was facing the Negro and his problems differently. A lengthy discussion of his views of the problems of the racial crisis, such as that in America, is contained in his essay "Race Problems and Modern Society," in *Problems of Civilization*, edited by Baker Brownell of Northwestern University. Toomer, at the time of publication of this article, had been enjoying popularity as a philosopher and lecturer in Chicago, and his opinions were esteemed by many critics. In this essay Toomer views the problem of race in America, not as a Negro, but as one who looks at the whole issue of race objectively. Taking the United States as a sufficiently representative example of modern society, he sees the causes of what is termed race prejudice as economic and political. He maintains that the term *race*, rather than applying to a clearly delimitable, homogeneous biological group, is rather a social classification and a confused and uncertain subject. "A race, it turns out, is a group of people that we treat as if they were one. You belong to a certain race, if you feel yourself to be a member, and if others treat you as if you were," he says.[1] He further states that race is a matter of public opinion, and not a question that can be easily settled by science, and that race problems are actually psychological and sociological in cause and in character. Toomer contends that both Negroes and whites are drawing lines between their own cultures and are, at the same time, following cultural patterns that "make the drawing of distinctions supposedly based on skin color or blood composition" more and more ridiculous. He concludes by saying that the solution of race problems can never be effected until there is a "fusion of racial and cultural factors in America, in order that the best possible stock and culture may be produced."[2]

Toomer was developing democratic ideas about the existence of races in America. He had already begun to see that his work was being judged (as well as being rejected) on the basis of race, and he therefore decided to devote his literary talents to an autobiography or perhaps a novel to promote an idea which he hoped would dissolve some of America's racial lines of demarcation. Waldo Frank, his longtime friend and confidante, had told Toomer that he did not write as a Negro but that he accepted his races naturally, just as any other American. This is precisely the manner in which Toomer had wanted to write—as an artist, not as a Negro artist. Toomer had said in 1931 in *Essentials*, "I am of no race, I am of the human race."[3] He reaffirmed this position later in a letter concerning the inclusion of his work in the category of "Negro literature":

> I am of the human race, a man at large in the human world, preparing a new race. This is an accurate statement of my position as it regards race. I am disassociating my name and self from racial classifications, as I believe that the real values of life necessitates it. This is my stand not only for myself, but for all Americans and for people in general.[4]

This idea, that all races of America have been fused into one race, is the ultimate position that Toomer assumed and to which he devoted his final literary efforts.

His ideas on the formation of a new race in America have been incorporated into two poems, "Brown River, Smile" and "Blue Meridian." "Brown River, Smile" appeared in *Pagany* in 1932 and was later expanded into the longer poem and called "Blue Meridian," which was published in *The New Caravan* (1936), an anthology edited by Alfred Kreymborg, Lewis Mumford, and Paul Rosenfeld.

In "Blue Meridian" Toomer visualized a "new America" which separates the old one that has been divided by the separation of men into races or national groups. Toomer says:

> It is a new America
> To be spiritualized by each new American,
> To be taken as a golden grain
> And lifted, as the wheat of our bodies,
> To matters uniquely man.[5]

He believes that Americans must outgrow the unbecoming and enslaving behavior associated with our prejudices and preferences which have impeded the progress of the nation. Americans and all countrymen must recognize that they obey the same laws and have the same goals and objectives and that all mankind possesses an "essence identical in all." Toomer visualizes America as a land in which "wave after wave" of European races have joined to grow towns on the rich soil of America; these towns, however, after a "swift achievement," have given way to a world of "crying men and hard women, a city of goddam and Jehovah, / Baptized in finance."[6]

Echoing the ideas of D. H. Lawrence, with whom he was closely associated while in New Mexico and California, Toomer deplores the statement that bloods of men in America cannot be mixed and that men have not been able to experience "birth above the body." Lawrence had maintained that modern men and women no longer experienced true communion with one another because of the death drive of civilization and that death of the ego-self and a resurrection of the bodily self were needed. Toomer pursues a similar theme in "Blue Meridian," that modern civilization has been responsible for the chaotic condition of the present-day world. He believes that a new people for whom America is waiting will throw off the separateness that has developed because of the different waves of races that have come to America.

> When the Spirit of mankind conceived
> A New World in America, and dreamed
> The human structure rising from this base,
> The land was as a vacant house to the new inhabitants,
> A vacuum compelled by Nature to be filled.
> Spirit could not wait to time-select,
> Weighing in wisdom each piece,
> Fitting each right thing into each right place,

But had to act, trusting the vision of the possible,
Had to bring vast life to this vast plot,
Drawing, in waves of inhabitation,
All the peoples of the earth,
Later to weed out, organize, assimilate.
And thus we are—
Gathered by the snatch of accident,
Selected with the speed of fate,
The alien and the belonging,
All belonging now,
Not yet made one and aged.[7]

"I would give my life," says the poet of Toomer's poem, to see the words "understanding, conscience, and ability" inscribed upon the life of everyone's consciousness so that all who wish might be able to "unbend dreams." He reminds the reader that lives of Americans are blighted by "mistakes and hates" that rush out of the past, blinding and sweeping.

The "pioneers and puritans," the poet says, who have passed on to us our legacy were themselves indentured; they have condemned those whom they subjugated to "Fill space and pass time/ Within a prison system." And he adds:

Nor can we eat, though food is here,
Nor can we breathe, though the universe is air,
Nor can we move, though the planet speeds,
Nor can we circulate, though Nature flows,
Nor can we love and bear love's fruit
Though we are living and life is everywhere.[8]

"Americans," he continues, "must outgrow themselves and their old places" and fix the "symbol of universal man" as their center of gravity. The poet's final plea is to "uncase all the races" from the "unbecoming and enslaving behavior" and to eliminate "prejudices and preferences," for, he says, all mankind is of the human race:

Uncase, unpod whatever impedes, until,
Having realized pure consciousness of being,
Sensing, feeling and understanding
That we are beings,
Co-existing with others in an inhabited universe,
We will be free to use rightly with reason
Our own and other human functions.[9]

The final section of the poem contains a narrative in which the poet relates how he, who had been praised and honored by the public, was attacked by public scavengers who had found a "river flowing backward into its source," obviously a reference to the ancestry of the poet. He tells us:

> I held a fair position as men rate things,
> Even enviable—
> I could taste flavors in a grain of sand,
> My eyes saw loveliness,
> And I learned to peal in the wind,
> In short, I was a lucky fellow,
> People shook my hand, said nice things,
> And sometimes slapped me on the back;
> Curious, then, that I, of all people,
> In the month of the nasty mouth,
> Should have found myself caught
> In a backbay leased by public and private scavengers;
> Such was the case—but I found
> A river flowing backward to its source.[10]

The poet concludes that the "new people" of America will mix their bloods, that they will suffer and create and "live in body," and that no man will be branded as a slave or a peon. The African races and the great red race will join with the waves of races from Europe and "aid the operation of the cosmos":

> We who exist today are the new people
> Born of elevated rock and lifted branches,
> A race called the Americans—
> Not to call this name but to live the reality,
> Not to stop at it, but to respond to man;
> And we are the old people; we are witnesses
> That behind us there extends
> An unbroken chain of ancestors, linking us
> To all who ever lived and will live;
> Of millions of fathers through a million years
> We are the breathing receptacles.[11]

The poet has faith that modern man will triumph over the "prejudices and preferences" which have been practiced in the past. The black and the white, the people of the East and the West, will all join to give to the "blue man," who represents those who have struggled through the ages to give rise to a new people.

This dream of a world in which all racial barriers would be eliminated represents the culmination of Toomer's views on race. Harassed by "public scavengers," as he called those who trace an individual's ancestry back to its sources, Toomer adopted the view that a new race had developed in America. This race, he said, could best exist in a new world which disregards racial ties.

"Blue Meridian" incorporates Toomer's final statement of his theory of the racial composition of America. It contains his plea that he be accepted as an American author and that his work be judged on its own intrinsic merits. This poem, which appeared in 1936, seems to be his last published creative work of consequence. In his earliest writing, he had attempted to treat Negro life as it existed in America as an integral part of the historical pattern of America. Then, he had found his identity with the Negro race and had satisfied his own emotional needs through writing about Negroes. But in time he expressed the belief that a literary artist should not limit his work's subject matter to any one group, in his case, the Negro race. He did not want his work to be labelled as "Negro literature." He insisted that literature ought to be on the plane of art and intelligence and that an author's racial identity ought not be considered when his work was evaluated.

It was useless for Toomer to try to disassociate his name from the Negro race. His singular success with *Cane* and his inclusion in discussions of works by Negro American authors could never be forgotten. His attempts to deny the existence of the Negro race in America as an entity led him into obscurity. Toomer lost contact with the world of reality. Rather than confine his literary endeavors to the literature of the Negro group, Toomer developed a new style, a half-convincing style that bordered on the psychological and the mystical. His later work was unconvincing. The promise that was shown by *Cane* was never fulfilled.

And Another Passing

DARWIN T. TURNER

A man died in a rest home near Philadelphia on March 30 of this year [1967]. There have been no editorials in newspapers, no reminiscences in magazines. Probably few knew the name when they read the brief obituary in his hometown paper. He deserved more. In 1923 he was the most promising of them all.

Editors of slick, little magazines begged for his stories and poems. A few years later, otherwise rational friends prophesied that he might be the next Messiah.

He was Jean Toomer. Actually, he was born *Nathan Eugene Toomer*, but, teased with the vanity of youth, he gave himself a French-sounding name. That is the way he was.

He was the grandson of P. B. S. Pinchback, the only self-proclaimed Negro to govern a southern state. (He served briefly as acting governor of Louisiana, was twice elected to Congress and twice denied his seat. But that's another story.) As a youth he searched not for identity but for the mission leading to the greatness he thought predestined. Agriculture, physical education, sociology, psychology, socialism, atheism—he tried them all with the frenzy of a secretary shopping for a hat during lunch hour.

In 1922 he seemed to have found it. In Georgia, where he worked briefly as an acting principal, Toomer found the content to match the style he had practiced for two years. In Georgia, in the Negro, he found his heritage. Inspired, he wrote the stories and poems later collected into *Cane* (1923), one of the most brilliant works ever written by an American Negro. In lyric lines he sketched haunting portraits of Negroes—especially southern Negro women—spiritually wounded in the conflict between human instinct and middle-class mores.

But *Cane*, which seemed a gate to glory, was only an oasis in the wilderness where he sought his destiny. Refreshed, invigorated, encouraged, he plunged onward, into oblivion.

Entranced with the mysticism of a Russian prophet named Gurdjieff, Toomer undertook to lead America to a new spirituality. His voice no longer hummed the plaintive echo of the soul. Harshly it ridiculed. Pedantically, it droned religio-psycho-philosophies.

He wrote; editors refused. Seeking an excuse for failure, he blamed his identification as a Negro. He denied that he came from Negro ancestry. Still the editors refused.

Depression starved and drove away the wealthy and the willing who had listened hypnotized while he preached for Gurdjieff's word. Scandal chased Gurdjieff in search of less puritanical shores. Toomer's marriage was soured by rumors about free love, polluted by scandal about miscegenation, and was ended tragically by his wife's death in childbirth.

He continued to write and rewrite: two novels, two books of poems, a collection of stories, books of nonfiction, two books of aphorisms. But editors never again accepted a book for publication.

Jean Toomer wrote his own epitaph in a letter to a friend* in 1951.

> Perhaps . . . our lot on this earth is to seek and to search. Now and again we find just enough to enable us to carry on. I now doubt that any of us will completely find and be found in this life.

---

*Editor's Note: Although Professor Turner does not identify this "friend" here, he tells us, in footnote number 90 to "Jean Toomer: Exile," that he "was Floyd M. Sandberg, the son-in-law of Marjorie Content Toomer." See Darwin T. Turner, *In A Minor Chord: Three Afro-American Writers and Their Search for Identity* (Carbondale and Edwardsville: Southern Illinois University Press, 1971), p. 131.

Jean Toomer,
Waldo Frank,
Sherwood Anderson,
and Hart Crane

Jean Toomer and Waldo Frank: A Creative Friendship

MARK HELBLING

In 1919 Jean Toomer attended his first literary party. He recounts this experience in one of his several autobiographical sketches, "Outline of the Story of the Autobiography," and notes that of the people in attendance he was most impressed with Waldo Frank. "One man stood out. He [Waldo Frank] had a fine animated face and a pair of lively active eyes. I felt there could be something between him and himself. I didn't know his name, but I marked him."[1] Soon after, Toomer returned to his birthplace, Washington, D.C., determined to be a writer.

Although Toomer singled out Frank as a person of consequence, he did not initiate a correspondence until three years later. As he comments, "It was not until I had begun to read more and felt worthy of publication that I had the courage to write to Frank."[2] However, once they began corresponding they soon became friends. They toured the South together, read and criticized one another's work, and became, in fact, something like surrogate brothers.

In Frank, Toomer found the critical intelligence and resonance of imagination he felt so lacking in others. In a moment of sudden courage, Toomer expressed his profound admiration for Frank and speculated as to their ultimate and collective significance:

I wrote that letter, and then considered what I had written. And my mind sanctioned my impulse by concluding that it was much better . . . to say exactly and truly what I felt rather than skimp to the strictly commercial. I cannot think of myself as being separated from you in the dual task of creating an American literature, and of developing a public, however large or small, capable of responding to our creations. Those who read and know me, should read and know you. So far as the people here are concerned, the path to both of us is blocked somewhat by a rigid moral conventionalism. . . . And, of course, as yet they are some distance from your art perceptions. But, underneath, the soil is good rich brown, and should yield splendidly to our plowing."[3]

At the same time, Toomer was an admirer of Sherwood Anderson and in a series of letters attempted to express to Anderson the important influence he had upon his own creative imagination. But Toomer's enthusiasm soon waned and was replaced by a sense that Anderson was congenial company but a person who lacked the tenacity of mind and depth of imagination to meet fully Toomer's intellectual and imaginative needs. At the same time, Anderson's insistence that Toomer remain true to his "Negro self" and that such "selfhood" was his true strength as a writer annoyed Toomer and strengthened his conviction that Anderson was essentially of a limited sensitivity and intelligence. In a letter to Frank, Toomer wrote:

Sherwood Anderson has doubtless had a very deep and beautiful emotion by way of the Negro. Here and there he has succeeded in expressing this. But he is not satisfied. He wants more. He is hungry for it. I come along. I express it. It is natural for him to see me in terms of this expression. I see myself that way. But also I see myself expressing myself, expressing *Life*. I expect artists to recognize the circle of expression. When they don't, I'm not disappointed, I simply know that in this respect they are second-rate. That in this respect they differ but little from the mass which must narrow and caricature if it is to grasp the thing at all. . . . The range of his sensitivity, curiosity, and intelligence is not very wide. One's admiration suffers, but one's personal liking need not be affected by this.[4]

And Frank, fully supportive of Toomer's own self-perceptions, assured him that his strength as a writer was fully the opposite of Anderson's counsel:

When your letter came, relative to what Sherwood Anderson had written you, I was too busy to answer it. But I want to say now: that

> the day you write as a Negro, or as an American, or as anything but a human part of life your work will lose a dimension. How typical that is of most recognition; that effort immediately to limit you, to put you in a cubby hole and stick a label underneath. I intend, possibly above all else, in my introduction to *Cane* to point out the important thing which has at length released you to the creating of Literature is that you do not write as a Negro.[5]

To some extent Frank's encouragement and interest in Toomer sprang from a shared feeling of disappointment in Sherwood Anderson. In 1916 Frank expressed the central concerns and demands he would expect of himself and others engaged in the creation of an imaginative literature:

> We do not expect an Apocalypse here in America. Out of our terrifying welter of steel and scarlet, a design must come. This design, a vision of wholeness as well as a symbol of wholeness in aesthetic form, must reflect as well as transcend all the energy and turmoil of the prevailing social order. Such a literature would be the beginning, the awakening, to a new and heightened sense of individual and national purpose.[6]

And in the person and writing of Sherwood Anderson, Frank proclaimed just such a greatness to have emerged in the American landscape.

> The significance of Sherwood Anderson, whose first novel, "Windy McPherson's Son," has recently appeared, is simply that he has escaped these two extremes [Van Wyck Brooks' high-brow, low-brow dichotomy], that he suggests at last a presentation of life shot through with the searching color or truth, which is a signal for a native culture.[7]

And yet, eight years later, in a postscript to this earlier article, Frank publicly expressed his disappointment with Anderson:

> [Anderson] lacked the spiritual power to hoist himself wholly into a more essential plane: the plane in which the materials of the phenomenal world are recreated into pure aesthetic forms. He is indeed more of a transitional artist than Dreiser. His work doesn't belong to the category of powerful reflective artists, nor yet does it win a place among the creators of sheer dynamic form. . . . His writing remains still a harbinger, rather than an experience of Emerging Greatness.[8]

In a more private way Frank expressed to Toomer the feelings of disappointment he felt toward Anderson:

> The violent antipathy of Munson and Burke [toward Anderson] is a bit hard for me to understand, although I think they are quite right not to be *satisfied* with him. My history with Sherwood is so intricate and subtle that I wonder if I'll ever have the energy to tell it to you. . . . But though he has hurt me very deeply and disappointed me doubtless, I am as alive as ever to his merits and as warmly moved by his genius. The Sherwood Anderson that counts is a tender, sensitive, pure human being. There's a strain of the girl in his brash masculinity—and hence doubtless have come not alone his beauties but as well all the troubles and contradictions.[9]

Thus, Anderson functioned as a kind of outside voice which helped both Toomer and Frank to define their own philosophic and artistic concerns. Initially impressed, each found in Anderson an answer to what he felt to be an impasse in modern literature. However, each soon felt something lacking. Anderson ultimately seemed ineffectual, a person stranded on the periphery of a depth of meaning he had as yet only glimpsed and begun to express. But in their disappointment, as in their celebration, Frank and Toomer each sensed what further had to be accomplished. In this way Anderson served as a link between the two, for the confidences exchanged were an important part of their deepening intellectual and personal friendship.

Frank's demand for "a vision as well as a symbol of wholeness" constitutes the aesthetic and philosophical basis upon which both he and Toomer discovered their common concerns and their common impatience with Sherwood Anderson. In a letter to Toomer, Frank attempted to define the meaning of experience and the sense in which experience was an act of the imagination, a construction of emotional and mental perception:

> Experience to me is a fusion of elements and essential knowledge, expressed in human terms, or possessed in a symbol. The base of this knowledge man has at birth. And from that base, he must proceed to build a conceptual structure in the form of personal life, which shall be the equivalent of the initial base. Thus, the true experience is but a body of birth. To the building of this symbol, man deploys all manner of tools: events of mind and body, reflections, reactions, actions, emotions, analyses, thoughts. To these various elements, as they occur to him, he is wont to give the name experience: for he is too often unaware that he is inexorably dedicated to the task of uni-

> fying all of them with and into the personal body. Indeed, were it not for this unifying process, he would be unable to retain, to gauge, or to assimilate the variety of what he calls his "experience." The one impossibility for the human mind is incoherence, since mind is above all an active agent of coherence. The word experience should be confined to the *form of that fusion* of the initial reality of a man's life with the unitary synthesis of what he knows his life, at every instant and every act, to be.[10]

Frank's definition of *experience* is the basis upon which he and Toomer presumed they were linked in the "dual task of creating an American literature." It is a moral as well as an aesthetic perspective, a means by which to link art to life and to judge the art that one or another sought to create.

Throughout their correspondence each pondered the ultimate relationship between life and art. At the same time, in terms of their own immediate writing, each consulted the other as to questions of form and eagerly awaited the other's reply:

> Here's the problem I face in the new Box Seat. The old one was under-written for many reasons, first of all I think because I was consciously shut down on Dan Moore. I wanted him to be sensitive, but weak. The minute I started to rewrite, Dan expanded. I could leave him blurred in the second half of the first Box Seat. In the second, he had to live during the boxing scene. The question is, can this new energy, this greater strength slough off up the alley? Would the ego and consciousness of the New Dan permit such an ending? I didn't feel that they would. A less balanced Jean Toomer, for instance, would raise all sorts of hell. Well, Dan sees Muriel is going to accept the rose from Mr. Barry. She didn't accept it from Dan. To save himself, both in terms of his ego and in terms of his energy, Dan reads wisdom and godliness into the dwarf's face, and shouts him into a possible Jesus. This new energy is ragged, dynamic, perhaps vicious. I don't see how I can channel it into the first rounded form. (I could do this, perhaps: after letting him shout, I could then lead him up the alley. Is this necessary? What do you think?) But I'll weigh the whole thing carefully by your criticism.[11]

Through form, experience had meaning and meaning could be experienced. And it was their task to provide the form(s) that would give to man a "sense of unity and at-homeness with an exterior world [so as to] save him from becoming a mere pathetic feature of it."[12]

To a great extent, Toomer's relationship with others was affected by their linking of his creative genius with his racial identity. As seen, Sherwood Anderson strained Toomer's patience thereby. And Waldo Frank, in contrast, proved inspiring in that he encouraged Toomer to reject such thinking. As a consequence, Toomer viewed Frank as a source of strength and liberation. Recently, however, Darwin T. Turner has argued that Toomer's ambivalence regarding his racial identity crippled and ultimately destroyed his creative ability:

> What is surprising is that during the summer of 1923 Toomer suddenly protested vehemently against a racial identification which a few months earlier he had accepted casually as a matter of slight importance. One looks for a significant occurrence between March and July. And one finds it. In June, finally accepting Waldo Frank's long-standing invitation to come to Darien, Connecticut, Toomer fell in love with Margaret Naumber[*sic*], Frank's wife. . . . Actually, however, it is not important to know what caused him to change; what matters is that Jean Toomer's stature diminished after he repudiated his African ancestry and rejected Afro-American subjects.[13]

To some extent, Toomer's own commentary regarding *Cane* supports Turner's comments and helps to explain his subsequent literary interests:

> Life had me tied in a knot, hard and fast. Even in Georgia I was horribly conflicted, strained and tense—more so here. The deep releases caused by my experience there could not liberate and harmonize the sum of me. Cane was a lyric essence forced out with great effort despite my knotted state. People have remarked its simple easy-flowing lyricism, its rich natural poetry; and they may assume that it came to bloom as easily as a flower. In truth, it was born in an agony of internal tightness, conflict, and chaos. It is true that some portions, after I had cleared the way, came forth fluently. Thus Fern came out, not without effort, but with comparative ease soon after I had labored to write Kabnis. But the book as a whole was somehow distilled from the most terrible strain I have ever known. I had to use my very blood and nerves to project it. The feelings were in me, deep and mobile enough. But the creations of the forms were very difficult. During its writing, and after it, I felt that I had by sheer force emptied myself and given to that book my last blood. I felt drained and dry, with no immediate or prospective source of recreation. Harvest Song, better than any other of the book's content, gives an idea of my state at that time. After finishing Cane, I swore that I

> would never again write a book at that price. Thus when people truly moved by Cane and valuing it have suggested that I write another book like it, I have smiled my appreciation of their response, but have firmly shaken my head. When they, in all good faith, have advised me, as Sherwood Anderson did, to keep close to the conditions which produced Cane, I have denied them. Never again in life do I want a repetition of those conditions. And of equal importance is the fact that Cane is a swan song.[14]

In one sense Toomer's comments are not very exceptional. Similar statements have been made by numerous others recalling the strain of creative work and the fear of having exhausted their imaginative powers. But more than this, Toomer seems to give voice to an aspect of his identity that is more profound and perplexing than simply a concern for his ability to function as a creative artist. In a letter to *The Liberator*, in answer to questions regarding autobiographical information, Toomer noted:

> Within the last two or three years, however, my growing need for artistic expression has pulled me deeper and deeper into the Negro group. And as my powers of receptivity increased, I found myself loving it in a way that I could never love the other. It has stimulated and fertilized whatever creative talent I may contain within me. A visit to Georgia last fall was the starting point of almost everything of worth that I have done. I heard folk-songs come from the lips of Negro peasants. I saw the rich dusk beauty that I had heard many false accounts about, and of which, till then, I was somewhat skeptical. And a deep part of my nature, a part that I had repressed, sprang suddenly to life and responded to them.[15]

Thus, in writing *Cane*, Toomer was forced to confront the deepest part of his nature—his blackness—and the experience proved both exhausting and disillusioning. Never again would he probe so deeply to the core of his identity. But do such remarks fully bear out Turner's claims? I do not think so.

It is important to note that at this very time *Cane* was on the threshold of being published. In August 1923 Horace Liveright offered his thoughts as to the best way to publicize Toomer's novel: "Second, I feel that right at the very start there should be a definite note sounded about your colored blood. To my mind this is the real human interest value of your story and I don't see why you should dodge it."[16] Toomer's reply was immediate and angry:

> Your letter of August 29th on hand. First, I want to make a general statement from which detailed statements will follow. My racial composition and my position in the world are realities which I alone may determine. Just what these are, I sketched in for you the day I had lunch with you. As a unit in the social milieu, I expect and demand acceptance of myself on their basis. I do not expect to be told what I should consider myself to be. Nor do I expect you as my publisher, and I hope as my friend, to either directly or indirectly state that this basis contains any element of dodging. In fact, if my relationship with you is to be what I'd like it to be, I must insist that you never use such a word, such a thought, again. As a B[oni] and L[iveright] author, I make the distinction between my fundamental position and the position which your publicity department may wish to establish for me in order that *Cane* reach as large a public as possible. In this connection I have told you, I have told Messrs. Tobey and Schneider to make use of what ever [*sic*] racial factors you wish. Feature Negro if you wish, but do not expect me to feature it in advertisements for you. For myself, I have sufficiently featured Negro in *Cane*. Whatever statements I give will inevitably come from a synthetic human and art point of view, not from a racial one.[17]

Thus, just as Toomer was on the verge of becoming a published author, a public figure, he is told that the real interest of his work is the fact that his great-grandmother was black.[18] For years after, Toomer flared at the way in which *Cane* was received. In a letter to James Weldon Johnson, Toomer states: "My poems are not Negro poems, nor are they Anglo-Saxon or white or English poems. My prose, likewise. . . . I take this opportunity of noting these things in order to clear up a misunderstanding of my position which has existed to some extent ever since the publishing of *Cane*."[19]

At the same time, Toomer's reluctance to be categorized in any manner is linked to a rather casual attitude toward racial groups of any kind. In 1922, a full year before his "fateful" involvement with Margaret Naumburg, Toomer explained to Frank something of his family history and his attitude toward his diverse genealogy:

> My own life has been equally divided between the two racial groups. My grandfather, owing to his emphasis upon a fraction of Negro blood in his veins, attained prominence in Reconstruction politics. And the family, for the most part, ever since, has lived between the two worlds, now dipping into the Negro, now into the white. Some

> few are definitely white; others definitely colored. I alone have stood for a synthesis in the matters of the mind and spirit analogous, perhaps, to the actual fact of at least six blood minglings.
>
> The history, traditions, and culture of five of these are available in some approximation to the truth. Of the Negro, what facts are known have too often been perverted for the purposes of propaganda, one way or the other. It has been necessary, therefore, that I spend a disproportionate time in Negro study. Recently, facts and possibilities discovered have led to an interest mainly artistic and interpretive.[20]

Here, Toomer plans something of a spectator's role. His interest in the Negro is described as disproportionate, an interest generated by others who have emphasized it at the expense of his other racial identities. But importantly, such interest, mainly "artistic and interpretive," is linked to his larger and more general commitment, "a synthesis in matters of mind and spirit." One hears here Frank's later definition of experience as a fusion of elements and essential knowledge.

What must be seen, I think, is that for Toomer all categories, all socially created definitions, were essentially unreal. For they were a denial of man's existential existence, his search to overcome the absurdity of his unrealized self:

> A being, dwelling on the planet Earth, with a being's possibilities, with a man's abnormalities, and limitations; somewhat aware that he exists in an inhabited intelligible Cosmos; somewhat sensing his responsibilities to Man, Nature, God and to himself; understanding . . . that the existence of all things has purpose, aim, meaning, and that it is possible for him to discover and fulfill this aim; knowing, yea, realizing with suffering that some power has hardened his heart and blinded his eyes, that some force incarnate as God or demon, for some purpose, presumably for cosmic necessity, has severed him, cut him from reality, arrested his reason and consciousness—a being existing in the twentieth century America by chance heard and responded to the call "Awake thou sleeper"![21]

As a consequence, when Toomer turned his attention to race he tended to treat the concept in a highly metaphoric way, since for him race had no meaning independent of social convention: "There is only one pure race—and this is the human race. We all belong to it—and it is the most and the least that can be said of any of us with accuracy. For the rest, it is mere talk, men labelling, merely a manner of speaking, merely a sociological, not a biological, thing."[22] Although race was no more divisive than other aspects of the prevailing social order, it tended to fragment man and to block a fuller realization of his deepest self. As a consequence, "racial, as all problems, depend for their solution upon the discovery or recovery and use of a method, a way of living, which will radically transform the whole make up of the individual and the nature of man as a whole."[23] Thus, Toomer's emphasis was on the individual and the inner essence of human consciousness—"for all human problems exist in the psyches of living men, existing nowhere else. Therefore, we must first understand the nature of the psyche."[24] And, as a consequence, Toomer was as ambivalent about his white self as he was about his black self. Both terms were essentially labels, social tags empty of human meaning.

Toomer's emphasis on inner states of human consciousness together with his sense of a transcendent completeness suggests both the elusiveness and the mystery of his own self-understanding. Such an emphasis, however, also helps one to understand the demands he would place upon himself and his art and the subsequent disillusionment he would ultimately experience. In a letter to Sherwood Anderson, Toomer wrote, "It seems to me that art in our day, other than in its purely aesthetic phase, has a sort of religious function. It is a religion, a spiritualization of the immediate."[25] As such it was the specific responsibility of the artist to unify into a whole the evanescent as well as the eternal, "And I, together with all other I's, am the reconciler." Thus, looking back on the immediate past, Toomer saw the energy and the chaos of discovery and innovation. But in the present he sensed a moment of pause before a truly timeless art was to be created:

> During the past decade the evident and vital literary energies of America were engaged in exploration and discovery, also in a loose, rapid, wasteful, or partial use of art materials. So insistent was the need for "digging up" that hitherto no surplus has been available for a valuing and ordering of those materials. I mean that there has been no clear and inclusive expository evaluation of them. I mean, further, that no creator has as yet completely purified, fused and incorporated them in a great work of literary art.[26]

But as stated earlier, upon finishing *Cane*, Toomer experienced a sense of exhaustion and incompleteness: "The deep release caused by my experience, here, could not liberate and harmonize the sum of me." And, in time, Toomer's faith in art would yield to skepticism and disillusionment, for he "saw that neither art nor literature were doing for [even] the men and women engaged in them what was most necessary in life—providing them with a constructive whole way of living."[27] That Toomer could make such a demand upon his experience and his art is fully consistent with his more general philosophic outlook. At the same time, however, such a demand and such a point of view renders problematic both the sustaining power of his art and/or the specific form or subject within which such a search might be located.

Beyond the wrenching experience of writing and the heightened sense that art had a sort of religious function, it is also important to see Toomer's conception of his subject as he journeyed south in 1921. In part, Toomer was excited by the sheer color and shape of daily life. But he was most struck by a sense of the impermanence and flux of what he saw. In a long letter to Frank, Toomer commented:

> There is one thing about the Negro in America which most thoughtful persons seem to ignore: the Negro is in solution, in the process of solution. As an entity, the race is losing its body, and its soul is approaching a common soul. If one holds his eyes to individuals and sections, race is starkly evident, and racial continuity seems assured. One is even led to believe that the thing we call Negro beauty will always be attributable to a clearly defined physical source. But the fact is that if anything comes up now pure Negro, it will be a swan song. Don't let us fool ourselves, brother: the Negro of the folksong has all but passed away: the Negro of the emotional church is fading. A hundred years from now these Negroes, if they exist at all, will live in art. And I believe that a vague sense of this fact is the driving force behind the art movements directed towards them today (likewise the Indian). America needs these elements. They are passing. Let us grab and hold them while there still is time.[28]

Toomer had no illusions that he was witness to a way of life that was irrevocably lost:

> The modern world was uprooted, the modern world was breaking down, but we couldn't go back. There was nothing to go back to . . . such peasantry as America had—and I sang one of its swan songs in Cain [*sic*] was swiftly disappearing, swiftly being industrialized by machines, motor cars, phonographs, movies. . . . Back to nature, even if desirable, was no longer possible, because industry had taken nature unto itself. Even if he wanted to, a city person could not become a soil person by changing his locale and living on a farm or

> in the woods. . . . Those who sought to cure themselves by a return to more primitive conditions were either romantics or escapists.[29]

But through art, Toomer attempted to incorporate into the consciousness of modern man the values he perceived in the human landscape of the black South:

> Up till now, most of the writers notably concerned with the American scene, its historical setting and the general forces that now influence or direct it, have omitted the peasant-adjustment rhythm of the Southern Negro. The non-pioneer rhythm of the South. They have isolated for consideration the extraverted restless, urging, forward-pushing rhythm of the pioneer. At most, the South has been a rather exotic and unrelated fragment. But in this work, the seed, after it has been blown and planted, will spring up in the South. And from the South it will bring the adjustment, the health and art and joy and beauty that, expanding, will determine the tone and content of the entire country. The foundation and real starting point of this work is the South.[30]

Thus, Toomer perfectly delineates his mood and his vision at the time of his writing *Cane*. *Cane* was a "swan song," but it was also a vision. And from this dialectic of the past and the future, Toomer sought, as he states, the creation of a human world which had meaning for modern man.

Toomer was and is an enigmatic figure. But any assessment that is to be made must be made in terms of the language and the art he shared with individuals such as Waldo Frank. For both men, art and life were essentially synonymous, and each sought to live on that fine plane of consciousness wherein art and life were fused into a unity. While living in Georgia, Toomer stressed in a letter to Frank that the rhythm, the motion, and the spirit of the place had a meaning for art—"the opportunity for a vivid symbolism." At the same time, "the region as a whole seemed a pulsating microcosm of a larger universe."[31] As long as the opportunity existed, each was interested and each sought to create a "vivid symbolism." And if the subject, the content of that symbolism, was "in the process of solution" it was necessary to "grab and hold" before the opportunity was lost. But once accomplished, each moved on to other subjects and other opportunities. After all, if sung well, a swan song need not perish, even if the singer has moved on to other concerns.

Toomer's relationship with Frank has been given little attention. Most who have written of either man and even bothered to mention the other merely note that for a short time the two journeyed through the South together. And in the most recent and only full-length study of the Harlem Renaissance, Nathan Huggins ignored their relationship altogether. But, as seen, the two were intimate friends and this was only possibly because they shared a common artistic vision. Out of Toomer's experience in Georgia came *Cane*, and out of Frank's experience in the South with Toomer came *Holiday*. Each novel was unquestionably the work of its author, but each was emotionally and intellectually dependent on the other. And the two novels would not have been the same without the other's criticism and encouragement. Even after the publication of *Holiday*, Frank continued to consult Toomer regarding the validity of the critical comments being made. Uncertain as to whether certain sections of *Holiday* should or should not be revised, Frank asked for Toomer's advice. Upon his reassurance that "*Holiday* is quite perfect as it stands," Frank was content to be satisfied with its achievement.[32]

> Your response to T. R. Smith's criticism of Holiday is so amazingly in tune with my own intuition that I am strengthened. The line you quote accurately from memory "it is your wound, John" appears to me the fulcrum and climax of the entire work: and that you should so light on it corroborates my feeling of success. Smith's reaction is merely valuable as an indication of what other "intelligent" persons will say. . . . The point is simply that the vile current realistic novel has spoiled all minds for the essential and pure lines of aesthetic form: they can't see anything except smudges: a true fine pencil stroke or brush-stroke makes no mark upon their retinas.[33]

For both men the ultimate consideration was the correctness of the aesthetic achievement. And the real test of one's literature was the achieving of a wholeness that had as yet not been realized in the existential present of human affairs. On this basis they continued to pursue a sense of meaning and purpose. Through the remainder of the decade and to the end of his life, Toomer would continue to seek such personal wholeness. For *Cane*, as Toomer understood it, was simply the beginning and not the conclusion of such a quest.

An Intersection of Paths: Correspondence Between Jean Toomer and Sherwood Anderson

DARWIN T. TURNER

In the fall of 1922 Sherwood Anderson scrawled[1] a brief commendation to a new author:

> Dear Jean Toomer,
>
> I read your Nora in September Double Dealer and liked it more than I can say. It strikes a note I have long been wanting to hear come from one of your race.
>
> More power to your elbow.
>
> Sincerely,
> Sherwood Anderson[2]

The unexpected praise must have delighted Toomer. At the age of twenty-eight, he could perceive in his past only a track of fallen hurdles marking the places at which he had tripped. The college degree, the agrarian or scholarly life, the reformer's mission, the musical career: all these seemed to lie behind him. Now, gazing upon the new path of a literary career, he was receiving unsolicited encouragement from Sherwood Anderson, who, the author of six books—including the highly praised *Winesburg, Ohio* (1919)—already enjoyed the kind of literary reputation which Toomer coveted. Even before Toomer found time to answer, Anderson sent a second, more critical reaction:

> I'm not so stirred by these things as I was [?] by the first thing I saw of yours in Double Dealer—and by one long thing—where you went to lie [?] beside a woman in the park at night. . . . The Double Dealer let me read.
>
> These present things seem to me real stuff but moulded by something outside yourself.
>
> I'll say no more about them. There seems to me something false—to yourself—not in the way you have felt them but in the way you have told them.
>
> If I'm wrong forgive me.[3]

From the preferences indicated in the two letters, one can infer the literary quality that Anderson esteemed in Toomer. "Nora"[4] lyrically, impressionistically fuses concrete details of setting with suggestive, symbolic images:

> Her soul is like a little thrust-tailed dog, that follows her, whimpering. I've seen it tagging on behind her, up streets where chestnut trees flowered, where dusty asphalt had been freshly sprinkled with clean water. Up alleys where niggers sat on low door-steps before tumbled shanties and sang and loved. At night, when she comes home, the little dog is left in the vestibule, nosing the crack beneath the big storm door, filled with chills till morning. Some one . . . eoho Jesus . . . soft as the bare feet of Christ moving across bales of southern cotton, will steal in and cover it that it need not shiver, and carry it to her where she sleeps: cradled in dream-fluted cane.[5]

The second piece praised by Anderson, "Avey," is less obviously impressionistic; nevertheless, it manifests its own lyricism. Against a backdrop of nature's beauty, Toomer softly illuminated the souls of the ambitious, idealistic young narrator and the attractive woman whose animalistic sensuality excites and frustrates him. Perhaps in favoring "Avey" above the more realistic pieces,[6] Anderson, responding to an echo of the familiar, unconsciously affirmed his appreciation of work resembling his own. Certainly, resemblances abound: similarities of character and thought between Toomer's narrator and Anderson's George Willard; similarities of style; the authors' suggestion that isolated vernal settings—the deserted Soldiers' Home in "Avey," the deserted Fair Grounds in "Sophistication"—offer an atmosphere which conjures Truth, whether of idea or of emotion; the writers' thematic emphasis that people must learn to express that intense passion which is both physical and supraphysical.

Such resemblances, of course, neither attest nor imply a copybook imitation of Anderson; however, they do not result from chance, as Toomer made clear when he finally responded to Anderson's letters:

> Dear Sherwood Anderson,
>
> Just before I went down to Georgia I read Winesburg, Ohio. And while there, living in a cabin whose floorboards permitted the soil to come up between them, listening to the old folk melodies that Negro women sang at sun-down, The Triumph of the Egg came to me. The beauty, and the full sense of life that these books contain are natural elements, like the rain and sunshine, of my own sprouting. My seed was planted in the cane- and cotton-fields, and in the souls of black and white people in the small southern town. My seed was planted in *myself* down there. Roots have grown and strengthened. They have extended out. I spring up in Washington. Winesburg, Ohio and The Triumph of the Egg are elements of my growing. It is hard to think of myself as maturing without them.
>
> There is a golden strength about your art that can come from nothing less than a creative elevation of experience, however bitter or abortive the experience may have been. Your images are clean, glowing, healthy, vibrant: sunlight on forks of trees, on mellow piles of pine boards. Your acute sense of the separateness of life could easily have led to a lean pessimism in a less abundant soul. Your Yea! to life is one of the clear fine tones in our medley of harsh discordant sounds. Life is measured by your own glowing, and you find life, you find its possibilities deeply hopeful and beautiful. It seems to me that art in our day, other than in its purely aesthetic phase, has a sort of religious function. It is a religion, a spiritualization of the immediate. And ever since I first touched you, I have thought of you in this connection. I let a friend of mine, a young fellow with no literary training but who is sensitive and has had a deep experience of life, read Out of Nowhere into Nothing when it first appeared in the Dial. After having finished it he came back to me with face glowing, and said, "When any man can write like that, something wonderful is going to happen." I think that there is. I think that you touch most people that way. And when my own stuff wins a response from you, I feel a linking together within me, a deep joy, and an outward flowing. . . .
>
> Naturally, my impulse was to write you when I first received your note. But at that time I was re-typing my stuff, writing three

> new pieces, and putting Cane (my book) together. I felt too dry to write. Now, the sap has again started flowing. . . .
>
> Wont you write and tell me more in detail how my stuff strikes you? And at the first opportunity I would certainly like to have a talk with you.[7]

Toomer's effusions of admiration failed to elicit the detailed critiques which he had requested, but they encouraged Anderson to articulate some of his views about Negroes:

> Your work is of special significants [*sic* ?] to me because it is the first negro [*sic*] work I have seen that strikes me as really negro. That is surely splendid. I wanted so much to find and express myself something clear and beautiful I felt coming up out of your race but in the end gave up. I did not want to write of the negro but out of him. Well I wasn't one. The thing I felt couldn't be truly done.
>
> And then McClure [editor of *The Double Dealer*] handed me the few things of yours I saw and there was the thing I had dreamed of—beginning. . . .
>
> In London I met a woman of your race with whom I had some good talk and with whom I have had some correspondence but in the end I felt she was a bit too negro.
>
> I felt something like this—that she was inclined to over-estimate everything done by a negro because a negro had done it.
>
> In you, that is to say in your work I have not felt anything of the sort. It is really an indication of a rather too great inner humbleness expressed [?] in an outer too great race boldness—isn't it.
>
> Anyway—thank God I haven't seen or felt it in any things of yours I've seen and I will be only too glad if you will let me see any of your other things. . . .[8]

At this stage of the correspondence, Anderson had not outlined his criteria for determining whether a work was "really Negro." A more cynical correspondent than Toomer might have questioned whether the "really Negro" could be defined by a white American who knew few blacks and who confessed an inability to write "out of" blacks.

But Jean Toomer did not wish to carp at Anderson, who intermingled his praise with offers to secure a publisher for the book that Toomer proposed, to write an introduction, or to serve in any other helpful way.[9] Toomer felt little need for such assistance; for Horace Liveright was examining the "Cane" papers for possible publication by Boni and Liveright, and Waldo Frank had promised to write an introduction.[10] Nevertheless, whether motivated by gratitude for Anderson's interest, by a natural courtesy, by an unwillingness to sever connections with a man who might prove helpful in the future, or merely by a desire to educate a respected white American, Toomer responded promptly and tactfully. Gently explaining how Anderson's black characters might be adjudged unreal, Toomer soothed any stings by praising, and expressing indebtedness to, Anderson's presentation of a genuine emotion and sense of beauty:

> In your work I have felt you reaching for the beauty that the Negro has in him. As you say, you wanted to write not of the Negro but out of him. "Well I wasn't one. The thing is that it couldn't be truly done." I guess you're right. But this much is certain: an emotional element, a richness from him, from yourself, you have artistically woven into your own material. Notably, in Out of Nowhere into Nothing. Here your Negro, from the standpoint of superficial reality, of averages, of surface plausibility, is unreal. My friends who are interested in the "progress" of the Negro would take violent exception to such a statement as, "By educating himself he had cut himself off from his own people." And from a strictly social point of view, much that they would say would be true enough. But in these pages you have evoked an emotion, a sense of beauty that is easily more Negro than almost anything I have seen. And I am glad to admit my own indebtedness to you in this connection.[11]

Toomer continued the letter even more delicately. Instead of merely accepting Anderson's willingness to distinguish Toomer from chauvinistic blacks, Toomer attempted to explain their psychological motivations, and his own desire to establish a magazine which, emphasizing consciousness of racial heritage, would eliminate Afro-Americans' feelings of inferiority:

> The Negro's curious position in this western civilization invariably forces him into one or the other of two extremes: either he denies Negro entirely (as much as he can) and seeks approximation to an Anglo-Saxon (white) ideal, or, as in the case of your London acquaintance, he over-emphasizes what is Negro. Both of these attitudes have their source in a feeling of (a desire not to feel) inferiority. I refer here, of course, to those whose consciousness and condition make them keenly aware of white dominance. The mass of Negroes, the peasants, like the mass of Russians or Jews or Irish or what not, are too instinctive to be anything but themselves. Here and there one finds a high type Negro who shares this virtue with his more

> primitive brothers. As you can imagine, the resistance against my stuff is marked, excessive. But I feel that in time, in its social phase, my art will aid in giving the Negro to himself. In this connection, I have thought of a magazine. A magazine, American, but concentrating on the significant contributions, or possible contributions of the Negro to the western world. A magazine that would consciously hoist, and perhaps at first a trifle overemphasize a negroid [*sic*] ideal. A magazine that would function organically for what I feel to be the budding of the Negro's consciousness. The need is great. People within the race cannot see it. In fact, they are likely to prove to be directly hostile. But with the youth of the race, unguided or misguided as they now are, there is a tragic need. Talent dissipates itself for want of creative channels of expression, and encouragement. My own means are slim, almost nothing. I have had and am still having a hard pull of it. But as I write these lines there are two young people whom I am barely keeping above surface by the faith and love I have for them.[12] I would deeply appreciate your thoughts in relation [to] this matter.[13]

This concluding section of the letter is startling, almost bewildering, to a reader who knows the path which Toomer subsequently followed. Here, at the risk of alienating Anderson, he championed the cause of blackness in a tone evidenced only in unpublished materials—a fictional manuscript about Harry Kennedy, letters to Mae Wright, and the play *Natalie Mann*. Writing to Anderson, he chided blacks for imitating whites and emphasized his determination to correct the psychological imbalances of blacks. In less than the time required to conceive and give birth to a child, however, Jean Toomer would be arguing vehemently that Boni and Liveright should not identify him as Negro.[14]

But that time had not yet come. Despite what Anderson might think, Toomer was determined to be a "race man." On the other path, blandly ignoring what might have seemed to be Toomer's implicit appeal for financial backing for the magazine, Anderson discouraged the idea:

> I'm afraid I am not enthusiastic about the magazine idea—at least not for the artist. It belongs to a field of effort outside the artist's life and as for yourself, I should think the important thing would be to go along the road you are traveling. If you can do so let someone else worry about the problem of bringing it to your own people and to the white race too.

> I'm sure I'm right about that. You can't make a living as a poet anyway and where, in God's name, are you going to get material to fill a magazine when you are the only negro [*sic*] I've seen who seems really to have consciously the artist's impulse.[15]

In his next letter, Anderson continued to protest against the idea:

> The only valid reason I can see for the magazine you suggest is covered by the suggestion—"and then too, there's the financial end."
>
> But isn't that a difficult and laborious way of making bread and butter. Seems to me it is. If someone were to give money for the project how much more healthy to give it to Jean Toomer.
>
> As you perhaps know I have always—until this year—made my own living as an advertising scribbler—a ghastly way—but it sufficed. The subject isn't I suppose too important. The artist has in some way to survive in the hodgepodge.
>
> The important thing is that there be artists of course and I believe you are one—and a negro [*sic*] artist—which is infinitely more important.[16]

Like many other ideas which Toomer conceived during his twenties, the magazine aborted. Perhaps it was covertly interred in a midnight ceremony attended only by Margaret Naumburg and Georges Gurdjieff, who lit the flares which distracted Toomer from the black world.

The correspondence resumed after Anderson received a copy of *Cane*. The book recalled for Anderson exotic memories of blacks he had seen at a distance; but the book's overtones of frustration—similar to those which he himself had sketched in *Winesburg*—informed Anderson of an unsuspected dimension in blacks and especially in Toomer:

> "Cane" came along to me at Christmas and last night, when I had got into bed, I plunged into it and finished it before I slept. It dances. It made me feel—what did it not make me feel? Once I lived in New Orleans and I'm going back there to live, for keeps, one of these days. There I used to spend hours on the docks, watching ships come in and most of all watching the blacks at work.
>
> They sang, their bodies sang. I used to go blessing [?] them—saying to myself it was glorious there was not a neurotic among [?] them but now I can no longer say that.
>
> You I am sure belong to us, nervous distraught one, us moderns, and it is quite wonderful to think you belong also to the men I saw working on the docks, the black men.

I never tried to talk to them, never approached them.
Perhaps I did not know how much I wanted a voice from them.
When I saw your stuff first I was thrilled to the toes. Then I thought—"He has let the intense white men get him. They are going to color his style, spoil him."
I guess that isn't true. You'll stay by your own, won't you.
It is just a little crack opened [?] of the thing you have got, that no one else can get—yet.
It is very very fine to me.
I've often wondered—do you paint! God what a painting story your people have got—for someone.[17]

Although Anderson subdued his raptures in a letter written less than a fortnight later, he continued to worry about Toomer's direction:

> My admiration for it [*Cane*] holds. Between our two selves I thought at one time you were going to fall under the influence of Waldo Frank and his style of writing—which may be all right for him but I thought would raise hell with you.
> In this book for example when you said of a negro [*sic*] woman that "Her mind was a meshbag of pink baby toes," I shivered.[18]
> I fancy I think you too first rate an artist to take your lead from anyone. And Lordy [?] God what a rich field you've tapped.
> Do write some more tales in the spirit in which you approached that wonderful story Kabnis.
> Please dear man do not let either the white high or low brows [?] get you.[19]

Anderson did not seem to realize how he was missing the point. Without informing Anderson, Toomer was moving along a path carrying him away from black people into a concern for the social-psychological dilemmas of white Americans. More important, even if he had remained the Jean Toomer of *Cane* days, he would not have been content to paint. What concerned him was not the sweat glistening on muscular black bodies, not the melodious song pouring through thick lips, not the laughter rising from souls that disdain a materialistic world—for Toomer, all these were the surfaces, the elements of local color. What interested him was the repression and the frustration that trouble blacks, as they trouble the whites of Anderson's stories.

In the letter which he had written immediately after reading *Cane*, Anderson had seemed to perceive Toomer's intentions. But almost as if he willed himself not to consider the psychological dimensions of blacks—including Toomer—Anderson returned to his myopic focus on the form and color of black life and to his suspicion that, beneath the form and color, lay a sensuality best known only to the darkest of races. Four days after the previous letter, he wrote to Toomer again:

> The ill health you speak of finding in New York has I fancy been in every capital of every civilization always—don't you think? Sometimes I think it is inherent in what we call intellectuality.
>
> A man like yourself can escape. You have a direct and glowing genius [?] that is, I am sure, a part of your body, a part of the way you walk, look at things, make love, sleep and eat. Such a man goes rather directly from feeling to expression. He has hellish times but keeps fairly well cleaned [?] out. I dare say you won't stay in New York. The warm south, no matter what its attitude towards you, will call you back.
>
> I have myself—having Italian blood in me, have a constant call southward. Something pagan and warm comes to me on a train going southward. I spent two long periods, one at Mobile, another at New Orleans. I dare say I had advantages there you couldn't have had. On the other hand I missed much.
>
> The negro [*sic*] life was outside me, had to remain outside me. That may have been why I wanted to paint. There was less mind, more feeling. I could approach the brown men and women through a quite impersonal love of color in skins, through the same kind of love of line as expressed in lazy sprawling bodies.
>
> That perhaps led me to the attempt to paint. I haven't done much with it since. Think I shall be back there next summer. Would like, I fancy, the breathless summer heat of it.
>
> It may be some day you will approach painting as you have writing—in those moments when you are so fully yourself. If one could forget what has been taught about painting much [?] might [?] be done.
>
> I myself had, I thought, an advantage as I could not draw. I went for lines and spaces only and the color I could lay into them. Subconscious things I fancy welled up. I owed [?] nothing to painting, to the traditions of painting, being no painter, being just a fellow with a brush in my hand and pots of color before me. I used water color. It's cheap. $12 or $15 would outfit me.
>
> What I got offered nothing, I dare say, to anyone but myself. There were, however, happy, excited hours, just the tenderness of a bit of color coming up—like the things in your book, where the smoke from the sawdust piles drifts over one of those terrible little Georgia mill towns at evening.[20]

> And the roads—your people laughing and walking in the roads, the significants [*sic?*] of roads in the south, to your people brought out like color in a painting.
>
> I speak of it at length only as a possible additional joy to you in life, something added.
>
> Your problem is bound to be hellish. That hellishness won't fail to come to any artist in our time but you are pioneering I think more than any of us. The ungodly ghastly emptiness. White men only about 11 or 12 years old, the best of them perhaps.[21]

The conversations almost ended here at the intersection of the paths of the two artists, whose lyric similarity John McClure, the editor of *Double Dealer*, had defined:

> As for Jean Toomer, I am thoroughly convinced that as a piece of literature, of durable writing, Karintha is far superior to Kabnis. I do not think that Toomer can't write short stories. I merely think that his finest work so far is lyrical and that if he ever does supreme work it must be in a lyrical manner. In my opinion he cannot handle dialect. He can do a certain sort of realistic story better than most and can rise to prominence in realism if wishes to. But the lyrical expression of his own moods he can accomplish, in his own fashion, better probably than nearly anyone. He can be an unusually good short story writer or a supremely fine lyrical rhapsodist, as he pleases. He should mould his stories into lyrical rhapsodies rather than attempt to present them realistically. I am sure if Toomer attempts realistic fiction as his lifework he will be merely one of a number of men. If he follows that African urge, and rhapsodizes, he will be a commanding and solitary figure. For his own sake, I feel that he ought to do that which he does best. You and I differ, of course, on what he does best. I am sure his dialect is weak. But his English, as he uses it out of his own heart, is founded on a rock.
>
> An honest confession, etc.: Contrary to the opinion of many good critics, I have the same attitude to *your* work. I am sure that the stories in which you have written simply out of your own heart with your own natural intonation of speech are incomparably better than those in which you have constructed the language to fit the character. In other words, I am sure that your genius is lyrical. "I am a Fool" and "I Want to Know Why" (which many people consider among your best) seem to me to be inferior to many things you have done. Not in conception, but in execution. You may disagree with me. I feel the same about Toomer. The moment he attempts to make characters talk in the accents of life he falls from his highest level. He can divine what they think and what they feel but the only way he

can express it is in his own language—by stepping into their shoes and then uttering his own words in quotation marks, or else by avoiding quotation marks altogether and simply telling in his own words, by indirect discourse, what is going on in the other fellow's mind. The lyrical genius is not restricted to poetry. A novel can be lyrical. Realism can be lyrical. I think you are a lyrical genius absolutely: You handle reality lyrically. I mean it is *your* mood, *your* point of view, *your* wonder or terror or perplexity or desire or affection, which permeates the work you do—it is Sherwood Anderson that stares at me out of the page. Now in Shakespeare what one sees is Falstaff, or Lear, or Iago, or a Clown, as the case may be. In Balzac, Cousin Pons or Cousin Bette. In Dickens, Mr. Micawber. In Thackeray, Pendennis. In Mark Twain, Huck Finn or Tom Sawyer. Those writers are realists—they work objectively. It seems to me that you, by nature, work subjectively—that however objectively you view a thing the natural approach to it for you, in literature, is subjective. And in the most detached story you do we find a lyrical expression of your own personality—a lyrical expression of some problem which you personally would like to solve. I think, sincerely, that you do your finest work when you are frankly lyrical, down to the very phraseology. When you present a situation or a problem or a fact precisely as you see it and in exactly your own words. You may disagree with me. I wonder if you feel that you are an objective realist?

My statement about Toomer is not based, I believe, on a fondness for poetry. "Poetry" as a state of mind does not exist, in my philosophy. Poetry is merely verse, rhythm in speech which reaches the condition of music. The human spirit expresses itself in many ways and verse is only one. Toomer's character seems to me to be lyrical—he is so intensely an individual that it is useless for him to attempt anything other than to express himself. He is not a sponge like Balzac. He is not a dramatist like Shakespeare or even like Eugene O'Neill, for that matter. He is Jean Toomer. Anything he touches will be transmuted into a personal expression. It seems to me he should not try to make his work anything other than an expression of himself, and devote his energies to making it as fine an expression as possible. . . .[22]

The paths intersected and diverged. From 1924 on, Jean Toomer obsessively focused on the neuroses of "the intense white men." On the other horizon Sherwood Anderson, in 1925, published *Dark Laughter*, a sympathetic but discordant paean to the race of innocent, sexually liberated, naturally wise, laughing primitives, whom he long had desired to paint.

One ironic note remained in the correspondence. A decade after they had passed and parted, Sherwood Anderson wrote to Jean Toomer to invite him to a baseball game in New York City.[23] If they had gone to watch the Yankees, they would have seen no black primitives on the field, of course; in 1934, "major league" baseball was still a white man's national pastime. But they might have seen the greatest of them all, George Herman Ruth—the uninhibited, happy-go-lucky Bambino—in his last year as a Yankee, but still legendary, not only for genius on the field, but also for the sensual and sexual appetites which he indulged off the field with none of the concerns which frustrated the intense Americans about whom Anderson and Toomer worried and wrote.

Sherwood Anderson and Jean Toomer

MARK HELBLING

In the literature which deals with the Harlem Renaissance, the name of Sherwood Anderson is given little if any attention. For the most part, Anderson's novel *Dark Laughter* is simply listed with a number of other novels written by whites that reveal a particular interest in and image of black Americans. Nathan Huggins, for example, notes that

> by 1926 the field [whites' writing of Blacks] was well worked, Eugene O'Neill had already startled New York with *Emperor Jones* (1920) and *All God's Chillun Got Wings* (1924). E. E. Cummings had already developed the child-primitive Black, Jean Le Negre in *The Enormous Room* (1922), to be followed a year later by Waldo Frank's in *Holiday*. In 1925 Sherwood Anderson published *Dark Laughter* and DuBose Heyward *Porgy*. And just two years later, Heyward completed *Mamba's Daughters*.[1]

Beyond such a listing Huggins gives Anderson no further attention. Such inattention is not without some justification.

Anderson was only marginally a part of the intellectual life of New York, white or black. He was most importantly involved in the Chicago Renaissance or Liberation and, like most of the men and women identified with this earlier movement, did not fully participate in that later period of intellectual and artistic expression.[2] In many ways New York was a quite different intellectual atmosphere, and much that seemed innovative and even daring to the earlier Chicago group was viewed in a somewhat indifferent and even condescending manner.[3] As a consequence, many felt out of place and uncertain as to where they belonged. In *A Story Teller's Story* Anderson openly expressed the ambivalence he felt regarding New York and what was taking place:

> I was in New York. . . . The New Movement in the Arts was underway. . . . I kept thinking of middle-western men like Dreiser, Masters, Sandburg and the others. There was something sincere and fine about them. Perhaps they had not worried, as I seemed to be doing, about the whole question of whether they belonged to the new Movement or not.[4]

As a consequence, Anderson remained an interested yet essentially distant figure.

Nevertheless, Anderson was not entirely divorced from New York intellectual interests and certain black intellectuals and artists who sought his advice and/or assistance. In 1922 Jean Toomer proposed starting a magazine that would champion black culture and feature black artists and intellectuals. As Toomer wrote, "[such a magazine] would concentrate on the significant contributions, or possible contributions, of the Negro to the Western World." For most importantly it would be "a magazine that would function organically for what I feel to be the budding of the Negro's consciousness."[5] However, Anderson declined to participate, and nothing came of Toomer's idea. In 1925 Alain Locke, whom Huggins calls "the father of the New Negro and the so-called Harlem Renaissance," inquired of Anderson whether or not he would contribute an article on "the value of the Negro material as a common body of material for American artists" for the forthcoming *New Negro*.[6] Anderson declined the offer. And in the following year Jessie Fauset asked if he would contribute to a series in the *Crisis* magazine concerning "what is acceptable material in the portrayal of the Negro."[7] Anderson agreed and offered the following:

> Naturally I think it is a great mistake for Negroes to become too sensitive. If, as a race, you were the ideal people sentimentalists sometimes try to make you how uninteresting you would be.

> Why not quit thinking of Negro art? If the individual creating the art happens to be a Negro and some one [*sic*] wants to call it Negro Art let them.
>
> As to Negroes always being painted at their worst I think it isn't true. Suppose I were to grow indignant every time a white man or woman were badly or cheaply done in the theatre or in books. I might spend my life being indignant.
>
> I have lived a good deal in my youth among the common Negro laborers. I have found them about the sweetest people I know. I have said so sometimes in my books.
>
> I do not believe the Negroes have much more to complain of than the white in this matter of their treatment in the arts.[8]

Anderson's casual dismissal of the question posed and his unwillingness to recognize, let alone explore, the complexities of meaning in such a concept as "Negro Art" deserves attention. But for the moment it is important simply to note that Anderson remained generally indifferent to such questions. For this reason, as well as his general indifference to New York, Anderson is given only passing attention by those whose center of interest is with the men and women of the Harlem Renaissance.

And yet, as the above correspondence might suggest, Anderson was not quite so marginal a figure as has generally been assumed. This is not to say that his involvement with black intellectuals and writers in any sense rivaled or can even be compared with that of Carl Van Vechten, "the undisputed prince of all the whites to become associated with black Harlem in the 1920's."[9] Such a role was neither his to choose nor his to want to choose. At the same time, the impact of black friends, intellectuals, and celebrities on his social and intellectual life doesn't compare with that upon Van Vechten. No one has asked of Anderson, as Huggins has rightly asked of Van Vechten, "It is at least as important . . . to ask how Harlem and the Negro served him."[10] But Anderson was indeed "served" by blacks. And Toomer, in particular, had a special importance that has seldom been acknowledged.

For a period of time both men corresponded with one another and shared several friends in common, most notably Waldo Frank and Alfred Stieglitz. During their friendship Toomer offered warm praise for Anderson's writing as well as constructive advice:

> In your work I have felt you reaching for the beauty that the Negro has in him. As you say, you wanted to write not of the Negro but

> out of him. . . . This much is certain: an emotional element, a richness from him, from yourself, you have artistically woven into your own material. Notably in Out of Nowhere into Nothing. Here your Negro, from the point of superficial reality, of averages, of surface plausibility, is unreal. . . . But in these pages you have evoked an emotion, a sense of beauty that is easily more Negro than almost anything I have seen.[11]

Anderson, in turn, reciprocated with encouragement and praise for Toomer's writing. When he learned that Toomer had recently finished writing a novel, *Cane*, he immediately offered to write an introduction and to help in its publication. However, their friendship soon cooled. Anderson could never fully appeal to Toomer's imaginative vision.[12] But what ultimately came between them was Anderson's peculiar insistence that Toomer acknowledge his black self and that he never abandon or forget his racial vision. The following letter is typical of many that Toomer received:

> The important thing is that there be artists of course and I believe you are one—and a Negro artist—which is infinitely more important. And o man keep clean your clear drift toward the sweetness and fineness in your own race. That I'm sure is the all important thing.[13]

And Toomer confided to Frank his feelings regarding Anderson's particular point of view:

> Sherwood Anderson and I have exchanged a few letters. I don't think we will go very far. He limits me to Negro. As an approach, as a constant element (part of a larger whole) of interest, Negro is good. But to try to tie me to one of my parts is surely to loose me. My own letters have taken Negro as a point, and from there have circled out. Sherwood, for the most part, ignores the circle.[14]

Why, one wonders, was Anderson, who was so condescending and cavalier in his response to the question posed by Jessie Fauset, so insistent that Toomer be known as a black writer? More important, why did he insist so strongly that Toomer list into artistic expression what he (Anderson) felt to be the underlying psychic meaning of Toomer's blackness? Anderson's attitude is all the more curious when one considers the fact that Toomer's genealogy was extremely mixed. His great-grandmother was black, but the rest of his ancestors were French, Dutch, Welsh, German, Jewish, and Indian. Because of this and because, as he recalls, he never felt that the particular circumstances of his childhood had anything to do with his being partly black, Toomer never developed a concept of self as a black individual:

> What did I think and feel and believe? As near as I can make out, I accepted myself and my family as I saw things. Without labels. Suppose, however, that someone asked me, "Are you white or colored?" I would have asked what this meant. If the explanation had been in terms of the usual racial divisions, and I could have been made to understand them, I would have answered, "White." I knew nothing of what my grandfather was called by some people. All of my family as I saw them were white. We lived in a white neighborhood. The children I had grown up with were white. I myself, though of darker complexion than my playmates, was white; against these facts the circumstances that I went to a colored school could have little or no weight. But I was never asked this question: so I had no cause to define myself to my environment there, thus fixing a self-view.[15]

It wasn't, then, that Anderson was seeking, in the manner of Carl Van Vechten, to introduce an obscure black writer of considerable talent to an as yet ignorant or indifferent white reading public. For while Toomer was generally unknown, Anderson's encouragement and his offer to help in the publication of *Cane* was part of a deeper need to remind (perhaps to convince) Toomer that he was, after all, black and that somehow this constituted the inner source of his unique creative vision. As to others, however, who consciously sought to create or articulate a black aesthetic, Anderson remained essentially indifferent.

At the same time, as Anderson wrote to Toomer, "the important thing is that there be artists." Such advice, as it applied to artists in general, had much to do with Anderson's conviction that the artist would serve to revitalize American society and to provide an aesthetic order for moral revision. It was in these terms, in an essay titled "Emerging Greatness," that Waldo Frank had earlier spoken of Anderson's real importance in American life.[16] And Anderson, if he hadn't yet quite perceived the meaning of the artist in exactly this way, fairly gushed with anticipation as to what could and must be done. Soon after the *Seven Arts* article, Anderson's letters to Frank and Van Wyck Brooks were an almost continuous commentary on the American scene, both past and present, and the role they could expect to play as artists in the forefront of cultural and social change. And yet, when it came to the question of "Negro art" and the role of the black artist, Anderson was all but silent.

In part, at least, Anderson's behavior toward Toomer can be understood as a kind of moral self-assurance or compensation for feelings of condescension he felt toward blacks in general. In an article titled "The South: The Black and White and Other Problems Below the Mason and Dixon Line," Anderson wrote, "In regard to the Negro I am Southern. I have no illusions about making him my brother. Liking Negroes—wanting them about—not wanting them too close. In me the Southern contradiction so puzzling to the North."[17] As for those who advocated reforms, he was contemptuous:

> The Negro race in America is something. The reformers are trying to make them race conscious, fight for their rights and all that. It's silly.[18]

Thus, just as Anderson could assure the reader of the *Crisis* magazine that he had associated with black people in his youth and even found them "the sweetest people I know," so too might Toomer—if he would only acknowledge his blackness—serve to assuage feelings of guilt Anderson might have about his own sense of racial superiority.

At the same time, however, Anderson responded to Toomer as a very special person with whom he happened to share, at least to his own mind, a uniquely similar sensitivity and understanding regarding literary form and artistic expression. Toomer, for example, had linked Anderson's creative vision with his own inspiration for what was to be *Cane*.

> Just before I went to Georgia I read Winesburg, Ohio. And while there, living in a cabin whose floorboards permitted the soil to come up between them, listening to the old folk melodies that Negro women sang at sun-down, The Triumph of the Egg came to me. . . . Winesburg Ohio and The Triumph of the Egg are elements of my growing. It is hard to think of myself as maturing without them.[19]

And Anderson was quick to see in *Cane* parallels to his own thoughts and intuitions.[20]

The sheer imaginative appeal that Toomer's writing had for Anderson should not be minimized. For this is certainly a major consideration as to why Toomer and not, say, Claude McKay, Nella Larsen, Wallace Thurman, or some other black writer could excite his interest. However, Anderson's relationship with Toomer eludes one's full understanding if primarily seen as a form of guilt and/or aesthetic fascination for another's creative talent. For Anderson's special insistence that Toomer acknowledge his blackness has a depth of meaning which transcends the immediate details of their specific relationship.

In 1920 Anderson left Chicago and went south to Mobile, Alabama. In his *Memoirs* he writes lyrically of this trip and the sense of release and inner freedom he now experienced. Central to his enthusiasm was his discovery of the blacks and his perception of the sensuous quality of their life:

> I heard soft voices, I heard laughter. There was a Negro woman's voice, perhaps speaking to her man. . . . It wasn't what the woman in the house said. It was the timbre of her voice, something I felt that night in the Negro street, something I wanted. It seemed to break in me.[21]

This was not Anderson's first journey to the South, and it was not the first time he had had contact with black people—as a boy in Clyde, Ohio, he had spent a great deal of time at the race tracks and loved both the spirit and the skill of black grooms and trainers. But now the South, and most important the blacks, became the special object of his search for emotional and artistic fulfillment:

> My own program is laid out. I'm going back to Alabama this winter and paint and write. . . . I'm going after the American nigger. He's got something absolutely lovely that's never been touched.[22]

As a consequence, *Cane* proved to be more than mere evidence that Toomer was indeed a writer with real talent. For in one sense Toomer's work served to sustain Anderson's own observations in the South and to strengthen his imaginative conception of the relationship between "the Negro and the warm fertile Southland." But most important, *Cane* served to confirm his innermost conviction that black Americans were essentially primitives who possessed a "truth that had never been touched."

Anderson's perception of the black as a primitive figure has roots deep in the cultural experience of America. However, whereas previous observers generally viewed blacks as a threat to the social order, Anderson perceived a figure of redemptive importance:

> Negroes have something—something physical—rhythm—something we want to get into ourselves—our work. . . . The Negro had something I wanted. All sensible white men want it. There is a kind of closeness to nature, trees, rivers, the earth—more primitive men have that less primitive men are all seeking.[23]

This particular understanding was itself shared by others at the time and was not uniquely Anderson's understanding. As Christopher Lasch has written, "The great discovery of the turn of the century was the existence of uncivilized man; the existence, that is, of a buried part of the psyche which had never accepted the restraints of adulthood nor consented to become a responsible member of society. Hence, the sudden interest not only in childhood but in primitive peoples."[24] However, though Anderson's thought is related to a larger and more general cluster of ideas and perceptions, it is important to give attention to specific elements of his point of view, most notably his conception of art and how this relates to his perceptions of blacks. For above all, blacks entered Anderson's consciousness in terms of his own imaginative and artistic concerns.

In his work *The Modern Writer*, Anderson wrote:

> The artist who works in stone, in color, sounds, words, building materials, and often in steel, as in the designing of bodies for some of the finer automobiles, is but the craftsman working in materials that are often elusive and difficult to handle and bringing into his work not only the skill of the craftsman but also the attempt at an expression of some need of his own inner being.[25]

In part, such a conception of the artist sprang from his understanding that the artist's primary concern was with art itself. But this point of view was more than a concern for art for art's sake. For the artist, as craftsman, through his concern for words, could best lift the inner life of his characters into conscious expression. The artist was not a reporter, he was a creator, and through his subjective creation he revealed more of the nuances and emotions of life than one who purported to be "realistic." More important, Anderson made craftsmanship, "the impulse in men to do good work," a universal urge, but an urge which too few had successfully realized. In part, man's inability to define his identity through the mastery of craft was due to the increasing mechanization and standardization of modern civilization. And this provided Anderson with a powerful basis for social criticism. But at the same time, modern man's inability to release his creative self was not simply social but psychological. And for this reason the artist, in his mastery of craft, released not only "some need of his own inner being" but held up to others the promise and the potential of their existential selves. The artist, then, served an important function, for he brought back to consciousness a primitive vitality (pretechnical and prerational) which man had all but lost or repressed. For Anderson, then, the concept of craft was both a basis for his critical thought and his understanding of art. As Bernard Duffey has written, "Craft in Anderson's view was not formalistic and not vitalistic, it was both. It was the element common to life and art."[26] It was also a basis for his conception of the black and the meaning he held for the general society.

In "Notes Out of a Man's Life," written while in New Orleans, Anderson contrasted his own sense of aimlessness with what he felt to be the fundamental completeness and inner peace of black Americans:

> I go to the river where men are loading ships. I sit watching two strong negroes [*sic*] who are putting great timbers into the hold of a ship. What they touch with their great black fingers is something definite. I am envious of them. . . . What would I not give to accomplish something definite—related to trees, the earth, the sky, the seas.
>
> What would I not give to be a man, not the shadow of a man.[27]

Here the black stands in contrast to Anderson's own psychic disharmony. But what is of interest is the context in which this contrast is made. For Anderson is writing from the point of view of the creative artist and his primary concern is with the creative process itself. Thus, he can identify with the black, for he perceived him to be a kind of natural craftsman whose very physical existence was itself a form of art. As a consequence, blacks had both a personal meaning and a larger cultural significance. But at the same time, given Anderson's understanding of art as craft, Anderson also perceived that the fate of the black was linked to the more general fate of the artist in modern society:

> Will the love of words be lost? Success, standardization, big editions, money rolling in . . . Words goin the way of the black, of song and dance.
>
> Can you imagine sweet words in a factory, sing them, dance them?

> In the end they will make factory hands of us writers too.
> The whites will get us. They win.[28]

Thus, as one who wrote poetically of rural Georgia, Toomer perfectly captured the spiritual and aesthetic qualities which Anderson saw most threatened by the emergent industrial order of the twentieth century.[29] For this reason, Toomer's future as a writer was for Anderson of more than passing interest. But most important, as a black writer, Toomer became in Anderson's eyes the very embodiment of what was most "fine" in the American black. *Cane*, then, was not simply the recording of a passing "folk-spirit." Rather, it was the essence of that spirit expressed by one who had succeeded in releasing through art the primitive depths of his, and his people's, racial soul. Toomer, as seen, did not view his accomplishment in exactly these terms. And as a consequence, he moved on to other concerns. But Anderson still clung to his vision of black primitivism as if to define as well as to forestall the changes that were fast taking place in American life.

The "Mid-Kingdom" of Crane's "Black Tambourine" and Toomer's *Cane*

VICTOR A. KRAMER

Crane's poem "Black Tambourine" (1921) may have been a source of inspiration for Jean Toomer in the composition of *Cane*,[1] published two years later. Several parallels exist, especially within "Kabnis," the climactic portion of *Cane*; however, even if Toomer made no conscious use of Crane's poem, the similarity of these works reinforces meaning in each. Recent studies illuminate the density of Toomer's amalgamation of prose and poetry. However, critical differences remain about what Toomer has achieved.[2] Critics agree that *Cane* is carefully planned, but how its many parts combine has not been completely explained, and some interpretations seem to force elements together. Charles W. Scruggs suggests that criticism about *Cane* which merely points out a division into sections or the contrast between a white, sterile world which has faith in technology and an opposed primitive black agrarian culture goes only halfway.[3] His point is that Toomer incorporated many threads into *Cane*, and he demonstrates how a relationship between *Cane* and the myth of the mark of Cain is one fundamental motif. The similarity in subject matter of Toomer's book and Crane's poem "Black Tambourine" does not conflict with this mythic reading, and it demonstrates how Toomer employed still another thematic element.

It is possible that "Black Tambourine" may have had an immediate influence upon the conception and execution of *Cane*, since Toomer and Crane seem to have known each other fairly well. They visited one another frequently, and Crane sketched a drawing of Toomer.[4] Toomer's name is mentioned in several letters by Crane. It is quite probable that Toomer would have been familiar with Crane's early poetry; and he must have been interested in how Crane sought to illuminate his prophetic vision of an emergent machine civilization. Toomer saw the same civilization and wondered if black people would be assimilated into it. Their mutual friend, Waldo Frank, to whom, incidentally, both *White Buildings* by Crane and "Kabnis" of *Cane* are dedicated, was also extremely interested in these artistic problems. Frank encouraged both Toomer and Crane. All three explored ways to incorporate the mythic into writing about modern America. The mild suggestion of hopefulness implicit in the closing pages of "Kabnis" is akin to the Whitmanian optimism of Crane and Frank.[5] Further, both writers were close friends with Gorham Munson, to whom they both wrote letters and with whom Crane lived in 1922. There is no doubt that Crane admired Toomer's writing, and it was at his suggestion that Allen Tate was urged to contact Toomer.[6] However, Toomer himself has not acknowledged direct literary influence from Crane. He stated in a letter to Gorham Munson that Sherwood Anderson, Waldo Frank, Robert Frost, and Carl Sandburg were the only modern writers who immediately influenced him.[7]

Whether Toomer knew Crane's poem before he wrote *Cane* may be impossible to determine, but the fact that black culture must span a gap between past and present is the preoccupation of both works. Crane and Toomer each perceived the condition of the American black man as that of someone in a dark hole yet confronted by the "closed door" of society. Toomer's book reveals his vision of the mixture of good and evil which constitutes the modern South. That landscape frames not just the geographical but the psychological and sociological position of black people. It is significant to recall that Toomer and Waldo Frank traveled through the South in the early 1920s. Their trip helped to generate *Cane*, as well as a novel by Frank entitled *Holiday*. Frank's novel is about a lynching. He and Toomer were evidently shocked by much of southern culture; but Toomer seems to have been equally fascinated by a realization that much of the older culture had not been eradicated. He saw the strength and power of an agrarian culture slowly being eaten away by urbanization and industrialization. The result was that many black people were left in an intermediate world. Society promised privilege but continued to relegate blacks to the role of menial; despite this many remained strong even while separated from the dominant culture.

Cane and "Black Tambourine" both stress how despite inequity many blacks do sustain themselves. The clearest emphasis of this in *Cane* is in episodes, in each of the book's major divisions, when a symbolic strong man is beheld by other Negroes. The first of these incidents occurs within a sermon preached by Barlo in the story "Esther." There Barlo recalls his earlier vision of a strong black man captured by "white-ant biddies" and taken away in chains. Barlo's symbolic reenactment of enslavement implies that the black man's strength is only temporarily lost. When he preaches his message, "to the people he assumes the outlines of his visioned African"; and he reassures his listeners: "Brothers an sisters, turn your faces t th sweet face of the Lord, an fill your hearts with glory. Open your eyes an see th dawnin of th mornin light. Open your ears—."[8] Black people, he urges, are in darkness, but light will come. Toomer ends *Cane* at dawn, and the implication is that black people have strength to carry on toward a new day. This strength is what frees them. A similar implication is at the core of Crane's "Black Tambourine." The tambourine is a small drum, reminiscent of Africa; but *tambourine* is, as well, a word which in the early nineteen twenties would have retained its popular meaning of minstrel performer. A minstrel-performing tambourine player is a grotesque representation of the true power of black people. Such a performer is a prisoner of other persons' conceptions of him. In Crane's poem the poetic figure sits in a darkened cellar but with a tambourine placed on the wall. Crane's representative figure no longer provides entertainment. Minstrel music is something of the past; and he also appears to be awaiting the coming of a new day.

A second important episode in *Cane* emphasizes the changing role and latent strength of black people. This occurs within "Box Seat," when Dan sees an old Negro beggar. This is the climactic story within *Cane's* middle urban section. The old man has been on the streets of Washington, D.C., for decades; and Dan realizes that he may have seen, or even been seen by, Walt Whitman, who sang of democracy and brotherhood. The old man, a symbol for the enslavement of black people, is also, surprisingly, a sign of strength. Evidently he earned his living by singing, probably spirituals. Dan realizes that this beggar, who appeared to remain enslaved, retained inner strength; Dan, who has rebelled against a society which attempts to force him into its mold, is taught by the old man. He realizes that man must first heal himself—before attempting to reform a crazy world. Driven to singing, the old man had become strong. And through his singing he survived. As will be suggested later, he is like the slave poet AEsop.

The final event of *Cane* which emphasizes the hidden strength of black people is manifested through the haunting presence of Old Father John. At the end of "Kabnis" he functions as a representative of the black man in his contemporary state—caught between worlds—apparently immobile—yet wise and able to communicate that knowledge. It is Father John who announces truth—the white man has made the Bible lie—and who illuminates the disillusioned Kabnis, the main character of the novelette. Father John, a bridge from past to present, passes judgment on the condition of black people in a world which has systematically denied them access. This judgment is similar to that made by Hart Crane's speaker within "Black Tambourine." Barlo's vision, Dan's realization, Father John's words, and Hart Crane's poetic figure—all emphasize the hidden strength which black culture possesses. Toomer imagines characters who live beneath the power of a dominant culture; but he implies that black men are strong enough to overcome the difficulties of such apparent enslavement. Religious faith is Toomer's metaphor for deliverance. Barlo says this; Dan sees it; and Father John lives this way. Through faith black people retain strength despite deprivation.

Both Toomer and Crane emphasize the alienation of black people. Old Father John of "Kabnis" marks judgment on a world which perpetrates a myth to exclude black people. That exclusion has placed Negroes in a region similar to the mid-kingdom of "Black Tambourine," a poem which suggests the atmosphere of the twentieth-century "Negro's place somewhere between man and beast." Crane's reference is to a sociological, not evolutionary position.[9] To relate "Black Tambourine" more closely to *Cane*, an overview of its quatrains is necessary. The poem combines metaphysical compactness with the implicatory imagery of the symbolists.

> The interests of a black man in a cellar
> Mark tardy judgment on the world's closed door.
> Gnats toss in the shadow of a bottle.
> And a roach spans a crevice in the floor.
>
> AEsop, driven to pondering, found
> Heaven with the tortoise and the hare;

Fox brush and sow ear top his grave
And mingling incantations on the air.

The black man, forlorn in the cellar,
Wanders in some mid-kingdom, dark, that lies,
Between his tambourine, stuck on the wall,
And, in Africa, a carcass quick with flies.[10]

Crane emphasizes the "sociological" position of the Negro. These are people suspended between a primitive past, its strength, and modern industrial democracy. Surprisingly, while in suspension enlightenment comes, and judgment about a "world's closed door" becomes possible. In the middle quatrain Crane recalls AEsop, the slave who made fables and who through poetry found heaven. Part of the legend of AEsop derives from the belief that he attained his freedom through cleverness. Forced into the dilemma of pondering his plight, AEsop drew wisdom in separation; and his fables continue into the present. Crane implies that the wisdom of the Negro will survive just as do AEsop's fables; the grave of AEsop is ironic because art triumphs.[11] (Probably the most popular of the fables is the tortoise and hare, and just as in that fable Toomer's strong characters persevere. Their strength and endurance will bring victory.) But today's black man is "forlorn," suggests Crane. He wanders in a mid-kingdom between what has been promised and the carcass of his earlier civilization, which is disintegrating. What had been his of Africa is decomposing; but importantly, humiliation and false role-playing are also in the past.

Crane's word *mid-kingdom* suggests, then, that the modern American Negro retains important qualities from his former culture. In that respect he is like a displaced king. Many similar ideas are also employed in *Cane*. The true meaning of Crane's mid-kingdom is understood when seen in contrast with "the 'black tambourine' of the present, which symbolizes the minstrel-like picture of the Negro in the public mind."[12] Any displaced man knows that the public image of him is impossibly distorted. It is this fact which Kabnis begins to learn when he comes in contact with Negroes like Halsey or Father John, men who have learned to accept their lives, but not a white conception of them. It is significant that throughout *Cane* other weaker characters are symbolically enclosed by ideas from the dominant culture. This is what happens to Muriel, Dan's girl friend, and what Toomer emphasizes in "Rhobert," a prose poem about a man who is drowning because he is submerged in his desire to own property. But it is the strength of other characters which allows them to retain integrity. Both Crane and Toomer emphasize that black men can retain integrity within a society which refuses to honor them; each saw the ironic fact that many retain an ability to be self-sufficient. However, with rapid cultural changes much of black culture is threatened. Toomer's poem "Song of the Son" emphasizes a realization that he should catch some of that beauty while it still exists. All of *Cane* does this. In "Kabnis" the hero (a young man like Toomer) slowly comes to realize the beauty of a culture from which he had earlier hoped to disassociate himself. A basic concern of Toomer is with how black people retain dignity when forced to surrender what they know, while simultaneously it remains impossible to be accepted by the dominant society. His vision of what can happen to those separated from what had given nourishment, while cut off from other forms of sustenance, is at the core of the book. Unless one is very strong, frustration inevitably results.

It is clear that the autobiographical element is strong in *Cane*. Toomer wrote in a letter to Waldo Frank, "Kabnis is *Me*."[13] His life has parallels with the experiences of the rural school teacher of "Kabnis." But if the autobiographical is important, there is no doubt that Toomer also thought of his book as an embodiment of the spiritual condition of all who lived in modern America. In still another letter to Waldo Frank, he complained that Sherwood Anderson had looked upon his work as only the work of a Negro artist and that therefore dimensions such as "a sense of the tragic separatedness, the tragic sterility of people . . ." were ignored.[14] Black people were therefore the inspiration, but ultimately he employs a vision of separated and sterile black lives to suggest what can happen to any person who becomes separated from the natural aspects of living which provide sustenance. Just as "Black Tambourine" provides a picture of a black figure waiting between worlds, much of *Cane* describes life as a limbo-like existence. Especially, urban people have lost contact with the best of their culture. The city degrades them. A similar fact is emphasized in "Kabnis." There, pressure from a dominant society makes some black people obsequious.

In the Crane poem a roach is employed as metaphor linked to the alienated black person who attempts to bridge a gap to modern society. But Crane and Toomer both emphasize that the Negro remains between his earlier culture and the modern world. Significantly, images similar to Crane's roach which "spans a crevice" are also effectively employed in "Kabnis." Hanby's characterization is the most obvious example. Kabnis continually thinks of Hanby as a cockroach. He is the kind of Negro who "to members of his own race . . . affects the manners of a wealthy white planter." And to "white men he bows, without ever completely humbling himself" (185). Hanby is the embodiment of a Negro who attempts to get along in a world by a double standard; but, of course, his gains are accomplished at the loss of self-respect. Kabnis becomes confused by his realization that there is beauty and strength in black people while he simultaneously fears that perhaps they are inferior. He wonders if it is necessary for Negroes to act like cockroaches if they are to be accepted. When Kabnis becomes angry he even asserts that old Father John is little more than a roach. During these moments Kabnis is extremely frightened and nervous. He is in a state of fear during the opening of the novelette because he sees how black people are suspended between cultures. Hanby, with his affectation of the mannerisms of a white planter, is repulsive to Kabnis because he assumes that Negroes are inferior. Other characters, like the artisan Halsey, do not act this way. Halsey can perform labor for white neighbors and not feel degraded. But when Ramsay, an inept white, comes to have his hatchet handle repaired, Kabnis "feels stifled. Through Ramsay, the whole white South weighs down upon him" (201).

Kabnis is psychologically in a midregion, and even his complexion suggests this. His is a "lemon" face. Most importantly, the setting of his story emphasizes that he feels trapped. Several times he thinks of the place where he lives as a "mud-hole," or a "mud-hole trap." His psychological situation is one of turmoil and rage. Essentially, Kabnis wants to accept the fact that he is Negro; but he cannot. He vaguely desires to be a poet, and he realizes that he might make poetry of his surroundings. In the midst of his rage about the "mud-hole" of his life, he is amazed at the beauty of the Georgia countryside. Cursing God he looks at the sky, "and the night's beauty strikes him dumb." He cries out:

> [D]ear God, dear Jesus, do not torture me with beauty. Take it away. Give me an ugly world. Ha, ugly. Stinking like unwashed niggers. Dear Jesus, do not chain me to myself and set these hills and valleys, heaving with folk-songs, so close to me that I cannot reach them.

> There is a radiant beauty in the night that touches and . . . tortures me.(161–62)

Toomer indicates that intuitively Kabnis knows that there is beauty to be beheld. But he also senses that he is chained (like a slave in prison) and cannot leave and cannot accept that fact. He cannot ponder his fate, accept circumstance, and sing. Other Negroes shout, sing, make music, and thereby cope with evil. Their art removes experience to a realm where it can be transcended: "To sing goes beyond resignation. It is a positive act, an artistic expression created not simply in the face of adversity, but because of it."[15] Such ability has made it possible to finger the jagged edge of pain and be comforted.[16] Everything in Georgia conspires to provide a poetic setting—"Night winds . . . are vagrant poets" (157). But Kabnis has to learn like AEsop to make poetry. He cannot do so when constantly frustrated by his situation. To transcend despair he has to first realize where he is. When he goes to work for Halsey, a man who has made peace with the difficulties of being a Negro in the South, he progresses further toward that necessary knowledge. Below Halsey's workshop is a cellar; and it is within that cellar that the final action of the book transpires. This is a setting similar to Crane's poem. This region functions symbolically like Crane's mid-kingdom. In the lower region depicted in the conclusion, old Father John stands as a link between past and present, a living illustration of the past and a prophetic warning of the difficulty of the future.

Kabnis advances toward a state of self-knowledge in the final part of the novelette. He comes closest to confronting the truth made up of distortions which both black and white people have accepted. Old Father John reveals a fundamental truth about American culture through his lamentation that white people have made the Bible lie. Because of this untruth Negroes accept an inferior role, and as has been suggested by Scruggs, because they come to believe untruths, they lose an ability to make poetry of living. It is not even necessary to be absorbed by an urban metropolis (Part 2) to lose contact with the positive aspects of one's culture. Kabnis himself is an example of what can happen when a black man is filled with self-doubt and hatred and cannot accept the ambiguity and complexity of race in the South.

After some weeks with Halsey, one evening Kabnis, Halsey, and others meet in the cellar for a party. The cellar seems like a prison that evening, and "there seems to be no goodtime spirit to the party. Something in the air is too tense and deep for that" (214). This is similar to the tenseness of Crane's mid-kingdom, where "gnats toss in the shadow of a bottle," an atmosphere where only the memory of a fly-covered carcass of an earlier culture lingers. The atmosphere of Halsey's party seems especially tense because Father John is present; and it is significant that when Kabnis spews out words at the old man, he not only unfairly calls him a cockroach, but his thought resembles Crane's: "Why I can already see you toppled off that stool . . . not beside me, damn you, by yourself, with th flies buzzin and lickin . . ." (233). The party does get underway; but Toomer's focus remains on the presence of the old man. Lewis, who is the kind of person a stronger Kabnis would have been, seats himself "so that his eyes rest upon the old man, merges with his source and lets the pain and beauty of the South meet him there" (214). Old Father John seems to represent the strength of black people who have not compromised themselves. One of the girls, Stella, says he reminds her of her father. When her father was too old to sing, he was carried to the church and placed before the pulpit where he led singing by swaying in front of it. (Crane's figure mingles "incantations on the air.") This is what Kabnis would also like to learn to do: to make music of his pain. He sees that others are able to transcend adversity and darkness. But it is so easy to be swallowed up by the darkness of this midregion. Too many words and too many untruths have made it difficult to see the truth. Too much has been said about the condition of black people; and since so much has been said, it is hard not to believe the distortions. Instead of being able to ponder the truth like AEsop or Father John, Kabnis is obsessed with distortions. His comments about language are crucial: "Th form thats burned int my soul is some twisted awful thing that crept in from a dream, a goddam nightmare . . . " (224). He wishes that a lynching white man would cut out the distortion and "pin it to a tree" (225).

Father John also realizes that there has been too much talking. But he sits and tolerates Kabnis, who cries out in anger at him: "Death . . . these clammy floors . . . just like th place they used t stow away the wornout, no-count niggers in th days of slavery . . . that was long ago"(231). Kabnis realizes that black people should not still be enslaved; yet the fact is, he begins to realize, that many remain suspended between the dignity of the past and the promise of the future. The question is, How do they learn to live with such disappointment? Kabnis does not even want to admit that his blood is related to old

Father John's: "He reminds me of that black cockroach over yonder. An besides, he aint my past. My ancestors were Southern blue-bloods" (217). But Lewis replies that there is not much difference between blue and black. He realizes that Father John has much to give anyone who listens: "Dead blind father of a muted folk who feel their way upward to a life that crushes or absorbs them" (212). But black culture is not completely absorbed or crushed. And for those who ponder those facts, sense can be made of existence.

Kabnis is close to being crushed as the book ends, but he learns from the old man, who seems in some ways like a displaced king, sitting "in [his] high-backed chair which stands upon a low platform" (211). It is true, as Scruggs asserts, that when Kabnis stumbles out of bed after the party the next morning, he is a parody of a poet. But he does wear the robe which hung on the wall, an object which functions like the tambourine of Crane's poem. It suggests the dignity of the past and also the possibility of deliverance. Crane's tambourine has been interpreted as a symbol for inactive creative expression. In Toomer's cellar the old robe worn by Kabnis may represent the older culture and an ability to sing. When Kabnis dons the robe the effect is laughable; but this does not mean he can deny his past. His "mock-solemnity" (213); the "mock curtsy" (220) toward Father John; and even the exaggerated ceremony with which he hangs up the robe in the morning: all indicate that Kabnis realizes honor is due the prophet, Father John. He goes to work with Halsey with a cynical sneer on his face, but he has learned from Father John and from Carrie, who comforts the old man. As he leaves the cellar "light streaks through the iron-barred cellar window. . . . The sun arises. Gold-glowing child, it steps into the sky and sends a birth-song slanting down gray dust streets" (239). Beauty is there, and poetry can be made of it. Toomer realized this, as did Crane, and while they both realized that in many ways black men are forlorn, each emphasized that black culture is strong enough to surmount temporary degradation. One remembers the girls of "Kabnis" doing up their hair on the morning after the party: "it is bushy hair that has gone through some straightening process. Character, however, has not all been ironed out. As they kneel . . . they are two princesses in Africa going through . . . ablutions [and] prayers" (229). We are reminded that there are "November Cotton Flowers";

"Brown eyes that loved without a trace of fear" (7). It is this strength which Toomer emphasizes in *Cane*. He and Hart Crane have each created works which emphasize that imprisonment or denial can not suppress the strength of black Americans.

The Toomer-Ouspensky-Gurdjieff Connection

The Influence of Ouspensky's *Tertium Organum* upon Jean Toomer's *Cane*

ALICE POINDEXTER FISHER

Since its publication in 1923, Jean Toomer's *Cane* has "presented an enigma" to the reading public and an interpretive challenge to the critics.[1] Part of the mystery of this important work, which heralded the inception of the Harlem Renaissance, lies in its language and the mood created therein. Toomer chooses his words with care, molding them into leitmotifs that unify the various themes. His recurrent images of dusk, pines, smoke, night, moon, sun, wind—all lend a timelessness and universality to the book that borders on the mystical. Indeed, Toomer lays the foundation for a visionary interpretation in the inscription—the cane is "oracular." What inspired Toomer to experiment with language and form as he did? Where did he develop a sense of "cosmic consciousness" as expressed in "Fern" and other sections of the book? Are there elements of mysticism in *Cane*, and whence do they spring? These questions will direct the following discussion of Jean Toomer's use of language in his unique work, *Cane*.

According to Robert Bone, Toomer "was a member of a semi-mystical group that included Hart Crane, Waldo Frank, Gorham Munson, and Kenneth Burke";[2] their avowed purpose was experimentation with words, "stretching them and refocusing them, until they became the pliant instruments of a new idiom."[3] That writers traditionally form literary coteries and discuss the theories underlying their art is not unusual; however, to be singularly influenced by a given work *is* unique. The opus that provided images for Hart Crane's poetry and influenced the personal philosophy of Waldo Frank; that led both Jean Toomer and Gorham Munson into a highly esoteric field of self-knowledge with the Gurdjieff Institute, was the philosophical, mystical *Tertium Organum—A Key to the Enigmas of the World* by Peter Demianovich Ouspensky, which was translated from Russian and published in English in 1920.[4]

Before exploring Ouspensky's influence on Toomer, it is necessary to establish that Toomer did come in contact with *Tertium Organum* before the publication of *Cane* in 1923. Bone asserts that Toomer was a member of the above-mentioned group in his "formative years" and that the group was "influenced philosophically by Ouspensky's *Tertium Organum*," forming a "bloc called art as vision" with catchwords such as "the new slope of consciousness," "the superior logic of metaphor," and "noumenal knowledge."[5] However, Bone does not date the year when these meetings were held.

Hart Crane's biographer, John Unterecker, notes Crane's interest in *Tertium Organum* as early as 1921 and mentions Crane's conversations first with Munson and "later with Jean Toomer and Waldo Frank" on the subject of Ouspensky's dogma.[6] Again, we are not given a specific date for the literary discussions, but we can suppose that they fell sometime in the year 1922, if we follow Unterecker's chronology of Crane's philosophical development.

One of the other members of Toomer's discussion group, Waldo Frank, is purported to have turned to Ouspensky specifically for an "up-to-date statement of mystical theories."[7] Robert Perry affirms Frank's "spiritual and mystical" influence on Hart Crane and records that "Ouspensky's *Tertium Organum* was a book that was familiar to many writers in the twenties. . . . The 1923 literary clique—Crane, Gorham Munson, and Jean Toomer—of which Frank served as patriarch, professedly considered Ouspensky's book to be their bible. Passages in Frank's novels and essays before 1923 seem to show that he had read the book much earlier than that, however."[8]

One can assume that Toomer read *Tertium Organum* much earlier than 1923, also, for several reasons: first, Frank and Toomer traveled through the South together in 1922 and must have had ample opportunity to discuss many ideas of interest to them both; second, Ouspensky was being read closely by two other friends of Toomer's; third, *Tertium Organum* became a bible for Toomer's literary group, indicating that it must have been read quite thoroughly by all members; fourth, Toomer's subsequent visits to the Gurdjieff Institute (Ouspensky's master) reflect the depth of his commitment to the philosophy; and last, there is evidence, both philosophically and imagistically, in *Cane* of Ouspensky's influence.

Who, then, is Ouspensky and what is *Tertium Organum*? To answer either question adequately is impossible within the scope of this paper, but a brief description of the book and its author will serve to clarify subsequent comments about Ouspensky's influence on Toomer's use of language and mysticism in *Cane*.

Peter Demianovich Ouspensky was born in Moscow in 1878 of highly cultured parents. He studied science, psychology, and mathematics but gradually developed an interest in theosophy and then the occult.[9] In 1912 he published *Tertium Organum*, a work that combines mysticism and mathematics in a system to discover the various levels of consciousness for man. Ouspensky's interest in the occult inspired him to travel to India in 1913, where he met Annie Besant, the leading advocate for theosophy, with whom he spent six weeks. Returning to Moscow, he met Georges Ivanovitch Gurdjieff in 1915, whose approach to the practical development of consciousness within man he admired. The Russian revolution interrupted their studies abruptly, causing Ouspensky to flee to Constantinople.

The subsequent history of the book's independent voyage from Russia into the hands of its translator, Claude Bragdon, would stimulate any skeptic's fancy.[10] Briefly, the English publication of *Tertium Organum* excited so much public interest that one Viscountess Rothermere demanded to know more of the author. After much sleuthing poor Ouspensky was discovered ailing and poverty-stricken in Constantinople. The kind countess immediately offered financial assistance, and in 1921 Ouspensky moved to London with his family, where he began conducting lectures. Gurdjieff rejoined him, and together they launched the Institute for the Harmonious Development of Man in Fontainebleau, France, in 1922. Jean Toomer began attending summer sessions at the institute in 1924.[11]

Tertium Organum, the third canon of thought (following Aristotle's *Organon* and Bacon's *Novum Organum*), is really a study of consciousness. Ouspensky maintains that man is asleep in his present state, but he can awaken to an objective consciousness in which prior limitations on his perception no longer exist. The intuitive faculty within the consciousness allows man to perceive ultimate truths.

One of the obstacles to "clear seeing," according to Ouspensky, is our perception of Time:

> We create time ourselves, as a function of our receptive apparatus, for convenience in perceiving the outside world. Reality is continuous and constant, but in order to make possible the perception of it, we must dissever it into separate moments; imagine it as an infinite series of separate moments out of which there exists for us only one. In other words, we perceive reality as if through a narrow slit, and what we are seeing through this slit we call the present; what we did see and now do not see—the past; and what we do not quite see but are expecting—the future.[12]

Time affects causality, motion, and dimension. The noumenal world is really the "Eternal Now of Hindu philosophy—a universe in which will be neither before nor after, in which will be just one present, known or unknown" (105). Everything participates in eternity and is animated by a common energy source. Consequently, individual differences give way to a common self. Ouspensky uses the Platonic comparison of man's relationship to his shadow-reflection as analogous to our imperfect perception of the noumenal world. However, contrary to Plato, the material world is not an illusion; it is merely misrepresented to us because of our own limitations. He says, "That world and our world are not two different worlds. The world is one. That which we call our world is merely our incorrect perception of the world: the world seen by us through a narrow slit" (242).

The nature of the world can really only be known through mysticism of which any type is acceptable. Certain people have been endowed with heightened consciousness which allows for spontaneous communication. "In mystical sensations all men feel definitely something in common, having a similar meaning and connection one with another. The mystics of many ages and many peoples speak the same language and use the same words" (277).

However, individual knowledge of the noumenal world is not enough. It must be expressed to the masses for universal enlightenment to be achieved. Ouspensky states that only a poet can communicate both the mystical, emotional feelings of an experience and the concepts inherent in that experience. Thus, "poetry endeavors to express both music and thought together. The combination of feeling and thought of high tension leads to a higher form of psychic life. Thus in art we have already the first experiments in a language of the future. Art anticipates a psychic evolution and divines its future forms" (73).

To conceive of one's artistic function as that of a prophet and mythmaker must inspire one to experiment radically with language and form in order to communicate that special insight. Thus, Toomer and his friends explored all the possibilities of a "new idiom," one that "was to recreate a sense of fundamental relatedness between art and experience, to make language once more a viable and powerful means of approaching reality."[13] But, as we have seen, reality has mystical overtones, because the artist is a visionary and clairvoyant as well as a poet.

Toomer delves into his racial heritage for his source of inspiration in creating a new idiom. That *Cane* is essentially a "celebration of blackness" is apparent; however, in light of the previous discussion, can we not also find evidence of Ouspensky's influence on Toomer in the elements of mysticism in *Cane*.

In the broadest sense *Cane* is an experiment in forming the "language of the future." The message is one of reintegration with one's spiritual and racial roots. Cosmic consciousness becomes racial consciousness. Most of the characters suffer from internal as well as external fragmentation; they do not fully understand their relationship to the world surrounding them; their eyes are veiled by dusk which creates a world of shadows and illusions. Toomer reaches the conclusion that love is the answer in the charitable, merciful figure of Carrie Kate, who attends to the blind father John with the understanding of one who has "seen."

More specifically, we immediately see Ouspensky's influence on Toomer in the concept of animated nature. Ouspensky devotes chapter twelve of *Tertium Organum* to a discussion of the rationality in the universe and maintains that if rationality exists, it must exist in everything, including "dead nature." In other words, nature is animated; life and feeling exist in everything; there is individuality of thought and feeling in all. Ouspensky's passage on this concept is worth noting:

> A strange individuality which is all their own is sensed in certain days. There are days brimming with the marvelous and the mystic, days having each its own individual and unique consciousness, its

> own emotions, its own thoughts. One may almost commune with these days. And they will tell you that they live a long, long time, perhaps eternally, and that they have known and seen many, many things.
>
> In the processional of the year; in the iridescent leaves of autumn, with their memory-laden smell; in the first snow, frosting the fields and communicating a strange freshness and sensitiveness to the air; in the spring freshets, in the warming sun, in the awakening but still naked branches through which gleams the turquoise sky; in the white nights of stars—in all these are the thoughts, the emotions, the forms, peculiar to itself alone, of some great consciousness: or better, all this is the expression of the emotions, thoughts and forms of consciousness of a mysterious being—Nature. (179)

Ouspensky goes on to make this statement:

> A MOUNTAIN, A TREE, A RIVER, THE FISH WITHIN THE RIVER, DEW AND RAIN, PLANET, FIRE—each separately must possess a psyche of its own. (179)

The relationship of Ouspensky's concept of animated nature to Toomer's imagery is strikingly obvious. In "Becky," a recurrent motif is "O pines, whisper to Jesus."[14] The pines are the only entities fully aware of Becky's suffering, which is evidenced by their whispered supplications to the savior for aid:

> The pines whispered to Jesus. (9)
> O pines, whisper to Jesus; tell Him to come and
> press sweet Jesus-lips against their lips and eyes. (10)
> Pines shout to Jesus! (12)

The direct address to the pines personifies them. In addition, the pine trees utter entreaties of their own.

The cane is animated and mystical, too, as seen in the inscription to the book:

> Oracular.
> Redolent of fermenting syrup,
> Purple of the dusk,
> Deep-rooted cane.

The canefields offer cooling solace to Bob Stone before he encounters Tom Burwell (62). "Time and space have no meaning in a canefield" (19). The soil itself that nurtures the cane has a psyche—". . . O soil, it is not too late yet / To catch thy plaintive soul, leaving, soon gone" (21).

Also animated is the smoke from the perennial sawdust pile. It "curls up and hangs in odd wraiths about the trees, curls up and spreads itself out over the valley" (4). The smoke expresses its own individual psyche by the form it takes. Always described as a "wraith," the smoke inspires a "creepy feeling" and fear in the people who see it, reminding us that Nature lives.

The "strange individuality" which exists in certain days, according to Ouspensky, is also present in Toomer. In "Fern," he describes the dusk:

> Dusk, suggesting the almost imperceptible procession of giant trees, settled with a purple haze about the cane. I felt strange, as I always do in Georgia, particularly at dusk. *I felt that things unseen to men were tangibly immediate. It would not have surprised me had I had vision.* (31—italics added)

Notice that the narrator does not say "a vision," but rather "vision," meaning insight into the order of the universe.

Perhaps "Blood-Burning Moon" is the best example of animated nature. It serves to punctuate each scene, but more than that, it elicits the unrest within each character. For example, "But for some reason, they jumbled when her [Louisa's] eyes gazed vacantly at the rising moon. And from the jumble came the stir that was strangely within her" (52). The same happens to Tom Burwell, when he leaves the company of friends at old David Georgia's: "Just then, the dogs started barking and the roosters began to crow. Tom felt funny. Away from the fight, away from the stove, chill got to him. He shivered. He shuddered when he saw the full moon rising towards the cloud-bank. He who didn't give a godam for the fears of old women" (55). The tragedy of murder and lynching completed, the moon still looks on: "They saw the full moon glowing in the great door. The full moon, an evil thing, an omen soft showering the homes of folks she knew" (67).

Animation is not just a characteristic of Nature, though. Material objects also possess a life of their own. Ouspensky states that "there cannot be anything dead or inanimate. In the world of causes everything must be alive, because it is life itself; the soul of the world" (176). In *Cane* this concept is used metaphorically, perhaps most dramatically in Rhobert, who "wears a house, like a monstrous diver's helmet, on his head" (73). The house is dead, but the "stuffing is alive." Why?

Because "God built the house. He blew His breath into its stuffing" (74). What better evidence is there than the last statement for animation of material objects. Surely, Toomer was familiar with this aspect of Ouspensky's philosophy.

The juxtaposition in *Cane* of nature and material objects with human and psychic qualities illustrates again and again Ouspensky's concept of a divine energy source permeating the universe. For example, "Houses are shy girls whose eyes shine reticently upon the dusk body of the street. Upon the gleaming limbs and asphalt torso of a dreaming nigger. Shake your curled wool blossoms, nigger. Open your liver lips to the lean, white spring" (104). Houses, girls, streets, bodies, sensuous lips—everything is seen as part of the order of things, with the vision of cosmic consciousness.

What is cosmic consciousness? Ouspensky quotes from Dr. Bucke, who affirms that it is "a consciousness of the cosmos, that is, of the life and order of the universe" (283). Our language inhibits a full description of what such a life and order is, because we see everything as dualistic and as influenced by time. The universe is becoming, evolving, continually moving. Ouspensky refutes this, affirming that the universe is eternally being (170). Everything exists now, simultaneously. Time is eliminated. The universe flows together into one unified whole with each object being a prism or facet of the entirety.

Toomer's statement of cosmic consciousness is expressed by the narrator in "Fern":

> Like her face, the whole countryside seemed to flow into her eyes. Flowed into them with the soft listless cadence of Georgia's South. (27)

Or,

> Saw her face flow into them [eyes], the countryside and something that I call God, flowing into them. (33)

"Calling Jesus" combines both animated nature and cosmic consciousness to produce a highly mystical selection on man's need to integrate his spiritual understanding and awareness with his physical being. The soul is likened to a whimpering dog, cast out and unrecognized by his mistress, whose awareness only extends to her physical environment.

Implicit to the philosophy of cosmic consciousness is "karma, the unbroken consecutiveness of phenomena. Each phenomenon, no matter how insignificant, is a link to an infinite and unbroken chain, extending from the past into the future, passing from one sphere into another, sometimes manifesting as physical phenomena, sometimes hiding in the phenomena of consciousness" (136). Every act carries with it its own retribution; acts are intrinsically attached, because we are all part of the whole.

Toomer has entitled one of the selections in *Cane*, "Carma." Surely, this is more than coincidence. Carma reaps the consequence of her own actions; she loses her husband and gains the reputation of being foolish. But on another level Toomer is discussing the karma of the slave. The act of bringing slaves from Africa to the states has produced its own disaster—loss of cultural heritage and creation of superstition which we see in the "juju men, greegree, witch doctors . . . " (18).

The cause and effect of karma is evident throughout *Cane*, especially in the appearance of Carrie Kate in "Kabnis," lost daughter of Karintha. The product of sensual love has become the exemplar of Christian love and the hope for the future. Ouspensky discusses love at great length in *Tertium Organum*, but since love is essential to many philosophical systems, I will not attempt to draw parallels here with Toomer.

More significant to an understanding of *Cane* is Ouspensky's view of sex. He divides man's consciousness into five parts: the intellectual, the emotional, the moving, the instinctual, and the sex functions. "The sex functions can be studied only after all the other functions are known; for they are the last ones to appear in man's life and they always depend on the other functions."[15]

Toomer definitely uses sex as a touchstone for each character's awareness of himself and his environment, especially in Part 1. It is possible that he, like Ouspensky, is reversing Freudian psychology and using sex as a measure of man's other functions. The question is interesting but too broad in scope for discussion here.

It would not do to end a discussion of the mystical elements in *Cane* without mentioning "Kabnis," which Toomer dedicated to Waldo Frank. While this last selection is primarily concerned with problems of identity and racial consciousness, it does embody a number of the influences derived from Ouspensky.

The mood of "Kabnis" is one of a dream, reminiscent of Ouspensky's statement that we all exist in a dream-like condition. "Ralph Kabnis is a dream" (158). The elements of fear, paranoia, artificiality—

all bespeak a condition in which Kabnis is out of touch with himself and his environment.

The understanding that would allow him to transcend the dream state is glimpsed momentarily when he encounters Lewis. "There is a swift, intuitive interchange of consciousness" (191). This interchange is comparable to Ouspensky's concept of the vision poets have and is seen more clearly in the meeting between Carrie Kate and Lewis:

> Their meeting is a swift sun-burst. Lewis impulsively moves towards her. His mind flashes images of her life in the southern town. He sees the nascent woman, her flesh already stiffening to cartilage, drying to bone. Her spirit-bloom, even now touched sullen, bitter. Her rich beauty fading . . . He wants to—He stretches forth his hand to hers. He takes them. They feel like warm cheeks against his palms. The sun-burst from her eyes floods up and haloes him. Christ-eyes, his eyes look to her. Fearlessly she loves into them. (205)

Lewis sees the past, present, and future simultaneously. He has opened up the slit of the present to reveal the timelessness of the universe.

Omnipresent in "Kabnis" is nature, offering a touchstone with reality against which the dream state is measured:

> Night winds in Georgia are vagrant poets, whispering. (157)

Or,

> Night, soft belly of a pregnant Negress, throbs evenly against the torso of the South. Night throbs a womb-song to the South. Cane- and cotton-fields, pine forests, cypress swamps, sawmills, and factories are fecund at her touch. Night's womb-song sets them singing. Night winds are the breathing of the unborn child whose calm throbbing in the belly of a Negress sets them somnolently singing. (208–9)

And finally, the language of the future, the experiment in form that will enlighten the masses, is part of the dream also:

> Those words I was tellin y about, they wont fit int th mold thats branded on m soul. Rhyme, y see? Poet, too. Bad rhyme. Bad poet. Somethin else youve learned tnight. Lewis dont know it all, an I'm atellin y. Ugh. Th form thats burned int my soul is some twisted awful thing that crept in from a dream, a godam nightmare, an wont

> stay still unless I feed it. An it lives on words. Not beautiful words. God almighty no. Misshapen, split-gut, tortured, twisted words. (224)

Perhaps this is the message Toomer wished to convey to Frank—that he is a victim of a dream-like state also, caught in a three-dimensional world with enough intuition to sense a greater meaning in the universe but without the tools to express it.

Jean Toomer's *Cane*

JAMES KRAFT

Jean Toomer in writing *Cane*[1] in 1923 was aware of the broad dimensions of his novel, which seeks in its last ambivalent dramatic section some reconciliation of the warring elements that still exist in the American experience. Yet, his first intention as a black writer is to describe the black American experience. What gives *Cane* its inner tension is that these two objectives are not mutually exclusive for Toomer: he finds it necessary to assert the black self set *within* a white world; racial "separateness" cannot contain the black or white truth. Toomer seeks to use the tension within race to find the truth that transcends races. This viewpoint is the result of a personal direction that can be traced to elements in Toomer's life, elements that gave him an unusual perspective and helped to make him in *Cane* the artist-seer of the black people—reflecting them as Hawthorne did the New Englander in *The Scarlet Letter* and as Faulkner did the Southerner in *The Bear*.

Toomer was able to move easily between black and white societies and was recognized in either as a member. This fact opened to him unusual perspectives, perspectives of a kind that few people can experience. His family had been once politically powerful: his grandfather, P. B. S. Pinchback, had been acting governor of Louisiana during

Reconstruction. Toomer was able to attend several universities, including Wisconsin, Chicago, and New York, although he did not complete a degree. Pulled as he was between black and white worlds, he sought something that would bring him a personal sense of unity, and he found this in the ideas of the Russian mystic Georges Gurdjieff. Basically, Gurdjieff saw the necessity of transforming the consciousness onto broader levels of awareness through discipline and the expansion of self-expression. In this process an individual would overcome all conventional forms of restrictive expression and thought, somewhat as Emerson believed that a comprehension of the oversoul transcends conventional forms. Toomer came to Gurdjieff's ideas as he was writing *Cane*, in the early 1920s, and it was immediately after the novel's publication that Toomer went to the Gurdjieff Institute in France. One can better understand the transformation in the novel of the black soul into a cosmic eye—neither black alone nor simply not white—if one understands his attraction to Gurdjieff. It helps to understand what this attraction is if one also bears in mind that for Toomer the all-embracing Whitman was one of the great American figures.

This synthesized vision that Toomer sought is not at once apparent in reading *Cane*. The difficulty is partly in the novel's symbols, which, as will be indicated here, are not always immediately clear, but the lack of clarity is also in Toomer himself. He never personally synthesized the elements of his nature. That he did not is not alone his fault, for as the novel suggests, the synthesis of our warring natures is an ideal, a goal, not necessarily a reality. Toomer knew that the tensions in him were part of his creative self, and they remained with him to his death in 1967 at the age of 73, but they were as much a source of his artistic failure, since they were too divisive to allow for productive creation. His most recent and thorough biographer-critic, Darwin T. Turner, considers Toomer's plays to have great experimental possibilities, but *Cane* remains Toomer's only major work, written at the start of his career.[2] What Toomer maintains in *Cane* is that a black man must know his earth-black roots, the land sense of life that is in the novel symbolically established in Georgia, but that no black man can ever forget that part of his blackness is in its contrast to the white world, the city sense of life symbolically expressed in the Washington and Chicago sections of the novel. The Chinese figure of the circle, equally divided in an S-curve between black and white, yet so mystically interweaving, seems to be the symbol for him and for his novel that is clearly so autobiographical of his life in Washington and Chicago and of the period he spent in the South as a schoolteacher.

The symbolic dimensions of *Cane* must be recognized if one is to understand the unity in diversity that Toomer is seeking to express. Robert Bone, the author of *The Negro Novel in America*, is aware of the symbolic quality of the novel.[3] Things are not what they seem; categories are broken; lines are crossed; symbols transform our vision until we are forced to break down all normal expectations. Cane is the black people, the black life, and black oppression, the black condition that becomes cosmic in its attempts to reach out of the earth to the sun, to something more than itself. The symbol "cane" is a symbol of man's life movements. The very style—richly expressive in inventive syntax and diction— becomes symbolic of this expansive sense of life. Finally, the form of the novel becomes creatively alive and noncategorical: in three sections it is never really a novel but is a collection of tales of five black women and one white Georgia country woman in Part 1, interspersed with poems of the black people and the land; a series of longer short stories of black city life in Washington and Chicago in Part 2; and a long final dramatic section, largely in dialogue, set in Georgia, about black men, but in particular about two young and contrasting black men, Kabnis, after whom the section is named, and Lewis. The form of the novel is kinetic, not static or limited, as is the style—the syntax and diction; as are the symbols—like the major symbol of the novel, the sugar cane, rich, lingering, sweet, sticky, heavy, oppressive, deep-rooted, oracular, all-pervasive.

The form of *Cane* suggests the kind of breadth and complexity that is in the novel and indicates the approach one must take to the symbols. Turner discusses briefly the form of the novel in "Jean Toomer's *Cane*," published in *Negro Digest*[4]. Here and in a letter to the author, Turner explains that *Cane* grew from pieces of shorter fiction—poems, short stories, character sketches, and a play—not originally written as parts of a novel.[5] Emphasis cannot, therefore, be placed upon the form as an original conception; however, Toomer has given the novel a formal unity through symbolic thematic development. But if it is thought that in the black aesthetic unity is organic, or self-creating, then the formal unity of *Cane* as a novel is not affected by Toomer's not originally conceiving of the parts as forming a whole. A recent article by Melvin Dixon in *Negro Digest*[6] suggests this aesthetic in discussing black theatre. Dixon maintains that the black aesthetic demands an organic, self-creating unity of forms, not something preconceived; the writer discovers form as he creates. The idea has a long history—one that includes Emerson's theory of poetry; it is controversial and goes beyond a critical review of the novel; yet, it is clear that, in part, the blackness of *Cane* is in its noncategorical and freely creative capacity to transform the forms of the "white" novel and create its own black existence. The form of *Cane*, whether created in thematic symbols or intuitively conceived, is expressive of the richness of life as seen within the black experience and must be understood on its several possible levels.

One begins now to approach the broad and complex symbolic nature of the novel, and it is in the future of the black man that this nature is most fully seen. He becomes a symbol of a man caught, struggling to be free of limitations of any life. As Robert Bone indicates, the polarities of white and black in the novel express the polarities of life: spirit and flesh, intellect and emotions, male and female. Kabnis, the dry, frightened, intellectual black of the final section, is caught in his black cellar in his southern black world of dead bodies, cold and inflamed with senseless passion, watched over by a repressive black, blind and deaf Tiresias, who pronounces sin and doom. Lewis, the other black, runs from this hole in the admission of the novel's central tenant—the necessity to accept the ambiguity of our condition and to live it out.

> "Cant hold them, can you? Master; slave. Soil; and the overarching heavens. Dusk; dawn. They fight and bastardize you. The sun tint of your cheeks, flame of the great season's multi-colored leaves, tarnished, burned. Split, shredded: easily burned. No use . . ."[7]

The scene and characters here are profoundly black, but this speech by Lewis is symbolically beyond the particular application. These are the ingredients that place *Cane* in relation to such works as Hawthorne's *The Scarlet Letter* and Faulkner's *The Bear*. A reader is in the realm of those individual literary works that can never be separated from their particulars—what is Hester Prynne without Puritan New England or Ike without his prejudiced South—yet are beyond simply being novels of their particulars. *Cane* can stand with those short and deeply symbolic works that are peculiarly expressive of aspects of our experience. And it is perhaps indicative of the novel's quality that one could also say that "Cane" is a major figure in our literary heritage, like Hester or Ike.

The novel might also be considered as the spiritual portrait or autobiography of Jean Toomer, the young black artist, and bears a similarity to Joyce's *Portrait of the Artist* in its searching through the self for a national and racial destiny. One can see Toomer wanting to publish the entire novel for the final section, in which he has earned the right to speak out, even to speak directly in the dialogue of a play. He had by then taken his reader through the female South and its rural rootless and passionate life, and through the North and its urban male streets that kill the roots and juices and intellectualize our emotional existence. Now, in the final section, back in the South, he is the artist in search of his emotional and aesthetic balance, in search of his selfhood. He begins to see the complexity of the problem. To be the self he seeks will be to be misunderstood, as Lewis is by the people of the small southern town, to be an enigma who can stay only a month in a place because there is no place for this transcendent kind of man, this artist. Lewis is in exile, as Toomer was for the rest of his life, and there is no question that as a novel of the artist, or black artist, *Cane* embodies the alienation inherent in man and especially in man's artists.

Toomer sets the particular problem in the black world, but he sees it as the true artist does, whatever his race. The problem is the eternal one man must confront: the mind is the source of insight and of any art in life, but the mind also destroys the blood and passions that feed the life of the mind. Here is the black-white war that this novel moves toward, a war that is in the particulars of race if one chooses but is also beyond race as well, in the realm that Toomer was himself in. It is something of this special war, personal, racial, religious, national, that Toomer meant when he had Lewis say "Master; slave." This is our condition whether we put it that way, or say "Father-son": we are all masters to someone and all slaves to someone—especially to ourselves; we are all fathers and all sons.

If we find this concept difficult to keep in mind, we should remember that Toomer precedes the phrase "Master; slave" with "Cant hold them, can you?" He challenges us. Why we cannot hold them does not appear, at first perhaps, the subject of the novel, yet it is this issue that is at the heart of the final mystical and strange pages of *Cane*. Here Toomer implies that the eternal conflict of self will be projected out onto the forms of our society *unless* we go beyond these forms in our internal transformation. Toomer puts the issue in this unusual phrase: "Mind me, the only sin is what's done against the soul." The phrase is, within its context, deeply important. The warring elements are there, "Mind me" and "soul," the two sides, yet they are also our means of transformation. The message here is in Toomer's sense that full cognizance of the separate self of men can lead to the loss of that selfhood in the greater awareness of the one soul of all man. The words *brother* and *sister* of these last pages are now in their own realm of special meaning. *Cane* is truly oracular, as Toomer says, if one reads its implications.

There is much more that can be said about this novel, particularly about the six stories of the first section, all but the last named after a woman, and as Robert Bone says, acting as critiques of white rationalism in their subject matter of infanticide, miscegenation, hysteria, mysticism, prophecy, and lynching. The central section on Washington and Chicago is also important and effective, as it blends the polarities of the novel; it sows and reaps for a sense of what does mean in this cold and harsh world. One pays a supreme compliment to Toomer when one acknowledges that he enlarges the area of the possible in so many ways, but especially in the ways in which he redefines for us the words we use so easily: *brother*, *sister*, *master*, *slave*, *transformation*, *rational*, *mind* and *spirit*, *body* and *soul*, *intellect* and *emotion*, *war*, *self*. The artist is expected to give us a vision not of where we have been, nor necessarily of where we are, but rather of where we might go if we could see differently—to be oracular.

Cane is not an easy book to read, as it demands that we submit our white and black selves to seeing again the commonplaces of our existence, and then, within a new definition of these, to redirect our lives. Toomer's manifesto is truly revolutionary, for it is, like Hawthorne's and Faulkner's, directed at the reformation not of external forms, but of the heart of man, and it is only when man has the humility and endurance to make this transformation that his human process might, indeed, change.

The Unity of Jean Toomer's *Cane*

CATHERINE L. INNES

When *Cane* was first published in 1923, it met with a variety of critical responses ranging from enthusiasm to bewilderment and caution. Waldo Frank, in his introduction to the book, praised Toomer as a true poet and saw *Cane* as marking the "dawn of direct and unafraid creation."[1] William Stanley Braithwaite was also enthusiastic, claiming that Jean Toomer was the first Negro writer to refuse to compromise artistic vision in writing about race, and the first to be truly "objective"[2]—a seemingly inappropriate description which is also used later by David Littlejohn, who informs us that Toomer views Negro life with "chilling objectivity" and then immediately adds that *Cane* is a book where "common things are seen as if through a strangely neurotic vision."[3] Although Littlejohn begins his two-page discussion of *Cane* by admitting it is an "esoteric work, difficult to grasp, define and assess,"[4] he ends by dismissing it as "too insubstantial to be remembered."[5]

Since 1930 *Cane* (except for one or two of its poems) has been largely ignored or dismissed as a seeming "hodge-podge of verse, songs, stories, and plays."[6] In the past decade, however, a few critics have begun to take a second look, and Robert Bone has hailed it "as a measure of the Negro novelist's highest achievement," ranking with

Native Son and *Invisible Man*.[7] Despite Bone's rather cursory study and a helpful article by Todd Lieber, "Design and Movement in *Cane*,"[8] the book remains an intriguing and enigmatic work whose full meaning and artistic significance await detailed exploration. As Arna Bontemps has pointed out, when *Cane* was first published, "the 'new criticism,' as we have come to recognize it, had scarcely been heard from then, and apparently it still has not discovered Toomer, but the chances are it may yet find him challenging."[9]

My aim in this paper is to try to take up that challenge, exploring *Cane* with the aid of P. D. Ouspensky's *Tertium Organum* and the "new" critical methods, concentrating on some of the recurring images and symbols in the book and tracing their relation to one another and to the theme and structure of the work as a whole. Limitations of time and space will permit me to point to only a few of the dominant *leitmotifs* in a work whose construction is more reminiscent of a musical composition such as Mussorgsky's *Pictures at an Exhibition* or Berlioz' *Symphonie Fantastique* than the conventional novel.[10]

The symbol which introduces the book and which dominates the whole of Part 1 is that of the dusk:

> Her skin is like dusk on the eastern horizon,
> O cant you see it, O cant you see it,
> Her skin is like dusk on the eastern horizon
> . . . When the sun goes down[11]

Many of the complex associations which surround this symbol are suggested in this first section: Karintha "carries *beauty*, perfect as the dusk when the sun goes down," and throughout the work there will be recurring references to the beauty of dusky skins. Dusk is associated also with ripeness, with "Purple of the dusk / Deep-rooted cane," with "Negro slaves, dark purple ripened plums," and with autumn and harvest time, "for the soul of her was a growing thing ripened too soon." Dusk also refers to the last glow of the setting sun, "just before an epoch's sun declines," that moment when the sun's glow is poignantly beautiful because it is fast disappearing. Finally, and perhaps most important, dusk represents a moment of fusion of dark and light, of past and future, a mingling of colors—the moment when it is neither day nor night but both, a moment which is matched by and reminds one of the dawn. It is the moment of intuitive apprehension rather than logical distinction: "I felt strange, as I always do in Georgia, particularly at dusk. I felt that things unseen to men were tangibly immediate" (31).

The significance of dusk as a central symbol of fusion, of a time when the invisible world and the aesthetic realm are most strongly felt (a connection expressed in "Georgia Dusk"), is, I believe, closely tied to Jean Toomer's study of the theories of P. D. Ouspensky, author of *Tertium Organum*, a book which also influenced Hart Crane, Kenneth Burke, Waldo Frank, and Gorham Munson, a group of writers with whom Toomer associated in the twenties.[12]

Ouspensky considered his work a successor to Aristotle's *Organon* and Francis Bacon's *Novum Organum*, replacing the laws of scientific observation and deduction with the "third Canon of Thought," or the logic of intuition. Whereas the scientists, exploring observable phenomena and the world of appearances, insist on distinctions between things ("Everything is either A or not-A"), Ouspensky insisted on the superior reality of the "noumenal," or subjectively felt, world long ago explored by Eastern sages and early Christian mystics, a world where "Everything is *both* A and Not-A."[13] The *Tertium Organum* urges the development of a new group of supermen capable of "cosmic consciousness," which involves the idea and sensation of a living universe in which the hidden meaning of all things will be realized and felt and the unity of all things understood. Such an understanding must come through the blending of emotional and intellectual modes of apprehension:

> Cosmic consciousness may develop in purely emotional soil . . . and is also possible of attainment through the emotion attendant upon creation—in painters, musicians and poets. Art in its highest manifestations is a path to cosmic consciousness.
>
> For the manifestation of cosmic consciousness it is necessary that the center of gravity of *everything* shall lie for man in the inner world, in self-consciousness, and not in the outer world at all.[14]

While Part 1 of *Cane* is suffused in the subjective, lyrical vision and is an implicit presentation of intuitive, nonlogical consciousness, the striving for a fusion of opposites, along with the consequences of failure to achieve it, is expressed most explicitly by Lewis in Part 3:

> Kabnis: Aint much difference between blue and black.
>
> Lewis: Enough to draw a denial from you. Cant hold them, can you? Master; slave. Soil; and the overarching heavens. Dusk; dawn. They fight and bastardize you. The sun tint of your cheeks, flame of

> the great season's multi-colored leaves, tarnished, burned. Split, shredded: easily burned. No use. . . (218)

A year before *Cane* was published, Jean Toomer wrote:

> Racially, I seem to have (who knows for sure) seven blood mixtures: French, Dutch, Welsh, Negro, German, Jewish and Indian. . . . I have strived for a spiritual fusion analogous to the fact of racial intermingling. Without denying a single element in me, with no desire to subdue one to the other, I have sought to let them function as complements. I have tried to let them live in harmony.[15]

The symbolism of racial fusion associated with striving for cosmic consciousness, though suggested in "Karintha," "Song of the Sun," and "Georgia Dusk," is most clearly developed in "Fern," an impression of Fernie May Rosen who unites Jewish and Negro, canticle and folk song, and into whose eyes flowed "her face, the countryside and something that I call God . . ." (33). She suggests the state in which "the center of gravity of *everything* lies in the inner world of self-consciousness." Fern is the passively receptive consciousness, responding to and becoming one with her world, which includes the anguished past of Jewish and African peoples—an anguish from which the narrator is unable to redeem her because he is unable to understand. His consciousness of himself as a separate entity prevents him from giving himself up wholly to Fern, from flowing into her, and so he remains perplexed, knowing only that the material, sensual things he might offer are inadequate.

The theme of the striving for racial fusion symbolizing spiritual harmony and of the failure of the passive female and active male to unite is taken up with some variations in "Esther," the story of a repressed girl who once catches a glimpse of the cosmic vision through the trance of King Barlo, whose image then becomes "the starting point of the only living patterns that her mind was to know" (40). Toomer stresses the contrast between Esther and Barlo. Her face is "chalk-white" and later becomes the "color of the gray dust that dances with dead cotton leaves" (43). Barlo, on the other hand, is "black. Magnetically so. . . . A clean-muscled, magnificent, black-skinned Negro" who in his trance "assumes the outlines of his visioned African."

Esther's dream of union with Barlo not only emphasizes the theme of fusion of opposites but also introduces another major motif which will be sounded more clearly and triumphantly at the end of the work—that of redemption—which is linked also with the imagery of dusk and dawn, and the connotations of a fading beauty and a new promise. Barlo speaks of his vision of past glory:

> "I saw a man arise, an he was big an black an powerful—". . .
>
> "—but his head was caught up in th clouds. An while he was agazin at th heavens, heart filled up with th Lord, some little white-ant biddies came an tied his feet to chains." (38)

Toomer reminds that dusk is "rapidly falling." Then comes the prophecy of dawn:

> Barlo rises to his full height. He is immense. To the people he assumes the outlines of his visioned African. In a mighty voice he bellows:
>
> "Brothers an sisters, turn your faces t th sweet face of the Lord, an fill your hearts with glory. Open your eyes an see th dawnin of th mornin light. Open your ears—." (39)

Inspired by this vision, a black woman drew a portrait in charcoal of a black madonna on the courthouse wall. Esther dreams of becoming that madonna, building fantasies of a child rescued from fire, claimed as her own. "She thinks of it immaculately."

The story of Esther also emphasizes the repression and prudishness which destroy her dream and finally make Barlo hideous to her—a theme which will receive full treatment in Part 2.

Two poems dealing with the perversion of religion and of sensual beauty lead into the grim story which ends Part 1, the story of the fatal competition between white Bob Stone and black Tom Burwell (whose name echoes Barlo), opposites between whom Louisa is forced to try and choose. For Louisa, Burwell's "black balanced, and pulled against the white of Stone when she thought of them" (52). It is significant, I think, that this episode takes place *after* dusk, in the false and ominous light of the "blood-burning moon," in a factory town, and that Tom is dragged into a factory to be killed. His head in the flames is compared to blackened stone. The lynching of Tom Burwell by "white men like ants upon a forge" not only recalls the vision of Barlo ("Some little white-ant biddies came an tied his feet to chains") but also looks forward to the migration North and to Toomer's depiction of the psychic destruction of black people, the conquest of subjective consciousness by white pragmatism and materialism in the industrial urban environment, the "factory town," to be portrayed in Part 2 of *Cane*. And, of course, "Blood-Burning Moon" is a fearful depiction of how whites had instigated a reign of terror in the South in an attempt to destroy black men physically and psychologically—a reign of terror which distorts the lives of those who are portrayed in Part 3.

Part 2 begins with an invocation of the contrast between "the white and whitewashed wood of Washington" and black inhabited Seventh Street, a wedge "thrusting unconscious rhythms, black reddish blood" into the "stale and soggy wood of Washington." "Seventh Street" serves as a transition between Part 1 and Part 2, moving the reader from South to North, from black Georgia soil and purple dusk to Washington's night life and hustling pace of the Prohibition era.

The next sketch, "Rhobert" (robot?), is a structural parallel to "Karintha," introducing the dominant theme and symbol for Part 2. Like "Karintha" it is also faintly elegaic in tone, but whereas the mode of "Karintha" is more purely lyrical, echoing the folk ballad, "Rhobert," like the whole of Part 2, is much more sardonic and intellectualized, and closer to the urban blues in tone.

Bone has discussed the importance of this section as "an attack on the crucial bourgeois value of home ownership."[16] The recurring house imagery implies this and much more, acquiring the complexity and thematic significance of the dusk imagery in Part 1. The house which Rhobert wears on his head and which slowly crushes him is a symbol not only of materialism but also of positivistic thinking, the dualistic logic, the separation of mind and body, soul and spirit, described by Ouspensky as characterizing the Third and inferior Form of Consciousness. Just as Becky in Part 1 was crushed by the cabin built by the community to hide her and her "sin," so the house becomes in Part 2 a symbol of repression and Puritanism, preventing the fusion of sense, emotion, and intellect, and representing a barrier to the open receptivity which is the concern of Part 1. It is significant that nearly all the scenes in Part 1 take place outside, in the light of the setting sun, imbued with the sounds and smells of the "whispering pines," the "rustling cane," the fragrance of fermenting syrup, the strain of folk songs, the sense of "soil and overarching heavens." In contrast, all the scenes in Part 2, with the important exception of "Avey," take place inside buildings, in houses, in theaters, in rooms, where the lighting is artificial or distorted.

As "Rhobert" forms a structural parallel and thematic contrast to "Karintha," "Avey" recalls and contrasts with "Fern." Both these sketches feature the first person narrator and his attempt to understand and come to terms with an enigmatic woman. As Fernie May Rosen is a symbol of racial/spiritual fusion and of emotional kinship between soil, land, and Negro people of the South, so Avey represents her people transplanted to the urban environment of V Street (she *is a* V Street), where "the young trees had not outgrown their boxes then. V Street was lined with them. When our legs grew cramped and stiff from the cold of stone, we'd stand around a box and whittle it" (76).

Like Fern, Avey remains indifferent to the narrator, who, gradually adopting the competitive spirit of the North, begins to condemn Avey for "her downright laziness. Sloppy indolence. . . . Among those energetic Swedes, or whatever they are, I decided to forget her" (82–83). But the narrator's attempt to forget and condemn his racial heritage as symbolized by Avey is futile. Once again we hear echoes of the opening motif in "Karintha": "One evening in early June, just at the time when the dusk is most lovely on the eastern horizon, I saw Avey, indolent as ever, leaning on the arm of a man, strolling under the recently lit arc-lights of U Street" (84).

Despite the winds from the South, despite his ardent talk sketched with wonderful self-irony by Toomer, the narrator cannot arouse Avey:

> I described her own nature and temperament. Told how they needed a larger life for their expression. How incapable Washington was of understanding that need. How it could not meet it. I pointed out that in lieu of proper channels, her emotions had overflowed into paths that dissipated them. I talked, beautifully, I thought, about an art that would be born, an art that would open the way for women the likes of her. I asked her to hope, and build up an inner life against the coming of that day. I recited some of my own things to her. (86–87)

The ending of "Avey" indicates that the narrator's hope for a new dawning, a new union with his blood heritage, has been a false one, for his dream, his "song," is not "sun-lit" but is based on an artificial and idealized conception of Avey, a purely cerebral "plotting of destiny" (to borrow a phrase from the next section), cut off from its southern roots. Avey remains an "orphan-woman," her face pale and lacking the "gray crimson-splashed beauty of the dawn" (88).

Two poems, "Beehive" and "Storm Ending," emphasize the contrast between the dreamed, artificial "silver honey" spun by "silver bees intently buzzing," and the rich refreshing "rain like golden honey" dripped from flowers "bitten by the sun." "Theater" takes up this contrast, modulating the silver dream and golden nature motifs in the figures of John and Dorris. John's mind and body function separately: "And as if his own body were the mass-heart of a black audience listening to them singing, he wants to stomp his feet and shout. His mind, contained above desires of his body, singles the girls out, and tries to trace origins and plot destinies" (92).

Dorris, depicted in the lemon, crimson, and purple colors of dusk, recalls the soul of her people as her dance transcends the mechanical, planned movements of the other chorus girls:

> Dorris dances. She forgets her tricks. She dances.
> Glorious songs are the muscles of her limbs.
> And her singing is of cane brake loves and mangrove feastings.
> (98)

But John's passion is "diluted" by his inability to merge mind and body; his dream, like the narrator's in "Avey," is an artificial thing composed of treeless streets where satin slippers tread dead autumn leaves, a dream bathed in melancholy. Dorris sees that her dance has become "a dead thing in the shadow which is his dream." She is left staring at the whitewashed ceiling of her drab dressing room.

Separation of soul from body is also the theme of "Calling Jesus," where the soul is imagined as a whimpering dog shut out of the "big house," able to steal in only at night "cradled in dream-fluted cane" (103).

"Box Seat," placed almost in the middle of the book, presents in surreal, often grotesque, terms the central conflict of the whole work. Dan Moore, who recalls Barlo and prefigures Lewis, is a precursor of the new redeemer: "Look into my eyes. I am Dan Moore. I was born in a canefield. The hands of Jesus touched me. I am come to a sick world to heal it" (105–6). He is able to feel the cosmic forces, vibrant rumbles from the earth's deep core, "the mutter of powerful underground races" (108). He is able to commune with the old slave, to feel the strong roots of the portly Negress, to penetrate the physical phenomenal world and pass beyond the dualistic thinking of his fellows. As he tells Muriel, "Life bends joy and pain, beauty and ugliness, in such a way that no one may isolate them. No one should want to. Perfect joy, or perfect pain, with no contrasting element to define them would mean a monotony of consciousness, would mean death. Not happy, Muriel. Say that you have tried to make them create. Say that you have used your own capacity for life to cradle them. To start them upward-flowing" (112).

But Dan, a representative of the southern heritage portrayed in Part 1, is unable to break down the walls, the bolts, the glass windows that imprison Muriel, who remains a "she-slave" shackled by the northern mode of thought and morality. Mrs. Pribby, with her steel blue eyes, represents Muriel's superego and remains constantly alert:

> Muriel: . . . Dan, I could love you if I tried. . . . I wont let myself. I? Mrs. Pribby who reads newspapers all night wont. What has she got to do with me? She *is* me, somehow. No she's not. Yes she is. She is the town, and the town wont let me love you, Dan. (110)

Whereas Muriel's Mrs. Pribby represents "the submission to the group consciousness of the family, of the clan, of the tribe, etc.," Dan, who won't "fit in," outraging Muriel and the theater audience by his behavior, looks forward to the return of the "law inside oneself."

Dan's manifestation of the new consciousness is followed by an even more explicit statement of Ouspensky's doctrine in the poem "Prayer," where the image of the "little finger" echoes these lines from the *Tertium Organum*:

> But we do not realize, do not discern the presence of rationality in the phenomena and laws of nature. This happens because we study always not the whole but the part, and we do not divine the whole which we wish to study—by studying the little finger of man we cannot discover his reason. It is the same way in our relation to nature: we study always the little finger of nature. When we come to realize this and shall understand that *every life is the manifestation of a part of some whole*, then only the possibility of knowledge of that whole opens to us.[17]

The final section of Part 2, "Bona and Paul," associates the protagonist with Paul's Epistle to the Corinthians and the famous chapter on the supreme importance of charity. Paul is described as looking through a "dark pane," cool and detached, and contemptuous of Bona and his companions. Paul's vision of love and unity between black and white comes too late: Bona has left him.

"Kabnis," the third part of Toomer's work, is a brilliant portrayal of the modern fragmented consciousness, uprooted from the traditions of the past and unable to find a place in which to grow naturally.

As Lewis perceives him, Kabnis is "a promise of soil-soaked beauty; uprooted, thinning out. Suspended a few feet above the soil whose touch would resurrect him" (191). Tormented by the fear of the white southerners, contemptuous of the Negroes who have remained in the South and the culture they have developed, denying his racial kinship with them, he can only turn to cynicism, self-contempt, alcohol, and self-conscious debauchery to conceal his pain.

A product of the northern experience, Kabnis is unable to return to that emotional consciousness of Part 1 which bathes Georgia in the rich after-glow of the setting sun. Projecting his own self-division, fear, and contempt upon his environment, Kabnis perceives it as opposed to him ("Hell of a mess I've got in: even the poultry is hostile." [159]). The pines "whispering to Jesus" are supplanted by the mocking songs of the night winds:

White-man's land.
Niggers, sing.
Burn, bear black children
Till poor rivers bring
Rest, and sweet glory
In Camp Ground.
(157, 167, and 209)

God has become an ugly, external force, "a profligate, red-nosed man about town" (161), who so torments him with the opposition between the ugliness (of white lynchers, cackling hens, and hogpens) and the beautiful serenity of the night that his bitterness erupts in the violent beheading of the cackling hen. The rich, mellow harvest time of Part 1 has become "gray, cold changed autumn weather" (167). "Georgia hills roll off into the distance, their dreary aspect heightened by gray spots of unpainted one- and two-room shanties" (169). The church, described as a "forlorn, box-like, whitewashed frame church," recalls the imagery which dominates Part 2. Here the "hysteria" of the spirituals echoes Kabnis's own hysteria and replaces the rich, elegaic outpourings of the songs in Part 1. As Kabnis scuttles back to his cabin, "a scarecrow replica of a man," sure that the southerners are about to run him out, the dusk imagery of Part 1 reappears in new form: "a false dusk has come early. The countryside is ashen and chill" (180).

After the cynicism and torment of Kabnis, we are offered a series of alternative reactions to the problem of existing in the white-controlled South. There is the school principal, Hanby, who represents in many ways the Booker T. Washington approach of "proving" to white folks that the Negro race is acceptable—on their terms. Asserting his power over black people while bowing to white men "without ever completely humbling himself," Hanby is the prototype of the college principal in Ellison's *Invisible Man* (as Father John is in some ways a precursor of the grandfather). Fred Halsey represents a second and more worthy alternative, a dignified artisan who takes pride in his work and refuses to be humbled by Hanby. Lewis, asked to describe Halsey, responds, "Fits here. Belongs here. An artist in your way, arent you, Halsey?" (200). But while Halsey is, as Sterling Brown points out, both "courageous and dignified,"[18] he is not capable of evolving into the man of cosmic consciousness. He can admire and appreciate Lewis but cannot become like him.

Lewis, "a tall wiry copper-colored man, thirty perhaps," is the real alternative to Kabnis. "He is what a stronger Kabnis might have been, and in an odd faint way resembles him" (189). Described on several occasions as Christ-like, Lewis is an extension of Barlo and Dan Moore, a man capable of the cosmic vision, of penetrating the world of appearances, and of fusing together past and present, anguish and joy, "soil and the overarching heavens. Dusk; dawn."

Along with Lewis, the possibility of a new dawning is offered by Carrie K., whose name echoes that first woman, Karintha, and whose soul is also in danger of ripening too soon ("Her spirit-bloom, even now touched sullen, bitter. Her rich beauty fading . . ." [205]). She can be saved by Lewis, but like Muriel and Esther is frustrated by the community mores; as she remembers "the sin-bogies of respectable southern colored folks," "her face blanches" and she steps back from Lewis.

Yet it is Carrie K. who feeds the old man in the cellar, who is concerned about his welfare, and who tries to communicate with him. To Kabnis this old man, "like a bust in black walnut," is merely a "tongue-tied shadow of the old," a symbol of the hell he wants to forget and disown. To Lewis he is "a mute John the Baptist of a new religion," "the symbol, flesh and spirit of the past" (211–17).

Although Kabnis remains till the end contemptuous of Father John and unwilling to hear him; although Lewis, no longer able to bear the anguish of his people in the South, leaves for the North, Toomer's final tableau suggests hope that a new consciousness will grow out of the African and southern heritage of black people, that the new dawning envisaged by Barlo will emerge for (and from) his "song-lit" race:

> Carrie's gaze follows him [Kabnis] till he is gone. Then she goes to the old man and slips to her knees before him. Her lips murmur, "Jesus come."
>
> Light streaks through the iron-barred cellar window. Within its soft circle, the figures of Carrie and Father John.
>
> Outside, the sun arises from its cradle in the tree-tops of the forest. Shadows of pines are dreams the sun shakes from its eyes. The sun arises. Gold-glowing child, it steps into the sky and sends a birth-song slanting down gray dust streets and sleepy windows of the southern town. (239)

This closing tableau also unites another pair of opposites whose struggle to achieve a harmonious and complementary relationship has been a central theme throughout the work: the male and female principles. The conflict is introduced in the "Karintha" section, where the male is depicted as impatient for Karintha's dusky beauty: "This interest of the male, who wishes to ripen a growing thing too soon, could mean no good to her." (1).

As *Cane* develops, it accumulates associations of the male principle with reaping, harvesting, cane-cutting, cotton-picking, working in the saw-mills—images which in turn link with the autumn/duck motif. Thus, the male relates to will, conscious purpose, action, and becoming (sense of past and future and power of prophecy), whereas woman connotes receptivity, passive ripening, emotion, and being in the present. Parts 1 and 2 depict a series of encounters in which the impatient male is unable to respond at the right time or in the right way to the questions raised in "Fern": What is the role of the male in regard to the passively receptive consciousness Fern symbolizes? What is that "something" he should do for her? What is the relation between emotion and intellect? The narrator's lack of understanding prevents him from helping her to evolve to a higher consciousness, and her anguish can only become more intense, remaining trapped and inarticulate. His impatience with Avey leaves her uprooted and orphaned without the soil needed to grow beautiful, and she remains sleepily unconscious of the need to change. Dorris's present being, her "soul" dance, is lost in John's intellectualized dream of the future. And Bona flees from the cool intellectual detachment of Paul, who learns too late the meaning of *caritas*. In "Harvest Song" we hear the anguished cry of the male harvester hungering for emotional sympathy, for the nourishment of the female, a cry echoed by Paul when he tells Bona, "I cant talk love. Love is a dry grain in my mouth unless it is wet with kisses" (144).

One of Ouspensky's main concerns was to stress that *both* the emotions and the intellect are organs of knowledge, and that the highest form of consciousness must include the fusion of both. He defined *spirituality* as a fusion of the intellect with the higher emotions: "The intellect is spiritualized from the emotions; the emotions are spiritualized from the intellect."[19] In order for cosmic consciousness to evolve, he claimed, the seed must be present, but it must be cultivated by a conscious effort of the will and intellect:

> A new order of receptivity grows in the soil of the intellect and higher emotions, but it is not created by them. A tree grows in the earth, but it is not created by the earth. A seed is necessary. This seed may be in the soul or absent from it. When it is there it can be cultivated or choked; when it is not there it is impossible to replace it with anything else.[20]

This imagery of soil, seed, and tree is taken up by Toomer in the "Song of the Son," which, as Todd Lieber points out,[21] is a central statement of *Cane's* purpose:

> Though late, O soil, it is not too late yet
> To catch thy plaintive soul, leaving, soon gone,
> Leaving, to catch thy plaintive soul soon gone.
>
> O Negro slaves, dark purple ripened plums,
> Squeezed and bursting in the pine-wood air,
> Passing, before they stripped the old tree bare
> One plum was saved for me, one seed becomes
>
> An everlasting song, a singing tree,
> Caroling softly souls of slavery,
> What they were, and what they are to me,
> Caroling softly souls of slavery.
>
> (21)

While "Song of the Son," with its play on song/sun/son and on soul/soil, focusses on the development of art, "a singing tree," the poem which immediately follows, "Georgia Dusk," emphasizes the development of religion, past and present, linked with art:

Meanwhile, the men, with vestiges of pomp,
  Race memories of king and caravan,
  High-priests, an ostrich, and a ju-ju man,
Go singing through the footpaths of the swamp.
. . . .
O singers, resinous and soft your songs
  Above the sacred whisper of the pines,
  Give virgin lips to cornfield concubines,
Bring dreams of Christ to dusky cane-lipped throngs.
(22–23)

These two poems in particular and the constant references to religious experience and to folk song throughout Part 1 relate to Ouspensky's claim that religion and art grow out of and are the organized forms of emotional knowledge.[22] Both Parts 1 and 2 also depict the degeneration of emotional consciousness and the perversion of religion and art when they are deprived of the conscious effort to cultivate and grow toward a higher form. Thus religion, which was a mystical unity with God and the universe for Fern, for Muriel has become a series of taboos and restrictions which prevent her from reaching Dan and the higher consciousness he represents. As mentioned earlier, Becky is buried by these same taboos, symbolized by the cabin built to hide and separate her from the community, a perversion of religion represented by the Bible leaves flapping idly on her mound, and recalled when Father John finally speaks his "truth" that "white folks made the Bible lie." Similarly, the rich folk songs and lyrical outpourings which suffuse Part 1 gradually dissipate into the mechanical routines and "tricks" of the chorus girls in "Theater," the grotesque boxing match and serenade staged by the dwarf in "Box Seat," and the Walpurgis-like caperings of Kabnis in Part 3.

So also the intellect deprived of emotion degenerates into the fragmented consciousness, cynicism, and egocentricity represented by Kabnis (and, to a certain extent, Hanby). In contrast to Part 1 where the focus is on women, on the lyric consciousness, with the form appropriately lyrical, permeated with feeling and sympathy, Part 3 is peopled and dominated almost entirely by men, portraying their attempts to "make it" in the South and their contemptuous treatment of women such as Stella and Cora. The semi-dramatic form of Part 3 and most of Part 2 is also appropriate to their emphasis on conflict, activity, and becoming. Only at the end, with the tableau of Carrie K.

and Father John, is a moment of stasis achieved, a moment which unites religion and art, past seed, and future promise.

My discussion of *Cane* has been limited to the metaphysical and symbolic level and has ignored other equally important and effective aspects of the book, such as fiction and characterization, the richly interwoven imagery, the word music and musical "texture" of Toomer's writing, the carefully wrought architecture. Part of the incredible achievement of Toomer's work is that it works brilliantly and subtly on *all* levels, so that the characters are both psychologically convincing and symbolic, the scenes depicted in prose and poetry are at the same time brilliantly painted landscapes and subjective projections, the words and sounds are sensuously heard, echoing and modulating other sounds and phrases without becoming mere sound. All these aspects deserve detailed study—which would, I believe, lead to the conclusion that *Cane* is one of the most brilliantly executed and richly complex works to have been written in America.

Selected Interpretations of *Cane*

Jean Toomer's *Cane* Again

W. EDWARD FARRISON

The first edition of Jean Toomer's *Cane* was published by Boni and Liveright in New York in 1923 with a foreword by Waldo Frank. There were a second printing of this edition with Boni and Liveright's imprint in 1927 and a third one in 1967 with the imprint of University Place Press, New York. A paperback edition with an introduction by Arna Bontemps was published by Harper and Row in the same city in 1969. The first two printings, which came early in the Harlem Renaissance, were very small because the demand for the book was very small and continued so for many years. The third printing was occasioned by the current interest in Negro literature, as were the paperback edition and also *The Merrill Studies in Cane*, which was compiled by Frank Durham and brought out by Charles E. Merrill Publishing Company of Columbus, Ohio, in 1971. This printing seems, however, not to have been generally noticed. Like several others who have recently written about *Cane*, in his research on the work Durham apparently missed seeing this printing. At least his volume just mentioned contains no reference to it.

During the forty-nine years which have passed since its first appearance, *Cane* has repeatedly been a subject of criticism. It has been this not because it has been a popular book, which it has never been, but because it was from the beginning and still is a uniquely interesting work. Its uniqueness consists primarily in the fact that it portrays phases of Negro life in places whence those phases had not previously received authentic, extensive literary treatment. In *Studies in Cane*, Durham brought together and thus made easily available more than twenty representative criticisms of various kinds belonging to the years from 1923 to 1969. "One of the purposes" of his compilation, he said in his preface, "is to bring together the documents which will enable the reader to trace the history of *Cane's* literary reputation" (iv).[1] This purpose is indeed commendable, even though some may find its reach beyond the grasp of this small volume. Among the selections in the volume are Frank's foreword (1923), Bontemps's introduction (1969), reviews by Montgomery Gregory (1923), W. E. B. Du Bois (1924), and Robert T. Kerlin (1926), and critical essays by Eugene Holmes (1932), Robert A. Bone, Bontemps (1966), and Durham himself.

In grouping the reviews and essays as he did according to whether their authors were whites or Negroes, Durham fell into what may be considered gross errors, according to who is doing the considering. He included Kerlin among the "Black Reviewers" and Bone among the "Black Critics." Kerlin (1866–1950), whose review Durham quoted from *Opportunity: Journal of Negro Life* for May 1926, was white; and so is Bone, from whose *The Negro Novel in America* (1958 and 1965) Durham quoted Bone's discussion of Toomer. Anyway, it was supererogatory to group the reviews and essays according to the race of their several authors, since the racial identity *per se* of the authors throws little or no light on what they said about Toomer and his book.

Since Durham completed his work, critical comments on *Cane* have continued to appear. The latest one which has come to my attention, and which is an important addition to scholarship on Toomer, is in Darwin T. Turner's *In a Minor Chord*.[2] One of the distinctive features of that work is the amount of biographical information it gives about Toomer—more than has heretofore been readily available.

In his foreword Waldo Frank described *Cane*, perhaps overenthusiastically, as "a harbinger of the South's literary maturity: of its emergence from the obsession put upon its minds by the unending racial crisis," and he further characterized the work as "the harbinger of a literary force of whose incalculable future I believe no reader of this book will be in doubt."

Although Frank's predictions concerning *Cane* can hardly be said to have come true, many have written about the book as if they did. In many of the selections in *Studies in Cane*, notably in the various comments of Montgomery Gregory, Eugene Holmes, and Arna Bontemps, *Cane* is repeatedly said to have influenced greatly the literature written by and about Negroes which has succeeded it. The same thing with some qualifications is said about the book in Durham's preface and in his essay, which is the last one in his compilation. "In *Cane*," said Eugene Holmes somewhat ecstatically in 1932, "raving critics and poetasters recognized a naturalism of such a distinctive kind that the applause was deafening," and "it [*Cane*] has also given the necessary influence and impetus to those younger Negro poets who did not know about what to write" (46). In 1966 and again in his introduction in 1969, Bontemps said that the reaction to *Cane* of "practically an entire generation of young Negro writers then [in the 1920s] just beginning to emerge" marked the awakening of what came to be called "a Negro Renaissance" (22 and 78–79). Also in 1966 Bontemps had remarked that "subsequent writing by Negroes in the United States as well as in the West Indies and Africa has continued to reflect its [*Cane*'s] mood and often its method, and, one feels, it also has influenced the writing about Negroes by others" (79). In Durham's opinion the influence which *Cane* has had upon Negro writers is the product of Toomer's having learned his craft of writing from such white writers and artists as Sherwood Anderson, Hart Crane, Waldo Frank, and others of their kind (viii–ix).

Interestingly enough, it is easier to maximize than to minimize literary influence and still easier to generalize than to be specific about it. Herein lies the probable reason why the influences by which *Cane* has been said to have been affected and the influence attributed to it have been generally left unexplained as well as overemphasized. Some clarification concerning both of these kinds of influence now seems well in order—in fact overdue.

As to the craft of writing, it is indeed probable that Toomer learned something especially from Anderson and Frank about the effective portrayal of folk life, but it is not improbable that he also learned something about this directly from Edgar Lee Masters's *Spoon River Anthology* (1915). From that work Anderson himself might have learned something about the art of portraying what a reviewer of his *Winesburg, Ohio* (1919) called "the inner individual life of a typical American small town." Also, since Frank and Toomer were closely associated while Frank was writing *Holiday* and Toomer was writing *Cane*, they might have influenced each other's writing. Moreover, Toomer, like many other writers, might have learned a great deal independently about writing by constant practice—by trial and error, by studious rewriting.

If Toomer was influenced by Masters, Anderson, Frank, and similar writers, it is at least probable that other Negro writers of his time, like non-Negro writers, were directly influenced by them rather than only indirectly through *Cane*. This probability is strengthened by the fact that *Cane* was never an easily available book until the paperback edition of it was published in 1969.

There seems to be no good reason to believe that *Cane*, which until recently was not widely circulated, could have had the extensive influence which some seem to think it has had. Nor is there any good reason for considering Toomer the father of the Harlem Renaissance, or a pioneering delver into and portrayer of "the soul of the Negro," "the Negro's psyche," "the Negro's spirit," "the race-soul," or "the great emotionalism of the race"—whatever these jargonistic phrases mean. It should be noted, by the way, that in *Cane* Toomer neither philosophized about Negroes nor made any of his characters do so. The Harlem Renaissance evolved from what became known at least as early as 1916 as "The Renaissance of the Negro Race" and also as the "New Negro" movement—long before Toomer's *Cane* or Alain Locke's *The New Negro* (1925) was published. Like other writers, Toomer the writer was as much the creation as the creator of the literary milieu in which he flourished. Doubtless the Harlem Renaissance helped to make him the writer that he became, and with other writers, probably he in turn helped to some extent, whether great or small, to make some of the writing of his time and afterwards what it became.

Cane has been frequently called a novel, which it certainly is not. It is a collection of thirteen prose sketches, fifteen occasional lyrics interspersed among them, and a closet drama. In addition there are occasional stanzas and fragments of folk verse which serve as headlinks or refrains of the several prose pieces. The subject matter of *Cane* is the imaginatively treated product of Toomer's actual experiences and observations in Washington, D.C., where he was born and where he made his home until late in the 1920s, in Chicago, where he studied briefly in a school of physical education, and in Sparta, Georgia, where he spent three months as a schoolteacher in the fall of 1921.

The first of the three parts into which the book is divided has its setting in Sempter, a semirural community in northeastern Georgia distinguished by the raising and processing of cane. Hence the title of the book. Sempter, of course, is a fictitious name for Sparta. The six sketches in this part, which are mainly the stories of six different women, reflect various phases of life in the community as Toomer had observed it.

Perhaps the most simply and most effectively written of these sketches, if not of all of those in the book, is the one entitled "Fern." Fernie May Rosen, its heroine, who was commonly called Fern, was a "cream-colored solitary girl," whose "face flowed into her eyes," and whose singing reminded one of that of "a Jewish cantor singing with a broken voice." Apparently her singing was more plaintive than beautiful but was still entrancing. Unsophisticated as she was, her personality commanded the interest of all who saw her even casually. Even her naiveté in conversation illustrated by her "yassur or nassur" in reply to whatever was said to her added to the naturalness of her disposition. Hers is a story of a young woman who existed in a narrow zone between hope and frustration.

The first six sketches in the second part of *Cane* have their setting in Washington early in the 1920s. The scene being incomparably larger and more varied than Sempter, Toomer could not encompass it in such a few sketches as he did the semirural community. What he did was to portray, sometimes effectively and sometimes ineffectively, isolated phases of life in the city.

The most convincing and most interesting of these sketches is "Avey," whose title is the same as the name of its heroine. Like Fern, Avey had sexual experience too early in life and thereafter became indifferent to romantic love. Meanwhile, having been educated and having taught school for a while, she lost her position and eventually degenerated into an "Orphan-woman." Had Avey lived in Sempter, Fern's story might have been Avey's; and had Fern lived in Washington, Avey's story might have been Fern's.

Recently Toomer has been credited with contrasting Washington as the North in the second part of *Cane* with the South in the first part. It is difficult to believe that Toomer would have been naive enough to attempt such a thing, for he certainly knew that Washington in the 1920s was not a part of the North vis-à-vis the South, but was in fact a part of the South. He knew that as far as matters racial were concerned, Washington then had much less in common with

New York than with Atlanta, and that Colonel James Crow was as much an habitué of Pennsylvania Avenue as of Peachtree Street. Moreover, none of the parts of *Cane* contain anything that suggests such a contrast.

"Bona and Paul," the last sketch in the second part of *Cane*, has its setting in Chicago. More so than any of the preceding sketches, this one is as much a story as a study of characters. It tells of a budding romance between Bona Hale, a southern white girl, and Paul Johnson, a southern Negro, who were students in a school of physical education in the city. Before the romance became a full-blown flower, the couple separated because both were too conscious that they were racially different.

The third part of *Cane* is "Kabnis," the closet drama, which, like the first part, has its setting in Sempter. The unifying agent in the drama is Ralph Kabnis, who figures prominently in all six of its scenes. A northern Negro with a southern ancestry, Kabnis loses his position as a schoolteacher in Sempter and for no clear reason becomes an apprentice in a local wagon shop, where he becomes a study in frustration. There is a variety of characters of uncertain principles who, along with Kabnis, are involved in much talk and some incidental action, all without very convincing motivation. Because of this fact, although the drama mirrors some phases of the life of the community, it has proved puzzling to many a reader.

Most of the lyrics in the several parts of *Cane* are associationally connected with the locales of the parts. In evidence of this fact, five of the lyrics in the first part are especially noteworthy. "November Cotton Flower," a sonnet, comments on the ravages of the boll weevil in Georgia during Toomer's sojourn there. "Face" and "Portrait in Georgia," two brief free-verse lyrics, impressionistically yet graphically describe two old women whom Toomer might have seen in Sparta. "Song of the Son," a poem of five stanzas, commemorates the songs which Negroes had learned from their slave forebears and still sang. In its second stanza "thy son" who had returned to Georgia need not be identified as Toomer, but as a persona who had returned there in time to hear these songs before they and their historical significance passed into oblivion. "Georgia Dusk," a slightly longer poem which immediately follows "Song of the Son," also deals with singing by Negroes such as Toomer probably had heard in Sparta. It contemplates the singing of Negro workmen at twilight after their day's work. Incidentally, none of the poems in the second part of the book—the third part contains no original poetry except a folk song—are comparable in thought and lyric qualities with the five just considered.

Cane is an unusually interesting book not only because of its subject matter but also because of the kind of writing it is. A most distinctive feature of the work is its emphasis on the realistic portrayal of characters rather than on action. In some instances, however, the characters are delineated mainly in simple recountings of their actions and their reactions to others and situations, as is true of Fern and Avey. In other instances the method of character revelation employed is a blending of associationism and the stream of consciousness. Both of these literary techniques have long been established. Toomer evinced extraordinary skill in using them, notably in the sketches entitled "Esther," "Blood-Burning Moon," "Theater," and "Box Seat," although the last-mentioned sketch leaves the reader somewhat befogged.

Another unusually interesting feature of the work is its gracious plenty of figurative language, much of which is spontaneous and natural and some of which is strained and artificial. All of it serves, nevertheless, to arrest the reader's attention and to keep his interest from flagging, as Toomer presumably intended for it to serve in addition to vivifying and clarifying his ideas. Uniquely interesting work of genius that *Cane* is, it was an auspicious beginning for Toomer's success as a writer of imaginative literature. Unfortunately, it also marked the end of that success, for it was his last as well as his first book of creative writing to be published.

Design and Movement in *Cane*

TODD LIEBER

Among the literature brought to attention by the current wave of rediscovery in the area of American Negro writing, few works are more worthy of critical study, or more exasperating, than Jean Toomer's *Cane*. Most critics have been impressed with the overall high quality of *Cane* and yet have left the book feeling somewhat baffled by it. "The book by which we remember this writer [Toomer] is as hard to classify as its author," writes Arna Bontemps,[1] and Robert Bone agrees that "a critical analysis of *Cane* is a frustrating task."[2] As one would expect, this perplexity has resulted in a wide range of critical opinion, and yet there are several major points of concurrence. Most critics, for example, agree that *Cane* is a highly personal work of art, inextricably linked to the mind and career of its creator, and that it is an exemplary statement of the assertive and idealistic affirmation of race that characterized black writing during the Harlem Renaissance. Furthermore, although Alain Locke, the most prominent of Toomer's contemporary critics, referred to it simply as a collection of short stories,[3] most later critics have sensed some kind of underlying plan or design, however vague or elusive that plan might be. As Edward Margolies writes: "*Cane* is very nearly impossible to describe. At first glance, it seems a hodge podge of verse, songs, stories, and plays, yet there is a thematic unity celebrating the passions and instincts of black persons close to the soil as opposed to the corruption of their spirit and vitality in the cities."[4]

With these basic points of agreement as a foundation, it is possible to go on to a more detailed and rewarding understanding of *Cane*. Although the book undeniably has its roots deep in Toomer's subjective experience, it is also highly representative of certain movements of the period in which it was written and can profitably be read in connection with two of the prevailing patterns of thought of the nineteen twenties: first, of course, the affirmation of race that formed the heart of the Harlem Renaissance, and second, the experimentation with form and language that dominated the work of the literary coterie of which Toomer was a part. Viewed from this perspective, the various fragments of *Cane* reveal more than merely the "thematic" unity that Margolies observes, and it becomes clear that the book has a comprehensive design that transcends and encompasses its separate bits and a progressive movement that is sustained from beginning to end.

The writers of the twenties with whom Toomer was intimate were, as Bone writes, "threshing and winnowing, testing and experimenting with words, stretching them and refocusing them, until they became the pliant instruments of a new idiom."[5] The function of this "new idiom" of which Bone speaks was to recreate a sense of fundamental relatedness between art and experience, to make language once more a viable and powerful means of approaching reality. Many of Toomer's closest friends, notably Hart Crane, felt keenly the gap between man's spiritual life and the materiality of a machine culture, and they were exploring the symbolic and mythical qualities of language, searching for a "usable past" out of which to create a new myth to replace the ones that had failed, a myth that would reestablish man's connection with his environment and his roots and give him a vital sense of his own identity and being.

For Toomer, a light-skinned racial hybrid who had lived in both white and black worlds without an integral sense of belonging to either, the need for such relatedness and identity had become crucial. In 1922, after a trip through the South with Waldo Frank, he wrote an optimistic letter to the editors of *The Liberator*, declaring that he had fulfilled his need through a communion with his Negro heritage:

> Within the last two or three years . . . , my growing need for artistic expression has pulled me deeper and deeper into the Negro group.

> And as my powers of receptivity increased, I found myself loving it in a way that I could never love the other. It has stimulated and fertilized whatever creative talent I may contain within me. A visit to Georgia last fall was the starting point of almost everything of worth that I have done. I heard folk-songs come from the lips of Negro peasants. I saw rich dusk beauty that I had heard many false accents about, and of which till then, I was somewhat skeptical. And a deep part of my nature, a part that I had repressed, sprang suddenly to life and responded to them. Now I cannot conceive of myself as aloof and separated.[6]

In the lives of southern Negroes and the heritage of slavery, Toomer found a reality to which his spirit could respond, a "usable past" from whose roots his art could grow and flower. It was in this mood that *Cane* was written, not only as a celebration of blackness but also as a record of Toomer's own search for blackness and a portrayal of the possibility of communion with the racial heritage that exists for every "lost" black man in America.

The central statement of Toomer's intentions is "Song of the Son," the poem that is placed in the center of Part 1. Toomer himself, or more accurately, the persona, is the "son" of the black race, and *Cane* is the "song" into which he will "pour that parting soul" which he senses within himself. The meaning of the poem hinges on the manipulation of three words: son, sun, and song. The natural sun once gave life to the "soul of slavery," but this life-giving force has almost set, and with its decline, the heritage of slavery is all but diminished, the sustenance of its tradition all but lost to the black man. The poet, however, one specific son, had embraced this heritage before the memory of it was gone completely, and by "pouring" his acceptance into art, he will make of his work a new life-giving force in the form of "an everlasting song"; and a race descended from slaves whose own songs once expressed their vitality will become "song-lit" again through the art of one of their sons:

> Now just before an epoch's sun declines
> Thy son, in time, I have returned to thee,
> Thy son, I have in time returned to thee.
>
> In time, for though the sun is setting on
> A song-lit race of slaves, it has not set;
>
> . . . .
>
> Passing, before they stripped the old tree bare

One plum was saved for me, one seed becomes

An everlasting song, a singing tree,
Caroling softly souls of slavery,
What they were, and what they are to me,
Caroling softly souls of slavery.
(21)

Cane is designed to function in both objective and subjective terms. In an objective sense it is a chronicle of what the "souls of slavery" were. In a personal sense it is a description of "what they are to me" and, by inference, what they can be to any man who accepts them and the heritage they represent: the substance of spiritual life and survival.

Such an acceptance, however, is not an easy task, for it must include the pain and suffering of the past along with its beauty, and the beauty that remains is rapidly being buried beneath the dominant, material culture of white America. As Margolies suggests in the passage quoted above, the basic structural principle of *Cane* is the conflict between two life-styles and systems of value, that of the South, which Toomer associates with the "soul of slavery" and to which his being responds, and that of the North, the industrial, white culture that threatens to create an unbreachable gap between the black man and his world as it destroys the inherent value of his racial heritage. The two are juxtaposed at virtually every point: the North is cold and passive, the South warm and full of emotion; sexual sterility and perversion are opposed to sexual consummation, cynicism to faith, transience to endurance, and spiritual death to the possibility of spiritual resurrection through an acceptance of self and race.

The efforts of the black man to break away from the engulfing white culture to an acceptance of his own racial heritage gives to *Cane* a unity and a continuous movement that progresses through its three major divisions. Part 1, in which the emphasis is on the black, southern style of life, is a portrayal of the inherent beauty, intimately mixed with pain and suffering, of this black culture, the culture that must be embraced if the black man is to attain spiritual life. Part 2, set amid the white, industrial culture, presents the consequences of the black man's failure to accept his own heritage: spiritual death among the "white and whitewashed wood" of the North. Part 3 contains a return to the South, a now successful reassertion of the search for an acceptance of blackness, and a portrayal of the spiritual rebirth that such an acceptance makes possible.

Part 1 takes place in the atmosphere of a setting sun, with a strong sense of the diminishing vitality of the "soul of slavery." Most of the stories and poems are set either at dusk or at night, and the dominant motif throughout is of beauty and value that have somehow been distorted and dissipated. The prevailing metaphor, running through and unifying all the stories, is that of the frustration or perversion of the sexual act. The valuable, passionate instincts and desires of men and women are in each case warped, and as a result, Part 1 appears, as Bone holds, much like an Andersonian gallery of grotesques.[7] Karintha is a creature of exquisite beauty, but her beauty is defiled by the impatience and lust of men who have no reverence for it, who "wish to ripen a growing thing too soon," and the fruit of her conception lies buried beneath a sawdust pile. Becky's union with a black man, an act which is in itself full of passion and value, renders her an outcast, adrift on an island between the railroad track and the road, and like Karintha's child, she ends up buried—beneath the pile of rocks that were her home. Carma's desire drives her to infidelity, and her fear makes a murderer of her husband. Esther and Fern spend their lives in frigid sterility. Louisa, whose story vies with Carma's for the title of "the crudest melodrama," is unable to limit her desire to one man, and as a result one of her beaux is murdered and the other is lynched.

Despite these distortions and perversions, however, there remains in each story a strong image of a potential value and beauty that remains vibrant and vital, although it has become intimately mixed with pain and suffering. Perhaps the best example is that of Karintha, who is described as a "November cotton flower," an image of potential beauty in the midst of degeneration and decay:

> Drouth fighting soil had caused the soil to take
> All water from the streams; dead birds were found
> In wells a hundred feet below the ground—
> Such was the season when the flower bloomed.
> Old folks were startled, and it soon assumed
> Significance. Superstition saw
> Something it had never seen before:
> Brown eyes that loved without a trace of fear,
> Beauty so sudden for that time of year.
>
> (7)

Fern is a similar figure. Despite her frigidity she remains almost a siren, a bewitching creature, for whom all men who know her wish to do "some fine, unnamed thing." Like the environment of which she is an integral part, and with which she seems to merge, Fern is able to endure with a kind of stoical beauty that encompasses and transcends her anguish. As the narrator rides past on a train, he describes her on her porch:

> From the train window I saw her as I crossed the road. Saw her on her porch, head tilted a little forward where the nail was, eyes vaguely focused on the sunset. Saw her face flow into them, the countryside and something that I call God, flowing into them. (33)

As a character, the narrator plays only a small part in the first section, but his role is a crucial one, for it illustrates the unwillingness of the black man to embrace the pain and suffering that have become an inseparable part of his heritage. This unwillingness is made clear in "Becky." The narrator recognizes Becky's vitality, and he is irresistibly drawn toward her; but at the last moment he is overcome by fear, and he turns and runs away:

> Barlo and I were pulled out of our seats. Dragged to the door that had swung open. Through the dust we saw the bricks in a mound upon the floor. Becky, if she was there, lay under them. I thought I heard a groan. Barlo, mumbling something, threw his Bible on the pile. (No one has ever touched it). Somehow we got away. My buggy was still on the road. The last thing I remember was whipping old Dan like fury. (12)

The narrator's avoidance is emphasized by Barlo, who is at least able to make a token gesture of sympathy and acceptance, and who, in "Esther," will appear as a prophetic voice, hearkening the black people to an acceptance of themselves and their race.

The failure of the narrator to achieve the communion he is seeking is portrayed again in "Fern." The narrator has a genuine feeling for her, and for a moment he seems very close to some kind of communion:

> I felt strange, as I always do in Georgia, particularly at dusk. I felt that things unseen to men were tangibly immediate. It would not have surprised me had I had vision. . . . From force of habit, I suppose, I held Fern in my arms—that is, without at first noticing it. Then my mind came back to her. Her eyes, unusually weird and open, held me. Held God. He flowed in as I've seen the countryside flow in. (31–32)

But at this point some force intervenes; the spell is broken, and the narrator is left hopelessly divorced from her: "I must have done something—what, I don't know, in the confusion of my emotion. She sprang up. Rushed some distance from me" (32). Thus separated, the narrator can only helplessly muse that there is "something I would do for her."

The sense of helplessness resulting from the failure to achieve communion is emphatically illustrated by Louisa in the closing story, "Blood-Burning Moon." Louisa has been close to consummation with Tom Burwell, but she, too, has been thwarted, unable to surmount the confusion placed in her mind by whiteness. Her song, which began as a song of courting and celebration, has become only a plaintive, empty wail, directed at the full moon, once a symbol of desire, but now the evil omen of tragedy:

> The full moon, an evil thing, an omen, soft showering the homes of folks she knew. Where were they, these people? She'd sing and perhaps they'd come out and join her. Perhaps Tom Burwell would come. At any rate, the full moon in the great door was an omen which she must sing to. (67)

Her song, like the entire first section of *Cane*, is a tale of woe and anguish, of loneliness, of a beauty and vitality that have become twisted and grotesque and yet remain, holding forth the possibility of spiritual life to the man who can love and accept them for what they are.

Part 2 of *Cane* is counterpoint. Set in the North, the stories and poems of this section reflect the spiritual sterility of black men and women cut off from their roots, lacking a sense of their heritage, trying to live with their minds the kind of life ordained by the dominant group, while their souls, divorced, lie buried. As Bone has noted, "during the second section of *Cane*, Toomer weaves [his] symbols into a magnificent design, so that his meaning, elusive in any particular episode, emerges with great impact from the whole."[8] Part 2 is dominated by two controlling themes: the divorce of mind from body and body from soul in the spiritually stifling environment of the North; and the result of this divorce, which is conveyed through images of burial and spiritual death.

"Seventh Street" and "Rhobert," the opening sketches, comprise a firm statement of the spiritual impotency that characterizes all the figures of this section. Toomer begins with an image of vitality that is wasted, power that is rendered useless by a debilitating environment:

> Seventh street is a bastard of Prohibition and the War. A crude-boned, soft-skinned wedge of nigger life breathing its loafer air, jazz songs and love, thrusting unconscious rhythms, black reddish blood into the white and whitewashed wood of Washington. Stale soggy wood of Washington. Wedges rust in soggy wood. (71)

Whitewashed, the key word in this passage, describes concisely the effect of the northern environment on the blacks of Part 2. Their own desires and needs become subordinated to the urge to act and live like the white man, and in the process their own essential identity is lost. Rhobert is the perfect example of such a figure. The white man has become his God, and his life is devoted to the task of fashioning himself in the image of his adopted deity. His life centers around paying the debt on his house: "God built the house. He blew His breath into its stuffing. It is good to die obeying Him who can do these things" (74). The image of burial established in "Seventh Street" with the wedge in the wood is repeated here, as Rhobert "sinks into the mud," and Toomer suggests with the bitter irony that characterizes the style throughout the section: "Lets build a monument and set it in the ooze where he goes down. A monument of hewn oak, carved in niggerheads" (75).

The causes of this spiritual death are developed more fully in some of the stories and poems that follow. "Theater" has the same motif as many of the stories of Part 1. John, the main character, is unable to bring himself to a spiritual or sexual communion with the soul of his race, represented here by Dorris, and the failure has disastrous consequences for both: the male force is impotent, and the female principle is unfulfilled and wasted. The cause of the failure lies in the separation of John's mind from the instincts of his body. His body responds to the dark, seething life of the theater, but his mind is pulled toward the shaft of white light that filters down from the ceiling:

> John's mind coincides with the shaft of light. Thoughts rush to, and compact about it. Life of the house and of the slowly awakening stage swirls to the body of John, and thrills it. John's body is separate from the thoughts that pack his mind. (92)

The fundamental conflict of *Cane* between the life-styles and value systems of North and South, white and black, is found in the tension between John's mind and body. His body is drawn to Dorris and all that she represents, but his mind is busy with reasons why the consummation should be avoided. Finally, the conflict itself overcomes John, and Dorris, unfulfilled, "falls down the steps into her dressing room. Pulls her hair. Her eyes, over a floor of tears, stare at the *white-washed* ceiling" (100—italics added).

"Calling Jesus," the brief sketch which follows, continues this theme of fragmentation. The woman, as Bone observes, is "urbanized and spiritually intimidated."[9] Her soul, "like a little thrust-tailed dog," exists in a no man's land between her house of "whitewashed" wood, which symbolizes her desire to achieve the values of the white, northern culture, and the soil of its ancestors, the South, a world that the woman permits herself to remember only in dreams. An even clearer statement of this theme is the poet's "Prayer" for some sense of self-integration and communion with his roots:

> My body is opaque to the soul.
> Driven of the spirit, long have I sought to temper
> it unto the spirit's longing,
> But my mind, too, is opaque to the soul.
> (131)

The spiritual corruption and fragmentation of the figures of Part 2 deprives them of all the vitality that typifies the characters of the first section. The dominant tone of Part 2 is not one of frustration, but simply one of hopelessness. The perversions and distortions of Part 1, of Karintha, Becky, Carma, Fern, Esther, Louisa, and of the narrator himself, are imbued with passion and an almost tragic sense of having almost grasped some essential value. The failures of Part 2, on the other hand, are little more than pathetic. Rhobert, John, the unnamed woman of "Calling Jesus," and Muriel of "Box Seat" are people so overburdened by northern culture that almost all sense of life and passion has been squeezed out of them; their vitality has, indeed, "rusted in the white and whitewashed wood of Washington."

The difference in the mood of the two sections is apparent in the contrast between Fern and Avey. Like Fern, Avey is an attractive, even bewitching, girl, admired from a distance by many, including the narrator, taken by many who derive little or no satisfaction from the experience. Like Fern, too, Avey maintains an air of personal detachment from all surrounding things and people. But whereas Fern's indifference reflects the ability to endure an inner anguish, Avey's indifference is merely nonchalance, reflecting a spirit that has no will and no life. The climactic event of "Avey" occurs in a situation almost identical to that of "Fern." The narrator has gone to her, as to Fern, seeking "the simple beauty of another's soul" (85); as with Fern, they lie in the grass, and the narrator approaches a moment of passion; as with Fern, the result is failure. But with Fern, the narrator is close to some kind of consummation, and Fern herself becomes embroiled in the agony of her trapped emotions. With Avey, the moment is characterized only by coldness and a complete lack of sexuality:

> An immediate and urgent passion swept over me. Then I looked at Avey. Her heavy eyes were closed. Her breathing was as faint and regular as a child's in slumber. My passion died. I was afraid to move lest I disturb her. Hours and hours, I guess it was, she lay there. My body grew numb. I shivered. I coughed. . . . I saw the dawn steal over Washington. The Capitol dome looked like a gray ghost ship drifting in from sea. Avey's face was pale, and her eyes were heavy. She did not have the gray crimson-splashed beauty of the dawn. I hated to wake her. Orphan-woman . . . (87–88)

Cut apart from her roots, left to drift aimlessly among the spiritual decay of a world that she hardly understands, Avey truly is an "orphan-woman."

A more optimistic figure in Part 2 is Dan Moore of "Box Seat." Like Barlo, Dan is a prophet of sorts, a man of visions, with a self-assumed mission: "Stir the root-life of a withered people. Call them from their houses, and teach them to dream" (104). The house imagery begun in "Rhobert" is maintained in "Box Seat," carrying with it the bulk of Toomer's meaning. Dan realizes that the beautiful vitality of the black women he knows has been locked within the frames of the houses. The women are stripped of emotion, unable to respond to him, and he himself can make no overtures to the lifeless houses:

> It is a sharp-edged, massed, metallic house. Bolted. About Mrs. Pribby. Bolted to the endless rows of metal houses. Mrs. Pribby's house. The rows of houses belong to other Mrs. Pribbys. No wonder he couldn't sing to them. (107)

Infuriated and sickened by the spiritual decay that he senses about him, feels in Muriel, and sees portrayed in the audience's reaction to the play they attend, Dan envisions himself as the agent of a purifying destruction:

> "I am going to reach up and grab the girders of this building and pull them down. The crash will be a signal. Hid by the smoke and dust Dan Moore will arise. In his right hand will be a dynamo. In his left, a god's face that will flash white light from ebony. I'll grab a girder and swing it like a walking stick. Lightning will flash." (126–27)

Dan's passion, however, results in nothing but his own frustration, and, unable to play his chosen role as a prophet of blackness, a savior and liberator of his people, he leaves the scene almost in a state of oblivion. He is free of his desire for Muriel, who has been "white-washed" beyond redemption. However, it is not freedom that he seeks, but rather love and communication. He is free, but, as Bone observes, he is also impotent and sterile.[10]

The denial of blackness that Dan senses and abhors, and which forms a major cause of all the liveliness portrayed in Part 2, is also responsible for the failure of Paul in the final story of the section. Bone correctly holds that Bona is attracted to Paul, a mulatto, precisely because of his blackness, and it is Paul's inability to assert his Negro self that makes the potential love affair an abortive one.[11] Within "Bona and Paul," however, there is a movement that is significant to the overall structure of the book. For Paul, in the closing pages of the story, realizes the cause of his failure and does try to assert his black selfhood. Rushing to the Negro doorman, he tells him:

> "I came back to tell you, to shake your hand, and tell you that you are wrong. That something beautiful is going to happen. . . . I came back to tell you brother, that white faces are petals of roses. That dark faces are petals of dusk. That I am going out and gather petals. That I am going out and know her whom I brought with me to these Gardens which are purple like a bed of roses would be at dusk." (152–53)

Paul has realized that to know Bona, he must first both know and acknowledge himself, that in order to gather "petals of roses," he must first gather to himself his own "petals of dusk."

Although Bona is gone when he returns, and his intentions are thus left unfulfilled, Paul has, at least, clearly recognized the cause of his frustration; he knows the consequences of the failure to fully espouse his own blackness. With this realization, he brings the second major movement of *Cane* to an end. Paul's final act is a symbolic reassertion of the search for a communion with the heritage of his racial past, but while Paul can make that reassertion, he cannot complete it.

The assertion can be completed only by a return to the native soil of the South, where the pain and beauty of the racial past continue to exist as an immediate reality. Away from these roots, in an alien and hostile world, the gesture remains empty and impotent.

Part 3 of *Cane* contains this return to the South. That Toomer dedicated this particular section to Waldo Frank is, I think, no accident, for, as Toomer wrote to the editors of *The Liberator*, his journey South with Frank "was the starting point of almost everything of worth that I have done." In the total experience of *Cane*, Part 3 performs the same function as Toomer felt the 1922 trip had performed in his own life, a reestablishment of contact and communion with his roots, the achievement of a new sense of life and creativity, and a resurrection from the death that overwhelms the spirit in Part 2. The focal point of Part 3, in fact the central symbol of the entire book, is Father John, the ancient patriarch who lives in the hole of Halsey's cellar and, as Bone says, "represents a link with the Negro's ancestral past."[12] Each of the main characters in the drama of "Kabnis" reacts to Father John in his own way, and the various reactions suggest several alternative attitudes which black men may adopt toward their own past. The main characters can be divided into two groups: Halsey, Hanby, and Lewis are members of an older generation whose attitudes are set and will not change; they represent the alternatives from which a younger generation, Carrie Kate and Kabnis, must choose. The decision that faces Carrie Kate and Kabnis forms the dramatic core of the play, and their choices bring the movement of *Cane* to its culmination.

Both Halsey, the handyman, and Hanby, the educator, have forsaken their sense of race and have been absorbed into the conception of reality put forth by the southern whites. Halsey is firmly in his "place" and is satisfied to be there, although the position requires him to settle for something less than full manhood.[13] His dialect as well as his thoughts reveal his character:

> "Give me th work and fair pay an I aint askin nothin better. Went over-seas an saw France; an I come back. Went t school; but there aint no books whats got th feel t them of them there tools. Nassur. An I'm atellin y." (200–1)

Hanby has been absorbed into the white frame of reference in another way. Unwilling to accept the "place" assigned to Halsey, he has dedicated his life to the task of making black men as "white" as they can possibly be in their own thoughts and behavior, implicitly accepting a sense of his own inferiority. He tells Kabnis:

> "The progress of the Negro race is jeopardized whenever the personal habits and examples set by its guides and mentors fall below the acknowledged and hard-won standard of its average member. This institution, of which I am the humble president, was founded, and has been maintained at a cost of great labor and untold sacrifice. Its purpose is to teach our youth to live better, cleaner, more noble lives. To prove to the world that the Negro race can be just like any other race." (186)

Both Halsey and Hanby are totally unaware of the significance of the old man who lives in the cellar. They view him simply as an unpleasant memory that is best kept buried and concealed and discussed as little as possible.

Among the members of the older generation, only Lewis has retained the pride and dignity of his manhood, and he alone has a sense of the importance and value of the old man. Consequently, the others refer to him as a "queer fellow." As Bone observes, Lewis is in many ways an extension of Dan Moore of "Box Seat."[14] But, able to give himself completely to his heritage, he succeeds where Dan finds only frustration. Lewis has a full sense of communion with the old man:

> Lewis, seated now so that his eyes rest upon the old man, merges with his source and lets the pain and beauty of the South meet him there. White faces, pain-pollen, settle downward through a cane-sweet mist and touch the ovaries of yellow flowers. Cotton-bolls bloom, droop. Black roots twist in a parched red soil beneath a blazing sky. Magnolias, fragrant, a trifle futile, lovely, far off . . . His eyelids close. A force begins to heave and rise. (214–15)

Only Lewis's attitude can bring true resurrection to the spirit of the black man; the other alternatives can result only in stagnation. Halsey and Hanby have already made their choices, and their lives are petty and without essential value. For Carrie Kate and Kabnis, however, the possibility remains of resurrection through an acceptance of the past that is represented by the old man. The choice that Carrie Kate and Kabnis must make is put to them explicitly by Lewis. Referring to the old man, he says to Kabnis:

> "Black Vulcan? I wouldnt say so. That forehead. Great woolly beard. Those eyes. A mute John the Baptist of a new religion—or a tongue-tied shadow of an old." (211)

In less allusive terms, Lewis is simply telling Kabnis that the memory of the racial past can either die an impotent and meaningless death, or it can become the sustaining, spiritual force behind a reawakened sense of race consciousness, pride, and dignity; and that its fate depends on whether Kabnis himself accepts or rejects it.

Kabnis, however, lacks the strength necessary for such an acceptance. Made fearful, timid, and cynical by his experiences in the North, he is, like the typical figures of Part 2, "a promise of soil-soaked beauty; uprooted, thinning out. Suspended a few feet above the soil whose touch would resurrect him" (191). Lewis reaches out spiritually toward Kabnis, encouraging him, but Kabnis decisively rejects him:

> There is a swift intuitive interchange of consciousness. Kabnis has a sudden need to rush into the arms of this man. His eyes call, "Brother." And then a savage, cynical twistabout within him mocks his impulse and strengthens him to repulse Lewis. His lips curl cruelly. His eyes laugh. (191–92)

When Lewis puts the question, Kabnis makes his decision immediately: "His tongue is tied all right, an I can vouch f that" (212). In his final words, his attitude remains unchanged, and he refuses to accept the old man as anything but an "old black fakir" (238).

Carrie Kate, however, presents another possibility. At first, she, too, rejects Lewis; as he reaches out to her,

> the sun-burst from her eyes floods up and haloes him. Christ-eyes, his eyes look to her. Fearlessly she loves into them. And then something happens. Her face blanches. Awkwardly she draws away. The sin-bogies of respectable southern colored folks clamor at her: "Look out! Be a *good* girl. A *good* girl. Look out!" (205)

Carrie Kate's rejection, however, is far from decisive. Her ability to love and feel is still present, and the possibility remains that her vitality may eventually break through the restrictions imposed by the "sin-bogies of respectability." In the final scene of the book, Carrie Kate achieves this breakthrough. In direct contrast to Kabnis, she chooses communion with the old man, goes to him, and, like Lewis, draws strength and sustenance from him. As Kabnis leaves,

> Carrie's gaze follows him till he is gone. Then she goes to the old man and slips to her knees before him. Her lips murmur, "Jesus, come."
>
> Light streaks through the iron-barred cellar window. Within its soft circle, the figures of Carrie and Father John. (239)

In writing *Cane*, Toomer set out to make his art "an everlasting song, a singing tree," which, by "caroling softly souls of slavery,/what they were, and what they are to me," might become a new myth for the black men to live by, a myth that would reinforce his sense of relatedness to his roots and save him from the isolation and impotency imposed upon him by life in a white-dominated society and culture to which he had little fundamental connection. With this final scene of communion, Toomer's goal has been achieved, and the achievement is symbolized by Carrie Kate's humble but loving acceptance of the old man, the pain and anguish and sin that he represents along with his intrinsic beauty and vitality. Toomer's "Song of the Son," which began in the atmosphere of a setting sun and moved through the spiritual death of northern exile, ends with the rising of a new sun, symbolizing the rebirth and resurrection of the Negro spirit, the new life-giving force that Toomer had attempted to create in *Cane*:

> Outside, the sun arises from its cradle in the tree-tops of the forest. Shadows of pines are dreams the sun shakes from its eyes. The sun arises. Gold-glowing child, it steps into the sky and sends a birth-song slanting down gray dust streets and sleepy windows of the southern town. (239)

The Spectatorial Artist and the Structure of *Cane*

SUSAN L. BLAKE

From the men in "Karintha" trying to turn a mysterious woman into a common prostitute, to the poet Kabnis longing to put the terrors of the night world into words, the characters in Jean Toomer's *Cane* are struggling to impose form on a world of chaos. They are all a little bit like Rhobert, the grotesque caricature of a striving homeowner, who "wears a house, like a monstrous diver's helmet on his head" to keep out "life . . . a murky wiggling, microscopic water that compresses him."[1] They fear, with increasing consciousness as the book progresses, that if they do not control chaos it will conquer them, leaving them as disordered and fragmented as the world appears to be. They do not realize that the disorder is within them already—not in the silent, mysterious, paradoxical universe—and that their efforts to impose their idea of order on life only compound their fragmentation. Despite Rhobert's efforts to keep out murky, wiggling, microscopic life, the stuffing in his house is "shredded life-pulp" (73).

Between Jean Toomer and these characters is a creative persona—represented sometimes by a narrator, sometimes simply by the narrative voice—who shares his characters' goals and whose story unifies the book. Like Kabnis, like any artist, he wants to give form to experience, and *Cane* is the record of his attempt. Gorham B. Munson has called this persona the "spectatorial artist,"[2] a term which suggests the artistic process outlined in the book: the persona progresses from a spectator in the first stories to an artist in "Kabnis." His progress is measured by his distance from his characters. Both the spectator and the artist are detached from their material, but the understanding that distinguishes the detached creator of the final story from the detached observer of the first comes from a transitional stage of involvement.

The central conflict in *Cane* is the struggle of the spectatorial artist to involve himself in his material. The characters in the individual stories are engaged in the same conflict. Their "material" is life; involvement for them means acceptance of its chaos. The protagonists in the first stories are unaware of the conflict; the men who try to buy Karintha do not know what they are missing, "do not know that the soul of her was a growing thing ripened too soon" (4). Kabnis knows; and the sight of "hills and valleys, heaving with folk-songs, so close to me that I cannot reach them" (161), drives him mad. For the spectatorial artist, involvement in his material means identification with his characters and recognition that the dilemma he is portraying in them is also his dilemma. The characters become more complex as they become more aware of their experience; they become more aware as their creator, becoming more involved with them, puts his own awareness into them. Thus, characters and creative voice develop in parallel in *Cane*, and the book resembles neither a novel nor a collection of short stories as much as it does a sketchbook—a record of artistic development.

In the first part of the book, the spectatorial artist maintains the distance of a reporter. The first four stories are anecdotes, local legends, related in the past tense from the point of view of an outsider. The artist's very presence in these stories as a distinct character, the narrator, emphasizes his emotional distance from the other characters. The struggle to comprehend chaos is represented in these stories as the struggle of men to possess the women—Karintha, Becky, Carma, Fern—whose names provide the titles. Superficially, the stories are about the women, but the real interest—the interest developed throughout the book—is in the men who labor to possess them. They are the active characters, artist figures with the will to limit, control, define experience. The women—silent, passive, elusive—represent the experience that the men are trying to grasp. They embody the beauty, suffer the pain, and above all accept the domination of the natural chaos. The spectatorial artist remains aloof from both the men and the women. He sees the mystery in the women, but intellectually, not sympathetically. He also sees that the men do not appreciate it and therefore feels superior to them. Only in the last two stories of Part 1, "Esther" and "Blood-Burning Moon," does the creative voice attempt to enter into the conflict.

"Karintha" dramatizes the essential conflict between the acceptance and limitation of being. By regarding her as a prostitute, the men who desire Karintha limit her to an existence defined by the tangible, measurable quantities of body and money. But Karintha is not to be confined in any way—physically, socially, or conceptually. "Her skin is like dusk on the eastern horizon" (1), not a texture to be touched or a warmth to be held, but a quality of light, far off and fleeting. Earth seems not to hold her down; when she was a child, her running feet did not flop in the dust like the other children's, "Karintha's running was a whir" (2). Social and moral laws are suspended for her sake: "even the preacher," the guardian of public morals, catching her stoning the cows and beating her dog, finds her "as innocently lovely as a November cotton flower" (2). Conceptually, Karintha exists outside the normal definition of words. Though she "has been married many times" and men "will bring their money," she is not a prostitute: "Karintha is a woman. She who carries beauty, perfect as dusk when the sun goes down" (3). Not only does Toomer refuse to apply to her a label like "prostitute," but the words with which he does describe her have no received meaning apart from the evocation of Karintha. "Carrying a burden," for example, is a concept with a restricted, because generally accepted, meaning, but "carrying beauty," the phrase applied to Karintha, is undefined and hence unlimited.

The "interest of the male," however, is the impulse to limit. Men respond to Karintha in the quantitative terms of time and money. First they "count time" until she will be old enough to mate with them; then they run stills and become salesmen and go to college to get money for her. Her attraction for them is of course her sexuality, and it is quite literally her sexual being that they measure in time and money. But Karintha's sexuality is intimately fused with her soul, which is "a growing thing ripening too soon." This metaphor, used in the context of reference to her sexual precocity (1) and to the birth of her child (4), links her soul to both her sexual potential and its fulfillment, to her reproductive capacity, to her femaleness. The men who try to buy her with money and define her as a prostitute get only half of what should be an indivisible unity of sexuality and soul: "Men do not know that the soul of her was a growing thing ripened too soon. They will bring their money; they will die not having found it out . . ." (4).

The money the men bring Karintha is only a symbol of the limited and fragmented world in which they try to confine her. They make her a prostitute not so much by bringing her money as by inflicting on her the personal fragmentation that the money implies. Ultimately, however, though Karintha's soul smoulders with her baby in the sawdust pile, it is the men who are left incomplete, who "will die not having found it out." Karintha at the end is still "perfect as dusk"—complete, part of the natural universe—and the men, having failed to know her soul, are still confined in the half-world of time and money.

In the stories of Becky, Carma, and Fern, we begin to see how the conflict dramatized in "Karintha" applies to the spectatorial artist, who functions in these stories as a narrator. There is something about each of these women that other people want to know and never find out. The narrator, experimenting, responds to the unknown in each story with a different pose. In "Becky" he is the bumbling innocent; in "Carma," the detached sophisticate; in "Fern," the earnest and worldly sophomore. His posing reflects his repeatedly unsuccessful attempts to deal with his material. At the end of each of these stories, an ironic comment about the limits of knowledge applies to the narrator as well as the other characters.

Becky, the white woman who had two Negro sons, has shattered the laws that the community wants to believe govern social behavior. The townspeople try to deal with the disorder she represents by pretending that she is not part of their world. They redefine her: "Common, God-forsaken, insane white shameless wench, said the white folks' mouths. . . . Poor Catholic poor-white crazy woman, said the black folks' mouths" (8). They imprison her in a one-room cabin on a narrow strip of ground "islandized between the road and railroad track" (9). They help her individually and secretly, so they will not have to admit responsibility for her even to themselves. Ultimately, they decide that she does not exist, "that if there was a Becky, that Becky now was dead" (10).

But Becky no more than Karintha will be held down to definitions. First she has a second Negro son; then smoke curling from her chimney proves she is not dead. The conflict between the town's determination to limit and Becky's refusal to be limited is represented stylistically in the interrupted sentence that characterizes this sketch—"A single room held down to earth . . . O fly away to Jesus . . . by a leaning chimney . . ." (9—ellipsis in text). The townspeople's need to define is precisely what prevents them from finding out anything that would satisfy that need: "Taking their words, they filled her, like a bubble rising—then she broke. Mouth setting in a twist that held her eyes, harsh, vacant, staring . . . Who gave it to her: . . . She wouldnt tell" (8). And the chimney by which the townspeople hold her down to earth is what in the end liberates her to fly away to Jesus.

The narrator of this story allies himself with the townspeople—"our congregation," "we, who had cast out their mother" (11)—and adopts their fears. All he can remember after seeing the rumbling of a ghost train collapse Becky's chimney is "whipping old Dan like fury" to get back to town. "I remember nothing after that—that is, until I reached town and folks crowded round to get the true word of it" (12–13). That these people who are so dependent on definitions could get the true word, or that this narrator could give it to them, is impossible. Their desire for the true word is as ironic as Barlo's Bible, true Word of the Puritanism with which they have cast Becky out, flapping "with an aimless rustle on her mound" (8,13).

Carma's story, the narrator tells us, is "crudest melodrama"—a term that suggests both sensational events and hollow characters. This story is made melodrama as much by the way the narrator tells it as by the way the characters in it act. Carma's husband, like Becky's persecutors, thinks truth is simple. Either Carma has had other men or she hasn't: "Bane accused her. She denied. He couldnt see that she was becoming hysterical" (18). When he loses his head and slashes his neighbor, he is reacting to the belief that he has been deceived—first by Carma's denial, then by her pretense of suicide, "Twice deceived, and one deception proved the other" (19). His concern with events rather than with Carma implies belief in a universe of fact, where everything may be known and a man has a right to expect not to be deceived.

By calling the story a melodrama, the narrator shows the same lack of sensitivity that characterizes Bane in the story itself. He is detached from Carma: he follows her down the red dust road, but only with his eyes. His interest is that of a storyteller in a bizarre sequence of events, or of a judge in a hypothetical case: "Should she not take others, this Carma, strong as a man, whose tale as I have told it is the crudest melodrama?" (20). The phrase "as I have told it" suggests, however—at the expense of absolute consistency in point of view—that there may be more to this story than the narrator knows to tell and that by the use of the word *melodrama* the detached sophisticate shows himself to be as naive as Bane.

The narrator flees from the scene of Becky's destruction, detaches himself from Carma's story, and attempts unsuccessfully to participate in Fern's life. He senses that Fern embodies the mystery of the universe; he sees "the countryside and something that I call God" flow into her eyes, hears the sorrow in her song as of a Jewish cantor singing, feels in her presence the immanence of "things unseen to men." He even half expects to enter into Fern's mystic communion with these things by having a vision. Instead, however, he makes some unconscious, automatic gesture that sends her off into her own world and away from him. She does not come to him on his terms, which are physical, and he does not come to her on hers, which are mystic.

Although the narrator takes Fern's side against the men who are "everlastingly bringing her their bodies" (25), he too brings her something she does not want. He brings his own world—his cosmopolitan experience, his successful friends, his rational approach to life:

> Or, suppose she came up North and married. Even a doctor or a lawyer, say, one who would be sure to get along—that is, make money. You and I know, who have had experience in such things. . . . (28)
>
> You and I who know men in these cities will have to say. . . . (29)

By making her a subject for sociological speculation and discussing her in a breezy, intimate, parenthetical tone of voice, the narrator detaches himself from Fern and associates with an audience which is, like himself, not-southern, not-mystic, and not-Fern. With his final remark—"Her name, against the chance that you might happen down that way, is Fernie May Rosen" (33)—he objectifies Fern's mystic sorrow and defines her in much the same way that the men who bring her money define Karintha. He shows that ultimately he is not trying to enter Fern's world, but to bring her into his. The narrator is not as different as he would like to think from the other men Fern has known. They brought her their bodies, were denied, and left thinking they would like to do something for her. He, too, has brought her something she rejects and leaves thinking, "Something I would do for her. Some fine unnamed thing . . ." (33). The narrator sees Fern's problem with her admirers, but he doesn't see that he is part of it.

In "Esther" and "Blood-Burning Moon," the spectatorial artist comes a little closer to his characters. Instead of simply relating what has happened to them, he gets inside their thoughts and looks at the world from their point of view. Both of these stories dramatize the personal fragmentation that results from the inability to deal with chaos, and the artist tries to present Esther's and Louisa's mental dislocation from the inside.

In "Esther" the conflict that has been represented so far as a struggle between two distinct groups—men (or, in the case of Becky, the community) and women—takes place within one person. Unlike the women in the first four stories, Esther is an artist figure; like the men, she is seeking personal wholeness through sexual union. But she is a more conscious artist even than the men, for the partner she seeks is largely a creation of her own imagination. Near white and sexually repressed, she decides she is in love with Barlo, who is black—"magnetically so"—and male—"Best man with his fists, best man with dice, with a razor" (42–43). She imagines that he could fulfill her racial and sexual needs by giving her a coal-black baby. But Esther idealizes both Barlo and sex. She pictures him as she saw him when she was nine—caught up in a religious trance, the embodiment of African spiritualism—and although the imaginary fire from which she rescues her imaginary baby suggests her unacknowledged physical passion, she envisions herself as a sort of madonna with an immaculately conceived baby nibbling at her breast. When she decides, at twenty-seven, to go to Barlo at Nat Bowle's place, it is partly, she rationalizes, to save him from the arms of the loose women there. There is nothing spiritual, however, about either Barlo or Esther's passion for him. Barlo has come back to town "as rich as anyone" (44), worshipping material gods. When Esther sees him he is drunk, hideous. And the loose women who hang around have Esther sized up better than she does herself: " 'So thats how th dictie niggers does it . . . Mus give em credit fo their gall' " (47). The shattering of her imaginary world leaves Esther with no world at all. When she steps out "there is no air, no street, and the town has completely disappeared" (48).

The chaos in "Blood-Burning Moon" results from the conflict between natural and social laws. Natural law allows Tom Burwell, black, and Bob Stone, white, to compete for the love of Louisa. Social law, however, prevents a black man from winning a fight with a white man—the white man may not win, but the black man must lose. The full moon, a natural deity, shining in the door of the factory, the social center of the community, becomes a symbol for the uneasy balance between the two laws: "The full moon in the great door was an omen. Negro women improvised songs against its spell" (51). Neither of the men can accept the mutual domination of contradictory laws. Bob Stone ignores natural law: "No sir. No nigger has ever been with this girl. He'd like to see one try" (60). Tom Burwell defies social law:

> "[W]hite folks aint up t them tricks so much nowadays. Godam better not be. Leastawise not with yo. Cause I wouldnt stand f it. Nassur."
>
> "What would you do, Tom?"
>
> "Cut him jes like I cut a nigger."
>
> "No, Tom—" (57)

Louisa, caught between the two men, senses the conflict between the two forces. Her "No, Tom—" may indicate fear for either or both of her lovers. But Louisa is powerless to prevent the disaster whose immanence she senses rather than sees. Just as there is no way for Louisa to live, as she would like to, with the love of both Bob and Tom, there is no concrete way to live between two powerful and conflicting laws. The people in factory town know this and, admitting the conflict, withdraw from life: "Negroes who had seen the fight slunk into their homes and blew the lamps out" (64). But Louisa withdraws instead from the knowledge of conflict. When the omen of the full moon shining in the factory door is fulfilled in the yell of the lynch mob slipping out the door, Louisa has lost both her lovers and all hold on objective reality. She still thinks Tom Burwell might come out to hear her sing to the moon. She cannot accept the reality of contradiction.

Though Esther is active and Louisa passive, both women experience the dilemma of living within a disordered world. In the previous stories, the narrator had observed the dilemma without suggesting that the characters feel it. The men are obtuse, the women inert. By locating the basic conflict of the book within a single character, the spectatorial artist not only gives the character a shade of complexity—which indicates a step in his artistic development—but also acknowledges that the conflict he observes is individual, psychological. By giving his characters some of the sensibility that so far has been his alone, he acknowledges their kinship with him, the artist; by putting himself imaginatively into their fragmented minds, he acknowledges his kinship with them. The spectatorial artist's identification with his characters, begun in "Esther" and "Blood-Burning Moon," increases in Part 2.

Everything in Part 2 conveys the intensity of the artist's involvement: the imperatives in the opening sketch—"Split it! In two! Again! Shred it!" (71); the direct appeal in "Rhobert"—"Lets open our throats, brother, and sing 'Deep River' when he goes down" (75); the grotesqueness of the imagery in all the sketches; and the mounting anxiety of the protagonists in the stories. The three sketches present images of the fragmentation dramatized in the four stories: Seventh Street, a "wedge of nigger life" splitting the "stale soggy wood of Washington," which in turn rusts the wedge (71); Rhobert's house stuffed with "shredded life-pulp"; the woman in "Calling Jesus" separated from her soul, which is like a little thrust-tailed dog that she locks in the vestibule at night. The protagonists in the stories become increasingly aware of their own fragmentation and increasingly anxious to unify themselves. Although they seek personal wholeness through sexual union, the conflict is clearly within the men; the women merely represent a part of life or themselves that the men cannot accept without first changing, analyzing, or idealizing, and as a consequence always lose. At the same time that the conflict centers in the individual, the individual becomes more like the spectatorial artist. No longer inarticulate peasants, the protagonists in these stories are artists and intellectuals. The frustration of the artist character trying to modify life into a rational form becomes an expression of the spectatorial artist's frustration at trying to shape life into art.

The narrator in "Avey" is the most naive of these characters. He represents his relationship with Avey as a series of encounters in which he has tried to win Avey by dominating her and always failed. He has tried to impress her by excelling in basketball and drill, teaching her to swim, dancing, talking—"I knew damned well that I could beat her at that" (80). He has tried to make her into an ambitious teacher instead of what he considers an indolent cow. Finally, when he meets her accidentally in Washington and takes her to his favorite spot on Soldiers' Home, he analyzes her: "I pointed out that in lieu of proper channels, her emotions had overflowed into paths that dissipated them. I talked, beautifully I thought, about an art that would be born, an art that would open the way for women the likes of her" (87). The narrator's expense of eloquence here is really an effort to remake

Avey in his own image—that of the artist anticipating a rebirth of art in which he would have a place. His speech stirs him to passion; it puts Avey to sleep. And when he looks down at Avey as she really is, asleep, his passion dies. As he regards her in the early-morning chill, he calls her "orphan-woman," which indeed she is, for though he insists on being paternal, he will not accept her for herself.

John, in "Theater," is also an artist; he imagines that he takes the chorus girl Dorris to his room after the show and reads her one of his manuscripts. His insistence on controlling experience results in his rejection not only of Dorris but also of himself. The dramatic conflict between Dorris, who throws herself into her dance, forgetting steps, whipping the whole stage to life, and John, who sits in the theater watching and imagining, parallels a personal conflict—symbolized by the division of his face into light and shadow—between John's body and his mind. His mind repeatedly represses the physical passion awakened in him by Dorris's dancing: "Her limbs in silk purple stockings are lovely. John feels them. Desires her. Holds off." His mind manipulates his identity to justify his retreat from action: "Stage-door johnny; chorus girl. No, that would be all right. Dictie, educated, stuck-up; show-girl. Yep. Her suspicion would be stronger than her passion. It wouldnt work. Keep her loveliness. Let her go" (94). When he rejects Dorris, John rejects the physical part of himself; at the end of the story, "his whole face is in shadow" (99). To have accepted Dorris would have been to integrate the two warring factions in himself; to reject her is to allow a part to take over for the whole.

When John rejects Dorris she rushes from the stage and bursts into tears, but he, unaware even of the contact Dorris has made with him, feels no loss. The narrator in "Avey," though he feels the separation between himself and Avey, attributes all the insufficiency to her. These characters, though they have tried unsuccessfully to fit experience into their sense of order, are complacent because, not understanding their experience, they do not understand their failure. But the protagonists in "Box Seat" and "Bona and Paul" do understand the complexity of life, so their failure to organize it results in anguish.

Dan Moore suffers the anguish of knowledge combined with impotence. He tries to live vicariously through Muriel, who simultaneously accepts and rejects life. She wears her hair bobbed, but keeps her hat on in the theater because teachers are not supposed to have bobbed hair. She has a certain "animalism, still unconquered by zoo-restrictions and keeper-taboos" (112), but she rejects pain and ugliness in life. When Dan comes to her to patch up an old quarrel, she refuses to talk about it and shifts the subject quickly to an impersonal one:

> "Lets dont mention that."
> "But why not, Muriel? I—"
> "Please."
> "But Muriel, life is full of things like that. One grows strong and beautiful in facing them. What else is life?"
> "I dont know, Dan. And I dont believe I care. Whats the use? Lets talk about something else. I hear there's a good show at the Lincoln this week." (109)

In this dialogue Muriel is running away from life to the imitation of life in the theater. Although the show she sees there later is more grotesque than anything she has encountered in real life, she can accept it as long as she feels she has no connection with it. When one of the bloody dwarf pugilists who have been battering each other for the entertainment of the audience reaches up to Muriel in her box, however, and offers her a blood-spattered rose, she shrinks in terror and revulsion.

Dan, moved to jump up and shout, "JESUS WAS ONCE A LEPER!" (129), understands intellectually what Muriel cannot accept, that "life bends joy and pain, beauty and ugliness, in such a way that no one may isolate them" (112), but he cannot live life. He cannot find the doorbell on a house he has visited often. He cannot get into his seat in the theater without treading on other people's corns and provoking a fight. In his mind he can save the world, but he cannot free Muriel from the influence of her landlady, Mrs. Pribby, or make the people in the theater understand his unwelcome proclamation. Muriel recognizes Dan's weakness; she thinks, "Timid lover, brave talker that you are. Whats the good of all you know if you dont know that [I love you]?" (110). Because Dan cannot free Muriel from the prison of Pribbyism and cannot live without her, he remains enslaved despite his understanding. "He-slave," he calls himself, "Slave of a woman who is a slave. I'm a damned sight worse than you are" (121). As the story closes he is walking away abstractedly from the fight he has provoked. Dan can dream, but he cannot act. He can conceive but not create.

In "Bona and Paul" the artist character finally acts, but his gesture is too hesitant to accomplish its purpose. As Paul sits in his room in afternoon reverie, he seems to see Bona in one of the room's two windows, himself in the other. The separation between them suggests to

Paul the paradox of his identity: "A Negress chants a lullaby beneath the mate-eyes of a southern planter" (138). As his mind returns from Georgia to Chicago, however, he and Bona come together—he finds himself at Bona's window.

All evening, out with Bona, Paul fights the union he has pictured in the window in the afternoon. He has suddenly realized, hearing his white roommate, Art, play jazz on the piano, that "nigger" is "different": "I've got to get the kid to play that stuff for me in the daytime. Might be different. More himself. More nigger. Different? There is. Curious, though" (142). The curious eyes of the white people around him at the Crimson Gardens reinforce his feeling of separation: "Suddenly he knew that he was apart from the people around him. Apart from the pain which they had unconsciously caused. Suddenly, he knew that people saw, not attractiveness in his dark skin, but difference" (145). He cannot accept the white girl he is attracted to without reconciling that difference, which separates him not only from Bona and his surroundings but also from himself.

For a moment, dancing with Bona, Paul forgets his preoccupation with the difference between white faces and black. Physical passion unites them. "They know that the pink-faced people have no part in what they feel. Their instinct leads them away from Art and Helen" (152) and out of the Crimson Gardens. By accepting Bona, Paul would be accepting the paradox of his identity and hence reintegrating his split self. But when he sees the leer on the black doorman's face that implies knowledge of why they are leaving and suspicion that Paul is passing for white, Paul rushes back to deny his instinct and replace it with a poetic rationalization: " 'Brother, youre wrong. . . . I came back to tell you, brother, that white faces are petals of roses. That dark faces are petals of dusk. That I am going out and gather petals. That I am going out and know her whom I brought here with me to these Gardens which are purple like a bed of roses would be at dusk' " (152–53). When he returns to the place where he has left her, however, Bona, and with her the opportunity for communion, is gone.

In Paul Johnson the characters in *Cane* have reached an impasse. Paul has all of the spectatorial artist's understanding of the complexity of life, but he cannot use it; when he tries, it betrays him. His very attempt to articulate a resolution between what he considers conflicting elements destroys the resolution and leaves him in the same isolation that signifies incompleteness in all the other characters. His situation mirrors the dilemma of the artist, who must limit life in order to express it but apparently cannot limit it without losing it.

It is as though, by the end of Part 2, the spectatorial artist has realized that this paradox is both his dilemma and his subject and is ready to examine it for itself. For in "Kabnis" the artist abandons the metaphor of sexual conflict and dramatizes the story of a frustrated artist whose conflict is literally what the sexual conflict stands for, that between the acceptance and limitation of being, and whose failure to accept life results not simply in the symbolic incompleteness of isolation but in the unmistakable fragmentation of a crack-up.

Kabnis is the self-conscious narrator of Part 1 seen from the outside instead of the inside. The spectatorial artist who did not know how much he was revealing about himself in the narrator-dominated stories of Part 1 is now examining himself as a subject. His ability to criticize himself in that earlier stage of development reveals his distance from it and hence his artistic growth.

As its length and development suggest, "Kabnis" is not simply the final step in the artist's progress, but the culmination of all that has gone before, the work that the spectatorial artist has been trying over and over again to write. Between Kabnis the artist and Halsey the artisan exists the same tension that has divided the spectatorial artist from the men in Part 1. Kabnis is sensitive; Halsey, like Karintha's admirers, is obtuse, deaf to the distant song Kabnis feels like a spark that sets the countryside ablaze:

> Kabnis: That song, Halsey, do you hear it?
> Halsey: Thats a man. Hear me, Kabnis? A man—
> Kabnis: Jesus, do you hear it.
> Halsey: Hear it? Hear what? Course I hear it. Listen t what I'm tellin y. (193)

Within Kabnis himself is the conflict between Dan Moore, who is acutely conscious of the chaos of life, and Muriel, who rejects it.

Every manifestation of mystery upsets Kabnis. The mingling of beauty and ugliness that the women in Part I passively accept tortures him:

> Dear Jesus, do not chain me to myself and set these hills and valleys, heaving with folk-songs, so close to me that I cannot reach them. There is a radiant beauty in the night that touches and . . . tortures me. Ugh. Hell. Get up, you damn fool. Look around. Whats beautiful there? Hog pens and chicken yards. (161–62)

The silence of the night world disquiets him:

> Still as a grave. Jesus, how still everything is. Does the world know how still it is? People make noise. They are afraid of silence. Of what lives, and God, of what dies in silence. There must be many dead things moving in silence. They come here to touch me. I swear I feel their fingers . . . Come, Ralph, pull yourself together. (164–65)

The unpredictability of southern race relations—"Nigger's a nigger down this away, Professor" (171)—petrifies him into thinking everyone is after him. The shouting in church upsets him so much he has to leave. Even a joke throws him off balance:

> Halsey: Is that th way youall sit on sisters up North?
> Kabnis: In the church I used to go to no one ever shouted—
> Halsey: Lungs weak?
> Kabnis: Hardly, that is—(175–76)

But disorder, like the murky, wiggling, microscopic water in "Rhobert," is only life. From the first scene, when he wrings the neck of a treading hen and picks her reproductive function to abuse—"get out of that, you egg-laying bitch" (159)—Kabnis rejects life. He rejects Lewis:

> There is a swift intuitive interchange of consciousness. Kabnis has a sudden need to rush into the arms of this man. His eyes call, "Brother." And then a savage, cynical twist-about within him mocks his impulse and strengthens him to repulse Lewis. His lips curl cruelly. His eyes laugh. (191–92)

He rejects Father John:

> "An besides, he aint my past. My ancestors were Southern blue-bloods—" (217)

Ultimately, he rejects himself, for Lewis is "what a stronger Kabnis might have been" (189), and Father John, as a memory of the pain and suffering of slavery, is a part of the chaos in Kabnis himself. Lewis identifies the rejection of Father John as Kabnis's inability to integrate the parts of a fragmented self:

> "Cant hold them, can you? Master; slave. Soil; and the overarching heavens. Dusk; dawn. They fight and bastardize you. The sun tint of your cheeks, flame of the great season's multi-colored leaves, tarnished, burned. Split, shredded: easily burned. No use. . . ." (218)

The inability to live within paradoxes leaves Kabnis shredded.

Kabnis lacks what the weakest characters, Father John and Carrie Kate, have—the courage to be. Kabnis is both fascinated by and abusive of Father John because the mute old man represents all that he both needs and fears. Father John is the incarnation of the silence of the universe that torments a man who cannot depend on himself. Yet his struggle to speak suggests that he has a secret that might help settle Kabnis's anxieties. The gnomic statement Father John finally utters, however—"O th sin th white folks 'mitted when they made the Bible lie" (237)—is closer to a truism than a truth. It exasperates Kabnis because it gives no answers: "So thats your sin. All these years t tell us that th white folks made th Bible lie. Well, I'll be damned" (238).

The difficult thing about truth, however, is not recognition but acceptance. "The sin the white folks 'mitted" does in fact apply to Kabnis, who has said himself, "Th whole world is a conspiracy t sin, especially in America, an against me. I'm the victim of their sin. I'm what sin is" (236). What Father John meant by his statement is anybody's guess, but the results of two ways in which white folks made the Bible lie are apparent in *Cane*: the Biblical justification of slavery and the corruption of religion into repressive moralism—the "sin-bodies" of "respectable southern colored folks." Both lies result in the repression of life. Of the first, Kabnis is, as he says, "the victim." Of the general repression he is "what sin is." His sin is the rejection of being, which prevents him from taking part in the symbolic Nativity scene that joins Father John and Carrie Kate in the end. As the sun "sends a birth-song slanting down gray dust streets and sleepy windows of the southern town," Kabnis, "with eyes downcast and swollen, trudges upstairs to the work-shop" (239), reduced in creative stature from a poet to a wagon-maker's apprentice. His inability to accept the irrationality of life like the passive young woman and the blind, deaf, immobile old man prevents the would-be artist from achieving creation.

In creating Kabnis, however, the spectatorial artist has transcended Kabnis's failure. Kabnis, who envisions himself the star of an old-time lynching, who thinks he is "th topic of conversation everywhere theres talk about this town" (222), who struts about pompously in an absurd robe that finally trips him, who insists one moment that the old man's tongue is tied, "an I can vouch f that" (212), and abuses him the next for talking—this Kabnis has absorbed and magnified the self-conscious posing of the narrator in Part 1. In the destruction of

Kabnis, the artist has exorcised the Kabnis in himself. The change is apparent in the narrative form.

As the artist character in *Cane* has become increasingly self-conscious, the creative artist has become less so. The narrative form of the stories develops gradually from the first-person journalism of Part 1 to the third-person narration of Part 2, to the semidramatic form of "Kabnis." In the first four stories, the characters' experience is sifted through the mind and expressed in the metaphors of an outsider: "Her soul was a growing thing ripened too soon" (4); "Nothing ever came to Fern, not even I." The better the persona knows his characters, the less he has to intrude on their lives. The present tense, adopted in "Esther" and used in all of the pieces in Part 2 except "Avey," and the internal monologues that characterize all of the stories after "Avey" develop into the immediate dramatic form of "Kabnis." The characters in drama are, according to the illusion, independent, free of authorial manipulation. The spectatorial artist, who in his final achievement has become Jean Toomer, the artist of the whole story of his development, allows Kabnis—as Kabnis does not allow himself—simply to *be*. Since the ability of a character to stand alone is the measure of the fullness of its creation, Kabnis's independence as a character represents the achievement of the spectatorial artist's creative goal.

The rather odd ending, in which a sympathetic character is allowed to destroy himself, signifies the artist's relinquishment of Kabnis's self-conscious anxiety and his placement of himself in the circle of soft light with Father John and Carrie Kate awaiting the epiphany. In separating himself from his character, the artist has created from his own struggle with that character's conflicts the work of art that frees him from the character's failure and consequent fragmentation. In *Cane* the spectatorial artist has discovered and demonstrated that creativity and self-unity depend on each other and that both depend, ironically, on submission to the apparent chaos of the universe.

The theme and structure of *Cane* indicate that Toomer was already motivated, as he put the book together, by convictions that his literary friend Gorham Munson recognized later:

> Shortly after writing *Cane*, he formed two convictions. One was that the modern world is a veritable chaos and the other was that in a disrupted age the first duty of the artist is to unify himself. Having achieved personal wholeness, then perhaps he would possess an atti-

> tude that would not be merely a reaction to the circumstances of modernity, merely a reflection of the life about him, but would be an attitude that could act upon modernity, dissolve away the remainder of an old slope of consciousness, and plant the seeds for a new slope.[3]

If in the theatrical and masochistic destruction of Kabnis, Toomer has "dissolved away the remainder of an old slope of consciousness," the dissolution is temporary, and there is no evidence, either in *Cane* or in Toomer's career thereafter, that he has "planted the seeds for a new slope." Symbolically, the union of Father John and Carrie Kate in a tableau suggestive of the Nativity represents the beginning of a new life, but dramatically, the union of an immobile old man and a passive young virgin is sterile. Lewis, the only other alternative to Kabnis, is a shadowy commentator whose successful adjustment to life is alluded to but never demonstrated. And Toomer himself, after reaching a statement of the artist's problem in "Kabnis," never progressed to its resolution. He discovered Gurdjieff, became absorbed in mysticism, and wrote transparently autobiographical and unpublishable formless fiction.[4] In the retreat into mysticism advocated in *Cane* Toomer achieved neither of the two conflicting requirements he had made of the artist—neither the ability of the wagon-maker to shape the chaos of experience nor that of a woman to submerge herself in it.

The Unifying Images in Part One of Jean Toomer's *Cane*

RICHARD ELDRIDGE

Although many of the poems and stories in Jean Toomer's *Cane*[1] were published separately in little magazines like *Broom*, *S4N*, and *Double Dealer*, the final compilation of Toomer's book was no random collection of writings. In July of 1922 Toomer wrote of his desire to put under one cover some of his writing because ". . . I feel a precipitant is urgently needed just at this time. The concentrated volume will do a great deal more than isolated pieces possibly would."[2] By December of that year, Toomer had compiled his writings into what he called a "circle design," the symbol of which he included into the book's format. The arcs on the frontpieces of each of the three sections theoretically blend into one circle.[3] The aesthetic relationship among the three parts, Toomer claimed, is from the simple design to the complex and back to the simple again. Regionally, the book moves from the South to the North and back to the South again. Spiritually, Toomer envisioned an entity which begins with "Bona and Paul (awakening), plunges into Kabnis, emerges into Karintha, etc., swings upward into Theater and Box Seat, and ends (pauses) in Harvest Song."[4] In other words, the spiritual unity begins at the end of Part 2, sweeps downward to the end of the book and returns to the beginning of the book, then climbs to an end at the penultimate piece of the second part. According to Toomer's description of the book's structure, then, Part 2 is the fulcrum of the first and third sections. The book does not conform to a linear structure associated with most novels or romances; rather, it is like a painting unified by a center of tension or like a piece of music embellished by a middle movement. Toomer's organization of his material is one of his most striking innovations.

After the publication of the book, Toomer continued to insist on the integrity of the whole, rather than considering it in parts. He was upset when anthologists wanted to select portions of *Cane* to be printed and refused at first to give permission to use a portion of the book separated from the whole. Nevertheless, *Cane* was known primarily by its fragments for many years in an occasional anthology; and it was not until recently that critics, beginning with Bone, began to view *Cane* with a totality that the book deserves. Bone was the first to call the book a novel, which gave *Cane* some stature as more than a collection of writings. Bell[5] and Lieber[6] both synthesize the tripartite structure by showing how Parts 1 and 2 act as antitheses to each other, while Part 3, "Kabnis," acts as a synthesis of both extremes. Reilly and Larson demonstrate how all three sections of the book, as well as the individual stories and poems, are linked together by ways that depart from the traditional. "In their place," says Reilly,

> he has adopted the compressed statement of images linked by their intrinsic associations, and he has represented those imagistic statements becoming synthesized either in the mind of a narrator, in the consciousness and unconsciousness of a character, or in the ambience of locale. Toomer, thus, links his various sketches and lyrics into a poetically structural record of a search for the route to self-expression and consequent redemption for the artist and his race.[7]

Similarly, Larson states that the unity of *Cane* is derived from a "narrative structured by images instead of the traditional unities" and containing a central character, a "narrator-observer who wanders throughout the book."[8]

Larson is correct on both accounts. The images of land, such as the cane, dusk, smoke from the sawmills, pines, the moon, intermingle throughout the stories and poems with images of people, such as their singing, praying, tilling, and reaping. The interlocking of man and nature creates a verbal tone-poem which reveals the mystery and spirituality that Toomer was so fond of describing. Toomer, in fact, establishes the ascendancy of the repeated image in his prefatory poem:

> Oracular.
> Redolent of fermenting syrup,
> Purple in the dusk,
> Deep-rooted cane.

Herein lie the central images of the book: dusk, the moment of mystery, equipoise, and deep (purple) feeling; cane, the profound grip into the earth that nurtures life; fermentation, the creative power that gives life purpose. These images are "oracular" through the medium of the prophet-poet, who reveals the mystery of the spiritual life to those who are in danger of losing it forever.

The setting in Part 1 of *Cane* is dominated by the pervasive atmosphere of the Georgia countryside. It is a setting where the land may still dominate the people, so that when land and person interact, each mirrors the other. To an outsider like Toomer, the land is invested with romantic beauty that belies the actual drudgery of the work-a-day life. The pastoral mode, as John Lynen notes,[9] has usually been the purview of the urban poet, and Toomer is no exception. In order to give the land its appropriate domination of mood, Toomer joins together a repeating flow of images that shape the feeling of the land and the people.

The poem "Reapers" is a fine example of Toomer's careful use of nature and man woven together to form a matrix of life and death, beauty and horror. Involved with the charm of the scene, yet detached enough to record with objectivity, the poem is the first in the book and establishes, along with the sketch "Karintha," the point of view of disengaged sympathy which is characteristic of the first section of the book. There is a Frost-like simplicity of diction contained in this highly structured poem. Toomer presents an informal picture of reapers sharpening scythes:

> Black reapers with the sound of steel on stones
> Are sharpening scythes. I see them place the hones
> In their hip-pockets as a thing that's done,
> And start their silent swinging, one by one.
> Black horses drive a mower through the weeds,
> And there, a field rat, startled, squealing bleeds,
> His belly close to ground. I see the blade,
> Blood-stained, continue cutting weeds and shade. (6)

The spectator-narrator is in the scene as a first-person witness and describes the action in easy iambic rhythm with a vernacular of simple words and casual connections: "as a thing that's done." And yet, because he is not a participant in the scene, he can also note occurrences on which he would not otherwise concentrate were he a reaper himself: "And there, a field rat, startled, squealing bleeds,/His belly close to ground." A partial result of the casual tone is the understatement for ironic effect. The blade, blood-stained, continues cutting indifferently; the momentary horror is covered over once more by the instrument of harvest and death.

The juxtaposition of man and nature is carefully balanced. First, Toomer presents a creature in the landscape, "the black reapers," then the sound made by the creature, "of steel on stones," then the explanation of the sound, "sharpening scythes." Toomer juxtaposes this presentation with that of the rat. There is a dramatic pause between the rat and its bleeding, just as there is a dramatic pause between the reapers and their sharpening. First we know that it is startled, then we hear it squealing, not unlike the whine of steel on stones. Finally the connection is made between the rat and blade, which, almost as an afterthought, is described as "blood-stained." The commentary continues in its easy-going manner, once more focusing on the reaping. The joining of "weeds and shade" is the final ironic view of the scene, for neither is truly the function of a harvest. The value of weeds and shade is to hide the rat; all three have been cut down.

The picture of the folk who work the land is little less startling in "November Cotton Flower." The poem uses Frost's device of connecting a subject in nature with a related general observation about mankind. In this case the premature flowering of a cotton plant in a barren landscape is related to the innocent boldness of premature love in a fallow society. The land is described as a wasteland. The boll-weevil is taking over; the soil has "robbed" the streams of water; dead birds are found "in wells a hundred feet below the ground." Then in the last lines the description of the flower moves into the realm of social commentary:

> . . . Superstition saw
> Something it had never seen before:
> Brown eyes that loved without a trace of fear,
> Beauty so sudden for that time of year. (7)

This sudden beauty may be astonishing, but beauty too suddenly flowered in a clime accustomed to waste has its tragic undertones.

For an explanation of that tragedy we must turn to the opening sketch of the book, "Karintha." The woman-child is as "innocently lovely as a November cotton flower," but "the soul of her was a growing thing ripened too soon." Whatever fresh beauty she might have had is destroyed by the eagerness of men to take her beauty to themselves. A girl so unexpectedly blooming in the bleak landscape of the human spirit would have the same effect as a flower that blooms so unexpectedly in a parched land. Karintha's soul, like the flower, is unnatural in its setting and thus is overprized. Expecting too much of her boldness, which is interpreted as innocence, men unwittingly kill the beauty that is in her and plunge her into a death experience: her baby is "dropped" on pine-needles for a grave. As a youth she taught people "how to live" because of her vitality; now when she is a woman men still expect her to teach them how to live, even while death presides, like the sun going down after the moment of dusk.

Dusk is an integral part of Karintha and is used throughout the rural scenes of Georgia to describe the mystery and depth of experience with which Toomer infuses *Cane*. The opening passage of the book relates Karintha with dusk: "Karintha carrying beauty, perfect as the dusk when the sun goes down." The reference to dusk most obviously describes the color of her skin, but duskiness also relates to the entire dark beauty that instills the experience of the "dusky cane-lipped throngs" (23—"Georgia Dusk"). Dusk contains a blend of secret meanings which a Zen Buddhist would call *shibui*, encompassing a hidden beauty which must be felt intuitively rather than perceived tangibly. In "Karintha" Toomer describes the sunset as a time when "there was no wind, and the pine-smoke from over by the sawmill hugged the earth, and you couldnt see more than a few feet in front" (1–2). Dusk is also the hiatus in people's lives between the activities of day and night, the moment of reflective pause "during the hush just after the sawmill had closed down, and before any of the women had started their supper-getting-ready songs . . ." (2). Out of the concealment of darkness darts Karintha, "a bit of vivid color, like a black bird that flashes in light." Karintha's voice is at this moment the corollary to the image of the black bird: "her voice, high pitched, shrill, would put one's ears to itching."[10] The contrast between the quiet of the day-night and the sheer force of her liveliness establishes her appeal, for Karintha is part of that dusk only as it reveals her fleeting appearance. Toomer states that she *carries* her beauty, as though beauty is an action—and Karintha is indeed more active than the rest of the scene. When one is active, one is elusive and therefore appealing. Without the stasis of dusk, Karintha cannot be known.

If dusk is the medium through which the subtle flux of nature is projected, then song is the human counterpart. The lyrical sketch "Karintha" illustrates the extent to which song shapes the style of much of *Cane*, for the opening piece was originally in the play *Natalie Mann*, to be recited with the accompaniment of drums and guitar. The description of Karintha is a mélange of repeated images, chants, songs, and prayers, the effect of which is a shadowy mood-piece. As in his later writings, Toomer in *Cane* seldom explores the inner reaches of character. Often those whom he describes are used as emblems for the greater meaning that Toomer has in mind. Karintha is such a person. We know little or nothing of her personality. Her motives and emotions remain as indistinct as the dusk which surrounds her. She becomes the embodiment of the tone-poem, the lyric which despairs over misused beauty. Making a song of Karintha does strange things to her, for the narrator, no less than the men who are described by the narrator, distances himself from the beauty he urgently wishes to have shared. The mystery of Karintha is indecipherable even to Toomer, who as the outsider in most interpersonal relationships, was best at describing tenuous rather than intimate relationships. Seen at dusk and interpreted through the dusk, Karintha, like Fern and Avey in other stories, remains self-contained and unfathomable to the most ardent of the illusionists, Toomer himself.

With this sense of mystery Toomer uses dusk as the image through which to express his song and the songs of others. Karintha is lyricized for her skin like dusk: the "Face" contains muscles which "are cluster grapes of sorrow purple in the evening sun" (14); Carma feigns shooting herself in the early night while someone sings a song about the wind in the cane. The poem "Georgia Dusk" praises a black and unknown bard "surprised in making folk-songs from soul sounds" (22). Fern and Louisa bewail their condition by singing at dusk.

The song element designs the sound of the prose with as much effectiveness as the poems, if not more so. "Karintha" illustrates the poetic cadences of Toomer's prose-writing in such passages as the contrast between the quietude of dusk and the energy of Karintha:

> At dusk, during the hush just after the sawmill had closed down, and before any of the women had started their supper-getting-ready songs, her voice, high-pitched, shrill, would put one's ears to itching. (2)

The opening is slow and peaceful, dominated by the low-pitched *u* sound in "dusk," "during," "hush," "just," and the voiced *d* sounds. These are combined with the relatively slow pace of the word combinations, such as "dusk, during," "hush just," and "closed down." The second part of the sentence, anticipating Karintha's entry, increases in speed and evenness of tempo, the women stirring themselves into action with "supper-getting-ready songs." Then, midst this even and ordered music, is interposed Karintha's voice, described as "high-pitched," "shrill," and "itching." The short *i* becomes a higher-pitched imposition on the middle-range *e* sound of "supper-getting-ready songs" and the deeper *u* sounds of the opening, and the *itch* sound drowns out the softer "sh" of "hush."

While the poetic quality of Toomer's prose is in many respects bolder and more successful than much of his poetry, the poems nevertheless are an essential part of his "song." As in his prose, many of his poems are dusk songs, reflecting not only the mood of the land but also the sense of the people. "Nullo" is a poem which shows the deep connection between the earth and sky at a time of day when limits are hard to define and therefore blend with the limitless:

> A spray of pine-needles,
> Dipped in western horizon gold,
> Fell onto a path.
> Dry moulds of cow-hoofs.
> In the forest.
> Rabbits knew not of their falling,
> Nor did the forest catch aflame.
>
> (34)

The poem places before the reader the merest glimpse of a moment when a spectacle occurs without notice but for the poet: the sun setting fire to the edges of a spray of pine-needles as it falls to the ground. The visual impression is precise; not only are we shown the path but the shapes in the path, "Dry moulds of cow-hoofs." The silence of such an eventful non-event protects it from all but the poet's eye: "Rabbits knew not of their falling,/Nor did the forest catch aflame." The pine spray catches the fire yet does not spread it beyond the spray's own beauty. The cows have parted till the next day, and the rabbits are unconscious of the passing. Such is the attraction of sunset, when the poet's eye can make the seemingly insignificant moment into a significant statement.

As in the sadness of Karintha's waste, Toomer's dusk poems often are commentaries on the sadness of a dying culture. "Song of the Son" has correctly been singled out as embodying the central idea of Toomer's southern experience.[11] In the poem dusk is connected most clearly with Toomer's thesis of the "swan-song" of the black folk heritage. The poem's message is that the narrator, ostensibly Toomer, has returned to his southern roots in time to record the rural life in art which will outlast the black man. A letter to Waldo Frank clarifies the point of view with which Toomer wrote the poem:

> There is one thing about the Negro in America which most thoughtful persons seem to ignore: the Negro is in solution, in the process of solution. As an entity, the race is loosing [*sic*] its body, and its soul is approaching a common soul. If one holds his eyes to individuals and sections, race is starkly evident, and racial continuity seems assured. One is even led to believe that the thing we call Negro beauty will always be attributable to a clearly defined physical source. But the fact is, that if anything comes up now, pure Negro, it will be a swan-song. The negro [*sic*] of the folk-song has all but passed away: the Negro of the emotional church is fading. A hundred years from now these Negroes, if they exist at all will live in art. . . . The supreme fact of mechanical civilization is that you become part of it, or get sloughed off (under). Negroes have no culture to resist it with (and if they had, their position would be identical to that of the Indians), hence industrialism the more readily transforms them. A few generations from now, the Negro will still be dark, and a portion of his psychology will spring from this fact, but in all else he will be a conformist to the general outlines of American civilization, or of American chaos. In my own stuff, in those pieces that come nearest to the old Negro, to the spirit saturated with folk-song: Karintha and Fern, the dominant emotion is a sadness derived from a sense of fading, from a knowledge of my futility to check solution. There is nothing about these pieces of the bouyant [*sic*] expression of a new race. The folk-songs themselves are of the same order. The deepest of them: "I ain't got long to stay here."[12]

If the expression of folk-roots is to be recorded in art, what better way to record it than by creating a pattern of song to drift from story to story, poem to poem, usually at dusk when toil and need are reflected upon with a soul-response? If the culture is dying, what better moment to frame that death than the moment of day which heightens life by the very imminence of darkness and, symbolically, death?

"Song of the Son" is just that: a song, too formal for blues but nevertheless a song of lamentation and hope, held together by the image of the setting sun. Though equating "son" with "sun" may be far-fetched,[13] there is a clear analogy between a departing sun and a departing race. The first stanza establishes the relationship of the race-soul with the sun:

> Pour O pour that parting soul in song,
> O pour it in the sawdust glow of night,
> Into the velvet pine-smoke air to-night,
> And let the valley carry it along.
> And let the valley carry it along. (21)

The "parting soul" pours out song like a setting sun pours out dark light into the "sawdust glow of night," the smoke and mist becoming the medium through which the slanted rays light the land in sunset colors. The smoke of the sawmill is man's labor; the mist is nature's. The combined forces couple man and earth at a moment when rest can come and songs can fuse the two forces into a glowing beauty. The traits of song, like the rays of light, are carried through the valley by the "velvet" smoke and mist, the muted reminder of the day's labor and of the dark, rich meaning that comes to life through song.

In the second stanza Toomer states: "Now just before an epoch's sun declines/Thy son, in time, I have returned to thee" (21). The message implies the coming of an anointed messiah, and in the third stanza he wears the mask of poet-prophet, the one who can save the "song-lit race of slaves" from oblivion by recording their culture in art, "to catch thy plaintive soul soon gone." In the final two stanzas Toomer uses the symbol of a tree to express the black experience, which has grown to a cultural fullness but is now being killed by absorption and neglect:

> O Negro slaves, dark purple ripened plums,
> Squeezed, and bursting in the pine-wood air,
> Passing, before they stripped the old tree bare
> One plum was saved for me, one seed becomes
>
> An everlasting song, a singing tree,
> Caroling softly souls of slavery,

What they were, and what they are to me,
Caroling softly souls of slavery.
(21)

The slave offspring, "purple ripened plums," have held on to their fertile heritage. Now, however, "they stripped the old tree bare," the inability of the Negro culture to stay alive being as inevitable as the setting of the sun. However, "one plum was saved for me"; that is, Toomer was able, at the last moment, to rediscover his roots and become the "seed," holding in time an "everlasting song" of the souls of black people. Thus, art for Toomer has purpose beyond the recording of experience: it is important that Toomer's song, like the urn, freeze experience into a timeless moment. While the urn stops the action in anticipation of fulfillment, Toomer's song stops the action just short of death; for the savior's task is to keep the sun permanently from setting.

In many ways Toomer's poems are more traditional in conception than are the poetic aspects of his prose. Poems like "Song of the Son" and "Georgia Dusk" are standard fare in terms of stanza, rhyme, line length, and imagery. "Evening Song," another of Toomer's dusk poems, is an uneven compromise between boldness and timid tradition. As in his other dusk poems and stories, Toomer tries to interchange images of nature with emotions of humans. Similar also to other pieces, "Evening Song" is about an attractive woman whom the narrator observes from a distance but never seems to touch closely.

Full moon rising on the waters of my heart,
Lakes and moon and fires,
Cloine tires,
Holding her lips apart.

Promises of slumber leaving shore to charm the moon,
Miracle made vesper-keeps,
Cloine sleeps,
And I'll be sleeping soon.

Cloine, curled like the sleepy waters where the moon-
waves start,
Radiant, resplendently she gleams,
Cloine dreams,
Lips pressed against my heart.
(35)

Each of the three stanzas has a standard rhyme scheme of *abba*. Nevertheless, the variation of line length in each stanza strengthens the simple declaration in the third line: "Cloine tires," "Cloine sleeps," and "Cloine dreams." The stanza winds down, as it were, from a long statement filled with imagery to a shorter commentary on the next line, to the declaration, and finally to the slightly longer line. There is, however, a fuzziness of imagery and a carelessness of word choice which mar the poem. Toomer is trying to establish the flow of emotion that is constantly moving from narrator to the self-contained Cloine. Cloine is the "Full moon rising on my heart," both of which join together with a detached passion: "Lakes and moon and fires." The first line of the second stanza, "Promises of slumber leaving shore to charm the moon," is weak. Apparently Toomer has in mind that not only does Cloine radiate attraction but the attraction is reciprocated. However, aside from the awkward sibilants and vowel combinations, little justification merits the "vesper-keeps" to charm the moon. The shore, not the water, charms the moon, thereby diluting the image of moon and water. Toomer uses his images too loosely in the third stanza as well. The line, "Cloine, curled like the sleepy waters where the moon-waves start," does once again connect the union between Cloine *née* moon and the narrator *né* water, but the subsequent line, "Radiant, resplendently she gleams," dissipates any concreteness of imagery that Toomer has achieved. All three major words in that line have similar meaning; thus the line is empty of refreshing imagery. While "lips pressed against my heart" effectively ties the first stanza with the last, the poem as a whole can best be described as a weak effort by a young poet.

At his best, though, Toomer links recurrent images together so that both are mutually reinforced, as he does with dusk and song. Another image closely connected with dusk which recurs throughout his Georgia sketches is the color of purple, which combines the dominant color of the evening half-light with the deepness of skin pigment and the profundity of the peasant's experience. The slave heritage is reflected in the "purple ripened plums," as we have seen, and the ongoing suffering of that heritage carves in a woman's face an image of "cluster grapes of sorrow/purple in the evening sun . . ." (14—"Face"). When Tom meets Louisa in "Blood-Burning Moon," the suffering which both are about to endure is hidden from view, even though there are premonitions in the air. While the moon moves "upward into the deep purple of the cloud-bank," an old woman starts singing the death-song in the dusk: "Blood-burning moon. Sinner!" (58)

In still another story, "Fern," the narrator is courting Fern, one of Toomer's poetic untouchables. The time for yet one more relationship filled with frustration and unexplained agony is, as expected, dusk:

> Through a canebreak that was ripe for cutting, the branch was reached. Under a sweet-gum tree, and where reddish leaves had dammed the creek a little, we sat down. Dusk, suggesting the almost imperceptible procession of giant trees, settled with a purple haze about the cane. I felt strange, as I always do in Georgia, particularly at dusk. I felt that things unseen to men were tangibly immediate. It would not have surprised me had I had vision. People have them in Georgia more often than you would suppose. A black woman once saw the mother of Christ and drew her in charcoal on the courthouse wall. . . . When one is on the soil of one's ancestors, most anything can come to one. . . . (31)

The sensuous intensity of imagery in a passage such as this shows Toomer at his most effective. The smell and taste of cane, which fill many scenes, the muted colors of red and purple, and the shadowy encroachment of dusk create an emotional pitch beyond conscious control. The sensate experience telescopes the past into the present and spins perception beyond ordinary limits, and in so doing becomes the catalyst for the spiritual emanation of songs, prayers, and visions. Fern, much to the distress of the narrator, has a religious vision of sorts a while later; one is tempted to believe that only under the conditions of dusk, purple, cane, and mist can the Georgia "soul" express itself.[14]

Another important element of the soul's response to the land is the religious expression, whether in song, sermon, prayer, or vision. The image of the Christ in a characteristically folk interpretation is part of the design of *Cane*. Toomer uses both "Christ" and "Jesus" in ways that depart from traditional church use. He does not, however, take the extremes in his treatment of the Christian religion which Fullinwider suggests in arguing that the poems and stories are anti-Christian, turning away from the "slave religion" to a more African-based religious experience.[15] Toomer makes clear in his autobiography that he is against organized religion, which includes the formal Christian churches, but he expresses the validity of the spontaneous religious experience that is identifiable with the soil. The worship of growth, harvest, continuity, and the hope of personal salvation are the extensions of the intuitive trust in the seasons' repetition. For those working the land, Jesus is an expression of that hope, for in Jesus lies the mythic embodiment of toil, suffering, death, deliverance, and forgiveness. Some critics, while tending to over-interpret certain religious connections, are not altogether wrong in making close analogies between the rural experience and the religious experience. Bernard Bell, for instance, interprets the poem "Face" as a "traditional typology of the suffering and sacrifice of Christ,"[16] while Mabel Dillard claims that "Face" reveals the suffering of the Virgin Mary.[17] "Face" is indeed a description of one who has suffered a life of pain and privation, and in that respect it is a face reflective of the archetypal Christian suffering. Relating the face too closely to that of a specific religious figure deprives it, however, of associations with the rural peasant and his personal struggle with the land and social forces, both of which try to dominate him. "Face" is, above all else, a description of an aged peasant whose life has been worn away:

> Hair—
> silver-gray,
> like streams of stars,
> Brows—
> recurved canoes
> quivered by the ripples blown by pain,
> Her eyes—
> mist of tears
> condensing on the flesh below
> And her channeled muscles
> are cluster grapes of sorrow
> purple in the evening sun
> nearly ripe for worms.
>
> (14)

As in traditional descriptions of women derived from the courtly love poems, Toomer itemizes various physical attributes and attaches an image to each one, usually with religious undertones. Toomer plays with the tradition in ironic ways, though with a beauty perhaps far more profound than that usually found in poems of the courtly tradition. The beauty of the woman is not derived from her static association with ideal and therefore spiritually "superior" attributes. Instead, her beauty is an inward growth of one who has loved and suffered for it, a beauty not of innocence, but of the deepest experience like that expressed in the *Pietà* or the *Caritas Romana.* Toomer also limits his description to a face rather than to the whole body, since a face expresses the inner life, while the rest of the body, especially in courtly poetry, complements the externalized ideal vision.

Toomer designs the impression of the woman by starting with her hair and continuing downward, a movement which expresses the burden of life which the woman has endured. The images therefore become heavier, beginning with the stars and ending with cluster grapes. The sense of flow, as in "Fern," from one part to the next is sustained by the water imagery. Her hair is like *streams* of stars, the downward flow already beginning and continuing with her eyebrows, which are likened to canoes "recurved," that is, the tips pointing downward rather than upward, the "ripples" of her forehead "blown by pain" ironically pushing the boat the wrong way like an upside-down picture. The eyes perpetuate the downward water-flow by "condensing" their "mist" onto the "flesh below." The "channels" in her sunken muscles, which in old people gather toward the jowls and under the chin, guide the tears and nourish the fruits of a lifetime, "grapes of sorrow." Her impending death is emblematic of the death of the entire peasant culture, which, as we have seen, is also "purple in the evening sun" and "nearly ripe for worms." In her death, as in the death of the entire culture, lies the embodiment of a folk religion, a calling upon the God of the Earth, so to speak, to deliver the peasant from his hardships of pain and sorrow.

This spontaneous, joyful-sorrowful supplication drives King Barlo to form visions of an African Jesus, inspires a woman to draw a black madonna on a wall, and sends Esther through a sexual-religious ordeal. But of all the characters in Toomer's book perhaps Becky comes closest to the religious experience by virtue of her role in society. Becky is a white woman whom the town rejects yet cares for, since she rests on their consciences for having mated with a black man. An isolate, spurned by the organized church to which she claims she belongs ("Poor Catholic poor-white crazy woman" [8]), she lives in a kind of concentration camp where society has placed her in order to put her out of their lives and therefore out of their minds. Yet guilt has created a concentration camp of their collective conscience, and all think about her willy-nilly. They "prayed secretly to God who'd put His cross upon her and cast her out" (8) and threw out of the train windows onto her property little pellets of paper inscribed with prayers. Thus, Becky's quite natural sexual experience has grown into a religious experience because she has been rejected. True to the rationalizations by which people justify their guilt-producing acts, those who have cast her out transfer the blame of rejection to God and pay homage to Becky as penance.

The natural act and the religious act coincide in other characters. Karintha, in a different way from Becky, engages in spontaneous sexuality which by its creative implications is religious. Her parents' loving she had perhaps "felt"; thus, ironically for Karintha, "one could but imitate one's parents, for to follow them was the way of God" (2–3). But the way of God is filled with pain and sorrow, as Karintha discovers, even though people still sing of her beauty. The songs nevertheless sustain a religious feeling that is a holy, albeit transient, transformation. That is why, in "Georgia Dusk," the singers not only can bring the miracle of "virgin lips to cornfield concubines" but also can "bring dreams of Christ to dusky cane-lipped throngs" (23). The laborer of the earth can be sanctified with a religious purity by the holiness of soul-song.

King Barlo, the preacher in "Esther," links the African pagan with the white Christian heritage. As in many mythical tales, Barlo's religious enlightenment is akin to sexual awakening. His vision is powerful because his physical attributes are powerful: he is the best cotton-picker, knifer, fighter, gambler, and lover in the area. To be invested with such physical strength gives one the spiritual command needed to be effective. His deep blackness, too, projects a power that a whiter complexion would not fulfill, for as he preaches he changes into the "outlines of his visioned African," the "big an black an powerful" man who, filled with the Lord, was captured by "white-ant biddies" (38). Barlo's incantation is pure folk preaching, capturing the rhythm and phrase rhyming of spontaneous oratory:

> "They led him t th coast, they led him t th sea, they led him across th ocean an they didnt set him free. The old coast didnt miss him, an th new coast wasnt free, he left the old-coast brothers t give birth t you an me. O Lord, great God, Almighty, t give birth t you and me." (38–39)

The chant is a powerfully designed rhythmic statement, which when broken into lines after each word that rhymes with "sea," creates four lines of iambic heptameters (including the spondaic first line) with a one-line refrain. The incremental repetition, slowly building the development of the black man's abduction to America and the eventual release from bondage by God, resembles the most typical of oral tales.

Barlo's preaching produces in his audience tears, "fragments of melodies," a hushed expectation. In the now-familiar Toomerian dusk Barlo implores his listeners to open themselves to the "dawnin of the mornin light," and Barlo effects his own salvation by inducing miraculous happenings. "Years after"—the required time for myth-making—"Esther was told that at that very moment a great, heavy rumbling voice actually was heard. That hosts of angels and of demons paraded up and down the streets all night. That King Barlo rode out of town astride a pitch-black bull that had a glowing gold ring in its nose" (39–40). Small wonder that Esther fantasizes Barlo to be her God-like Deliverer! Barlo is the soil, the earth, the sexual urgency of physical procreation which is the mythic basis of religion. That Barlo is crass and lustful is not a matter of concern. As the "primitive" progenitor of faith, Barlo, like God, is King.

Esther, however, is too detached from the soil, which provides physical and spiritual growth. Like Kabnis, Esther finds union with the earth too repugnant; the reality of making love to Barlo other than in her mind makes her sick. This reaction is not Barlo's fault. Barlo's appeal has been the very blackness of his skin representing the sexuality which she, bland in spirit as well as in skin, can only daydream about. A god has sexual attributes; Esther dreams of having a child by him, glorifying it in defiance of the townspeople's mockeries. As she is accused at the end, Esther is indeed "dictie," attempting in artificial ways to attain refinement and higher sensibilities even while engaged in sexual dreams. She "decides" that she loves Barlo, as though love is a rational decision weighed by the intellect. Her resolution is kept as a prim secret, a "wedding cake for her to tuck beneath her pillow and go to sleep upon" (43). Hope is a pale sort of consummation, but it assuredly is all that Esther can handle.

Esther's physical passion has as its image the flame of desire, related to the setting sun, which "swings low" like the death-chariot. The fire is but a reflection in McGregor's store windows, but the mirror image is enough for her. When Esther is sixteen the flame sets in her dream an imaginary fire from which she saves her and Barlo's baby. Fearing that she is sinning, she "puts away" the dream, only to have it break out into new sexual fantasies in which the baby, "ugly as sin," latches itself to her willing breast. Eleven years later Barlo in the flesh appears before her, at the time of day when again the setting sun leaves a "pale flame" of reflection in McGregor's windows. Esther is reborn momentarily—"suddenly is animate"—and against her rational wish, desires to be "sharp" and "sporty" so that she can "possess" Barlo. The thought of sin disengaged from actuality appeals to Esther, but when she tests her desires on reality the dream on which she wasted her youth dissolves. The "dull flame" of McGregor's windows follows her a third time, to the whorehouse where Barlo is spending the evening. There reality is palpable: crude voices, heavy smoke, smell of liquor. Unable to reconcile the intensity of sensate experience with her delicate sensitivity of the mind, Esther becomes "violently dizzy," and "blackness rushes to her eyes." The blackness is Barlo, the physical and spiritual force that his own color represents. Her sensibilities are shocked; the exotic at close range becomes repugnant. The black savior turns into the devil himself, for Esther cannot accept the blackness that at first made him so appealing. Her one dream shattered, she stumbles into the street as one dead: "There is no air, no street and the town has completely disappeared" (48). Esther, having always been spiritually deadened, requires a confrontation with the living god of fecundity to realize her emptiness. There is not even a pale flame any more, for there is no air or town to feed it.

King Barlo is not just the apotheosis of an African god, nor does he necessarily represent a contrast between pagan and Christian religious thought. In a sense Barlo is a pagan Christian, fusing his spontaneous folk outbursts with a Christian view of God as deliverer. He is godly in a classical Greek sense: less holy than grandiosely human, and therefore worthy of admiration if not reverence. In a similar way the poem "Conversion" casts an image of the fusion of African zest with Christian ideology. Like King Barlo, the "African Guardian of Souls" has moved into a new culture which, though debasing him, has not deprived him of his liveliness and joy. Each line increases the African's assimilation into the white culture:

> Drunk with rum,
> Feasting on a strange cassava,
> Yielding to new words and a weak palabra
> Of a white-faced sardonic God—
>
> (49)

It is not a complimentary picture of the noble guardian, having changed his drinking, eating, and—most fundamental of all—speaking habits[18] in the face of a new religion that derides him. Though the

African "yields," he has adjusted to a seemingly weaker cultural force. "Strange cassava" is not cassava at all, and thus by implication a poor substitute, while the voices of God are weak in comparison to those of his African heritage. Yet the African converts not with slavish passivity but with a zeal that enlivens an old religion with new vitality. He is "drunk," and he "feasts," neither act connoting a dull communion. The unpremeditated thrill of religious celebration is still part of the African past. The new religion is powerful because it belongs to those in power, but paradoxically the conquered Guardian has increased the power of the Christian religion because his conversion has forced Christianity to be converted, in style at least, to the African Guardian.

The mixture of the two cultures into an African-American blend brings us once again to the metaphor of dusk, for that time not only is expressive of the southern landscape and of the imminent absorption of African culture into American culture but also is, as Philip Royster notes, the symbol of the mulatto trapped between two worlds, like dusk between day and night.[19] Toomer never forgets the white element in his characters. In a letter written in 1923 to Sherwood Anderson, Toomer states that his seed was planted both in the cane and cotton fields and "in the souls of the *black and white* people in the small Southern town" (italics added). Toomer's portrayals in Part 1 range in hue from the deep-black Barlo to the purely white Becky. Most are somewhere in the dusk between, the mulatto acting out Toomer's struggle to accommodate both worlds.

Aside from Bob Stone in "Blood-Burning Moon," Becky in the sketch "Becky" is the only white person developed in Part 1. Nevertheless, Becky has intertwined her fate with the black man and suffers persecution from both races. Having had a son with Negro blood, Becky, a white woman, has breached the strongest of southern taboos. Males of both races participate in the mystique of the inviolable white "lady," even when the "lady" is of questionable rank or beauty. Becky, in fact, is not a particularly beautiful woman: "Her eyes were sunken, her neck stringy, her breasts fallen . . ." (8). Nevertheless, any white woman who breaks the taboo of miscegenation inspires an occult fascination containing part hate, part jealousy, and part admiration. The "damn buck nigger" who was the father might have been lynched had Becky told who he was. Becky's defiance of the pressures of the town, however, makes her rise above the normal scorn heaped upon such a woman. She carries the secret of the union of the races which for some reason renders blacks and whites incapable of doing anything but helping her, much as they are horrified by her violation of southern mores. Becky ironically unifies the races because she dared break the taboo. Instead of turning on her, the "white folks and black folks built her a cabin, fed her and her growing baby . . ." (8). The house, built between a road and railroad tracks, is the stationary reminder to those who are life's travelers of their innermost urges and deepest levels of conscience. Banned from society, she nevertheless remains true to herself while the rest of the town participates in a troubled exile which they had intended for Becky.

From the same twist of human behavior, the object of scorn is more like an object of praise. By their prayers, which are actually a mark of their guilt, the townspeople revere her, in recognition of the awesomeness of the secret sin which they all share. The pines constantly whispering to Jesus make the house and ground on which it stands seem hallowed. Passersby throw pellets of paper inscribed with prayers at the cabin, like pilgrims who attach written prayers to trees surrounding Buddhist temples. Becky's emanation of sacredness is derived at least in part from her never having been seen outside the cabin for several years. One knows that the goddess of racial union is still fertile only when another baby appears in the arms of the older brother.

The two children are the archetypal mulattoes: rootless, defensive, sullen loners, born of both races yet accepted by neither.

> White or colored? No one knew, and least of all themselves. . . . We, who had cast out their mother because of them, could we take them in? They answered black and white folks by shooting up two men and leaving town. "Godam the white folks; godam the niggers," they shouted as they left town. (11)

The children are the new Americans in the old value system of black and white, destined to suffer and to be hostile toward two societies that made them outcasts.

So Becky continues to be the town's "untouchable" even after the day when the shack crumbles on top of her. The collapse of the chimney onto Becky carries with it the weight of an entire town's guilt. Becky is heard to groan beneath the rubble, but so awesome is the fear which she engenders, that Barlo (one assumes, perhaps wrongly, that it is King Barlo) can only throw his Bible onto her grave and flee. Further, "no one has ever touched" the Bible, as though the site were too sacred to approach. In effect, Becky has functioned in the capacity of scapegoat for the town. The townspeople have driven her away as the receptacle of their sins—actually the receptacle of *the* southern sin—and, true to mankind's irrational behavior, they worship what they abhor.

Just as Becky's whiteness flows into the black world, so also in the short story "Fern" do Fern's contrasting qualities blend into each other. Toomer felt that racial mingling is a "flowing" of one part into another, making "white" or "black" characteristics an impossibility.[20] Fern represents that type of fluidity, for it is hard to categorize her. Her languid beauty arises from the "creamy brown" of her skin, an ambiguous racial color. Her whiteness combines with her blackness so that she has equal appeal to both races; the narrator wonders if the viewer who passes her on a train—either in the Pullman or the Jim Crow—will stop at the next town and return. Fern is a blend of other things as well. Though she makes an appeal to Christ and the Virgin Mary, she sings like a Jewish cantor, her nose is Semitic, and her last name is Rosen. As if to complicate her even more, she "became a virgin," a reversal of the natural sequence of experience. Finally, there is Fern's marvelous passivity, which lures men looking for the mystery they assume lies embedded in indifference.

The key to Fern's appeal is the blend, for the dominant metaphor is that of flowing. The description of Fern begins with, "Face flowed into her eyes" (24), revealing little beyond the soft, hidden lines of her features. The "creamy foam" of her skin is liquid like the "plaintive ripples" of her face. The "soft suggestion of down" reinforces her indefinite features, which form the basis of her attraction. One's eyes, the narrator states, must inevitably flow back into her eyes, the "common delta" toward which the curves of her body run "like mobile rivers."

The eyes are so appealing because of a paradox: while they search for nothing, they deny nothing. Such exotic indifference drives men wild. To deny nothing implies a need for something, yet Fern appears to have no needs; she is self-contained, and therefore impenetrable. If the male urge is to violate sexually, self-containment is the essence of virginity, since the male cannot penetrate to the spiritual core of the woman. Man relies on woman's need; hence men's awe of Fern, who takes the gift of their bodies without desire.

The contrasts that grip Fern hardest are sexuality and religiousness. These qualities, as we know from King Barlo, are forces springing from the same source, opposite though they may seem. The narrator, a northerner trying to fathom the tremendous attraction which Fern has for him, has taken her to a remote part of the stream beyond the canebreak. It is dusk, the time for visions. A vision is the flux between things seen and unseen, and it is through the medium of the eyes that a vision occurs. Toomer has already verified the power of Fern's eyes, like a sucubus drawing the whole countryside into her with "the soft listless cadence of Georgia's South" (27). There, by the stream, the narrator's expectation of a vision is transmitted into Fern. Her eyes hold the seen vision of the narrator, who is at that moment a sexual attraction, and they also hold the unseen vision of God. Suddenly repulsed by the narrator, she rushes away and falls to her knees in a trance. The "torture" she undergoes is the tension between the sexual rage of "boiling sap" in her body seeking an outlet and the desire for salvation through Jesus Christ. The union of sexuality and chastity is like the miracle of immaculate conception, and indeed "God flowed into her" at the moment of orgasmic joy and pain. Innocence and experience coupling in her body force her voice to express both: "A child's voice, uncertain, or an old man's" (32).

Ultimately, the problem with Fern, as it is with many of Toomer's women, is that everything flows into her but nothing flows back out. Toomer's women who have most appeal have little urge to reciprocate, and Toomer's men become victims of the unreturned gift. Fern's body "was tortured with something it would not let out" (32); therefore, even though God, the landscape, and seemingly every man who passed her way flowed into her, "nothing ever really happened. Nothing ever came to Fern, not even I." The one who inspires so much worship is the goddess of impotence. Men will constantly worship what they fail to understand, and they will bear the sacred symbol of fertility to whoever offers the challenge of barrenness.

While individuals like Carma, who drives her husband momentarily insane, Karintha, and Fern can be grouped together as exotic and somewhat pitiable *femmes fatales*, the most terrifying goddess of all is the southern white woman who attracts the black man, for in her inviolability lies the seed of horrendous destructiveness: In "Georgia Portrait" Toomer describes the white woman with bitter irony:

Hair—braided chestnut,
  coiled like a lyncher's rope,
Eyes—fagots,
Lips—old scars, or the first red blisters,

Breath—the last sweet scent of cane,
And her slim body, white as the ash
  of black flesh after flame.
(50)

In each line the opening refers to the object of physical desire: hair, eyes, lips, breath, slim body. Yet each portion of the body generates an image of a lynching scene. The effect is one of uniting passionate desire with ugly violence. Each physical attraction brings the black man closer to the consummation of death instead of love. The braid of hair is really the lyncher's rope; the eyes kindle not only his passion but the fagots to set him on fire. Her lips turn into his lesions, the "old scars" of fears and the "red blisters" of his burning flesh. The agitated breath of passion is his last breath, for to touch her flesh is to burn his. The connection of white and black, implied throughout the poem, is finally yoked in the last line, for the whiteness of her appealing flesh is the same color as his black flesh once it has been burned. The message is clear in all its grim aspects: white woman, symbol of life and beauty, is equally the symbol of violence and death. "Georgia Portrait" presents a picture of sexual and racial frustration, like Toomer's other portraits of women who ultimately impose destruction upon those who love them.

"Blood-Burning Moon," the final piece in Part 1, is the story that typifies most dramatically the conflict and the union of black and white. A black and a white male, inseparable enemies, destroy each other over a woman who wants them both. Louisa, the focus of both men's love, stands as yet one more woman in Toomer's tales whose passivity, indecision, and self-directed concerns wreak destruction. The fulcrum of a seesaw courtship, she equally desires, and is equally desired by, her black and her white lover. The white Bob Stone and the black Tom Burwell are but reflections of each other; their significance is their togetherness. Louisa feels their complementary pull as she is returning home from work: Tom's "black balanced, and pulled against, the white of Stone, when she thought of them" (52). Her "strange stir," the foreboding of evil to come, is caused by both: "she tried to fix upon Bob or Tom as the cause of it" (52). Trying to separate Bob's courting her in the canebrake from Tom's marriage proposal makes each lover that much more important: together they shrouded her confidence like the clouds about to cover the moon and sent her to sing and the dogs to howl.

The dogs and chickens, like other beasts of intuition, anticipate imminent danger and form a constant link among the fates of Bob, Tom, and Louisa. The animals hoot and cackle as they pick up the significance of Louisa's worrying "tremor." When Tom Burwell becomes filled with rage because his friends laugh about Bob and Louisa's liaison, the dogs again start barking, and the roosters crow. Bob, himself burning with jealousy, stumbles over a dog, sending yelps, cackles, and crows reverberating across the countryside. When the threesome are about to converge, however, all noise has stopped, as though the animals are waiting for the final battle.

The link between Bob and Tom is not only through Louisa's thoughts and the animals' alarm. Tom and Bob are mirrors of each other even in their actions. Much as their background and social expectations differ, they are bound together because they love the same woman. Bob Stone claims racial superiority, yet he is an emotional mixture which reflects the white and the black of the southern society: "The clear white of his skin paled, and the flush of his cheeks turned purple" (59). Toomer's color-image of the black peasant's experience, I have noted, is dusk, and fruit-purple. Bob Stone pales and purples simultaneously; the whiter he gets the darker he gets. Having arrived at his meeting place but not finding Louisa, Bob is enraged that Tom "had her." Bob bites his lips so hard that he tastes blood: "not his own blood; Tom Burwell's blood" (62). Bob is too overwhelmed with jealousy to think about the incongruity of tasting his enemy's blood in his own veins. Rage has formed a union closer than brotherhood; Bob *is* Tom through the bond of hate.

Though both love Louisa, neither accepts the truth that she has an alternate lover. Both Tom and Bob hear the news from the same source, the men boiling cane at the canebreak. Both flee from the men uncontrollably angry, refusing to believe the truth about her disloyalty and immediately attempting to seek her out. Tom tells Louisa, "I dont believe what some folks been whisperin. . . . Bob Stone likes y. Course he does. But not th way folks is awhisperin" (57). Tacitly he knows differently, for Louisa must get her frilly gifts from some lover's source. Bob, too, has been plagued with hints of her unfaithfulness, for "Cartwell had told him that Tom went with Louisa after she reached home." Protesting too much he immediately thinks, "No Sir. No nigger had never been with his girl. He'd like to see one try" (60). In a similar way Tom has overreacted to Louisa's innocent claim that she has no connection with Bob: "Course y dont. Ise already cut two niggers. Had t hon, t tell em so" (57). Jealousy, then, has reduced both men to the same human condition, irrespective of race or caste. Bob is ready to defend his woman in the same way that the antebellum white gentry would defend the purity of a belle. Likewise, Tom Burwell is ready to kill his "master's" son "jes like I cut a nigger" (57). Charged to action by irrational forces, they can no longer delay the inevitable clash, hard as Louisa may try to put it off. Tom's shyness and Bob's secretiveness vanish in preparation for aggressive claims of ownership. The fight is unavoidable, for both have as their "game" the ability to fight with their knives. And, just as inevitably, the killing of one equates the killing of the other. It is not surprising that Bob Stone's last words are "Tom Burwell," or that the last view of Tom is one with "stony" eyes and a head like a "blackened stone."

Except for the stilted, utterly unbelievable speech that Tom Burwell delivers to Louisa, and for the implausible fragment of folk song which is chanted twice to foreshadow the final scene, "Blood-Burning Moon" is among the more effectively constructed short stories in the collection. In Louisa he fuses with dramatic intensity the love and hate, beauty and ugliness that live side by side in the twilight zone of the interracial South. "Blood-Burning Moon" embodies the very elements that so attracted, and so repelled, Jean Toomer in his sojourn to find lasting roots in the soil of the South.

There is no doubt that Toomer saw his work, if not in terms of a novel, at least in terms of a unified entity which in many ways is undefinable according to traditional book-length works. However, the recurrent imagery, such as that found in the first section of the book, helps to unify the tale wherein Jean Toomer seeks a reprieve from the seemingly soulless human state by retreating to nature for an identity that she often cannot provide.

Jean Toomer's *Cane*: A Modern Black Oracle

BOWIE DUNCAN

In his introduction to Jean Toomer's *Cane*, Arna Bontemps says, "It does not take long to discover that *Cane* is not without design, however,"[1] noting that the book is divided into three parts. However, the many characters, the variety of literary forms, and the myriad perspectives of reality seem to leave the book with little traditional design, and Bontemps refrains from being too specific about the design he perceives. The book resembles Fred Halsey's ancestor's picture in "Kabnis," for like her, the book "seems to shift before one's gaze—now ugly, repulsive; now sad, and somehow beautiful in its pain" (168). The unique ambiguity that is the design and the experience of the book is reflected as well in the poem on the title page:

> Oracular.
> Redolent of fermenting syrup,
> Purple of the dusk,
> Deep-rooted cane.

The oracle speaks analogically of a relative and multifaceted reality which can be perceived through reflexive thought which arranges in retrospect the contradictory images and planes of such a seemingly disassociated reality. *Cane* can be called, among other things, an elaborate jazz composition, for Toomer seems to compose by laying down a theme and doing variations on it, without defining a rigid progression. The result is a composition that is continuously in process, and the reader must continuously seek out the relations of the variations or planes of the piece during and after experiencing it. It almost has to be read over for the second time to be understood for the first time. It is a very modern concept of reality that informs the design of the oracle's message.

In *Cane* there is a definite break with traditional linear thought about composition which perceived of literature as pertaining to a time sequence composed of the past, present, and future, each entity separate and unique, strung together on the narrative line. Toomer employs a perspective of reality similar to that found in modern sciences where, as Sigfried Giedion says, "space in modern physics is conceived of as relative to a moving point of reference, not as the absolute and static entity of the baroque system of Newton."[2] The new reality, being fluid and impermanent, is dependent for perception on the relative position of both the observer and the object observed. A sense of simultaneity is also an aspect of this reality, for the delineation of a reality that is so amorphous demands it be refracted into planes perceived synchronically. The old three-dimensional reality which emanates from a set point of reference seeing reality isolated at points on a sequence of lines emanating from the center point is no longer valid. What is real is, as Wylie Sypher puts it,

> a structure of "emergent relationships"—emerging, according to our point of view, from the substrate neutral activity which must be called process because it has no feature of itself and is like a fog out of which appear the various objects taking form for us depending on our prehension. . . . Things are merely an area of tension in constantly emerging conditions.[3]

A way to perceive this new reality so apparent in *Cane* is offered by Joseph Frank's discussion of modern poetry:

> Aesthetic form in modern poetry, then, is based on a space-logic that demands a complete reorientation in the reader's attitude toward language. Since the primary reference of any word-group is to something inside the poem itself, language in modern poetry is really reflexive. The meaning-relationship is completed only by the simultaneous perception in space of word-groups that have no com-

> prehensible relation to each other when read consecutively in time. Instead of the instinctive and immediate reference of words and word-groups to the objects or events they symbolize and the construction of meaning from the sequence of these references, modern poetry asks its readers to suspend the process of individual reference temporarily until the entire pattern of internal references can be apprehended as a unity.[4]

Word-groups in literature are equivalent to planes in cubist painting, and in both art forms, the observer must put reality together himself, reflexively, being careful that he takes each image or plane as unique while he defines it in terms of those planes comprising the nexus of that plane. Sypher clarifies the new perspective, saying it is "no one perspective, but synchronization or jazz syncopation with rhythms stated in sharp profiles brought up into the foreground."[5] With this new sensibility in mind, *Cane*'s design can be perceived and its oracle understood.

The unity or organic quality of *Cane* can be approached through a discussion of the planes in the first study, a comparison of the first three pieces, and a comparison of the three sections of the book. In that manner, the texture of the book can be appreciated and a method for further appreciation indicated. In "Karintha" we find the first image of Karintha one of purity, a plane that is "as innocently lovely as a November cotton flower" (2). When she is so pure, the introductory poem sings a hymn to her flawless nature. However, there is a hint of danger to her, for "Men had always wanted her," men who wish to "ripen a growing thing too soon" (2). Thus, the initial image is refracted when contrasted against the hint of a new identity, for she might fall from the old men's knees, falling from grace into untimely corruption.

The second plane or image is forcefully presented and juxtaposed to the first when she "played 'home' with a small boy," thereby transforming her purity. The poem is repeated, but now it reflects her fall into darkness as the sun goes down. Her dusky skin is no longer pure, but impure as she becomes defined by the physical as opposed to the ideal world.

A third plane is presented when her child is born like a wild animal or flower, cribbed in a natural setting suffused by sacred smoke that carries souls to Jesus. The dusk of evening and the smoke from the mill unite and drift heavenward. Comprised of the ideal and the real, Karintha becomes a deeper, more complex person than when she sat on the old men's knees or when she played house. It is her soul as well as her womb that is ripened bearing holy fruit, flowering none too soon. The poem is repeated a third time, framing a now multifaceted Karintha, full of images that are in contradiction and tension, but all of which are necessary to her organic identity. The unity of the whole has to be comprehended through reflexive thought, for Toomer has opened up Karintha's experience, giving her a diversity and unity that make her a uniquely organic being.

The first three pieces seem too much more disassociated than the elements in "Karintha," different both in structure and experience. However, like the planes in "Karintha," the three pieces are organized in a special way, for "Reapers" reflects the holy, natural Karintha, hinting that as a natural element, she can be reaped and is not out of harm's way; the fall into grace is not an absolute condition. However, the flower in "November Cotton Flower" is both Karintha as she bears a new purity as well as an anomaly that negates both the scythe of autumn and the "Reapers." The flower blooms as does Karintha, out of a seemingly fallen condition; thus, the triumph of the cotton flower over the season is as complete as Karintha's triumph over her fall. "Brown eyes that lowered without a trace of fear, / Beauty so sudden for that time of year" (7), confound the passage of time, transcending the scythe of the season as does Karintha the young men. The tension between the various contradictory planes of existence slowly builds up into an increasingly complex and tenuous vision of reality, a reality that gains depth and significance and identity as it gains facets.

Relating the three sections of the book is a considerable problem, for larger planes must be organized from smaller ones drawn from the various pieces in each section. In the first section the flowering of passion seems to confer salvation or divinity: in "Karintha" the soul blooms from giving birth; in "Becky" the outcast's humanity and unseen, but apparent, passion prevail over the townspeople's weak hypocrisy; in "Carma" the girl rises above the "crudest melodrama" by her natural passion; in "Blood-Burning Moon" Tom's passion rises above the power of the white "ants" who burn him, the passion of his righteous fury rivaling and superseding the fire that consumes him. In "Fern" it is a passionate religion that makes the "virgin" Fern conceive heat for the first time in her life, bearing Christ in such a manner that her blood becomes like "boiling sap." Some pieces do not focus on passion, as in "Esther," but for the most part, the physical world is the dominant image, generally bringing life and freedom.

In the second section physical relationships that are divine are seldom achieved, making the section different from the first both in location and in experience. Washington, not Georgia, is the scene, and though "Seventh Street" indicates that the passion is there, most of the pieces find such passion and vitality curiously unattainable. Rhobert is like one of Eliot's "Hollow Men" or Esther in his need of life-giving vitality. His body is the shell of an animal out of water, and he is dying; in Washington there is no salvation because there is no union of the real and the ideal. In "Avey," "Theater," "Calling Jesus," "Box Seat," and "Bona and Paul," the planes of the ideal and the real are juxtaposed as they were in the preceding section, but there is never a union of the two. Thus, it seems that the second section, at least in terms of its major images or chords, is unique, for conflicts end in arid frustration which only passion can soothe.

In the third section Ralph Kabnis is introduced as a weak, idealistic teacher who can't cope with the South but who seeks roots into it. He lives in a world of thought, dreaming like Esther, wishing, "Give what I know a bull-neck and a heaving body, all would go well with me, wouldnt it sweetheart?" (158). Dismissed from his position, he becomes a manual laborer, sinking into Fred Halsey's cellar to drink and make love with a "bull-neck," wearing the robe of his ancestors. However, he hasn't their glory, for he seems a dissolute cynic, and things don't "go well." When he comes out of the hole at the end of the story, he is still not united and is unredeemed, even after having heard the old man's secret. He never does perceive the unity between his African, his southern, his northern, his real, and his ideal identities. The planes of his identity clash without unity, and the story ends with Carrie's, not Ralph's, beatification. The story seems to be a proof of a certain sort of existence, one in which discord prevails for the most part. The unity of King Barlo and Tom is not available to Kabnis, and the robe of his ancestors does not fit well even when he achieves a "heaving body." The curse of the white man who makes the Bible lie might blight Kabnis's attempt at salvation, but whatever the reason, he is no closer to Karintha's type of unity at the end of the story than in the beginning, even though he is as alternately ideal and real as she is.

In relating the three sections, it is apparent that they, too, have a discordant relationship and that the experience gained in perceiving them as a whole is more bewildering than that gained in perceiving some of the individual pieces. The section on Georgia reflects Ralph's physical nature and his descent into the hole, while the section on Washington reflects his days as a teacher and his ideal self. However, Ralph's experience in the hole is contrary to the proof of the first section and the implication of the second, and Ralph serves as a contrast to them both. His alienation is complete, though he does relate to the first two sections.

Thus, it seems that in the book as a whole the variations on the theme of the relationship between the past and the present, the ideal and the real, are infinite, and there seems to be no resting place for the composition or the audience. The process of perceiving the elements of existence in different relationships continues, and it is the unending variations on certain themes that become the experience Toomer conveys. Each plane of existence offers its version, but like the narrator in "Avey," the reader is continually shifting points of view. Thus, the composition continues without specific direction, though it is guided somewhat by the themes. *Cane* is multifaceted, like an onion or a Chinese puzzle, and as an oracle it speaks of a reality like itself, something to be experienced without absolute finality.

The oracular cane and its many messages of no one cane reveal a new depth to reality that would be concealed if there were a reconciliation or compromise among the various contending planes. Perhaps a way of seeing *Cane*'s final unity can be found in Sypher's description of the cubists' world which

> knows both change and permanence; it is a region of process, arrest, transition, where things emerge into recognition, then revise their feature; an Uncertainty Principle operates here. . . . 6

Such an "Uncertainty Principle" makes *Cane*'s disunity its unity, and the meaning of its oracle is its multiplicity and uncertainty of meaning.

Dan Moore, who in "Box Seat" says "the hands of Jesus touched me. I am come to a sick world to heal it" (106) is of no avail to Ralph Kabnis, and Dan's balm of passion leaves Ralph as empty as Mrs. Pribby. The uncertainty of an absolute design for the oracle is Toomer's message, for as S. P. Fullinwider says, Toomer

> confronted his readers with the pain of reality unmitigated by the pleasant knowledge of having in hand The Answer.[7]

Even as the formal structure of the book suggests a fractured reality, the experience Toomer reveals is equally fraught with tension. He was dealing with a reality whose old categories had broken down, and he undertook to reconstitute a world of his own. The contradictory tensions of a multifaceted and reverberating reality are bound up in the image of a piece of cane refracted into a book which is alive.

According to Sir James George Frazer in *The Golden Bough*, particularly in the sections "Dying and Reviving God" and "Spirits of the Corn and Wild," peopled with Adonis, Attis, Osiris, and Dionysus who were emblematic of, among other things, the seasons' and the animal and vegetable kingdoms' growth patterns, primitive man was inherently bound up in the rhythms of an organic life and all its integral variations. Much of man's literature through the ages reflects some perspective of such patterns, and Jean Toomer's *Cane* is one such example which is at the same time traditional and very modern. Whatever one says about the influence that spawned *Cane*—whether the book is attributed to the English literary tradition of Spenser's *Faerie Queen*, Pope's *An Essay on Man*, and Eliot's *The Wasteland*, or the African tradition Toomer so often elicits, speaking of juju men and the folk soul, or his own experience in Washington and Georgia—the book is informed by a substance, cane, that is the center of things as was Spenser's "strond" and the ancients' Dionysus. It is this emblem or substance that must be understood to know the message of the oracle.

The attempt to create such a universal view of reality and to speak it or reveal it could well be a killing ambition, and looking at the little critical acclaim the book has received, Toomer's ambition might seem to have been his undoing. The book is disjointed and not unified in a traditional sense of either the cycle of the seasons or literary form. There are no neat distinctions and progressions to follow. One of the many things which allows Toomer to speak successfully, laying the blame of his obscurity on his critics and not himself, is the emblem cane that gives the book its title. Cane is the center of the book, controlling all facets of the experience the book reveals, but it is highly ambiguous and full of agitation due to very modern tensions within it. The agitation that pervades the cane makes it unique, not at all like older representations of the organic life.

The introductory poem offers a traditional view of the organic emblem, for like Dionysus, cane is

> Oracular.
> Redolent of fermenting syrup,
> Purple of the dusk,
> Deep-rooted cane.

Cane is very much of the physical world, tending to death and destruction as is the woman in "Face," whose "channeled muscles / are cluster grapes of sorrow / purple in the evening sun / nearly ripe for worms" (14). Further refracting the first glimpse of cane, we find it is the sign of Carma and freedom, like Dionysus, for the cane in the poem that introduces "Carma" says:

> Scratching choruses above the guinea's squawk,
> Wind is in the cane. Come along.
> Cane leaves swaying, rusty with talk,
> Wind is in the cane. Come along. (17)

We see Carma, who "is a song. She is in the forest, dancing. Torches flare . . . juju men, gree-gree, witch-doctors . . . torches go out . . . the Dixie Pike has grown from a goat path in Africa" (17–18). Here, the cane and passion and freedom and Carma are planes of one complex but similar identity, quite contrary to the hint of death that taints the woman in "Face." The notion that the fermented sap of cane is life-giving is further refracted in "Fern," when it is religious fervor, not sexual fervor, that affects Fern: "Like boiling sap it flooded arms and fingers till she shook them as if they burned her" (32). Here, as with Dionysus and the juju men, cane is a religious symbol, capable of transcending the physical world. At this point the woman in "Face" is not so threatened by her morality.

The multiple facets of cane are refracted throughout the book on many levels. One example is in the conflict between blacks and whites. It is the deep-rooted, black King Barlo, fermenting from too much liquor, who contrasts so sharply with the almost white Esther, highlighting her impotent fantasy and weakness, giving the lie to her pale and lifeless dreams. The essence of the cane-like Barlo is also social, sexual, moral, and regional. Similar to Barlo is Dan Moore in "Box Seat," who says, "I was born in a canefield" and seeks to "stir the root-life of a withered people." He doesn't succeed, but his effort is proof of a certain form of life that the Mrs. Pribbys of the world must have in order to have a more complete existence.

The Dionysiac quality of cane dominates the book only sporadically, however. In the last story Ralph Kabnis goes underground, seeking the roots of his existence after finding his intellectual life lacking in essential ingredients. However, he fails to find salvation in passion and in the end, "with eyes downcast and swollen, trudges upstairs to the workshop" (239). For him the passion is not liberating, and he never finds the goat path to Africa where his robe might fit more splendidly. He finds no salvation in the earth, manual labor, the folk soul, or his physical nature of which he dreamed early in the story, and the message the oracle brings of the Kabnis facet of cane is bleak and hollow, redolent of despair and disillusionment.

As the center of things, cane resembles traditional emblems, but in Toomer's hand its message is one of agitation, not fruition. Somehow, the rhythm of death and rebirth is disjointed in *Cane*, and the oracle sings of ecstasy only intermittently, as in "Conversion" and "Georgia Dusk." Often, the oracle sings of aridity, echoing "The Hollow Men" and "The Wasteland," as in "Harvest Song." The grain of life, a refracted plane of cane, is parched, and Rhobert and Kabnis find no rebirth anywhere.

The complete message of the oracle is complex and often baffling due to its contradictions, but such contradiction is the result of Toomer's honesty in perceiving reality plagued by relativity. He presents no propaganda for either the ideal or the real world, the North or the South, the white or the black man, the educated or the folk black man, agape or eros love. Individual pieces are variations of the cane emblem that embraces and anchors the variety, releasing itself and the book from categories and narrow definitions. Even though he is Dionysiac himself, Dan Moore in "Box Seat" reveals a perspective that can appreciate and understand such an ambiguous oracle as *Cane* when he says to Muriel:

> "There is no such thing as happiness. Life bends joy and pain, beauty and ugliness, in such a way that no one may isolate them. No one would want to. Perfect joy, or perfect pain, with no contrasting element to define them, would mean a monotony of consciousness, would mean death." (112)

Here, he reveals an essential part of modern consciousness which makes ambiguity essential to existence, threatening the linear concept of reality. Dan's perspective informs the emblem cane and the entire book, for it conceives of a multifaceted reality in process which would be destroyed if categorized and segmented. It is this perspective which makes *Cane*'s ancient rhythm very modern.

Toomer does not copy or reflect old material or aspects of reality; rather he refracts reality in a modern way, each of the resulting planes being unique to his experiences as well as to the black man in America and universal man. The unsettling tension that swells Toomer's *Cane* is an honest response to a modern predicament and particularly the modern American black man's sense of alienation from any safe "strond" with an answer to the alienation. Thus, the emblem cane is more than part of a tradition; it is a unique expression in its own right, revealing a modern struggle between belief and disillusionment. *Cane* deserves to be known better than it is, for it is at the same time universal, part of the black experience in America, and, most important, unique as a special vision of that universe and America by a long-slighted black writer, Jean Toomer.

Toomer's *Cane*: The Artist and His World

GEORGE C. MATTHEWS

Critics have generally hailed *Cane* as a high point among fictional works of the Harlem Renaissance. Alain Locke, a chief spokesman of the Renaissance, exclaimed that *Cane* "soared above the plane of propaganda and apologetics to a self-sufficient presentation of Negro life in its own idiom and gave it proud and self-revealing evaluation."[1] *Cane* is the single work on which Jean Toomer's reputation as a literary figure hinges; yet, ironically, it is the work that Toomer called a "swan song."[2] He could not understand why people expected him to write "a second and a third and a fourth book like Cane."[3] Perhaps it is moot to argue such a point; but, on the other hand, it is known that Toomer's subsequent involvements with the Gurdjieff Institute and the Friends generated interests and attitudes markedly different from those expressed in *Cane*. The fact remains, though, that his ability to transcend stereotypical images of black literary characters enabled him to depict life in the sensitive and artistic manner suggested by Alain Locke.

In ascertaining how *Cane* "soars" in its depiction of black people in the North and South, it is helpful to refer to Toomer's unpublished letter to Waldo Frank dated December 12, 1922, in which he explains that *Cane* should be viewed from three critical angles:

> Aesthetically, from simple forms to complex ones, and back to simple forms. Regionally, from the South up into the North, and back into the South, and then a return North. From the point of view of the spiritual entity behind the work, the curve really starts with Bona and Paul (awakening), plunges into Kabnis, emerges in Karintha, etc., swings upward into Theatre and Box Seat, and ends (pauses) in Harvest Song.[4]

Examined from these perspectives, *Cane* illuminates themes ultimately concerned with questions relating to aesthetics, society, and the individual.

Toomer himself looked upon writing as an elusive and exacting mistress. Before composing *Cane* he had written literally a "trunk full" of manuscripts with which he was not especially pleased.[5] Although his ability and ideas caught the attention of John McClure of *Double Dealer* and Helena McKay of *Broom*, Toomer was unsure of his footing in the literary world. It was not until he came under the influence of Waldo Frank and Sherwood Anderson that his writing gained some equilibrium. Bolstered by his reading of Frank, Anderson, Frost, Dostoyevsky, Baudelaire, and Freud, among others, Toomer began to get the "feel" for literature. He was able, as he said, to "get inside literature."[6] In reading Frost and the imagists he became aware that "their insistence on fresh vision and on the perfect, clean economical line was just what I [Toomer] had been looking for. I began feeling," he said, "that I had in my hands the tools for my creation."[7]

Toomer used his "tools" expertly in fashioning his unique creation of *Cane*. For it was shortly after his "discovery" of literature that he undertook a position as a substitute principal of a school in Sparta, Georgia. It was here that he was inspired to create *Cane*. In the unpublished "Outline" of his autobiography, Toomer describes the background:

> The setting was crude in a way, but strangely rich and beautiful. I began feeling its effects despite my state [Toomer was terribly drained—physically and mentally at this time], or perhaps, just because of it.
>
> There was a valley, the valley of Cane, with smoke-wreaths during the day and mist at night . . . So I realized with deep regret, that the spirituals, meeting ridicule, would be certain to die out. With Negroes also the trend was towards the small town and then

> towards the city—and industry and commerce and machines. The folk-spirit was walking in to die on the modern desert. That spirit was so beautiful. Its death was so tragic. Just this seemed to sum life for me. And this was the feeling I put into *Cane*.[8]

That he was able to describe this feeling cannot be denied. After reading "Song of the Son" Jessie Fauset was moved to write Toomer that she "almost cried" to think that she was unable to write like that.[9] Matthew Josephson, a reviewer with *Broom*, a magazine which published several of the *Cane* pieces, told Toomer that he had been "bowled over by the power in [Kabnis]."[10] Countee Cullen called *Cane* "a classical portrayal of things as they are."[11] In his letters to Toomer, Sherwood Anderson encouraged him repeatedly to continue writing in his own style, a style that made *Cane* such a "painting story."[12] Certainly, praise from his contemporaries indicates the esteem and regard in which Toomer's ability and achievement were being held.

In reflecting upon the formal excellence of *Cane* of which his critics spoke, mention should be made of the economy of expression and the versatility that Toomer employs in his vignettes. "Karintha" begins: "Men had always wanted her, this Karintha, even as a child, Karintha carrying beauty, perfect as dusk when the sun goes down."[13] The story of Karintha is told in that full sentence. From the statement that "men had always wanted her," Toomer adds that "this interest of the male, who wishes to ripen a growing thing too soon, could mean no good to her" (1). The story unfolds from a kernel truth about Karintha the child to a blossomed reality about Karintha the woman who "at twenty [was still] carrying beauty, perfect as dusk when the sun goes down" (5).

Other sketches proceed in a similar fashion, that is, with unalloyed but artful expositions of central figures. Note the precision in "Becky": "Becky had one Negro son. Who gave it to her? Damn buck nigger, said the white folks' mouths. She wouldnt tell. . . . Poor Catholic poor-white crazy woman, said the black folks' mouths" (8). Basically, this is the story of Becky, whose eventual death evokes no words of sympathy from blacks or whites because she was kept "islandized between the road and railroad track" (9). Her only memorial is a Bible which "flaps its leaves with an aimless rustle" (13) on her cabin grave of brick and mortar.

Toomer's ability to manage his prose with poetic cadence appears throughout many of the sketches. For example, in "Fern" he is able to describe and highlight the beauty of Fern's face by the use of such mellifluous terms as "flowed," "soft," "cream," "foam." The suggestion of mobility of expression, the softness of her color—caught in the liquid quality of her eyes—is exquisitely captured in these opening lines:

> Face flowed into her eyes. Flowed in soft cream foam and plaintive ripples, in such a way that wherever your glance may momentarily have rested, it immediately thereafter wavered in the direction of her eyes. The soft suggestion of down slightly darkened, like the shadow of a bird's wing might, the creamy brown color of her upper lip. (24)

On the other hand, Toomer was able to employ his prose as a cutting edge. In "Esther" he writes:

> Esther's hair falls in soft curls about her high-cheek-boned chalk-white face. Esther's hair would be beautiful if there were more gloss to it. (36)

Instead of the suggested softness, Esther's hair takes on a brittle, artificial quality that adds to the rigidness of her high-cheek bones and further augments the death-like pallor of her "chalk-white face."

The interweaving of the simple and complex forms that shuttle through the fabric of *Cane* is perhaps most closely woven in "Portrait in Georgia." In this imagistic poem the simple and complex mesh to form a collage rather than a symmetrical portrait:

> Hair—braided chestnut,
> coiled like a lyncher's rope
> Eyes—fagots
> Lips—old scars, or the first red blisters,
> Breath—the last sweet scent of cane,
> And her slim body, white as the ash
> of black flesh after flame. (50)

Esther's hair has been described as soft, but it could just as well be "coiled like a lyncher's rope." The beautiful, flowing eyes of Fern can be pitted against the "blood-hot eyes"—the fagots—in "Georgia Dusk." the tempting, parted lips of Cloine in "Evening Song" can be juxtaposed against the searing, blistered lips of Tom in "Blood-Burning Moon." Again, in "Blood-Burning Moon" there is not only the heavy scent of "boiling cane" but also the stench of Tom's burning body "white as the ash of black flesh after flame" (50). "Portrait in Georgia," then, highlights the technical complexities and ambiguities not only of the first section but of *Cane* generally. Toomer's ability to weave patterns that are at once simple yet complex, obvious yet mysterious, earthy yet ethereal puts in bold relief his acknowledged distinction as a notable literary craftsman.

In stating that *Cane* may be interpreted "regionally, from the South up into the North, and back into the South again," Toomer specifies the locales—replete with diverse attitudes and customs—that are within the province of *Cane*. The South of the first section of Cane embodies the spirit of the "valley of Cane," while the world of Kabnis—also set in the South—has the sense of a physical, regimented community. Alien to both these settings is northern society with its trappings of machinery, industry, and sophistication.

In the southern, rural setting, in which such women as Carma, Becky, and Louisa find themselves, there is a noticeable stability founded on respect for tradition and order. When the order is disturbed, cruelty, violence, and even bloodshed erupt. A smoothly functioning society is one in which the past is esteemed and even emulated. There is a place for everything. We are told in "Karintha" that "homes in Georgia are most often built on the two-room plan. In one, you cook and eat, in the other you sleep, and there love goes on" (2). Toomer's words are very nearly prescriptive—this is the way things are done. "One could but imitate one's parents, for to follow them was the way of God" (2–3). If one goes outside the designs of Providence, then we will surely be alienated on "ground islandized between the road and railroad track. Pushed up where a blue-sheen God with listless eyes could look at it" (9). Placed in such a precarious position—as was Becky—one experiences ostracism from a society in which compliance with codes and customs admits of no exceptions. Both blacks and whites disown and condemn the "insane white shameless wench . . . poor Catholic poor-white crazy woman" (8) who *dared* to have children by a black man. This divine and societal disapproval of miscegenation again appears in "Blood-Burning Moon," in which Louisa—moved by a black man and a white man—provokes the scorn of the blacks and the wrath of the whites for her part in precipitating the tragic deaths of Tom Burwell and Bob Stone. She is left alone to pine:

Red nigger moon, Sinner!
Blood-burning moon, Sinner!
Come out that fact'ry door.
(67)

The women in this first section are much like Louisa in that they do not protest against the injustices or outrages they suffer. Rather they resign themselves to their fate. If anything, they lapse into a past that is as far off as a "goat path in Africa." The closer they are to their African past, the more mystifying they seem to be. Becky—a poor white woman—is the most overtly abused. Her predicament is readily recognized and labeled by her society. Esther, a mulatto [perhaps more white than black], is also abused and ignored by whites and blacks. Louisa—who identifies with both blacks and whites—is left to herself to suffer the pangs of her haunting "crime." Fernie Mae Rosen—half-black, half-Semitic—combines the folk spirit of the southern black and the spirit of the Hebrew people of old who dared to dream their "wild" dreams. Carma is more mystifying. Although her tale is the "crudest melodrama," her role in that melodrama is cloaked with primitive and supernal references. Driving her "Georgia chariot" along "a goat path in Africa," she is illuminated by "the sun which . . . shoots primitive rockets into her mangrove-gloomed, yellow flower face. . . . God has left the Moses-people for the nigger" (16). Most mystifying of all is Karintha. She is other-worldly; she is a "wild flash that told the other folks just what it was to live. . . . Her sudden darting . . . was a bit of vivid color, like a black bird that flashes in light" (1–2). She is detached, ethereal, "perfect as dusk when the sun goes down" (1).

Fern, Carma, and Karintha seem removed from their surroundings. For them "time and space have no meaning in a canefield" (19). They are like primitive spirits in close touch with another world, far removed from their own hostile environment. Their mysterious demeanor and occultness suggest that Toomer's attitude is one of detachment from racial and civil entanglements *per se*. It is an attitude that bespeaks a view of the person as a human being whose associations with the present are linked with his past, the strings of which are secured deeply within himself. Southern society has erected certain restrictions that necessarily qualify the extent and influence of those distant ties, but characters in touch with their past are able to function within the confines of those restrictions. If one is able to respond to "vibrations" from the past to see beyond strictures of the present, then he is on the threshold of an "awakening." Unlike Dan Moore of "Box Seat," none of the women in this first section experiences such an awakening.

Although the North is supposedly a foil to southern society, it, too, honors and preserves traditional societal demarcations. Censure is in store for those who attempt to leave their "waxen cell in the world comb" (89). It is apparent in "Theater" that John and Dorris suffer from the pressure of "white walls" and the restrictions of "dictie" values that prevent their love from being realized. John desires to reach out to Dorris, but he understands that such a step would be folly. In his mind his "heart beats tensely against her dancing body, [but] walls press his mind within his heart" (98). His "mind" restrains his "heart," and his face is hidden in shadow.

Muriel in "Box Seat" is no better off than John. She, too, has come under the influence of the "Mrs. Pribbys" of her society who have denied her the free expression of her feelings. Muriel has become a *part* of the town; she has been fixed in her place—bolted in her slot—as a member of a well-ordered, "tidy" world. Dan, however, does not fit into a pre-cast mold. He is a free spirit, "born in a canefield" (105) who hears the rumble and roar of "powerful underground races" coming from the "earth's deep core" (108). Unlike Muriel, who is left defeated and disillusioned, Dan removes himself from the metallic world around him. He is on the verge of an awakening, one that does not include robots or mannequins. In walking away from Muriel, "he is as cool as a green stem that has just shed its flower" (129). Unfortunately, we do not know what happens to Dan after he walks away from the theater. Perhaps like Muriel—the "flower" he had shed—he, in turn, is destined to wither in a cruel environment. Whatever his destiny he has awakened to the cold emptiness of the hollow world around him.

The vignettes set in the North—similar to the cameos of life in rural Georgia—emphasize the *status quo* of society. Toomer's characters are not successful in coming to grips with the world around them. They either opt to retain the established, accepted norms of conduct, or else, like Dan, they are called into account for challenging them. Given this somewhat staid attitude toward society, it is not surprising that "Kabnis" follows much along the same lines in its delineation of attitudes toward education and religion.

As one who participated in northern urban living and goes to teach in rural Georgia, Ralph Kabnis has the apparent background to comment on both worlds. But his exposure to the values of northern life has left him confused and disoriented. He even feels tortured by the beauty that surrounds him. In the midst of one of his reveries, he falls to his knees and cries to heaven: "Whats beauty anyway but ugliness if it hurts you?" (162). He sees himself as "an atom of dust in agony on a [Georgia] hillside" (162). His agony is indicative of his position in a society of extremes. His cabin on the hillside is in the midst of an ordered world dominated by "the large frame house, squatting on brick pillars, where the principal of the school, his wife and the boarding girls sleep" (163). In contrast to this spacious house is "a cabin silhouetted on a knoll about a mile away. Peace. Negroes within it are content. They farm. They sing. They love. They sleep. Kabnis wonders if perhaps they can feel him. If perhaps he gives them bad dreams. Things are so immediate in Georgia" (164). This description is reminiscent of an earlier one of a Georgia cabin-home in which people cook, eat, sleep, and love. In Kabnis's world, as in Karintha's, the society is part of a neatly arranged, "peaceful" system in which boundaries are clearly defined and life-styles prescribed.

Mr. Hanby, the principal, lives in the "big house," which stands as an imposing structure over the "contented" Negroes living in their two-room cabins. It is in this world of contorted values that Kabnis lives and tries to function. But his attempts are futile. He sees himself ill-equipped to satisfy Mr. Hanby's idealistic codes of conduct. Hanby, who "to members of his own race . . . affects the manners of a wealthy white planter" (185) discharges him and explicitly informs him that "the progress of the Negro race is jeopardized whenever the personal habits and examples set by its guides and mentors fall below the acknowledged and hard-won standard of its average member" (186). Kabnis is a stumbling block to Hanby, whose goals and aspirations are inextricably committed to education, whose purpose, he says, is "to teach our youth to live better, cleaner, more noble lives. To prove to the world that the Negro race can be just like any other race" (186).

Kabnis cannot accept Hanby's view of education, but he is powerless to do anything about it. He is weak, "uprooted, thinning out. Suspended a few feet above the soil whose touch would resurrect him" (191). That touch would seem to be contact with the "rumbling and roar" coming from the heart of the earth. Kabnis's own belief is that education and culture elevate a man no matter his color or background. But Mr. Layman, "a teacher and preacher who has traveled in almost every nook and corner of the state and hence knows more than would be good for anyone other than a silent man" (169), tells Kabnis that a "nigger's a nigger down this away, Professor. An only two dividins: good an bad. An even they aint permanent categories. They sometimes mixes um up when it comes t lynchin. I've seen um do it" (171–72).

In the eyes of Layman, people like Kabnis, and, especially Hanby, are ludicrous, for they are trying to emulate the "ways of white folks." We are told that "when he [Hanby] is up North, he lets it be known that his ideas are those of the best New England tradition" (185). Although Layman does not think that Kabnis is an "Uncle Tom" like Hanby, he nonetheless tells him: "Teachin in th South aint th thing fer y" (194). He sees that Kabnis must get to know himself better before he can attempt to teach others about themselves.

In a sense Kabnis is a weaker version of Dan Moore in "Box Seat." He is on the verge of an awakening, but, unlike Dan, he does not have the necessary spirit or drive—that "rumbling and roar"—to effect his own conversion. His lethargy is augmented by the static society in which he is placed, that is, with people who either deceive themselves or who are helpless about the deception perpetrated upon them.

In his frustration and anxiety Kabnis lashes out at the "preacher-ridden race. Pray and shout. Theyre in the preacher's hands. Thats what it is. And the preacher's hands are in the white man's pockets" (174). This condemnation of institutionalized religion and its effects on society—black people in particular—is again brought out in the description of the church: "The church bell tolls. Above its squat tower, a great spiral of buzzards reaches far into the heavens. An ironic comment upon the path that leads into the Christian land" (169). Kabnis concurs with the narrator—Christianity has failed in the South. It has been unable to effect a true conversion in the hearts of either blacks or whites. Whites have exploited the tenets of Christianity by making the black man think that he is an inferior being whose salvation can only be found in faithful servitude. Even Kabnis, who looks askance at the southern version of religion, has been turned around and upside down by his confrontation with Christianity in the person of Father John.

Father John is an enigma to Kabnis. He calls him a "done-up preacher" (217), yet he is strangely attracted by the spirit of the past that seems to emanate from the old man. Father John says that the sin fixed upon white folks is the sin they committed when they made the Bible lie. Kabnis ultimately rejects Father John, but he nonetheless applies to himself what the old man proclaimed. He sees religion as a conspiracy against society, one that has so muddled his own position that he is unable to distinguish between "master; slave. Soil; and the overarching heavens. Dusk; dawn. They fight and bastardize [him]" (218). He is unable to place his own ancestry. He looks upon his ancestors as southern blue-bloods, denying that there is "much difference between blue and black" (218). It is this inability to distinguish differences—this unwillingness to commit himself—that leaves Ralph Kabnis a "weakenin man" for whom "th axle an th beam's all ready waitin" (238). His cross has been fashioned by a society in which he is unable to function. Crucified by his own inaction, he sees that "th whole world is a conspiracy t sin, especially in America, an against [him]" (236).

In the final analysis, Kabnis's world is a society that has perpetuated the myths of the past. It has subsumed values of white southern education and religion into its own thought patterns and mores. The black society, as Toomer pictures it, had changed slightly in outlook or design since Emancipation. Although Toomer may not argue for a change of societal structures, he does suggest a refurbishing of spirit and a growth of inner awareness that will enable one to set himself free. This liberating awareness is the spiritual entity behind *Cane*.

In tracing the spiritual cycle in *Cane*, Toomer begins his curve with "Bona and Paul (awakening), plunges into Kabnis, emerges in Karintha, etc. swings upward into Theatre and Box Seat, and ends (pauses) in Harvest Song."[14] In "Bona and Paul" it is Paul's awakening that is of primary importance. His conversion is precipitated by his quickening perception of himself and others. The two windows in his room, close to and parallel with the Chicago "L," provide his points of vision from which he looks out on the world around him. One window symbolizes himself and the other Bona. Through his own window Paul "follows the sun to a pine-matted hillock in Georgia" (137). He sees a scene strangely reminiscent: "the gray unpainted cabins tinted lavender . . . a Negress chanting a lullaby" (137–38). This vision fades into the recesses of his mind as "Paul follows the sun into himself in Chicago" (138). When Paul tries to see through Bona's window, "he looks through a dark pane" (138). Since the South has no meaning for Bona, there are no recollections of a dimmed past there for Paul.

Through Bona's window Paul can see only the immediate murkiness of his present world.

As the sun sets and dusk closes in, Paul becomes more conscious of his identity. Later that night in the midst of the conviviality of Crimson Gardens, he is suddenly struck by the thought "that people saw, not attractiveness in his dark skin, but difference. Their stares, giving him to himself, filled something long empty within him, and were like green blades sprouting in his consciousness. There was fullness, and strength and peace about it all. He saw himself, cloudy, but real" (145). Bona's window was a cold dark pane; Crimson Gardens is warm and clear. A fertile and productive awareness begins to grow inside him. This newly discovered knowledge of himself—however nebulous it may be—fills Paul with joy. He senses that he no longer can be the same person. If he had met Bona earlier, he might have taken pleasure in her love, but now a greater joy is found in the revitalized image of himself. He glows within, content with the thought that his eyes are finally opened.

The awakening that Paul experiences in Crimson Gardens, an awakening that lay dormant since his earlier realization in his room, fills Paul with an evanescence that confuses and frustrates Bona. Paul reassures Bona that she will know more of him before long. As he prepares to leave Crimson Gardens on the verge of relating his conversion to Bona, he is struck by another thought. Lost in wonderment he leaves Bona outside Crimson Gardens and darts back to the Negro doorman to relate to him how his "thoughts were matches thrown into a dark window" (153). He feels uplifted by his symbolic confession, but when he returns to where Bona was waiting, he finds that she has left. If we are left to speculate on the permanence of Paul's conversion, we are nonetheless struck by his awakening, a spiritual realization that Toomer saw fit to place at the beginning of his wheel of awareness.

As the wheel turns we see that Ralph Kabnis is another character who gains an insight into his inner life. But, unlike Paul, who is initially illumined by the rays of Georgia sunlight glowing within him, Kabnis becomes increasingly insular and pessimistic. He is unable to appreciate either his community or companions. He is tortured by the beauty around him. Wherever he turns in the academic, social, or workaday world, he feels himself degraded or abused. He is unable to own up to his own identity. As a foil to Kabnis, Lewis appears to be "what a stronger Kabnis might have been and in an odd faint way resembles him. . . . He seems to be issuing sharply from a vivid dream" (189–90). Kabnis has difficulty realizing his own dream. He says: "If I, the dream (not what is weak and afraid in me) could become the face of the South. How my lips would sing for it, my songs being the lips of its soul" (158). The approximating of this dream is the measure of success that Kabnis's awakening takes. Perhaps in this respect Kabnis is one step ahead of Paul. Paul does not know what will be the outcome of his conversion. Kabnis does—at least he has an idea what the consequences could be. It is his confrontation with history that frightens him. He would rather delude himself into believing that he is an offspring of southern blue-bloods than think that he or his ancestors could have been conceived in sin. Kabnis is beside himself with rage when Father John keeps repeating "sin." It pains him to think that he has been the "victim" of sin, that he is "what sin is."

Yet Father John's words effect a catharsis in Kabnis. He vents his pent-up contempt on Father John, calling him an "old black fakir," and then slumps to the ground in front of the young girl, Carrie Kate. "Kabnis crumbles. He sinks to his knees before her ashamed, exhausted" (238). Carrie cools his fever and hot cheeks with her reassuring hands. She is about to pray with him when Halsey interrupts this moment of decision by recalling Kabnis to his mechanical existence. On the threshold of a conversion, but unable to pass through it completely, Kabnis picks up a bucket of dead coals and "trudges upstairs to the work-shop" (239). He leaves "The Hole" for Father John to dream his dreams and for Carrie Kate to delight in her visions. For Kabnis his dreams and visions are as alive as the coals he carries.

It is the frustrating of dreams and the rejecting of visions that characterize those at the beginning of the spiritual cycle. As the curve progresses it passes through tales of the South regarding Karintha, Fern, and Carma. It has already been suggested that they are primitive spirits for whom "time and space have no meaning." Their detachment from a hostile environment denotes their degree of spiritual awareness. They are mystifying in that they seem not to respond to forces about them, but rather to other vibrations shooting up like wild flashes from the "earth's deep core." They are in touch with a past that only their primitive spirits seem to detect.

As the wheel revolves through stages of frustration, rejection, and transcendence, it begins to "swing upward into 'Theater' and 'Box Seat.' "[15] These sketches are perhaps the most positive in terms of spiritual realization in that the characters test their awareness. Although

Dorris becomes disillusioned and Dan disenchanted, they have nevertheless ventured forth into the "real" world. In this respect they experience a growth or develop an awareness that other characters in *Cane* do not. They are symbolic of a promise—however nebulous or disconcerting—that the future may be different from the past. Although John represses the desires and dreams aroused by Dorris's dance, Dorris is able to act out her wishes in dance. "Glorious songs are the muscles of her limbs. And her singing is of canebrake loves and mangrove feastings" (78). It is not the dance or the dancer that has been found wanting; the lack is in John, who, like Kabnis, is "tortured" by the beauty around him.

Dan Moore discovers himself the hard way in his relationships with Muriel. He tries to remove or at least soften the metallic tone of Muriel's actions. His advice to Muriel is perhaps the most comprehensive statement in *Cane* on how to arrive at a full awareness of life:

> There is no such thing as happiness. Life bends joy and pain, beauty and ugliness, in such a way that no one may isolate them. No one should want to. Perfect joy, or perfect pain, with no contrasting element to define them, would mean a monotony of consciousness, would mean death. . . . Say that you have tried to make them [people] create. Say that you have used your own capacity for life to cradle them. To start them upward-flowing. Or if you cant say that you have, then say that you will. My talking to you will make you aware of your power to do so. Say that you will love, that you will give yourself in love. (112–13)

Dan hopes that his message of love will seep into the cold chambers of Muriel's heart and fill her with warmth and sensitivity for others. He wants to start an "upward-flowing" motion in her consciousness that will culminate in an awakening. His hopes are shattered, however, when Muriel shrinks back into her rigid box seat when the dwarfish actor offers her a rose from the stage. Muriel's obvious rejection of the deformed actor and her revulsion at being coerced into accepting the rose prompts Dan to spring from his seat to shout: "JESUS WAS ONCE A LEPER!" (129). In essence, Dan is saying that love knows no bounds. If one cannot accept others, he cannot accept himself. In failing to respond to the dwarf, Muriel has failed not only to see the humanity in the "leper" before her but also to come alive to the love she has to give. Dan storms out of the theater "cool as a green stem that has just shed its flower" (129). He leaves the theater "alive," rooted to the soil from which he had sprung.

As the curve comes round a full 360 degrees, the cycle of spiritual awareness is brought to a close or "pauses" in "Harvest Song." In this remarkable poem a reaper stands alone at the end of the day in the field he has been harvesting. He longs to see the other reapers who are as "dust-caked and blind" (132) as himself. He "hungers" for knowledge of them but at the same time is afraid of that knowledge. He hesitates to call for fear of being heard; "what should they hear me, and offer me their grain, oats or wheat, or corn?" (132). He fears the knowledge of his "hunger." In actuality, this holding back, this fear of the unknown is the same type of fear that prevented Paul and Kabnis from either communicating or alleviating their "hungers" effectively. Caught up in their own "fields," they hesitate to look beyond their own needs. Like the reaper they prefer to beat their palms "against the stubble of [their own] harvesting" (133). But neither they nor the reaper will benefit from this insularity, for it will not bring them knowledge of their needs. They will be left alone in their own fields to sow the seeds and reap the harvest cultivated through spiritual frustration and deprivation.

As he brings his cycle full circle, Toomer seems to take a strangely ambiguous stand on the implication of spiritual or inner awareness in the individual. In "Bona and Paul" and "Kabnis" the spiritual awakenings are indefinite or short-lived. On the other hand, in "Karintha," "Fern," and "Carma" a sense of awareness is as alive as burning coals, but they are fanned by winds from a distant shore. The "fire" is most intense in "Theater" and "Box Seat," but in "Harvest Song" the flame dies and remains only a glow in the reaper as it had been in Paul. The characters generally seem poised for a celebration, but there is none in sight.

In some ways *Cane* defies analysis. Perhaps appreciation of its haunting poetry and mystifying prose is reward enough. Yet, if we accept the guide Toomer has given us for reading his work, then we can at least suggest the patterns of thought that run through the stories and poems.

Aesthetically, Toomer employs clean, economical lines in his poetry and prose whose apparent clarity leads ironically to ambivalence and mystification. Regionally, he delineates attitudes of the North and South that suggest the need for a balanced, well-ordered society in which misfortune and deprivation result when customs are violated. Spiritually, Toomer seems to point in the direction of an awakening while at the same time he appears to show the impossibility of realizing it fully. In the final analysis *Cane* is a great work of art that attempts to reckon with life, but like life, leaves many questions unanswered.

Jean Toomer as the *Cane* Short-Story Writer

Three Enigmas: Karintha, Becky, and Carma

WILLIAM L. DUTCH

The three short stories or sketches "Karintha," "Becky," and "Carma" have many similarities—in tone, theme, structure, and language. However, their interest for readers probably lies in the fact that the protagonist in each of them is an enigma. The narrator tells how they got to this point in life, but the reader wants to know where the characters go from here. Toomer has succeeded in establishing interesting, viable characters, but he leaves them at that. What motivates these people? Do they evolve or is this where they begin and end?

The basic structural pattern in the three character sketches is a prose story enclosed in a frame. The frame is a stanza that summarizes the story or sets the mood for the story that follows. Here Toomer is making use of a literary convention often used by authors of long poems, especially epics. In "Karintha" and "Carma" the stanzas emphasize sensuality; in "Becky" the frame summarizes the plot. Internally, the three short stories or sketches are organized into sections resembling three- or four-act dramas.

"Karintha" is informed by irony and paradox. Sex has always been a part of Karintha's life: she has experienced phallic symbols all of her life. Old men have fondled her, and the young men who have danced with her have continued the physical stimulation as she has grown. Karintha's home also has been a source of sexual stimulation or cultivation. The narrator points out: "Homes in Georgia are most often built on the two-room plan. In one, you cook and eat, in the other you sleep, and there love goes on. Karintha has seen or heard, or perhaps she had felt her parents loving."[1]

Up to this point in the story, Karintha has been passive: a picture, a flower, a stalk of "sugar cane." At the age of twelve, at puberty, she exchanges the symbol for the object symbolized: "She played 'home' with a small boy who was not afraid to do her bidding. That started the whole thing" (3). This act announces her nubility: "Karintha is a woman" (3). With this statement the narrator changes from past to present tense to tell the remainder of the story.

"She has been married many times" (3), the narrator tells us, but "married" is probably a euphemistic way to say that she has had many lovers. What motivated her to have many lovers? Two things in her life stand out: sexual stimulation from early childhood and the pursuit of lovers. A third is implied: a desire to ripen fruit (become a mother). She rejects the old men because they are not good candidates for fatherhood but accepts the young men because they are. Neither old nor young men understand her, however. The narrator tells us, "Men do not know that the soul of her was a growing thing ripened too soon" (4). The tragedy of her life is the death of her child. This sketch ends with Karintha giving her ripened-too-soon offspring as a burnt offering to Jesus (4).

Karintha can be viewed as a stalk of cane growing in the field along with other cane plants. People look forward to her ripening for their pleasure and use. She wants to ripen so she can bear fruit. The tension is between her desire and the desires of the people who cultivated her. "Old men rode her hobby-horse upon their knees. Young men danced with her at frolics when they should have been dancing with their grown-up girls. . . . Even the preacher, who caught her at mischief, told himself that she was as innocently lovely as a November cotton-flower. . . . They [the young men] all want to bring her money" (1–3). This plant motif is continued with Karintha dropping her seed: "A child fell out of her womb onto a bed of pine-needles in the forest" (4). The biblical symbolism of the seed dropping to the ground implies that there will be rebirth, but this seed falls on pine-needles.

The two poems—"Reapers" and "November Cotton Flower"—which serve as a bridge between "Karintha" and "Becky," support the interpretation that the two women of these stories, and Carma, in the story to follow, can be viewed as nature's stalks growing in a field.

The frame for "Becky" reveals Becky's story in four prose sentences. Unlike Karintha, Becky—"the white woman who had two Negro sons"—is not an object of affection for the people in the community. She is an object of both hatred and charity. Although she is not cultivated, she is permitted to grow: "Trainmen, and passengers who'd heard about her, threw out papers and food. . . . Folks from the town took turns, unknown, of course, to each other, in bringing corn and meat and sweet potatoes. Even sometimes snuff" (9–10). Becky, therefore, exists in a world where all contraries are true. Love (charity) and hate, attraction and repulsion exist concurrently. The community is ambivalent toward her. The narrator comments, "When the first was born, the white folks said they'd have no more to do with her. And black folks, they too joined hands to cast her out" (9). Yet these same people built her a cabin in which to raise her offspring.

Symbolically, the central action in this sketch can be understood as a people building a temple for their goddess and bringing gifts to her. The cabin is built in a central location in the town, on a narrow strip of land between the railroad and the road. All traffic passes it. Like God, Becky is never seen, but people leave their offerings. Paradoxically, Becky's miscegenetic act unites the blacks and whites in this community—through their hatred and charity toward her—but it separates her from the community. The temple symbolism is further pointed out in Becky's end: "The chimney (spire) fell into the cabin. . . . Barlo, mumbling something [prayers], threw his Bible on the pile. (No one has ever touched it.)" (12).

Both Becky and Karintha can be looked upon as goddesses, each with her votaries. Karintha's worshipers are propelled by her sensual beauty. In contrast, Becky's ". . . eyes were sunken, her neck stringy, her breast fallen . . ." (8). Yet, she is able to hold a lover for at least a five-year period. Moreover, Becky's followers are moved by their common hatred and charity toward her. Unlike Karintha, Becky never speaks nor is the reader given an insight into her mind. However, the reader can surmise that her thoughts are those expressed by her two sons: "'Godam the white folks; godam the niggers'" (11).

Carma, the third goddess in Toomer's pantheon, like Karintha and Becky, leads a life that is lascivious. Moreover, her lasciviousness is more enigmatic because the narrator describes her as possessing masculine attributes and doing masculine work. The first sentence in the tale contains a phrase describing Carma as "strong as any man" (16), and the last sentence repeats the phrase. Between these two sentences Carma's crudest melodrama, informed by her attractiveness to men and her desire for and willingness to have sexual relations with many men, is acted out: "She had others. No one blames her for that" (18).

The narrator's statement that "Carma's tale is the crudest melodrama" (18) is accurate. It is crude in that the subject matter is adultery and violence. It is melodramatic in that the plot is sensational, and it contains violent acts, threats of violence, deception, and the occult. Although it is related in a sketchy manner, there is enough information provided to make the tale coherent and enjoyable to read. However, there is no conventional happy ending. Or is there a happy ending for Carma now that her husband is in the gang? (20).

All art exaggerates; it distorts through its emphasis and selection of material. Toomer has demonstrated his ability to create art out of subject matter that could offend many readers. His laconic narrators tell just the bare essentials, just the highlights which give the stories a folktale quality. This folktale quality is especially evident in the verses that frame each sketch. Furthermore, this "little information" given artfully by the narrators is consonant with the enigmatic nature of Karintha, Becky, and Carma.

Jean Toomer's "Fern": A Mythical Dimension

HARGIS WESTERFIELD

Although a recent study of Jean Toomer's "Fern" roundly asserts that her last name of Rosen is "irrelevant,"[1] I contend that Toomer uses the name Rosen to point up the Jewish and Christian myth of the story. For Toomer reserves her last name for the final position, which is the position of emphasis. The last word in the story is *Rosen*. Actually, appearance of this usually German-Jewish name anywhere in this southern black story ought to startle the reader. For the provenance of names used by black Americans in the South is usually British or west European—not Jewish. Moreover, references to Jewishness regarding Fern begin with the fifth sentence in the story and occur throughout. And accompanying evidences reveal that Toomer has exalted this charming Fern with the mythos of the Jewish Mother of God.

Besides the name Rosen, unmistakably Jewish references occur again and again.[2] Five sentences from the start, Toomer says, "Her nose was aquiline, Semitic" (24). In the next sentence he says that if one has heard a Jewish cantor sing, he will know the narrator's feelings when he looks at her face. Later, our narrator says that at first sight of her, he felt as if he had heard a Jewish cantor sing (28). And in the epiphany where Fern rejects carnal love, she sings like "a Jewish cantor singing with a broken voice" (32).

Such are Toomer's plainly Jewish references. But Toomer structures "Fern" to suggest what for Christians is the greatest event in the Holy Land—the Incarnation of God in Mary. Toomer begins "Fern" with a lengthy character sketch replete with allusions which are connected with Mary—at least connected for Christians. Toomer follows this sketch with the concentrated impact of the tremendous mystic experience of Fern with God. Toomer's brief epilogue points up this Judeo-Christian exaltation of Fern.

The story beings with a character sketch as if to provide an assured documentation of the coming experience of the Incarnation. This sketch takes up over half of the story. Toomer tells us that young men "took her" but had no pleasure from the union. As she grew up, new men came to town. These new men felt like almost everyone else who saw her; they would not be denied. "Men were everlastingly bringing her their bodies" (25). But something in her grew tired of men—although the narrator is certain that Fern herself could not tell why she began to turn them off. The strangest part of this rejection is that the would-be lovers were not merely baffled and ashamed. Instead, they vowed one day to do something for her—give her rich gifts or rescue her from some unworthy fellow who had married her (25–26).

"A sort of superstition" crept into these men's minds that Fern stood somewhere above them. In paradox, Toomer says, "She became a virgin" (26). And Toomer pauses to stress his opinion that a virgin in a small southern town is unusual (26).

This opening character sketch has associated Fern with Jewishness (24), then brought out her rejection of men and her becoming a virgin. Now Toomer associates Fern's rejection of the narrator with the experience of the Incarnation.

On the evening of this mystic occurrence, the narrator has walked out at dusk with Fern. He says that he feels strange—that he would not be surprised to have "vision." For Georgia people have more visions than one might expect. Once, for example, a black woman saw the Mother of Christ and drew a charcoal picture of her on the courthouse wall (31).

He is now alone at dusk with Fern. From force of habit he finds himself embracing her. And Fern goes into a trance. Unusually weird and open, these eyes hold the narrator. And they hold God! God flows into her. In his confusion the narrator believes that he has done something to cause a wild outburst from Fern. She falls to her knees, sways back and forth. She calls "Jesus Christ" and sings brokenly, "a Jewish cantor singing with a broken voice." She seems to pound her head on the ground and faints (32).

In the epilogue the narrator says that there was some talk of making him leave town—from some self-appointed protectors. But he leaves unmolested. From the train he sees her for the last time, and something he calls "God" flows from her face into the countryside and the sunset. Like the men who had known her sexually, he wishes to do some "fine unnamed thing" for her. And he names her for the first time in full—"Fernie May Rosen" (33).

Since the myth of the Incarnation is clear in the story, perhaps the nail has symbolic associations. Twice Toomer mentions this nail, which appears at an unbelievable position in connection with Fern's body. At any time of day, Fern sits listlessly on her porch railing. She props her back against a post; her head she tilts forward because of the nail behind her head. For some unknown reason she has never bothered to pull this nail out (26–27). In the narrator's last view of Fern, he sees her again on the porch—"head tilted a little forward where the nail was" (33). Fern sits as if to commemorate the sufferings of Christ when he incurred the nails of Calvary.

Nowhere does Toomer explicitly state that the Mother of God has reappeared as an avatar in Georgia. But with his skilled Judeo-Christian allusions, he has made Fernie May Rosen a character to exalt and adore.

The Search for Identity in Jean Toomer's "Esther"

EDWARD E. WALDRON

As are all of his works, Jean Toomer's short story "Esther," which appears in his novel-poem *Cane*,[1] is a story of many levels. On the surface is the rather obvious interpretation that Robert Bone gives briefly in his *The Negro Novel in America*. Bone dismisses the story as a tale of a frigid girl's longing for the open masculinity of "King" Barlo, her subsequent failure to give herself to him, and her return to frigidity.[2] Beneath this superficial level, however, lie at least two more intense and, for Toomer, more personal interpretations. One deals with the relationship of a light-skinned American Negro to the black community in which he (she) must try to function, and the other has to do with a common theme of the Harlem Renaissance, the relationship between the American Negro and Africa.

On the surface level of the story, Esther has problems in her dealings with her own people. Because she is so near-white and because her father is "the richest colored man in town," she is set above the common black folk of the town; and, since she is obviously excluded from the company of the town's white folks, she is, in fact, alone. The theme of the tragic mulatto, isolated from both the worlds from which he is created, is a recurring one in Afro-American literature, but it is a theme that carries a special power when the writer himself suffers from the dilemma of racial duality. In some ways Jean Toomer must have felt as isolated as his Esther, and this story serves as a search for an answer to the mulatto's plight.

Esther apparently never considers trying "to pass." Given the size of her town and her obvious lack of mobility or *desire* to move, this would be out of the question anyway. It is in her witnessing of Barlo's visionary trance that Esther finds the link that ties her to *something*—and that something is blackness. Just as she is "chalk-white," Barlo is a "magnificent, black-skinned Negro" (36). In his color she finds a solidity that appeals to her, even in her nine-year-old child mind. Later, she is to dream of having Barlo's black baby, even though her concern with his religious vision forces her to dream of an immaculate conception. And, although she is at first repelled by the ugly, "tobacco-juiced baby" of her dream, she finds it "sweet" when she puts it to her breast. The baby gives her comfort, and she forgets the jeers turned to jealousy of the townspeople and finds peace in her dream.

This dream, the product of her loneliness and her attraction to Barlo's blackness, dominates her life until Barlo returns in the flesh eleven years after she began the dream. She has wasted away and has lost the bloom of her youth, but Barlo's arrival stirs the old dreams, and she vows to see him. For years she has bolstered herself by "telling herself of his glories," and the first of these is always: "Black. Magnetically so" (12). Comes the night, she slips away to the house of sin where her man of faith has been "lured." As she goes, the familiar world around her fades into nothingness and becomes a ghostly companion to her. She has decided her fate, and she needs nothing else but Barlo. Her confrontation with the vulgar reality of Barlo, drenched in a tobacco-liquor stench, shatters her, however, and she leaves Nat Bole's place completely empty—no dream is left to comfort her. Even the street belonging to the world to which *she* never belonged is gone. Only emptiness is left.

Given Toomer's denial of his Negro background in later years, one begins to see something of personal importance to the author in the plight of Esther Crane. While the works of poetry and fiction that he wove together to make *Cane* show an extremely sensitive awareness of the life of the American Negro in all its complexities and paradoxes, Toomer obviously had difficulty accepting his own blackness, perhaps because that blackness was, in his case as in Esther's, of the spirit rather than of the flesh. In other words, what Toomer has given us in

"Esther" is a brilliantly condensed, overpoweringly poignant portrait of a human being reaching desperately for something that will tell her (him) who she (he) is and where she (he) belongs in the scheme of creation.

The answer is not pretty. Caught between two worlds, one which she denies herself—a world of mixed-color reality—and one which is denied *her*—the world of total blackness/Purity, a dream world which can only exist in her desperate mind—Esther finds nothing. She is left in Limbo, with not even a Hell in sight. If Toomer felt this despair himself, small wonder he denied part of himself in order to salvage something of himself.

If this were all that was working in "Esther," Toomer would have done well by his readers: yet, beneath the individual seeking consciousness of Esther lies a racial search that has also been dominant in the thematic structure of Afro-American literature: the search of the American Negro for his link with Africa, the cultural mother from which he was torn centuries ago. In the Harlem Renaissance this theme was particularly strong, in life as well as in the arts. Garvey's Back to Africa movement could not have existed if the urge to know the past had not been present in the black community. The answer to whether or not the American Negro still had a viable link with Africa was constantly sought in the literature of the time. Langston Hughes's "The Negro Speaks of Rivers," as others of his works, speaks of a continuing chain of black identity, while Countee Cullen's "Heritage" expresses an ambivalent reaction. Cullen sees his blackness and Africa's as from a common source, but he also realizes his changed nature after centuries of Westernized culture and religion have been bred into him.

In "Esther" Toomer appears to agree more with Cullen than with Hughes. That Barlo can be taken to represent Africa is easily observable both in Barlo's vision and in the people's vision of him: "To the people he assumes the outlines of his visioned African" (39). His mystery and blackness are, for Esther, the "almost-white" product of generations of racial-cultural mixing, a force that she can only dream about, not confront. On this level of meaning, the analysis works very much as it does for the level discussed above, except that Esther now represents the American Negro, and Barlo becomes Africa. In rejecting the earthy primitiveness of Barlo, then, Esther, as the American Negro, is rejecting the strange, lost world that is Africa.

Does this mean that Toomer saw the American Negro as the hopeless victim of circumstance, caught in limbo, without a country *or* a culture? I think not. He is saying, however, that the search for an identity, when it denies reality in favor of a more attractive and less painful dream, is doomed to achieve nothing. Any man is limited by his realities; the question is whether he accepts them and works with them to mold his own identity, or whether he chooses to escape reality by chasing after false dreams. That is not to say that Africa is not part of the black American's identity. Toomer's lesson is for those who decide to seek in Africa their all when, in fact, the very nature (accident) of their birth forces upon them an other-than-African reality.

Toomer once said: "I am of no particular race, I am of the human race, a man at large in the human world, preparing for a new race."[3] Unfortunately, he lived in a society that would not allow him the dignity of being of the human race *only*; he was categorized, fought the categorization, and lost himself in an identity that was not his whole being. In "Esther" he gives warning to us all of the danger and tragedy that mark our concerns with "race" in this country. If Esther could have accepted herself as a human being, she could have lived a complete life in the world of real people; her search for blackness might have continued, but its urgency would be lessened by the knowledge that she was an entity unto herself, independent of color, race, or other ties. She could have belonged and not had to face a life of emptiness and despair.

Central Conflict Between Rural Thesis and Urban Antithesis in Jean Toomer's "Avey"

BURNEY J. HOLLIS

It is generally conceded—despite the fact that Jean Toomer did not conceive of *Cane* as a novel and added the second section of the book only to appease publishers' complaints that the work was too brief[1]—that Part 2 of *Cane* shares with the other two sections of the book consistency of theme and structure, and that it carries forth, as much as the other sections, the central conflict of the novel. Much discussion has been generated to underscore Toomer's claim that the design of the novel is circular, and one of the more convincing arguments has been Bernard Bell's description of *Cane* as patterned on the Hegelian dialectic, the Freudian theory of personality, and the Gurdjieffian triad. Bell claims that Part 1 of *Cane* focuses on the slave past, the libido and the rural thesis; Part 2 on the modern world, the superego and the urban antithesis; and Part 3 on the synthesis or reconciliation of the two.[2] He fails, however, to emphasize that this central conflict, despite the particular emphasis in each individual section of *Cane*, is acted out in all three sections. This is so in Part 2 as much as in the others, even though it was not part of Toomer's original plan for the book. As Susan Blake has demonstrated in considerable detail, this central conflict is seen through the struggle of the spectatorial artist-narrator in *Cane* to comprehend and accept the chaos of life and, thereby, to achieve self-knowledge, which is manifested in a recurring war between the women and men of the novel.[3] Following Bell's schemata, the women represent the rural thesis, the slave past and the intuitive, emotional component of experience, while the men represent the modern, urban antithesis, with its emphasis on mind and logic. With multiple levels of meaning, the women symbolize the libido, the closeness to nature, the natural, instinctive, uninhibited, chaotic, animalistic, amoral side of the human and black experience, with which the superego, the warped social conscience, the striving to superimpose order upon experience (symbolized by the men) must be reconciled before the synthesis or redemptive self-knowledge can be achieved. This struggle is dramatized most vividly in the stories that explicitly explore the male-female relationship, and in none is it more apparent and conscious than in "Avey."

In some respects "Avey" is a pivotal story in *Cane*. It may be that having written "Avey" after composing the first and third parts of *Cane*, Toomer was able to synthesize and to cast in sharper relief in "Avey" the issues and ideas which are somewhat less clear in the segments composed earlier. At any rate its delineations of that central conflict and its portrait of the characters involved in the struggle for self-knowledge are more poignant than in any other part of the book.

As Blake has argued, Toomer's presentation of this central conflict, this circular journey toward self-knowledge, has a double focus. It focuses, first, on the titular heroines of the stories in which this struggle is dramatized, and second, sometimes with equal or greater importance, it focuses on the spectatorial artist, or creative persona, who narrates the tales and the men who struggle to possess these women.[4] In "Avey" Toomer's portrait of these two factions reaches a pinnacle.

The character Avey is Toomer's consummate statement about the rural thesis. Like her antecedents in the novel, Avey symbolizes the life essence, the predominance of emotion and heart over mind, of the libido over the superego. She is, according to Patricia Chase, strange yet real, indifferent, capable of both love and lust, mysterious and somewhat inaccessible to the man who would possess her.[5] Like the indolent cow to which the narrator repeatedly compares her, she is carefree and akin to animated nature. Closeness to her brings the sweet smell of clover and "a salt tang, a stale drift of sea-weed."[6] More than any of her antecedents, Avey is perfect like dusk on the eastern horizon, and it is to the likes of her that *Cane*, "the swan-song," is being sung. Toomer makes Avey singular among the women in the novel, for it is she who, in a sense, embodies the resolution of the conflicts presented. It is she who survives through acceptance and indifference, and it is she whom he apotheosizes because of her endurance. The apotheosis is suggested by her name.

The choice of the name "Avey" appears to have multiple meanings and to hold a possible key to the significance of the character. The name is strikingly similar to *ave*, a Latin word with two denotations. On one hand, *ave* means to welcome, to acclaim, or to greet with shouts, and *Cane* is, in fact, an encomium to, and an acclaim for, the rural thesis and closeness to nature that Avey and the other amoral women in the novel symbolize. Above all else this story and the novel argue for the liberation of such women from the restrictions imposed by society and praise them for retaining their beauty in spite of society's efforts to subdue or transform it. On the other hand, *ave* means farewell, or adieu, and as Toomer himself admitted, *Cane* is a swan-song. It bids adieu to the folk spirit of the rural South, which the advance of commerce and machines threatened to destroy. It is "a song of the end," says Toomer, "[to something] strangely rich and beautiful."[7] Avey, the character, is the embodiment of that strange and baffling beauty, and in the end of the story she sinks, symbolically, into a deep slumber and, for all practical purposes, fades irretrievably before the reader's eyes.

The most important aspect of the title "Avey" is its religious association with "Ave Marie" (Hail Mary), the first words in the Latin version of a prayer to the Virgin Mary used in the Roman Catholic Church. By subtle implication Avey is being compared with the Madonna. Such a comparison may seem a bit farfetched, but there are images and motifs in the story that lend support to this interpretation. Like most of Toomer's women, Avey cannot be possessed by the man who pursues her. She is somehow more spiritual than physical, and notwithstanding repeated attempts, the narrator cannot kindle her passion or possess her. In fact, there is very little physically that occurs between them, and her love for the narrator is immaculate. Avey, in her relationship with the narrator, at least, remains a creature inviolable and inviolate. Furthermore, at times her regard for the narrator seems purely maternal. She offers him an asexual love which he cannot understand. The image invoked during one of their encounters is especially significant:

> She took me in hers [arms]. And I could feel by the touch of it that it wasnt a man-to-woman love . . . She ran her fingers through my hair and kissed my forehead. I itched to break through her tenderness to passion. I wanted her to take me in her arms as I knew she had that college feller. I wanted her to love me passionately as she did him. I gave her one burning kiss. Then she laid me in her lap as if I were a child. Helpless. (30)

The image that is invoked in this passage is strikingly similar to the Pietà, where Mary mourns over the body of Christ, and the moaning that the persona hears coming from her on another occasion gives credence to the notion that this story, as well as the novel, is a *lamentation* for the "parting soul" to which Toomer alludes continually in *Cane*. It is a lament for the inability of the men and the society and the values that they symbolize to comprehend either the chaos of experience or themselves. It is the same lament that might be raised by Karintha, Esther, Carma, and Fern in stories that appear earlier in the book.

Moreover, consistent with Toomer's reversal of the traditional attitude toward the women that appear in *Cane*, he appears to be alluding to Mary Magdalene, as well as to the Virgin Mary, in the title "Avey." It is in this allusion that the central conflict of the story becomes clearest. Even on the surface, Mary Magdalene, who also mourned over the body of Christ, bears a closer resemblance to Avey, since she, according to social definition, was guilty of sin. She is the repentant and forgiven woman who, according to society's laws, should be cast out, but according to the laws of nature and nature's God, as it were, she bears neither guilt nor shame. When Avey is viewed in this context, her battle with the narrator becomes more clearly a battle between her natural, amoral, folk spirit and the efforts of society (represented by the narrator) to impose its control and its values on her. And this central struggle of the novel is acted out consummately in "Avey."

Blake argues that in *Cane*, "superficially the stories are about the women, but the real interest—the interest developed throughout the book—is in the men who labor to possess them."[8] In "Avey," this observation seems to hold true, for the reader sees little of Avey in the story. He sees her only as she is filtered through the mind and conscience of the narrator. Consequently, his attention becomes riveted upon the narrator to such an extent that the narrator becomes the central focus of the story. This shift of focus lends support to Bell's notion that Part 2 of *Cane* is the antithesis of Part 1, which focuses on the women.

In "Avey" Toomer draws a clearer portrait of the male narrator than he does of Avey. Such a focus allows him to criticize sharply the values of urban society which that narrator represents. In effect, Toomer's overall purpose in *Cane*—as he admits it to be in all of his writing—is to translate "his philosophy into an idiom comprehensible to the uninitiated."[9] The construct of the book requires not only that he convince the reader of the worth of his philosophy but also that he make a convert of its narrative voice, a voice which, in its fundamental perception, represents many of the prejudices against which his philosophy must struggle for survival.

This narrative voice, poet-narrator, or "spectatorial artist," as one critic[10] labeled him, is present throughout *Cane*. But in "Avey" his role is more crucial than in stories which appear earlier in the book. As Blake points out, in the first part of *Cane*, the spectatorial artist is an observer who maintains the distance and detachment of a reporter and an outsider. He stands aloof not only from the women but also from the men and their struggle to possess the women's elusive beauty.[11] However, in "Avey" the narrator becomes more than a spectator somewhat remote from the central conflict. He becomes the participatory artist, intimately involved in the struggle to possess and comprehend Avey. And in stepping to the forefront to participate in the struggle, he intensifies and magnifies the central conflict between the rural thesis and libido, on one hand, and the urban antithesis and superego, on the other. In addition, the conflict is further enhanced by the narrator's youth and naiveté, and "Avey" becomes essentially Toomer's portrait of the artist as a young man.

As a symbol of urban society and of the artist's impulse to create his own reality, the young raconteur is reminiscent of the unreliable narrators of many of Poe's tales of terror. Subject to romantic flights of fancy and limited in his perception, he cannot be relied upon as the sole source of truth. An analysis of him is often more revealing than an analysis of the subjects that he perceives, for it is often his shortsightedness that reveals the truth and is the object of the reader's interest. The narrator of "Avey" reflects the social censureship of and prejudice against the rural folk spirit. His attitude is at once romantic and limiting, no matter how sincere, and prevents him from achieving the redemptive self-knowledge and knowledge of Avey that he seeks. Toomer analyzes and satirizes this cultural naiveté in five episodes in which the narrator attempts to possess and comprehend the fleeting, elusive beauty and soul of Avey and of the rural thesis.

In the opening episode the narrator and several friends are seated on a street curb in front of an apartment house awaiting Avey's departure from a top-floor apartment, where she is apparently making love to a college fellow. Ned is the oldest among them, and he has just begun to wear long pants. The narrator and the others respect his maturity and "smutty wisdom" about women. Ned, Doc, and the narrator collectively voice society's judgment of Avey's amorality, which they see as immorality. Ned, whom the narrator misjudges as one who knows all there is to know about women, is fervent in his desire to possess Avey sexually:

> He dilated on the emotional needs of girls. Said they werent much different from men in that respect. And concluded with the solemn avowal: "It does em good." (77–78)

He boasts that Avey will marry him one day. Doc, on the other hand, is worried about Avey's "immorality" and wonders how she gets away with it. The collective decision of the three is that they will stone the college fellow and run him out of town.

However, the narrator's attitude toward Avey is a bit more complicated. He is convinced that Avey's activities are immoral, but he grows indignant at Ned's lustful contempt for her and finds himself mysteriously drawn to her. He says, "Just how I came to love her . . . I do not know" (76). The reader, however, does know, from Toomer's portrait, that the narrator is drawn to her mainly out of his messianic ideal, his artist's impulse to make of Avey his alter ego, a reflection of his cultural and moral values. He sees himself as her savior, her liberator, who will come to understand and control her and raise her above her immorality. He fancies Avey to be one of the young trees planted in the boxes before the apartment house:

> The young trees had not outgrown their boxes then. V Street was lined with them. When our legs grew cramped and stiff from the cold of the stone, we'd stand around a box and whittle it. I like to think now that there was a hidden purpose in the way we hacked with our knives. I like to feel that something deep in me responded to the trees, the young trees that whinnied like colts impatient to be let free . . . (76)

What the narrator-artist does not realize is that Avey is already free and that his efforts are really aimed at freeing himself from the cold stones and asphalt of the urban antithesis—at acquiring redemptive self-knowledge. He is the young, cramped tree, the impatient colt who has not yet outgrown his box. He has outgrown neither Doc's moral judgments nor Ned's "smutty wisdom" and has not come, like Avey, to accept the amoral chaos of the folk spirit. Thus, he concludes this first episode by naively picturing himself married to Avey—a dream totally inconsistent with reality. But in his moral and intellectual self-righteousness, he sees marriage to her as saving her from men like Ned and the college fellow, both of whom are motivated by lust.

In the second, very brief episode, the narrator attempts to penetrate Avey's indifference to him. Actually, she seems unaware of him and never calls him by name, but he dreams, self-deceptively, that he is breaking through her resistance to him. He tries to impress her with traditional displays of masculinity and maturity. He executes clean shots in a basketball game and fancies that she applauds louder for him than for the other players. During a drill he lowers his voice into a deep tone to call for a complicated maneuver, but she only smiles indifferently at him. These surface trappings of masculinity, then, do not give the narrator access to the soul that seems to lie buried so deeply beneath the surface of Avey.

In the third, more symbolic, episode, the first direct battle between Avey and the narrator takes place, and Toomer's portrait of the narrator's frustrated efforts at redemption become poignantly clear. In this episode the narrator and Avey embark upon an excursion to Riverview, and symbolically it is a journey toward self-knowledge. Like Langston Hughes in his poem "The Negro Speaks of Rivers," Toomer uses the river as a symbol of the black man's soul, of Avey's soul. Therefore, this journey to Riverview—to view the river—will bring the narrator face-to-face with the soul of Avey. At first, the narrator's delusions about himself as Avey's savior and teacher prevent him from reaching her. Ironically, he tries to teach her to swim, when it is he who needs to learn to swim at Riverview, and he tries to teach her to dance. He sees dancing especially as a means of drawing closer to Avey. Though dancing brings him physically closer, when he holds her tightly in his arms, she seems far, far away. Only later, in the quiet and serenity of a moon-lit river, is the narrator able to glimpse the soul of Avey, and even then that vision is not achieved without struggle.

Proximity to the soul of Avey brings with it the natural smells that Toomer associates with the folk spirit and the rural thesis: "The air was sweet like clover. And every now and then, a salt-tang, a stale drift of sea-weed" (80). The smell of clover, of course, is alluring for the impatient, restless colt and the smell of sea-weed equally so for the would-be swimmer. Therefore, the narrator, being both of these, is spurred on by this sense of closeness to his goal. Instead of yielding to this natural order, however, he attempts to gain control and impose his definitions upon it. When Avey takes him in her arms, his social conscience causes him to feel shame, for he senses that the love she offers is not the kind that would satisfy his definition. Her love is maternal rather than passionate, and he hopes to reach her through passion. He gives her a burning "kiss," but instead of returning his passion, she lays him in her lap like a child and hums a lullaby. He tries to escape from her hold but fails, then tries to disarm her with conversation (his intellect), to talk, explain, rationalize, and define experience, but she finds his efforts to control and define her irrelevant. Defeated, the narrator permits her to love him in her own way, and when he does so, the smell of clover and sea-weed becomes stronger. Temporarily, then, the rural, amoral folk spirit triumphs partially over the urban impulse to subdue it. Nevertheless, the triumph is incomplete because the narrator does not become an initiate to Toomer's philosophy, nor does he come any closer to knowledge of self or of Avey, as a result of this experience.

The fourth episode takes the narrator to a similar setting:

> The next time I came close to her was the following summer at Harpers Ferry. We were sitting on a flat projecting rock they give the name of Lover's Leap. Some one is supposed to have jumped off it. The river is about six hundred feet beneath. (81)

Once again he is brought to the bank of the river to take the apocalyptic plunge into Avey's soul. And once again he manages not to move any closer to redemptive self-knowledge. Instead, he rationalizes and fantasizes about her amorality and once again projects himself in the role of her savior, reviving his earlier noble intention of somehow liberating her tormented soul. Evening after evening the two sit at Lover's Leap holding hands; he tries to get her to talk about her life, while she remains mysterious, remote, and unreachable by him. His social consciousness makes him uneasy about her indifference to gossip and her lack of ambition about getting a job as a teacher. In other words, she is indifferent to social respectability and status—a fallen and unregenerate woman in desperate and pitiable need of salvation by him. As he hears the whistling of a train going through the valley, he fancies that its echoes resemble "iterated gasps and sobs . . . crude music from the soul of Avey" (81). He sees her as one with pent-up, aching emotions that need release. Unconsciously, he imagines himself the mechanistic force of urban society that blasted away part of the mountain at Harpers Ferry so that the train could proceed through the valley—the creative artist who must pave the way for the likes of her. Although he comes to realize that Avey is greater than the young trees boxed before the Washington apartment house, he still thinks himself capable of controlling and redefining her:

> Avey was as silent as those great trees whose tops we looked down upon. She has always been like that. At least, to me. I had the notion that if I really wanted to, I could do with her just what I pleased. Like one can strip a tree. (82)

However, because he has no success in stripping her on these occasions, his quest becomes a frustrated one, and he turns—as society does—to creating his own definitions and explanations to compensate for his failure. He describes her as lazy, sloppy, and indolent like a cow, but he has to admit that making love to the best Wisconsin girls was not equal to holding Avey's hand. The narrator's growing intransigence and irredeemable commitment to the urban ethos paves the way for the swan-song that Toomer presents in the final episode of the story.

The last episode takes place five years later, with Avey and the narrator once again in a peaceful, serene natural setting, Soldiers' Home. It is a place where the narrator goes, he thinks, when he wants "the simple beauty of another's soul," of Avey's soul. Though he feels older and comes to Avey with a modified view toward her and her folk and rural ethos, he remains essentially the unrepentant voice of urban society attempting to impose a definition upon her. He consciously suppresses the impulse to interpret her actions as indifferent and indolent because he has convinced himself that her folk spirit is the stuff that can be transformed and remolded into art, with him as the artistic recreator:

> I described her own nature and temperament. Told how they needed a larger life for their expression. How incapable Washington was of understanding that need. How it could not meet it. I pointed

> out that in lieu of proper channels, her emotions had overflowed into paths that dissipated them. I talked, beautifully I thought, about an art that would be born, an art that would open the way for women the likes of her. . . . I recited some of my own things to her. I sang, with a strange quiver in my voice, a promise-song. (86–87)

Like many white and black patrons of Afro-American folk art during the Harlem Renaissance, the narrator still has not penetrated the surface and does not understand the soul of Avey. He has come to accept only the surface reality. As he sits with Avey cradled in his arms, humming a folk tune, he wants to hear the Howard Glee Club sing "Deep River" from the roadside. He is attracted to the romantic, surface charm of such an experience, and he does not realize that the deep river for which that spiritual laments is indeed, like Avey, far, far away over Jordan. The artist's dream of remolding Avey is self-deluding. It stirs his passion and makes him want "to get up and whittle at the boxes of young trees" (87) again. However, it only lulls Avey to sleep, this time irretrievably from him. She is left lying on the grass asleep, while Washington drifts in from the sea like a gray ghost ship and the usual beauty of the dawn fades from her face. The narrator's effort at possessing Avey, at being a patron of the art into which he hoped to transform her, fails, leaving her an "orphan-woman." And the ending of this story sings more loudly than any of the others Toomer's central thesis in *Cane*:

> . . . for though the sun is setting on
> A song-lit race of slaves, it has not set;
> Though late, O soil, it is not too late yet
> To catch thy plaintive soul, leaving, soon gone,
> Leaving, to catch thy plaintive soul soon gone.
> (21)

For the most part, Part 2 of *Cane* is the antithesis of the rural folk thesis presented and emphasized in Part 1, and in "Avey" Toomer has held to that schema. Nevertheless, as is the case with most of the segments of the novel, in this story both the rural thesis and the urban antithesis are engaged in battle. In "Avey," clearly there is an emphasis on satirizing and examining the urban ethos, as represented by the male narrator, but significantly he is pitted against a female who is the culmination and epitome of the folk spirit that Toomer's women symbolize. For this reason the struggle between the two becomes one of the most intense and revealing battles in *Cane*.

The Tensions in Jean Toomer's "Theater"

GEORGE KOPF

"Theater," a short story which appears in Jean Toomer's *Cane*,[1] is the product of its author's perception of tensions and countertensions in the reality of the black experience in the United States. For Toomer, who had lived in both the South and the North both as a Negro and a white man by the time of *Cane*'s publication in 1923, a phrase like "the reality of the black experience" was a challenge which he brought to bear on all of his writing about black people. In fact, it is his effort to record the truth of the human condition for black people in America which shaped his work, and the story "Theater" in particular, into what it is.

Yet, for his interest in recording a truth, Toomer's work is not realistic. Nor do his methods resemble those prescribed by either James or Zola. His prose does not depend on complications of details, recordings of events and place. His places themselves can be as animate as his characters, even more so, and, most significantly, his thoughts and attitudes toward characters are not the product of those characters' behavior as "observed" by the artist's imagination. In other words, Toomer's characterization is not the objective product of a sequence of fictive developments within the story, but represents, instead, given values which he brings to the story.

This type of thinking in a fiction writer is far from literary realism. Yet, paradoxically, when one turns to a story like "Theater," or for that matter *Cane* as a whole, one discovers a type of realism rising to the surface of Toomer's prose despite the imagery and lyricism of the language itself.

All this has to do with Toomer's perception of the reality of the black experience. While fully worked out in *Cane*, and especially in the relationship of the book's various parts, sections and pieces of poetry and prose to one another, a significant portion of the author's vision can be found in "Theater." In this story Toomer approaches black reality not as simply what is happening to individuals (not even, as the realist might have it, representative individuals). His characters are, instead, archetypes, and his settings are archetypical. "Theater" is not only a story about Negroes; it forms a statement about a race.

Toomer's interest in the direction of the Negro race as a collective experience brings his focus around to archetypes in *Cane*. Take the book's archetypal strains as a whole, and Toomer leads one ultimately to a myth of black sexuality as a fertility power drawn from the soil and to another myth of a Negro race consciousness. These objectives naturally color the language one finds in "Theater." They account for both its poetic quality and grand proportion. When Toomer opens the story, he does not open on a mere theater, but on life:

> Life of nigger alleys, of pool rooms and restaurants and near-beer saloons soaks into the walls of Howard Theater and sets them throbbing jazz songs. Black-skinned, they dance and shout above the tick and trill of white-walled buildings. At night, they open doors to people who come in to stamp their feet and shout. At night, road-shows volley songs into the mass-heart of black people. Songs soak the walls and seep out to the nigger life of alleys and near-beer saloons, of the Poodle Dog and Black Bear cabarets. (91)

By personifying, really anthropomorphizing, elements of his setting and by using such sexually suggestive diction as the phrase "Songs soak . . . and seep out to . . . life," Toomer introduces a value, sex, into his narrative. Literally, he injects an impression of it into the story, offering the reader images of the sex value by way of a careful attention to the weight of his words. Prose deliberate in its effect as Toomer's can only be manufactured by a poet. Note the multiple tensions of color and audible shape in "dance and shout" against "tick and trill" and the phrase "Black-skinned" set against "white-walled."

But what motivates this contrast between black and white? Why the tension? The story "Theater" is set in the North, Washington, D. C., in apposition to rural Georgia, which is the setting for two-thirds of *Cane*. Although the narrative concerns black people, Toomer's Washington blacks have been urbanized, vulgarized by white capitalism. One, John, "the manager's brother" (91), sits in the theater. It is day, and he is coaching a chorus line. Everything Toomer tells us about this John respects a dualism in his character. "One half his face is orange. . . . One half his face is in shadow" (91). His body "is separate from the thoughts that pack his mind" (92). He is, in a word, man-divided. John is a twentieth-century hero in a twentieth-century predicament. While his social role calls for professionalism, his physical self is aroused by the girls who "clog the floor in rhythm" (92). He must remain apart, and for this the girls call him "dictie" (95), that is to say, stuck-up.

There is nothing new about this first level of sexual tension in "Theater," nor is the problem particularly a black one. But Toomer injects a third voice into his dialogue of appearances and realities, a voice which is central to an understanding of this theme. As John sits in his chair, willing "thoughts to rid his mind of passion" (93), Toomer records his interior monologue by way of third-person omniscience. John watches the girls and muses:

> Soon the director will herd you, my full-lipped, distant beauties, and tame you, and blunt your sharp thrusts in loosely suggestive movements appropriate to Broadway. (O dance!) Soon the audience will paint your dusk faces white, and call you beautiful. (O Dance!) Soon I . . . (O dance!) I'd like . . . (92–93)

The remainder of the story's action can be read as a quest for identification of the third voice which appears in John's monologue. But its expression "O dance!" is parenthetical. Is John conscious of these words, or does he merely feel them somewhere below the point of recognition? One knows that dancing can be a release of sexual tension, even a sexual expression, and Toomer assures us that John is aroused. "I'd like . . . ," he says. Soon his emotions focus on Dorris, a dancer. She is beautiful and apparently mulatto. Toomer pictures her as "bushy, black hair bobbing about her lemon-colored face. Her lips are curiously full and very red. Her limbs in silk purple stockings are lovely" (94). John, a man-divided, "holds off" (94). He reasons that she is "dictie, educated, stuckup; show girl. . . . Her suspicion would be stronger than her passion. It wouldn't work" (94).

Ironically, Dorris is becoming interested in John at this point. Toomer enters her thoughts into the story; they also reveal an attempt to reason with passion:

> Nothin doin? How come? Aint I as good as him? Couldnt I have got an education if I'd wanted one? Dont I know respectable folks, lots of em, in Philadelphia and New York and Chicago? Aint I had men as good as him? Better. Doctors and lawyers. Whats a manager's brother, anyhow? (95)

The significant factor in this mental outburst is not Dorris's attraction to John, which provides the story with the mechanics of an irony, but her words. Dorris thinks in terms of a class-oriented society. She envisions a world which is urban, competitive, and she sees her place in it as a combatant on a social field of play, the boundaries of which are dictated by the white establishment and its values.

As the rehearsal progresses so does John's passion as he watches Dorris. In his mind he pleads with her to dance "just a little more" (97). "Dance from yourself" (97), he asks. Dorris's thoughts, as if reaching the same plane as John's and communicating with his, respond. She dances, and as she dances she thinks. As she considers John as a lover in the following passage, note how Dorris's thoughts curve from the materialistic to the personal until finally she begins to speak from her emotional self:

> I'd get a pair of silk stockings out of it. Red silk. I got purple. Cut it, kid. You cant win him to respect you that away. He wouldnt anyway. Maybe he would. Maybe he'd love. I've heard em say that men who look like him . . . will marry if they love. O will you love me? And give me kids, and a home, and everything? (I'd like to make your nest, and honest, hon, I wouldnt run out on you.) (97–98)

If Dorris's conscious formulation of her desires read like an American dream, such a response to sexuality is not inappropriate for an urban creature who is half-black, divided, mulatto. But when Dorris's passions move away from concepts, words, and values to another side of her nature, her dream is no longer materialistic. Dorris's blackness goes deeper than concepts of value. "She forgets her tricks" (98), says Toomer. Instead, "She dances" (98).

Now the dance prompts an explosion of images suggestive of Toomer's conception of the myth at the root of the black experience. Toomer's language transfers his action to the green South as the dance outgrows the stage of the Howard Theater and becomes allied with the principle of sexuality which has pulled on John and Dorris like a third voice. As Dorris dances her limbs are "glorious songs" (98), and her singing is of canebrake loves and mangrove feastings" (98). John watches and dreams. He dreams that he takes Dorris from the stage door to a place where "the air is sweet with roasting chestnuts, sweet with bonfires of old leaves" (98–99). Leaves are underfoot, and Dorris's face "is tinted like . . . a southern canefield" (99). The summit of John's dream is an image of Dorris dancing. As he dreams, the real Dorris dances on the stage of the Howard Theater, Washington, D. C. Toomer offers a moment of synthesis, and then collapse.

The piano stops. The music halts. The rehearsal is ending. Dorris stops dancing and looks to the man she has been dancing for. "His whole face is in shadow. She seeks for her dance in it. She finds it a dead thing in the shadow which is his dream" (99). Crushed, Dorris flees the room and collapses, sobbing. The story ends.

What type of life is this a slice of? At the heart of this story is a tension between North and South as two human conditions. The materialistic blacks of the theater, whitewashed with urban values, make fairly convincing characters. While they are archetypes, they also respond to critical realism. Toomer depicts Dorris especially well; her dress and her speech seem life-like and whole. She appears to represent a character-type which Toomer observed in the North. John is less satisfying as a realistic character. His speech is less colloquial and more pompous. One questions whether a manager's brother would say, "Her whom I'd love I'd leave before she knew I was with her" (93). Additionally, Toomer does not make an effort to describe John, convincingly or otherwise. The theater itself, as a setting, is not rendered in any detail. As literary realism then, Toomer's "Theater" is not a satisfying record of sexual conflict.

Yet, there is power in this story, a great deal of it. It lies in Toomer's ability to bring an ordinary story of a theater in Washington, D.C., to terms with another story, one that cannot be explicated as a realistic narrative. Toomer does not narrate this other story; he only suggests it. It explains John's third voice and Dorris's impassioned dance. Not narrative, not even knowledge, it is a force, a presence which the characters share. Call it racial consciousness, or, better still, racial subconsciousness. It is black sexuality. Its source is a state of affinity with the rhythms of nature and the sensuous southern landscape which, Toomer believed, blacks in the U. S. shared and lost as a mutual experience. A large concept, it is in fact a mythic assumption, a concentration of experience into two principles, sexuality and mutuality. Obviously, a literary impulse on this scale cannot be expressed as ordinary experience corroborated against consensus reality, for the idea itself hinges on the fact that it is broader than any individual experience, even any representative experience. It must be totally collective. Fortunately, Toomer resorts to what he does best and culls from his language suggestive images of canebrake and mangrove, love and dance, sweet air and roasting chestnuts, or blood and flesh and "footfalls softened on the leaves" (99). The total impact of these suggestions must exceed their sum as entities, for they supply the tension on which the story operates, and the story "Theater" holds together.

"Nora" is "Calling Jesus": A Nineteenth-Century European Dilemma in an Afro-American Garb

UDO O. H. JUNG

In his latest book on Afro-American short fiction Robert Bone takes the position that black short story writers are inescapably indebted to "Western literary *forms*."[1] In this paper I shall argue that in the particular instance of Jean Toomer's sketch "Calling Jesus,"[2] the indebtedness goes somewhat beyond form and extends to content as well. To do so, it is necessary to relate how successive versions of the story evolved from each other.

In September or October 1922 Toomer received a letter from Sherwood Anderson. He was full of praise for one of Toomer's very early pieces: "I read your Nora in September *Double Dealer* and liked it more than I can say. It has a note I have been wanting to hear come from one of your race. More power to your elbow."[3] Toomer had tried to publish two other stories of his, "Karintha" and "Fern," in the New Orleans *Double Dealer*, but the editor, John McClure, had declined to do so on account of the bigotry and prejudice permeating his subscription list.[4] "Nora," however, was accepted, and one wonders what the qualities might have been that caused "Nora" to appear more palatable to the readers of the *Double Dealer*.

"Nora" is a very short sketch[5] of some twenty-six lines. In modern parlance Nora is a split personality, for her soul has been separated from her body. A whimpering, thrust-tailed (holding the tail between the legs as a gesture of submission or a sign of fear) dog, the soul follows the shell of Nora wherever she goes, pleadingly, always trying to catch up. Theoretically, Nora could find a warm spot for it, since in the author's words "she is large enough" (102). But the soul-dog is denied access, and when she comes home it is left in the vestibule, "filled with chills till morning" (102). Home for Nora is a large stone mansion in a northern city with a big outside storm door. Dogs are not allowed inside. The woman thus conforms to the etiquette of a well-to-do class of house-owners, conforms to the values of a bourgeois society, which insists on the separation of two complementary entities. Despite herself and her submission to the rules of conduct, this unnatural separation of body and soul is miraculously alleviated during the night. An unidentified someone *steals in* and *carries* the dog to where Nora sleeps "upon clean hay cut in her dreams" (102). This someone is associated with reminiscences of a pastoral[6] setting and the spiritual landscape of a fervent identification with the religious practices of the "emotional church."[7] The mention of him or her provokes an outcry of ". . . eoho Jesus . . ." and we learn that he is "soft as a cotton boll brushed against the milk-pod cheek of Christ" (102). In her dreams Nora has returned to a locality, where the hay is still "clean" and where there is "no need for vestibules" or "for swinging on iron hinges, storm doors" (103).

Nearly the same thing happens when you meet Nora in the daytime, but not until after she has "forgotten" her present surroundings. In such a situation the little dog keeps coming, and a sensitive observer literally feels "a soft thing like fur" rubbing his limbs, he hears a "scared voice, lonely, *calling*" (102) and he sees Nora's eyes "*carry*" toward the South, down home (italics added). The fragments of Nora's dreams delineate a composite picture of the vegetative and the spiritual. It is characterized by the immediate presence of the Saviour. This suffusion of all and everything by the spiritual element, which Toomer believed to be the hallmark of life in the Old South, he also declared to be the poet's foremost task. As he explained to Sherwood Anderson: "It seems to me that art in our day, other than in its purely aesthetic phase has a sort of religious function. It is a religion, a spiritualization of the immediate."[8]

Since January 20, 1880, when Ibsen's play *Ett Dukkehjem* (*A Doll's House*) was premiered in Oslo, Nora has been a classical figure of suppressed womanhood. Nora Helmer, the wife of a well-to-do lawyer, has faked a signature in order to save her ailing husband's life. Nora's main concern is to keep her husband in the dark about her financial transactions, while secretly and regularly economizing on her household money in order to repay the financial shark she obtained the loan from; for the husband prefers to look upon Nora as his little plaything, a doll, unexperienced in the ways of the world. When as a consequence of unpropitious circumstances Nora's illegal transactions come to light, the doll's house collapses. Nora discovers that she is not being loved for what she is and does. She leaves her family, shutting the door with a bang.

Admittedly, this is a simplified account of the intricate, multifaceted dramatic pattern of Ibsen's play. Even so, it is obvious that certain parallels exist.[9] The point is that both Ibsen's and Toomer's Nora are denied self-fulfillment. For Ibsen's Nora this involves emancipation from the values and constraints of a male-oriented bourgeois society with the suppressor personified by a domineering husband. Toomer's Nora suffers from an anonymous oppressor; she seems to be alone in the world, cut off from her roots and without support.

In reply to Sherwood Anderson's communication of September 1922 Toomer sent a long letter in December explaining: "Naturally, my impulse was to write you when I first received your note. But at the time I was retyping my stuff, writing three new pieces, and putting *Cane* (my book) together."[10] In the case of Nora, this implied a few typographical corrections and the substitution of the title: *Nora* became *Calling Jesus*.

The question arises as to why Toomer deleted the allusion to the European dramatist's work. The reasons are twofold: First, Toomer must have known all the while or recently become aware of the fact that he had been paraphrasing, albeit inversely, a Negro Spiritual: "Steal away to Jesus":

> My Lord, He calls me,
> He calls me by the thunder,
> The trumpet sounds within-a my soul,
> I ain't got long to stay here.[11]

The spiritual expresses the bondsmen's worldly and other-worldly longings: Freedom from slavery and a distinct death-wish. In *Calling Jesus*, written some sixty years after Emancipation and in the midst of the Great Migration northward, we note a complete change of direction and a reversal of the actor-action pattern. Just as the soulless body of Nora leads and the soul-dog follows when they walk through the streets of the big city, so Jesus is no longer calling the poor sinner, Jesus is being called; the slave no longer steals *away* to Jesus, someone is stealing *in*. And yet this someone is not Jesus.

Fortunately, we are not without clues as to the identity of this someone. A close reading of Toomer's sketch reveals that Nora's (the unnamed lady's) eyes *carry* to the South, and this is no coincidence. The author has deliberately used identical lexical units to describe the action of identical actors. When Nora, in the daytime, is closest to a dreamlike state, her eyes *carry* to the South in the same way as someone steals into her house during the night in order to *carry* her soul-dog to her "dreamfluted (cane)" bedstead. It is her former whole self who performs the reunification of body and soul. Only in her (American) dream can the wound inflicted by American society be healed.

For Toomer this is not an unusual device. The human beings depicted in his stories and poems possess an innate psychic quality which helps them to bridge distances, both temporal and spatial. Insofar as they have not been completely spoiled by the blessings of Western civilization they bring to bear this faculty on their daily problems and conjure up their African heritage: jujumen, greegree, and witch-doctors.[12]

Another reason for renaming *Nora* is that only by disengaging his solitary lady from the European model could the true impact of the Afro-American dilemma be brought into the open. Ibsen's Nora is suppressed because of her sex. Ibsen's theme is the role of women in a bourgeois society. Toomer's Nora has been alienated from her racial and cultural background. The main and only figure in *Calling Jesus* just happens to be a nameless female heroine; she could have been replaced by a male. In her namelessness, however, she stands for a whole group of people. In order to acquire this symbolic value, Nora has to be dechristenized. *Nora* was a misnomer.

Ibsen's Nora has been degraded, and so has Toomer's. However, there is a way out of the dilemma for the Norwegian dramatist's heroine. By disentangling herself from the past she can become herself again. Not so Toomer's race figure. Her humanity depends upon the possibility of reestablishing a link with the past. But her past is in a rapid process of dissolution. "As an entity, the race is losing its body, and its soul is approaching a common soul."[13]

Jean Toomer's "Box Seat": The Possibility for "Constructive Crisises"

ELIZABETH SCHULTZ

Jean Toomer's *Cane* has once again come into its own. Recognized by a handful of critics shortly after its publication in 1923 as a masterpiece, it fell into neglect until the late sixties when a flurry of articles began to appear on Toomer in general and on *Cane* in particular. Many of these discussions, noting the disparate structure of the work, focus on its thematic, imagistic, or philosophical unity.[1] Several of them also identify "Box Seat," the short story at the center of the work, as a pivotal piece in terms of *Cane*'s unity. Although the story's importance to the work as a whole has thus been acknowledged, "Box Seat" has scarcely been recognized as a piece with an integrity of its own, which in addition reinforces *Cane*'s basic intentions.[2] Whereas *Cane* as a whole exposes Toomer's concern for the artificial divisions of race and class and of body and soul which have so brutally rent twentieth-century human life, "Box Seat" seems the work's most concise and dramatic expression of Toomer's yearning for these antagonisms to be healed.

In the autobiography "Earth-Being," which Toomer composed between 1927 and 1934, he establishes the resemblance between his own character and the modern city of Chicago; both embrace "a juxtaposition of extremes." Of himself in Chicago, he writes:

> In it I am an ascetic and a lover. I am an alien; yet to no place do I so belong. I am rejected. I am accepted. I live with people in a common existence. I stand alone. I want to leave it. I want to go back. I die in it. I live in it. I suffer. I enjoy. I degenerate and am reborn. I do nothing at all and seem about to fall to pieces. I do the greatest things of my life so far.[3]

Spelling out the full nature of the extremes in himself, he continued: "I am both pessimistic and optimistic, a realist and an idealist. I am an egotist; I can be genuinely humble. I am promiscuous; I am single. I have regard for nothing; I am devoted and sincerely deeply care."[4] Although written earlier than "Earth-Being," "Box Seat" is the lyrical and dramatic expression of this "juxtaposition of extremes" in human character, not only as it is particularly exacerbated by a modern urban setting but also as it describes humankind in general. Toomer's story insists that life can be fully realized only when we are conscious of the contrasting elements in our characters and our circumstances; such realization is the only means of salvation for the urban characters in *Cane* and in "Box Seat."

To some "a juxtaposition of extremes" might imply a static condition, but Toomer does not endorse that position in either *Cane* or "Earth-Being." Assuming an almost Hegelian stance, he explains in his autobiography his belief that from the tension which occurs between extremes, resolution may evolve:

> Life, and any living organism such as human society, is a field of force, a situation of tensions of forces. In society these tensions must exist. . . . The tensions should arise from natural oppositions—force against inertia, value against valueless, the essential against the non-essential, the new against the old, reason against the irrational and stupid, will against body, feeling against the feelingless, one type of man against another type, the individual against the mass. They should eventuate in constructive crisises [*sic*], namely, in periods of especially active creation during which the culture of man is greatly advanced.[5]

In "Box Seat" Toomer seems to have anticipated his theory of tensions arising from "natural oppositions" and eventuating in "constructive crisises," for the dynamic of this story repeatedly sets up the conditions for a constructive crisis, with a thesis evoking an antithesis which in turn seeks to precipitate a synthesis of these very oppositions.

Narrative method and theme consequently seem to reinforce each other, giving "Box Seat" full organic unity.[6]

The basic conflict in "Box Seat" and in *Cane* as a whole is made apparent in the opening pages of this story. Toomer sets in jarring opposition to a dream of the creative potentialities of nature a nightmare of the restrictive probabilities of a materialistic and mechanistic social life. In his idealized view of reality, it is spring; the chestnut trees are budding and blossoming; it is obviously a time for human as well as natural rebirth. Animating the artificial urban environment, Toomer assigns masculine qualities to the streets and feminine qualities to the houses; he imagines that the houses will awaken the streets and that the streets will then woo the houses: "Houses are shy girls whose eyes shine reticently upon the dusk body of the street. Upon the gleaming limbs and asphalt torso of a dreaming nigger."[7] In this springtime vision Toomer imagines a communion between sexual opposites, psychological opposites, and class opposites.

The antithesis to this vision is immediately established in the story. Houses are no longer animated but become weight as dead as that of Rhobert's house in the second vignette in Part 2 of *Cane*, crushing the life out of its occupants. With iron gates and thick glass doors, these houses enforce the separation of people from each other and of their minds from their emotions; communication can't begin without the ringing of a doorbell. In this environment Toomer's characters are so concerned with propriety, with "fitting in," that they become bolted into their seats, each individual having a specific slot, each person locked into the mass. Movements are mechanized; like machines, people click or gyrate or ratchet. Stagnation is set against fecundity, isolation against communion, mechanization against sensuality, enclosure against space. Although the mass of humankind comes to react with violence against its own restrictions, it does so unconsciously; it produces crises, consequently, which are life-denying rather than life-giving, destructive rather than constructive. Without consciousness, "a juxtaposition of extremes" *is* merely static.

Epitomizing the natural opposition to this mechanized social world is the story's central character, Dan Moore. Critics of *Cane* who acknowledge the importance of "Box Seat" usually identify Dan with the powerful prophets of apocalypse in other parts of the work, such as Barlo in "Esther" and Lewis in "Kabnis," or with its ineffectual, alienated heroes, such as the unnamed narrator of "Avey" and Kabnis himself.[8] They do so justifiably, but Dan is not simply a prophet or an outcast. He is both. Does Dan contradict himself? Very well, then, he contradicts himself. If he represents the idealized natural world in antithesis to the mechanized social world, he also harbors oppositions in himself, for he recognizes that synthesis may emerge from the confrontation of thesis with antithesis. A foreshadowing of Toomer's description of himself in "Earth-Being," Dan both embodies and gives voice to his creator's sense of "a juxtaposition of extremes" and, because he is conscious of these extremes, of his belief of creative conflict.

We learn at the story's outset that Dan's personal history contains contradictions. He was " 'born in a canebrake,' " and therefore, like the characters in Part 1 of *Cane*, he is associated with the sweet, full life of the rural Afro-American community. As the story begins, however, he is alone: " 'a poor man out of work' " (105) in the city. Uprooted, he nevertheless remembers his roots. And because he remembers he does not suffer the disease of disassociated sensibilities as do other urbanites in *Cane*; his mind, his body, and his soul always react in relation to each other. In the vignette immediately preceding "Box Seat," Toomer describes a young woman whose soul—her spiritual and her sensual life—has atrophied as a result of her lonely, frigid life in a city house with iron-hinged storm doors; she has rejected the blossoming chestnut trees and the "niggers [who] sat on low doorsteps before tumbled shanties and sang and loved" (103), and only at night do dreams of cane return; although she has no name, Toomer gives us here an early sketch of Muriel, the woman whom Dan, out of love, attempts to save. In "Prayer," the poem which follows "Box Seat" and can be considered its epilogue, Toomer expresses his own longing to be attuned to the mysterious harmony of mind, body, and soul.[9]

In addition to his memory, Dan's principal assets are his eyes and ears; both help him to translate a material reality into a spiritual reality. With his eyes he is able to read souls in the eyes of others; he claims he "never miss[es] eyes" (125). Thus, he sees that even houses may have shining eyes. He sees that Mrs. Pribby's eyes are weakened from reading banalities in newspapers; yet their very weakness has power to control; like her house her eyes are steel, and they "gimlet" Dan. In his beloved Muriel's eyes Dan sees a lost self, a self once brimming with confidence and exuberance. In the eyes of a former slave he remembers seeing the Afro-American past—the anguish of slavery and the arrival of the industrial age, the hope of Whitman's prophetic vision for America and the promise implicit in natural changes. He looks finally into the eyes of a dwarf and sees himself and all humanity, deformed with hatred and ennobled with tenderness. If only others would look into Dan's eyes as he demands at the beginning of the story—" 'Take your hands off me, you bull-necked bears. Look into my eyes' " (105)—they would see not only Dan Moore but also their own contradictory human nature.

With his ears Dan is able to hear the rhythms of a different drummer. As he strolls down the street at the beginning of the story on his way to Muriel, he feels and hears the vibrations of spring. He hears "a forgotten song" which stirs his old passion. He also hears the call to begin a mission: "Stir the root-life of a withered people. Call them from their houses, and teach them to dream. . . . Come on, Dan Moore, come on" (104). In Mrs. Pribby's house he interprets the sound of a streetcar as a "rumble [that] comes from the earth's deep core. It is the mutter of powerful underground races" (108). In the theater to which he goes following Muriel's rejection, although the crowd only roars, he continues to hear this rumble and to imagine that others might hear it, too. He has caught the hidden beat of Langston Hughes's 1951 "Dream Boogie":

> Good morning, daddy!
> Ain't you heard
> The boogie-woogie rumble
> Of a dream deferred?
> . . . .
> Listen to it closely:
> Ain't you heard
> something underneath
> Like a—[10]

While the crowd at the theater is captivated by the cacophony of jazz and sentimental songs, of boxing match gongs and its own uproar, Dan remembers the spirituals and listens for Gabriel's trumpet. He who can articulate the signs he reads with his senses may become either prophet or artist; Dan appoints himself to the former role; Toomer chooses the latter, at least for the time being.[11] Both Toomer and his character, however, share a similar vision: black American life once had an integrity in which natural contradictions, such as those which exist between mind, body, and soul, are harmonized; salvation—a restoration of that integrity—now lies only through crises which activate the imagination to synthesize these contradictions anew.

In the first section of "Box Seat," Toomer shows Dan going through the paces of thesis, antithesis, and synthesis in terms of his personal relationship with Muriel inside the enclosed arena of the house of Mrs. Pribby, her landlady. In this section Dan shifts from an expression of love and beauty to an expression of fear and brutality, making intermittent attempts to resolve these contradictory feelings. He initially perceives a life in which people have not been mixed up, separated from each other into racial and class hierarchies, with their souls separated from their bodies. Yet, because his perception of life's creative possibilities seems denied by the reality of Muriel's behavior and circumstances, it is repeatedly transformed into an expression of violence and a desire for personal power. Thus, as the story opens, Dan, responding to the vision of spring's loveliness, feels "Girl-eyes within him widen upward to promised faces" (104) and tries eagerly to sing. But his song of love, like the spirituals, whose loss Toomer mourns in the lives of black people through *Cane*, can't be sustained. His song becomes a shrill whistle as he confronts the oppressive nature of materialistic, hierarchical twentieth-century urban life.

Dan realizes in the opening scene in the first section of the story that the residential area in which he is walking does not welcome him. The houses are fortresses, not shy girls, and he, a poor, black man, is regarded as an intruder, not a poetic dreamer. As he approaches Mrs. Pribby's thick glass door, he becomes like the narrator of Claude McKay's 1922 poem, "The White House":

> A chafing savage, down the decent street;
> And passion rends my vitals as I pass,
> Where boldly shines your shuttered door of glass,
> Oh, I must search for wisdom every hour,
> Deep in my wrathful bosom sore and raw.[12]

From dreaming and singing he catapults to envisioning himself as slashing and stealing. He fancies himself stereotypically as the "bad nigger"—"Jack the Ripper. Baboon from the zoo"—the Bigger Thomas that middle-class society fears he is. Immediately, however, he turns to denying these exaggerated self-images to describe himself as he is: " 'I'm a poor man out of work. . . . I am Dan Moore' " (105). From this straightforward assertion of self, he goes on to claim an association with Christ, " 'come to a sick world to heal it' " (106), a claim which he then attempts to validate self-righteously and self-consciously by pointing out that " 'a dope fiend' " had recently brushed against him. Such antithetical self-images may be understood in terms of Toomer's theory of the "juxtaposition of extremes"; yet, at this point in the story, Dan's vacillations seem to be confused reactions. Self-conscious rather than conscious, he fantasizes rather than exercizes his imagination. Involved in his own ego, slightly paranoid, he doesn't yet see a vision of humanity.

In the second scene in the first section of the story, Dan's feelings fluctuate more dramatically from one extreme to another, for he realizes that the girl he loves does not welcome him. Muriel has become bound by the propriety of the woman in whose house she lives, and Dan has become a stranger to her. She fits into her slot, but he can fit no slot. He is growing, and growing takes a different kind of room from that in which he has to meet Muriel in Mrs. Pribby's house. He shifts from murderous thoughts about Mrs. Pribby to a premonition of the apocalypse with a " 'new-world Christ' " walking the treacherous waters. When Muriel makes her appearance, he feels first "the pressure of the house, of the rear room, of the rows of houses"; then "he is light. He loves her"; then "he is doubly heavy" (109). In the presence of Muriel's beauty and in the repressed atmosphere of Mrs. Pribby's sitting room, Dan's rhetoric becomes saturated with urgent sexual imagery. When Muriel rejects him he again is charged with feelings of violence. His fingers and arms "are fire to melt and bars to wrench and force and pry" (113) her away; he wants to kill " 'whats weak in both of us and a whole litter of Pribbys' " (115); aware of the absurdity of his strong-man tactics, he nevertheless persists, thrusting, grabbing, demanding, until the clock strikes and Mrs. Pribby raps, until propriety and machinery reassert themselves.

In the midst of these emotional vacillations, Dan again has a moment of clarity. As earlier he had not lost sight of his simple identity, here he does not lose sight of the necessarily contradictory nature of his life; he sets forth his thoughts to Muriel, as Toomer himself might have, by way of elucidating his belief in "a juxtaposition of extremes":

> "There is no such thing as happiness. Life bends joy and pain, beauty and ugliness, in such a way that no one should isolate them. No one should want to. Perfect joy, or perfect pain, with no contrasting element to define them, would mean a monotony of con-

> sciousness, would mean death. Not happy, Muriel. Say that you have tried to make . . . [people] create. Say that you have used your own capacity for life to cradle them. To start them upward flowing." (112)

Dan's understanding of the synthesis of opposites here, however, seems to have been reached intellectually. His statements might even be considered platitudinous in reaction to the platitudes he has had from Muriel; important as they are to both Dan's and Toomer's philosophy, the statements seem abstract rationalizations of Dan's feelings, his mind having overpowered his emotions. In the second section of the story, Dan's imagination extends the basis of his understanding; it goes beyond ego and race and draws him into alliance with other misfits, giving his theoretical explanation of the synthesis of opposites a human face and character.

The second section of "Box Seat" is set in the Lincoln Theater; Toomer repeatedly identifies the theater audience as "the house," with its functions being the same as those of Mrs. Pribby's house in the first section of the story: to confine and to separate humanity into artificial categories. Having described the paralyzing effects of social pressure upon individuals, Toomer now describes these effects upon a people as a whole. In this house, ironically named for the "Great Emancipator," individual black people now become a "mass"; freed, they have become slaves again, this time to a system of false values. The conversation at the theater is completely dominated by a concern for appearances. Although one large woman may evoke the dream of spring and new life, Dan finally discovers only hostility in her eyes:

> A soil-soaked fragrance comes from her. Through the cement floor her strong roots sink down. They spread under the asphalt streets. Dreaming, the streets roll over on their bellies, and suck their glossy health from them. Her strong roots sink down and spread under the river and disappear in bloodlines that waver south. Her roots shoot down. Dan's hands follow them. Roots throb. . . . He is startled. The eyes of the woman dont belong to her. They look at him unpleasantly. (119)

Muriel is the most obvious victim of the new slavery. Made so conscious of her appearance, she keeps her coat on in order to prevent a clash of colors between her lovely dress and the draperies in her box seat; she keeps her hat on so that her thick, bobbed hair will not compromise her status as a schoolteacher. Toomer suggests, however, that she has not become altogether bolted into her brass box seat; her mind is still in flux between extremes as she thinks of Dan and of the theater: "He makes me feel queer. . . . Upsets me. I am not upset. . . . I am going to enjoy the show. Good show. . . . This damn tame thing. O Dan. Wont see Dan again. Not alone. Have Mrs. Pribby come in. She *was* in. Keep Dan out. If I love him, can I keep him out? Well then, I dont love him. Now he's out. Who is that coming in? . . . Looks like Dan" (117–18). As soon as she turns around in her seat and faces the theater audience, however, the full weight of convention falls upon her, and she resolves the anguish of contradiction and the fear of sexuality which Dan's presence arouses in her by wishing him dragged into the back alley and beaten with a whip butt—a wish nearly granted at the story's conclusion.

The program for the evening's entertainment is mixed: a jazz overture, a boxing match between dwarfs, an encore of sentimental songs. This juxtaposition of staged events suggests a parody of the "juxtaposition of extremes" which Toomer and Dan believe underscore life. In the opening of the story's second section Toomer expresses his doubt that the house could respond to the rich culture of the Afro-American past; he doubts that this audience would hear the Lord's questions or Gabriel's trumpet. This audience can only roar out its enthusiasm for a cheap thrill, substituting gratuitous emotional pleasure for the direct and total involvement which is demanded by the spirituals and gospel preaching.

The source of the gratuitous pleasure which the audience derives from the boxing match is its violence, with the brutality of the fight evoking the crowd's own latent brutality, ordinarily kept in confinement by the restrictions of society. As the dwarfs pound each other, the audience—including Muriel—pounds its box seats, and the house which had held the potential for being a shy girl is now animated as a roaring beast. Roger Rosenblatt makes clear the ironic resemblance of the dwarfs to the crowd: The fight is "akin to the battle royal in *Invisible Man*; the savagery of the dwarfs is meant to amuse an audience which already had to have reached a savage condition and level of apprehension in order to regard the dwarfs as amusing. The fact that the black audience cheers on the dwarfs perpetuates a cycle of brutality in which each group of the down-trodden seeks only to find solace or satisfaction in the humiliation of another."[13] In addition, the actions of the audience, which stand in terrifying antithesis to their concern for propriety and appearance, fully demonstrate the separation of mind from emotion. Expressions of violence which emanate from fear, such as Muriel's in thinking of Dan, or from amusement, such as the crowd's, are blind emotional reactions. Dan, too, swings from calm to violence; yet he comes to understand the extremes in himself consciously and to synthesize them imaginatively. One extreme never swings completely out of sight of the other.

Dan is as much a misfit at the theater as he was at Mrs. Pribby's. He stumbles to get into his seat, and he squirms once he is there. He is emphatically differentiated from the mass, however, largely because he is conscious. During the dwarfs' fight, he does not become part of the crowd's blind emotionalism; instead the dwarfs "pound and bruise and bleed each other, on his eyeballs" (123), and he is moved to think of alternatives to the brutality of their fight and the crowd's response. Although his thoughts run a course parallel to the fight's, in the arena of his mind he seems to be struggling toward a victory for himself and his people.

At one level during the fight, Dan's thoughts reflect the pure desire of the powerless for power. Rejected by the woman he loves and the people he loves, he wants control over them. Thus he imagines in explicitly sexual terms men horizontally poised over women, dominating "until women learn their stuff" (124). And he imagines himself tearing down the theater and appearing with a dynamo—symbol of the machine age—in one hand and a flashing black god's face—symbol of a primitive age—in the other. His image of himself as a baboon smashing into Mrs. Pribby's has become expanded to that of colossus. His visions here may be seen as defensive, as violently destructive. But they may also be seen as creative, for Dan imagines a unity of man and woman, of technological present with spiritual past. His visions are saved from being paranoiac hallucinations by the fact that on another level Dan's thoughts reflect his recognition of the marvel of his people's capacity for style, vitality, and survival and his refusal to despair in the face of the fact that his people seem to have lost this capacity. He remembers Muriel's glorious talent for dancing and the eagerness of a former slave, paralyzed in a wheelchair, to keep on dreaming of greater changes coming. Seeing into Muriel's and the old man's eyes in his mind's eye, seeing what was, Dan is able to envision what can be. His thoughts therefore become apocalyptic; if he has grandiose notions of his own prowess, he also longs for Muriel to "burn clean . . . burn clean . . . BURN CLEAN!" (123) and for the old man to become a Moses who will shout "LET MY PEOPLE GO!" (125).

The pattern of vacillation in Dan's thoughts in the theater repeats the pattern of thesis versus antithesis which his thoughts took as he stood both outside and inside Mrs. Pribby's house. But here the dimension of contradictory impulses is enlarged as he alternates between destructive and creative desires, between despair and hope, between memory of the past and dreams of the future. During the program's final event, however, Dan at last is able to synthesize these contradictions, to extend them beyond his own ego, and to make them pulsate in the present moment. He comes finally to be able to transcend the intellectualization of his former synthesis and the fantasizing of his ego to exercise his imagination. For Dan the tension caused by oppositions within himself and his individual opposition to the mass becomes constructive.

In his narrative, Toomer had reflected the dwarfs' fight on Dan's inner eye by setting up contrasting paragraphs describing first the public contest, then the private one in Dan's mind. At the fight's conclusion, however, one of the bloody dwarfs is brought forward to sing a sentimental song, and Dan's eyes are suddenly opened to his full kinship with the dwarf. The dwarf bears a bloodied rose in one hand and in the other a mirror, which he flashes at members of the audience; Dan at this moment appears on the stage of his mind bearing the dynamo and the god's face. As he imagines himself catching the world's attention with the flashing mask, his attention is caught by the dwarf's flashing mirror. He is uncomfortable, for he must realize that the dwarf's devices are his own. He must realize, too, that the philosophy of "joy and pain, beauty and ugliness," which he had tried to present to Muriel, is identical to the blood-stained rose which the dwarf is now attempting to give to her in the theater. He seems no longer self-conscious about contact with dope fiends, for like the dwarf, he knows that he, too, has been brutalized. Like the dwarf, he, too, can bristle with hate and melt with serenity. He notes the dwarf's deformed brow: From being hideous, it grows in Dan's vision to seem "profound . . . a thing of wisdom and tenderness, of suffering and beauty" (128).

The concept of synthesis which Dan expresses in the first part of "Box Seat" seems the intellectual hypothesis for the complex human reality which he finally perceives in the dwarf's face. Gazing at this face, he imagines a dialogue with the dwarf; and in italic phrases, his imagination begins translating the unspoken personal yearnings in the dwarf's eyes into a general truth about human nature:

Do not shrink. Do not be afraid of me.
Jesus
See how my eyes look at you.
the son of God
I too was made in His image.
was once—
I give you the rose. . . .
(128)

Finally he shouts out his completed thought to the theater audience: " 'JESUS WAS ONCE A LEPER!' " (129). His final vision seems to be one of personal epiphany rather than universal apocalypse. Through the power of his imagination to suspend his ego and to synthesize opposites, Dan has seen the crowd's similarity and his own similarity to the dwarf; he has seen that, if the deformed and brutalized dwarf may share divinity with Christ, so may a deformed and brutalized humanity. He has seen that the dope fiend, the dwarf, the leper, the misfits, as well as the son of God coexist in himself and in others. He is not, therefore, as he had earlier fantasized, " 'the next world-savior . . . the new-world Christ' " (108); if he has saved anyone, it has been himself.[14] Thus the conflict with the house has stretched his imagination; he sees now with Keats's "negative capability," not simply in terms of himself or even of his own race, but in terms of our common humanity. Salvation, Toomer implies through his description of Dan's experience, can only come as a result of a prophetic revelation in the consciousness of the individual.

At the conclusion of "Box Seat," Dan is once again on the street, out of the house, in contact with nature. The story has come full cycle. As Charles Scruggs has observed, Toomer, reacting to the industrialism of his age, is committed to organic form, and *Cane* itself, having been composed in organic terms, has a continuous cyclical movement.[15] The dynamic of thesis versus antithesis without synthesis does not lead to change in the story. Repeated synthesis, however, becomes the basis for a process of growth. Thus in "Box Seat," the spring which opened the story flows into summer, and Dan leaves the theater continuing to grow.

At the beginning of the story, chestnut buds and blossoms surrounded Dan; at the conclusion of the story, Toomer's continued use of flower imagery suggests the perpetuation of the natural process. Dan, on his way out of the theater, is described as being "as cool as a green stem that has just shed its flower" (129). Rather than implying that he has become sterile and impotent, as Robert Bone has suggested,[16] the image indicates that Dan has attained a maturity of vision: "Ripeness is all." Just as spring passes and flowers fade, so do the fantasies of youth; the alley to which Dan goes is filled with the smell of garbage and trash, and "in the morning, singing niggers will drive by and ring their gongs . . . Heavy with the scent of rancid flowers and with the scent of flight" (130). In contrast to the hopeful image at the beginning of the story of the "dreaming nigger" who could "stir the root-life of a withered people," and whom Toomer clearly intended to be associated with Dan, this concluding image of "singing niggers," which must also be associated with Dan, sounds an elegaic note. Like the dwarf, Dan may now sing as he was initially unable to do, but in a desolate world, he reeks of inevitable decay and struggle. Thus Toomer's final natural image in "Box Seat" blends together "joy and pain, beauty and ugliness" and fulfills the movement toward synthesis in the story.

As he later noted, Toomer may have written *Cane* as a swan song for the Negro "folk-spirit" and consciously saturated the book with sadness.[17] Yet the character of Dan Moore suggests that Toomer did not "go gentle into that good night." At the conclusion of "Box Seat," Dan, having seen the dwarf in himself and having sought to share his vision of humanity with the house, realizes that the house can only judge him as the antithesis of their restricted lives—as a lunatic. His vision has neither qualified him to be Christ nor has it made him a new man, but he is not crazy. He continues to react, and in outrage against the unseeing house, he steps on a man's toes, tweaks his nose, and punches him. The man insists on slugging it out with Dan in the back alley, and the house roars its approval. But in the story's last line, "Dan . . . keeps going on" (130). Man keeps going on. The process of thesis, antithesis, and synthesis keeps going on.

By exercising his imagination to synthesize opposites, Dan may have saved himself; with difficulty he has found "wisdom . . . deep in [his] bosom sore and raw." He does not simply react to the crowd's desire to perpetuate brutality. But walking away from the theater, he is alone, his only companionship the unknown tribe with whom Toomer associates himself on the first leaf of "Earth-Being":

> *It is our task to suffer*
> *a conscious apprenticeship*

in the stupidities
and abnormalities of mankind.[18]

Yet with the mass of humankind oblivious to either their "*stupidities and abnormalities*" or to their wondrous creative potentialities, "Box Seat," like *Cane* itself, is finally a poignant expression of Toomer's yearning for an advanced human culture to evolve from "constructive crisises."

Jean Toomer's "Bona and Paul": The Innocence and Artifice of Words

JACK M. CHRIST

Jean Toomer's *Cane* has defied analysis ever since it was first published in 1923, partly because it behaves like a mob of imagistic poems masquerading as a novel. Its significance is embedded in an intricate web of metaphors, puns, and allusions, the whole of which reverberates to a touch anywhere on its fragile surface. Some of the most important of these metaphors, puns, and allusions are biblical. The ever-present imagery of the cane echoes the name of history's first murderer: the world of *Cane* is the world of Cain—a primitive, murderous world long before the advent of any redeemer. The opening story, "Karintha," ironically echoes St. Paul's letter of love to the people of Corinth. The last story, "Kabnis," depends largely on a verbal trick: the title character's name read backwards is "Sinbak." There are dozens of other instances of wordplay in *Cane*, but the point need not be labored here: Toomer's multidimensional language expands the focus of our attention beyond the particular setting and links the fate of his characters with the timeless themes of our biblical and mythological heritage.

Of all the stories in *Cane*, I find "Bona and Paul" the most elusive. To begin with, it deals with characters who are unlike the others in *Cane*. Most of the characters here are white, of northern European extraction; Paul Johnson, the main character, is the only mulatto in *Cane* who even tries to "pass" for white; and the only legitimate black character in "Bona and Paul" is the doorman of the Crimson Gardens. Thus, while "Bona and Paul" rather clearly culminates the theme of absorption of black Americans into the philistine urban life of white northern, Jazz Age America, it also complicates our perspective on that theme. But the language of this story is even more difficult than the characters to pin down. It is so complex as to prove more baffling with every reading. The complexity of language, in fact, is a major theme of the story.

In order to establish some kind of context for closer analysis of the language of this story, we must go back to "Box Seat," the story which immediately precedes "Bona and Paul." The main character of "Box Seat," Dan Moore, sees himself as a black redeemer "come to a sick world to heal it."[1] The metaphor of rampant sickness in the world defines the larger context for "Bona and Paul"—and, by extension, for all of *Cane*. The latter story opens:

> On the school gymnasium floor, young men and women are drilling. They are going to be teachers, and go out into the world . . . thud, thud . . . and give precision to the movements of sick people who all their lives have been drilling. (134)

Several themes are immediately established. The metaphor suggests the regimentation and repression of physical, instinctive energy. The central characters—Paul Johnson, Bona Hale, Art Carlstrom, and Helen—are preparing themselves for what is commonly called "real life," and yet they are also preparing to perpetuate an artificial conception of life.

The narrative continues: "One man [Paul Johnson] is out of step. In step. The teacher glares at him. A girl in bloomers [Bona Hale] seated on a mat in the corner because she has told the director that she is sick, sees that the footfalls of the men are rhythmical and syncopated. The dance of his blue-trousered limbs thrills her" (134). Throughout this story, Bona and Paul are instinctively attracted to each other, and both exist on the fringes of this artificial, regimented life. Paul in particular is by turns in and out of step.

Bona's first thoughts about Paul establish another major theme. When she thinks "He is a candle that dances in a grove swung with pale balloons" (134), she is attempting to capture Paul in metaphor, to know him intuitively rather than analytically. She sees him in images which express her own romantic and erotic fantasies but which may have nothing to do with the real Paul Johnson. As Paul himself claims later, their knowledge of each other is "mostly a priori" (151); both related immediately, as if instinctively, to the preconceived expectations of a pretty white southern girl and a dark-skinned handsome man. Nor is this problem limited to Bona and Paul. Nobody seems really to know Paul (or anyone else, for that matter) in this story. Helen, who resents Paul's friendship with Art, but who is also perversely attracted to Paul, explains him to herself "by a piece of information which a friend of hers had given her: men like him (Paul) can fascinate. One is not responsible for fascination. Not one girl had really loved Paul; he fascinated them" (150).

Helen may presume to understand Paul in some tentative way because her vocabulary includes the word *fascination*; but that word itself is nothing more than a signpost staking out a territory which can be mapped only by metaphor, pun, or allusion. Wordplay is itself a major theme of "Bona and Paul." The relationships between words and things trouble all the characters at one point or another. All the white characters, for example, worry over the word *nigger* in relation to Paul. Art Carlstrom tries to account for Paul's eccentricity partly by playing with words: "God, he's a good straight feller, though. Only, moony. Nut. Nuttish. Nuttery. Nutmeg" (147). On the way to the Crimson Gardens, Bona is puzzled by Paul's refusal to tell her in words that he loves her. Twice she tells him that he is cold, then thinks: "Colored; cold. Wrong somewhere" (144). And when Paul remembers that Bona is a southern white girl, he thinks:

> From the South. What does that mean, precisely, except that you'll love or hate a nigger? That's a lot. What does it mean that in Chicago you'll have the courage to neither love or hate. A priori. But it would seem that you have. Queer words, arent these, for a man who wears blue pants on a gym floor in the day-time. Well, never matter. You matter. I'd like to know you whom I look at. Know, not love. Not that knowing is a greater pleasure; but that I have just found the joy of it. (148)

Throughout this story, thoughts, emotions, things and words collide, slide past each other, and rebound at odd angles. Bona, Paul, Art, and Helen are constantly talking at cross-purposes or interrupting each other's internal monologues. The passage just quoted, for example, continues for another half page or so; then Paul turns to Bona and says:

> "And you know it too, don't you, Bona?"
> "What, Paul?"
> "The truth of what I was thinking."
> "I'd like to know I know—something of you."
> "You will—before the evening's over. I promise it." (148–49)

Paul's promise, however, is never fulfilled—at least not as he intends.

As we might expect, wordplay is significant in the names of the four characters. Their names, in fact, imply the central conflicts of the story. Art Carlstrom, whose last name reduces to Scandinavian for "colorless man," represents art that is bloodless, effete, and artificial. His girlfriend, Helen, suggests the conventional, self-indulgent, sentimental heroine who might easily imagine herself as the fatal Helen of Troy. For Art and Helen, the exotic, erotic, urban, jazzy Crimsom Gardens is a symbol of primitive life, in the sense that it stimulates and provides a setting for the release of instinctive energy, an escape from the regimentation of school. Bona and Paul stand in ironic contrast with Art and Helen. Although she is also spoiled and self-indulgent, Bona Hale's first name puns with the Latin word for *good*, and her last name is a double pun on *healthy* and *hail*, as in "Hail, Mary." The link between Bona Hale and the mother of Christ is confirmed by several other women in *Cane* who represent, in complex ways, the hope for salvation through sexual creativity. Bona is an ironic reincarnation of Karintha, Becky, Carma, Fern, Esther, Avey ("Ave"), Muriel in "Box Seat," and Carrie Kate and Mame Lamkins in "Kabnis."

Paul Johnson's name conjures several more echoes. His last name foreshadows Father John and all that he represents in "Kabnis." His first name puns first on *pall*, a dark mourning cloth, and thus suggests his impact on those around him. It also alludes to St. Paul, Christianity's first great missionary and literary man. Paul Johnson is an aspiring artist, and he wishes to quicken the world with his words. His special mission seems to be to the dominant white world rather than to black Americans; he is thus unlike Toomer's other aspiring artist-redeemers Dan Moore and Ralph Kabnis. Paul Johnson ministers to the dominant culture just as St. Paul, a Jewish Christian and Roman citizen, aimed the missionary zeal of early Christianity at the pagan Roman Empire. Bona and Paul also see the Crimson Gardens as a symbol of primitive life, of escape and release; but Paul at least is dimly aware that the Gardens is not all that it seems.

The full significance of the action in the Crimson Gardens can best be understood in terms of these puns and allusions. Mary Kathryn Grant has noted that "the northern section closes with an interesting irony: the final scene is in 'The Gardens,' a title reminiscent of the Edenic myth of the South."[2] The ironic complexities of this allusion need closer attention. Chicago's Crimson Gardens is patently artificial and theatrical, like everything else in Toomer's northern stories. Paul toys with the name of the Gardens in his mind and wonders about the Gardens' true colors:

> Come where? Into life. Yes. No. Into the Crimson Gardens. A part of life. A carbon bubble. Would it look purple if he went out into the night and looked at it? (146)

The color symbolism here helps to reveal the significance of the Gardens in Paul's imagination. He associates red or crimson with the instinctive passional life of white people: Bona, for example, flushes crimson whenever Paul momentarily excites her. But that crimson turns purple at night. When black folks in Georgia are singing and making love, white folks in Chicago are listening to someone else sing and chatting in nightclubs. While Paul and Art are preparing for their night on the town, Art's face is

> a healthy pink the blue of evening tints a purple pallor. Art is happy and confident in the good looks that his mirror gave him. Bubbling over with a joy he must spend now if the night is to contain it all. His bubbles, too, are curiously tinted purple as Paul watches them. Paul, contrary to what he had thought he would be like, is cool like the dusk, and like the dusk detached. His dark face is a floating shade in evening's shadow. He sees Art curiously. Art is a purple fluid, carbon-charged, that effervesces beside him. He loves Art. But is it not queer, this pale purple facsimile of a red-blooded Norwegian friend of his? Perhaps for some reason, white skins are not supposed to live at night. Surely, enough nights would transform them fantastically, or kill them. And their red passion? Night paled that too, and made it moony. Moony. That's what Art thought of him. Bona didnt, even in the day-time. Bona, would she be pale? Impossible. Not that glow. But the conviction did not set his emotion flowing. (140–41)

Paul thinks of Art and the Crimson Gardens in identical images; red-blooded passion faded to a purple pallor and "a purple fluid, carbon-charged." The Crimson Gardens implicates all that these four characters represent and all that they desire. It is an artificial garden, a false Eden, a fragile carbon bubble, a kind of monstrous incubator in which white Americans protected from moral responsibility can nurse their own innocence over cocktails and jazz in the exotic glow of pink spotlights.

Paul half-wittingly attempts to burst this carbon-bubble, to deliver himself and at least one white American girl (aptly, a southern girl) from this artificial innocence. The full significance of his intent is revealed early in the story, as he muses about his roommate:

> He's going to Life [to the Crimson Gardens] this time. No doubt of that. Quit your kidding. Some day, dear Art, I'm going to kick the living slats out of you, and you wont know what I've done it for. And your slats will bring forth Life . . . beautiful woman. (139)

As an aspiring artist wishing to quicken the world's art, Paul alludes to God's creation of Eve from Adam's rib in Eden, as if he wishes to incarnate in art the feminine principle of creativity itself—which ultimately implies temptation and moral knowledge. And as moral knowledge led to the expulsion of Adam and Eve from Eden, so Bona and Paul must leave the artificial innocence of the Crimson Gardens.

But Paul, like virtually all of Toomer's male characters, finally fails his own dream. The world's sickness is too complex and too far gone; and Paul is too thoroughly infected to bring his own vision to life. The story ends as Bona and Paul, after a confused quarrel on the dance floor, are swept by passion and hastily decide to leave the Gardens for a tryst outside. Significantly, the door of the Gardens is guarded by the only black character in the story, a doorman in a crimson uniform who seems to leer at them as they leave. Once outside, Paul fatally acts like so many of Toomer's men: he lets the moment of instinctive passion die and returns to lecture the polite but bewildered doorman in a compulsive rationalization charged with the colors and metaphors of his own confused imagination:

> "I came back to tell you, to shake your hand, and tell you that you are wrong. That something beautiful is going to happen. That the Gardens are purple like a bed of roses would be at dusk. That I came into the Gardens, into life in the Gardens with one whom I did not know. That I danced with her, and did not know her. That I felt passion, contempt and passion for her whom I did not know. That I thought of her. That my thoughts were matches thrown into a dark

> window. And all the while the Gardens were purple like a bed of roses would be at dusk. I came back to tell you, brother, that white faces are petals of roses. That dark faces are petals of dusk. That I am going out and gather petals. That I am going out and know her whom I brought here with me to these gardens which are purple like a bed of roses would be at dusk." (152–53)

Paul shakes hands with the black doorman, as if to acknowledge his own dark intuitive, passional nature—but intuitive self-recognition does not satisfy him. He is compelled to intellectualize that self-recognition, even though it is paradoxically a recognition of nonintellectual forces. And in the process, he loses Bona Hale: "When he reached the spot where they had been standing, Bona was gone" (153). Seduced by his own need to express himself in words, he finds himself but loses her; thus, he loses himself again. Paul had desired to "know" Bona in all the implications of that biblical verb; but he is left at the end, outside the Gardens, as alone as Adam before his "slats" gave birth to Eve.

Paul's self-defeating desire to know and his failure to love must finally be considered in their larger contexts. Within *Cane*, the pattern of "Bona and Paul" is the recurring pattern of every story from "Karintha" to "Kabnis." Hopes for fulfillment or redemption are repeatedly inflated, like carbon bubbles, only to be punctured in the end. And in the even larger context defined by Toomer's agile and evocative metaphors, puns, and allusions, Paul's fate is the fate of all fallen human beings who can accept neither the mindless innocence of any artificial Eden nor the purgatory of moral knowledge, and whose dark intuitive love is sicklied by the pale cast of words.

Jean Toomer as Poet of the *Cane* Poems and of "Blue Meridian"

A Key to the Poems in *Cane*

BERNARD BELL

In the wake of the rising tide of interest in Afro-American literature and the acquisition of the Jean Toomer manuscripts by Fisk University in 1963, critics began digging into their libraries to take a closer look at *Cane* (1923)—the book that launched the Harlem Renaissance. But insofar as the poems in the book are concerned, the rediscovery of *Cane* seems to have generated more heat than light. Critics either, like Robert Bone, completely ignore them or, like Darwin Turner and Todd Lieber, fail to explore their full implications to the integrity of the thematic and structural concerns of the work.[1] This paper attempts to explicate the meaning of these poems and to outline briefly how they are interwoven into one of the most innovative novels of the twentieth century.

On one level *Cane* is a deeply religious quest—a book whose search for the truth about man, God, and America takes its nameless narrator on a circular journey of self-discovery. At the time he was writing *Cane*, Toomer was on the road to becoming an essentialist. "I am not a romanticist," he declared in his autobiography. "I am not a classicist or a realist, in the usual sense of these terms. I am an essentialist. Or, to put it in other words, I am a spiritualizer, a poetic realist."[2] Basically this means two things. First, it reveals Toomer's belief in the idea that metaphysical essences, especially the soul, really subsist and are intuitively accessible. After the publication of *Cane*, Toomer became deeply involved with the teaching of Gurdjieff, but he continued to express in writing his conviction "that in each human being there is an undying essence or soul that survives the death of the perishable body, and persists ultimately to fulfill God's purpose."[3] Second, it means that as a writer, he tried, in his own words, "to lift facts, things, happenings to the planes of rhythm, feeling, and significance . . . to clothe and give body to potentialities."[4]

Cane is an intricately structured, incantational book. Divided into three major parts, it progresses from a highly poetic to a heavily dramatic form. "Karintha," the opening sketch of Part 1, is barely five pages in length and depends on the refrains of a song for its haunting effects, while "Blood-Burning Moon," the sixteen-page concluding sketch of the same section, finds its unity and force in its narrative structure. Similarly, the striking metaphorical style of the brief first sketch in Part 2, "Seventh Street," culminates in the symbolism and dramatic internal monologue of "Bona and Paul." "Kabnis," the single sketch that comprises the whole of Part 3, is cast in the form of an allegorical play.

The structure of the book also reveals the influence of Toomer's reading in psychology and philosophy. Its three major divisions might be compared to the Freudian theory of personality, an Hegelian construct, or the Gurdjieffian triad. As I argue elsewhere,[5] Toomer anticipates the mystical theory of Gurdjieff in that he too believed that man was composed of three nearly independent forces: the intellect, emotions, and body.[6] Toomer further believed that it was imperative for man to synthesize or harmonize these apparently disparate elements. Thus, Part 1 of *Cane*, with its focus on the slave past and the libido, presents the rural thesis, while Part 2, with its emphasis on the modern world and the superego, offers the urban antithesis. Part 3 then becomes a synthesis of the earlier sections, with Kabnis representing the black writer whose difficulty in reconciling himself to the dilemma of being a black American prevents him from tapping the creative powers of his soul. Unlike the appeal to the logic of an Hegelian construct, however, Toomer attempts to overwhelm the reader with the truth of his mystical theory of life through images and symbols whose appeal is more to the senses than to the intellect.

Contrary to Turner's observation, none of the fifteen poems in Parts 1 and 2 are "exquisite only in the sharpness and suggestiveness of their imagery."[7] They are all functional, serving to elucidate or to set the stage or to provide a transition between the sketches. "Reaper" and "November Cotton Flower," for example, are companion poems to the first sketch. They reinforce the haunting appeal and religious core of "Karintha." In the first, Toomer depicts "Black reapers" and "Black horses" cutting down "weeds" and "a field rat." In addition to its emblematic representation of death as a timeless source of tension in life, this image of harvest alludes to the cyclical rhythm of Nature. "November Cotton Flower" continues to develop this pastoral image of the tension between life and death, while at the same time clarifying the relationship between Karintha and the cotton flower. Neither the "boll-weevil's coming" nor "the winter's cold" nor the scarcity of cotton nor the "drouth" prevents this delicate, ephemeral flower from blooming:

> Old folks were startled, and it soon assumed
> Significance. Superstition saw
> Something it had never seen before:
> Brown eyes that loved without a trace of fear,
> Beauty so sudden for that time of year.[8]

On the one hand, these lines reinforce the mysterious power of Karintha's beauty by comparing it to that of the cotton flower that blooms in a hostile environment; on the other, they suggest by the contrast between the reaction of the old folks to the flower and that of the men to Karintha that those who stand in awe of Nature possess not only a lust for life but a greater capacity for love.

The poems "Face" and "Cotton Song" extend the religious symbolism of "Becky." Portraying the "channeled muscles" of a woman's face as "cluster grapes of sorrow/purple in the evening sun/nearly ripe for worms" (14), "Face" draws on the traditional typology of the suffering and sacrifice of Christ. "Cotton Song" complements this image of the Crucifixion with a subtle reference to the Resurrection as black stevedores call for strength to roll a bale of cotton aboard ship. The obvious biblical analogue here is the huge boulder that was miraculously rolled away from the tomb of Christ. In the refrains "Come, brother, roll roll!" and "We aint agwine t wait until th Judgment Day" the exhortative mood of the poem reaches a crescendo.

The next two poems, "Song of the Son" and "Georgia Dusk," expand on the regional imagery and metaphysical meaning of

"Carma." The opening stanza of "Song of the Son" picks up the "sad strong song" of the singing girl in "Carma":

> Pour O pour that parting soul in song,
> O pour it in the sawdust glow of night,
> Into the velvet pine-smoke air to-night,
> And let the valley carry it along.
> And let the valley carry it along.
>
> (21)

In the plaintive cry of these lines we discover Toomer, the poet-novelist, turning to his folk heritage and slave past for spiritual inspiration:

> O land and soil, red soil and sweet-gum tree,
> So scant of grass, so profligate of pines,
> Now just before an epoch's sun declines
> Thy son, in time, I have returned to thee,
> Thy son, I have in time returned to thee.
>
> (21)

The desolation of the red soil "scant of grass" contrasts with the abundance of pines, and the decline of "an epoch's sun" points up the nostalgic return of the black artist to his roots.

The key to the irony and yoking together of disparate elements in the poem is found in the play on the word *son* in the last two lines of the stanza. The pun is a subtle allusion to the Son of God, which in the context of the rapid association of ideas in the poem, stresses the Christian paradox that in death there is life. This is particularly true of the slaves and their songs:

> O Negro slaves, dark purple ripened plums,
> Squeezed, and bursting in the pine-wood air,
> Passing, before they stripped the old tree bare
> One plum was saved for me, one seed becomes
>
> An everlasting son, a singing tree,
> Caroling softly souls of slavery,
> What they were, and what they are to me,
> Caroling softly souls of slavery.
>
> (21)

More than anything else, these lines celebrate the slave spirituals as sorrowful and joyous songs. Spirituals, Toomer seems to say, are the "one seed" of the past that enabled the slaves to transcend the grim hardships of their bondage. Moreover, since these songs embody the spirit of the many thousand gone, they, like the mythical tree of life, possess the power to arouse the eternal soul of man.

Toomer looked on his experiences as a school administrator in Georgia, the home state of his grandfather, P. B. S. Pinchback, as a return to his folk past. A lyrical expression of this feeling is found in "Georgia Dusk," which deals with the tradition of Afro-American spirituals and folk songs. In the opening two stanzas of the poem, the similarity between a southern barbecue and a Bacchanalian feast is clear:

> The sky, lazily disdaining to pursue
>   The setting sun, too indolent to hold
>   A lengthened tournament for flashing gold,
> Passively darkens for night's barbecue,
>
> A feast of moon and men and barking hounds.
>   An orgy for some genius of the South
>   With blood-hot eyes and cane-lipped scented mouth,
> Surprised in making folk-songs from soul sounds.
>
> (22)

The word that stands out in these two stanzas is *genius*. Stirred by the ritual of the feast, the first black genius of the South wove the sights and sounds of his African past and his bitter-sweet slave experience into soulful music.

The imagery of the final three stanzas of "Georgia Dusk" are equally striking in their archetypal ethnic allusions:

> Meanwhile, the men, with vestiges of pomp,
>   Race memories of king and caravan,
>   High-priests, an ostrich, and a juju-man,
> Go singing through the footpaths of the swamp.
>
> Their voices rise..the pine trees are guitars,
>   Strumming, pine-needles fall like sheets of rain..
>   Their voices rise..the chorus of the cane
> Is caroling a vesper to the stars..
>
> O singers, resinous and soft your songs
>   Above the sacred whisper of the pines,
>   Give virgin lips to cornfield concubines,
> Bring dreams of Christ to dusky cane-lipped throngs.
>
> (22–23)

Like the magical powers attributed to precolonial African rituals, the voices of the men blend with the rhythmic sounds of the New World and become mystical agents of transformation.

Two cryptic nature poems follow "Fern." "Nullo" gives an aura of wonder and mystery to the common, everyday phenomenon of "A spray of pine-needles / Dipped in western gold" falling in the quiet forest. "Rabbits knew not of their falling, / Nor did the forest catch aflame" (34). In "Evening Song" the metaphysical forces of life are represented by the image of a pastoral character "curled like the sleepy waters where the moon waves start," dreaming with her "Lips pressed against my heart" (35). In its waxing and waning the moon is the traditional symbol of the cyclical pattern of life, its changing phases influencing the cycle of fertility in humans and Nature alike.

Like the other poems in the novel, "Conversion" and "Portrait in Georgia" are closely related to the themes and imagery of the sketches they connect. "Conversion" heightens the meaning of the parable in Barlo's sermon by exposing the Christian deception of substituting "a white-faced sardonic god" for the "African Guardian of Souls." The grim image of a woman in "Portrait in Georgia" forcefully establishes the sexual link between the southern ritual of lynching and the myths of white purity and black bestiality.

In contrast to the ten poems in Part 1, there are only five in Part 2. However, they are characterized by the same dramatic tensions between either the body, emotions, and intellect or man and modern social conventions. In an extended cosmic metaphor, "Beehive" depicts man's failure to develop his intellectual and spiritual potential by associating the mechanical activity of human life with that of bees. "Storm Ending" captures the insensitivity of man to the awesome beauty of Nature, while "Her Lips are Copper Wire" focuses on the lips, the breath, and the tongue as transmitters of the electrical current of the soul. "Prayer" continues this theme with the plea: "O Spirits of whom my soul is but a little finger, / Direct it to the lid of its flesh-eye" (131). In "Harvest Song," the last of the poems, the image of a reaper overpowering the knowledge of his hunger by beating the palm of his hand against a stubble of grain communicates the delicate balance that exists between the mind, emotions, and body. Indeed, the primary focus of Part 2 is on the corruption of the mind when it is enslaved by the genteel mores of society as well as the mind when it has rid itself of that form of oppression. Properly used, mind, emotions, and body can be one. Spirituals, folk songs, jazz, and poetry are vehicles for the attainment of this end.

Finally, Part 3 is "Kabnis," the most symbolical part of the book. Its six subsections are more dramatic than poetic and bring the quest of Kabnis, the poet-narrator, full circle. His journey carried him through the Edenic garden of the South, then on to the cities of Babylon in the North, and finally back to the fertile soil of his father's father, Georgia. Throughout his odyssey Kabnis seeks to know the mystery of life, to contain within himself the beauty and the pain of his Afro-American heritage, and to capture all this in the magic of the word. However, despite his contacts with others, especially Father John, the indomitable spirit of the black American's past, and Carrie Kate, the fragile hope of the future of the race, Kabnis remains at the close of the book only "a promise of soil-soaked beauty; uprooted, thinning out. Suspended a few feet above the soil whose touch would resurrect him" (191). As for the poems in the earlier sections, they communicate the spiritual core of *Cane* and suggest the metaphysical forces necessary to bring the crass materialism of American society and the sensuality of man's nature into harmony.

"Spirit-Torsos of Exquisite Strength": The Theme of Individual Weakness vs. Collective Strength in Two of Toomer's Poems

UDO O. H. JUNG

The great majority of the people in Jean Toomer's stories and poems have one thing in common: They cannot come together in any real sense. Their encounters are of a superficial nature. All attempts to the contrary fall short of complete union. Karintha remains single, despite frequent contacts with the opposite sex; Fern *becomes* a virgin, although "men were everlastingly bringing her their bodies."[1] Kabnis and Lewis cannot be brothers, and the split in the personality of the black lady who lives in a fine Washington mansion ("Calling Jesus") can only be healed in her dreams, when the little soul-dog is permitted to come close enough to effect a reintegration of her former self. Interpersonal and intrapersonal separation and the ways and means of overcoming such isolation is Jean Toomer's theme. "Cotton Song" and "Prayer" are two fine examples—on different levels of abstractness—of how Toomer thought the problem might be solved.

COTTON SONG

Come, brother, come. Lets lift it;
Come now, hewit! roll away!

Shackles fall upon the Judgment Day
But lets not wait for it.

God's body's got a soul,
Bodies like to roll the soul,
Cant blame God if we dont roll,
Come, brother, roll, roll!

Cotton bales are the fleecy way
Weary sinner's bare feet trod,
Softly, softly to the throne of God,
"We aint agwine t wait until th Judgment Day!

Nassur; nassur;
Hump.
Eoho, eoho, roll away!
We aint agwine t wait until th Judgment Day!"

God's body's got a soul,
Bodies like to roll the soul,
Cant blame God if we dont roll,
Come, brother, roll, roll!

(15)

"Brother" is a connective by means of which a sense of communality is established between speakers of different codes right from the start. What brings them together is a common problem in the face of an unnamed object, a stumbling block in their way that can only be removed if they pool their resources. The partners seem to have an understanding as to its identity, the reader is left to guess. Not before stanza three is the object of their concern revealed to him.

Lines two and three are not only typographically at the center of stanza one. The peripheral lines in their colloquial style stand out against the proverbial sententiousness of the central couplet. Sententiousness and the problem of unravelling the rather complicated structure and discovering the true meaning of apparently unconnected utterances is at the core of this poem. The essential part of stanza two is a string of such causally unconnected statements—or so it seems. How could God possibly have a body? Can the material part of man assume leadership over its spiritual counterpart?

For by one Spirit are we all
baptized into one body, whether

we be Jews or Gentiles, whether
we be bond or free; . . . [3]

Toomer extends the semantic spread of the word *body* in the same way as the Holy Bible does. *Body* here is an abstract concept, which potentially includes all mankind. But *body* also represents the physical part of man and man-made institutions, which by their simple presence can exert pressure on and influence the way people look upon themselves and others. The material part of man and the "peculiar institutions" he creates can easily disinherit and supersede its spiritual overlord, can reverse roles and assume a leading position. The verb *like* expresses this *tendency* immanent in things.

This is exactly what had happened to the Negro inhabitants of the Deep South when Toomer came there to "catch thy [the race's] plaintive soul" (21). (The whites were beyond hope; southern history—as evidenced by the white faces Toomer saw—consisted of nothing else but the never-changing circularity of evil.) The cotton bale is Toomer's symbol of the Negro's way of life. The poet does not describe its physical outlines, but the way it was composed. How the self-image of the Negro was shaped in a process that lasted for centuries is indicated by the tense contrast ("are" . . . "trod").

"Fleecy Way" is easily discernible as a "derivation" from Milky Way. (According to an age-old myth the souls of the deceased proceed to the throne of God on the Milky Way.) Toomer is not interested in describing reality as such; he prefers to describe the way something has come about. The removal of this symbol of a modest, nonrefractory way of life is what the partners set their shoulders to. They announce their willingness to discontinue a behavioral pattern that has as its distinctive features meekness, endurance, patience.

Associations with jazz, "one of the inherent expressions of Negro life in America,"[3] are by no means accidental. On the contrary, F. L. Olmsted, who toured the antebellum South, observed a "loading gang of negroes [*sic*]" from a railroad passenger train. He reports:

> "After a few minutes I could hear one urging the rest to come to work again, and soon he stepped towards the cotton bales, saying, 'Come, bredern, come; let's go at it; come now, eoho! roll away! eeoho-eeoho-weeioho-i!!'-and the rest taking it up as before, in a few moments they all had their shoulders to a bale of cotton, and were rolling it up the embankment."[4]

This report might well have been Toomer's source. The resemblances are too great to assume that the poet heard these shouts exactly the same way during his visit to Sparta, Georgia. Compare:

TOOMER	OLMSTED
Come, brother, come.	Come, bredern, come;
Let's lift it;	let's go at it;
Come now, hewit!	Come now, eoho!
roll away!	roll away!

The change of register at the end of stanza three and the emphatic negation at the beginning of the next clearly indicate the brotherhood's intention of freeing themselves of the shackles and in the act freeing God Himself. "God is a synthetic personality of the whole people, taken from its beginning to its end."[5] Only through the collective efforts of—at least—two partners can God manifest Himself. He depends on the meaningful interaction of His congregation. Its members must destroy the web that has been spun around and which has distorted their self-image by words and maxims according to which freedom can only be had at the price of death. Shackles do fall before the judgment day if the manacled are willing to accept the challenge. For God can be reconstructed. He regains His ideal figure when the elements that constitute His body and thus partake of His divine nature turn toward each other and realize their immanent divinity, and with that a new kind of freedom. That is the "motto"; that is why stanza two is repeated.

The theme returns on a higher level of abstractedness in "Prayer."

PRAYER

My body is opaque to the soul.
Driven of the spirit, long have I sought to temper it
  unto the spirit's longing.
But my mind, too, is opaque to the soul.
A closed lid is my soul's flesh-eye.
O Spirits of whom my soul is but a little finger,
Direct it to the lid of its flesh-eye.
I am weak with much giving.
I am weak with the desire to give more.
(How strong a thing is the little finger!)
So weak that I have confused the body with the soul,

And the body with its little finger.
(How frail is the little finger.)
My voice could not carry to you did you dwell in
stars,
O Spirits of whom my soul is but a little finger . .
(131)

The speaker notices that the two extremes of his personality—body and soul—are discrete units, separated from one another by unilluminated blackness. But while the first element is clearly marked, the second lacks such preciseness. We do not know what "*the* soul" is. The language of lines one, four, and five—that is where the caesura occurs and the first part ends—is matter-of-fact. Lines two and three differ from them in that the speaker assumes a "poetical" stance. They contain the only lengthy passage of part one; the inversion of the adjective "long" and the archaic use of the preposition, as well as the tense, all contribute to the impression of continuity and a certain timelessness. These lines could have sprung directly from Alfred Tennyson's "Ulysses" ("For always roaming with a hungry heart, much have I seen and known"); the author displays what T. S. Eliot calls the "historical sense." In Eliot's words:

> The historical sense involves a perception, not only of the pastness of the past, but of its presence; the historical sense compels a man to write not merely with his own generation in his bones, but with a feeling that the whole of the literature . . . has a simultaneous existence and composes a simultaneous order.[6]

It might be worthwhile to remember that as a young man Toomer was "fascinated by the idea of self-improvement by body building"[7] and also that "temper" is "a solution containing lime or some alkaline substance serving to neutralize the acid in the raw cane-juice and clarify it." Transparency, to penetrate the material part of man and suffuse it with spiritual identity, is the aim, "the Big Light" a central concept in Toomer's later poetry. The force behind all these attempts is an unidentified entity, "the spirit," which is present in the person and there unfolds its activities.

The laconic statement of line four abruptly terminates this bit of self-indulgence. Even the logical part of man is no sure guide. As any other human being the author-speaker of this soliloquy is not autonomous. Without help from outside he will be doomed. This is summed up neatly in the closing line of part one. "Lid" is a synecdoche that stands for what his benighted physical existence is: A windowless urn. (The parts of speech may not be permuted. Only by permuting them would a superficial correspondence between "eye-lid" and "flesh-eye" be obtained.) But Toomer means what he says. Of primary importance is the identification of a part with the whole. The complement contains the elements "body" and "mind." It describes the speaker's physical existence. Notice that a careful separation is maintained between "*my* body," "*my* mind," "*my* soul's flesh-eye" and "*the* soul," "*the* spirit," "*the* spirit's longing."

Part two begins with an apostrophe of the "Spirits." The plural *-s* points to the manifold sources (one of the spirits was found to operate in the speaker) of the addressee, while the capital letter shows that it is conceived of as a single *Gestalt*. It is an aggregation of many spirits, but once its formation has been achieved, the sum total is detached from its origins and leads a life of its own, as it were.

The speaker now describes *his* soul and its relation to the "Spirits." It is part of that whole, "a little finger" in comparison with an oversized, not yet delineated Super- or Over-Soul with physical attributes. This Over-Soul is more powerful than a single soul in isolation, a little finger. It has power to direct this organ to the—after all—moveable lid in order to let the light in. By incorporating the strengths of individual souls the Over-Soul gains power and effects the illumination of its component parts. The individual becomes seeing, the opaqueness disappears.

Personal pronouns at the beginning of lines eight and nine are clear indicators of the self-centeredness formerly indulged in by the individual. (Possibly, the short, one-line utterances are reflexes of the resulting weakness.) The exclamation mark of line ten, however, directs our attention to the fact that the speaker no longer speaks to himself but addresses his remarks to an audience. The soliloquy becomes a monologue, the philosopher turns agitator. He invites his hearers to realize the potential power of their individual souls in cooperative effort. And he becomes aware of his error, which consisted in futile attemps to temper the body ("*his* body") and in the misguided effort to place a higher value on *his* soul than on the community of souls which constitute *the* body. In the light of recently acquired knowledge his preference for his own soul reveals itself as egoistic. And besides, how could a single voice cover the distance that stretches between it and the infinite, the "Spirits," were they as otherworldly as they are sometimes conceived of?

The newly won strength in the community of souls seems to enable the speaker forthwith to form longer sentences. He abdicates his egotism. The divinity of man, his share of it, constitutes itself in spiritual group interaction. It is well known that in 1931 Toomer "undertook a psychological experiment with a group of friends living in a cottage in Portage, Wisconsin."[8] Although, as Arna Bontemps reports, "not too much is known about this," we may assume that it was not only "in line with Gurdjieff aims"[9] but also with aims that Toomer had developed more or less independently before he met the Russian in New York and later on in Fontainebleau, and as they have been described here on the basis of two of his poems. "Brook Farm" and "Fruitlands" come to mind immediately, particularly so, since Emerson's concept of the Over-Soul returns on the pages of Jean Toomer's poetry. Of course, the Spiritus-Mundi concept as developed by W. B. Yeats could also be at the root of Toomer's idea of an Over-Soul. Freud has left his imprint on the work of Toomer, and the influence of C. G. Jung's psychological theories can be felt at every step.[10] Still, an authoritative biography of Toomer is missing. The importance of such a desideratum can hardly be overemphasized.

Jean Toomer's Vision: "Blue Meridian"

HARRY L. JONES

According to his own testimony, Jean Toomer was a man in whose veins flowed the blood of many nations, many races. Unfortunately, he lived in an America which did not acknowledge such an admixture and which made people subconsciously choose and declare a racial identity. Toomer seemed incapable of making such a declaration permanently; he tried both black and white but was satisfied with neither. All the while he sought a faith, if not an ideology, to unify the various strains warring in him and in America.

It was no doubt this search that led to his interest in the Quakers, in the thought of Ouspensky, and the mysticism of Georges I. Gurdjieff, the Russian founder of unitism. The number of years that Toomer spent teaching and preaching unitism seems to indicate that he found this system to be the most satisfactory solution to his own dilemma of identity. In it he found the basis to support his description of himself as a man of no particular race, at large in the human world preparing a new race. His attempt to poeticize this sentiment appears in the poem called "Blue Meridian."

"Blue Meridian" is a long poem, running some 739 lines. Fortunately, it is essentially lyrical and does not attempt to force upon the reader that much of the idea of unitism. Actually, the poem's basic message (and the fundamental principle of unitism) is philosophically quite simple: through transcending the multiplicity of particularities and individualities, one can arrive at a new oneness (unity) where all differences are reconciled. There is nothing new in this. In the West it is the starting point of one Milesian school of Greek philosophy, and, ironically, it is also the *E Pluribus Unum* of the American creed.

What is new is the poetic method Toomer uses to present his idea. The poem is a philosophical statement presented as a vision in stages. The first statement, which is presented as the first stage of the vision, later becomes a lyrical refrain and enhancement of the second stage or statement of the vision. Here is really a kind of expanded technique of incremental repetition. Toomer applies this technique so deliberately that the refrains finally outweigh the new substantive passages, so that the last 69 lines of the poem are all repetitions or whole lyric refrains.

Mystics have long known of (and psychologists have recently discovered) the effect of repetition in the chant or incantation. In "Blue Meridian" mysticism is presented through Toomer's use of three of the five traditional steps of the mystical journey from longing to union. The "meridians" are Toomer's symbols for the three steps on this journey: black meridian for longing, a stage before awakening; white meridian, birth or awakening, the mystical re-birth; and blue meridian, transcendent unity or mystical union. Whereas mystics think of these steps as part of an individual journey, Toomer thinks of them as part of a group or national journey.

The poem begins with an assertion:

> It is a new America,
> To be spiritualized by each new American.[1]

and the assertion ends with an invocation to the "Radiant Incorporal."

> O thou, Radiant Incorporal
> The I of earth and of mankind, hurl
> Down these seaboards, across this continent,
> The thousand-rayed discus of thy mind,
> And above our walking limbs unfurl
> Spirit-torsos of exquisite strength!
>
> (507)

The "Radiant Incorporal" becomes the moving force (*primum mobile*) in Toomer's scheme, moving all from black through white to blue meridian. As previously mentioned, all of these lines are repeated as chants at the poem's end.

In a poem that is so clearly the poet's *credo* and vision, one ought to look for matters autobiographical or statements beyond those found in philosophical doctrine that apply to the poet himself. It seems so obvious that the vision presented in the poem is a personal plea for acceptance, that it is safe to construe most of the *I's* in the poem as empiric rather than as *fictive personae*. That is, they refer to Toomer himself rather than to an assumed voice.

If the assumption is that the voice of the poem is empiric rather than fictive, then the poem contains elements that are highly autobiographical—settings, actions, feelings, and thoughts of Toomer himself. So when the voice says:

> I would give up my life to see inscribed
> Upon the arch of our consciousness
> These words: Understanding, Conscience,
> Ability.
> (509)

or later,

> We're all niggers now—get me?
> Black niggers, white niggers—take your choice . . .
> (509)

the voice is Toomer's.

The largest autobiographical section begins at line 485 and covers some 68 lines. It begins by mentioning the recognition bestowed on Toomer because of his achievements (possibly *Cane*), and his turning his back on comrades and accomplishments. The climax of the section is a reference to an unsuccessful love affair—

> I met a woman—
> Much that I am I owe to her,
> For she was going where I was going
> . . . .
> Except that on the way we parted.
> (512)

The effect of the affair—

> She divided us, she divided me,
> So that had I stayed or tried to follow
> I would have stopped, lost my way, lost
> myself . . .
> (512)

And the aftermath—

> Upon my phonograph are many records
> . . . .
> And some rare times
> I hear myself, the unrecorded,
> Sing the flow of I . . .
> (512)

From this approximation of the mystical dark night of the soul, the poem moves toward its end, stating again the principles of unitism and chanting the previously stated refrains. One final time Toomer inserts his own voice, saying:

> My life is given to have
> Fixed in our consciousness,
> Materialized in life without celebrity,
> This actual: wisdom empowered.
> (514)

The poem ends with a vision of the "*Blue Meridian, banded-light, / Dynamic atom-aggregate . . .*" (514) awaking upon the earth, and a final chanting of the refrain:

> O thou, Radiant Incorporal,
> The I of our universe, hurl
> Down these seaboards, across these continents,
> The thousand-rayed discus of thy mind,
> And above our waking limbs unfurl
> Spirit-torsos of exquisite strength!
> (514)

There is much more in "Blue Meridian" than is covered in this brief essay. There is a parade of immigrants bringing their contributions to the American melting pot. There is sympathetic treatment of Native Americans and use of elements of Indian culture, including the chant of the Ghost Dance. Black Americans get equal cultural representation through echoes of blues and work songs. Even the autobiographical elements are richer than presented here. Thus, "Blue Meridian" will reward any serious and careful reader, because in it all of these significant elements are expressed artistically in powerful poetic lines, both beautiful and lyrical. Toomer effectively presents his vision of a new race to incorporate all races and colors in a new land of such great promise—our own America.

Jean Toomer's "Blue Meridian": The Poet as Prophet of a New Order of Man

BERNARD W. BELL

It may come as a surprise to many of his new admirers, but Jean Toomer viewed himself as a cultural aristocrat, not a cultural nationalist. Recalling how the discovery of Goethe's *Wilhelm Meister* helped him to pull together the scattered pieces of his life, he wrote in 1918:

> I was lifted into and shown my real world. It was the world of the aristocrat—but not the social aristocrat; the aristocrat of culture, of spirit and character, of ideas, of true nobility. And for the first time in years and years I breathed the air of my land. . . . I resolved to devote myself to the making of myself such a person as I caught glimpses of in the pages of *Wilhelm Meister*. For my specialized work, I would write.[1]

More like the avant-garde of the Lost Generation than the vanguard of the Harlem Renaissance, Toomer was deeply involved in creating a synthesis of new forms and themes. In the wake of World War I he completely devoted himself to the task of learning the craft of writing. During this period he confessed to being strongly influenced by two approaches to literature. First, he was attracted to those American writers and works that used regional materials in a poetic manner, especially Walt Whitman, Robert Frost, and Sherwood Anderson.[2] Second, he was impressed by the imagists. "Their insistence on fresh vision and on the perfect clean economical line," he wrote, "was just what I had been looking for. I began feeling that I had in my hands the tools for my creation."[3] The artistic fusion in *Cane* of symbols of the black American's African and southern experience and the Afro-American tradition of music bears witness to this influence and establishes the book as a landmark in modern American literature.

Following the publication of *Cane*, Toomer, convinced by personal experience and extensive reading that "the parts of man—his mind, emotions, and body—were radically out of harmony with each other,"[4] discovered the method for unifying these three centers of being in the teachings of Georges Ivanovitch Gurdjieff, the "rascal sage." A synthesis of Western science and Eastern mysticism, Gurdjieff's system was a rigorous discipline that taught self-development and cosmic consciousness through self-awareness, sacred exercises, temple dances, and various psychic feats.[5] In 1934 Toomer began making annual retreats to the Institute for the Harmonious Development of Man, Gurdjieff's headquarters in Fontainebleau-Avon, France. He returned as a Gurdjieffian prophet to spread the gospel in Harlem—where his sessions included such talented artists as Aaron Douglass, Wallace Thurman, Harold Jackman, Nella Larsen, and Dorothy Peterson—and in Chicago. He also continued writing voluminously, but most of these writings, which repudiate racial classifications and celebrate a Gurdjieffian vision of life, were rejected by publishers.

The most significant exception is "Blue Meridian," a long Whitmanesque poem. "Blue Meridian" is the poetic zenith of Toomer's quest for identity. It represents the resolution of a long process of agonizing emotional and intellectual turmoil over the problems of race and aesthetics as viewed through the prism of his own personal crisis. Toomer began grappling with the question of race in high school and began the first draft of the poem, then entitled "The First American," in the early 1920s. Completed in 1930, a section of the poem appeared as "Brown River, Smile" the following year in *The Adelphi*. But the entire poem was not published until 1936, when it appeared in Kreymborg, Mumford, and Rosenfeld's *The New Caravan*.[6]

Toomer the poet-prophet sings exultantly of a new world order in "Blue Meridian." Neither black nor white, Eastern nor Western, the new order of man is "The blue man, the purple man"; the new people are the "race called the Americans," and the new society is America, "spiritualized by each new American." Through evolution the regenerated American is also the harmoniously developed, universal man, free of definition and classifications that restrict or confine the vitality of his being. For Toomer, as for Whitman, America was, in Whitman's exuberant words, "the greatest poem," "a teeming nation of nations," and "the race of races."

"Art," writes Toomer, "is a means of communicating high-rate vibrations," and the artist is he "who can combine opposing forms and forces in significant unity."[7] Toomer splendidly fulfills both the letter and spirit of these definitions in "Blue Meridian." As with *Cane*, the chief symbol of "Blue Meridian is implicit in its title. In the context of the poem, the meridian, which generally denotes the highest point of prosperity, splendor, and power, symbolizes the spirit of mankind. On the geographical and astronomical planes it also represents the imaginary circles which connect both geophysical poles and the circle passing through the celestial poles. Other important symbols relating to the spiritual power of the new American include the Mississippi River, a pod, a grain of wheat, a waterwheel, crocks (i.e., earthenware receptacles), and the cross. The title of the poem thus generates a series of symbols which reinforce the themes of potential wholeness, evolution, and cosmic consciousness. So intricate is the symbolic pattern that the color progression of the meridian from black to white to blue corresponds to the movement of the poem through different stages of man's historical and organic development to a higher form.

Retracing the stages of man's development and the process by which the new American was born, Toomer invokes the primeval forces of life waiting to energize select men to a higher form of being. In the first section of the poem primal darkness is upon the face of the deep:

> Black Meridian, black light,
> Dynamic atom-aggregate,
> Lay sleeping on an inland lake.[8]

In order to elevate himself man must let the "Big Light" in to awaken his dormant potential. Neither Christian nor mystical in the traditional sense, the genesis is an eclectic yet harmonious blend of Darwinian evolution and Gurdjieffian mysticism. The poet invokes the "Radiant Incorporal / The I of earth and of mankind" to crash through confining barriers, across the continent and spiral on into the cosmos:

Beyond plants are animals,
Beyond animals is man,
Beyond man is the universe.
(633)

At this stage the Mississippi River, sister of the Ganges and main artery of the Western World, has the potential for becoming a sacred river, a potential which is realized in the White Meridian section of the poem. Similarly, each form that appears in the first section, the Black Meridian stage, contains the seed for its future growth. For since Adam, man has been in a state of becoming, ready to unite parts and reconcile opposites into a moving whole of total body and soul:

Men of the East, men of the West
Men in life, men in death,
Americans and all countrymen—
Growth is by admixture from less to more,
Preserving the great granary intact,
Through cycles of death and life,
Each stage a pod,
Perpetuating and perfecting
An essence identical in all,
Obeying the same laws, unto the same goal,
The far-distant objective,
By ways both down and up,
Down years ago, now struggling up.
(633)

The poet is firm in the conviction that the capacity for growth is common to all men and has always been present in America. Past generations, however, have not fully realized their human potential and, by extension, the promise of the nation and the universe.

Toomer's purpose, then, is not the glorification of the common man but the celebration of "A million million men, or twelve men," the result of a long process of natural selection and self-realization. Elitist in nature, Toomer's view of modern man in "Blue Meridian" is essentially Gurdjieffian. Comparing man to an acorn, Gurdjieff says:

> Nature make many acorns, but possibility to become tree exist for only few acorns. Same with man—many men born, but only few grow. People think this waste, think Nature waste. Not so. Rest become fertilizer, go back into earth and create possibility for more acorns, more men, once in while more tree—more real man. Nature

> always give—but only give possibility. To become real oak, or real man, must make effort.[9]

For both Gurdjieff and Toomer, the real man, the new man, must manifest understanding, conscience, and ability. Defective men—those who lack or fail to acquire these three attributes—become the fertilizer for perpetuating the promise of eternally awake souls.

Included among the defectives in "Blue Meridian" are old gods and old races. The old gods, "led by an inverted Christ / A shaved Moses, a blanched Lemur, / And a moulting Thunderbird," have failed to transform the soul of man. All that remains of their existence is "Their dust and seed falling down / To fertilize the seven regions of America." The waves of old people have similarly failed. The European races, "displaced by machines" and "Baptized in finance," could not rise above materialism: the African races—moaning "O Lord, Lord, / This bale will break me— / But we must keep the watermelon"—were weighted down by racism and a negative self-image; and the red race, whose organic relationship with Nature was ruptured when its members were "serpentined" into reservations and towns, was annihilated by an alien culture. These were the early inhabitants of the New World, great races of nondescript persons waiting to be fused into the first Americans:

> Drawing, in waves of inhabitation,
> All the peoples of the earth,
> Later to weed out, organize, assimilate,
> Gathered by the snatch of accident,
> Selected with the speed of fate,
> The alien and the belonging,
> All belonging now,
> Not yet made one and aged.
>
> (637)

The creation of the new man is a long evolutionary process engineered by Nature. This is the myth of America as told by a twentieth-century Gurdjieff poet-priest.

In the past America did not fulfill its promise because each American did not lift himself "to matter uniquely man." Out of a past blind to the transcendent value of understanding, conscience, and ability—words the poet would give his life "to see inscribed / Upon the arch of our consciousness"—comes the hell of the depression. The vital material and spiritual forces of mankind have gone wrong:

An airplane, with broken wing,
In a tail spin,
Descends with terrifying speed—
"Don't put me on the spot!"—
From beings to nothings,
From human beings to grotesques,
From men and women to manikins,
From forms and chaoses—
Crash!
(640)

The eagle, majestic symbol of American extremes of production and destruction, has degenerated into a one-wing plane of death. And the heroic daring of a Lindbergh—"Flight symbol of the alone to the Alone"—is displaced in newspaper headlines by the unheroic exploits of Al Capone. Because man is responsible for his own downfall and spiritual blight, he must follow the poet's example and assume the responsibility for his own regeneration.

In the second section of the poem Toomer lustily calls forth the new American and shows him the highway to love and "unstreaked dignity." This stage opens with a heavenly white light, as the symbol of hope and emerging consciousness:

White Meridian, white light,
Dynamic atom-aggregate,
Lay waking on an inland lake.
(642)

The poet exhorts modern man to break from a moneyed and machined death, urging him to move on to a new level of consciousness:

Walk from it,
Wake from it,
From the terrible mistake
That we who have power are less than we should be.
Join that staff whose left hand is
Demolishing defectives,
Whose right is setting up a mill
And a wheel therein, its rim of power,
Its spokes of knowledge, its hub of consciousness—
And in that same heart we will hold all life.
(643)

Breaking free from his islandized condition and fixing his sight on universal man, Toomer, like Whitman, becomes the Creator calling into being a new world order:

> Uncase the races,
> Open this pod
> Free man from this shrinkage,
> Not from the reality itself,
> But from the unbecoming and enslaving behavior
> Associated with our prejudices and preferences.
> Eliminate these—
> I am, we are, simply of the human race.
>
> Uncase the nations,
> Open this pod
> Keep the real but destroy the false:
> We are of the human nation.
>
> Uncase the regions—
> Occidental, Oriental, North, South—
> We are of Earth.
>
> Free the sexes,
> I am neither male nor female nor in-between;
> I am of sex, with male differentiations.
>
> Open the classes;
> I am, we are, simply of the human class
>
> Expand the fields—
> Those definitions which fix fractions and lose wholes—
> I am of the field of being,
> We are beings.
>
> Uncase the religions;
> I am religious.
>
> Uncase, unpod whatever impedes, until,
> Having realized pure consciousness of being,
> Sensing, feeling and understanding
> That we are beings
> Co-existing with others in an inhabited universe,
> We will be free to use rightly with reason
> Our own and other human functions.
>
> (644–45)

Unlike Whitman's bombast and the unqualified democratic strain of his America, Toomer's social imperatives and expansive mood affirm a Gurdjieffian world of beings who have realized the value of intelligence, conscience, and ability.

But were it not for his imaginative use of concrete symbols, we would surely be lost in a sea of abstractions. In this section of the poem a waterwheel becomes the agent for invigorating the soul. But first the poet acknowledges the regenerative influence of a special woman in his life, probably Margaret Naumburg:

> Much that I am I owe to her,
> For she was going where I was going,
> Except that on the way we parted.
> She, individualized and beautiful,
> Remarkable beyond most,
> Followed, at one turn, her picture of herself—
> (647)

The poet does not follow for fear he might lose himself and betray "the task of man." Instead he responds to the music of "sacred and profane extremes" and the song of himself:

> And some rare times
> I hear myself, the unrecorded,
> Sing the flow of I,
> The notes and language not of this experience,
> Sing I am,
> As the flow of I pauses,
> Then passes through my water-wheel—
> And these radiant realities, the living others,
> The people identical in being.
> (648)

After invoking the waterwheel, "its rim of power, / Its spokes of knowledge, its hub of conscience," to transform their lives, the poet and his nameless female companion experience the White Meridian:

> Sun upon clean water is the radiance of creation—
> And once, far out in the vast spread,
> Our eyes beheld a sacrament;
> Her face was marvelously bright,
> My brain was fiery with internal stars,
> I felt certain I had brought
> The gods to earth and men to heaven;
> I blessed her, drawing with the fingers
> Of my spirit the figure of the cross;

I said to her—
"All my senses will remember you as sweet,
Your essence is my wonder."
(648)

This mystical experience marks the spiritual rebirth of the poet.

The poem now approaches its final stage, the Blue Meridian, with the poet heralding the dawn of a new people, the synthesis of contrasting and conflicting forces:

A strong yes, a strong no,
With these we move and make drama,
Yet say nothing of the goal.
Black is black, white is white,
East is east, west is west,
Is truth for the brain of contrasts;
Yet here the high way of the third,
The blue man, the purple man
Foretold by ancient minds who knew,
Not the place, not the name,
But the resultant of yes and no
Struggling for birth through ages.
(651)

Earlier lines and images of the poem reappear in transfiguration, spiritualized by the regeneration of the poet, "America among Americans, / Man at large among men." While the Mississippi River fulfills its sacred potential, a fusion of Christian and Gurdjieffian symbols reflects the crowning achievement of an unbroken chain of millions of ancestors:

Mankind is a cross,
Joined as a cross irrevocably—
The solid stream sourcing in the remote past,
Ending in far off distant years,
Is the perpendicular;
The planetary wash of those now living
Forms the transverse bar . . .
(652)

For Toomer, America was the majestic base "of cathedral people," a people who were genuinely interracial and capable of cosmic consciousness. Thus, as the streams of humanity merge, as the forces of

Nature are reconciled and all divisions harmoniously resolved, the poem reaches its final stage:

> Blue Meridian, banded light,
> Dynamic atom-aggregate,
> Awakes upon the earth;
> In his left hand he holds elevated rock,
> In his right hand he holds lifted branches,
> He dances the dance of the Blue Meridian
> And dervishes with the seven regions of America.
>
> (653)

At the end of *Cane*, the apparent analog for the Black Meridian section of the poem, Toomer left us with only the promise of self-realization. In "Blue Meridian" he moved beyond race to become the Prophet of a New Order of Man known as the American. But rather than a betrayal of race for a cheap chauvinism, Toomer's poetic resolution of his private and public quest for identity represents a genuine effort to cast off all classifications that enslave human beings and inhibit the free play of intelligence and goodwill in the world.

Jean Toomer as Playwright

Design in Jean Toomer's *Balo*

MICHAEL J. KRASNY

Balo, a one-act sketch written by Jean Toomer the year before the publication of his masterpiece, *Cane*, was published in 1924 and performed by the Howard Players that same year. It was the only dramatic piece of Toomer's besides *Topsy and Eva*, a later work, to see production. Like Toomer's *Kabnis*, *Balo* is a drama of black life in Georgia; the play has psychological and racial implications. In *Balo*, Toomer is again concerned with revealing the social forces which have separated black people from their emotions. In contrast to his earlier drama, however, the crux of these forces is explicitly seen as white Christianity.

Balo takes place in rural Georgia during cane-harvesting time. Will Lee, a Negro farmer and aspiring preacher, and his sons Tom and Balo must work long and hard because it is a lean year for the crops. Toomer goes to great lengths to emphasize the fact that Will has a nest egg laid away from the more productive years that precede the time of the play and that he is a landowner. Will is thus ostensibly no different from his white neighbor Jennings, and there are many parallels between the two men. Jennings's dialect is almost indistinguishable from Will's, and the two men openly assist one another in this time of scarcity. Toomer says of the Jennings's family:

> . . . a poor white family . . . who would, but for the tradition of prejudice and coercion of a rural public opinion, be on terms of frank friendship growing out of a similarity of occupations and consequent problems. As it is, there is an understanding and bond between them little known or suspected by northern people.[1]

The irony here is that "rural public opinion" separates the races from true comradeship. It also tends to inhibit behavior. We see, for example, that Susan, Will's wife, sits stolidly in the company of Jennings and does not speak unless he directly addresses her. She has revealed herself to be an animated woman of needs that will never be fulfilled:

> There's somethin' more'n life besides all the money in th' world. I want that somethin' else; an' folks say I might could get it if I went up north. (271–72)

Friends and relatives of the Lees arrive on the scene, including blind old Uncle Ned, a sterile Tiresias figure who resembles Father John of *Kabnis*. Almost everyone hopes that a "frolic" will ensue. Sam, who accompanies Uncle Ned, takes out cards, and Will stares into the fire, tacitly giving his approval. The guests begin to play, though their enjoyment is swiftly cut off by the more somber reminders of religion evoked by Uncle Ned's entrance. In the context in which these people have come to understand Christianity, it is considered wrong to give vent to natural impulses; hence it is necessary to look to Will, the preacher, for approval. Will and the rest of the company are reminded even more of the fears they have come to associate with religion by the frenziedly devout Balo, who experiences a somnambulistic outburst of religious passion in which he begs God for mercy on his sinner's soul. The party atmosphere reemerges, only again to be stifled by Uncle Ned's homilies on the wages of sin and the necessity for rebirth. Balo soon falls into paroxysms of an even more frenzied outburst, precipitated like the previous one by a spiritual melody. As though possessed by a vision, Balo screams, "Jesus, Jesus, I've found Jesus. One mo' sinner is a-comin' home" (285). All the cardplayers file out "in sheepishness and guilt" (286) as Uncle Ned lovingly embraces the wildly sobbing Balo.

The key to this in many ways brilliant though poorly constructed dramatic sketch lies in what Jennings tells Will he observed before the action of the play:

> Saw Balo there a while back actin' like he was crazy. An' what do yer think he said? An' kept on repeatin' it. "White folks ain't no more'n niggers when they gets ter heaven." (Laughs) (277)

Despite Jennings's "bond" with the Lees, the white man cannot comprehend the seriousness of Balo's vision. The vision has indeed affected Balo's psyche; yet he recognizes the kinship shared by all men regardless of race. Balo's vitality and irrepressible response to the spirituals are both potentials for great joy and creativity. The potential has been perverted into a spiritual mania by an ambience which makes black men feel inferior and views the free and unfettered expression of joy or pleasure as sinful. Despite the fact that the Lees and the Jenningses live in apparent harmony, they still cannot have an open and unbridled friendship because of the inculcation of prejudice and stifling mores, wrought by the same white culture which has fostered the notion of sin. The desire for a joyous and communal experience is thwarted and perverted, as is the enormous reservoir of energy which Balo possesses. In this sense, *Balo*, though it is subtitled merely "A Sketch of Negro Life," is an intense dramatization both of Toomer's poem "Conversion" in *Cane* ("a white-faced sardonic god")[2] and of Father John's seemingly incoherent declaration: "O th sin th white folks 'mitted when they made th Bible lie."[3] Toomer's central concern is the forces which inhibit, pervert, and destroy innate spirituality.

Jean Toomer's Ralph Kabnis: Portrait of the Negro Artist as a Young Man

WILLIAM J. GOEDE

S. P. Fullinwider's recent attempt to solve the mystery of Jean Toomer provokes still more questions.[1] Toomer's "Second Conception" probably did mean, as he says, the birth of philosophical certitude and the death of art, but, curiously, Fullinwider's biographical discovery fails to unlock the mystery of Toomer's novel *Cane*.[2] One supposes he is right about Toomer's ambivalence toward being *Negro*, yet his ambivalence imparts the peculiar power of *Cane*. It is a misreading of the novel and simplification of Toomer's thought to say that, in the story "Kabnis," Lewis represents Toomer's hopes and Kabnis his doubts toward the race, with the novel ending in a deadlock. Rather, we see an artist working in materials over which he has total control, materials which, perhaps more profoundly than any other, express our great belief in humanity, in whatever shape and color it comes. The novel is about something else, and until we understand *Cane*, we cannot be sure that we know Toomer.

Moreover, it is a simple case of oversight to accept the decision of Ralph Ellison's Invisible Man to leave partisan politics for literature as unprecedented in writing by Negroes. "There is an implied change of role from that of a would-be politician and rabble-rouser and orator to that of writer," says Ellison,[3] and in turning away from protest writing, he only follows a course Jean Toomer took some thirty years before. We might also hastily conclude that *Invisible Man* is a kind of first attempt at a Negro *Portrait of the Artist as a Young Man*. But Negro novelists have portrayed themselves richly: along with Toomer's Ralph Kabnis, there is Claude McKay's Ray in *Home to Harlem* and *Banjo*, Langston Hughes's Sandy Rogers in *Not Without Laughter*, Countee Cullen's Negro literati in *One Way to Heaven*, Wallace Thurman's "niggerati" in *Infants of the Spring*, and Chester Himes's Jessie Robinson in *The Primitive*.

Clearly, none of these portraits equals Ellison's; only Toomer's project themselves imaginatively beyond the material. But while critics are constantly rediscovering the work, it remains obscure.[4] One of the reasons is our refusal to bring to *Cane* the kind of critical insights we train on Hemingway and Joyce. I intend briefly and generally to look at themes and technique and to concentrate specifically upon "Kabnis," because this surprising novella both offers the first portrait of a Negro writer in American literature and illustrates the problems Toomer himself faced as a Negro writer.

James Baldwin's main complaint about writing by Negroes is that, for the sake of politics, it avoids making Negro characters human:

> In most of the novels written by Negroes until today (with the exception of Chester Himes' *If He Hollers Let Him Go*) there is great space where sex ought to be; and what usually fills this space is violence.[5]

Although there is a great deal of violence in *Cane*, sex is where sex should be. The first generation of Negro writers set about to make their own characters behave, not as ciphers in a racial conflict, but as fully developed humans. (Toomer's people thrive upon their conditions.) They believe that not only were Negroes human beings but when contrasted to white Americans, more human. The characters in *Cane* are possessed of a force that struggles with the imposition of white restrictions, which are too often antilife. White society is symbolized in "Avey" by the view through the Washington dawn: "The Capitol dome looked like a gray ghost ship drifting in from sea" (88). Essentially, Negroes are crushed in white society. This theme runs throughout the stories and poems, as for example, "Beehive":

Within this black hive to-night
There swarm a million bees;
Bees passing in and out the moon,
Bees escaping out the moon,
Bees returning through the moon,
Silver bees intently buzzing,
Silver honey dripping from the swarm of bees
Earth is a waxen cell of the world comb,
And I, a drone,
Lying on my back,
Lipping honey,
getting drunk with silver honey,
Wish that I might fly out past the moon
And curl forever in some far-off farmyard flower.
(89)

Throughout the stories, roots, flowers, and natural objects are poised against heavy picture frames, vestibules, auditoriums, basements, passenger cars, and other "womb-tombs" of modern life which shackle the spirit of Negroes. In many stories, Negroes burst free, like the Invisible Man, into a resurrected life.

The first story, "Karintha," for instance, essays the indestructible beauty of life. Because her skin is like "dusk on the eastern horizon," Karintha soon becomes the sex object of all men. As a result, she bears an illegitimate child whom she buries under a pyramid of sawdust. When the pile burns, it is "so heavy you tasted it in water" (4). Now a grown woman, she is still as "perfect as dusk when the sun goes down" (5) despite the dehumanization of men.

The other girls—Dorris, Avey, and Fern—in various ways represent the same beauty. Their stories reveal the mystery of the Negro woman: a deep, natural child who, though made for love, should not be unthinkingly violated. The narrator of "Fern," for instance, passing her one day on the train, is hypnotized by her strange dark beauty and, after he meets her, walks alone with her into a canebrake:

> Her eyes, unusually weird and open, held me. Held God. He flowed in as I've seen the countryside flow in. Seen me. I must have done something—what, I dont know, in the confusion of my emotion. She sprang up. Rushed some distance from me. Fell to her knees, and began swaying, swaying. Her body was tortured with something it could not let out. Like boiling sap it flooded arms and fingers till

> she shook them as if they burned her. It found her throat, and spattered inarticulately in plaintive, convulsive sounds, mingled with calls to Christ Jesus. (32)

"Becky," on the other hand, is the story of a white girl who had two Negro sons, and whose tragedy is in terms of racial conflict but whose meaning is supremely personal. Becky is, like Hester Prynne, made to pay for the collective sense of guilt of the community: after whites and Negroes exile her, they secretely build her a house which both sustains and finally buries her. The house, on the other hand, built between the road and the railroad, confines the girl until the day when the roof falls through and kills her.

"Avey," "Box Seat," and "Kabnis," are possibly the greatest short stories of white and Negro confrontation ever written. Their strength lies in their skill at symbolizing the racial experience without sacrificing either the metaphor or Negro life.

In "Avey," Toomer's theme is similar to F. Scott Fitzgerald's in *The Great Gatsby*: the unnamed Negro writer-narrator, having been rejected by Avey as a young boy, searches for the instruments of social prestige which will restore his favor with the young girl who offers only indifference to him. Like Jay Gatz, the narrator turns in desperation to basketball, swimming, dancing, the University of Wisconsin, and the business world in order to win her affections, but to no avail. Unlike Daisy Buchanan, Avey is worthy of his quest but seems unimpressed by his deeds; conversely, the narrator, like Gatsby, has pursued phantoms in his desire to impress Avey. The narrator's pursuit of "civilization" only separates him further from her. Avey symbolizes the fertility of the Negro soul; he is, on the other hand, "unnatural" and sterile. He cannot reach her even when they are alone:

> I should have taken her in my arms the minute we were stowed in that old lifeboat. I dallied, dreaming. She took me in hers. And I could feel by the touch of it that it wasnt a man-to-woman love. (80)

He tries to gain his "birthright" and assert his manhood, but she remains curiously inaccessible, treating him as a child:

> I gave her one burning kiss. Then she laid me in her lap as if I were a child. Helpless. I got sore when she started to hum a lullaby. She wouldnt let me go. I talked. I knew damned well that I could beat her at that. (80)

But his talking only draws them further apart. The irony is that, although he believes she is cold, he fails to become human. When he returns from a five-year absence, having accumulated academic degrees and money—like Gatsby—he meets her by chance, and, lying together in the dark on the lawn of the Soldiers' Home in Washington, he tries to woo her by chanting his deeds and showing off his new intelligence:

> I traced my development from early days up to the present time, the phase in which I could understand her. I described her own nature and temperament. (86)

To understand her is to win her, and to go to a university and become a responsible worker is to offer her things she needs. The narrator is also the Negro writer and knows the Harlem Renaissance is beginning. His poetry would win her:

> Told how they needed a larger life for their expression. How incapable Washington was of understanding that need. How it could not meet it. I pointed out that in lieu of proper channels, her emotions had overflowed into paths that dissipated them. I talked, beautifully I thought, about an art that would be born, an art that would open the way for women the likes of her. I asked her to hope, and build up an inner life against the coming of that day. I recited some of my own things to her. (86–87)

The narrator has hoped college would teach him how to write and how to feel: technique and "trust" will win beauty. But as he continues to talk, he begins to note that Avey is not responding to his epic recitation which was, after all, working up a great deal of self-admiration. His Renaissance poems succeed only in putting Avey to sleep!

> An immediate and urgent passion swept over me. Then I looked at Avey. Her heavy eyes were closed. Her breathing was as faint and regular as a child's in slumber. My passion died. (87)

Sadly, he leaves her to sleep away on the grass; he drifts toward the "gray" world, his aesthetic sensibility equipped perhaps to endure that world, but without having won beauty, love, and the Negro soul.

Like the narrator of "Avey," Dan Moore, in "Box Seat," is also the Negro writer, not so much impressed with the flowering new art about to be born but with the "mission" of Negro writing. As the story begins, he calls upon Muriel, who, unlike Avey, is an inmate of civilization. He has just come up from the South, and, in an attempt to rescue her from "zoo-restrictions and keeper-taboos" performed by her landlady, Mrs. Pribby, and white men's Washington, waits for her in Pribby's living room. When she comes, he tries to take her from this tomb, but she fails to overcome her "keepers." Later, in a theater, he watches her capitulate totally to the white world and flees, like Avey's lover, into the world without having won Muriel, without having rescued the Negro soul through his "committed" art from white America.

Unlike Avey's lover, Dan Moore is not a knight-errant in search of the symbols of white power; rather, he comes from the deep South to reclaim the fallen Muriel. He has come from the soil to redeem his ghetto people:

> Look into my eyes. I am Dan Moore. I was born in a canefield. The hands of Jesus touched me. I am come to a sick world to heal it. (105–6)

A "new-world Christ," Dan is also in effect the Negro writer, for he is one of the many "invisible men" coming up from their slavery:

> That rumble comes from the earth's deep core. It is the mutter of powerful underground races. Dan has a picture of all the people rushing to put their ears against walls, to listen to it. The next world-savior is coming up that way. Coming up. A continent sinks down. The new-world Christ will need consummate skill to walk upon the waters where huge bubbles burst . . . (108)

Muriel, unlike Avey, is wavering between two worlds but has tentatively accepted Pribby. She is a librarian-teacher struggling very hard to return to her true Negro heritage. She wants to love Dan, but the ironclad Pribby world will not allow her to leave her "pen":

> Dan rises. His arms stretch towards her. His fingers and his palms, pink in the lamplight, are glowing irons. Muriel's chair is close and stiff about her. The house, the rows of houses locked about her chair. (113)

The more he pushes his suit, the more she retreats; then she runs away, and Pribby reclaims her. Because he has not been able to save her now, Dan plans to try again in the evening at the theater.

The theater is a giant iron maiden: people are robots locked into a massive machine: each is "a bolt that shoots into a slot, and is locked there" (117). With Bernice ("who is a cross between a washerwoman and a blue-blood lady" [116]) Muriel enters under Dan's searing glance to her box seat. The entertainment resembles Ellison's "Battle-Royal" scene, in which Negro midgets battle for the heavyweight crown, pounding each other so that the audience can have fun. In "Box Seat," the battle is rendered in surrealistic terms: "The dwarfs pound and bruise and bleed each other, on his eyeballs" (123). Muriel and Bernice behave like Negro schoolteachers are expected to when they are in public. The champion then offers Muriel a white, blood-specked rose, which she tries to refuse:

> Arms of the audience reach out, grab Muriel, and hold her there. Claps are steel fingers that manacle her wrists and move them forward to acceptance. (128)

When she is constrained to accept, Dan jumps to his feet and shouts: "JESUS WAS ONCE A LEPER!" (129). He is "cool as a green stem that has shed its flower" (129) as he races into the night.

Critics, except for Robert Bone, have been reluctant to work out the implications.[6] Dan Moore is the writer who maneuvers within society, disillusioned with the promises of the Pribbys, but also, in the end, blind. Dan's eyes are symbols of "vision" that exceeds sight; often the world makes him "half-blind" by its actions. The unusual number of verbs and nouns of sight are to be noted in a passage like the following: (Dan dreams of an incident in which he came to see his connection with the Negro past.)

> Dan: Strange I never really noticed him before. Been sitting there for years. Born a slave. Slavery not so long ago. He'll die in his chair. Swing low, sweet chariot. Jesus will come and roll him down the river Jordan. Oh, come along, Moses, you'll get lost; stretch out your rod and come across. LET MY PEOPLE GO! Old man. Knows everyone who passes the corners. Saw the first horse-cars. The first Oldsmobile. And he was born in slavery. I did see his eyes. Never miss eyes. But they were bloodshot and watery. It hurt to look at them. It hurts to look in most people's eyes. He saw Grant and Lincoln. He saw Walt—old man, did you see Walt Whitman? Did you see Walt Whitman! Strange force that drew me to him. And I went up to see. The woman thought I saw crazy. I told him to look into the heavens. He did, and smiled. I asked him if he knew what that

> rumbling is that comes up from the ground. Christ, what a stroke that was. And the jabbering idiots crowding around. And the crossing-cop leaving his job to come over and wheel him away . . .
>
> The house applauds. The house wants more. The dwarfs . . . (125–26)

Dan tried to free Muriel from the chains of the white civilization: his quest, unlike that of Avey's lover, is to keep the Negro soul from going white. He will destroy to rebuild: "Sometimes I think Dan Moore, that your eyes could burn clean . . . burn clean . . . BURN CLEAN!" (123). But when Muriel capitulates and accepts the venal rose, stained by convention, Dan is outmaneuvered by both white and Negro worlds. At that point, he jumps up in the theater (of life?) and shouts, "JESUS WAS ONCE A LEPER!" (129).

The meaning of Dan's tortured cry is central to the understanding of the story, and yet it is not yet clearly understood within the context of the story. On one hand, it might signify Dan's severance from Christ's "world": Christ was not—apparently—a leper. Dan sees the destruction of Negroes in Muriel's act, which is worthy only of his curse. On the other hand, as Bone suggests, Dan completes the subconscious poem that the fighter is thinking as he extends the rose to Muriel:

> Words form in the eyes of the dwarf:
> Do not shrink. Do not be afraid of me.
> *Jesus*
> See how my eyes look at you.
> *the Son of God*
> I too was made in His image.
> *was once—*
> I give you the rose.
>
> (128)

Muriel, tight in her revulsion, sees black, and daintily reaches for the offering. As her hand touches it, Dan springs up in his seat and shouts: "JESUS WAS ONCE A LEPER!"

To Dan, the Christian world of both whites and Negroes is so leprous that he goes underground to avoid his responsibilities to either race. He gives up, it seems to me, his hope to "stir the root-life of a withered people" (104). If this is so, Bone is then only partially correct in saying that Dan "is free at last of his love for Muriel—free, but at the same time sterile. . . ."[7] Dan is, like Avey's lover, a victim of race who must travel without having freed the Negro soul. This is Toomer's portrait of the Negro protest writer, so seared by his experiences that he is unable to write a novel that is not a racial tract.

Ralph Kabnis is easily the most complex character in the writing of Negroes before the Invisible Man. In him, Jean Toomer has expressed the universal anxiety of modern man, and it is precisely because he is Negro that his experiences formulate, rather than limit, distinctly and honestly the tragedy of all life. More significant is that Kabnis is also Toomer's portrait of the Negro writer, who, like the Invisible Man, is trying somehow to reduce his chaotic impressions and fears of Negro life into metaphor.

At the outset he is teaching at a Negro school in Sempter, Georgia, a graduate of a northern university and an aspiring writer. As the story opens, Kabnis is trying to read himself to sleep but the winds whisper in the cracks of his cabin, and he thinks, "Night winds in Georgia are vagrant poets, whispering." Kabnis listens to the words of the wind:

> White-man's land.
> Niggers, sing.
> Burn, bear black children
> Till poor rivers bring
> Rest, and sweet glory
> In Camp Ground.
> (157)

He fears the surrounding, huge, inexplicable world much as do the protagonists in Richard Wright's novels. He lies still, attempting to come to grips with his inability to write what he feels, to make any order out of the chaos about him:

> Ralph Kabnis is a dream. And dreams are faces with large eyes and weak chins and broad brows that get smashed by the fists of square faces. (158)

He does not seem to be able to join reality—the world as it is—to his ideals:

> The body of the world is bull-necked. A dream is a soft face that fits uncertainly upon it. . . . God, if I could develop that in words. Give what I know a bull-neck and a heaving body, all would go well with

> me, wouldnt it, sweetheart? If I could feel that I came to the South to face it. If I, the dream (not what is weak and afraid in me) could become the face of the South. How my lips would sing for it, my songs being the lips of its soul. (158)

Kabnis's crisis, like that of other Negro writers in 1923, is his inability to animate his vision; he cannot, in Kabnis's words, fit the artist's soft-faced dream to the bull-necked Negro experience. His art is unable to tame Negro life, to transcend and so to affirm its vitality.

Kabnis also feels uneasy about being a Negro and a writer, which is miscegenation between earth and God. In Toomer's symbols, the earth represents Negroes, God whites: thus, Kabnis is symbolically the tragic mulatto summed up in Langston Hughes's lines:

> My old man died in a fine big house.
> My ma died in a shack.
> I wonder where I'm gonna die
> Being neither white nor black?[8]

But God is "a profligate red-nosed man about town" and so Kabnis, as a bastard son, feels he has "a right to curse his maker" (161). Kabnis feels keenly his sense of being trapped by race. First, he prays to Christ not to torture him with the beauty of the countryside: "Dear Jesus, do not chain me to myself and set these hills and valleys, heaving with folk-songs, so close to me that I cannot reach them" (161). In other words, he asks that he be allowed to preserve what he erroneously believes to be a necessary distance between his own art and nature, the hills and valleys, Negroes, the folk-songs. Second, as he looks out over the silent pine-covered hills of Georgia, he sees the white courthouse tower and knows the "justice" which threatens his life:

> It is dull silver in the moonlight. White child that sleeps upon the top of pines. Kabnis' mind clears. He sees himself yanked beneath that tower. He sees white minds, with indolent assumption, juggle justice and a nigger . . . (163)

In between a warm, moist Negro breast of mother Georgia and the cold white justice, or injustice, of the phallic courthouse tower, Kabnis knows he must live and write.

The following day, Sunday, Kabnis visits the parlor of Fred Halsey. Looking out the window, he sees the church again and, noting the buzzards circling the scene, he listens to Halsey and Professor Layman—both of whom fit in comfortably with Georgia—expatiate upon the weird ways of white men and Negroes. Toomer, as one of the New Negroes, takes as a target not only the cruelty of whites, but also Halsey and Layman, men who observe advice to stay in their "place" and accept the old moral codes. Layman says, for instance, "Nigger's a nigger down this away, Professor. An only two dividins: good an bad. An even they aint permanent categories" (171–72). In the midst of their discussion, a rock bearing a note is tossed through the window. It reads: " 'You northern nigger, its time fer y t leave. Get along now' " (179). Believing he is the intended victim, Kabnis panics and races into the woods.

In the third section, after they find Kabnis hiding out in his own cabin, Halsey and Layman try to revive him with some "corn licker," though of course it is forbidden on school grounds. Halsey notes that the liquor might resemble the kind of art that Kabnis wants to create:

> "Th boys what made this stuff—are y listenin t me, Kabnis? th boys what made this stuff have got th art down like I heard you say youd like t be with words." (184)

At that moment Samuel Hanby enters. He is the first in a continuity of portraits of the southern school principals that culminate in The Founder in *Invisible Man*.

Whereas the city librarian and teacher often are culture heroes in writing by Negroes of the twenties, the principal is often perhaps the enemy of the people. To the Negro writer, the southern principal is often the symbol for Booker T. Washington, who in turn symbolizes everything repugnant to the life of modern Negro intellectuals. Hanby is very quickly sketched:

> He is a well-dressed, smooth, rich, black-skinned Negro who thinks there is no one quite so suave and polished as himself. To members of his own race, he affects the manners of a wealthy white planter. Or, when he is up North, he lets it be known that his ideas are those of the best New England tradition. To white men he bows, without ever completely humbling himself. Tradesmen in the town tolerate him because he spends his money with them. He delivers his words with a full consciousness of his moral superiority. (185)

His words echo the Washington tradition: when one Negro steps out of line, the race is threatened, and since Kabnis is drinking, he must leave the school. Halsey unexpectedly defends Kabnis by telling Hanby that Kabnis will be working in his wagon works. At that point

Lewis enters: he is "what a stronger Kabnis might have been, and in an odd faint way resembles him" (189). Lewis will play a larger part in the story than this introduction admits. He is the first portrait of "the race man" who, like W. E. B. Du Bois, will shake a timetable of civil rights in the face of whites.

But Lewis's character is not yet fully developed. He is mysterious: both Hanby and Halsey are attracted to him, but the Negroes in the area who threw the stone through the window to frighten him out of town are apparently being pushed by the whites who for unknown reasons dare not attack him. He is not going to be frightened out of town by whites or Negroes. "I'm on a sort of a contract with myself" (191) he says. Yet Lewis is attracted to Kabnis, who realizes his own predicament:

> In the instant of their shifting [Lewis's eyes], a vision of the life they are to meet. Kabnis, a promise of a soil-soaked beauty; uprooted, thinning out. Suspended a few feet above the soil whose touch would resurrect him. Arm's length removed from him whose will to help . . . There is a swift intuitive interchange of consciousness. Kabnis has a sudden need to rush into the arms of this man. His eyes call, "Brother." (191–92)

But, unlike Lewis, whose life is ordered because he is rooted to the soil, and whose vision is intact, Kabnis realizes the futility of his life and recognizes his own worthlessness:

> And then a savage, cynical twist-about within him mocks his impulse and strengthens him to repulse Lewis. His lips curl cruelly. His eyes laugh. They are glittering needles, stitching. (192)

The occasional obscurity and intense contraction of Toomer's images are both provocative and dissatisfying. What is it that keeps Kabnis from lifting himself into a meaningful life with Lewis? How is it that his eyes are "glittering needles" and how do they, what do they stitch? Does Toomer imply that Kabnis is blinding himself?

A month later Lewis enters Halsey's workshop and talks to Halsey, Kabnis, and Layman. His "contract" up, Lewis is returning to the North. Halsey tells Lewis that he had a talk with one of the local Negroes who thought Lewis was "a queer one"; Lewis responds in a way which can be understood only within the context of the Black Power movement:

> "I remember him. We had a talk. But what he found queer, I think, was not my opinions, but my lack of them. In half an hour he had settled everything: boll weevils, God, the World War. Weevils and wars are the pests that God sends against the sinful. People are too weak to correct themselves: the Redeemer is coming back. Get ready, ye sinners, for the advent of Our Lord. Interesting, eh, Kabnis? but not exactly what we want." (199)

What exactly Lewis wants is clear: Negroes should militantly oppose segregation. He feels Negro education, as represented by Professor Layman, could have helped him, "but the incentive to his keeping quiet is so much greater than anything I could have offered him to open up . . ." (199). When he confronts Kabnis, however, Halsey interferes: "Tell him, Lewis, for godsake tell him. I've told him. But its somethin else he wants so bad I've heard him downstairs mumbling with th old man" (200). That "somethin else" is, for the moment, unclear.

But Lewis expects no help out of Kabnis because life "has already told him more than he is capable of knowing. It has given him in excess of what he can receive. I have been offered. Stuff in his stomach curdled, and he vomited me" (200). He means that Kabnis is unable to deal with his own racial experience, and Lewis's "contract" for racial advancement "curdles" this kind of writer. Like the mules tethered to the trees behind Halsey's shop, Kabnis is "burdened with impotent pain" (205). Kabnis is unable to make anything out of his predicament, and, as a way of cursing his blackness, is forced to verbally abuse the old Negro slave in the cellar.

Halsey, on the other hand, "fits" in the South and will not march for the rights of Negroes; he says, "there aint no books whats got th feel t them of them there tools" (200–1). To give emphasis to this point, a white man, bearing a broken hatchet, enters; he gives it to Kabnis, who cannot fix it, while Halsey, with a few strokes, repairs and returns it without charge to white Ramsay, who says, "Yer daddy was a good un before y. Runs in th family, seems like t me" (202). At that moment Carrie Kate, Halsey's sister, enters with food for the old man in the cellar; she is confronted by Lewis. Instinctively, they turn toward each other—the southern masses and the new leader—but puritanism overcomes:

> He stretches forth his hands to hers. He takes them. They feel like warm cheeks against his palms. The sun-burst from her eyes floods

> up and haloes him. Christ-eyes, his eyes look to her. Fearlessly she loves into them. And then something happens. Her face blanches. Awkwardly she draws away. The sin-bogies of respectable southern colored folks clamor at her . . . (205)

Nonetheless, the party scheduled for the evening in "The Hole," a kind of farewell event for Lewis, will go on as planned.

They all meet the old man, "a bust in black walnut," whom Lewis calls Father John. Throughout the evening, the old slave silently broods upon their drinking and love making. Lewis is drawn immediately to Father John, blind and cabinned, deaf and speechless; Halsey, on the other hand, keeps remembering the oak-beam he is supposed to put on a wagon. Kabnis, however, wants to forget Lewis's past and Halsey's future: he wants to get drunk and make love:

> "What in hell's wrong with you fellers? You with your wagon. Lewis with his Father John. This aint th time fer foolin with wagons. Daytime's bad enough f that. Ere, sit down. Ere, Lewis, you too sit down. Have a drink. Thats right. Drink corn licker, love th girls, an listen t th old man mumblin sin." (214)

But the party fails. Lewis becomes preoccupied with "John the Baptist of a new religion—or a tongue-tied shadow of an old" (211); and the young man "merges with his source and lets the pain and beauty of the South meet him there" (214). Kabnis cannot enjoy himself either, and as he drinks, his feelings of anxiety and guilt drive him to the old man. He screams at him:

> "Whatsha lookin at me for? Y want t know who I am? Well, I'm Ralph Kabnis—lot of good its goin t do y. Well? Whatsha keep lookin for? I'm Ralph Kabnis. Aint that enough f y? Want th whole family history? Its none of your godam business, anyway." (216–17)

Moreover, while Lewis argues that Father John is "symbol, flesh and spirit of the past," Kabnis angrily retorts, "He aint my past. My ancestors were Southern blue-bloods—" (217). Kabnis dissociates himself from Father John's history.

After a while, overhearing Halsey and Lewis talking about him behind his back, he jumps up to confront the two men with his confession:

> "I've been shapin words after a design that branded here. Know whats here? M soul. Ever heard o that? Th hell y have. Been shapin words t fit m soul. Never told y that before, did I? Thought I couldnt

> talk. I'll tell y. I've been shapin words; ah, but sometimes theyre beautiful an golden an have a taste that makes them fine t roll over with y tongue. Your tongue aint fit f nothin but t roll an lick hog-meat." (223)

Kabnis is drunk but articulate; he continues to try to explain himself, telling about the resistance of his artistic materials:

> "Those words I was tellin y about, they wont fit int th mold thats branded on m soul. Rhyme, y see? Poet, too. Bad rhyme. Bad poet. Somethin else youve learned tnight. Lewis dont know it all, an I'm atellin y. Ugh. Th form thats burned int my soul is some twisted awful thing that crept in from a dream, a godam nightmare, an wont stay still unless I feed it. An it lives on words. Not beautiful words. God Almighty no. Misshapen, split-gut, tortured, twisted words. Layman was feedin it back there that day you thought I ran out fearin things. Niggers, black niggers feed it cause theyre evil an their looks are words. Yallar niggers feed it. This whole damn bloated purple country feeds it cause its goin down t hell in a holy avalanche of words." (224)

In other words, while Halsey was shaping ax handles and Lewis was drumming up a political organization—one subscribing to Booker T. Washington's theory, the other to W. E. B. Du Bois's—Kabnis has been feeding the "form thats burned into my soul" and the words that will apparently grow into literature. He seems to have succeeded at times, for some are "beautiful an golden an have a taste that makes them fine. . . ." As yet, however, we do not know the source of Kabnis's strength.

When he awakes the following morning, he continues to fulminate in the dark against the old mute slave. In the midst of his torrent of abuse, Carrie Kate enters. She rebukes him, but Kabnis hastens to correct her:

> "Great God Almighty, a soul like mine cant pin itself onto a wagon wheel an satisfy itself in spinnin round. Iron prongs an hickory sticks, an God knows what all . . . all right for Halsey . . . use him. Me? I got my life down in this scum-hole. Th old man an me—" (234–35)

The old man, he says, is a good audience. And, in talking to him, he has discovered his identity:

> "Mind me, th only sin is whats done against th soul. Th whole world is a conspiracy t sin, especially in America, an against me. I'm the victim of their sin. I'm what sin is." (236)

Kabnis is the very definition of sin, since the whole world has discovered its own guilt in him. It is, after all, the only word the old man has ever been heard to utter; Kabnis believes that, when the old man uses the word, history defines him.

But the old man, urged on by Carrie, talks for the first time: "O th sin th white folks 'mitted when they made th Bible lie" (237). Carrie cries, but Kabnis is shocked. All along he had believed the old man had been judging Negro life, whereas he had meant the whites. Kabnis faints, and Carrie, as symbol of the Negro time-present, holds him affectionately. As Kabnis goes up to work, Carrie Kate falls on the old man's knees and prays, "Jesus, come" (239). Outside, the sun "sends a birth-song slanting down gray dust streets and sleepy windows of the southern town" (239).

In light of this quite obvious recommitment of the writer Kabnis to the Negro people, Bone's analysis of Kabnis's last act is curious.[9] He believes that Kabnis cannot be reconciled with the old man, whereas in fact, Kabnis, through his splenetic poetry against the old man, is feeding his soul the words it needs to grow. "I get my life down in this scum-hole. Th old man an me," he says, meaning he is, wrongfully, defining himself in protesting against Negro life. Bone also believes that the curve of the plot is the "progressive deterioration of the protagonist," who becomes a clown "without dignity or manhood, wallowing in the mire of his own self-hatred." On the other hand, Carrie Kate, he believes, "may yet be redeemed through her ties with Father John."[10] Yet I suggest that Carrie Kate, when she met Lewis, was unable to overcome her puritan ties, and Kabnis, surely a suffering man and at times a sad clown, is, in the darkness of the cellar, arriving at an understanding, not only of himself, but also of the weird old man who symbolizes the past, and of the white-Negro, hostile world outside. Kabnis, if he comes up and helps Lewis in the end, will perhaps be unable to overcome his tremendous experience and to give shape to his branded soul. But at least he is wrestling with it, trying to come to terms with the world by questioning it. In this respect, Kabnis is an Invisible Man: he too is underground, in the dark night of the soul, wrestling with the old habits of mind, struggling to fit the dream to the bull-neck, to forge his experience into new metaphor.

In Kabnis Jean Toomer has discovered an appropriate symbol of the Negro writer who hopes to stir "the root-life of a withered people." Like Ellison's hero-writer, Toomer's hero-writer senses at least the first, tentative steps upward from the underground and toward a commitment, through art, to the racial experience of Negroes.

The Failure of a Playwright

DARWIN T. TURNER

In 1922 Sherwood Anderson wrote to a twenty-seven-year-old poet and short story writer, "You are the only Negro I've seen who seems really to have consciously the artist's impulse."[1] One might quibble that Mr. Anderson revealed his ignorance of or disdain for Paul Laurence Dunbar and Charles Chesnutt, but his tribute only faintly echoed the praise lavished on Jean Toomer in the early 1920s by Waldo Frank, Gorham Munson, William Stanley Braithwaite, Allen Tate, and Robert Littell, literary figures whose pronouncements commanded respect. For the general reader, Toomer's reputation rests upon *Cane* (1923), a collection of stories, sketches, and poems of such high quality that historians of literature by American Negroes mourn his failure to produce more books. Almost unknown, however, is his struggle to succeed as a dramatist. For more than a decade Jean Toomer experimented with dramatic form and technique in order to blend social satire with lyric expression of modern man's quest for spiritual self-realization. It was, as Waldo Frank wrote, an aim so new that it required a new form.[2]

Editor's Note: This essay is based on research made possible by a study grant from the American Council of Learned Societies.

The 1920s were so marked by experimentation in the American theater that pioneering playwrights and set-designers seem to have conspired to revolt against the form, language, and staging of conventional drama, which purported to imitate or represent the actualities of life. But when Toomer completed his first plays in the spring of 1922, the "revolution" was little more than sniper-fire. The Provincetown players had produced Eugene O'Neill's *The Emperor Jones* (1920) and *The Hairy Ape* (1922); Elmer Rice's expressionistic *The Adding Machine* and John Howard Lawson's *Roger Bloomer* would not be produced until 1923. Two to seven years away were other experimental dramas by O'Neill and Lawson, by George Kaufman and Marc Connelly, by John Dos Passos, e. e. cummings, Sophie Treadwell, and Channing Pollock. Toomer, therefore, did not imitate a literary fad; he was sufficiently far ahead of his time that success would have assured him an important place in the annals of American drama.

Unlike Rice, Kaufman and Connelly, and some of the other dramatists, he did not exploit the novelty of dramatic techniques which had been popularized in other countries. He sought to perfect a technique by which he might most effectively use his artistic talent to objectify mankind's spiritual struggle and to ridicule the society which chains man with false moral standards and false values. Toomer's unique talent, as he later demonstrated in *Cane*, was a lyric impressionism which demanded language more flexible than the patter imitating actual conversations. He needed intensity to express the powerful emotions of his protagonists; but he also needed stylized artificiality to reflect the dullness and superficiality of the guardians of middle-class morals. The emotional impact of the scenes often depends not on the words but on the tone created by the words. Because he was concerned with mankind rather than with private men, he imitated the German expressionistic playwrights who posited each character for a human type. And he elevated dance from its customary functions of spectacle and mood; literally and symbolically, it is the rhythmic means by which characters release themselves from inhibiting forces. To achieve these effects, he needed the flexibility of nonrepresentational technique and form. His, therefore, was no deliberate rebellion against the dramatic conventions of his time; those forms simply were inadequate to express his intention.

In his first drama, *Natalie Mann* (1922), Toomer argued for the freedom of the young, middle-class Negro women. Nathan Merilh, a Christ-like representation of Jean Toomer, seeks to free Natalie from middle-class morés and from her dependence upon him. After defying convention by living with him in New York, she achieves total self-realization when, after he has collapsed at the climax of a dance ritual evolving individual personality from national and social origins, she comprehends his divinity and the meaning of his sacrifice of himself.

Natalie's success is contrasted with the failure of Mertis, product of the same society. Having failed to choke the life force by teaching, engaging in social work, and fighting for Negroes' rights, she timidly enters a self-developing relationship with Law, Nathan's friend. Her search begins too weakly and too late; she dies from chill.

Lyric intensity characterizes the lovers and the soul-releasing dances of Nathan and Etta, a primitivistic Negro, who has discovered an ethic untainted by her fathers' repressive morality or the destructive lusts of white men. Contrasted with this lyric freedom are scenes of dullness, seeping from artificial, banal, self-appointed guardians of public morality, who plan to destroy any Negroes unwilling to obey their code. Having dedicated themselves to reshaping their race to fit the mold sanctioned by white society, they deplore the rowdy habits of some Negroes, extol the moral superiority of Negro women, and condemn spirituals and other reminders of the Negro's past. Convinced that natural expression of emotion is improper, they reflect their sterility in painfully self-conscious phraseology larded with allusions to the best writers and philosophers.

Toomer, however, does not attribute the repression to the racial characteristics of the Negro, but to his desire to be accepted in American society. For three hundred years, Nathan Merilh says, "An unsympathetic and unscientific white posture has gestured with scorn and condemnation at what it calls the benighted moral looseness of the Negro."[3] Lacking the self-assurance of the French, who have ridiculed the moral pretensions of the Anglo-Saxon,

> the Negro, cursed by his ignorance of moral evolution, of moral relativity, and lack of any sense of autonomous development, has not been so fortunate. He has knuckled to. . . . What should be the most colorful and robust of our racial segments is approaching a sterile and denuded hypocrisy. . . .[4]

The Negro woman, Toomer argues, has been restricted even more severely than the male. She is limited to marriage or prostitution, for white society blocks artistic, industrial, or political careers of all except the few Negro geniuses insensitive to pain.

Not surprisingly, faint echoes of George Bernard Shaw haunt the play: the style and thought of Shaw's plays had inspired Toomer's first serious considerations of a literary career.[5] Toomer's experiments with symbolic uses of character and of dance are more original. Except in *The Hairy Ape* and *The Emperor Jones*, symbolic uses of characters were uncommon in American drama in 1922, although they constituted a major characteristic of the expressionistic drama which Georg Kaiser and Ernst Toller were writing in Germany. Toomer's concept of characterization, however, probably did not derive from a specific literary source but from his inclination to abstract meaning from particulars. In the set for Nathan Merilh's room, for instance, he symbolized Nathan's harmonious blending of racial elements by a portrait which is an idealized blending of a picture of Tolstoy and a picture of a powerful African. The dance, for Toomer, symbolized the rhythmic freedom of the emotion through which self-realization must be achieved. Although symbolic uses of dance are common in ballet, American dramatists of the twenties generally overlooked such possibilities. The nearest approximations to Toomer's device are less imaginative uses of jazz in John Howard Lawson's *Processional* (1925) and John Dos Passos's *The Moon is a Gong* (1926). Lawson marched striking workers to jazz cadences; Dos Passos symbolized the relationship of characters by their dances. Both later dramatists made dance a vivid accessory; Toomer used it to express meaning.

Despite his imaginative techniques, Toomer did not fully realize his intention. After examining a draft of the play, Waldo Frank advised Toomer that the texture of the "teaparties, the talk of the incidental" was dead.[6] The obtuseness of Frank's criticism reveals the cardinal weakness of the drama. If Frank, sophisticated in literary symbolism, failed to comprehend the tonal implications of the contrived artificiality, keener judgment could not be expected from theatergoers habituated to the realistic, the comic, and the melodramatic. Toomer apparently abandoned the play when he could not improve the form, for there is no record that he attempted to publish it or to have it produced.

He evidenced more faith in a second play, *Kabnis*, which, a companion piece to *Natalie Mann*, had been written before April 1922. Published in revised form in *Cane*,[7] *Kabnis* negates the possibility that an intellectual Negro can achieve self-realization in the South.

Ralph Kabnis, a northern Negro who has been teaching in a southern school, is discharged when his principal sees him intoxicated. Choosing to remain in the South despite the fears which motivate his drinking, he becomes a handyman and an apprentice in a blacksmith shop. Although he has hoped to root himself in that section of the country which he posits for the ancestral soil of his race, he cannot imitate the natives. Uneducated Negroes reject him because they know that he is different. Unlike Principal Hanby, Kabnis cannot compensate for his lost self-respect by abusing less powerful Negroes. Trained to a middle-class respect for education and humiliated to a fear of white southerners, he cannot pattern after blacksmith Halsey, who, contemptuous of formal education, enjoys manual labor, and, secure in his self-esteem, loses no dignity when he greets his white customers deferentially. Poetically sensitive and easily shocked, Kabnis cannot imitate Layman, a jackleg preacher, who preserves his own life by mutely observing the abuse, the injustice, and the violence inflicted upon Negroes while he safeguards his income by offering them relief through the fervor of a primitive religion which he knows to be impotent. Insufficiently sensual to control Stella, who has been born of the lust of white men and victimized by the lust of leaders of the Negro community, Kabnis must content himself physically with Cora, whose sensuality is imitative, and spiritually with Carrie K, a youthful, pure, mother-image. Debauched, impotent himself, cognizant of the impotence of education and religion, he awaits inspiration and guidance to come from the message of Father John, an incoherent babbler from the Negro's past. But when Father John finally mumbles something which can be understood, it is merely the banal, the white people sinned "when they made th Bible lie."[8] As the play ends, Kabnis, carrying a bucket of dead coals to his workshop, trudges upward from the basement where Father John is dying in the arms of Carrie K.

The only scintillating ray in this morbid allegory of Negro impotence is Lewis, who, like Nathan Merilh, is both an ectype of Jean Toomer and a Christ-figure. Reared in the North, educated, sensitive but not poetically ineffectual, he can control his actions by will and reason, or can respond naturally to emotional impulse, the life-force, which orders the spiritual and physical union of male with female. Having contracted with himself to remain among his people for a month, he observes them compassionately and communicates satisfactorily with all of them. Sympathetic but emotionally detached, he offers help but is forced to leave when they seek instead the anodynes of drink and sex.

Lacking *Natalie Mann's* lyric language, exciting dances, and satirical social commentary, *Kabnis* has the somber tone of a medieval morality play, written in the style of twentieth-century expressionism. For Toomer the play proved a disappointment. For two years he tried unsuccessfully to arrange a staging, but producers' reactions can be defined by the rejection by Kenneth Macgowan, one of the most daring experimental producers of his generation:

> It won't do as it stands. The dialogue is good dialogue, the characters are exceedingly good. The incidents are most of them very interesting. But I feel that the play lacks the one thing a play can't lack—a general dramatic design.[9]

Unfortunately for Toomer, he and Macgowan preceded the Theater of the Absurd. Macgowan could not see beyond Eugene O'Neill, who experimented with plot construction, language, setting, and sound, but who worked within a clearly defined plot which had both beginning and end. Toomer's efforts anticipated the dramas of Samuel Beckett and Ionesco. Like *Waiting for Godot*, *Kabnis* is a spectacle of futility and impotence. Like Ionesco's *The Chairs*, it suspensefully prepares for a trenchant summation of life, which will give meaning to the play and to life itself; but the expected explosion is muted in both plays to the wet-sack whisper of a banal restatement of the obvious. Judged by the standards of 1922, *Kabnis* is a pale form of the expressionism which had not yet become familiar in America; judged by the standards of 1966, it is good Theater of the Absurd.

In 1923, when Alain Locke asked for a work to be included in *Plays of Negro Life*, Toomer sent him the already completed *Balo*, which is the least comprehensible of all his dramas. Nondramatic and plotless, *Balo* seems to be an experiment with dialogue rather than a completed play.

Using dialect for the first time, Toomer pictured the morning and the evening of a Negro family in Georgia. Idled by lack of work, the father—a preacher and a farmer—spends the morning reading theology. In the evening the family entertains relatives.

Balo suggests the essences of daily living and of the Negro folk: the friendliness and the cooperation of the interrelationships among neighbors, the pleasantness of a meal shared with relatives, the emotional enthusiasm of a spiritual, the saintliness of Uncle Ned (a healthier, more articulate Father John), and the religious fervor of Balo, a young son in the family. Lacking dramatic or emotional tension, however, *Balo* seems an experiment to achieve greater flexibility and freedom for prose forms rather than a work intended for the stage. Ironically, however, *Balo*, unlike Toomer's other dramas, has been produced on the stage.

His early efforts exhausted and his plays apparently unwanted, Toomer abandoned drama for a few years. By the time he wrote *The Sacred Factory* (1927), expressionism had become so familiar to American critics and audiences that the term was freely used to describe almost any experimentation with nonrepresentational techniques. In starkly simple expressionism comparable to that of Ernst Toller's *Man and the Masses*, Toomer found form for his most artistically successful drama, which reveals the dull existences of the working classes and the frustrated, repressed lives of the middle class.

For the first time, Toomer used a nonrepresentational stage set. Pillars divide the stage into three chambers not separated by walls. The domed central chamber resembles a religious structure, dominated by blue lighting. The adjacent chambers represent the homes of the workers and the cultured people.

After a choral incantation, the workers pantomime their lives. Having completed the stiff, awkward ritual dance of marriage, the man leaves for work, the woman moves in circles, the man returns; they eat, become sleepy, go to bed, arise; the man goes to work, the woman circles. Children are born; after circling briefly with their mother, they leave. The man dies, the woman mourns, the woman dies. Like robots, they have lived and died without interest, desire, hope, or possibility.

In the chamber of the middle class, John and Mary, awakening to life, are joined by a child who wonders where she is. The mother's imaginative explanation that they are on "a little speck of dust on a great vast elephant full of stars" elicits ridicule from the chorus. When the child poses additional questions about life and about God, the physician-husband, interrupting, lowers the tone from metaphysical to mundane by arguing with the wife. Accusing the wife of being a perfectionist who seeks ideal existence with a new husband, he charges that she sublimated her emotional needs in intellectual activities at the age of eighteen instead of satisfying them by marrying. Education, philosophy, morality, he continues, are drugs destroying mankind.

Having responded by chant and dance to each accusation made by the husband, the chorus now sings its worship of the drugstore which dispenses art, science, and religion. Its appeal to religion and God is ignored, however, by the scientist-husband and by the saint who has separated herself from the chorus.

Estranged from her husband, the wife regrets their failure to become a single blend of her faith and his knowledge. Separated from him spiritually, she remains with him physically because she will not desert her child.

The mood of the final act is established by the chorus's acclaiming the joy and the horror of war. Looking back to the early years of the marriage, the husband asserts that their first estrangement developed from the conflict between his intellect and her emotion. After the conflict became apparent, he dedicated himself to pleasure, which mankind calls "God." Having risen to protest the scientist's allegation that men seek only pleasure, the chorus kneels and chants its worship of the Madonna. When Being enters the room, John refuses to die because he has not lived. Confused, the child enters the central chamber and seats herself.

Despite the abstractness and despite the ambiguous conclusion, it is somewhat surprising that Toomer failed to find a producer for *The Sacred Factory*. The play certainly is as artistic as some of the pseudo-expressionism shown to New York audiences in 1927. Perhaps, however, producers feared the absence of a conventional protagonist with whom the audience might sympathize. Mary, a symbol of emotion and of Woman, compels more sympathy than any other individual figure, but she is too obviously designed merely to be the target for John's tirades. Mankind is the actual, pathetic protagonist; but a protagonist abstracted from abstractions evokes intellectual rather than emotional response. And intellectual appeal alone does not form lines at ticket windows.

When publishers rejected *The Gallonwerps*, a satirical novel, Toomer rewrote it as a play for gigantic marionettes. Earlier in the century, designer-director Gordon Craig had proposed using gigantic marionettes as actors to transcend the limitations of human actors. Toomer, however, conceived of the marionettes as a dramatic, visual emphasis of his thesis that the world is a puppet-show manipulated by a master puppeteer.

In *The Gallonwerps* (1928), the master is enigmatic, mystical, cultured, worldly Prince Klondike of Oldrope, an expert "diker" or practitioner of the art of tricking people in such a way that they enjoy being tricked. The drama itself is the tale of a necessary "dike."

Under the pretext of helping Wimepime Gallonwerp assemble an audience to listen to the philosophical ideas of Wistwold, her husband, Prince Klondike plans to steal Little Gasstar from the watchful nurse Elginbora. Assisted by the confusion attending one of the many arguments of the guests, Klondike succeeds with his plan. Later, having hidden Little Gasstar, he returns to the Gallonwerp home to take Wimepime and Wistwold with him.

A dramatization of the ego's rescue of the id from the superego, *The Gallonwerps* depends too heavily upon satiric caricatures and quips. Some of the character-types are interesting. The prince, more Mephistophelean than Nathan Merilh or Lewis, is the familiar extension of Jean Toomer. Wimepime, a world-famous beauty of Billboa of Baaleria (Chicago of America), has her prototype in Natalie Mann, the female who must be awakened by self-realization. Wistwold, an idealist and a dreamer, hopes to save the world by appealing to reason. Wimepime and Wistwold thus symbolize the awakened emotion and the intellect which, Toomer believed, must be merged within a fully realized individual.

Some character types earn recognition from the prince: Limph Krok, a sensitive pedant who is sickened by contact with the world of sweating bodies and mundane thoughts; Breastbuck Coleeb, a sarcastic but genial naturalist who, perhaps, had his prototype in Clarence Darrow; and Boldkire Kigore, a masterbuilder, a leader of men, almost worthy to be a rival of the prince. Those whom the prince condemns are the female leader who, with chains of Approval, binds society to her fixed and shallow ideas; the poseur who pretends originality for the philosophic ideas which he has gathered from books; the artificially sophisticated world traveler; the mindless woman who repeats her lover's ideas; the tasteless nouveau-riche being groomed for her sale into European nobility; the prim and officious busybody; the effeminate artist; and the man who assumes authority on every subject.

Successful drama, however, must offer audiences more than interesting stereotypes. As Gorham Munson warned, Toomer had failed to assume the possibility of a disinterested reader or spectator.[10] Actually, Toomer had been misguided by the effusive praises he had received from friends. Circulated in manuscript form among them, *The Gallonwerps* had been pronounced a success by those who recognized themselves among Toomer's caricatures and by some who respected him as a published author and worshipped him as their spiritual leader. Exalted by these, Toomer was unprepared for the uninformed reader who would neither laugh at the intimate joke nor comprehend the philosophical and psychological doctrines. Although he tried to rewrite *The Gallonwerps* during the early thirties, publishers and producers who had feared to introduce it during the booming twenties scarcely considered it during the depression.

After an abortive attempt at more realistic drama, *A Drama of the Southwest* (1935), based on his experiences in New Mexico, Toomer abandoned efforts to write drama for stage production but continued to write dialogue. In 1937 and again in 1941, he published Socratic dialogues in the *New Mexico Literary Sentinel.* As late as 1947, he attempted magazine sale of a brief satirical drama of modern man, who, deserted by a wife preoccupied with meetings, solaces himself with the sympathetic companionship of the robot who serves as a maid. Rejection of this drama ended Toomer's unsuccessful flirtation with drama.

Despite imaginative techniques, occasionally striking characterizations, and frequently brilliant dialogue, Toomer failed to sell his nonrepresentational drama to producers of his generation. Accustomed to looking for a plot in even the most abstract expressionistic drama they knew, they were irritated to find only a lecture by Jean Toomer, masked as Christ or Mephistopheles. At least two of the plays—*Kabnis* and *The Sacred Factory*—merit, however, a sympathetic reading by a contemporary producer of off-Broadway theater. Conditioned by Beckett, Ionesco, Genet, and Albee to the intellectual excitement of spending a few hours puzzling out the meaning of a play, audiences of the sixties are sufficiently sophisticated to appreciate Jean Toomer's expression of the futility and the frustration of man's existence.

Women and Male-Female Relationships in *Cane*

The Women in *Cane*

PATRICIA CHASE

If the fabric of *Cane* is the life essence and its meaning behind absurdity, then Toomer's women characters are the threads which weave *Cane* together. Like the form in which Toomer chose to express himself, his women characters are no less rare and sensual. Perhaps they are all the same woman, archetypal woman, all wearing different faces, but each possessing an identifiable aspect of womanhood. Each is strange, yet real; each wears a protective mask of indifference; each is as capable of love as well as lust; and each is guilty of or victimized by betrayal—of herself or of a man. There is no aspect of woman that Toomer does not weave inextricably into his archetypal woman, and in the end, through Carrie K., he has fashioned out of flesh and also failure his vision of womankind.

Toomer moves his women characters, as he changes the locus of *Cane*, from South to North and back to the South again. All of the women reflect their environment, are mirrored in it and react to it. Some belong to themselves (Carma, Karintha, Avey); others belong to the rich earth of Georgia (Fern, Becky, Esther, Louisa); and the rest belong to the whitewashed conformity and death-in-life of the North (Dorris, Muriel, Bona). If Toomer poses a question through one woman, he often answers that same question, or makes his statement through another. If Carma, in her ferocity and natural drive, does not understand her responsibility for her actions and their consequences, then Louisa most clearly does. If Karintha and Fern are the existential questions, of being or nonbeing, of identity vs. nonentity, then Avey is the statement of survival through acceptance and indifference. If Becky is reality in the face of absurdity, then Esther is absurdity in the face of reality. If Dorris mirrors the question of finding life sustenance in the North, then Muriel is the answer.

Toomer's thread of meaning begins weaving itself in Karintha, who is "perfect as dusk when the sun goes down." If Toomer is fashioning an archetypal woman, he begins with the first feminine quality, beauty:

> *Her skin is like the dusk on the eastern horizon,*
> *O cant you see it, O cant you see it,*
> *Her skin is like dusk on the eastern horizon*
> *. . . When the sun goes down.*[1]

Karintha is passionate and fierce, bursting with vitality and life, but she grows ripe too soon. She is suffused, even as a child, with an almost tangible sexuality and sensuality, but she suspends herself just out of reach of those who want her. Like many of Toomer's women, she is not to be possessed. Toomer paints Karintha in gentle brushstroke words: "Her sudden darting past you was a bit of vivid color, like a black bird that flashes in light" (2). Karintha seems to be holding the promise of life's secret, but just out of reach. Like the baby that "fell out of her womb," she exists in a haze of sweet smoke. In the rural South, poor, with nothing to *do*, she is very much free to *be*. She belongs simply to herself and to "the Georgia dusk when the sun goes down." Karintha is a question, a provocative overture to a rehearsal of human experience.

If Karintha is Toomer's existential question, then Fern and finally Avey are the statement to that question. In Fern Toomer expands on the quality of beauty in a woman. Her face "flowed into her eyes. Flowed in soft cream foam and plaintive ripples, in such a way that wherever your glance may momentarily have rested, it immediately thereafter wavered in the direction of her eyes" (24). Fern is alluring yet elusive. Through Fern, Toomer deals with the concept of beauty for its own sake in a woman. Men see in her eyes what they want to see, mystery and a yet unfulfilled desire. In his desire and fascination, the young man says of her: "They were strange eyes. In this, that they sought nothing—that is, nothing that was obvious and tangible and that one could see, and they gave the impression that nothing was to be denied. . . . Fern's eyes desired nothing that you could give her; there was no reason why they should withhold. . . . When she was young, a few men took her, but got no joy from it" (24–25). Perhaps behind her beauty there was nothing else. Her promise, it appeared, was just out of reach, and: "As you know, men are apt to idolize or fear that which they cannot understand, especially if it be a woman" (26). In Fern, Toomer is building a myth of woman, endowing her with mysticism and an ineluctability that make men want to do some "fine, unnamed thing" for her. But Fern lacks external identity. She *is* her beauty. It is her only gift from life. Yet Fern is the only one who accepts this. Others weave myths about her to sustain themselves, and then with vague guilt, having used her to escape oppressive passion or ennui, or perhaps to escape—for a moment—themselves, they weave myths and dreams protectively about her in payment for their use of her. "A sort of superstition crept into their consciousness of her being somehow above them" (26). In her dissertation, "Jean Toomer: Herald of the Negro Renaissance," Mabel Mayle Dillard makes the point that men are "struck by an attachment to Fern that transcends all reality." But no one really touches Fern, if there is anything to touch. She is waiting, it seems, for something that will never come, and she knows it. She belongs to the soil of Georgia and the scent of the cane. There is no choice involved. So in waiting, Fern has *become* all that life has given her—her beauty—and her being is dreamy and drugged by the day-to-day life that is her reality and her prison. Said Toomer in a letter to his friend, Waldo Frank. "In Karintha and Fern the dominant emotion is a sadness derived from a sense of fading, of a knowledge of one's futility to check solution . . ." In the same letter he says, "The supreme fact of mechanical civilization is that you become part of it or get sloughed off or under."[2] Fern's song is one of loneliness; in the canefield she goes into a trance and "her body was tortured by something it could not let out. . . . And then she sang brokenly. A Jewish cantor, singing with a broken voice. A child's voice, uncertain, or an old man's" (32). In the canefield, Fern is alone with the pattern of her existence, her loneliness, and sameness of her life, over which she has no control, but nevertheless accepts.

> Anyone, of course, could see her, could see her eyes. If you walked up the Dixie Pike most any time of day you'd be most like to see her resting listless-like on the railing of her porch, back propped against a post, head tilted a little forward because there was a nail in the porch post just where her head came which for some reason or another she never took the trouble to pull out. Her eyes, if it were sunset, rested idly where the sun, molten and glorious, was pouring down between the fringe of pines. Or maybe they gazed at the grey cabin on the knoll from which an evening folksong was coming. . . . Wherever they looked, you'd follow them and then waver back. Like her face, the whole countryside seemed to flow into her eyes. Flowed into them with the soft, listless cadence of Georgia's South. (26–27)

What he hints at in Karintha and Fern, Toomer states outright through Avey, the existential woman. Unconcerned, indifferent, living in the here and now, "lazy and easy as anything," she is an earthy but enigmatic woman. Like Karintha and Fern, Toomer describes Avey in terms of her allure and her elusiveness. She is a mystique to the adolescent boys who see her as floating among, but somehow above, them. Avey is a woman already, but they are not yet men and cannot have her. The young man in love with Avey says, "I'd meet her on the street, and there'd be no difference in the way she said hello. She never took the trouble to call me by my name. . . . She'd smile appreciation, but it was an impersonal smile, never for me" (78–79). Later, when they are older, he says wistfully, "But though I held her tightly in my arms, she was way away" (79). Like Karintha and Fern she came and went as she pleased, leaving always a scent of unfulfilled promise behind her. She is silent and knowing, surprised by none of life's traps and betrayals. Like Fern and Karintha men are tempted to weave myths about her and to "idolize and fear that which they cannot understand, especially if it be a woman." Avey, like Fern and Karintha, seems to hold the key to some secret, that if men only knew what, would make them free. However, if Avey is heavy with sensual promise, it is not through her own design. It is simply what men *choose* to see in her, not being able to understand her for what she is. Not being able to really know Avey or possess her, the persona (perhaps speaking for the author) wishes to protect her from the sordid side of life to explain her to herself. But she has already experienced life and has come to grips with it on her own terms. Life has been real enough and brutal enough for Avey that she has seen it for its absurdity and hypocrisy, come to workable terms with it, and thus can no longer be wounded by it. She has been so blown about willy-nilly by life that she knows her powerlessness against circumstance. But to her would-be lover she is "lazy and indolent . . ."

> As time went on her indifference to things began to pique me; I was ambitious. . . . The more I thought of it, the more I resented, yes, hell, thats what it was, her downright laziness. Sloppy indolence. There was no excuse for a healthy girl taking life so easy. Hell! She was no better than a cow. (82–83)

If Avey is unconcerned and indifferent it is because she must be in order to survive. It is this quality, this refusal to compete in a competitive world that men misunderstand and resent in Avey. But Avey's life is valid and real; she is living it and she has no illusions. It is *they* who choose to weave myths about her. It is *their* vision that is sharply limited. Men seem only able to view women as a self-created alter ego. In other words, "If there is nothing to take and nothing to protect, then how else can one react to woman?" Thus, their perplexity and anger at Avey's indifference and refusal to "play the game" is merely the shadow of their own limited vision.

In moving from the black world (the South) to the white world (the North) in *Cane*, Toomer passes consciously through the grey world of Esther and Becky, a purgatory of miscegenation. Through both Becky and Esther, Toomer limns women who bear the burden of society's vision of race mixing. In Becky he is dealing with the creator; with Esther, the creation. If Becky is reality in the face of absurdity, then Esther is absurdity in the face of reality. Becky, who is white, is rejected because she bears two illegitimate black sons; Esther is rejected because she is neither black nor white, and her mind becomes equally gray. Becky is relegated to her world through her actions; Esther fashions a world of fantasy for lack of a real one. Becky is reality. Esther is illusion.

Becky has borne two blacks sons. As a result she is ostracized by both the black and white communities. In their guilt for rejecting her, they scurry desperately but furtively to provide her with food, shelter, and a cloak of anonymity. Those who weave a myth of mysticism about Fern and Avey also endow Becky with a supernatural myth, laying their burden of guilt upon her. She is feared by them since she is the mirror within which they must see their own narrowness and cruelty. Becky is said to exude "vitality," but it is nothing so qualitative as that; hers is simply bone-hard determination to survive. Her survival for so long in the face of rejection and scorn proves her strength and the validity of her existence. The author's description of Becky is merely a sketchy framework for his purpose, for "Becky" reveals the bleak reality of the human experience, more than the woman. In Toomer's style, she *is* the experience. Of course, the crumbling of Becky's house is most symbolic; perhaps it caves in from the oppressive weight of a whole town's guilt. And it is interesting that in the face of rejection and ostracism, Becky chooses to stay in this rural southern town while it is the people of the community who really flee from Becky, who holds the mirror of their weaknesses.

Toomer's other "grey world" woman, Esther, is a woman without racial or sexual identity. She lacks the color, both literally and figuratively, of Fern, Karintha, Louisa, Carma, and Avey. Having been bleached of the color to which she has birthright, black, she has also been robbed of its quality. She is of neither world in color and neither world in mind. Belonging nowhere, Esther builds her own world through fantasy. All of her plans are sketchy and unsure. Even her dreams are bits and pieces of fantasy, never whole or complete. In her loneliness and emptiness, both as a person and as a woman, she reaches out for depth and the reality of living, personified for her by King Barlo, but she has little save fantasy to offer him. She sees Barlo as her deliverer—from loneliness to love, from barrenness to fulfillment, from greyness to blackness, from nonentity to identity. In her solitude, and out of her need, she creates an impossible myth about Barlo, and in the end, it is the myth she desires, not the man. Face-to-face with King Barlo (fantasy faced with reality) she sees that he is a man, not a myth, and since her life is built on myths and fantasy, she cannot relate to him. Esther leaves with numb acceptance of her life stretching out before her empty and meaningless. She "steps out" then of whatever shreds of realness she may have had into a world where "there is no air, no street, and the town has completely disappeared" (48). With no alternative left, Esther steps finally into the world of madness, where no identity is required. Her mind is indeed a "pink meshbag filled with babytoes." Perhaps Esther symbolizes that part of woman that needs myth to survive in an alien and frightening world, sexual myth as well as male myth. For many women these myths are reality. Society makes them reality, and many cannot choose but believe. And like Esther, for them, the myth becomes the man. And the life. Everlasting.

It was stated earlier that if Carma does not grasp the meaning of taking responsibility for her actions, then Louisa does. In practicing her right to be a free human being, Carma becomes involved in the "crudest melodrama" wherein someone else pays the price of her infidelity. Through Carma, Toomer is juggling the effects of pride, in man and woman, and the price that is exacted when men and woman play at power and pride in their relationships. Carma, like the other women in Part 1 of *Cane*, is earthy and sensual, more apt to follow the natural impulses of her being than the unnatural, dictates of society. She is bone-tough, "strong as any man," arrogant and sensual. With her husband away much of the time, "She had others. No one blames her for that" (18). She feels free to give herself to whomever she chooses, for is her body not hers to give? But Carma's vision is somewhat limited. She thinks only in terms of what she wants without considering the effects of her actions on others. In his hurt pride and wrath at discovering Carma's infidelity, her husband, Bane, confronts her. Suddenly she is faced with the consequence of her actions. In her simplicity, it had not occurred to her that she should be questioned. She defends. He advances. In fear and confusion, and in a sudden impulse of female wile, she flees into the canefield with a gun, hoping to put Bane on the defensive by making him feel responsible for a faked suicide. It is a crude melodrama within a crude melodrama, and its effects are catastrophic. Bane and his friends follow her into the canefield after they hear a shot ring out and find her lying near the gun. They carry her home, fearful that she has killed or wounded herself.

> They placed her on the sofa. A curious, nosey somebody looked for the wound. This fussing with her clothes aroused her. Her eyes were weak and pitiable for so strong a woman. Slowly, then like a flash, Bane came to know that the shot she fired, with averted head, was aimed to whistle like a dying hornet through the cane. Twice deceived, and one deception proved the other. His head went off. Slashed one of the men who'd helped, the man who'd stumbled over her. Now he's in the gang. Who was her husband. (19–20)

Carma is responsible for her husband's acts and his imprisonment, but others than Carma have taken the consequences. Carma is still herself, belonging to no one, living free in the here and now. "Should she not take others, this Carma, strong as any man, whose tale as I have told it is the crudest melodrama?" (20).

If Toomer leaves us with this question in Carma, his statement is clear in Louisa, who pays, as well as Tom Burwell and Bob Stone, the price of pride. In describing Louisa, Toomer begins again with beauty—soft, sensual, warm. His description of Louisa is lyrical and sweet with the scent of the cane:

> Her skin was the color of oak leaves on young trees in fall. Her breasts firm and up-pointed like ripe acorns. And her singing had the low murmur of winds in the fig trees. (51)

Enjoying woman's rare advantage, Louisa has two men in love with her—and does not care to choose between them. But as the "blood-burning" moon symbolizes, all is not calm. One man is black, like Louisa, and the other is white. There is a price to pay that Louisa hasn't considered. Louisa becomes caught in a web of events over which she no longer has control. Lulled by the heat, the heavy, sweet scent of the sugar cane, which carries the aura of death and violence, as well as love, and drugged by the "blood-burning" moon, Louisa has not considered the effects of her actions in the light of her environment and the ways of men. She lives, like many of Toomer's women, in the here and now. In factory town, only here and now. She is young and reckless, which is youth's gift. Thus how can she comprehend when the past crashes together with the present before her? Not wishing to choose between Tom and Bob, and in her glory, she has forgotten the pride of men.

> Separately, there was no unusual significance to either one. But for some reason, they jumbled when her eyes gazed vacantly at the rising moon. (52)

Quickly, over before they begin, violence and death snap Louisa from her dreamy indecision to stark reality.

> Blue flash, a steel blade slashed across Bob Stone's throat. Blood began to flow. . . . Negroes who had seen the fight slunk into their homes and blew the lamps out. Louisa, dazed, hysterical, refused to go indoors. She slipped, crumbled, her body loosely propped against the woodwork of the well. (64)

With gruesome finality, Tom Burwell is murdered by a white mob for killing a white man, refusing in their fear and hate to investigate the circumstances. They are driven, "blood-burning" with mindless hate, to evil and insane acts of violence. They are the hint of violence that fills the air, always waiting behind the sweet smell of the cane for the scent of blood and the chance to destroy what they cannot understand.

> Stench of burning flesh soaked the air. Tom's eyes popped. His head settled downward. The mob yelled. Its yell echoed against the skeleton stone walls and sounded like a hundred yells. Like a hundred mobs yelling. . . . It fluttered like a dying thing down the single street of factory town. Louisa, upon the step before her home, did not hear it, but her eyes opened slowly. They saw the full moon glowing in the great door. The full moon, an evil thing, an omen, soft showering the homes of folks she knew. Where were they, these people? She'd sing and perhaps they'd come out and join her. Perhaps Tom Burwell would come. (67)

The horror is more than Louisa can bear. The fear, the injustice, the evil, and the finality are more than she can comprehend, and she loses her mind. Her powerlessness and the consequences of her naiveté become for a moment clear to her and exact a price—her sanity. Like Esther, Louisa withdraws to a world beyond the real, where she can no longer be wounded. She has cost a man his life.

In her dissertation, Mabel Dillard has referred to Louisa, Avey, Carma, Karintha, Fern, Esther, and Becky as Toomer's "primitive" women, due to their earthiness, and particularly because they are a reflection of rural America, forgotten in the industrial crush of a growing nation. They are closer to the earth, the life, and themselves because they are not tied up in the artificiality and desperation of the industrial North.

If it is difficult for us to understand these women, and the way they react, it is because we live in a society and a century in which there is little left which is spontaneous and natural, where plastic reigns supreme god, and the price of freedom is death. In turning our backs to the soil and building concrete jungles for homes, we have raped the land, misused its resources, and destroyed its wildlife. We have eliminated the real and replaced it with the unreal. We have sold our souls for colored television sets, and IBM computers find our lovers for us. In place of love, joy, and human feeling we have accepted a bag of cement on credit and a lust for things instead of life.

From the depth and natural life force of the South, Toomer moves his women characters and their lives to the fast-moving world of the urban North—industrial, cold, anonymous. If Toomer characterizes through primitive woman a reaction to life in the South, then Dorris, Muriel, and, to an extent, Bona typify the life of the whitewashed North.

Dorris, with her beauty and vitality, exemplifies all that the North represents, but in "Theater," she takes up arms in her dancing and passionately presents herself to the world, asking for love in return. She gives herself over to the rhythms of life, through her dancing, hoping to draw John into the dance of life and into her:

> I've heard em say that men who look like him (what does he look like?) will marry if they love. O will you love me? And give me kids, and a home, and everything? . . . Dorris dances. She forgets her tricks. She dances. Glorious songs are muscles of her limbs. And her singing is of canebrake loves and mangrove feastings. (97–98)

Dorris tries with all her being to clutch the feelings of the man, John, whose black body is separated from his consciousness, which is white-washed and melancholy like the North. As Lieber[3] points out, John does not accept or rejoice in his black heritage, is estranged from it, and cannot love Dorris on her terms. His mind is a prison of the shaft of white light; he has been white-washed by the white people, standards, and racism of the North, where, because of his blackness, his manhood is denied. Thus he cannot love, and without love, Dorris is in turn robbed of her womanhood. The dank whiteness of the North, its cold, its people, and its "dry smell of dry paste and paint and soiled clothing" (100) will make Dorris dry and brittle herself. She will become, without love, a dancing doll, groping for feeling and empathy, laboring to survive as a woman where there is no survival possible.

Muriel is John's counterpart in a woman. Starched, retreating, disguising her selfness behind the walls of a prim, white house, Muriel worries constantly about "what people think" and becomes the prisoner of that cliché. At the first hint of something real and of value, Dan and his desire, she backs away in fear. Dan, trying desperately to retain his identity in the disgusting conformity of urban life, tries to free Muriel from her prison of fear. "For once in your life youre going to face whats real, by God—" (115). But Muriel pushes him away.

> Muriel fastens on her image. She smoothes her dress. She adjusts her skirt. She becomes prim and cool. Rising, she skirts Dan as if to keep the glass between them . . . (115)

Muriel has sold herself to play a minor part in a sham, white-washed world. She wants Dan, but not in a real or honest way. She wants him sexually, but is not free enough to enjoy her own sexuality. Since she is not free enough to give herself to him, she fantasizes rape and violence, anything but real loving. Like an adolescent, she wants to call what she wants by another name. Dan recognizes her for what she is, a slave to convention.

> Muriel—bored. Must be. But she'll smile and she'll clap. Do what youre bid, you she-slave. Look at her. Sweet, tame woman in a brass box seat. Clap, smile, fawn, clap. Do what youre bid . . . (120–21)

For the real sexual love that she wants, Muriel accepts the symbolic grappling of midgets on a stage. "They charge. . . . They pound each other furiously. Muriel pounds" (124). And for her orgasm she sees "cut lips and bloody noses." For love, she accepts hate; for sex, blood. In a grotesque parody of afterlove, a battered midget comes out holding flowers and a mirror, within which Muriel is refused her reflection, since she has none. Instead, the midget presents her with bloody roses as a mocking memento.

Like Muriel and Dorris, Bona, a white girl from the South transplanted to the North, is colorless and washed by conformity. In her search for meaning in life and in the "white experience," she is in love with Paul's blackness, but not Paul himself. Like John, a victim of white-washing, Paul has not embraced his racial identity and all that it involves. As Robert Bone asserts in *The Negro Novel in America*, it is Paul's inability to assert his Negro self that makes the potential love affair "an abortive one."[4] As the white woman face-to-face with, and attracted to, the black man, Bona is confused and unsure. She symbolically dances about Paul on the basketball court, testing her feelings and measuring his.

> She whirls. He catches her. Her body stiffens. Then becomes strangely vibrant, and bursts to swift life within her anger. . . . He look at Bona. Whir. Whir. They seem to be human distortions spinning tensely in a fog. Spinning . . dizzy . . spinning . . . Bona jerks herself free, flushes a startling crimson, breaks through the bewildered teams, and rushes from the hall. (136–37)

An extrovert herself, Bona is irresistibly drawn to Paul, who is quiet, pensive, and deep. She wants to know him, but with her preconditioned vision of him, she does not see him at all. Their experiences and their lives have been kept so rigidly apart for so long by society that they are strangers and do not know how to reach out to each other as man and woman. The gulf between them is far too wide, from black to white, from man to woman, and from real to real. In "Bona and Paul" Toomer is no longer dealing with absurdity in the face of reality, or reality in the face of absurdity, but one reality in the face of another.

> "And you know it too, dont you Bona?"
> "What Paul?"
> "The truth of what I was thinking."
> "I'd like to know I know—something of you."(148–49)

In the only way they know, they grapple mentally with their estrangement, both trying to understand, and both unable. Finally, through desire, they let their bodies carry the passion of their feelings. "Passionate blood leaps back into their eyes" (151). They leave to go make love, to find each other. But the contempt and the knowing glances of those who watch bring Paul back to himself, and he embraces at last his own unique being and his blackness. He goes back to explain to the black doorman, who looked "knowingly" at them.

> "I came back to tell you, brother, that white faces are petals of roses. That dark faces are petals of dusk. That I am going out and gather petals." (153)

But Bona, who in reality wants Paul's essence, and not Paul, is gone. The shell of her conformity and fear, which she had left on the dance floor in a moment of discovery, has caught up with her outside. She is not yet enough woman or comfortable enough with her womanhood to take what life offers. Bona wishes to embrace the color, not the man, or the man, not the color. Life offers her, for a moment, both, but she flees in fear. The novelty, depth, and uniqueness of Paul's experience frighten her. Like Muriel, she too is a prisoner of convention.

With his statement in "Bona and Paul" and with Paul's realization (perhaps a reflection of Toomer's own agonizing battle with identity), Toomer is ready to move back again to the source—the deep South. Here, through Kabnis, he extends his question of identity to a statement through woman. Quietly and surely, through Carrie K., Toomer makes his final statement of woman and her role. Carrie K., unlike some of the other women characters in *Cane*, is able to accept herself and her cultural experience totally, with action as well as reaction. She is young and shy, yet knowing. She is able to understand equally the young man, Kabnis, denying yet searching for his identity, as well as she understands the old man, Father John, who is the container and the reflector of the black experience for which Kabnis searches: "She is lovely in her fresh energy of the morning, in the calm, untested confidence and nascent maternity . . ." (233). Carrie K. believes not only in herself, but in the validity of all human experience. She is the bridge between the old and the new, and between fantasy and reality. Toomer seems to present, through Carrie K., his total vision of woman—not withdrawing, but advancing toward the future carrying the relevant past, i.e., Father John, with her. Through her Toomer makes his final statement of woman as a bridge, not only between man and man, but as a bridge between man and himself. This is most evident when Father John, the "mute John the Baptist of a new religion—or tongue-tied shadow of an old," vouchsafes ". . . th sin th white folks 'mitted when they made th Bible lie" (211, 237). Infuriated, Kabnis retorts,

> "So thats your sin. All these years t tell us that th white folks made th Bible lie. Well, I'll be damned. Lewis ought t have been here. You old black fakir –"(238)

Carrie K. then responds to Kabnis:

> "Brother Ralph, is that your best Amen?" She turns him to her and takes his hot cheeks in her firm cool hands. Her palms draw the fever out. With its passing, Kabnis crumples. He sinks to his knees before her, ashamed, exhausted. His eyes squeeze tight. Carrie presses his face tenderly against her . . . (238)

Without fear and with intuitive perception, Carrie K. accepts the validity of *all* human experience without judgment or contempt. She is, in her compassion and acceptance, the link between the man and his soul.

Toomer begins with Karintha and her beauty, and ends with Carrie K. and her profundity, as *Cane* culminates in the vision and meaning of human experience. Through his reflections of a woman's reaction to living, through many women and the faces they wear, Toomer has woven a vision of woman that is real and valid, because they are.

This vision culminates in Carrie K. She is all of his women in one self-actualizing woman. She is *Cane*.

> *Her skin is like the dusk on the eastern horizon,*
> *O cant you see it, O cant you see it,*
> *Her skin is like dusk on the eastern horizon*
> *. . . When the sun goes down.*
>
> (1)

Frustrated Redemption: Jean Toomer's Women in *Cane*, Part One

J. MICHAEL CLARK

One stumbles upon a number of problems in studying Toomer's *Cane*: not only are the bits and pieces of response and criticism deceptively similar, like a crazy quilt whose pieces turn out to be patterned, only different in size or shade, but also the bulk of Toomer criticism has occurred in the last decade. The purpose of this essay, then, will be to survey this material in order to elucidate *Cane*'s portrayal of the frustrated search for redemptive self-knowledge through women whom men cannot genuinely meet or understand.

Born in 1894, Toomer did not begin writing seriously until after a period of post-adolescent wandering from school to school and job to job—an abortive journey of self-discovery—ended about 1920.[1] Under the mixed influences of the philosophies of atheism, naturalism, and socialism and of writers such as Shaw, Goethe, Hugo, and Whitman, he began writing in a manner which would become a lifelong problem of trying to communicate "his philosophy into an idiom comprehensible to the uninitiated."[2] *Cane* (1923) was both the first and the last published product of this struggle, for after its publication he disclaimed any identification with the Negro race, deciding via his light skin and mixed blood to "pass," and joining white society from which his literary skills never again came together.[3] *Cane* was really first conceived during his journeying. The town of Part 1, "Sempter," is really the town of Sparta in northeast Georgia, where Toomer taught physical education for three months in 1921, a town then characterized by its involvement in the raising and processing of sugar cane.[4] This was the Valley of *Cane*; says Toomer of his experience there:

> With Negroes also the trend was towards the small town and then towards the city—and industry and commerce and machines. The folk spirit was walking in to die on the modern desert. That spirit was so beautiful. Its death was so tragic. Just this seemed to sum up life for me. And this was the feeling I put into *Cane*.[5]

This pilgrimage toward a "wasteland" of modernity was ultimately seen as a loss of the passional, redemptive aspects of human interaction and illustrated in the structure and title of *Cane*, the stories of Toomer's visiting in the South.

Part 1 shows the South's passionality through its portraits of instinctively natural sexuality, of irrationally embraced tradition and social order, and of the tragedy which erupts when these conflict.[6] Part 2, in contrast, illustrates order rationalized and idolized; machinery, industry, and sophistication have repressed and purged persons of any genuine passion.[7] Despite its also offering tragedy, then, that the South at least experiences the passions of love, lust, anger, and murderous hate is preferred to the sterility of the North; Part 3, then, shows the incompatibility of the northern life-style in the South.[8] Roberta Riley summarizes the structure of *Cane*:

> The first section of the book, which includes pictures of rural Georgia life, primarily descriptions of women, who despite painful hardships have managed to endure because of their closeness to their roots, contrasts with the second section of the book, which provides portraits of the urbanized Negro, whose culture has sunk into lifeless, white-washed sterility.[9]

The title then further suggests a southern favoritism for Toomer's *Cane*: not only does the title signify the Georgian land of sugar cane, but also it is thought to be a pun on Canaan or the Promised Land.[10] However, as one turns from observing structure to a thematic overview, the South is hardly a panacea. Its own tragedy ultimately yields ambivalence, and the metaphor of blacks in America gels more as the Hebrews in the wilderness, circling and quarreling for forty years, than as having arrived at promised wholeness.[11]

Ambivalence and ultimately failure in human interrelationships seems to characterize not only the episodes of Part 1 but also those of the entire work as expressed by Patricia Watkins: "Toomer is saying throughout *Cane* that man is a creature alone and apart, unable to share and commit himself with another, and after many abortive attempts to do so, he finds that nothing has happened and nothing has changed."[12] The episodes then yield a whole cloth of strangers who meet and yet fail to commune. Examples in Part 1 would include Becky and the community, or Karintha and Fern, who seek one thing from men but are ever offered something else.[13] The intensity of this failure is tragic; almost all encounters—which proves "man's inability to communicate and interact with fellow human beings, the inability to understand and therefore to love, the inability to quicken another human soul,"[14]—ultimately end "in torture and pain so deep that it demands the victim's escape from [further] human interaction"—to wit, Karintha's contempt, Becky's death, Esther's and Louisa's insanity, and Fern's mysticism.[15]

This tragedy is so deep because of the meaning that interaction has for Toomer, for his characters, seeking wholeness in relationships, are "struggling to impose form on a world of chaos," never realizing that the chaos is within themselves and is further fragmented by their superimposed order.[16] It is, then, a struggle for involvement in life, acceptance of chaos. To illustrate this, Toomer uses the device of men (as limits, controls, definitions) seeking to possess women (as instinctive, silent, passive, elusive).[17] Women represent "the experience men are trying to grasp" (beauty in suffering, acceptance of the dominance of chaos) and are finally a mystery which men in seeking only their bodies (the possessiveness of materialism, rationalism, and ordering) fail to find.[18] The intended redemptive outcome, could these two forces—sexes—come together, would be self-knowledge. This seems to depend on instinctual spontaneity of the self, which has been repressed in the North—in men—and reduced to sex in the South—in women—whereas mutuality of passions in balance to rationality could produce salvation.[19] That encounter remains merely carnality between strangers is essentially out of fear; though self-knowledge is desired and necessary for interpersonal wholeness, fear of its disclosure is stronger.[20] A secondary theme within this abortive quest for self-knowledge occurs at the level of equally unrequited striving for racial fusion and spiritual harmony against the damning social order, which is also shown as a conflict of active males and passive females: colorless Esther cannot have black, black Barlo, and Louisa cannot intermingle with both a black and a white lover, and Becky is condemned for crossracial mating and progeny. A world which is above color distinctions is impossible; fragmentation-chaos withstands.[21]

Although Susan L. Blake argues that the men who seek are Toomer's focus,[22] the women in Part 1 actually stand in the forefront, the men serving only as ploys in the conflicts the women incarnate. The women *are* the frustration of the dreams and visions of self-knowledge,[23] the instinctive, passional victims of both men's and society's inability to transcend depersonalizing orders, for "if the fabric of *Cane* is the life essence and its meaning behind absurdity [chaos], then Toomer's women characters are the threads which weave *Cane* together" into a whole cloth, a single archetypal woman whose only refuge is indifference.[24] This indifference becomes their passivity, their resignation to fate, their lapsing into a far-removed past.[25] This latter prepares them for transcendence; spiritually removed from their hostile environments, they teeter on the threshold of awakenings to self-knowledge and wholeness, but the male discord of order and carnality shatters catharsis; seething ambivalence continues unresolved, a death within life.[26] Finally, even as woman cannot neutralize man, nor passionality be harmonized by rationality, neither is Toomer's God-Messiah in natural processes able to embrace the ordering materialism of non-natural, mechanized society.[27] The women also incarnate and express this hopeless, natural Jesus-God, whether in Dionysian acts or Jewish chanting. Thus, seeing the scope of Toomer's women, generalized out of his themes, a detailed character-by-character study will give this flesh, incarnating the tragedy of Toomer's *Cane*-quilt vision, the impossibility of genuine I-Thou human interrelationships and their consequence, the frustration of redemptive self-knowledge-in-relationship.

Karintha is the first of Toomer's elusive women who "personified the physical beauty for which men yearn" and who, because she is only a sex object to them but knows herself to be more, cannot be possessed:[28]

> Men had always wanted her, this Karintha, even as a child, Karintha carrying beauty, perfect as dusk when the sun goes down. . . . This interest of the male, who wishes to ripen a growing thing too soon, could mean no good to her.[29]

She "carries beauty" as if carrying a burden, a conflict "between acceptance and limitation of being."[30] Because of her burdening beauty, men restrict her to prostitution against her own wish not to be so defined. Her very being defies this earth-binding role:[31]

> Karintha at twelve was a wild flash . . . Her sudden darting past you was a bit of vivid color, like a black bird that flashes in light. . . . Karintha's running was a blur. (1–2)

Moreover, because one's sexuality is ultimately linked to one's personal wholeness or soul, men who seek only her beauty are never made whole and, tragically, their materialistic carnality finally fragments Karintha, whose stillbirth is like a jettisoning of her depreciated soul:[32] "A child fell out of her womb onto a bed of pine needles in the forest" (4).

Bowie Duncan sees three stages in Karintha's development, the first being that of purity "as innocently lovely as a November cotton flower" (2).[33] The second is of the loss of purity in too early ripening when "she played 'home' with a small boy who was not afraid to do her bidding. That started the whole thing" (3).[34] Finally is the triumph over fallenness, as in birth "she bears a purity."[35] Duncan's vision of this movement as an affirmation of redemption overlooks certain clues. First of all, Karintha's innocence is one of the men's myths, an illusion which disguises fallenness and precludes distinguishing good from bad and thereby the possibility of repentence-redemption. Even the symbol of Christianity perpetrates this damning illusion:

> No one ever thought to make her stop. . . . She stoned the cows, and beat her dog, and fought the other children. . . . Even the preacher, who caught her at her mischief, told himself that she was . . . innocently lovely. . . . (2)

Second, after her initial sexual experiment, she becomes a victim, less fallen than raped, because "that started the whole thing" (3). Most severely has Duncan failed to see the birth as a stillbirth, a depositing; certainly the images of smouldering sawdust, of smoke curling and infecting the water for weeks are images of death (4).[36]

If redemption is not in the stages Duncan has suggested, perhaps its *potential* lies in Karintha's power (like Fern's) to bring out the altruistic self-sacrifice in men. The irony and the frustration of redemption occur in that the men who seek a material thing (sex) can only offer a material thing (money) (3). Ultimately, genuine encounter on a higher level than carnality is not achieved; unable to interact wholly and ambivalent about her sexuality because of men's limiting of it, she retreats for survival, soulless, into a mystery ever unperceived:

> Karintha is a woman. Men do not know that the soul of her was a growing thing ripened too soon. They will bring their money, they will die not having found it out . . . (4)

"Becky" and "Esther" provide two further examples of women's singular tragedies brought about by restrictive sexual identities, although Becky's story may be the less tragic. Becky knew that white women's sex must be kept to white men, but she chose to shatter that social restriction and in so doing cut herself off from human encounter with either race.[37]

> Becky had one Negro son. . . . God-forsaken, insane white shameless wench, said the white folks' mouths . . . Poor Catholic poor white crazy woman, said the black folks' mouths. (8)

Eventually, Becky had another presumably Negro child (10), suggesting the biblical Rebecca, whose sons, Jacob and Esau, quarrelled over the stolen birthright.[38] Her sons' birthrights had been stolen by the town who denied them; they rebelled:

> They answered black and white folks by shooting up two men and leaving town. "Godam the whitefolks; godam the niggers," they shouted as they left town. (11)

On a theological level, Becky becomes, for the town, a scapegoat, an unrecognized Christ-figure. Again, other people create a myth centering on her social evil and use that both to restrict her from social interaction and as a scapegoat for their own "narrowness and cruelty."[39] The town actually needs her for this function, and so they do not liberate but sustain her in secret—

> White folks and black folks built her cabin, fed her and her growing baby, prayed secretly to God who'd put His cross upon her and cast her out. (8)

Ultimately, as God is wont to do for the God-forsaken, He vindicates her. She stays and persists, thereby proving her strength and validating her existence; it is really the town which "flees," "because they had a fear" (11).[40] Her vindication is complete in that when her chimney becomes too heavy under the weight of the town's guilt, the blue-sheen God with one eye effects its falling and liberates her to the sweet consolation of Jesus (12).[41] Thus, while redemption in Toomer's sense of genuine human encounter is frustrated by the town's punitive sexual-mores restriction of Becky, hope lies in her endurance and her release, albeit to an otherworldly salvation not so unlike Karintha's earthly mystery: "The pines whisper to Jesus. The Bible flaps its leaves with an aimless rustle on her mound" (13).

Esther's tragedy stems primarily from buying into the masculine perception, assuming wholeness of identity (both personally and racially) to be equivalent to mere sexual union.[42] On the one hand, like Toomer himself, her light color and better-than-average financial status isolate her from blacks as much as from whites (because of immobility she cannot seek a place to "pass"):[43] "Esther looks like a little white child, starched, frilled, as she walks slowly home from her father's grocery store" (36). On the other hand is her actual sexual innocence. Enraptured by the very black Barlo's religious trance (37–39), she idolizes him as the key to both racial and sexual wholeness.[44] But because of this particular and very exceptional encounter with Barlo and because of her innocence, she "begins to dream" her Freudian fantasies of sex as ecstasy; a union with Barlo, she anticipates, would be like an immaculate conception, for she sees herself as the "black madonna on the court-house wall" (40–41).[45] But even this kind of sexuality seems sinful to her, and the envisioned baby is an aberration—"black, singed, woolly, tobacco juice baby—ugly as sin"; both stand against the purifying flames of her vision and her own whiteness-purity (41).[46] The illusion deepens.

Years later, upon Barlo's return, she—the whitish, virginal, saving Mother of God—goes after Barlo to redeem his blackness and his sexuality from the house of "sin" (46–48).[47] She confronts a reality she cannot accept and, unlike the biblical queen, is rejected by "king" Barlo.[48] On the racial level, she is not afforded a mixed-color world and is denied by the black, by Barlo; she is left in an empty limbo worse than Hell, for "in rejecting the earthy primitiveness of Barlo, Esther, as the American Negro [like Toomer after *Cane*], is rejecting the strange lost world that is Africa."[49] On the personal level she reaches out to Barlo for sexuality-life but has nothing to offer but the fragmented fantasies which have become her identity.[50] Faced with reality, she sees her fantasy world crumble, with nothing to fill it but madness; "her mind is a pink meshbag filled with baby toes" (45),[51] which is the devastating nonbeing Toomer described: "There is no air, no street, and the town has completely disappeared" (48).[52] Finally, on a cosmic level, Esther symbolizes the ambivalence of woman—needing the self-deceptive myth for survival, yet finding the myth she has incommensurate with reality.[53] Esther, by accepting the materialist-male view of sexual union alone as the answer for racial and personal wholeness and identity, isolates herself from genuine, realistic interrelationships and exchanges all her inward, albeit unnurtured, redemptive resources for the void.

Juxtaposed against these three women (Karintha, Becky, Esther) Toomer has interspersed two whose sexually related tragedies reach out to overtly harm their men, the stories of Carma and Louisa ("Blood-Burning Moon"). Carma again invokes memories of the African preslavery bluntness and a sexuality little at ease in the Western order:[54]

> From far away, a sad strong song. Pungent and composite, the smell of farmyards is the fragrance of the woman. She does not sing; her body is a song. She is in the forest, dancing. Torches flare. . . . Juju men, greegree, witchdoctors. . . . Torches go out. . . . The Dixie Pike has grown from a goat path in Africa. (17–18)

Defying man's order of facts, when caught for infidelity she must use deception; her pretended suicide is the reincarnation of her name (Karma) (19).[55] Her sexual liberty, then, is not without its price. Bane first accused her and sought to hurt her: "He would like to take his fists and beat her" (18).[56] Fear becomes frenzied anger and mocking deception. Thus, not only deceived in sex but in her "suicide," he loses control and kills an innocent companion to avenge himself:[57]

> Twice deceived, and one deception proved the other. His head went off. Slashed one of the men who'd helped, the man who'd stumbled over her. Now he's in the gang. Who was her husband. (19–20)

Ultimately this crude melodrama points simply to the limited vision of sexual freedom in its disregard for consequences (Carma's husband's crime and imprisonment).[58] If there is any redemption here, it is only in her primitive perseverance to continue defiantly free. "Should she not take others, this Carma . . . ?" (20).[59]

"Blood-Burning Moon" deals even more with the men's tragedy in its plot, treating Louisa only peripherally until the end. Again there is a strong conflict between nature and social law. White Bob Stone is hopelessly drawn to Louisa's African beauty. "It was because she was nigger that he went to her. Sweet . . ." (61). Nature makes any color lover seem right; society forbids it, and yet society also forbids a black man's attacking a white man who crosses that barrier—Tom Burwell is doubly trapped.[60] The scapegoat, however, is again the woman who pays the price. Her instinctive sexuality, which would condone multiple lovers of either race, is, like Carma's, seen as an indifference to the reality of its consequences: her independence of consequences, her unwillingness to meet the collision of the African past (natural sexuality) with the present (social mores) causes tragedy, the death of both men, against which she is powerless.[61] But the tragedy does not end with the murder and the lynching; it turns in upon Louisa, "her powerlessness and the consequences of her naïveté become for a moment clear to her and exact a price—her sanity."[62] Louisa loses her grip on reality and withdraws; simultaneously with Tom's death she expects his return and reassurance:[63]

> Tom's eyes popped. His head settled downward. The mob yelled. . . . Louisa, upon the step before her home, did not hear it, but her eyes opened slowly. They saw the full moon . . . an evil thing, an omen soft showering the homes of folks she knew. Where were they, these people? She'd sing, and perhaps they'd come out and join her. Perhaps Tom Burwell would come. (67)

So far as possibility for redemption is concerned, both for Carma and for Louisa, it is precluded, frustrated at the core, because genuine relationship, being with another, includes responsibility, awareness of consequences, and in both instances this is forfeited for freedom in the realm of sex (Carma's flaunting freedom, Louisa's fickle freedom), to which both women's identity has been reduced.

Saving the best for last, as it were, Toomer includes Fern, who is the most often interpreted of his women: elusively beautiful like Karintha, racially mixed like Becky's sons, ecstatically religious and rarified like Esther, but also as affected by sexual-identity delimitation as Carma or Louisa.

In the Fern story Toomer expands on the beauty which men see in mystery and its unfulfilled desire:[64]

> Face flowed into her eyes. . . . The soft suggestion of down slightly darkened, like the shadow of a bird's wing might, the creamy brown color of her upper lip. Why, after noticing it, you sought her eyes, I cannot tell you. . . . They were strange eyes. In this, that they sought nothing—that is nothing—that was obvious and tangible. . . . (24)

This mystery of Fern, though, lies much deeper than physical beauty, for, "like her face, the whole countryside seemed to flow into her eyes" (27); through her eyes she is filled, informed and incarnates the mystery of the universe.[65] Her embracing the world of her vision, "the listless cadence of Georgia's South," suggests on a racial level the "emotional kinship between soil, land, and Negro people of the South."[66] Yet because it is a cosmic or universal wholeness, it transcends race, as is suggested by her mixture of Africa, Georgian South, and Judaism—her Semitic nose, Jewish cantor songs, and last name (Rosen)—mingled with tribal mysticism and Christian invocations.[67] Finally, her beautiful mystery may be seen as *kenotic*, Christlike, as in Phil.2:6–11—by mystical self-emptying she is able to be filled by the world. Like Christ she is ripe for redeeming and for redemption. Her tragedy ultimately is in being filled by carnality, money, and rationality.

This materiality was all that was offered Fern—"men were everlastingly bringing her their bodies," and later gifts and money (25). Consequently no genuine *self*-sacrifices occurred; their giving was not altruism but lust.[68] Ultimately the men of Sempter realize her mystery as an otherness they—as carnal orderers—cannot meet. They cannot meet her either on their physical terms or on her spiritual terms.[69] As order is afraid of mystery, so Toomer's men justify their gift giving by the exonerating myths of her mystery and elusiveness to the extent that their having been unsatisfied by her becomes virginity:[70]

> As you know, men are apt to idolize or fear that which they cannot understand, especially if it be a woman. She did not deny them, yet the fact was that they were denied. A sort of superstition crept into their consciousness of her being above them. Being above them meant that she was not to be approached by anyone. She became a virgin. (26)

Thus, Fern is really more whole, even as their scapegoat (a virgin Christ), than the men, but she knows they have still reduced her to her beauty, failing to understand her elusive wholeness. Unable to find spiritual realization in the physical reality of sex, she succumbs, as it were, to the men's myth of her; she becomes her beauty and lapses into a mystical waiting.[71] It is at this point, of mystical waiting for redemption amidst the hopelessness of men's delimitation, that the narrator arrives.

The narrator, however, is little better than the town's men. Although he is not so much interested in her body, he still responds with a materialist urge to give her other unwanted gifts—his rationality, his northern sophistication, his empty words—rather than human understanding.[72] His spiritual impotence is expressed as pettiness, as triviality, as something not worth mentioning but which disenables his being part of the hoped-for, redemptive encounter. Fern retreats into a frenzy, reseeking the shalom of her mysticism. She finally returns to her Jewish hope for a Messiah who still hasn't come, sitting on her porch, eyes filled with the cosmos:

> I must have done something—what, I dont know, in the confusion of my emotion. She sprang up. Rushed some distance from me. Fell to her knees, and began swaying, swaying. Her body was tortured with something it could not let out. Like boiling sap it flooded arms and fingers till she shook them as if they burned her. It found her throat, and spattered inarticulately in plaintive, convulsive sounds, mingled with calls to Christ Jesus. And then she sang, brokenly. A Jewish cantor singing with a broken voice. A child's voice, uncertain, or an old man's. Dusk hid her; I could hear only her song. It seemed to me as though she were pounding her head in anguish upon the ground. . . . Shortly after, I came back North. From the train window I saw her as I crossed her road. Saw her on her porch, head tilted a little forward where the nail was, eyes vaguely focused on the sunset. Saw her face flow into them, the countryside and something that I call God, flowing into them. . . . Nothing ever really happened. Nothing ever came to Fern, not even I. (32–33)

Fern then embodies the spirituality necessary for redemption, but it is not tapped. Hers is the mystic, "passively receptive consciousness, responding to and becoming one with her world, which includes the anguished past of Jewish and African peoples—an anguish from which the narrator is unable to redeem her because he is unable to understand."[73] Therefore, he cannot help her "to evolve to a higher state of consciousness, and her anguish can only become more intense, remaining trapped and inarticulate."[74]

Hargis Westerfield offers an alternative, more optimistic view playing out the theological symbols in the story. Noting the Judaisms which resonate throughout the story, he believes Toomer exalts Fern as *the* Virgin, as the Mother of God, not only in his descriptions of her beauty but also in the townsmen's myth and the reference to the courthouse-wall madonna.[75] He goes on to interpret the men's gift-bearing as magi-adoration and her climactic mystical experience as a sensual union with God which produces an incarnation—the narrator. Westerfield, to illustrate his interpretation, quotes the narrator: "Her eyes, unusually weird and open held me, held God " (32).[76] Noting her return to her porch to sit by the nail, he says, "Fern sits as if to commemorate the sufferings of Christ when he incurred the nails on Calvary."[77]

Westerfield, buying into the male egotism of the Toomer-narrator, overlooks several important facts. Fern does not incarnate/birth the narrator; she flees from him. Her cries at the end are *to* Christ Jesus in anguish, not birth announcements (31). Moreover, to pick up the *kenotic* motif, aforementioned, if Fern *is* the Christ figure ripe for redemption, then any allusion to the porch post and the nail at her head does not "commemorate" Christ; she *is* Christ (33). The tragedy is that she remains on that cross waiting for some God-man-Messiah to come and vindicate her; but since nothing ever came to Fern, least of all the narrator, she is a Jewess on the threshold of Easter who somehow never sees the redeeming dawn. Attributes of the other women in *Cane*, Part 1, come to a focus in Fern: perhaps more than any of the others, Fern has the inner seeds of redemption (and these do not completely leave her—she has her touch with reality in anger at the gossips and the shalom of her mysticism, of another, greater reality) (32), but like the other instances these do not and cannot come to fruition but are frustrated because she is also, like them, denied any genuine I-Thou relationship.

As a way of further responding, I should like to briefly comment upon a couple of overall interpretive conclusions. Important in the present context is Toomer's use of women. Darwin T. Turner comments on the unreality of *Cane's* view of the feminine essence:

> They all loved as Toomer thought women should . . . each in her own way is an *elusive* beauty, who charitably or indifferently or inquisitively offers her body to men who will never understand her soul.[78]

Toomer's women *are* one-sided. They basically all stand under the rubric of sex object, whether as passive (Karintha, Becky, Fern), or as active (i.e., irresponsible—Carma, Louisa), whether as Virgin (Esther, self-defined by sex) or as mother (Becky). Equally objectionable, however, is his one-sided treatment of men. Men are no more generalizable as coldly rational, ordered, and carnal than women are all passional, chaotic, and ethereal. From a feminist perspective, one can appreciate that at least women carry the seeds of redemption; men apparently do not and are by inference hopeless, damned. Unfortunately, many, although not all, men and women, especially in the South, do still see themselves in this way. Toomer's use of this motif cannot further the demise of stereotypical self-punishment whose results are tragic (e.g., Esther). Perhaps, however, Toomer is to be actually credited, for he does indeed portray not only stereotypical caricatures but also the tragedy accruing to them—frustrated redemption for all. His, then, is a prophetic call to transcend our stereotypes and roles and enter into genuine relationships.

On this note is one more comment on the work as a whole. Patricia Chase has said:

> Toomer begins with Karintha and her beauty, and ends with Carrie K. and her profundity, as *Cane* culminates in the vision and meaning of human experience. . . . This vision culminates in Carrie K. She is all of his women in one self-actualizing woman.[79]

Unfortunately, this seems again only to ignore the actual frustration of redemptive self-knowledge—Man-Kabnis ascends to his drudgery, and Woman/Carrie K. remains in awe but virtually holding her meal-bucket, her ball and chain of menial subservience to the men (238–39). Carrie K. does have her faith and is much akin to Fern, perhaps the most whole of Part 1; but as has been shown in every case, stereotypical situations, only slightly varied, leave each of Toomer's women only on the brink but never at the Easter dawn.

Male and Female Interrelationship in Toomer's *Cane*

RAFAEL A. CANCEL

Jean Toomer's *Cane* is a much praised but much misunderstood literary work. Critics initially received it with a mixture of awe and puzzlement. Its style was magnificent, they said; its structure, puzzling. Thus, Elizabeth Sergeant praises it as "the outstanding artistic performance of the young Negro in prose," where Toomer "had joined to the bitter objective truths of the Georgia earth and expressed through his style a kind of folk music, folk ecstasy."[1] Another critic, Robert Littel, says that *Cane* does not resemble any of the trite, superficial views of the South. "On the contrary," he states, "Mr. Toomer's view is unfamiliar and bafflingly subterranean, the vision of a poet far more than the account of things seen by a novelist—lyric, symbolic, oblique, seldom actual."[2] Langston Hughes, in turn, points out the indifferent reception accorded to *Cane* by white and Negro alike. The whites, he says, did not buy it; the colored people were afraid of it.[3]

They were afraid of the implications of *Cane*'s themes. According to Robert Bone, Toomer speaks of man's essential goodness, of his sense of brotherhood, of his creative instincts as they are overwhelmed and stifled by the modern industrial society.[4] Toomer's positive values spring from the soil, Bone says; he is concerned with universality rather than with provinciality, with the deeper issues rather than with "the conundrums of mixed blood and racial loyalty."[5] James Weldon Johnson, however, sees in *Cane* a reaffirmation of the Negro's values in the face of the materialism and barbarism of white America. Toomer's *Cane* demonstrates that the Negro has brought culture to America; through his folk songs and folk customs he has balanced America's materialism.[6] S. P. Fullinwider interprets *Cane* as the author's religious conflict and his eventual conversion. He points out that the key to the understanding of *Cane* lies in Toomer's religious experience: from denial of God to final assent.[7] On the other hand, Bone notes that Toomer's struggle is not religious, but racial. The decisive factor in Toomer's life was his ambivalence toward his blackness. At times Toomer regarded his blackness as a category to transcend, a limitation to overcome; at other times, as in *Cane*, Toomer was inspired to affirm rather than deny his blackness.[8] Another critic, William Goede, envisions *Cane* as the progressive steps of the young Negro writer struggling for expression and ultimately attaining a renaissance.[9]

If *Cane*'s themes have so confused the critics that they went prying into the life of the author, its structure has baffled them even more. For Bone, *Cane* is a "miscellany of stories and sketches, interspersed with poems, and culminating in a one-act play. . . . It belongs to no genre; it simply is. . . ."[10] However, he observes that the book has a structural and stylistic unity. The style is highly metaphorical because Toomer's vision of the world, Bone implies, was not conceptual but imagistic. Bone divides *Cane* into three parts: Part 1, a series of female portraits; Part 2, the black ghetto of Washington, D. C.; and Part 3, the black writer's quest for a usable past.[11] Littel, however, believes that *Cane* has two principal parts: the first, a series of character sketches, and the second, a long short story, "Kabnis," which is quite different from the sketches and peculiarly interesting.[12] Arna Bontemps observes that the changes in setting—from the black peasantry in Georgia to the Negro community of Washington, D. C., back to rural Georgia, again—reveal a more subtle change in the consciousness of the characters.[13]

These different views witness *Cane*'s richness and complexity and provide one with a challenge as one approaches the book for the first time. My response to *Cane* is a very personal one. For me *Cane* speaks as a poetic drama, a sort of Negro *comédie humaine*. Because *Cane*'s main emphasis is on character portrait, I propose to study the characters as they incarnate Toomer's themes. I concur with most critics that *Cane* is an affirmation of the Negro soul in an increasingly crushing industrial civilization. I think that Toomer, along with other Negro and white writers of his age, notably Allen Tate and the Agrarians, shows through his search for primitive roots, through his emphasis on proximity to the soil, and through his search for the past, redemption from the materialism of his age. For him, as for the Agrarians, the only possible way to forestall the disintegration of character and the dissociation of personality is through attachment to the soil and to one's culture. Love of the land, a return to the past, a loyalty to one's instincts as they are transmitted from one generation to the other by means of the blood are themes common to Allen Tate's *The Fathers*, Stark Young's *So Red the Rose*, Toomer's *Cane*, and other works of the Agrarians. Bontemps regrets the fact that Toomer never came in direct contact with Allen Tate.[14] In spite of this failure to meet, Toomer's themes are indeed very similar to those of the Fugitives.

His search for values, however, went beyond the soil and the South to the Negro soul itself. Nowhere is this Negro soul better portrayed than in Toomer's female characters. Like writers of other nationalities, such as Federico Garcia Lorca, Toomer sees in the female all the beauty and the sensitivity of his race. Just as Lorca regards the Spanish female as a symbol of fertility, of the life-giving force, of the Mother earth, so Toomer envisions the Negro woman as possessing all the primitive instincts and the lust for life that refuses to be contained in a sterile and mechanistic world. In contrast to the male, the female in Toomer is rich with sensibility, beauty, and fertility. The effect of modern civilization, however, is the atrophy of that sensibility. Dwarfed and enslaved by white society, the Negro female succumbs to corruption and loses her finest instincts. Ironically, as the female loses her awareness, the male becomes more conscious of the loss and attempts to rescue her. Finally, Toomer reconciles both male and female through an acceptance of the past and the healing contact of the soil. This juxtaposition of Negro male and female unfolds throughout *Cane*, providing unity of theme and structure.

To begin with, "Karintha" is the story of a lively, lovely, innocent young girl, "a November cotton flower" (2). Watching her the old men who ride her hobby-horse become lascivious, and the young men anxiously wait for the days when they will mate with her. Unaware of her attractive female power, she plays and runs "like a black bird that flashes in light" (2). She behaves like any other child her age, stoning the cows, beating her dog, and fighting the other children. Awareness of her body comes, however, as she overhears her parents making love. Loss of innocence follows shortly after. As she grows to be an enticing, irresistible female, she has only contempt for the old men. In order to "bring her money" and make love to her, the young ones "go to the big cities and run on the road" or "go away to college" (3). One day she gives birth to an unwanted baby and burns him. But guilt, symbolized in the smoke, "so heavy you tasted it in water," burdens her conscience, and she prays for forgiveness. Her loss of innocence is brought about by the insensibility of the men who did "not know the soul of her was a growing thing ripened too soon" (4). The story emphasizes the corruption of the female beauty, the desecration of a young, premature female soul by male insensitivity.

"Becky" has the same theme. Like Karintha, Becky is a victim of the hypocrisy of white and black men alike. A white woman, she has two Negro sons who grow up to be sullen and rebellious against the town which has ostracized them along with their mother. Soon, they shoot two men and have to leave. Just as Karintha is made to prostitute herself and even to kill, so Becky becomes insane. Ashamed of their sin, both black and white men build her a shack by the railroad and bring her food. The insane Becky's prayer, "pines whisper to Jesus," recalls Karintha's baby fallen from her womb onto a bed of pine-needles in the forest. The blue-sheen God of the hypocritical townspeople has listless eyes. The Bible they throw on the wooden pile which buried Becky when the shack fell down on her means nothing to them. It is just an aimless rustle on her mound.

Carma, the next female figure, shows the primitive richness of the Negro woman. Bane, her husband, works with a contractor and is away most of the time. His neglect prompts her infidelity. Carma is as full of life as the singing girl in the "yard of a whitewashed shack" whose feminine fullness goes out to other men:

> Her voice is loud. Echoes, like rain, sweep the valley. Dusk takes the polish from the rails . . . Pungent and composite, the smell of farmyards is the fragrance of the woman. She does not sing; her body is a song. (17)

Even the narrator rejoices in Carma's beauty because "God has left the Moses-people for the nigger" (16). In her zest for life, Carma is just obeying the invitation of nature, "Wind is in the cane. Come along" (16). A jealous, impulsive man, Bane kills a man and goes to jail.

Carma continues to receive other men. Her quarrel and her feigned suicide in the forest is a smart strategy to get rid of her husband.

Like the previous female figures, Fern is both an inscrutable mystery to men and a life-giving force that cannot be enclosed. She enslaves every man she comes in contact with. Because they cannot understand her and because she is "above them," she isolates herself from men and becomes a "virgin" (26). Her mysterious eyes possess the soil and the countryside which flow into them. Men, likewise, are hypnotized by her. Meant for the contemplation of Georgia's dusk, the narrator observes, her eyes would be vacant and lost in Harlem's indifferent throngs. In their obtuseness, men reach for her body but fail to touch her soul. Even when the narrator attempts to reach her soul, "that unnamed thing," he, too, fails. His efforts only sharpen her pain and isolation, and she becomes hysterical and faints in his arms.

A nine-year-old girl with a chalk-white face, Esther, too, fashions a dreamworld of her own where Barlo, black and noble like an enslaved African King transplanted to America, becomes the hero. However, Barlo disappears but not without first impressing in Esther's mind "the only living patterns that her mind was to know" (40). At sixteen, still the dreamy girl whose maternal instincts are beginning to awaken, she dreams that she gives birth to a baby whom she loves "frantically." At twenty-two, she is neither attracted to nor attractive to men. As she assists her father in his grocery store, Barlo is the only subject of her dreams. When she is twenty-seven, Barlo returns to town. Her mind "a pink meshbag filled with baby toes" (45), she becomes jealous and possessive about Barlo. When she discovers that the real Barlo is not the noble black African of her dreams and that he consorts with whores, she sees him as repulsive and hideous. Built upon a dream, now broken, her world disappears. Thus, the blunted male figure once again fails to respond to the female's susceptibility.

In "Blood-Burning Moon," the last episode of the first part, Bob Stone, a white man, and Tom Burwell, a black man, fight to the death over Louisa, a Negro girl. Stone feels an undefinable attraction toward Louisa, who is lovely in her "nigger way" (60). In Louisa we find the same mysterious force met in the earlier females so incomprehensible to the men: "Beautiful nigger gal. Why nigger? Why not, just gal? No, it was because she was nigger that he went to her" (61). She is sweet like the scent of boiling cane. Tom, in turn, must fight for his girl, and when he cuts Bob's throat, he is lynched and then burned. In this story, the conflict is not racial, but even more primitive. Animal, irrational forces, symbolized in the blood-burning moon, "the full moon, an evil thing," involve two men in a struggle for the possession of a woman. On another symbolic level, the story points toward the slow surrender of both the white and the Negro male to the destructive civilization of the North. Neither Bob, whose family was once so wealthy that the men could have all the female slaves they wanted but whose fortune has been swallowed by modern industrialism, nor Tom, "from factory town," can truly possess Louisa, a symbol of the land.

"Seventh Street" is a transitional piece describing the new setting—Washington, D. C. Its images establish the main conflict of *Cane*. The "nigger life" in Washington's Negro ghetto pours itself into the "white and whitewashed wood of Washington." There, the Negro is drained of his dignity and corrupted. The Negroes, wedges "brilliant in the sun," stand in sharp contrast to the whites, "ribbons of wet wood" which "dry and blow away." However, "the black reddish blood" is poured forth and wasted for the "soft skinned life" (71) of the whites. The narrator grows indignant at the corruption of the Negro, "Money burns the pocket, pocket hurts" (72).

This decadent civilization claims a slave in Rhobert who, like so many whites, is possessed by his house and works himself to death to make money. Materialism has completely degraded Rhobert, who should have stayed in the South with his wife and children instead of coming North to become the lifeless slave of a house.

A Negro "orphan-woman," Avey symbolizes, as Goede aptly points out, the fertility of the Negro soul.[15] The narrator loves her, but she does not pay attention to him. Like Karintha, she passes from innocence to awareness of her womanhood and to corruption in a white man's world. At first, she has intercourse with a college student whom she visits in his flat. She never reciprocates the narrator's infatuation with her, however. Like the other previous males, he cannot fathom the mystery of the female soul because he deals in superficialities. Unperceptive of her real need, he mistakes her indifference for indolence. He cannot understand that, unlike the other earlier females, she is displaced, out of her natural environment. Like Rhobert, she belongs to the South, to the soil of which she is a mere extension. In New York, or in Washington, the Negro female loses her dignity and sensibility. The sophisticated narrator, a product of the northern civilization, cannot comprehend that Avey has lost her soul, that she is no more than a walking zombie. When he tries to approach her again, he bores her with his irrelevant monologues. He pours forth platitudes about "an art that would open the way for women the likes of her" (87), and "a larger life for their expression" (86). He speaks about her "need" and her "emotions," but he cannot understand that her seeming laziness is ennui with the world that surrounds her. Soon, his passion betraying his chivalric mood, he tries to make love to her but obtains no response from her. The pattern of the sensitive female and the imperceptive male is once again repeated in this story.

This design is also found in "Theater." The setting is the Howard Theatre, but the action really takes place in the mind of John, the manager's brother. His face is partly orange from the light that filters through a window and partly shadow—a reflection of the conflict and division of his mind. In his body, "separate from the thoughts that pack his mind" (92), he loves Dorris, a show girl who has crisp-curled, bushy black hair and lips curiously full and very red. But in his mind her dance becomes "a dead thing in the shadow which is his dream" (99). Toomer's description of John's revery moves with the same rhythm and swiftness of the jazz. It also blends the meaningless real world where these Negroes live and lose their identity, with their wistful dreamworld. In contrast to John's imaginary world, where everything gleams beautiful and satisfying, we are faced with this dreary place. The staleness of their lives "of nigger alleys, of pool rooms and restaurants and near-beer saloons" (91) forces these Negroes to seek relief in daydreaming. Like Avey, Dorris has lost the robustness and lustiness of the earlier females. The male, in turn, has suffered a change. John is no longer the subservient slave of the female of the earlier stories. Though a very selective dreamer, he still lacks total awareness of his situation.

"Calling Jesus" reiterates the theme of the female soul oppressed by the environment of the North. In this story there is also the nostalgia for the past. The soul of this nameless Negro woman is "like a little thrust-tailed dog that follows her whimpering" (102). Smothered in her surroundings, her soul yearns for the "clean hay cut" and the "dream-fluted cane." Her soul calls to Jesus, too, like Becky's, for salvation lies not in the oppressive North, but in the South where "the bare feet of Christ" move "across bales of southern cotton" (103).

From these bales of cotton comes Dan Moore of "Box Seat" to reclaim the lost Muriel, who, like the female in the previous story, is a slave of white society. Having capitulated to both white and Negro materialistic civilization, Muriel has no will of her own. She is a prisoner in Mrs. Pribby's house. In fact, she has become her property like the other houses of Mrs. Pribby. Like Rhobert, Muriel has metamorphosed into the house she lives in, "The house, the rows of houses locked about her hair" (113). Tamed and shy, she has lost her identity by surrendering her soul to Mrs. Pribby, "She [Mrs. Pribby] is me somehow!" (112). Her spirit has been conquered by "zoo-restrictions and keeper-taboos" (112). In the theater, where "the seats are bolted houses" (117), she is intimidated by the people around her: "Teachers are not supposed to have bobbed hair. She'll keep her hat on" (116). Bernice, her shallow friend, is another slave. Muriel, however, has kept some semblance of struggle in the presence of Dan. Her primitive instincts are "still unconquered."

To these instincts Dan, "A new-world Christ" come to rescue her, appeals:

> Shake your curled wool-blossoms, nigger. Open your liver lips to the lean, white spring. Stir the root-life of a withered people. Call them from their houses, and teach them to dream. (104)

He dreams of smashing the tenement houses that contain his people—the prisons of the Negro soul. "Baboon from the zoo," he will break in and "smash in with the truck . . . grab an ax and brain em" (105). He is very conscious of his mission of redemption:

> I was born in a canefield. The hands of Jesus touched me. I am come to a sick world to heal it . . . Give me your fingers and I will peel them as if they were ripe bananas. (105–6)

With his bare hands, he will strip free the Negro soul once again. When he knocks at Mrs. Pribby's door, "the tension of his arms makes the glass rattle" (106). Although he is strong with the strength of the southern soil, he encounters resistance from the start. First, his lusty voice cracks when he tries to sing to the houses which belong to Mrs. Pribby, "No wonder he couldn't sing to them" (107). Once inside, he "feels the pressure of the house, of the rear room, of the rows of houses" (109). Under this pressure the spirit of Muriel, and of every Negro who lives here, labors and is eventually crushed.

Unable to cope with this influence, Muriel finally capitulates in the theater. She surrenders even her passion by accepting the blood-stained rose from Mr. Barry, the dwarf, after the brutal fight. Ironically, this kind of entertainment is the refinement for which Muriel, Bernice, and the rest of the Negroes who live in Mrs. Pribby's prison-houses have sold their souls. Dan, who still sees himself as the new Samson who will "reach up and grab the girders of this building and pull them down" (126), or as the new Moses who cries to the white masters, "Let my people go!" rises from his seat and utters the protest of the whole Negro race throughout the ages, "JESUS WAS ONCE A LEPER!" Goede believes that this represents Dan's rejection of the white man's Christianity, his "severance from Christ's world."[16] To me, however, this is not a rejection, but a reaffirmation in new terms of the true Christianity. Christ is not, Dan implies with his cry, created in the image of a white dwarf. Rather, taking upon himself the sickness of the world, echoes of St. Paul, Christ indeed became a leper. To accept the rose from this white anti-Christ, as Muriel does, is to deny oneself. Defeated in his purpose, Dan contemplates the hopeless ruin: "Eyes of houses, soft girl-eyes, glow reticently upon the hubbub and blink out" (130). With Muriel still a prisoner, Dan realizes that there is no reason to fight and, unconcerned, walks away.

Like Muriel and Dan, Paul Johnson in "Bona and Paul" is a displaced Negro whose ambivalence of identity is reflected in his "red-brown face." "An autumn leaf," he is a mulatto who still feels the strong pull of the southern past preventing him loving Bona, a white girl: "Paul follows the sun to a pine-matted hillock in Georgia" (134). In his dreams, he feels the slanting roofs of gray unpainted cabins tinted lavender where "a Negress chants a lullaby beneath the mate-eyes of a southern planter." With breasts "ample for suckling of a song" (138), she is a picture of the fertile female. But Paul's dreamy vision of the southern past does not last, and he must follow the sun back to the world of Chicago. Paul's friend Art tried to cheer him up, but to no avail. Paul suffers the melancholy of a past that is out of reach; he has "dark blood."

Though Art has arranged a double date with Bona and Helen, Paul still dreams of the Negro woman who sends the suckling of a song "curiously weaving among lush melodies of cane and corn" (138). For him, the Negro female is "life . . . beautiful woman." For this reason, during the date Paul's eyes are very critical of Bona. Though she confesses her love for him, he feels that he is isolated:

> Apart from the pain which they had consciously caused. Suddenly he knew that people saw, not attractiveness in his dark skin, but difference. (145)

Their attitude toward his color stirs in him a dormant pride: their stares "filled something long empty within him, and were like green blades sprouting in his consciousness" (145). When he finally seems to have solved the conflict for himself and to have found reconciliation in Crimson Gardens, Bona leaves him. His attempt to reach her comes too late. Like the preceding males, Paul ultimately fails to achieve success with a female. His immersion in himself prevents him from knowing Bona's soul.

Significantly, the reconciliation which is finally obtained in *Cane* takes place on southern soil. Kabnis, like Paul, has a conflict between his acceptance of the past and his identity. A teacher educated in a northern school, Kabnis is both disgusted with and afraid of his new environment. He cannot sleep because of his nervousness. In an outburst of rage, he kills a cackling hen, but even then the silence is too much for him. Talk of lynching and of the southerners' sadism toward Negroes scares him more. He feels disgust for the Negro's religious expression which teaches submission to his kind of cruelty. But he is too frightened to reveal his thoughts to his friends. In a land where the whites get the boll and the Negroes the stalk, "a great spiral of buzzards reaches far into the heavens. An ironic comment upon the path that leads into the Christian land . . ." (109). Not discriminating between good and bad Negroes, whites hang both. Their brutality, as narrated by Layman, terrifies Kabnis:

> "Seen um shoot an cut a man t pieces who had died th night befo. Yassur. An they didnt stop when they found out he was dead—jes went on ahackin at him anyway." (173)

A rock thrown through one of the windows into their midst sends Kabnis running through cotton fields until he locks the door of his shack behind him. The conflict within Kabnis, like that within Paul, veers between his white education and his Negro roots. His refusal to accept his past weighs him down. The presence of Father John, "a symbol of the flesh and spirit of the past" (217), is irksome to him.

Like Dan Moore, Kabnis regrets the surrender that both the Negro male and female have allowed in the South. Stella and Cora, for instance, have straightened their hair. There is still some hope in them:

> Character, however, has not all been ironed out. As they kneel there, heavy-eyed and dusky, and throwing grotesque moving shadows on the wall, they are two princesses in Africa going through the early-morning ablutions of their pagan prayers. (229)

Finally, Kabnis accepts his past as manifested in the words of Father John, but also in the "firm, cool hands" of Carrie K., an uncorrupted female:

> Her palms draw the fever out . . . Carrie presses his face tenderly against her. The suffocation of her fresh starched dress feels good to him . . . Carrie notices his robe. She catches up to him, points to it, and helps him take it off. (238–39)

Thus, through the help of Carrie K., Kabnis is able to put away his robe, a symbol of sophistication and the negation of his blackness.

The full cycle, then, has been completed. Groping for affirmation, the male finally attains it in the female who, in spite of the hardening of her sensibility brought about by the white civilization, rises from her degradation. Acceptance of the past finally is achieved through the female who is also a symbol of mother earth. Kabnis obtains reconciliation because he reaches toward the very soul of the female, of the earth "whose touch would resurrect him" (191). As the sun "is rising from its cradle" (239), both male and female are reunited. Their harmony brings peace and integrity to a disjoined, dissociated race.

Celebration and Biblical Myth; Surrealism and the Blues in *Cane*

Images of Celebration in *Cane*

SISTER MARY KATHRYN GRANT

One does not expect to find much celebration appearing in the writing of an oppressed people. However, even a cursory survey of the literature of such groups reveals that this spirit cannot be entirely suppressed: Jean Toomer's *Cane* is one such illustration of this spirit of celebration. Depicting the life of blacks in the North and in the South, *Cane* is replete with images of celebration.

Defined as affirmation, an urge to dance and sing the mysteries of life, a sense of identity, a spirit of play, celebration is an essential part of man's experience. However, etched into every human life are the intersecting and converging patterns of celebration and of sorrow. In the tension between these conflicting forces, man becomes fully himself. Aware of this inescapable reality, Dan carefully instructs Muriel in the "Box Seat" section of *Cane*:

> "There is no such thing as happiness. Life bends joy and pain, beauty and ugliness, in such a way that no one may isolate them. No one should want to. Perfect joy, or perfect pain, with no contrasting element to define them, would mean a monotony of consciousness, would mean death. Not happy, Muriel. . . . Say that you have used

your capacity for life to cradle them. To start them upward-flowing. Or if you can't say that you have, then say that you will. My talking to you will make you aware of your power to do so."[1]

Earlier he had also explained to her:

> "Dont know, Muriel—wanted to see you—wanted to talk to you—to see you and tell you that I know what you've been through—what pain the last few months have been—"
> "Lets dont mention that."
> "But why not, Muriel. I—"
> "Please."
> "But Muriel, life is full of things like that. One grows strong and beautiful in facing them. What else is life?" (109)

Harvey Cox, noted contemporary theologian, has observed that the Puritan Protestant ethic has stifled the spirit of celebration in American culture.[2] At the same time, he insists that man universally experiences this need to celebrate. If it cannot be expressed publicly or openly, the need does not diminish. It must be met to some degree in all human life.

Cox calls particular attention to the American Negro, whose church has preserved this life-affirming characteristic.[3] Despite, if not because of, oppression, a sense of celebration, although often evanescent and overshadowed, permeates the culture. A refrain repeated in "Kabnis" epitomizes the situation: "White-man's land. / Niggers, sing" (167, 209). However, the song continues: "Burn, bear black children / Till poor rivers bring / Rest, and sweet glory / In Camp Ground." Celebration is nurtured on hope—in something yet to be realized.

The most prevalent motif or image of celebration is that of singing and dancing. In one of the interchapter songs, the blacks are described thus:

> A song-lit race of slaves . . .
> . . . .
> O Negro slaves, dark purple ripened plums,
> Squeezed, and bursting in the pine-wood air,
> Passing, before they stripped the old tree bare
> One plum was saved for me, one seed becomes
>
> An everlasting song, a singing tree,
> Caroling softly souls of slavery,

> What they were, and what they are to me,
> Caroling softly souls of slavery. (21)

The valleys and fields sing as well. Among the earliest references to this is the song, "Georgia Dusk" (22), which describes a "feast of moon and men . . . surprised in making folk-songs from soul sounds." The song continues:

> Meanwhile, the men, with vestiges of pomp,
> Race memories of king and caravan,
> High-priests, an ostrich, and a juju-man,
> So singing through the footpaths of the swamp.
>
> Their voices rise . . . the pin trees are guitars
> Strumming, pine-needles fall like sheets of rain . . .
> Their voices rise . . . the chorus of the cane
> Is caroling a vesper to the stars.
> (22–23)

Returning to the South in his search for identity, Kabnis laments, "If I, the dream . . . could become the face of the South. How my lips would sing for it, my song being the lips of its soul" (158). He longs for the hills and valleys to heave with folk-songs (161), for man and nature sing in celebration.

Structurally, *Cane* is cyclic; the novel begins and ends in the South. Images of celebration in the southern section are many; they are also natural and earthy. The central section, occurring in the North, is noticeably lacking in such images, an omission which tends to support the opinion that oppression and celebration are not necessarily mutually exclusive. Celebration, in the North, is usually generated by a memory, a recollection of the South. In the "Theater" section, when Dorris dances, "glorious songs are the muscles of her limbs. And her singing is of canebrake loves and mangrove feasting" (98). In the same section, when John dreams of Dorris, "her face is tinted like the autumn alley. Of old flowers, or of a southern canefield, her perfume. 'Glorious Dorris.' So his eyes speak" (99).

The anonymous woman in "Calling Jesus" also dreams of the South. Her soul, "like a little thrust-tailed dog" (102), is carried

> to . . . where she sleeps upon clean hay cut in her dreams. . . . Her breath comes sweet as honeysuckle whose pistils bear the life of coming song. And her eyes carry to where builders find no need for vestibules, for swinging on iron hinges, storm doors. . . . Some one . . .

> eoho Jesus . . . soft as the bare feet of Christ moving across bales of southern cotton, will steal in and cover it that it need not shiver, and carry it to her where she sleeps: cradled in dream-fluted cane. (102–3)

The earthy celebrations of the rural, Georgia scenes—the cane-brakes and mangrove feastings—are replaced in the North by the artificial world of the theater. There are only memories of southern times, reveries of the past where sadness and celebration existed together. In the North, celebration is a futile effort to "Stir the root-life of a withered people . . . and teach them to dream" (104).

The central section, which could be a migration piece, contains conflicting themes: the North, which politically and socially is less hostile to the blacks is also a mechanistic, mercantile, depersonalized world. "Life of nigger alleys, of pool rooms and restaurants and near-beer saloons soaks into the walls of Howard Theater and sets them throbbing jazz songs. Black skinned, they dance and shout above the tick and trill of white-walled buildings. . . . At night, road-shows volley songs into the mass-heart of black people. Songs soak the walls and seep out to the nigger life of alleys and near-beer saloons . . ." (91). Valleys which once rang out with song are replaced by white-washed walls. Fine is the contrast between this scene and the southern one in which Kabnis hears a woman singing. And "her song is a spark that travels swiftly to the near-by cabins. Like purple tallow flames, songs jet up. They spread a ruddy haze over the heavens. . . . Now the whole countryside is a soft chorus" (192). From hills and knolls, Fern's people also listen for the evening folk-song (27).

Life, too, is viewed differently in the North and in the South. Karintha dances and teaches "other folks just what it was to live" (1). The "November cotton flower" (2,7), taught them at least a kind of life—beautifully different from the life Rhobert knew in the city, a life that is a "murky, wiggling, microscopic water that compresses him. . . . Life is water that is being drawn off" (73). The inversion of the water image powerfully underlines the death-life of the North.

The aspect of celebration which affirms life, both human and natural life, also occurs most frequently in the southern sections of the novel. Women are described in images of nature: Karintha is a cotton flower, Carma is the "forest, dancing" (17). Women are linked directly with the earth, with the life-giving force of nature, the act of creating and bringing forth: Karintha ripens (4), Becky bears two sons (8).

In *Cane*, night is an occasion of celebration. This natural phenomenon is also linked with woman: "Night, soft belly of a pregnant Negress, throbs evenly against the torso of the South. Night throbs a womb-song to the South. Cane and cotton-fields, pine forests, cypress swamps, sawmills, and factories are fecund at her touch. Night's womb-song sets them singing" (208–9).

The northern section closes with an interesting irony: the final scene is in "the Gardens," a title reminiscent of the Edenic myth of the South. ". . . That I came into the Gardens, into life in the Gardens with one whom I did not know. . . . I came back to tell you, brother, that white faces are petals of roses. That dark faces are petals of dusk. That I am going out and gather petals. That I am going out and know her whom I brought here with me to these Gardens which are purple like a bed of roses would be at dusk" (153).

Immediately after this section, the section of the novel returns to the South. Both literally and figuratively, the parentheses close. The themes of identity, of celebration, of loving and being loved are brought together as Kabnis's life parallels the structure of the novel. Kabnis must go South to discover his identity and to discover celebration. Tormented with his searching, one night he goes out to a cabin. "Peace. Negroes within it are content. They farm. They sing. They love. They sleep" (164). Kabnis, however, can't sleep (164).

Linked with the need to celebrate is the need to play.[4] In addition to the images of singing and dancing in *Cane*, the song "Georgia Dusk," quoted previously, speaks of a game in which, with "vestiges of pomp, / Race memories of king and caravan, / High-priests . . . and a juju-man" (22) are staged. This masque-like game is repeated in the "Kabnis" section. "Kabnis, with great mock-solemnity, goes to the corner, takes down the robe, and dons it. He is a curious spectacle, acting a part, yet very real" (213). In the cellar room, with his friends, Kabnis wrestles for identity. When he is finally capable of emerging from the womb-like room, he removes the robe and "hangs it, with an exaggerated ceremony on its nail in the corner" (239). Through his game, Kabnis is reborn.

The final scene of the novel encapsulates these images of celebration and rebirth. Kabnis ascends the stairs, leaving the cellar room as Carrie, remaining behind, watches. "Outside the sun arises from its cradle in the tree-tops of the forest. Shadows of pine are dreams the sun shakes from its eyes. The sun arises. Gold-glowing child, it steps into the sky and sends a birth-song slanting down gray dust streets and sleepy windows of the southern town" (239). Kabnis has reclaimed his identity, and a birth-song resounds.

Throughout the novel a second motif has been working: purple dusk. It is introduced in the epigraph on the title page and is woven throughout the narrative sections and interchapters. However, as the novel closes, dusk becomes dawn, purple becomes gold, an inversion which reenforces the informing motif of celebration. Toomer chooses to end *Cane* with the hopeful image of the dawn.

There is no exuberance in *Cane*—no frivolous, carefree mood. There is searching and sadness, pain and death. Despite this, there is an underlying spirit of hopeful celebration. There are canebrakes and mangrove feastings (98), because man, imaged in the "deep-rooted cane" (title page), celebrates not with tawdry show and paltry amusements but with a birth-song (239) which announces a new day.

Jean Toomer's *Cane* and Biblical Myth

LOUISE BLACKWELL

When Jean Toomer published *Cane* in 1923, he made a significant statement on the theme "Black Is Beautiful." Now, fifty years later, *Cane* is still one of the most profound statements on that theme. As pleasant as it is to read the book in this context, however, this is not all that can be said about it. At this point the word *book* is used deliberately, since there is still argument as to whether *Cane* is a novel. Writing in 1969, Darwin T. Turner said: "It [*Cane*] is not a novel, not even the experimental novel for which Bone[1] pled to justify including it in his study. It is, instead, a collection of character sketches, short stories, poems, and a play, which form one of the distinguished achievements in the writings of Negro Americans."[2]

This is the same type of argument that still centers on James Joyce's *Ulysses*, some critics contending that the work is not a novel because it lacks unity, with others offering equally good arguments that it is a novel. In this essay, *Cane* is assumed to be an experimental novel of the 1920s. Published just a year after *Ulysses*, it continues to be just as pleasing and surprising as its Irish counterpart.

As for unity in *Cane*, a good case was made in the fall of 1970 by John M. Reilly, who writes:

> The means of unity may be briefly described. In *Cane* Toomer has dropped from his narrative the conventional dependence upon causal sequence, continuous presence of leading characters, and chronological progression. In their place he has adopted the compressed statement of images linked by their intrinsic associations, and he has represented those imagistic statements becoming synthesized either in the mind of a narrator, in the consciousness and unconsciousness of a character, or in the ambience of locale. Toomer, thus, links his various sketches and lyrics into a poetically structured record of a search for the route to self-expression and consequent redemption for the artist and his race.[3]

Reilly is using the word *redemption* in a secular sense to identify the search for identity through self-discovery. He writes: "Toomer conceives of self-discovery as an intuitive experience which must be described or, rather, transmitted in a way that will preserve the content of feeling. The prose in *Cane*, therefore, is impressionistic and nondiscursive."[4]

The gist of Reilly's essay is that Toomer was pointing back to the folk experience of black people in America and contending that redemption comes through "spontaneous expression of their inner selves."[5] In other words, when irrational feeling is expressed instinctually, it is redemptive, but if a person is socially conditioned to repress instinct or to exploit it in others, it is nonredemptive. All of this is true, since a central interest of the writers and artists in the Harlem Renaissance, with which Toomer was identified, concerned the folk, their racial past, and the culture of black folk in America. Reilly makes the statement that this "book is a symbolic record of the sensitive author's attempt to relate his personal past."[6] Certainly Reilly's reading of *Cane* is valid.

The full beauty and power of this novel, however, cannot be appreciated without consideration of Toomer's mythical method. Just as Joyce, in *Ulysses*, published a year before *Cane*, drew upon Homeric myth to imply analogies and correspondences, so Toomer drew upon biblical myth to make vivid the experience of his people. Central to the meaning of *Cane* is the majestic and compelling metaphor which identifies the black people in America with the Hebrew children wandering in the wilderness. Toomer is not the first to use this metaphor, but his use is more comprehensive and poetic than any other author's, and *Cane*, by this metaphor, is lifted into the realm of prophecy. The metaphor is sustained by the biblical style, which includes a mixture of poetry and prose, religious symbols, biblical themes, and characters with biblical names. With regard to individual characters, Toomer draws parallels from both the Old Testament and the New Testament.

Here it should be pointed out that Jean Toomer knew the Bible well and that as a poet, he was completely aware of his achievement in *Cane*. He had a lifelong interest in religion, moving at an early age into mysticism. In 1924, he spent a summer at the Gurdjieff Institute in Fontainebleau, France, and from then on he devoted most of his time and writing to Gurdjieff's beliefs. Earlier, before writing *Cane*, he had gone from Washington, D. C., to Georgia to superintend a small Negro industrial school. There he became familiar with the folk, his racial past, and in 1922 he wrote to the editor of *The Liberator*: "Within the last two or three years . . . my growing need for artistic expression has pulled me deeper into the Negro group. . . . I found myself loving it in a way that I could never love the other."[7] Jean Toomer could, and often did, pass for white, yet his deepest feeling of identification was for the instinctive, natural people of the Negro race, and out of this identification grew *Cane*.

Any analysis of this novel should begin with the title. Although the title is spelled C-A-N-E, it has, by its sound rather than the spelling, a biblical ring. The title refers to a land of sugar cane, the land being Georgia. But Georgia is only one part of the setting. Washington, D. C., and Chicago are part of the setting, and sugar cane does not grow there. The allusion, therefore, seems to be to Canaan Land, or the promised land. One is reminded also, by textual allusions, of Cain, the son of Adam, and of the city of Cana. One is also reminded of the bulrushes and of the baby Moses.

Very early in the book,[8] there is a section entitled "Carma," Carma being a beautiful black woman. But the allusion is to "Karma," which has to do with reincarnation. This prose passage is introduced by a short poem:

> Wind is in the cane. Come along.
> Cane leaves swaying, rusty with talk,
> Scratching choruses above the guinea's squawk,
> Wind is in the cane. Come along.
>
> (16)

The poem is intended to alert the reader, since there are voices in the cane and since the guinea, which symbolizes the human soul in biblical mythology, is squawking. In any event, Carma is a regal woman, driving a mule and wagon, "driving a Georgia chariot down an old dust road. Dixie Pike is what they call it" (16). And a few lines further on one finds: "God has left the Moses-people for the nigger" (16). This statement is followed by a long, parenthetical passage which begins as follows: "The sun is hammered to a band of gold. Pine-needles, like mazda, are brilliantly aglow" (17). In this passage, the sun, as in Christian symbology, is Christ. In the sentence, "Pine-needles, like mazda, are brilliantly gold," the word *mazda* means "great wisdom." This word derives from the Sanskrit, originally referring to part of the name of Ahura Mazda, the one God.

The remainder of the tale is quite realistic, with descriptions of the sawmill, the railroad, the farmyard, and the general community. In fact, just as in the Bible, God's chosen people are portrayed with all of their strengths and weaknesses, their sins and their beauty. The realism, however, is interspersed with moving symbolism. For instance, the moon, which is the eye of God in Christian symbology, is almost always referred to when anything significant is occurring. In "Carma," as night comes on, "Foxie, the bitch, slicks back her ears and barks at the rising moon" (18). And just before Carma pretends to shoot herself, "there, in quarter heaven shone the crescent moon" (19). According to the narrator, "Carma's tale is the crudest melodrama" (18), since she is responsible for her husband going to prison, but through allusion and symbolism, the story is very moving. Immediately following the incident of Foxie barking at the moon, the poem at the beginning of the tale is repeated, and it is repeated at the end, when the narrator tells us again that Carma's tale "is the crudest melodrama" (20). In other words, he had told what he knew and understood, nothing more.

In "Blood-Burning Moon," we find these lines: "Up from the dusk the full moon came. Glowing like a fired pine-knot, it illumined the great door and soft showered the Negro shanties aligned along the single street of factory town. The full moon in the great door was an omen" (51). The story involves Louisa, a black woman, who works for a white family. Bob Stone, the young son in that family, is in love with her. Tom Burwell, a young and powerfully built black man, is also in love with her. After Tom is chided by his friends about Louisa and Bob Stone, he decides that he has had enough and leaves to find Bob Stone. He then "shuddered when he saw the full moon rising toward the cloud-bank" (55). Before going to Bob Stone, however, he stopped to talk to Louisa on her front steps. At that point, "the full moon sank upward into the deep purple of the cloud-bank" (58). And various people on the street began to sing:

> Red nigger moon. Sinner!
> Blood-burning moon. Sinner!
> Come out that fact'ry door.
> (58)

Finally, after Bob came to look for Louisa, finding her with Tom Burwell, it was the white man who attacked first, with Tom cutting him so badly that he barely made it back to Broad Street before collapsing. That same night white men lynched Tom by tying him to a stake inside the abandoned factory and burning it down. From where she sat, Louisa could not hear the yelling of the lynchers, but she opened her eyes and "saw the full moon glowing in the great door. The full moon, an evil thing, an omen, soft showering the homes of folks she knew" (67). She wondered where these people were, and decided to sing, hoping "they'd come out and join her" (67). Anyway, she had to sing to the moon, for "the full moon in the great door was an omen" (67).

While this tale is a realistic account of the lynching of a black man, there is constantly present the mysticism that has surrounded the moon forever. There is also what most people today would call "superstition," which is made explicit when Tom, after watching the moon move "towards the cloud-bank" (55), thinks to himself that he "didnt give a godam for the fears of old women" (55). And, as mentioned previously, the moon symbolizes the eye of God as it sinks "upward into the deep purple of the cloud-bank" (58). Clouds symbolize the presence of God, while "purple" is symbolically the color of sorrow and penitence. The blood-red moon is frequently used, as in some of the works of Flannery O'Connor, to symbolize the Host drenched in blood. According to the Old Testament, sacrifices, both human and animal, were made under certain forms of the moon, which are frequently explained in the Bible. In this story, the moon is rising toward a dark cloud. Thus God is symbolically trying to hide his face from the evil that is about to take place. When she begins to sing after the lynching, Louisa hopes that her people will come out to join her, and she thinks that perhaps Tom Burwell might come, too. This suggests a Christ-like sacrifice with the possibility of resurrection.

In the story entitled "Fern," an enchanting and unexplainable young black woman is described as having an "aquiline, Semitic" nose. And immediately the narrator states: "If you have heard a Jewish cantor sing, if he has touched you and made your own sorrow seem trivial when compared with his, you will know my feeling when I follow the curves of her profile, like mobile rivers, to their common delta" (24). Later, he states: "But at first sight of her I felt as if I heard a Jewish cantor sing" (28). Her name, finally, is revealed as Fernie May Rosen.

The theme of the Prodigal Son is suggested by a poem, "Song of the Son." This poem, in the context of the book, suggests that slavery and bloodshed have made the land barren. The prophecy is here, too. That is, even though the end seems to be near, it has not come yet, because "before they stripped the old tree bare / One plum was saved for me, one seed becomes / An everlasting song, a singing tree" (21). The bare tree is symbolic of the cross, but the singing tree is symbolic of the inexhaustible life process, and in this instance it is more than this; it is the black man's contact with the Almighty. The plum is a symbol of fidelity and independence in the Christian context. When considered in this way, the Son that has returned to the barren land may be the Son of God. This is a moving poem that, given more space than this paper permits, would lend itself to line-by-line explication.

In the poem "Beehive," the black city is compared to a beehive, with numerous symbols denoting the relationship between black people and God. Bees have been used, symbolically, in various ways in the Bible and in biblical art. In this poem, however, the beehive symbolizes the unity and religious attitude of the black community. Other symbols used here are the words *moon*, *silver*, *honey*, and *flower*, all of which contribute to the religious effect of the poem.

A few of the readily recognizable biblical names in *Cane* are Becky, an allusion to Rebecca; Esther; Dan, alluding to the son of Jacob, an ancestor of the Hebrew Tribe; Paul; and John, used in two different stories, with direct reference to John the Baptist. In *Cane*, Becky is a white woman who has two black sons; in the Bible, Rebecca had two sons, Esau and Jacob. The biblical Esther was a Queen, one of the wives of Ahasuerus; Esther in *Cane*, however, is rejected by a black man named King Barlo, although she is characterized as a queenly person. In the story, "Box Seat," Dan Moore is admonished to "Stir the root-life of a withered people" (104), thus suggesting the biblical Dan. Paul, in the story "Bona and Paul," is a deep, mysterious young black man who terms himself a philosopher. At the end of an evening at a night spot, the Crimson Gardens in Chicago, with another young man and two girls, all white, Paul becomes aware that he is looked upon as different and somewhat out of place. The black doorman gives him a knowing look as the party walks out. Once outside, Paul runs back to the doorman and says:

> "I came back to tell you, to shake your hand, and tell you that you are wrong. That something beautiful is going to happen. That the Gardens are purple like a bed of roses would be at dusk. That I came into the Gardens, into life in the Gardens with one whom I did not know. That I danced with her, and did not know her. That I felt passion, contempt and passion for her whom I did not know. That I thought of her. That my thoughts were matches thrown into a dark window. And all the while the Gardens were purple like a bed of roses would be at dusk. I came back to tell you, brother, that white faces are petals of roses. That dark faces are petals of dusk. That I am going out and gather petals. That I am going out and know her whom I brought here with me to these Gardens which are purple like a bed of roses would be at dusk." (152–53)

Much can be made of the symbolism of the Garden, the roses, the gathering of petals, the coming to life in the Garden, etc. In "Theater," John, the brother of the theater manager, is seated in the theater watching dancers and musicians rehearse. "His mind, contained above desires of his body, singles the girls out, and tries to trace origins and plot destinies" (92). Dorris, in the role of Salome in the Book of Matthew, dances her heart out in an effort to win the attention of John, but he ignores her. Dorris, of course, can only weep, since she is in no position to demand his head on a platter. In "Kabnis," one black man is called Father John. He is described as a "slave boy whom some Christian mistress taught to read the Bible. Black man who saw Jesus in the ricefields, and began preaching to his people" (212).

Kabnis, the last piece in *Cane*, is a play about an intellectual Negro named Ralph Kabnis, who left the city and went to Georgia to teach school. Like Jonah, whom the Lord sent to Nineveh to teach the people, he is afraid and wishes to flee. After considerable suffering, abuse, and finally adjustment to the strange land, Kabnis, having been ousted from his teaching position, becomes a laborer in a workshop owned by another black man. *Kabnis*, the longest piece in *Cane*, is rich with religious references and allusions.

Since *Cane* contains twenty-eight poems, short stories, and vignettes, and one play, suffice it to say that no attempt is made here to cite every instance of biblical analogies and parallels in the work. It is hoped, however, that this brief essay will invite new readers and new interest on the part of old readers of *Cane*. If further enticement is needed, the reader's attention is called to the statement by Clifford Mason, who contends that Jean Toomer created "a dramatic and revolutionary prose in sheer mastery of English fiction as craft and style that has been matched for achievement both in content and technique only once in the history of the American novel, and that work, *The Sound and the Fury*, was still eight years away from publication!"[8] Indeed, *Cane* is in the class with William Faulkner's *The Sound and the Fury*, as well as James Joyce's *Ulysses*.

As John M. Reilly pointed out, there was, in the Harlem Renaissance, a search for self-identity, but there was more. There was an effort to identify the race, to salvage a people, and to reveal the rich culture of black people in America. What Toomer was saying is that black people are beautiful and good just as they are; they do not have to imitate white people. And by his use of biblical myth, he lifted *Cane* to the level of prophecy in the vein of the Old Testament.

Jean Toomer and Surrealism

SUE R. GOODWIN

Arna Bontemps has said that "*Cane* and Jean Toomer, its gifted author," present "an enigma"[1] and that the book and its author are best characterized by a quality of "elusiveness."[2] Darwin Turner has called Toomer and his work "poetically ambiguous,"[3] and Robert Bone has stated that attempted analysis of Toomer's work is a "frustrating task."[4] Moreover, the critics do not seem to agree on the genre of Toomer's major work. Bone has insisted that *Cane* is an experimental novel,[5] while Turner has stated "It is not a novel. . . . It is, instead, a collection of character sketches, short stories, poems, and a play."[6] George E. Kent described *Cane* as "a group of narratives and poetry,"[7] but Waldo Frank has simply called it a "book" and its author a "poet."[8]

There is even more disagreement concerning the reasons for Toomer's failure to fulfill the hopes of the first readers of *Cane* for a long and productive literary career for its author. Several critics have alleged that he lost his ability to write when he denied his African ancestry. Bone believes Toomer stopped writing because *Cane* was poorly received and proved an economic failure.[9] Turner, who has worked extensively with Toomer's unpublished letters and other manuscripts, has called attention to the various weaknesses he found in

Toomer's unsuccessful work following *Cane*. He has attributed Toomer's failure largely to his devotion to the cult of Georges Gurdjieff (37). Furthermore, Larry Thompson has postulated that Toomer's plays were unsuccessful, not because of the artistic failure of the playwright, but because "society was not ready for his themes and experimentations."[10]

Each of these scholars obviously has spent many hours analyzing and studying Toomer's work, both published and unpublished. At least two of them, Turner and Bontemps, enjoyed a personal relationship with Toomer. Although they agree that Toomer is an enigma, perhaps it is possible, nevertheless, that some pattern might be found in his elusiveness. It is interesting to notice that in the broad definitions of the social, psychological, political, and artistic principles of the surrealists much can be found which seems to correspond with the themes, concerns, and style of both the life and work of Toomer.

Surrealism was a movement in literature and the plastic arts which reached fruition in France in the 1920s. In 1924, the poet André Breton formulated the philosophy of the movement in his *Manifeste du surréalisme*. In it he stated that the aim of the surrealists was to resolve the "two seemingly contradictory states, the cold dry tool of logic and the magic of the unconscious and the dream world, into a sort of absolute reality."[11]

Sir Herbert Read, a very able apologist for the surrealists, says that the movement was a "spontaneous generation of an international organism, in contrast to the artificial manufacture of a collective organization."[12] He further describes surrealism in general as the romantic principle in art, but "romanticism is understood in a certain strict and not too comprehensive sense" (21). Read also states the belief that the surrealist is an integral artist whose philosophy of life embraces painting, poetry, philosophy, and politics (59).

It must be emphasized that in the material available no evidence has been found to link Toomer directly with the surrealist movement, other than as a pattern in his life and work which seems to establish a philosophic and artistic kinship with the surrealists. Nevertheless, given his special eagerness for new ideas and the general intellectual atmosphere in which he lived, it is certainly not unreasonable to suppose that he was aware of the movement.

At any rate, even the briefest definitions of surrealism include the influence of Sigmund Freud and Karl Marx on the movement, as well as mention of the admiration of the surrealists for the romances of

Victor Hugo. Darwin Turner lists among the extensive reading done by Toomer from 1916 to 1921 works by Freud, Coleridge, Blake, and Hugo, as well a works in the fields of sociology, socialism, occultism and atheism (7–11).

Read explains that one of the basic tenets of the surrealists is their belief in the principle of dialectical materialism—that the most striking characteristic of the natural world is continuous change and development. In terms of human society, the theory becomes the socialism of Marx (38–40). Turner describes Toomer's conversion from lukewarm Catholic to atheist and ardent socialist, after hearing a lecture by Clarence Darrow in 1916. Turner also mentions the tremendous impression made on Toomer by Lester Ward's *Dynamic Sociology*, which inspired Toomer to go to New York University to study sociology (7–8).

Toomer's belief in the application of dialectic reasoning to human society appears in various ways in his work. In the first portion of *Cane* he records his impressions of rural southern blacks with a sort of unsentimental nostalgia for a simple, close-to-the-earth life-style which he believed would inevitably pass away. "Song of the Son" expresses this theme as it speaks of the "parting soul" and the decline of the "epoch's sun" (21). The long poem, "The Blue Meridian," published in 1936, is a further development of the theme of evolution in human society. In it Toomer visualizes himself, not as the "new Negro," but as the ultimate American—the first of a new race of men evolved from a combination of all the races in the New World.

Perhaps a reason for the rather plaintive, almost funereal, tone of much of the first section of *Cane* can be found in the collection which makes up the second section, which deals with themes of the urban black society that perhaps Toomer saw replacing the more innocent and unrepressed rural life. One of the major themes of the second section deals with the paralyzing effects of the cult of capitalist materialism on the individual, the most striking example being the sketch "Rhobert," in which the title character is shown slowly sinking in the mud while trying to support a gigantic house on his head (74–75). Turner notices this same criticism of capitalist society as the major theme of two of Toomer's later unpublished works, the experimental dramas *The Sacred Factory* and *The Gallonwerps* (39–42).

Another tenet supported by the surrealists, according to Read, is opposition to the current code of morality—a belief that the social aspect of the whole system of organized control and repression is "psychologically misconceived and positively harmful." He affirms that the moral code of the surrealist is based on liberty and love (86). All three sections of *Cane* contain examples of men and women who fail to find fulfillment, peace, and full self-realization because of the repressive moral and social codes with which they live. For example, Bona and Paul repress their instinctual feelings for each other because of society's codes governing relationships between white women and black men (134–53). The same code of society leads a whole town to pretend to ignore the existence of Becky, "the white woman who had two Negro sons" (8). In the story "Box Seat," Dan Moore is unable to lead Muriel away from the superficial moral code of the Miss Pribbys of the world. Dan's plea to Muriel is perhaps Toomer's own plea for a moral code based on liberty and love:

> ". . . Your aim is wrong. There is no such thing as happiness. Life bends joy and pain, beauty and ugliness, in such a way that no one may isolate them. No one should want to. Perfect joy, or perfect pain, with no contrasting element to define them, would mean a monotony of consciousness, would mean death. Not happy, Muriel. Say that you have tried to make them [the people she meets] create. Say that you have used your own capacity for life to cradle them. To start them upward-flowing. Or if you cant say that you have, then say that you will. My talking to you will make you aware of your power to do so. Say that you will love, that you will give yourself in love—" (112–13)

The poem "November Cotton Flower" is Toomer's lyric description of the beauty of this kind of spontaneity of spirit, rarely found in his urban characters:

> Boll-weevil's coming, and the winter's cold,
> Made cotton-stalks look rusty, seasons old,
> And cotton, scarce as any southern snow,
> Was vanishing; the branch, so pinched and slow,
> Failed in its function as the autumn rake;
> Drouth fighting soil had caused the soil to take
> All water from the stream; dead birds were found
> In wells a hundred feet below the ground—
> Such was the season when the flower bloomed.
> Old folks were startled, and it soon assumed
> Significance. Superstition saw
> Something it had never seen before:

Brown eyes that loved without a trace of fear,
Beauty so sudden for that time of year.
(7)

Besides discussing the moral code of the surrealists, Read describes the surrealist's vision of the artist:

> To a certain extent the mental personality of the artist is originally determined by a failure in social adaptation. But his whole effort is directed towards a reconciliation with society, and what he offers to society is not a bagful of his own tricks, but rather some knowledge of the secrets to which he has had access, the secrets of the self which are buried in every man alike, but which only the sensibility of the artist can reveal to us in all their actuality. (27)

The surrealists, therefore, viewed the artist as priest in much the same way as did Emerson and the transcendentalists. In this light, Read considers St. Francis of Assisi and Sir Thomas More to be more poets than priests (37).

On several occasions in his life it would seem that Toomer's image of himself was that of priest. Turner tells us that Toomer, after his conversion to socialism while a student at the University of Chicago, immediately "offered evening lectures on philosophy and economics in classrooms at the university" (8). Turner also tells of Toomer's crusade as a socialist reformer in New York, in 1919 (9), and describes the experiment in spiritual growth Toomer led in Portage, Wisconsin, in 1931, with a group of male and female followers of Gurdjieff (50). Langston Hughes satirized Toomer's failure as a Gurdjieff priest in uptown New York: "He returned to Harlem, having achieved awareness, to impart his precepts to the literati." When this failed, he "left his Harlem group and went downtown to drop the seeds of Gurdjieff in less dark and poverty-stricken fields."[13]

It may be argued that Read's summary of the surrealist's stance is a bit too general and all-inclusive; and certainly, to try to categorize Toomer as a surrealist artist simply because he happened to agree with other surrealists politically and philosophically would be ridiculous. Nevertheless, all the descriptions (including Read's) of purely artistic precepts, principles, and methods of the surrealists also mention certain common characteristics which I believe can be found in abundance in Toomer's work. One of these is the belief in the primacy of the imagination of the artist (as opposed to the world of sensation) as a source of art. Imagination of the surrealist means the unconscious mind, the dream world, and occult and mystic experiences, not as outside forces, but as integral parts of the total or "super" reality of life. One art book states that "the imagination of the artist discovers associations between disparate things, resulting, not only in surprising juxtapositions, but also in visual puns. By evoking different things at the same time he implies the possibility that one of those things might be metamorphosed into another or others."[14]

One example of this kind of surrealistic image can be found in Toomer's poem "Storm Ending" in *Cane*"

> Thunder blossoms gorgeously above our heads,
> Great, hollow, bell-like flowers,
> Rumbling in the wind,
> Stretching clappers to strike our ears..
> Full-lipped flowers
> Bitten by the sun
> Bleeding rain
> Dripping rain like golden honey—
> And the sweet earth flying from the thunder.
>
> (90)

Another extended surrealistic image occurs in the description of "Seventh Street," which begins the second section of *Cane*. Toomer paints the grotesque picture of "black reddish blood. . . . Eddying on the corners? Swirling like a blood-red smoke up where the buzzards fly in heaven?" (71–72).

In another sketch from *Cane*, "Calling Jesus," the character has no name, but "her soul is like a little thrust-tailed dog that follows her, whimpering . . . each night when she comes home and closes the big outside storm door, the little dog is left in the vestibule, filled with chills till morning" (102).

A surrealistic image occurs in the imagination of the character Dan Moore, in the story "Box Seat," as he sits down beside a huge Negro woman in the Lincoln Theater:

> A soil-soaked fragrance comes from her. Through the cement floor her strong roots sink down. They spread under the asphalt streets. Dreaming, the streets roll over on their bellies, and suck their glossy health from them. Her strong roots sink down and spread under the river and disappear in blood-lines that waver south. Her roots shoot down. Dan's hands follow them. Roots throb. Dan's heart beats vio-

> lently. He places his palms upon the earth to cool them. Earth throbs. (119)

A very striking example of a surrealistic image which undergoes several metamorphoses in the mind of the reader is "Portrait of Georgia," near the end of the first section of *Cane*:

> Hair—braided chestnut,
>   coiled like a lyncher's rope,
> Eyes—fagots,
> Lips—old scars, or the first red blisters,
> Breath—the last sweet scent of cane,
> And her slim body, white as the ash
>   of black flesh after flame.
> (50)

The visualization of the woman (perhaps a white woman in whose name a lynching has taken place) and the picture of the lynching and burning itself are actually superimposed, somewhat like a photographic double exposure, except that one is an integral part of the other. A second metamorphosis might also take place, in which the portrait becomes a reproduction of a primitive African ceremonial mask. Even though Toomer, Aaron Douglass, Zora Neale Hurston, and other participants in the Harlem Renaissance, as well as members of the surrealist movement, were interested in primitive African culture, it is impossible to say that Toomer intended the mask image in the poem; but it is difficult not to see it there. I was reminded of "Portrait in Georgia" upon reading the following chant of the Sigi festival of the African Dogon tribe:

> The mask with burning eyes, burning bright, is coming to the
>   village;
> The eyes of the mask are the eyes of fire;
> The eyes of the mask are the eyes of the sun;
> The eyes of the mask are the eyes of the arrow;
> The eyes of the mask are the eyes of the axe;
> The eyes of the mask are the eyes of the antelope;
> The eyes of the mask are the eyes of the serpent;
> Burning, burning, burning bright.[15]

Turner has stated that Toomer, at his best, "sang and painted" pictures (27). I believe that quite often the pictures he painted were surrealistic. Toomer himself stated that "as for writing . . . I am an essentialist. Or, to put it in other words, I am a spiritualizer, a poetic realist."[16] I choose to think that Toomer's definitions of *essentialist*, *spiritualizer*, and *poetic realist* would not be very different from the definitions of those terms by André Breton and the surrealists.

Cane as Blues

BENJAMIN F. MC KEEVER

A pregnant excerpt from Jean Toomer's classic contains this image:

> Oracular.
> Redolent of fermenting syrup,
> Purple of the dusk,
> Deep-rooted cane.[1]

To be oracular is to be prophetic, for an oracle is not simply a messenger but a harbinger. The oracle vouchsafes a prediction which is not merely a forecast but a talisman, a way of dealing with the fate foreseen. *Cane* is oracular, documenting as it does a southern milieu, naming a certain malaise but proffering only the alembic of experience coupled with the vision of the artist.

Cane is "redolent," indeed, resplendent with the imagery of Georgia and with the burden of human history that this spiritual-physical region lives.

Georgia is the "blood-burning moon" rising to illuminate "the Dixie Pike [which] has grown from a goat path in Africa" (18). Georgia is also

A feast of moon and men and barking hounds,
  An orgy for some genius of the South
  With blood-hot eyes and cane-lipped scented mouth,
Surprised in making folk-songs from soul sounds.
(22)

And Georgia is the blues, ". . . An everlasting song, a singing tree / Caroling softly souls of slavery . . ." (21).

The blues is not a state of chronic melancholia but a mood ebony for a condition which can only be described as chaos. This mood, this attitude of mind, signifies man's attempt, in the words of Ralph Ellison, "to endow his life's incidents with communicable significance."[2]

Toomer appears to be replete with questions and bereft of answers about the history and destiny of black humanity. However, the reader is surfeited with symbols which upon examination yield a tacit certainty which is life—life in all its comedy and tragedy, humanity and pathos, soul and blues.

Comedy is said to be life viewed at a distance, while tragedy is life seen close at hand; life is supposed to be comedy to the man who thinks and tragedy to the man who feels. *Cane* is a vision of life. But Toomer's black exposure gives him a different perspective, for *Cane* is the blues.

Ellison explains in *Shadow and Act* that "the blues is an impulse to keep the painful details and episodes of a brutal experience alive in one's aching consciousness, to finger its jagged grain and transcend it, not by the consolation of philosophy but by squeezing from it a near-tragic, near-comic lyricism" (78).

What Ellison says about the blues is an appropriate description of *Cane*, "an autobiographical chronicle of personal catastrophe expressed lyrically" (79). *Cane* is not the autobiography of a man, but rather the chronicle of the fate of an idea, an idea whose time has come.

Cane is autobiographical because it represents the apotheosis of one man's attempt to bear witness to the reality and the power of an idea. The idea that the Negro is not an apprentice to equality but a journeyman in suffering. The idea that the choice is always and everywhere between freedom and death.

Cane is the oracle of this idea offered in blues. It contains the blues of Karintha, a madonna bereft of a child who engages then imprisons "this interest of the male, who wishes to ripen a growing thing too soon" (1); the blues of Avey, the "orphan-woman" whose "emotions had overflowed into paths that dissipated them" (87); the blues of Becky, the outcast white woman who had two Negro sons, and died in a solitude crowded with loneliness; and the blues of Carma, a beloved infidel whose primal strength and passion drove her husband to murder and then to the chain gang.

Cane describes the blues of Fern, a veritable black Medusa—one look into whose eyes turned men into slaves who could never fill the loveless void that was her life; and also the blues of Esther, the virgin aged-in-youth whose infatuation for a picaresque-quixotic King Barlo rests upon her like an incubus until his return, when she realizes that he can offer her only cheap desire and ersatz satisfaction.

Perhaps the most telltale blues is that of Kabnis, the protagonist in the novella written like a play that climaxes *Cane. Kabnis* rehearses the fate of a "dream deferred," an inanimate idea held by a weakling idealist, trapped in Hamletesque stasis.

Kabnis is the portrait of the artist as a northern Negro teaching school in Georgia. Here is the black artist as educator who can only intellectualize his blues. For example, Kabnis describes his alienation in the South in terms of "loneliness, dumbness, awful, intangible oppression" (162); and he feels himself to be "an atom of dust in agony on a hillside" (162).

The blues refrain, "sometimes I feel like a motherless child," is reiterated by his calling himself "Earth's child," "Bastardy . . . me," and by his designating God as "a profligate red-nosed man about town" (161). Kabnis exclaims, "A bastard son has got a right to curse his maker. God" (161). Nevertheless, on the debris of his despair, Kabnis must build phoenix-like his character.

"Through Ramsay [a prototype of the southern white] the whole white South weighs down upon him" (201). And Kabnis is "burdened with an impotent pain" (205).

Lewis, a prototype of the artist as leader, organizer, activist, who is a colleague of Kabnis, is "a tall wiry copper-colored man, thirty perhaps. His mouth and eyes suggest purpose guided by an adequate intelligence. He is what a stronger Kabnis might have been, and in an odd faint way resembles him" (189).

During a conversation, Lewis turns his eyes to Kabnis:

> In the instant of their shifting, a vision of the life they are to meet. Kabnis, a promise of a soil-soaked beauty; up-rooted, thinning out.

> Suspended a few feet above the soil whose touch would resurrect him. Arm's length removed from him whose will to help . . . There is a swift intuitive interchange of consciousness. Kabnis has a sudden need to rush into the arms of this man. His eyes call, "Brother." And then a savage, cynical twistabout within him mocks his impulse and strengthens him to repulse Lewis. (191–92)

Kabnis cannot embrace Lewis and, thereby, accept himself. He knows intimately, inescapably what the black experience has been; but this knowledge had merely driven him to cynicism and dissipation.

Lewis declares later, "Life has already told him [Kabnis] more than he is capable of knowing. It has given him in excess of what he can receive. I have been offered. Stuff in his stomach curdled, and he vomited me" (200).

Nevertheless, the link between Kabnis and Lewis is represented in the person of Father John, "gray-bearded, gray-haired, prophetic, immobile" (211); Father John is a blind, deaf black man in the twilight of life. Lewis originally calls John "father," but he is the spiritual and metaphorical father of Kabnis as well. In the dirt basement of an artisan's workshop, which is his corner of the world, Father John appears as a "Black Vulcan, a mute John the Baptist of a new religion—or a tongue-tied shadow of an old" (211).

However, Kabnis rejects and denies the old man, insisting that "he aint my past. My ancestors were Southern blue-bloods—" (217). Then he admits, "Aint much difference between black and blue" (218), which is a virtual equation of blackness with the blues.

Lewis supplies the climactic indictment of Kabnis by saying to him:

> Cant hold them, can you? Master; slave. Soil; and the overarching heavens. Dusk; dawn. They fight and bastardize you. The sun tint of your cheeks, flame of the great season's multi-colored leaves, tarnished, burned. Split, shredded: easily burned. No use . . . (218)

Thus Lewis delivers surrealistically a cryptic commentary on the South's "peculiar institution."

Kabnis confesses in his own defense:

> "I've been shapin words after a design that branded here. Know whats here? M soul. Ever heard o that? Th hell y have. Been shapin words t fit m soul. Never told y that before, did I? Thought I couldnt

> talk. I'll tell y. I've been shapin words; ah, but sometimes theyre beautiful an golden an have a taste that makes them fine t roll over with y tongue. . . .
>
> "Cant keep a good man down. Those words I was tellin y about, they wont fit int th mold thats branded on m soul. Rhyme, y see? Poet, too. Bad rhyme. Bad poet. Somethin else youve learned tnight. Lewis dont know it all, an I'm atellin y. Ugh. Th form thats burned int my soul is some twisted awful thing that crept in from a dream, a godam nightmare, an wont stay still unless I feed it. An it lives on words. Not beautiful words. God almighty no. Misshapen, split-gut, tortured, twisted words. . . . White folks feed it cause their looks are words. Niggers, black niggers feed it cause theyre evil an their looks are words. Yallar niggers feed it. This whole damn bloated purple country feeds it cause its goin down t hell in a holy avalanche of words. I want to feed th soul—I know what that is; th preachers dont—but I've got to feed it." (223–24)

He explains, "Mind me, th only sin is whats done against th soul. Th whole world is a conspiracy t sin, especially in America, an against me. I'm th victim of their sin. I'm what sin is" (236). Here we have poignantly presented the datum of the black experience: the consciousness of having been more sinned against than sinner.

Kabnis is born into the midst of an oppressed and persecuted people. He is one of them—a part of them and apart from them. He knows the unique experience of being the rejected and despised of men: sometimes one feels like a "motherless child" and other times like a "manchild in the promised land" on the eve of the death of God, when only one's enemies have received the uncovenanted revelation of God's demise.

Thus, it is difficult to "sing the Lord's song in a strange land." But he must decide to be or not to be a man. Consequently, Kabnis recognizes that "a soul like mine cant pin itself onto a wagon wheel an satisfy itself in spinning round" (234). For he knows and he feels that a man's life is not supposed to be a chronicle of personal catastrophe but rather a celebration: perhaps a poem, a song, a dance, a bacchanalia, a saturnalia, a romantic interlude before the final elegy. However, the difference between the possibility of black life and the reality of black life is the blues. Yet the blues idiom itself celebrates life; it celebrates the will to endure and the necessity to survive, to "keep on keepin on."

Kabnis does not realize the possibility of saving himself and the opportunity of redeeming his ideal until the Sphinx-like Father John vouchsafes that the white folks sinned when they made the Bible lie (237), which is to say that "things are not what they seem."

Perhaps black folks are not the prodigal descendants of Cain; maybe they represent the personae of the "eternal Adam in the new world garden," the only true sons of God. For black folks are the only people, at this time, in this place, who have paid their dues in blues.

Jean Toomer, the Artist—An Unfulfilled American Life: An Afterword

NELLIE MC KAY

Almost two decades have gone by since the rediscovery of *Cane* and Jean Toomer, who wrote that one astonishing book and then disappeared from the landscape of American arts and letters for almost forty years. Published to loud applause in 1923, *Cane* reached only a small self-selected audience, primarily those men and women who saw themselves in the avant-garde of American literature. Toomer was described by many as the "most promising Negro author" of his day. However, the promise of such an illustrious beginning was never fulfilled.

Since the late 1960s, a new generation of critics has sought to reinterpret *Cane* and to find answers to the enigmas of Toomer's literary career. During these years of revival, a great deal has been written about both the book and its author by critics who have made pilgrimages to Fisk University to sift through the many thousands of pages of his unpublished manuscripts and by those who have not looked beyond his early unpublished work.

The search for new insights into *Cane* and for an explanation of Toomer's brief sojourn in the world of letters followed the discovery of his vast collection of unpublished manuscripts shortly after his death in 1967. Housed at Fisk University in Nashville, Tennessee, the collection confirmed that he had continued to write for many years after *Cane* was published in 1923. After 1923, until the early years of the 1930s, a few of his poems and short stories appeared, but his longer literary works, several novels and full-length plays, were subject to numerous rejections from publishers. Changes in his writing style after the publication of *Cane* contributed to his failure to achieve further literary recognition, for by the middle of 1923 Toomer had turned away from the literary muse to search for the meaning of life in religion and philosophy and had sacrificed the art and brilliance that characterized *Cane* for the didacticism of a variety of dogma.

Toomer's obsessive quest for personal harmony was largely responsible for the stylistic changes that he made in his writings. In its pursuit, he came to believe that religion and philosophy held higher potentials for the success of his goal. From his autobiographical writings we know that he expected to find all-inclusive answers to the large questions of human existence through these mediums. When he was twenty-one, he thought he had discovered a source of harmony in socialism but soon found that socialism would not bear the full weight of his need for an "intelligible scheme" to direct his life. Socialism gave way to Buddhist philosophy and Eastern teachings, which gave way to Western literature and art, which, in turn, gave way to the Gurdjieff philosophy, followed by the words of the Holy Men of India, the Society of Friends, and, finally, scarcely a decade before his death at age seventy-three, dianetics (Scientology). None of these, individually, was sufficient to meet the needs of the single system he sought. The grand epiphany he awaited eluded him throughout his life.

When *Cane* was published it was, for many, the beacon that stood at the gateway to the Harlem Renaissance, unsurpassed during that period and for a long time after in its artistic craftsmanship. After a small reprint edition was published in 1927, both the book and its author disappeared from the eyes of their early admirers and critics. In the 1960s, when he was very ill, his wife, Marjorie Content Toomer, turned over his manuscripts to Fisk University. The late Arna Bontemps was chief librarian there at the time, and he had been among the first people to hail Toomer in the early 1920s. His presence at that institution made it a good place for the deposit of the manuscripts. University Place Press, New York, published a third edition of *Cane* in 1967, and in 1969 Harper and Row issued a paperback edition with a new introduction by Bontemps. It was the latter edition that informed the larger public of what had happened to Toomer's star: it had fallen in its ascendency.

Cane immediately recaptured its former prestige in the world of letters and propelled itself and its author into the spotlight. This came in the wake of the black revolution of the 1960s, the rise of black studies programs in colleges and universities across the country, and a reawakened interest in the black American's cultural past. *Cane* was mandatory on many reading lists. In a position of preeminence in Afro-American letters, it was unanimously applauded by its new critics as an outstanding depiction of the Afro-American experience. At the same time, scholars had always been intrigued and curious about those issues that might have been responsible for the unfulfilled career of this brilliant writer, and these arose anew.

A study of Toomer's life and work between 1923 and 1967 reveals that this man spent his life searching for the fullest meaning of human existence. However, it was an unsuccessful quest, not only because of his failings but also because of the failings of the world in which he lived. One problem that arose for Toomer early in his brief literary career concerned the link between the success of *Cane* and himself as a "Negro" writer. He never considered himself a Negro, not because he considered himself a white man, but because he aspired in his life and writings to create a synthesis of the many blood lines that flowed through his veins. He aspired, he said, to obliterate the notion of racial superiority or inferiority among a nation of people who were, in a majority proportion, the offspring of many different racial groups. Consequently he rejected the "Negro" writer label in all of its connotations and turned his back on those things that had made the book the splendid achievement it had been. After *Cane* he wrote nothing in which he used, exclusively, those materials related to black American life, but he went beyond this. He deliberately rejected his previous literary ambitions and the modes of expression through which these could have been achieved. His later works were not intended for artistic acclaim. Had the sales of *Cane* been large in 1923 and 1924, his decision to retreat from the literary world might have been different, but, in general, the small sales were not particularly disturbing to him because he had made his withdrawal from that part of his life before the book was published. To his great distress, his later writings went unnoticed because publishers were unsympathetic to the change in his course and to his undisguised discipleship of the Gurdjieff philosophy.

In his heart Toomer was always a philosopher and a mystic. After *Cane* he also wanted to be prophet-priest. He was committed to working toward an America in which all Americans would transcend the errors of past history and move into a new and glorious day of national harmony. In his early writings, he was influenced by Waldo Frank, now one of the forgotten men of American letters, but in the 1920s an influential figure in the group that included Sherwood Anderson, Alfred Stieglitz, Van Wyck Brooks and Randolph Bourne. Frank's philosophy was akin to the creative strivings of the young Toomer.

Toomer broke allegiance with Frank at the same time that he repudiated the merits of art for the salvation of America and Americans. It was then that he turned to Georges I. Gurdjieff, an Eastern mystic who promised his followers that his program would lead them to achieve internal harmony. Toomer was intrigued by Gurdjieff's ideas, for the question of perfect accord between the physical, intellectual, and moral qualities of the human being was one with which he had struggled for a long time. Most of Toomer's writings after *Cane* were products of the Gurdjieff influence, and although his underlying philosophic concerns altered only mimimally between those two periods of his life, there was a marked difference in the way in which he expressed them. The former years were ones of the artist-poet, the latter, those of the prophet-priest. Through all the changes, however, he never gave up the idea of writing as a vocation.

Although there is no question that Toomer's turning away from art was partly connected to his rejection of a racial designation and that it was also partly a rebellion against carrying the burdens of racial and cultural alienation, he was not blameless in his failure as a writer. He read a great deal, and he pondered, but he never formulated his own philosophical theories. He spent his life appropriating whatever was convenient for him from the ideas of others. In a pattern of beginnings and endings, he spent much of his life pursuing ends which never fully materialized for him. He attended half a dozen colleges and universities but never earned a degree, and he adopted a variety of views on how to achieve internal harmony, but all eventually led to disappointment for him. He was led to literary art by his association with Frank and other members of that group. His wish to transcend the "Negro" label led him to the Gurdjieff philosophy and the exploration of higher consciousness, but he discarded this in time because it too failed to fully satisfy his expectations of it. His inability to accept the limitations and failings of human systems and endeavors kept him searching for a perfection that he was never to find. Jean Toomer's failure to fulfill his early promise as a writer is one in which the responsibility must be shared between himself and his society. On his side, in time, his vision, his desire to transcend all limits, lost touch with reality. He died an unhappy man, for he had found no resolution to the dilemma of the human condition. But Toomer's story is not one of only failure, for he was courageous in his personal struggle to strive for the highest ideals of the human imagination, and for this he deserves credit. He was a gifted writer whose vision was of a world in which all people belong to the family of the human race and in which the attainment of spiritual, intellectual, and physical harmony is the ultimate goal to which each should aspire. He was striving to make this a reality. In pursuit of his ideals, he wandered through many doors of inquiry, but sadly, his dream had little chance of fulfillment. The world was not willing to validate his philosophical ideas by publishing his works. Although he could not single-handedly resolve the problem life raised for him, he never turned aside from it. His personal trials reveal that he believed in the potential in himself and in all of America to bring the world closer to the ideal he imagined.

Cane and a number of his lesser known pieces are sufficient to prove that Toomer had the eye and the ear of a poet, and he had the gift and genius of an artist. When he turned aside from art it was a great loss for American literature, as well as a tragedy for the man himself. But the larger critical concern that his life raises transcends Jean Toomer or the individual, for it is the universal issue of the artist and society. His failure to achieve his personal goals proves that when any society attempts to place limits on the creative will of the artist there is a tragic loss of cultural vision, and all mankind is poorer for that loss.

NOTES

BIBLIOGRAPHY

CONTRIBUTORS

INDEX

Notes

Jean Toomer in His Time: An Introduction

NELLIE MC KAY

1. Jean Toomer, "Earth-Being," Jean Toomer Collection, Fisk University Archives,* Nashville, Tennessee, Box 19, Folder 3, p. 1. Subsequent material from the collection will be designated "J.T.C." "Earth-Being" is also reprinted in part in *The Wayward and the Seeking: A Collection of Writings by Jean Toomer*, ed. Darwin Turner (Washington, D.C.: Howard University Press, 1980), pp. 15–27.

2. *Ibid.*

3. Bernarr MacFadden, *The Virile Powers of Supreme Manhood* (New York: Physical Culture Publishing Company, 1900).

4. Toomer, "Why I Entered the Gurdjieff Work," J.T.C., Box 14, Folder 1, p. 26.

---

*Editor's Note: In the notes to this volume, contributors cite Fisk University Library as the depository for the Jean Toomer Collection. In 1985, however, Jean Toomer's papers became a part of the Yale Collection of American Literature, Beinecke Rare Book and Manuscript Library, Yale University.

5. Gorham Munson, interview with India M. Watterson, The Wellington Hotel, New York City, 27–28 June 1969, The Amistad Collection, Dillard University, New Orleans.

6. Toomer to Waldo Frank, 24 March 1922, J.T.C., Box 1, Folder 3.

7. Toomer to Frank, ca. May 1922, J.T.C., Box 1, Folder 3.

8. Toomer to Sherwood Anderson, 1922, J.T.C., Box 1, Folder 1.

9. Toomer to Mae Wright, August 1922, J.T.C., Box 1, Folder 10.

10. Toomer to Frank, March 1922, J.T.C., Box 1, Folder 3.

11. *Ibid.*

12. Toomer to Anderson, 1922, J.T.C., Box 1, Folder 1.

13. Toomer, "Why I Joined the Gurdjieff Work," J.T.C., Box 66, Folder 8, p. 29.

14. *Ibid.*

15. James Weldon Johnson, "The Dilemma of the Negro Author," *American Mercury* 28 (December 1928): 481.

Jean Toomer: Lost Generation, or Negro Renaissance?

S. P. FULLINWIDER

1. Jean Toomer, "Book of Parents," Jean Toomer Collection, Fisk University Archives, Nashville, Tennessee (ca. 1934), pp. 17–37. Subsequent material from the collection will be designated "J.T.C."

2. Jean Toomer, "Outline of Autobiography," J.T.C. (unpublished ms., ca. 1934), p. 2.

3. *Ibid.*, p. 8.

4. *Ibid.*, p. 26.

5. *Ibid.*, handwritten note on reverse of p. 25.

6. *Ibid.*, pp. 27–55.

7. Jean Toomer, "Essentials: Prose and Poems," J.T.C. (unpublished ms., 1930), pp. 70, 112–18.

8. Walter H. Sokel, *The Writer in Extremis: Expressionism in Twentieth-Century German Literature* (Stanford, 1959), pp. 85–118.

9. Jean Toomer, *Work Ideas* I, Mill House Pamphlet, Psychological Series, No. 2 (Doylestown, Penn.: 1937), p. 13.

10. Jean Toomer, *Living Is Developing*, Mill House Pamphlets, Psychological Series, No. 1 (Doylestown, Penn.: 1937), p. 14.

11. Toomer, "Autobiography," pp. 58–59.

12. Jean Toomer, "Box Seat," *Cane* (New York: Boni and Liveright, Inc., 1923), pp. 104–30.

13. Jean Toomer to editor of *The Liberator*, J.T.C., 19 August 1922.

14. Toomer, "*Autobiography*," p. 63.

15. Gorham B. Munson, "The Significance of Jean Toomer," *Opportunity* 3 (September 1925): 262–63.

16. Jean Toomer, "From Exile into Being," J.T.C. (unpublished ms., 1938), p. 1 of prescript.

17. See, for example, Jean Toomer, unpublished mss. of novels: "The Gallonwerps," ca. 1927; "York Beach," ca. 1928; "Transatlantic Crossing," ca. 1930; "Eight-Day World," ca. 1932; unpublished ms. of a philosophic work, "Essentials: Definitions and Aphorisms," 1931; unpublished ms. of a psychological experiment, "Portage Potential," 1931, J.T.C.

18. Toomer, "Essentials: Prose and Poems," p. 63.

19. *Ibid.*, p. 46.

20. Toomer, "Eight-Day World," pp. 324–25.

21. Jean Toomer to Overseers, Buckingham Meeting (Lahaska, Penn.: August 28, 1940), J.T.C.

22. Jean Toomer to James Weldon Johnson, J.T.C., 11 July 1930.

Jean Toomer and Mae Wright: An Interview with Mae Wright Peck

THERMAN B. O'DANIEL

1. May Wright changed the spelling of her first name to *Mae* during her first year at Tufts University. There was a classmate whose name was *Amy* Wright, and though different from *May*, there was always confusion. Mae Wright hoped that the slight change would be helpful in solving the problem.

2. Three formal meetings, a number of informal meetings, and many telephone conversations went into the preparation of this interview. The formal meetings were specifically arranged to discuss the subject; the informal meetings refer to times when Mrs. Peck and I saw each other at various events and chatted briefly about new information she had thought of or anything

else pertinent to the subject; and the many telephone conversations were used to verify or clarify innumerable details. All of this was conveniently possible because Mrs. Peck and I both live in Baltimore, we are good personal friends, and she was very cooperative at all times. The formal meetings were held on Wednesday, January 30, 1980 (a dinner meeting at the O'Daniel home); on Friday, June 6, 1980 (a second dinner meeting at the O'Daniel home); and on Sunday, June 22, 1980, at Mrs. Peck's home. In between these formal meetings, the many informal meetings and telephone conversations occurred, and several drafts were prepared, corrected, and revised. The final manuscript was completed on Wednesday, July 2, 1980.

3. Harpers Ferry, West Virginia, is a small, mountain town, located in the extreme eastern part of West Virginia. It is situated on bluffs overlooking the place where the Potomac and Shenandoah Rivers meet and flow together. The town was incorporated in 1763, but in 1747 Robert Harper established and operated a ferry there—thus, the name. The United States located an arsenal there in 1796, which John Brown seized in his raid of October 16, 1859. Storer College, now closed, was founded there in 1867.

4. The first line of Toomer's poem "Glaciers of Dusk." See John C. Griffin, "Two Jean Toomer Poems: 'For M.W.' and 'Glaciers of Dusk'," *Pembroke Magazine* 6 (January 1975).

5. Lover's Leap is described by Toomer in his story "Avey" and is used as the setting for one of his scenes. Toomer, *Cane* (New York: Boni & Liveright, 1923).

6. Toomer, *Cane* (New York: Boni & Liveright, 1923).

7. Toomer dedicated the third part of *Cane*, "Kabnis," to his friend Waldo Frank.

Jean Toomer's Life Prior to *Cane*: A Brief Sketch of the Emergence of a Black Writer

MICHAEL J. KRASNY

1. I have found no information specifically linking Miss Grimké and Toomer. There are some provocative parallels between several of her more widely published poems, such as "The Black Finger" and "Clarissa Scott Delaney," and early Toomer poetry. Her three-act play *Rachel* was published in 1921, the year Toomer wrote his first drama. Black poet Sterling Brown was also a graduate of M Street High School but was five years [*sic*] younger than Toomer.

2. From periodic conversations between the author and Darwin Turner, March 1969 to January 1970.

3. From an autobiographical note in the author's own hand (ca. 1934) in an unpublished manuscript belonging to Mrs. Marjorie Content Toomer.

4. Information obtained from the Office of the Registrar, University of Wisconsin, Madison, Wisconsin.

5. The woman may have served as a model for Avey in the prose piece of the same name in *Cane* (New York: Boni & Liveright, 1923). The chronology is altered in "Avey," however, because Toomer's narrator goes to Harpers Ferry before entering the University of Wisconsin and spends two years at the University (Toomer was there for only one year). Nevertheless, one can probably make the connection because, significantly enough, the woman Toomer pursued, like Avey, was black (from conversations with Darwin Turner).

6. The setting for "Bona and Paul" in *Cane* (New York: Boni & Liveright, 1923) is a training center for physical education teachers.

7. Transcript obtained from the Office of the Registrar of the Community College of New York, Mr. George Papoulas. It was about this time that Toomer began to call himself *Jean*, apparently to stress the French pronunciation of the name.

8. From an autobiographical note in the author's own hand (ca. 1934) in an unpublished manuscript belonging to Mrs. Marjorie Content Toomer.

9. It is of interest to note how the narrator of "Fern" in *Cane* characterizes himself as one who has "knocked about from town to town too much not to know the futility of mere change of place" (*Cane*, New York: Harper & Row, 1969, p. 28).

10. This is probably another biographical link to "Avey." The narrator in that piece gets work in a shipyard after he leaves Wisconsin to seek Avey in New York.

11. Gorham Munson, *Destinations* (New York: J. H. Sears and Company, 1928), p. 186; and S. P. Fullinwider, "Jean Toomer: Lost Generation, or Negro Renaissance?" *Phylon*, 27: 4 (Winter 1966): 396–403 (reprinted in this volume) and S. P. Fullinwider, *The Mind and Mood of Black America* (Homewood, Ill.: The Dorsey Press, 1969).

12. Mabel M. Dillard, "Jean Toomer: Herald of the Negro Renaissance" (Ph.D. diss., Ohio University, 1967). In their introduction to *On Being Black* (New York: Fawcett World, 1970), Charles T. Davis and Daniel Waldon make a number of broad, though nonetheless accurate, generalizations about the works of early black writers, all of which, interestingly enough, apply to *Cane*.

13. See King Barlo's sermon in "Esther," *Cane* (New York: Harper & Row, 1969), pp. 38–39.

Jean Toomer in Wisconsin

NELLIE MC KAY

1. Jean Toomer, "Why I Entered the Gurdjieff Work," Jean Toomer Collection, Fisk University Archives, Nashville, Tennessee, Box 66, Folder 8, p. 2. Subsequent material from the collection will be designated "J.T.C."

2. *Ibid.*, p. 4.

3. Toomer, "Outline of an Autobiography," J.T.C., Box 16, Folder 1, p. 116.

4. *Ibid.*, p. 25(a).

5. Toomer, *Cane* (New York: Harper & Row, 1969), pp. 44–45.

6. *Ibid.*, p. 8.

7. Toomer, "Portage Potential," J.T.C., Box 41, Folder 1, p. 64.

8. *Ibid.*

9. Margery Latimer Toomer to Meridel Le Seur, June 1932, J.T.C., Box 7.

"Just Americans": A Note on Jean Toomer's Marriage to Margery Latimer

DANIEL P. MC CARTHY

1. See especially S. P. Fullinwider, "Jean Toomer: Lost Generation, or Negro Renaissance?" *Phylon* 27 (Winter 1966): 396–403. (Reprinted in this volume.)

2. *Ibid.*, p. 402.

3. Robert C. Hart, "Black-White Literary Relations in the Harlem Renaissance," *American Literature* 44 (January 1973): 621.

4. Abraham Chapman, ed., *Black Voices* (New York: New American Library, 1968), p. 381.

5. Fullinwider, "Jean Toomer," p. 400.

6. Darwin T. Turner, *In a Minor Chord: Three Afro-American Writers and Their Search for Identity* (Carbondale: Southern Illinois University Press, 1971), p. 50.

7. William A. Titus, *Wisconson Writers: Sketches and Studies* (Chicago: privately printed, 1930), p. 87.

8. "Margery Toomer, Novelist, Dies in West," *New York Times*, 18 August 1932, p. 19.

9. "Just Americans," *Time*, 28 March 1932, p. 19. (All subsequent references to *Time* in the text are to this article and page number.)

10. *TLS*, Margery Latimer to Richard Johns, University of Delaware Special Collection. (Although undated, the letter can be approximately fixed in April 1932.)

11. Turner, *In A Minor Chord*, pp. 51ff.

12. Fullinwider, "Jean Toomer," p. 401.

13. *TLS*, Mark S. Schorer to Richard Johns, 29 October 1967, University of Delaware Special Collection. (The author thanks Mr. Stuart Dick, Special Collections Curator at the University of Delaware, for his assistance.)

Jean Toomer's Contributions to *The New Mexico Sentinel*

TOM QUIRK AND ROBERT E. FLEMING

1. Darwin T. Turner, *In a Minor Chord: Three Afro-American Writers and Their Search for Identity* (Carbondale: Southern Illinois University Press, 1971), pp. 27–30.

2. Alfred Kreymborg *et al.*, eds., *The New Caravan* (New York: The Macaulay Company, 1936).

3. Turner, *In a Minor Chord*, p. 38.

4. See John C. Griffin, "A Chat with Marjorie Content Toomer," *Pembroke Magazine* 5 (January 1974): 14–27.

5. Turner, *In a Minor Chord*, p. 141.

6. All but a few scattered issues of *The New Mexico Sentinel*—missing from the microfilmed files at the University of New Mexico—have been checked for Toomer contributions.

7. *The New Mexico Sentinel*, 20 July 1937, p. 6.

8. *Ibid.*, pp. 6–7.

9. *Ibid.*, 31 August 1937, p. 8.

10. *Ibid.*, 7 September 1937, p. 8.

11. *Ibid.*, 17 November 1937, p. 7.

12. *Ibid.*, 12 January 1938, p. 6.

13. *Ibid.*, 24 July 1938, p. 8.

Jean Toomer—The Veil Replaced

MABEL M. DILLARD

1. Jean Toomer, "Race Problems and Modern Society," in Baker Brownell, ed., *Problems of Civilization*, Man and His World Series, Vol. 7 (New York: D. Van Nostrand, 1929), p. 78.

2. *Ibid.*, p. 108.

3. Toomer, *Essentials*, private edition (Chicago: Lakeside Press, 1931).

4. Extract from a letter from Jean Toomer to Miss Catherine Latimer (ca. 1934), Jean Toomer Collection, Fisk University Archives, Nashville, Tennessee.

5. Toomer, "The Blue Meridian," *The New Caravan*, ed. Alfred Kreymborg *et al.* (New York: The Macaulay Company, 1936), p. 638.

6. *Ibid.*

7. *Ibid.*, p. 637.

8. *Ibid.*, p. 640.

9. *Ibid.*, p. 645.

10. *Ibid.*, pp. 646–47.

11. *Ibid.*, pp. 651–52.

Jean Toomer and Waldo Frank: A Creative Friendship

MARK HELBLING

1. Jean Toomer, "Outline of the Story of the Autobiography," Jean Toomer Collection, Fisk University Archives, Nashville, Tennessee (ca.

1934), p. 48. Subsequent material from the collection will be designated "J.T.C."

2. *Ibid.*, p. 53.

3. Toomer to Waldo Frank, 2 August 1982, J.T.C.

4. Toomer to Frank, undated, J.T.C.

5. Frank to Toomer, ca. August 1923, J.T.C.

6. Waldo Frank, "A Prophet in France," *Salvos* (New York: Boni & Liveright, 1924), p. 89. Frank's quarrel with most of the prevailing literature and art was that they caught only glimpses of life and failed to provide an awakened sense of "a common experience and a common purpose." See, for example, "Pseudo Literature," pp. 139–42; "Utilitarian Art," pp. 142–46; "Art in Our Jungle," pp. 146–49; and "The Artist in Our Jungle," pp. 149–53 in *In the American Jungle* (New York: Farrar & Rinehart, Inc., 1937). See also "Vicarious Fiction," pp. 53–67, and "A Note on the Novel," pp. 223–31, in *Salvos*.

7. Frank, "Emerging Greatness," *Salvos*, p. 32.

8. *Ibid.*, p. 40.

9. Frank to Toomer, ca. March 1923, J.T.C.

10. Frank to Toomer, 30 May 1924, J.T.C.

11. Toomer to Frank, 20 September 1922, J.T.C.

12. Frank, "Vicarious Fiction," *Salvos*, p. 55.

13. Darwin T. Turner, *In a Minor Chord: Three Afro-American Writers and Their Search for Identity* (Carbondale: Southern Illinois University Press, 1971), pp. 35–37.

14. Toomer, undated commentary, J.T.C.

15. Toomer to *The Liberator*, 19 August 1922, J.T.C.

16. Horace Liveright to Toomer, 29 August 1923, J.T.C.

17. Toomer to Liveright, 5 September 1923, J.T.C.

18. Toomer's grandfather, P. B. S. Pinchback, whose own father was of Scotch-Welsh-German stock, but whose mother was black, is the "Negro blood mixture" to which he refers.

19. Toomer to James Weldon Johnson, 11 July 1930, J.T.C.

20. Toomer to Frank, 24 March 1922, J.T.C.

21. Toomer, unpublished ms., p. 1, J.T.C.

22. Toomer, "The American Race," unpublished ms., p. 2, J.T.C.

23. Toomer, "The Crock of Problems: Race Problems—A Psychological Approach," unpublished ms., p. 5, J.T.C.

24. *Ibid.*, p. 31.

25. Toomer to Sherwood Anderson, 18 December 1922, J.T.C.

26. Toomer, *Notebook: 1923–24*, J.T.C.

27. Toomer, "Outline of the Story of the Autobiography," p. 62, J.T.C.

28. Toomer to Frank, 19 July 1922, J.T.C.

29. Toomer, "On Being an American—Autobiography," 19 November 1934, p. 45, J.T.C.

30. Toomer to Frank, 19 July 1922, J.T.C.

31. *Ibid.*

32. Letter from Toomer to Frank, Summer 1923, J.T.C.

33. Letter from Frank to Toomer, Summer 1923, J.T.C.

An Intersection of Paths: Correspondence between Jean Toomer and Sherwood Anderson

DARWIN T. TURNER

1. Anyone who has struggled to decipher Anderson's handwriting will agree that the term *scrawled* is appropriate. Because I cannot be certain that I have always guessed correctly what word Anderson intended, I have bracketed question marks throughout the text to designate those words that are most questionable.

2. Sherwood Anderson to Jean Toomer, 1922, No. 43, Jean Toomer Collection, Fisk University Archives, Nashville, Tennessee. Subsequent material from the collection will be designated "J.T.C."; the numbers refer to the numbering of materials in the Toomer Collection. This letter and all subsequent quotations are reprinted by permission of Harold Ober Associates, Inc., copyright 1974 by Eleanor Copenhaver Anderson.

3. Anderson to Toomer, 1922, J.T.C., No. 46.

4. Later published in *Cane* (New York: Boni & Liveright, 1923) as "Calling Jesus."

5. Toomer, "Calling Jesus," *Cane* (New York: Harper & Row, 1969), p. 103. All subsequent quotations from *Cane* have been taken from this edition.

6. Later published in the second part of *Cane*.

7. Toomer to Anderson, December 1922, J.T.C., No. 43. The catalog number is an erroneous duplication by the cataloger. This letter and all subsequent quotation from Toomer's letters are reprinted by permission of Mrs. Marjorie Content Toomer. Copyrighted 1974 by Mrs. Marjorie Content Toomer.

8. Anderson to Toomer, 22 December 1922, J.T.C.

9. *Ibid.*

10. Toomer to Anderson, 29 December 1922, J.T.C.

11. *Ibid.*

12. Possibly Harry Kennedy and Mae Wright.

13. Toomer to Anderson, 29 December 1922, J.T.C. It is interesting to speculate about the kind of magazine that Toomer might have founded. Although *The Crisis* and *Opportunity* championed racial consciousness and afforded outlets for black literary talent, neither was as significant a literary outlet at this time as each would become later in the decade. Despite the efforts of *The Crisis* and *Opportunity*, the continuing need for additional showcases in the twenties is evident in attempts to establish such new magazine as *Fire* and *Harlem*.

14. Equally ironic is Anderson's appraisal of Waldo Frank, whom Toomer later blamed for the "misunderstandings" about Toomer's racial ancestry and attitude. Anderson wrote, ". . . of course Waldo Frank is . . . the ideal man to introduce you. He wrote the first understanding article about my own work and you may absolutely depend on him for understanding and sympathy toward any . . . effort." (Anderson to Toomer, 1923, J.T.C.)

15. Anderson to Toomer, 1923, J.T.C. Anderson unconsciously echoed William Dean Howells's appraisal of Paul L. Dunbar a generation earlier.

16. *Ibid.*

17. Anderson to Toomer, 3 January 1924, J.T.C.

18. Anderson misquoted Toomer. The sentence from "Esther" reads, "Her mind is a pink meshbag filled with baby toes" (*Cane*, p. 45). The matter may be unimportant, but Anderson's transposition of *pink* adds a racial coloring to the sentence.

19. Anderson to Toomer, 14 January 1924, J.T.C.

20. In "Karintha."

21. Toomer to Anderson, 19 January 1923, J.T.C.

22. John McClure to Anderson, No. 53.

23. Anderson to Toomer, 19 April 1934, J.T.C., No. 55.

Sherwood Anderson and Jean Toomer

MARK HELBLING

1. Nathan Irvin Huggins, *Harlem Renaissance* (London and New York: Oxford University Press, 1973), p. 116.

2. Bernard Duffey, *The Chicago Renaissance in American Letters: A Critical History* (Ann Arbor: Michigan State College Press, 1954), pp. 258, 262; and Dale Kramer, *The Chicago Renaissance: The Literary Life in the Midwest, 1900–1930* (New York: Appleton-Century, 1966), pp. 309–20.

3. Henry F. May, *The End of American Innocence* (Chicago: Quadrangle Books, 1959), pp. 219–48.

4. Sherwood Anderson, *A Story Teller's Story* (New York: B. W. Huebsch, Inc., 1924), p. 304.

5. Jean Toomer to Sherwood Anderson, 29 December 1922, Jean Toomer Collection, Fisk University Archives, Nashville, Tennessee. Subsequent material from the collection will be designated "J.T.C."

6. Alain Locke to Anderson, 25 June 1925, Yale University.

7. Jessie Fauset to Anderson, 21 January 1926, Yale University.

8. Anderson, "The Negro in Art—How Shall He Be Portrayed?" *Crisis* 32 (May 1926): 36.

9. Huggins, *Harlem Renaissance*, p. 93.

10. *Ibid.*

11. Toomer to Anderson, 29 December 1922, J.T.C.

12. In a letter to Frank, Toomer indicated the limits he felt in Anderson's writings: "He is pleasant reading, no doubt of that. Pleasant, middle aged. His . . . narrative gift swings along like a carriage-dog noseing [*sic*] the dust and flowers of a mid-Western road-side. Its mind glimpses the tragedy of unpainted clapboards and closed doors. But its nose keeps to the dust and flowers of the road, and its heart beats regularly as it lopes along. . . . In direct contact I am certain that I would like him. His notes have a full hearted warmth and ease about them. But I need something more" (Toomer to Frank, Summer 1923, J.T.C.).

13. Anderson to Toomer, ca. 1922–1923, J.T.C.

14. Toomer to Frank, ca. Summer 1923, J.T.C.

15. Toomer, "On Being an American—Autobiography," 19 November 1934, J.T.C.

16. Frank, "Emerging Greatness" (1916), *Salvos* (New York: Boni & Liveright, 1924), p. 32.

17. Anderson, "The South: The Black and White and Other Problems below the Mason and Dixon Line," *Vanity Fair* 9 (1926): 49–50.

18. Anderson to Lucile Blum, 24 December 1920, in *Letters of Sherwood Anderson*, ed. Howard Mumford Jones and Walter B. Rideout (Boston: Little Brown and Company, 1953), p. 69.

19. Toomer to Anderson, 18 December 1922, J.T.C.

20. Anderson to Toomer, 3 January 1924, J.T.C.

21. Anderson, *Memoirs* (New York: Harcourt, Brace and Company, 1924), p. 268.

22. Anderson to Jerome and Lucile Blum, July 1920, in Jones and Rideout, *Letters*, p. 58.

23. Anderson, *Vanity Fair* 9 (1926): 50.

24. Christopher Lasch, *The New Radicalism in America—1889–1963* (New York: Vintage Books, 1967), pp. 143–44.

25. Anderson, *The Modern Writer* (San Francisco: The Lantern Press, 1925), p. 31.

26. Duffey, *The Chicago Renaissance in American Letters*, p. 103.

27. Anderson, *Sherwood Anderson's Notebook* (New York: Boni & Liveright, 1926), pp. 130–31.

28. *Ibid.*, p. 135.

29. Toomer's evaluation of his novel *Cane* could, for the most part, just as well be Anderson's: "With Negroes also the trend was towards the small town and towards the city—and industry and commerce and the machines. The folk-spirit was walking in to die on the modern desert. That spirit was so beautiful. Its death was so tragic. Just this seemed to sum life for me. And this was the feeling I put into *Cane*. *Cane* was a swan-song. It was a song of an end" (Toomer, "Outline of the Story of the Autobiography," J.T.C., ca. 1934, pp. 58–59).

The "Mid-Kingdom" of Crane's "Black Tambourine" and Toomer's *Cane*

VICTOR A. KRAMER

1. I am indebted to John Neal, whose original insight has prompted this essay.

2. See Donald G. Ackley, "Theme and Vision in Jean Toomer's *Cane*," *Studies in Black Literature* 1 (Spring 1970): 45–65; Todd Lieber, "Design and Movement in *Cane*," *CLA Journal* 13 (September 1969): 35–50 (reprinted in this volume); Darwin T. Turner, "Jean Toomer's *Cane*," *Negro Digest* 18 (January 1969): 54–61 (reprinted in this volume); and William C. Fischer, "The Aggregate Man in Jean Toomer's *Cane*," *Studies in the Novel* 3 (Summer 1971): 190–215.

3. Charles W. Scruggs, "The Mark of Cain and the Redemption of Art: A Study in Theme and Structure of Jean Toomer's *Cane*," *American Literature* 44 (May 1972): 277.

4. *The Letters of Hart Crane*, ed. Brom Weber (New York: Hermitage House, 1952), p. 149.

5. See Robert L. Perry, *The Shared Vision of Waldo Frank and Hart Crane*, University of Nebraska Studies, N.S., no. 33 (Lincoln, Neb.: University of Nebraska Press, 1966).

6. Arna Bontemps, Introduction to *Cane*, by Jean Toomer, (New York: Harper & Row, 1969). p. xvi.

7. Letter to Gorham Munson, Jean Toomer Collection, Fisk University Archives, Nashville, Tennessee, Box 7, Folder 12. Cited by Scruggs, "The Mark of Cain." Subsequent material from the collection will be designated "J.T.C."

8. Jean Toomer, *Cane* (New York: Harper & Row, 1969), p. 39. All subsequent references are noted parenthetically in the text.

9. Weber, *The Letters of Hart Crane*, p. 58.

10. Hart Crane, *The Complete Poems of Hart Crane* (Franklin Center, Pa.: The Franklin Library, 1979).

11. Samuel Hazo, *Hart Crane* (New York: Holt, Rinehart, 1963), p. 26. See also R. W. B. Lewis, *The Poetry of Hart Crane* (Princeton: Princeton University Press, 1967), p. 29.

12. Hazo, *Crane*, p. 25.

13. Toomer to Waldo Frank, J.T.C., Box 3, Folder 7. Cited by Scruggs in "The Mark of Cain," p. 282.

14. Toomer to Frank, J.T.C. Box 3, Folder 7. Cited by Scruggs in "The Mark of Cain," p. 276.

15. Scruggs, "The Mark of Cain," pp. 284–85.

16. Ralph Ellison, *Shadow and Act* (New York: Random House, 1964), p. 78.

The Influence of Ouspensky's *Tertium Organum* upon Jean Toomer's *Cane*

ALICE POINDEXTER FISHER

1. Arna Bontemps, Introduction to *Cane*, by Jean Toomer (New York: Harper & Row, 1969), p. vii.

2. Robert A. Bone, *The Negro Novel in America* (New Haven, Conn.: Yale University Press, 1958), p. 81.

3. *Ibid.*, p. 80.

4. Peter Demianovich Ouspensky, *Tertium Organum—The Third Canon of Thought—A Key to the Enigmas of the World*, tran. by Nicholas Bessaraboff and Claude Bragdon, (New York: Random House, First Vintage Books Edition 1970).

5. Bone, *The Negro Novel*, p. 81.

6. John Unterecker, *Voyager—A Life of Hart Crane* (New York: Farrar, Straus and Giroux, 1969), p. 247.

7. Robert L. Perry, *The Shared Vision of Waldo Frank and Hart Crane*, University of Nebraska Studies, N.S., no. 33 (Lincoln, Neb.: University of Nebraska Press, 1966), p. 11.

8. *Ibid.*

9. *Theosophy* is defined as a belief about God and the world held to be based on mystical insight.

10. For a full account of this story, see Claude Bragdon, "The Romance and Mystery of *Tertium Organum*," *Merely Players* (New York: Alfred A. Knopf, 1905), pp. 197–204.

11. S. P. Fullinwider, "Jean Toomer: Lost Generation, or Negro Renaissance?" *Phylon* 27 (Winter 1966); 396–403. (Reprinted in this volume.)

12. Ouspensky, *Tertium Organum*, p. 33. All subsequent references are noted parenthetically in the text.

13. Todd Lieber, "Design and Movement in *Cane*," *CLA Journal* 13 (September 1969): 35–50. (Reprinted in this volume.)

14. Jean Toomer, *Cane* (New York: Harper & Row, 1969), p. 10. All subsequent references are noted parenthetically in the text.

15. Rom Landau, "War Against Sleep—P. D. Ouspensky," *God Is My Adventure—A Book on Modern Mystics, Masters, and Teachers* (New York: Alfred A. Knopf, 1936), pp. 201–23.

Jean Toomer's *Cane*

JAMES KRAFT

1. Jean Toomer's *Cane* was reissued in 1969 by Harper & Row with an introduction by Arna Bontemps.

2. Darwin T. Turner, "The Failure of a Playwright," *CLA Journal* 10 (June 1967): 308–18. This article discusses Toomer's many attempts to be a playwright and is important here for the biographical facts and for the critical comments on the "Kabnis" section of *Cane*, a section originally written as a play. (Reprinted in this volume.)

3. Robert A. Bone, *The Negro Novel in America* (New Haven, Conn.: Yale University Press, 1958), pp. 80–89.

4. Darwin T. Turner, "Jean Toomer's *Cane*," *Negro Digest* 18 (January 1969): 54–61. (Reprinted in this volume.)

5. Dr. Turner has seen a letter from Toomer to Waldo Frank (now in the Jean Toomer Collection in the Fisk University Archives in Nashville, Tennessee) that explains this fact.

6. Melvin Dixon, "Black Theater: The Aesthetics," *Negro Digest* 18 (July 1969): 41–44.

7. Jean Toomer, *Cane* (New York: Harper & Row, 1969), p. 218.

The Unity of Jean Toomer's *Cane*

CATHERINE L. INNES

1. Quoted by Arna Bontemps, "The Negro Renaissance: Jean Toomer and the Harlem Writers of the 1920's," in *Anger and Beyond: The Negro Writer in the United States*, ed. Herbert Hill (New York: Harper & Row, 1966), pp. 25–26.

2. *Ibid.*, p. 23.

3. David Littlejohn, *Black on White* (New York: Grossman, 1966), p. 59.

4. *Ibid.*, p. 58.

5. *Ibid.*, p. 60.

6. Edward Margolies, *Native Sons: A Critical Study of Twentieth-Century Negro American Authors* (Philadelphia: J. B. Lippincott Company, 1968), p. 39.

7. Robert A. Bone, *The Negro Novel in America*, rev. ed. (New Haven, Conn.: Yale University Press, 1965), p. 81.

8. Todd Lieber, "Design and Movement in *Cane*," *CLA Journal* 13 (September 1969): 35–50. (Reprinted in this volume.)

9. Hill, *Anger and Beyond*, p. 29.

10. Gorham B. Munson, in "The Significance of Jean Toomer," *Destinations* (New York: J. H. Sears and Company, 1928), does analyze the musical structure of "Karintha" and points out that Toomer had wanted to be a composer. I suspect that a detailed analysis of the whole book might show a very close analogy with late nineteenth century symphonic structure.

11. Jean Toomer, *Cane* (New York: Harper & Row, 1969), p. 1. All subsequent references are noted parenthetically in the text.

12. Bone, *The Negro Novel*, p. 81.

13. Peter Demianovich Ouspensky, *Tertium Organum—The Third Canon of Thought—A Key to the Enigmas of the World* (New York: Alfred A. Knopf, 1922), pp. 262–65.

14. *Ibid.*, pp. 330–31.

15. Quoted by Arna Bontemps in his Introduction to Jean Toomer's *Cane* (New York: Harper & Row, 1969), p. viii.

16. Bone, *The Negro Novel*, p. 84.

17. Ouspensky, *Tertium Organum*, p. 215.

18. Sterling Brown, *The Negro in American Fiction* (Washington, D.C.: Associates in Negro Folk Education, 1937), p. 153.

19. Ouspensky, *Tertium Organum*, p. 218.

20. *Ibid.*, p. 219.

21. Lieber, "Design and Movement in *Cane*," p. 37. (Reprinted in this volume.)

22. Ouspensky, *Tertium Organum*, pp. 230–31.

Jean Toomer's *Cane* Again

W. EDWARD FARRISON

1. Frank Durham, *Studies in Cane* (Columbus, Ohio: Charles E. Merrill Publishing Company, 1971), p. iv. All subsequent references are noted parenthetically in the text.

2. Darwin T. Turner, *In a Minor Chord: Three Afro-American Writers and Their Search for Identity* (Carbondale: Southern Illinois University Press, 1971). See Chapter 1, "Jean Toomer: Exile." Also, see Todd Lieber "Design

and Movement in *Cane*," *CLA Journal* 13 (September 1969): 35–50 (reprinted in this volume); and Bernard Bell, "A Key to the Poems in *Cane*," *CLA Journal* 14 (March 1971): 251–80 (reprinted in this volume).

Design and Movement in *Cane*

TODD LIEBER

1. Arna Bontemps, "The Negro Renaissance: Jean Toomer and the Harlem Writers of the 1920's," in *Anger and Beyond: The Negro Writer in the United States*, ed. Herbert Hill (New York: Harper & Row, 1966), p. 27.

2. Robert A. Bone, *The Negro Novel in America*, rev. ed. (New Haven, Conn.: Yale University Press, 1965), p. 88.

3. Alain Locke, *The New Negro: An Interpretation* (New York: Albert & Charles Boni, 1925), p. 49.

4. Edward Margolies, *Native Sons: A Critical Study of Twentieth-Century Negro American Authors* (Philadelphia: J. B. Lippincott, 1968), p. 39.

5. Bone, *The Negro Novel*, p. 80.

6. Arna Bontemps, Introduction to *Cane*, by Jean Toomer (New York: Harper & Row, 1969), pp. viii–ix. All subsequent references are noted parenthetically in the text.

7. Bone, *The Negro Novel*, p. 82.

8. *Ibid.*, p. 84.

9. *Ibid.*, p. 85.

10. *Ibid.*, p. 86.

11. *Ibid.*, p. 87.

12. *Ibid.*, p. 88.

13. *Ibid.*

14. *Ibid.*, p. 87.

The Spectatorial Artist and the Structure of *Cane*

SUSAN L. BLAKE

1. Jean Toomer, *Cane* (New York: Harper & Row, 1969), p. 73. All subsequent references are noted parenthetically in the text.

2. Gorham B. Munson, "The Significance of Jean Toomer," *Opportunity* 3 (September 1925); 263.

3. *Ibid.*

4. Darwin T. Turner, "Jean Toomer: Exile," *In a Minor Chord: Three Afro-American Writers and Their Search for Identity* (Carbondale: Southern Illinois University Press, 1971).

The Unifying Images in Part One of Jean Toomer's *Cane*

RICHARD ELDRIDGE

1. Jean Toomer, *Cane* (New York: Harper & Row, 1969). All page references are noted parenthetically in the text.

2. Jean Toomer to John McClure, 22 July 1922, Jean Toomer Collection, Fisk University Archives, Nashville, Tennessee. Subsequent material from the collection will be designated "J.T.C." Toomer sent a similar letter to Waldo Frank on 19 June 1922.

3. With the printing of the book, the arcs did not in fact meet to make an entire circle as Toomer had intended. Charles Larson erroneously attributed the incompleteness of the circle to an intentional lack of closure symbolizing the instability of lives that cannot become whole because of their inability to understand the past. See Charles Larson, "Reconsideration: *Cane* by Jean Toomer," *The New Republic* 174 (19 June 1976): 32

4. Toomer to Waldo Frank, December 1922, J.T.C.

5. Bernard Bell, "A Key to the Poems in *Cane*," *CLA Journal* 14 (March 1971): 251–58. (Reprinted in this volume.)

6. Todd Lieber, "Design and Movement in *Cane*," *CLA Journal* 13 (September 1969): 35–50. (Reprinted in this volume.)

7. John M. Reilly, "The Search for Black Redemption: Jean Toomer's *Cane*," *Studies in the Novel* 2 (Fall 1970): 313.

8. Larson, "Reconsideration: *Cane*," pp. 31–32.

9. John F. Lynen, *The Pastoral Art of Robert Frost* (New Haven, Conn.: Yale University Press, 1960), pp. 8–12. Lynen's commentary on how Frost uses the pastoral mode could apply equally to Toomer.

10. It is well known that the imagists studied at great length the literature of the Far East. In that light, it is interesting to compare Toomer's technique of blending visual-aural images with one of Bassho's haiku:

The lightning flashes!
And slashing through the darkness,
A night-heron's screech.
(Translated by Earl Miner)

Toomer experimented with the haiku form and content in his early poetry.

11. Lieber, "Design and Movement," pp. 35–39.

12. Toomer to Frank, undated but probably written in 1923, J.T.C.

13. Lieber, "Design and Movement," p. 39.

14. Evidence in Toomer's unpublished works shows that he was not altogether restrictive in the use of his *Cane* imagery to reflect exclusively the rural peasant's experiences in Georgia. For instance, except for the fact that the following poem is written about Harpers Ferry, the imagery and attitude could be from a Georgia poem:

Tell me, dear beauty of the dusk,
When purple ribbons bind the hill,
Do dreams your secret wish fulfill,

Do prayers, like kernels from the husk
Come from your lips? Tell me if when
The mountains loom at night, giant shades
Of softer shadow, swift like blades
Of grass seeds come to flower. Then

Tell me if the night winds bend
Then towards me, if the Shenandoah
As it ripples past your shore
Catches the soul of what you send.

(J.T.C., Box 50, Folder 57)

15. S. P. Fullinwider, "Jean Toomer: Lost Generation, or Negro Renaissance?" *Phylon* 27 (Winter 1966): 400. (Reprinted in this volume.)

16. Bell, "A Key to the Poems," p. 254.

17. Mabel Dillard, "Jean Toomer: Herald of the Negro Renaissance" (Ph. D. diss., Ohio University, 1967), p. 45.

18. The word *palabra* seems to be a typographical error for *palavra*, the Portuguese word from which *palaver* is derived. Toomer suggests that the gift for oratory, parleys, and verbal parries is undeveloped in a literate culture, fettered by sermons and hymns which must be followed according to script.

19. Philip Royster, "Book Review of *Cane*," *BANC!* 2 (Nashville, Tenn.: Fisk University Library, June 1972): 14.

20. Jean Toomer, "Earth-Being," unpublished autobiography, ca. 1930, J.T.C., Box 19, Folder 3.

Jean Toomer's *Cane*: A Modern Black Oracle

BOWIE DUNCAN

1. Arna Bontemps, Introduction to *Cane* by Jean Toomer (New York: Harper & Row, 1969), p. xii. All subsequent references are noted parenthetically in the text.

2. Sigfried Giedion, *Space, Time and Architecture* (Cambridge, Mass.: Harvard University Press, 1956), p. 432.

3. Wylie Sypher, *Rococo to Cubism in Art and Literature* (New York: Vintage Books, 1950), p. 247.

4. Joseph Frank, *The Widening Gyre* (New Brunswick, N.J.: Rutgers University Press, 1963), p. 13.

5. Sypher, *Rococo to Cubism*, p. 277.

6. *Ibid.*, p. 270.

7. S. P. Fullinwider, "Jean Toomer: Lost Generation, or Negro Renaissance?" *Phylon* 27 (Winter 1966): 402. (Reprinted in this volume.)

Toomer's *Cane*: The Artist and His World

GEORGE C. MATTHEWS

1. Alain Locke, "From *Native Son* to *Invisible Man*: A Review of the Literature of the Negro for 1952," *Phylon* 14 (March 1953): 34.

2. Jean Toomer, "Outline of Autobiography," Jean Toomer Collection, Fisk University Archives, Nashville, Tennessee, Box 14, Folder 1, p. 59. Subsequent material from the collection will be designated "J.T.C."

3. *Ibid.*

4. Jean Toomer to Waldo Frank, 12 December 1922, J.T.C., Box 3, Folder 6, Letter 800.

5. Toomer, "Outline of Autobiography," p. 53.

6. *Ibid.*

7. *Ibid.*, p. 55.

8. *Ibid.*, p. 58.

9. Jessie Fauset to Toomer, J.T.C., Box 3, Folder 3, Letter 743.

10. Matthew Josephson to Toomer, J.T.C., Box 1, Folder 6, Letter 209.

11. Countee Cullen to Toomer, J.T.C., Box 1, Folder 12, Letter 386.

12. Sherwood Anderson to Toomer, J.T.C., Box 1, Folder 1, Letter 50.

13. Jean Toomer, *Cane* (New York: Harper & Row, 1969), p. 1. All subsequent references are noted parenthetically in the text.

14. Toomer to Frank, 12 December 1922, J.T.C., Box 3, Folder 6, Letter 800.

15. *Ibid.*

Three Enigmas: Karintha, Becky, and Carma

WILLIAM L. DUTCH

1. Jean Toomer, *Cane* (New York: Harper & Row, 1969), p. 2. All subsequent references are noted parenthetically in the text.

Jean Toomer's "Fern": A Mythical Dimension

HARGIS WESTERFIELD

1. Marian Stein, "The Poet-Observer and Fern in Jean Toomer's *Cane*," *The Markham Review* 2 (October 1970): 64–65.

2. Jean Toomer, *Cane* (New York: Harper & Row, 1969). All page references are noted parenthetically in the text.

The Search for Identity in Jean Toomer's "Esther"

EDWARD E. WALDRON

1. Jean Toomer, *Cane* (New York: Harper & Row, 1969). All page references are noted parenthetically in the text.

2. Robert A. Bone, *The Negro Novel in America* (New Haven, Conn.: Yale University Press, 1958), p. 81.

3. Toomer, *Essentials*, private edition (Chicago: Lakeside Press, 1931).

Central Conflict Between Rural Thesis and Urban Antithesis in Jean Toomer's "Avey"

BURNEY J. HOLLIS

1. Darwin T. Turner, Introduction to *Cane*, by Jean Toomer (New York: Liveright, 1975), p. xxi.

2. Bernard Bell, "A Key to the Poems in *Cane*," *CLA Journal* 14 (March 1971): 252–53. (Reprinted in this volume.)

3. Susan L. Blake, "The Spectatorial Artist and the Structure of *Cane*," *CLA Journal* 17 (June 1974): 516–17. (Reprinted in this volume.)

4. *Ibid.*

5. Patricia Chase, "The Women in *Cane*," *CLA Journal* 14 (March 1971): 259–63. (Reprinted in this volume.)

6. Jean Toomer, "Avey," *Cane* (New York: Harper & Row, 1969), p. 80. All subsequent references are noted parenthetically in the text.

7. Turner, "Introduction," p. xxiii.

8. Blake, "The Spectatorial Artist," p. 517.

9. J. Michael Clark, "Frustrated Redemption: Jean Toomer's Women in *Cane*, Part One," *CLA Journal* 22 (June 1979): 319. (Reprinted in this volume.)

10. Gorham B. Munson, "The Significance of Jean Toomer," *Opportunity* 3 (September 1925): 263.

11. Blake, "The Spectatorial Artist," p. 517.

The Tensions in Jean Toomer's "Theater"

GEORGE KOPF

1. Jean Toomer, *Cane* (New York: Harper & Row, 1969), pp. 91–100. All subsequent references are noted parenthetically in the text.

"Nora" is "Calling Jesus": A Nineteenth Century European Dilemma in an Afro-American Garb

UDO O. H. JUNG

1. Robert A. Bone, *Down Home: A History of Afro-American Short Fiction from Its Beginnings to the End of the Harlem Renaissance* (New York: G. P. Putnam's Sons, 1975), p. xvi. (Italics are mine.)

2. Jean Toomer, "Calling Jesus," *Cane* (New York: Harper & Row, 1969), pp. 102–3. All subsequent references are noted parenthetically in the text.

3. Sherwood Anderson to Jean Toomer, September 1922, Jean Toomer Collection, Fisk University Archives, Nashville, Tennessee.) Subsequent material from the collection will be designated "J.T.C." This letter is quoted from Mabel M. Dillard, "Jean Toomer: Herald of the Negro Renaissance" (Ph. D. diss., Ohio University, 1967), p. 14.

4. See U. O. H. Jung, "Jean Toomer, 'Fern'," in *The Black American Short Story in the Twentieth Century*, ed. Peter Bruck (Amsterdam: B. R. Grüner, 1977).

5. It is not, as Mabel Dillard maintains, "one of Toomer's earliest poems" (Dillard, "Jean Toomer: Herald," p. 3).

6. For a more complete treatment of the pastoral element in Afro-American short fiction during the Negro Renaissance, see Bone, *Down Home*.

7. Toomer to Waldo Frank, undated but written ca. 1922, J.T.C. This letter is quoted from Dillard, "Jean Toomer: Herald," p. 19.

8. Toomer to Anderson, 22 December 1922, J.T.C. This letter is quoted from Dillard, "Jean Toomer: Herald," p. 15.

9. This holds true even though Mrs. Marjorie Content Toomer informs me that she has no evidence whatsoever that her husband had read Ibsen.

10. Toomer to Anderson, 18 December 1922, J.T.C. This letter is quoted from Dillard, "Jean Toomer: Herald," p. 15.

11. J. Jahn, ed., *Negro Spirituals* (Frankfurt am Main: Fischer Bücherei, 1963), p. 184.

12. See Toomer, "Carma," *Cane*, p. 18 and "Georgia Dusk," *Cane*, p. 22.

13. Toomer to Waldo Frank, undated but written ca. 1922, J.T.C. This letter is quoted from Dillard, "Jean Toomer: Herald," p. 19.

Jean Toomer's "Box Seat": The Possibility for "Constructive Crisises"

ELIZABETH SCHULTZ

1. See, for example, Todd Lieber, "Design and Movement in *Cane*," CLA *Journal* 13 (September 1969): 35–50 (reprinted in this volume); Catherine L. Innes, "The Unity of Jean Toomer's *Cane*," *CLA Journal* 15 (March 1972): 306–32 (reprinted in this volume); Bernard W. Bell, "Portrait of the Artist as the High Priest of Soul: Jean Toomer's *Cane*," *Black World* 23 (September 1974): 4–19, 92–97; Charles W. Scruggs, "The Mark of Cain and the Redemption of Art: A Study of Theme and Structure in Jean Toomer's *Cane*," *American Literature* 44 (May 1972): 276–91.

2. The only full critical treatment of "Box Seat" appears in Roger Rosenblatt, *Black Fiction* (Cambridge, Mass.: Harvard University Press, 1974), pp. 55–59.

3. Jean Toomer, "Chapters from *Earth Being*: An Unpublished Autobiography," *The Black Scholar* 2 (January 1971): 12.

4. *Ibid.*

5. *Ibid.*

6. Scruggs discusses Toomer's interest in organic form at length. (See Scruggs, "The Mark of Cain," pp. 279–80.)

7. Toomer, *Cane* (New York: Harper & Row, 1969), p. 104. All subsequent references are noted parenthetically in the text.

8. Innes sees Dan as "a precursor of the new redeemer." See Innes, "The Unity of Jean Toomer's *Cane*," p. 314. (Reprinted in this volume.) Houston A. Baker calls him "the bringer of dreams." See Houston A. Baker, *Singers of Daybreak* (Washington, D.C.: Howard University Press, 1974), p. 73. Contrarily, Lieber notes that Dan's passion "results in nothing but his own frustration." See Lieber, "Design and Movement," p. 45. (Reprinted in this volume.) Robert A. Bone describes Dan as "free—but at the same time, sterile." See Bone, *The Negro Novel in America*, rev. ed. (New Haven, Conn.: Yale University Press, 1965), p. 86.

9. Innes demonstrates the importance of P. D. Ouspensky's philosophy to an understanding of *Cane*, noting that "one of Ouspensky's main concerns was to stress that *both* the emotions and the intellect are organs of knowledge, and that the highest form of consciousness must include the fusion of both." See Innes, "The Unity of Jean Toomer's *Cane*," p. 318. (Reprinted in this volume.) S. P. Fullinwider quotes Toomer as writing in 1937 that "'Themosense (thought and emotion and sensing) is the inner synthesis of functions, which represents the entire individual and gives rise to complete action'." See

Fullinwider, "Jean Toomer: Lost Generation, or Negro Renaissance?" *Phylon* 27 (Winter 1966): 398. (Reprinted in this volume.)

10. Langston Hughes, "Dream Boogie," *Selected Poems* (New York: Alfred A. Knopf, 1959; reprint, New York: Vintage Books, 1974, p. 221.

11. Robert A. Bone notes that under the later influence of Georges Gurdjieff, Toomer became more of a philosopher than a poet: "Toomer's style becomes increasingly abstract. The vivid images that were its crowning glory give way to windy generalities. The pungency of *Cane* is nowhere to be found. . . . [In] Toomer's later fiction . . . dramatization is this, and incessant sermonizing takes the place of narrative. As imagination falters, the dry rot of abstraction sets in. The rich concreteness of experience is sacrificed to the pursuit of philosophical Absolutes" (See Bone, *Down Home: A History of Afro-American Short Fiction from Its Beginning to the End of the Harlem Renaissance* [New York: G. P. Putnam's Sons, 1975], p. 237).

12. Claude McKay, *Selected Poems of Claude McKay* (New York: Harcourt, Brace & World, 1953), p. 78.

13. Rosenblatt, *Black Fiction*, p. 57.

14. Scruggs indicates that "what Dan learns at the Lincoln Theater is that he must first heal himself." See Scruggs, "The Mark of Cain," p. 288.

15. In discussing Toomer's interests in organic form, Scruggs quotes from a 1922 letter Toomer wrote to Waldo Frank, in which he identifies the position of "Box Seat" in the cyclical scheme of *Cane*: "'From three angles, *Cane*'s design is a circle. Aesthetically, from simple forms to complex ones, and back to simple forms. Regionally, from South up into the North, and back into the South again. Or from the North down into the South and then a return North. From the point of view of the spiritual entity behind the work, the curve really starts with Bona and Paul (awakening), plunges into Kabnis, emerges in Karintha, etc. swings upward into Theater and Box Seat and ends (pauses) in Harvest Song'." See Scruggs, "The Mark of Cain," p. 279.

16. Bone, *The Negro Novel*, p. 86. All other critics, however, seem to ignore the troubling simile at the conclusion of "Box Seat."

17. Bone, in *Down Home*, quoting from Toomer's "Outline of an Autobiography," points to Toomer's sense that "'the folk-spirit was walking in to die on the modern desert. That spirit was so beautiful. Its death was so tragic. Just this seemed to sum up life for me. And this was the feeling I put into *Cane*. *Cane* was a swan-song. It was a song of an end'" (p. 207). In a letter to Frank, written in 1923, from which Bone also quotes, Toomer had also expressed his feeling that, "'if anything comes up now, pure Negro, it will be a swan-song'" (p. 218).

18. Toomer, "Chapters from *Earth Being*," p. 2.

Jean Toomer's "Bona and Paul": The Innocence and Artifice of Words

JACK M. CHRIST

1. Jean Toomer, *Cane* (New York: Harper & Row, 1969), p. 106. All subsequent references are noted parenthetically in the text.

2. Sister Mary Kathryn Grant, "Images of Celebration in *Cane*," *Negro American Literature Forum* 5 (Spring 1971): 34. (Reprinted in this volume.)

A Key to the Poems in *Cane*

BERNARD W. BELL

1. See Robert A. Bone, *The Negro Novel in America*, rev. ed. (New Haven, Conn.: Yale University Press, 1965); Darwin T. Turner, "Jean Toomer's *Cane*," *Negro Digest* 18 (January 1969): 54–61; and Todd Lieber, "Design and Movement in *Cane*," *CLA Journal* 13 (September 1969): 35–50. (The Lieber article is reprinted in this volume.)

2. Jean Toomer, "Earth Being," Jean Toomer Collection, Fisk University Archives, Nashville, Tennessee, Box 19, Folder 3, p. 18. Subsequent material from the collection will be designated "J.T.C."

3. See Toomer, *The Flavor of Man* (Philadelphia: The Young Friends Movement of the Philadelphia Yearly Meeting, 1949), p. 18. See also the philosophical works: *Essentials* (Chicago: Lakeside Press, 1931); the novels: "The Gallonwerps" (unpublished ms., ca. 1927), "Caromb" (unpublished ms., ca. 1932), and "Eight-Day World" (unpublished ms., ca. 1933); and the short stories: "Love on a Train," "Drackman," "Fronts," "New Beach," "Pure Pleasure," and "Winter on Earth," J.T.C.

4. Toomer, "Earth-Being," p. 18.

5. Bernard W. Bell, "*Cane*: A Portrait of the Black Artist as High Priest of Soul" (unpublished ms., 1969), later published as "Portrait of the Artist as the High Priest of Soul: Jean Toomer's *Cane*," *Black World* 23 (September 1974); 4–19, 92–97.

6. Toomer, "On Being American," J.T.C., p. 48.

7. Turner, "Jean Toomer's *Cane*," p. 60.

8. Toomer, *Cane* (New York: Harper & Row, 1969), p. 7. All subsequent references are noted parenthetically in the text.

"Spirit-Torsos of Exquisite Strength"

UDO O. H. JUNG

1. Jean Toomer, *Cane* (New York: Harper & Row, 1969), p. 25. All subsequent references are noted parenthetically in the text.

2. I Corinthians 12:13.

3. Langston Hughes, "The Negro Artist and the Racial Mountain," *The Nation* 122 (23 June 1926): 694.

4. Frederick L. Olmsted, *A Journey in the Seaboard Slave States* (New York: Dix and Edwards, 1856), pp. 394 ff.

5. See Malcolm Cowley, *Exile's Return: A Narrative of Ideas* (New York: W. W. Norton & Co., 1934, 1954), p. 92. Cowley attributes this statement to the Russian writer Dostoeyevsky.

6. T. S. Eliot, *Selected Essays* (London: Faber, 1932).

7. Arna Bontemps, Introduction to *Cane*, by Jean Toomer, p. xiii.

8. *Ibid.*

9. *Ibid.*, pp. xiii–xiv.

10. However, as Mrs. Marjorie Content Toomer has kindly informed me, Jean Toomer did not think much of psychoanalysis.

Jean Toomer's Vision: "Blue Meridian"

HARRY L. JONES

1. Jean Toomer, "Blue Meridian," in *Black Writers of America: A Comprehensive Anthology*, ed. Richard Barksdale and Keneth Kinnamon (New York: The Macmillan Company, 1972), p. 507. All subsequent references are noted parenthetically in the text.

Jean Toomer's "Blue Meridian": The Poet as Prophet of a New Order of Man

BERNARD W. BELL

1. Jean Toomer, "Outline of the Story of the Autobiography," Jean Toomer Collection, Fisk University Archives, Nashville, Tennessee. Subsequent material from the collection will be designated "J.T.C."

2. *Ibid.*, pp. 43–55.

3. *Ibid.*, p. 55.

4. Toomer, "On Being American," (unpublished ms.), J.T.C.

5. India Watterson, "Gorham Munson on Jean Toomer," unpublished interview in the Amistad Research Center, Dillard University, New Orleans, Louisiana, p. 10. See also Georges I. Gurdjieff, *Beelzebub's Tales to His Grandson: An Objectively Impartial Criticism of the Life of Man* (1950; reprint, New York: E. P. Dutton, 1973) and Kathleen Riordan Speeth, *The Gurdjieff Work* (1976; reprint, New York: Pocket Books, 1978).

6. Alfred Kreymborg, Lewis Mumford, and Paul Rosenfeld, eds., *The New Caravan* (New York: Macaulay, 1936), pp. 107–33.

7. Toomer, *Essentials* (Chicago: Lakeside Press, 1931), p. iv.

8. Toomer, "Blue Meridian," *The New Caravan*, ed. Kreymborg, Mumford, and Rosenfeld, p. 633. All subsequent references are noted parenthetically in the text.

9. Quoted in Fritz Peters, *Boyhood with Gurdjieff* (1964; reprint, Baltimore: Penguin Books, 1972), p. 42.

Design in Jean Toomer's *Balo*

MICHAEL J. KRASNY

1. Jean Toomer, "Balo," *Plays of Negro Life*, ed. Alain Locke and Montgomery Gregory (New York: Harper and Brothers, 1927). All subsequent references are noted parenthetically in the text.

2. Jean Toomer, *Cane* (New York: Harper & Row, 1969), p. 49.

3. Toomer, *Cane*, p. 237.

Jean Toomer's Ralph Kabnis: Portrait of the Negro Artist as a Young Man

WILLIAM J. GOEDE

1. S. P. Fullinwider, "Jean Toomer: Lost Generation, or Negro Renaissance?" *Phylon* 27 (Winter 1966): 396–403. (Reprinted in this volume.)

2. Jean Toomer, *Cane* (New York: Harper & Row, 1969). (All page references are noted parenthetically in the text.) The author has chosen to call it a novel for the same reason as Robert Bone had. See Robert A. Bone, *The Negro Novel in America* (New Haven, Conn.: Yale University Press, 1958).

3. Allen Geller, "An Interview with Ralph Ellison," *Tamarack Review* 32 (Summer 1964): 11.

4. See, for example, Eugene C. Holmes, "Jean Toomer—Apostle of Beauty," *Opportunity* 10 (August 1932): 252–54, 260; Sterling Brown, *The Negro in American Fiction* (Washington, D.C.: Associates in Negro Folk Education, 1937); and Hugh M. Gloster, *Negro Voices in American Literature* (Chapel Hill: University of North Carolina Press, 1948).

5. James Baldwin, "Alas, Poor Richard," *Nobody Knows my Name* (New York: Dial Press, 1961), p. 188.

6. Bone, *The Negro Novel*, pp. 85–86.

7. *Ibid.*, p. 86.

8. Langston Hughes, *Selected Poems of Langston Hughes* (New York: Alfred A. Knopf, 1959), p. 158.

9. Bone, *The Negro Novel*, pp. 85–86.

10. *Ibid.*

The Failure of a Playwright

DARWIN T. TURNER

1. Sherwood Anderson to Jean Toomer, undated but probably written ca. 1923, Jean Toomer Collection, Fisk University Archives, Nashville, Tennessee. Subsequent material from the collection will be designated "J.T.C."

2. Waldo Frank to Toomer, 25 April 1922, J.T.C.

3. From a manuscript copy of *Natalie Mann*.

4. *Ibid.*

5. Toomer gave Shaw this credit in an unpublished journal written about 1936.

6. Frank to Toomer, 25 April 1922, J.T.C.

7. Jean Toomer, *Cane* (New York: Harper & Row, 1969), p. 237.

8. *Ibid.*

9. Kenneth Macgowan to Toomer, 22 September 1923, J.T.C.

10. Gorham Munson to Toomer, 19 March 1928, J.T.C.

The Women in *Cane*

PATRICIA CHASE

1. Jean Toomer, *Cane* (Harper & Row, 1969), p. 1. All subsequent references are noted parenthetically in the text.

2. Toomer to Waldo Frank. This letter is reprinted in Brian Joseph and Mabel Mayle Dillard, *Jean Toomer* (Boston: Twayne Publishers, 1980), pp. 25–26.

3. Todd Lieber, "Design and Movement in *Cane*," *CLA Journal* 13 (September 1969): 42–43. (Reprinted in this volume.)

4. Robert A. Bone, *The Negro Novel in America* (New Haven, Conn.: Yale University Press, 1958), p. 87.

Frustrated Redemption: Jean Toomer's Women in *Cane*, Part One

J. MICHAEL CLARK

1. Darwin T. Turner, "Jean Toomer: Exile," *In a Minor Chord: Three Afro-American Writers and Their Search for Identity* (Carbondale: Southern Illinois University Press, 1971), p. 10.

2. *Ibid.*, pp. 10, 13.

3. *Ibid.*, p. 30.

4. W. Edward Farrison, "Jean Toomer's *Cane* Again," *CLA Journal* 15 (March 1972): 299. (Reprinted in this volume.)

5. George C. Matthews, "Toomer's *Cane*: The Artist and his World," *CLA Journal* 17 (June 1974): 544. (Reprinted in this volume.)

6. *Ibid.*, p. 547. See also Turner, *In a Minor Chord*, p. 20.

7. Matthews, "Toomer's *Cane*," p. 547.

8. Turner, *In a Minor Chord*, p. 23.

9. Roberta Riley, "Search for Identity and Artistry," *CLA Journal* 17 (June 1974): 480.

10. Louise Blackwell, "Jean Toomer's *Cane* and Biblical Myth," *CLA Journal* 17 (June 1974): 537. (Reprinted in this volume.)

11. *Ibid.*, p. 536.

12. Patricia Watkins, "Is There a Unifying Theme in *Cane?*" *CLA Journal* 15 (March 1972): 303.

13. *Ibid.*, pp. 303 ff.

14. *Ibid.*, p. 305.

15. *Ibid.*, p. 304.

16. Susan L. Blake, "The Spectatorial Artist and the Structure of *Cane*," *CLA Journal* 17 (June 1974): 516. (Reprinted in this volume.)

17. *Ibid.*, p. 517.

18. *Ibid.*, pp. 517, 519; Riley, "Search," p. 481; and Turner, *In a Minor Chord*, p. 24.

19. Blackwell, "Biblical Myth," p. 535; and Bowie Duncan, "Jean Toomer's *Cane*: A Modern Black Oracle," *CLA Journal* 15 (March 1972): 326–27. (Reprinted in this volume.)

20. Matthews, "Toomer's *Cane*," p. 558.

21. Catherine L. Innes, "The Unity of Jean Toomer's *Cane*," *CLA Journal* 15 (March 1972): 310–11 (reprinted in this volume); Patricia Chase, "The Women in *Cane*," *CLA Journal* 14 (March 1971): 263 (reprinted in this volume); and Turner, *In a Minor Chord*, p. 27.

22. Blake, "Spectatorial Artist," p. 517.

23. Matthews, "Toomer's *Cane*," p. 556.

24. Chase, "The Women in *Cane*," p. 259.

25. Matthews, "Toomer's *Cane*," pp. 548 ff.

26. *Ibid.*, pp. 549, 555.

27. Turner, *In a Minor Chord*, p. 29.

28. *Ibid.*, p. 15. See also Chase, "The Women in *Cane*," p. 260.

29. Jean Toomer, *Cane* (New York: Harper & Row, 1969), p. 1. All subsequent references are noted parenthetically in the text.

30. Blake, "Spectatorial Artist," p. 518.

31. *Ibid.* See also Turner, *In a Minor Chord*, p. 27 and Matthews, "Toomer's *Cane*," p. 549.

32. Blake, "Spectatorial Artist," p. 519 and Turner, *In a Minor Chord*, p. 15.

33. Duncan, "Black Oracle," p. 325.

34. *Ibid.*

35. *Ibid.*, p. 326.

36. Turner, *In a Minor Chord*, p. 15; and Blake, "Spectatorial Artist," p. 519.

37. Turner, *In a Minor Chord*, p. 27; and Blake, "Spectatorial Artist," p. 519.

38. Blackwell, "Biblical Myth," p. 540.

39. Blake, "Spectatorial Artist," pp. 519 ff; and Chase, "The Women in *Cane*," p. 264.

40. Chase, "The Women in *Cane*," p. 264.

41. Turner, *In a Minor Chord*, pp. 16, 29; Blake, "Spectatorial Artist," p. 520; and Chase, "The Women in *Cane*," p. 264.

42. Blake, "Spectatorial Artist," p. 522.

43. Edward E. Waldron, "The Search for Identity in Jean Toomer's 'Esther'," *CLA Journal* 14 (March 1971): 277. (Reprinted in this volume.)

44. *Ibid.*

45. *Ibid.*, p. 278; Turner, *In a Minor Chord*, p. 27; and Blake, "Spectatorial Artist," p. 523.

46. Turner, *In a Minor Chord*, pp. 19–20.

47. Waldron, "The Search for Identity," p. 278.

48. Blackwell, "Biblical Myth," p. 541.

49. Waldron, "The Search for Identity," p. 279.

50. Chase, "The Women in *Cane*," p. 264.

51. *Ibid.*, p. 265.

52. Waldron, "The Search for Identity," p. 278.

53. Chase, "The Women in *Cane*," p. 265.

54. Matthews, "Toomer's *Cane*, pp. 549.

55. Blake, "Spectatorial Artist," p. 521; and Blackwell, "Biblical Myth," pp. 537–38.

56. Turner, *In a Minor Chord*, p. 27.

57. *Ibid.*, pp. 18, 20.

58. Chase, "The Women in *Cane*," pp. 265 ff.

59. *Ibid.*, p. 266.

60. Blake, "Spectatorial Artist," p. 523.

61. *Ibid.*, p. 524; Chase, "The Women in *Cane*," p. 267; and Turner, *In a Minor Chord*, pp. 20, 27.

62. Chase, "The Women in *Cane*," p. 268.

63. *Ibid.*; Blake, "Spectatorial Artist," p. 524.

64. Chase, "The Women in *Cane*," p. 260.

65. Blake, "Spectatorial Artist," p. 521.

66. Innes, "Unity," p. 312.

67. *Ibid.*, pp. 309, 312; Blackwell, "Biblical Myth," p. 540; Matthews, "Toomer's *Cane*," p. 548; and Hargis Westerfield, "Jean Toomer's 'Fern': A Mythical Dimension," *CLA Journal* 14 (March 1971): 274. (Reprinted in this volume.)

68. Turner, *In a Minor Chord*, p. 17; and Chase, "The Women in *Cane*," p. 261.

69. Blake, "Spectatorial Artist," p. 521.

70. Chase, "The Women in *Cane*," p. 261; and Turner, *In a Minor Chord*, p. 17.

71. Turner, *In a Minor Chord*, pp. 27, 29; and Chase, "The Women in *Cane*," p. 261.

72. Blake, "Spectatorial Artist," p. 521.

73. Innes, "Unity," p. 521.

74. *Ibid.*, p. 319.

75. Westerfield, "Jean Toomer's 'Fern'," p. 274; and Turner, *In a Minor Chord*, p. 17.

76. Westerfield, "Jean Toomer's 'Fern'," p. 275.

77. *Ibid.*, p. 276.

78. Turner, *In a Minor Chord*, p. 16.

79. Chase, "The Women in *Cane*," p. 273.

Male and Female Interrelationship in Toomer's *Cane*

RAFAEL A. CANCEL

1. Elizabeth Sergeant, "The New Negro," *The New Republic* 46 (12 May 1926): 371.

2. Robert Littel, "*Cane*," *Literary Review* (8 December 1925): 126.

3. Langston Hughes, "The Negro Artist and the Racial Mountain," *The Nation* 122 (23 June 1926): 693.

4. Robert A. Bone, *The Negro Novel in America*, rev. ed. (New Haven, Conn.: Yale University Press, 1965), p. 84.

5. Bone, "The Black Classic that Discovered 'Soul' Is Rediscovered after 45 Years," *New York Times Book Review* (19 January 1969): 3.

6. James Weldon Johnson, "Race Prejudice and the Negro Artist," *Harper's Magazine*, 157 (1928): 769–76.

7. S. P. Fullinwider, "Jean Toomer: Lost Generation, or Negro Renaissance?" *Phylon* 27 (Winter 1966): 402. (Reprinted in this volume.)

8. Bone, "The Black Classic," p. 3.

9. William J. Goede, "Jean Toomer's Ralph Kabnis: Portrait of the Negro Artist as a Young Man," *Phylon* 30 (Spring 1968): 73–85. (Reprinted in this volume.)

10. Bone, "The Black Classic," p. 3.

11. *Ibid.*

12. Littel, "*Cane*," p. 126.

13. Arna Bontemps, "The Negro Renaissance: Jean Toomer and the Harlem Writers of the 1920's," in *Anger and Beyond: The Negro Writer in the United States*, ed. Herbert Hill (New York: Harper & Row, 1966), pp. 27–28.

14. Bontemps, Introduction to *Cane*, by Jean Toomer (New York: Harper & Row, 1969), p. xvi. All subsequent references are noted parenthetically in the text.

15. Goede, "Jean Toomer's Ralph Kabnis," p. 75.

16. *Ibid.*, p. 78.

Images of Celebration in *Cane*

SISTER MARY KATHRYN GRANT

1. Jean Toomer, *Cane* (New York: Harper & Row, 1969), pp. 112–13. All subsequent references are noted parenthetically in the text.

2. Harvey Cox, "Corita: Celebration and Creativity," *Sister Corita* (Philadelphia: United Church Press, 1968), p. 17.

3. *Ibid.*

4. See Robert Neale, *In Praise of Play* (New York: Harper & Row, 1970) and Johan Huizinga, *Homo Ludens: A Study of the Play Element in Culture* (Boston: Beacon Press, 1950).

Jean Toomer's *Cane* and Biblical Myth

LOUISE BLACKWELL

1. Robert A. Bone, *The Negro Novel in America* (New Haven, Conn.: Yale University Press, 1958), pp. 80–89.

2. Darwin T. Turner, "Jean Toomer's *Cane*," *Negro Digest* 18 (January 1969), 55.

3. John M. Reilly, "The Search for Black Redemption: Jean Toomer's *Cane*," *Studies in the Novel* 2 (Fall 1970): 313.

4. *Ibid.*, p. 315.

5. *Ibid.*, p. 314.

6. *Ibid.*, p. 323.

7. Reprinted in Arna Bontemps, Introduction to *Cane*, by Jean Toomer (New York: Harper & Row, 1969), pp. viii–ix. All subsequent references are noted parenthetically in the text.

8. Clifford Mason, "Jean Toomer's Black Authenticity," *Black World* 20 (November 1970); 72–73.

Jean Toomer and Surrealism

SUE R. GOODWIN

1. Arna Bontemps, "The Negro Renaissance: Jean Toomer and the Harlem Writers of the 1920's," in *Anger and Beyond: The Negro Writer in the United States*, ed. Herbert Hill (New York: Harper & Row, 1966), p. 23.

2. *Ibid.*, p. 36.

3. Darwin T. Turner, Introduction to *Cane*, by Jean Toomer (New York: Liveright, 1975), p. x.

4. Robert A. Bone, *The Negro Novel in America*, rev. ed. (New Haven, Conn.: Yale University Press, 1965), p. 88.

5. *Ibid.*, pp. 80–81.

6. Darwin T. Turner, *In a Minor Chord: Three Afro-American Writers and Their Search for Identity* (Carbondale: Southern Illinois University Press, 1971), p. 14. All subsequent references are noted parenthetically in the text.

7. George E. Kent, "Patterns of the Harlem Renaissance," *The Harlem Renaissance Remembered*, ed. Arna Bontemps (New York: Dodd, Mead & Company, 1972), p. 38.

8. Waldo Frank, Introduction to *Cane*, by Jean Toomer (New York: Boni & Liveright, 1923), p. vii. All subsequent references are noted parenthetically in the text.

9. Bone, *The Negro Novel*, pp. 88–89.

10. Larry E. Thompson, "Jean Toomer: As Modern Man," *The Harlem Renaissance Remembered*, p. 57.

11. Quoted in J. J. Sweeney, *Plastic Redirections in Twentieth Century Painting* (Chicago: University of Chicago Press, 1934), p. 87.

12. Sir Herbert Edward Read, *Surrealism* (New York: Praeger, 1971), pp. 21–22. All subsequent references are noted parenthetically in the text.

13. Langston Hughes, *The Big Sea* (New York: Alfred A. Knopf, 1940), pp. 241–42.

14. David Sylvester, ed., *Modern Art from Fauvism to Abstract Expressionism* (New York: Grolier, 1959), p. 280.

15. Dmitry Olderogg and Werner Forman, *The Art of Africa: Negro Art*, trans. Philippa Hentges (London: Paul Hamlyn, 1969), pp. 21–22.

16. From Toomer's unpublished autobiography, "Earth-Being," quoted by Larry Thompson in "Jean Toomer: As Modern Man," p. 55.

Cane as Blues

BENJAMIN F. MC KEEVER

1. Jean Toomer, *Cane* (New York: Harper & Row, 1969), poetic epigraph on the title page. All subsequent references are noted parenthetically in the text.

2. Ralph Ellison, *Shadow and Act* (New York: Random House, 1964), p. 78. All subsequent references are noted parenthetically in the text.

Jean Toomer: A Classified Bibliography

THERMAN B. O'DANIEL

I. Works by Toomer

A. BOOKS

Cane. Foreword by Waldo Frank. New York: Boni and Liveright, Inc., 1923.
Cane. Second Printing. New York: Boni and Liveright, Inc., 1927.
Essentials: Definitions and Aphorisms. Chicago: Privately printed by H. Dupee's Lakeside Press, 1931.
Cane. Third Printing. New York: University Place Press, 1967.
Cane. Intro. Arna Bontemps. New York: Harper and Row, 1969.
Cane. Intro. Darwin T. Turner. New York: Liveright, 1975.
The Wayward and the Seeking: A Collection of Writings by Jean Toomer. Intro. and ed. Darwin T. Turner. Washington, D.C.: Howard University Press, 1980.

B. POEMS BEFORE *CANE*

"Song of the Son." *Crisis* 23 (April 1922): 261.
"Banking Coal." *Crisis* 24 (June 1922): 65.
"Storm Ending." *Double Dealer* 4 (September 1922): 146.
"Georgia Dusk." *The Liberator* 5 (September 1922): 25.
"Harvest Song." *Double Dealer* 4 (December 1922): 258.

C. POEMS IN THE YEAR OF *CANE*

"Georgia Portraits." *Modern Review* 1 (January 1923): 81.
"Gum." *The Chapbook*, no. 36, April 1923, p. 22.
"Her Lips Are Copper Wire." *S4N*, May–August 1923, n.p.
"November Cotton Flower." *The Nomad*, Summer 1923.

D. POEMS AFTER *CANE*

"Reflections." *Dial* 86 (April 1929): 314.
"White Arrow." *Dial* 86 (July 1929): 596.
"Brown River Smile." *The Adelphi* 2 (September 1931).
"Brown River Smile." *Pagany* 3 (Winter 1932): 29–33.
"As the Eagle Soars." *Crisis* 41 (April 1932): 116.
"The Blue Meridian." In *The New Caravan*, 107–33. *See* Kreymborg, Mumford, and Rosenfeld, 1936.
"See the Heart." *Friend's Intelligencer* 104 (9 August 1947): 423.
"Five Vignettes." In *Black American Literature: Poetry*, 58. *See* Turner, 1969.
"The Lost Dancer." In *Black American Literature: Poetry*, 58–59. *See* Turner, 1969.
"At Sea." In *Black American Literature: Poetry*, 59. *See* Turner, 1969.
"The Blue Meridian." In *The Poetry of the Negro, 1746–1970*, 107–33. *See* Hughes and Bontemps, 1970.
"Blue Meridian." In *Black Writers of America: A Comprehensive Anthology*, 507–14. *See* Barksdale and Kinnamon, 1972.
"Glaciers of Dusk." *Pembroke Magazine* 6 (January 1975): 68.
"For M.W." *Pembroke Magazine* 6 (January 1975): 68.
"The Blue Meridian." In *The Wayward and the Seeking*, 214–34. *See* Turner, 1980.
"And Pass." In *The Wayward and the Seeking*, 201. *See* Turner, 1980.
"Angelic Eve." In *The Wayward and the Seeking*, 203. *See* Turner, 1980.
"Honey of Being." In *The Wayward and the Seeking*, 204. *See* Turner, 1980.
"Sing Yes!" In *The Wayward and the Seeking*, 205–7. *See* Turner, 1980.
"Men." In *The Wayward and the Seeking*, 210. *See* Turner, 1980.
"Peers." In *The Wayward and the Seeking*, 211. *See* Turner, 1980.
"Mended." In *The Wayward and the Seeking*, 212. *See* Turner, 1980.
"One Within." In *The Wayward and the Seeking*, 213. *See* Turner, 1980.

E. STORIES BEFORE *CANE*

"Nora" ["Calling Jesus"]. *Double Dealer* 4 (September 1922): 132.
"Carma." *The Liberator* 5 (September 1922): 5.
"Becky." *The Liberator* 5 (October 1922): 26.

"Fern." *The Little Review* 9 (Autumn 1922): 25–29.
"Seventh Street." *Broom* 4 (December 1922): 3.

F. STORIES IN THE YEAR OF *CANE*

"Esther." *Modern Review* 1 (January 1923): 50–55.
"Karintha." *Broom* 4 (January 1923): 83–85.
"Blood-Burning Moon." *Prairie*, March–April, 1923, p. 18.

G. STORIES AFTER *CANE*

"Easter." *The Little Review* 11 (Spring 1925): 3–7.
"Mr. Costyve Duditch." *Dial* 85 (December 1928): 460–76.
"Winter on Earth." In *Second American Caravan*, 694–715. *See* Kreymborg, Mumford, and Rosenfeld, 1928.
"York Beach." In *The New American Caravan*, 12–83. *See* Kreymborg, Mumford, and Rosenfeld, 1929.
"Of a Certain November." *Dubuque Dial*, 1 November 1935, pp. 107–12.
"Withered Skin of Berries." In *The Wayward and the Seeking*, 139–65. *See* Turner, 1980.
"Winter on Earth." In *The Wayward and the Seeking*, 166–81. *See* Turner, 1980.

H. AUTOBIOGRAPHIES

"Chapters from Earth-Being: An Unpublished Autobiography." *Black Scholar* 2 (January 1971): 3–13.
"Autobiographical Selections" [From "Earth-Being," "Incredible Journey," "Outline of an Autobiography," and "On Being An American"], as ed. Darwin T. Turner. In *The Wayward and the Seeking*, 7–133. *See* Turner, 1980.

I. PLAYS

Kabnis. First Part. *Broom* 5 (August 1923): 12–16.
Kabnis. Second Part. *Broom* 5 (September 1923): 83–94.
Kabnis. In *Cane*. New York: Boni and Liveright, Inc., 1923. 157–239.
Balo. In *Plays of Negro Life*. Ed. Alain Locke and Gregory Montgomery. New York: Harper and Brothers, 1927. 269–86.
Natalie Mann: A Play in Three Acts. In *The Wayward and the Seeking*, 243–325. *See* Turner, 1980.
The Sacred Factory: A Religious Drama of Today. In *The Wayward and the Seeking*, 327–410. *See* Turner, 1980.

J. ESSAYS

"Race Problems and Modern Society." In *Problems of Civilisation*. Vol. 7 of *Man and His World* series. Ed. Baker Brownell. New York: D. Van Nostrand, 1929. 67–111.

"The Hill." In *America and Alfred Stieglitz: A Collective Portrait*. Ed. Waldo Frank, Lewis Mumford, and Paul Rosenfeld. New York: Doran and Company, 1934. 295–303.

"A New Force for Cooperation." *The Adelphi*, October 1934, pp. 25–31.

K. LITERARY CRITICISM AND BOOK REVIEWS

"An Open Letter to Gorham Munson." *S4N*, March–April 1923.

"Notations on *The Captain's Doll*" (Review-Article). *Broom* 5 (August 1923): 47–48.

"[Review of] Zona Gale's *Faint Perfume*." *Broom* 5 (October 1923): 180–81.

"Waldo Frank's *Holiday*." *Dial* 75 (October 1923): 383–86.

"The South in Literature." *The Call* (1923).

"The Critic of Waldo Frank." *S4N*, September–January 1923–1924.

"Oxen Cart and Warfare" (Review-Article). *The Little Review*, Autumn–Winter 1924–1925, pp. 44–48.

L. DIALOGUES: *THE NEW MEXICO SENTINEL* CONTRIBUTIONS

"J. T. and P. B." *The New Mexico Sentinel*, 20 July 1937, 6.

"Make Good." *The New Mexico Sentinel*, 20 July 1937, 6–7.

"From a Farm." *The New Mexico Sentinel*, 31 August 1937, 8.

"Evil." *The New Mexico Sentinel*, 7 September 1937, 8.

"Good and Bad Artists." *The New Mexico Sentinel*, 1937.

"A Skunk Used as an Example." *The New Mexico Sentinel*, 17 November 1937, 7.

"Imprint for Rio Grande." *The New Mexico Sentinel*, 12 January 1938, 6.

"Socratic Dialogue." *The New Mexico Sentinel*, 1941.

M. PAMPHLETS

Living is Developing. Mill House Pamphlets. Psychological Series, No. 1. Doylestown, Pennsylvania, 1937.

Work-Ideas I. Mill House Pamphlets. Psychological Series, No. 2. Doylestown, Pennsylvania, 1937.

Roads, People, and Principles. Mill House Pamphlets. Doylestown, Pennsylvania, 1939.

The Flavor of Man. Philadelphia: The Young Friends Movement of the Phileadelphia Yearly Meeting, 1949.

N. CONTRIBUTIONS TO THE *FRIEND'S INTELLIGENCER*

"The Other Invasion." *Friend's Intelligencer*, 1 July 1944, pp. 423–24.
"The Presence of Love." *Friend's Intelligencer*, 25 November 1944, pp. 771–72.
"Today May We Do It." *Friend's Intelligencer*, 13 January 1945, pp. 19-20.
"Keep the Inward March. *Friend's Intelligencer*, 30 June 1945, pp. 411–12.
"The Uncommon Man." *Friend's Intelligencer*, 9 March 1946, pp. 147–48.
"Love and Worship." *Friend's Intelligencer*, 14 December 1946, pp. 695–96.
"Authority, Inner and Outer." *Friend's Intelligencer*, 5 July 1947, pp. 352–53.
"Chips." *Friend's Intelligencer*, 27 December 1947, p. 705.
"Something More." *Friend's Intelligencer*, 25 March 1950, pp. 164–65.
"Blessing and Curse." *Friend's Intelligencer*, 30 September 1950, pp. 567–77.

II. Works About Toomer

A. SOME ANTHOLOGIES

Adams, William, Peter Conn, and Barry Slepian, eds. *Afro-American Literature: Poetry*. Boston: Houghton Mifflin, 1970. 117, 127.

Adoff, Arnold, ed. *The Poetry of Black America: Anthology of the 20th Century*. New York: Harper and Row, 1973. 29–35, 536.

Baker, Houston A., Jr., ed. *Black Literature in America*. New York: McGraw-Hill, 1971. 159–65, 431.

Barksdale, Richard, and Keneth Kinnamon, eds. *Black Writers of America: A Comprehensive Anthology*. New York: Macmillan, 1972. 500–14.

Barnet, Sylvan, Morton Berman, and William Burto, eds. *Nine Modern Classics: An Anthology of Short Novels*. Boston: Little, Brown, 1973. 351, 445–49.

Bell, Bernard W., ed. *Modern and Contemporary Afro-American Poetry*. Boston: Allyn and Bacon, 1972. 2, 4, 5, 17–19, 184.

Bontemps, Arna, ed. *American Negro Poetry*. New York: Hill and Wang, 1963. 32–37, 193.

Brown, Sterling, Arthur P. Davis, and Ulysses Lee, eds. *The Negro Caravan*. New York: Dryden Press, 1941. 15–16, 41–54, 355–57.

Calverton, V. F., ed. *Anthology of American Negro Literature*. New York: Modern Library, 1929. 11, 21–26, 202–3, 534.

Chapman, Abraham, ed. *Black Voices: An Anthology of Afro-American Literature*. New York: New American Library, 1968. 63–73, 375–81.

Cullen, Countee, ed. *Caroling Dusk: An Anthology of Verse by Negro Poets*. New York: Harper, 1927. 93–99.

Cunard, Nancy, ed. *Negro: An Anthology.* Edited and abridged, with an introduction, by Hugh Ford. New York: Frederick Ungar, 1970. 64, 81, 91, 92.

Davis, Arthur P., and Saunders Redding, eds. *Cavalcade: Negro American Writing from 1760 to the Present.* Boston: Houghton Mifflin, 1971. 233–34, 285–91.

——, and Michael W. Peplow, eds. *The New Negro Renaissance: An Anthology.* New York: Holt, Rinehart and Winston, 1975. xxvi, xxviii, 28–36.

Dreer, Herman, ed. *American Literature by Negro Authors.* New York: Macmillan, 1950. 79–81.

Emanuel, James A., and Theodore L. Gross, eds. *Dark Symphony: Negro Literature in America.* New York: The Free Press, 1968. 95–109, 579–80.

Ford, Nick Aaron, ed. *Black Insights: Significant Literature by Black Americans 1760 to the Present.* Waltham, Mass.: Ginn, 1971. 150–54, 299.

Hayden, Robert, ed. *Kaleidoscope: Poems by American Negro Poets.* New York: Harcourt, Brace and World, 1967. 50–55.

Hughes, Langston, and Arna Bontemps, eds. *The Poetry of the Negro, 1746–1970.* Rev. ed. Garden City, New York: Doubleday, 1970. 107–33.

Hughes, Langston, ed. *The Best Short Stories by Negro Writers: An Anthology from 1899 to the Present.* Boston: Little, Brown, 1967. vii, x, 30–34, 505–6.

James, Charles L., ed. *From the Roots: Short Stories by Black Americans.* New York: Dodd, Mead, 1970. 62–70.

Kearns, Francis E., ed. *The Black Experience: An Anthology of American Literature for the 1970s.* New York: Viking, 1970. 405–11, 648–49.

Lomax, Alan, and Raoul Abdul, eds. *3000 Years of Black Poetry.* New York: Dodd, Mead, 1970. 193, 211–12.

Long, Richard A., and Eugenia W. Collier, eds. *Afro-American Writing: An Anthology of Prose and Poetry.* 2 vols. New York: New York University Press, 1972. Vol. 2, pp. 393–402.

Meserole, Harrison T., Walter Sutton, and Brom Weber, eds. *American Literature: Tradition and Innovation.* 2 vols. Lexington, Mass.: D. C. Heath, 1969. Vol. 2, 3119–26.

Schorer, Mark, ed. *The Literature of America: Twentieth Century.* New York: McGraw-Hill, 1970. 528–34.

B. DISSERTATIONS

Antonides, Chris. "Jean Toomer: The Burden of Impotent Pain." Michigan State University, 1975.

Bell, Bernard W. "The Afro-American Novel and Its Tradition." University of Massachusetts, 1970

Brown, Robert Michael. "Five Afro-American Poets: A History of the Major Poets and Their Poetry in the Harlem Renaissance." University of Michigan, 1971.

Christian, Barbara. "Spirit Bloom in Harlem: The Search for a Black Aesthetic During the Harlem Renaissance, The Poetry of Claude McKay, Countee Cullen, and Jean Toomer." Columbia University, 1970.

Collins, Paschal Jay. "Jean Toomer's *Cane*: A Symbolistic Study." University of Florida, 1978.

Crewdson, Arlene Joan. "Invisibility: A Study of the Works of Toomer, Wright and Ellison." Loyola University of Chicago, 1974.

Dillard, Mabel Mayle. "Jean Toomer: Herald of the Negro Renaissance." Ohio University, 1967.

Eldridge, Richard Leethe. "Jean Toomer's *Cane*: The Search for American Roots." University of Maryland, 1978.

Ellison, Curtis William. "Black Adam: The Adamic Assertion and the Afro-American Novelist." University of Minnesota, 1970.

Goede, William J. "Tradition in the American Negro Novel." University of California, Riverside, 1967.

Griffin, John Chandler, Jr. "Jean Toomer: American Writer." University of South Carolina, 1976.

Harris, Trudier. "The Tie That Binds: The Function of Folklore in the Fiction of Charles Waddell Chesnutt, Jean Toomer and Ralph Ellison." Ohio State University, 1973.

Hayashi, Susanna Campbell, "Dark Odyssey: Descent into the Underworld in Black American Fiction." Indiana University, 1971.

Helbling, Mark Irving. "Primitivism and the Harlem Renaissance." University of Minnesota, 1972.

Hunter, Raymond Thomas. "Black Naturalism: A Philosophy and Technique Used by Black Novelists in the First Half of the Twentieth Century." Wayne State University, 1978.

Kousaleos, Peter G. "A Study of the Language, Structure and Symbolism in Jean Toomer's *Cane* and N. Scott Momaday's *House Made of Dawn*." Ohio University, 1973.

Krasny, Michael J. "Jean Toomer and the Quest for Consciousness." University of Wisconsin, 1972.

Matthews, George Christopher. "Subjects and Shadows: Images of Black Primitives in Fiction of the 1920's." University of Iowa, 1977.

McKay, Nellie Yvonne. "Jean Toomer, the Artist: A Portrait in Tragedy." Harvard University, 1977.

McNeely, Darrell Wayne. "Jean Toomer's *Cane* and Sherwood Anderson's *Winesburg, Ohio*: A Black Reaction to the Literary Conventions of the Twenties." University of Nebraska, Lincoln, 1974.

Rubin, Lawrence. "The Castaways: A Study of Three Poets of the Negro Renaissance." Columbia University, 1974.

Rusch, Frederick Lunning. "'Every Atom Belonging to Me as Good Belongs to You': Jean Toomer and His Bringing Together of the Scattered Parts." State University of New York, Albany, 1976.

Shaw, Brenda Joyce Robinson. "Jean Toomer's Life Search for Identity as Realized in *Cane*." Middle Tennessee State University, 1975.

Smith, Cynthia Janis. "Escape and Quest in the Literature of Black Americans." Yale University, 1974.

Smith, James Frederick, Jr. "From Symbol to Character: The Negro in American Fiction of the Twenties." Pennsylvania State University, 1972.

Taylor, Carolyn G. "'Blend Us with Thy Being': Jean Toomer's Mill House Poems." Boston College, 1977.

C. BOOKS, ARTICLES, AND REVIEWS

Ackley, Donald G. "Theme and Vision in Jean Toomer's *Cane*." *Studies in Black Literature* 1 (Spring 1970): 45–65.

American Negro Writer and His Roots, The. Selected Papers from the First Conference of Negro Writers, March 1959. New York: American Society of African Culture, 1960.

Anderson, Sherwood. "The Negro in Art, How Shall He Be Portrayed: A Symposium." *Crisis* 32 (May 1926): 36.

Angoff, Allan, ed. *American Writing Today: Its Independence and Vigor*. New York: New York University Press, 1957. 98, 101–2.

Anonymous. "A Review of *Cane*." *Boston Transcript*, 15 December 1923, p. 8.

_____. "Literary Vaudeville." *Springfield Republican*, 23 December 1923, 9a.

_____. Review. *Dial* 76 (January 1924): 92.

_____. Review. *Salient* 2 (February 1929): 18–19.

_____. Review. New Orleans *Times-Picayune*, 12 April 1931, p. 30.

_____. Review. Buffalo *Courier Express*, 21 June 1931.

_____. New York *World-Telegram*, 17 March 1932, p. 1.

_____. New York *Herald Tribune*, 18 March 1932, p. 9.

_____. "Just Americans." *Time* 19 (28 March 1932): 19.

_____. St. Louis *Argus* (March 1932).

_____. "Obituary." *New York Times*, 18 August 1932, p. 19.

_____. Baltimore *Afro-American*, 27 August 1932.

_____. Baltimore *Afro-American*, 24 November 1934.

_____. Editorial. New York *Age*, 24 November 1934.

_____. Baltimore *Afro-American*, 1 December 1934.

_____. Review. *Choice* 5 (December 1968): 1312.

Armstrong, John. "The Real Negro." *New York Tribune*, 14 October 1923, p. 26.

Aubert, Alvin. "Jean Toomer." A poem in *Obsidian* 1 (Spring, 1975): 66.

Baker, Houston A., Jr. "Journey Toward Black Art: Jean Toomer's *Cane*." *Singers of Daybreak: Studies in Black American Literature*. Washington, D.C.: Howard University Press, 1974. 53–80, 107–8.

Bardolph, Richard. *The Negro Vanguard*. New York: [1959] Vintage Books, 1961. 202, 203, 204, 206, 294.

Barthold, Bonnie J. *Black Time: Fiction of Africa, the Caribbean, and the United States*. New Haven: Yale University Press, 1981.

Barton, Rebecca Chalmers. *Race Consciousness and American Negro Literature*. Greifswald, Prussia: H. Dollmeyer, 1934. *Passim*.

Bell, Bernard. "A Key to the Poems in *Cane*." *CLA Journal* 14 (March 1971): 251–58.

_____. "Portrait of the Artist as the High Priest of Soul: Jean Toomer's *Cane*." *Black World* 23 (September 1974): 4–19, 92–97.

_____. "Literary Sources of the Early Afro-American Novel." *CLA Journal* 18 (September 1974): 29–43.

_____. *The Folk Roots of Contemporary Afro-American Poetry*. Detroit: Broadside Press, 1974. 14, 46.

_____. "Jean Toomer's 'Blue Meridian': The Poet as Prophet of a New Order of Man." *Black American Literature Forum* 14 (Summer1980): 77–80.

Berghahn, Marion. *Images of Africa in Black American Literature*. Totowa, N.J.: Rowman and Littlefield, 1977. 122, 137, 140–46, 191, 218n.

Berzon, Judith R. *Neither White Nor Black: The Mulatto Character in American Fiction*. New York: New York University Press, 1978. 63, 68–70, 76, 220–22, 226, 243–44.

Bigsby, C. W. E., ed. *The Black American Writer*. 2 vols. Deland, Fla.: Everett/Edwards, 1969. Rpt., Baltimore: Penguin, 1971.

Blackwell, Louise. "Jean Toomer's *Cane* and Biblical Myth." *CLA Journal* 17 (June 1974): 535–42.

Blair, Walter, Theodore Hornberger, James E. Miller, Jr., and Randall Stewart. *American Literature: A Brief History*. Glenview, Ill.: Scott, Foresman, 1974. 202, 343.

Blake, Susan L. "The Spectatorial Artist and the Structure of *Cane*." *CLA Journal* 17 (June 1974): 516–34.

Bone, Robert A. "Jean Toomer." In *The Negro Novel in America*. New Haven: Yale University Press, 1958. Rev. ed., 1965. 56 , 60, 80–89.

_____. "The Black Classic that Discovered 'Soul' is Rediscovered after 45 Years." *New York Times Book Review*, 19 January 1969, p. 3.

_____. "Jean Toomer." In *Down Home: A History of Afro-American Short Fiction from Its Beginnings to the End of the Harlem Renaissance*. New York: G. P. Putnam's, 1975. 204–38, *passim*.

Bontemps, Arna. "The Harlem Renaissance." *Saturday Review* 30 (22 March 1947): 12–13, 44.

———. "The Negro Renaissance: Jean Toomer and the Harlem Writers of the 1920's." In *Anger and Beyond: The Negro Writer in the United States.* Ed. Herbert Hill. New York: Harper and Row, 1966. 20–36.

———. "Remembering *Cane.*" *BANC!* 2 (May–June 1972): 9–11.

———. *The Harlem Renaissance Remembered.* New York: Dodd, Mead, 1972. 1–2, 38–39, 51–52, 64–65, *et passim.*

Bowen, Barbara E. "Untroubled Voice: Call-and-Response in *Cane.*" *Black American Literature Forum* 16 (Spring 1982): 12–18.

Bradley, David. "Looking Behind *Cane.*" *The Southern Review* 21 (Summer 1985): 682–94.

Braithwaite, William Stanley. "The Negro in American Literature." In *The New Negro.* Ed. Alain Locke. New York: Albert and Charles Boni, 1925. 29–44.

Brawley, Benjamin. "The Negro Literary Renaissance." *Southern Workman* 56 (April 1927): 177–84.

———. *The Negro in Literature and Art in the United States.* New York: Duffield, 1929. Rpt., New York: Dodd, Mead, 1934. 123.

Brickell, Herschell. Review. *Literary Review of the New York Evening Post*, 8 December 1923, p. 333.

Brinkmeyer, Robert H., Jr. "Wasted Talent, Wasted Art: The Literary Career of Jean Toomer." *The Southern Quarterly* 20 (Fall 1981): 75–84.

Bronz, Stephen H. *Roots of Negro Racial Consciousness, the 1920s: Three Harlem Renaissance Authors.* Roslyn, New York: Libra, 1964.

Brown, Lloyd W., ed. *The Black Writer in Africa and the Americas.* Los Angeles: Hennessey and Ingalls, 1973. 86–96, 121.

Brown, Sterling A. *Negro Poetry and Drama.* Washington, D.C.: The Associates in Negro Folk Education, 1937. 67–68.

———. *The Negro in American Fiction.* Washington, D.C.: The Associates in Negro Education, 1937. 153–54.

———. "A Century of Negro Portraiture in American Literature." *The Massachusetts Review* 7 (Winter 1966): 73–96.

Bruck, Peter, ed. *The Black American Short Story in the 20th Century: A Collection of Critical Essays.* Amsterdam: B. R. Grüner, 1977. 8, 53–69.

Bryfonski, Dedra, ed. *Contemporary Literary Criticism*, vol. 13. Detroit: Gale Research Company, 1980. 550–56.

Bush, Ann Marie, and Louis D. Mitchell. "Jean Toomer: A Cubist Poet." *Black American Literature Forum* 1 (Fall 1983): 106–8.

Butcher, Margaret Just. *The Negro in American Culture.* New York: Alfred A. Knopf, 1956. 126, 127, 184.

Byrd, Rudolf P. "Jean Toomer and the Afro-American Literary Tradition." *Callaloo* 8 (Spring–Summer 1985): 310–19.

Caldeira, Maria Isabel. "Jean Toomer's Cane: The Anxiety of the Modern Artist." *Callaloo* 8 (Fall 1985): 544–50.

Calverton, V. F. *The Liberation of American Literature.* New York: Charles Scribner's, 1932. 446.

Cancel, Rafael A. "Male and Female Interrelationship in Toomer's *Cane.*" *Negro American Literature Forum* 5 (Spring 1971): 25–31.

Carter, Paul J. *Waldo Frank.* New York: Twayne, 1967. 44, 54.

Chandler, Sue P. "Fisk University Library Archives: Jean Toomer Collection, List of Published Works." *BANC!* 2 (May–June 1972): 15–16.

_____. "Books by Jean Toomer in the Fisk University Library Special Collections." *BANC!* 2 (May–June 1972): 17.

_____. "Material on or Writings by Jean Toomer to be Found in Selected Titles in Special Collections." *BANC!* 2 (May–June 1972): 17–18.

Chapman, Abraham. "The Harlem Renaissance in Literary History." *CLA Journal* 11 (September 1967): 38–58.

Chapman, Dorothy. *Index to Black Poetry.* Boston: G. K. Hall, 1974. 366 *et passim.*

Chase, Patricia. "The Women in Cane." *CLA Journal* 14 (March 1971): 259–73.

Christ, Jack M. "Jean Toomer's 'Bona and Paul': The Innocence and Artifice of Words." *Negro American Literature Forum* 9 (Summer 1975): 44–46.

Clark, J. Michael. "Frustrated Redemption: Jean Toomer's Women in *Cane,* Part One." *CLA Journal* 22 (June 1979): 319–34.

Clarke, John Henrik. "The Origin and Growth of Afro-American Literature." *Negro Digest* 17 (December 1967): 54–67.

Cooke, Michael G. "The Descent into the Underworld and Modern Black Fiction." *The Iowa Review* 5 (Fall 1974): 72–90.

Corrigan, Robert A. "Bibliography of Afro-American Fiction, 1853–1970." *Midcontinent American Studies Journal* 11 (Fall 1970): 114–35.

Cowley, Malcolm. *Exile's Return: A Literary Odyssey of the 1920's* New York: Viking Press, 1951. 179–80.

Davenport, Franklin. "Mill House." *BANC!* 2 (May–June/1972): 6–7.

Davis, Arthur P. "Jean Toomer." *From the Dark Tower: Afro-American Writers 1900 to 1960.* Washington, D.C.: Howard University Press, 1974. xiv, 44–51 *et passim.*

_____. "Growing Up in the New Negro Renaissance: 1920–1935." *Negro American Literature Forum* 2 (Fall 1968): 53–59.

Davis, Charles T. "Jean Toomer and the South: Region and Race as Elements Within a Literary Imagination." *Studies in the Literary Imagination* 7 (Fall 1974): 23–37.

D.E.D. Review. *Brooklyn Life* 68 (10 November 1923): 3.

Dickerson, Mary Jane. "Sherwood Anderson and Jean Toomer: A Literary Relationship." *Studies in American Fiction* 1 (Autumn 1973): 162–75.

Dillard, Mabel Mayle. "Behind the Veil: Jean Toomer's Esthetic." From "Jean Toomer: Herald of the Negro Renaissance" In *Studies in Cane.* Comp. Frank Durham. Columbus, Ohio: Charles E. Merrill, 1971. 2-10.

———. "Jean Toomer—The Veil Replaced." *CLA Journal* 17 (June 1974): 468–73.

Du Bois, W. E. B., and Alain Locke. "The Younger Literary Movement." *Crisis* 27 (February 1924), 161–62.

Du Bois, W. E. B. "Mencken." In "Postcript." *Crisis* 34 (October 1927): 276.

Durham, Frank. "The Poetry Society of South Carolina's Turbulent Year: Self-Interest, Atheism, and Jean Toomer." *Southern Humanities Review* 5 (Winter 1971): 76–80.

———, comp. *Studies in Cane.* Columbus, Ohio: Charles E. Merrill, 1971. xiv–113.

———. "Jean Toomer's Vision of the Southern Negro." *Southern Humanities Review* 6 (Winter 1972): 13–22.

Duncan, Bowie. "Jean Toomer's *Cane:* A Modern Black Oracle." *CLA Journal* 15 (March 1972): 323–33.

Edwards, Sister Ann. "Three Views on Blacks: The Black Woman in American Literature." *CEA Critic* 37 (May 1975): 14–16.

Eldridge, Richard. "The Unifying Images in Part One of Jean Toomer's *Cane.*" *CLA Journal* 22 (March 1979): 187–214.

Elias, Robert H. *"Entangling Alliances with None": An Essay on the Individual in the Twenties.* New York: Norton, 1973. 151, 153–56.

Emanuel, James A. "The Challenge of Black Literature: Notes on Interpretation." In *The Black Writer in Africa and the Americas,* ed. Lloyd W. Brown. Los Angeles: Hennessey and Ingalls, 1973. 85–100.

Farrison, W. Edward. "Jean Toomer's *Cane* Again." *CLA Journal* 15 (March 1972): 295–302.

———. "Much Ado About Negro Fiction: A Review Essay." *CLA Journal* 19 (September 1975): 90–100.

Faulkner, Howard. "The Buried Life: Jean Toomer's *Cane.*" *Studies in Black Literature* 7 (Winter 1976): 1–5.

Ferguson, Blanche E. *Countee Cullen and the Negro Renaissance.* New York: Dodd, Mead, 1966. 51, 82.

Fischer, William G. "The Aggregate Man in Jean Toomer's *Cane.*" *Studies in the Novel* 3 (Summer 1971): 190–215.

Fisher, Alice Poindexter. "The Influence of Ouspensky's *Tertium Organum* Upon Jean Toomer's *Cane.*" *CLA Journal* 17 (June 1974): 504–15.

Ford, Nick Aaron. "Jean Toomer and His *Cane.*" *The Hughes Review* 2 (Spring 1983): 16–27.

Frank, Waldo. "Foreword" to *Cane* by Jean Toomer. New York: Boni and Liveright, 1923. vii–xi.

_____. *The Rediscovery of Man: A Memoir and a Methodology of Modern Life.* New York: George Braziller, 1958. 425.

Franklin, John Hope. "A Harlem Renaissance." In *From Slavery to Freedom: A History of Negro Americans*, 3rd ed. New York: Alfred A. Knopf, 1967. 503–4.

French, Warren. "Fiction: 1900 to the 1930's." *American Literary Scholarship*, no. 9. Durham, N. C.: Duke University, 1971. 209–44.

Fuller, Hoyt W., ed. "The Harlem Renaissance Revisited." Special Number of *Black World* 20 (November 1970): 130 pp.

Fullinwider, S. P. "Jean Toomer: Lost Generation, or Negro Renaissance?" *Phylon* 27 (Winter 1966): 396–403.

_____. *The Mind and Mood of Black America.* Homewood, Ill.: Dorsey, 1969. 133–44.

Gayle, Addison, Jr., ed. *Black Expression: Essays by and About Black Americans in the Creative Arts.* New York: Weybright and Talley, 1969.

_____, ed. *The Black Aesthetic.* Garden City, New York: Doubleday, 1972.

_____. "Strangers in a Strange Land." *Southern Exposure* 3 (Spring-Summer 1975): 4–7.

_____. *The Way of the New World: The Black Novel in America.* Garden City, New York: Anchor Press/Doubleday, 1975. xvi, 83, 98–104, *et passim.*

Gibson, Donald B. "Jean Toomer: The Politics of Denial." *The Politics of Literary Expression: A Study of Major Black Writers.* Westport, Conn.: Greenwood Press, 1981. 155–81.

_____., ed. *Modern Black Poets: A Collection of Critical Essays.* Englewood Cliffs, N.J.: Prentice-Hall, 1973. 1–17.

Gilpin, Patrick J. "Charles S. Johnson: Entrepreneur of the Harlem Renaissance." In *The Harlem Renaissance Remembered*, ed. Arna Bontemps. New York: Dodd Mead, 1972. 215–46.

Gloster, Hugh M. *Negro Voices in American Fiction.* Chapel Hill: University of North Carolina Press, 1948. 111, 114, 117, 128–30, *et passim.*

Goede, William. "Jean Toomer's Ralph Kabnis: Portrait of the Negro Artist as a Young Man." *Phylon* 30 (Spring 1969): 73–85.

Golding, Alan. "Jean Toomer's Cane: The Search for Identity through Form." *Arizona Quarterly* 39 (Autumn 1983): 197–214.

Goode, Stephen H. *Index to American Little Magazines 1920–1939.* Troy, New York: Whitson, 1969. 307.

Graham, James D. "Negro Protest in America, 1900–1955: A Bibliographical Guide." *South Atlantic Quarterly* 67 (Winter 1968): 94–107.

Grant, Sister Mary Kathryn. "Images of Celebration in *Cane.*" *Negro American Literature Forum* 5 (Spring 1971): 32–34, 36.

Gregory, Montgomery. Review of *Cane. Opportunity* 1 (December 1923): 374–75.

Green, Elizabeth Lay. *The Negro in Contemporary American Literature*. Chapel Hill: University of North Carolina Press, 1928. Rpt., College Park, M.D.: McGrath, 1968. 51–52.

Griffin, John C. "A Chat With Marjorie Content Toomer." *Pembroke Magazine* 5 (January 1974): 15–27.

_____. "Two Jean Toomer Poems: 'For M. W.' and 'Glaciers of Dusk'." *Pembroke Magazine* 6 (January 1975): 67–68.

_____. "Jean Toomer: A Bibliography." *South Carolina Review* 7 (April 1975): 61–64.

Gross, Seymour L., and John Edward Hardy, eds. *Images of the Negro in American Literature*. Chicago: University of Chicago Press, 1966. 14, 268, 312.

Gross, Theodore L. "The Negro Awakening: Langston Hughes, Jean Toomer, Rudolph Fisher, and Others." In *The Heroic Ideal in American Literature*. New York: The Free Press, 1971. 137–47.

Gysin, Fritz. *The Grotesque in American Negro Fiction: Jean Toomer, Richard Wright, and Ralph Ellison*. Bern, Switzerland: Franke Verlag, 1975.

Harrison, Paul Carter. *The Drama of Nommo*. New York: Grove Press, 1972. 26, 112–18, 165.

_____, ed. *Kuntu Drama*. New York: Grove Press, 1974. 9, 20, 31–77.

Hart, Robert C. "Black-White Literary Relations in the Harlem Renaissance. *American Literature* 44 (January 1973): 612–28.

Hayden, Robert, David J. Burrows, and Frederick R. Lapides. *Afro-American Literature: An Introduction*. New York: Harcourt Brace Jovanovich, 1971. 3, 5–12, 110, 303.

Helbling, Mark. "Jean Toomer and Waldo Frank: A Creative Friendship." *Phylon* 41 (Second Quarter 1980): 167–78.

_____. "Sherwood Anderson and Jean Toomer." *Negro American Literature Forum* 9 (Summer 1975): 35–39.

Hemenway, Robert E. *Zora Neale Hurston: A Literary Biography*. Urbana: University of Illinois Press, 1977. 61, 106.

Henderson, Stephen. *Understanding the New Black Poetry*. New York: William Morrow, 1973. 47, 393–94.

Hicks, Granville. "Balm in Gilead." *Hound & Horn* 3 (January–March 1930): 276–80.

Holmes, Eugene. "Jean Toomer, Apostle of Beauty." Opportunity 10 (August 1932): 252–54, 260.

_____. "Alain Locke and the New Negro Movement." *Negro American Literature Forum* 2 (Fall 1968): 60–68.

Horton, Philip. *Hart Crane: The Life of an American Poet*. New York: Viking Press, 1937. 110, 149, 154, 155ff.

Houston, Helen Ruth. *The Afro-American Novel 1965–1975: A Descriptive Bibliography of Primary and Secondary Material.* Troy, New York: Whitson, 1977.

Howell, Elmo. "Jean Toomer's Hamlet: A Note on *Cane.*" *Interpretations: Studies in Language and Literature,* 9:70–73.

Huggins, Nathan Irvin. *Harlem Renaissance.* New York: Oxford, 1971. 172, 179–87, 220–21, *et passim.*

Hughes, Langston. "The Negro Artist and the Racial Mountain." *Nation* 122 (23 June 1926): 692–94.

_____. *The Big Sea.* New York: Knopf, 1940. Rpt., New York: Hill and Wang, 1963. 241–43.

_____. "The Twenties: Harlem and Its Negritude." *African Forum* 1 (Spring 1966): 11–20.

Inge, M. Thomas, Maurice Duke, and Jackson R. Bryer, eds. *Black American Writers: Bibliographical Essays.* 2 vols. In volume 1: "The Beginnings Through the Harlem Renaissance and Langston Hughes." New York: St. Martin's Press, 1978. 163, 165–66, 182–86, *et passim.*

Innes, Catherine L. "The Unity of Jean Toomer's *Cane.*" *CLA Journal* 15 (March 1972): 306–22.

Jackson, Blyden, and Louis D. Rubin, Jr. *Black Poetry in America: Two Essays in Historical Interpretation.* Baton Rouge: Louisiana State University Press, 1974. x, 26, 33–34.

Jackson, Blyden. "Jean Toomer's *Cane*: An Issue of Genre." In *The Twenties: Fiction, Poetry, Drama,* ed. Warren French. Deland, Fla.: Everett/Edwards, 1975. 317–33.

_____. *The Waiting Years: Essays on American Negro Literature.* Baton Rouge: Louisiana State University Press, 1976. 189–97.

Jahn, Jahnheinz. *A Bibliography of Neo-African Literature From Africa, America, and the Caribbean.* New York: Praeger, 1965. 309.

_____. *Geschichte der neoafrikanischen Literatur.* Dusseldorf-Koln: Eugen Diederichs Verlag, 1966. Trans. from the German by Oliver Coburn and Ursula Lehrburger as *Neo-African Literature: A History of Black Writing.* New York: Grove Press, 1968. 189, 191, 195–96, 211.

Jellinek, Roger. Review. *New York Times,* 21 January 1969, p. 45.

Johnson, Abby Arthur, and Ronald Maberry Johnson. *Propaganda and Aesthetics: The Literary Politics of Afro-American Magazines in the Twentieth Century.* Amherst: University of Massachusetts Press, 1979. 43, 54, 71, 83, 147–48.

Johnson, James Weldon. "Race Prejudice and the Negro Artist." *Harper's Magazine* 157 (1928): 769–76.

_____. *Black Manhattan.* New York: Alfred A. Knopf, 1930. 274.

_____. *Along This Way.* New York: Viking, 1968. 375–76.

Jones, Howard Mumford, ed., with Walter B. Rideout. *Letters of Sherwood Anderson.* Boston: Little, Brown, 1953. 118–20.

Jones, LeRoi. "Philistinism and the Negro Writer." In *Anger and Beyond*, ed. Herbert Hill. New York: Harper and Row, 1966. 51–61.

———. "The Myth of a 'Negro Literature'." *Home: Social Essays.* New York: Morrow, 1966. 105–15.

Jones, Norma Ramsey. "Africa, as Imaged by Cullen & Co." *Negro American Literature Forum* 8 (Winter 1974): 263–67.

Jones, Robert. "Jean Toomer as Poet: A Phenomenology of the Spirit." *Black American Literature Forum* 21 (Fall 1987): 275–87.

Joost, Nicholas. "Some Primitives in *The Dial* of the Twenties, Part II." *Forum* (Houston) 11 (Spring 1973): 12–18.

Josephson, Matthew. "Great American Novels." *Broom* 5 (October 1923): 178–80.

Jung, Udo O. H. "'Spirit-Torsos of Exquisite Strength': The Theme of Individual Weakness vs. Collective Strength in Two of Toomer's Poems." *CLA Journal* 19 (December 1975): 261–67.

———. "'Nora' is 'Calling Jesus': A Nineteenth Century European Dilemma in an Afro-American Garb." *CLA Journal* 21 (December 1977): 251–55.

———. "Jean Toomer, 'Fern' (1922)." In *The Black American Short Story in the 20th Century*, ed. Peter Bruck. Amsterdam: B. R. Grüner, 1977. 53–69.

Keller, Frances Richardson. "The Harlem Literary Renaissance." *North American Review* 5 (1968): 29–34.

Kent, George E. *Blackness and the Adventure of Western Culture.* Chicago: Third World Press, 1972. 24, 26, 55.

Kerlin, Robert T. "Singers of New Songs." *Opportunity* 4 (May 1926): 162.

———. "A Decade of Negro Literature." *Southern Workman* 59 (May 1930): 221–29.

———. *Negro Poets and Their Poems.* 2nd ed. rev. and enl. Washington, D.C.: Associated Publishers, 1935. 282–84, 334–35.

Kerman, Cynthia E. "Jean Toomer?—Enigma." *Indian Journal of American Studies*, 7–i:67–78.

Kesteloot, Lilyan. "Negritude and Its American Sources." *Boston University Journal* 22 (Spring 1974): 54–64.

Kopf, George. "The Tensions in Jean Toomer's 'Theater'." *CLA Journal* 17 (June 1974): 498–503.

Kraft, James. "Jean Toomer's *Cane.*" *Markham Review* 2 (October 1970): 61–63.

Kramer, Victor A. "The 'Mid-Kingdom' of Crane's 'Black Tambourine' and Toomer's *Cane.*" *CLA Journal* 17 (June 1974): 486–97.

Krasny, Michael J. "Design in Jean Toomer's 'Balo'." *Negro American Literature Forum* 7 (Fall 1973): 103–4.

_____. "Jean Toomer's Life Prior to *Cane*: A Brief Sketch of the Emergence of a Black Writer." *Negro American Literature Forum* 9 (Summer 1975): 40–41.

_____. "The Aesthetic Structure of Jean Toomer's *Cane*." *Negro American Literature Forum* 9 (Summer 1975): 42–43.

Kreymborg, Alfred. *Our Singing Strength, An Outline of American Poetry 1620–1930*. New York: Coward-McCann, 1929. 561, 573, 575.

Kulii, Elon A. "Literature, Biology and Folk Legal Belief: Jean Toomer's Kabnis." *The USF Language Quarterly* 25 (Spring–Summer): 5–7, 49, 54.

Larson, Charles. "Reconsideration: *Cane* by Jean Toomer." *The New Republic* 174 (19 June 1976): 30–32.

Lasker, Bruno. "Doors Opened Southward." *The Survey* 51 (1 November 1923): 190–91.

Lee, Brian. "American Literature: The Twentieth Century." In *The Year's Work in English*, ed. Geoffrey Harlow *et al.*, for The English Association. London: John Murray, 1971. Vol. 50 (1969). 396.

_____, and David Murray. In *The Year's Work in English Studies*, ed. James Redmond *et al.*, for The English Association. London: John Murray, 1974. Vol. 53 (1972). 461, 469–70.

Lewis, David Levering. *When Harlem Was in Vogue*. New York: Alfred A. Knopf, 1981.

Lewis, Thomas S. W., ed. *Letters of Hart Crane and His Family*. New York: Columbia University Press, 1974. 152, 167n, 169, 215–16, 378–79, *et passim*.

Lieber, Todd. "Design and Movement in *Cane*." *CLA Journal* 13 (September 1969): 35–50.

Littel, Robert. "*Cane*." *Literary Review* 8 December 1923: 126.

Littlejohn, David. *Black on White: A Critical Survey of Writing by American Negroes*. New York: Grossman, 1966. 58–60.

Locke, Alain. "Negro Youth Speaks." *The New Negro*, ed. Alain Locke. New York: Albert and Charles Boni, 1925. 47–53.

_____, ed. *The New Negro: An Interpretation*. New York: Albert and Charles Boni, 1925. Rpt., New York: Johnson Reprint Corporation, 1968. 49, 96–104, 136–37, 415.

_____. *Four Negro Poets*. New York: Simon and Schuster, 1927. 5–6

_____. "Self-Criticism: The Third Dimension in Culture." *Phylon* 11 (Fourth Quarter 1950): 391–94.

_____. "From *Native Son* to *Invisible Man*: A Review of the Literature of the Negro for 1952." *Phylon* 14 (First Quarter 1953): 34–44.

Lonn, Ella. "Pinckney Benton Stewart Pinchback (May 10, 1937–December 21, 1921)." In *Dictionary of American Biography*, ed. Dumas Malone. New York: Charles Scribner's, 1934. Vol. 7, Part 1, p. 611.

Ludington, C. T., Jr. "Four Authors View the South: A Symposium—Introduction." *Southern Humanities Review* 6 (Winter 1972): 1–4.

McKay, Nellie Yvonne. *Jean Toomer, Artist: A Study of His Literary Life and Work, 1894–1936.* Chapel Hill: University of North Carolina Press, 1984.

Margolies, Edward. "The Image of the Primitive in Black Letters." *Midcontinent American Studies Journal* 11 (Fall 1970): 67–77.

———. *Native Sons: A Critical Study of Twentieth-Century Negro Authors.* Philadelphia: J. B. Lippincott, 1968. 38–40, 48, 54.

———. ed. *A Native Sons Reader.* Philadelphia: J. B. Lippincott, 1970. 10, 57, 360.

Martin, Odette. "*Cane:* Method and Myth." *Obsidian* 2 (Spring 1976): 5–20.

Mason, Clifford. "Jean Toomer's Black Authenticity." *Black World* 20 (November 1970): 70–76.

Matthews, George C. "Toomer's *Cane:* The Artist and His World." *CLA Journal* 17 (June 1974): 543–59.

Mellard, James M. "Solipsism, Symbolism, and Demonism: The Lyrical Mode in Fiction." *Southern Humanities Review* 7 (Winter 1973): 37–52.

Miller, Ruth. *Blackamerican Literature, 1760–Present.* Beverly Hills, Calif.: Glencoe Press, 1971. 373–81, 767–68.

——— and Peter J. Katopes. "The Harlem Renaissance: Arna Bontemps, Countee Cullen, James Weldon Johnson, Claude McKay, and Jean Toomer." In *Black American Writers: Bibliographical Essays, I: The Beginnings Through the Harlem Renaissance and Langston Hughes. See* Inge, Duke, and Bryer, 1978. 161–86.

Mintz, Steven. "Jean Toomer: A Biographical Sketch." *BANC!* 2 (May–June 1972): 1–3.

Moore, Gerald. "Poetry in the Harlem Renaissance." In *The Black American Writer,* Vol. 2, ed. C. W. E. Bigsby. Deland, Fla.: Everett/Edwards, 1969; Rpt., Baltimore: Penguin, 1971. 67–76.

Munro, C. Lynn. "Jean Toomer: A Bibliography of Secondary Sources." *Black American Literature Forum* 21 (Fall 1987): 275–87.

Munson, Gorham. *Waldo Frank: A Study.* New York: Boni and Liveright, 1923.

———. "The Significance of Jean Toomer." *Opportunity* 3 (September 1925): 262–63.

———. *Destinations: A Canvas of American Literature Since 1900.* New York: Sears, 1928. 178–86.

———. Review. New York *World-Telegram,* 7 April 1931, p. 25.

———. Correspondence. *New York Times Book Review,* 16 February 1969, p. 54.

MacKethan, Lucinda H. "Jean Toomer's *Cane:* A Pastoral Problem." *Mississippi Quarterly* 28 (Fall 1975): 423–34.

McCarthy, Daniel P. "'Just Americans': A Note on Jean Toomer's Marriage to Margery Latimer." *CLA Journal* 17 (June 1974): 474–79.

McConnell, Frank D. "Black Words and Black Becoming." *Yale Review* 63 (Winter 1974): 193–210.

McKeever, Benjamin F. "*Cane* as Blues." *Negro American Literature Forum* 4 (July 1970): 61–63.

McPherson, James M., Laurence B. Holland, James M. Banner, Jr., Nancy Weiss, and Michael D. Bell. *Blacks in America: Bibliographical Essays*. Garden City, New York: Doubleday, 1971. 244, 251–53.

Naylor, Carolyn. Review of *The Wayward and the Seeking: A Collection of Writings by Jean Toomer*. Ed. Darwin T. Turner. *Black Scholar* 11 (September–October 1980): 96–98.

Nower, Joyce. "Foolin' Master." *Satire Newsletter* 7 (Fall 1969): 5–10.

Noyes, Sylvia G. "A Particular Patriotism in Jean Toomer's 'York Beach.'" *CLA Journal* 29 (March 1986): 288–94.

Nyren, Dorothy, Maurice Kramer, and Elaine Fialka Kramer, comps. and eds. "Toomer, Jean (1894–1967)." In *A Library of Literary Criticism: Modern American Literature*, Vol. 4, Sup. to 4th ed. New York: Frederick Ungar, 1976. 478–83.

Olsson, Martin. *A Selected Bibliography of Black Literature: The Harlem Renaissance*. Exeter, England: University of Exeter, 1973.

Otto, George Edward. "Religious Society of Friends." *BANC!* 2 (May–June 1972): 8.

Ouspensky, Peter Demianovich. *Tertium Organum—The Third Canon of Thought—A Key to the Enigmas of the World*, trans. Nicholas Bessaraboff and Claude Bragdon. New York: Random House, First Vintage Books Edition, 1970.

Oxley, Thomas L. G. "The Negro in the World's Literature." New York *Amsterdam News*, 28 March 1928. Rpt. as "The Black Man in the World of Literature." Philadelphia *Tribune*, 25 June 1936.

Page, James A. "Black Literature." *English Journal* 62 (May 1973): 709–17.

_____, comp. *Selected Black American Authors: An Illustrated Bio-Bibliography*. Boston: G. K. Hall, 1977. 266–67.

Parsons, Alice Beal. "Toomer and Frank." *The World Tomorrow* 7 (March 1924): 96.

Payne, Ladell. *Black Novelists and the Southern Literary Tradition*. Athens: University of Georgia Press, 1981.

Perry, Margaret. *Silence to the Drums: A Survey of the Literature of the Harlem Renaissance*. Westport, Conn.: Greenwood Press, 1976. 27, 32–43, 110.

Perry, Robert L. *The Shared Vision of Waldo Frank and Hart Crane*. *University of Nebraska Series*, 33. Lincoln: University of Nebraska, 1966.

Phylon, XI. (Fourth Quarter, 1950), 293–394. Entire issue devoted to the Negro writer and his literature.

Popkin, Michael, ed. *A Library of Literary Criticism: Modern Black Writers.* New York: Frederick Ungar, 1978. 412–19.

Porter, Dorothy. *The Negro in the United States: A Selected Bibliography.* Washington, D.C.: Library of Congress, 1970. 180.

Quirk, Tom, and Robert E. Fleming. "Jean Toomer's Contributions to *The New Mexico Sentinel.*" *CLA Journal* 19 (June 1976): 524–32.

Rampersad, Arnold. *The Art and Imagination of W. E. B. Du Bois.* Cambridge: Harvard University Press, 1976. 187, 189, 192, 199.

Rankin, William. "Ineffability in the Fiction of Jean Toomer and Katherine Mansfield." In *Renaissance and Modern: Essays in Honor of Edwin M. Moseley,* ed. Murray J. Levith. Saratoga Springs: Skidmore College, 1976. 160–67.

Redding, J. Saunders. *To Make A Poet Black.* Chapel Hill: University of North Carolina Press, 1939. 103, 104–6.

——. *They Came in Chains.* Philadelphia: J. B. Lippincott, 1950. 265, 266, 285.

——. "The Black Arts Movement in Negro Poetry." *The American Scholar* 42 (Spring 1973): 330, 332, 334, 336.

Redmond, Eugene B. *Drumvoices: The Mission of Afro-American Poetry, A Critical History.* Garden City, New York: Doubleday, 1976. 2, 145, 146, 169–70, 174–79, *et passim.*

Rexroth, Kenneth. "Panelizing Dissent." *Nation* 194 (7 September 1964): 97–99.

Reidl, Hal. Review of *When Harlem Was in Vogue,* by David Levering Lewis. *Baltimore Sun,* 9 August 1981, D-5.

Reilly, John M. "The Search for Black Redemption: Jean Toomer's *Cane.*" *Studies in the Novel* 2 (Fall 1970): 312–24.

——. "Jean Toomer: An Annotated Checklist of Criticism." *Resources for American Literary Study* 4 (Spring 1974): 27–54.

Rice, Herbert W. "An Incomplete Circle: Repeated Images in Part Two of *Cane.*" *CLA Journal* 29 (1986): 442–61.

——. "Repeated Images in Part One of *Cane.*" *Black American Literature Forum* 17 (1983): 100–5.

Richmond, Merle A. "Jean Toomer and Margery Latimer." *CLA Journal* 18 (December 1974): 300.

Riley, Roberta. "Search for Identity and Artistry." *CLA Journal* 17 (June 1974): 480–85.

Roberts, Evelyn H. *American Literature and the Arts Including Black Expression.* New York: Heath Cote, 1977. 27, 29, 52–56.

Robinson, Clayton. "Gilmore Millen's *Sweet Man:* Neglected Classic of the Van Vechten Vogue." *Forum* (Houston) 8 (Fall–Winter 1970): 32–35.

Rosenblatt, Roger. "*Cane.*" *Black Fiction.* Cambridge: Harvard University Press, 1974. 54–64, *et passim.*

Rosenfeld, Paul. "Jean Toomer." *Men Seen: Twenty-Four Modern Authors.* New York: Dial Press, 1925. 227–33.

Royster, Philip. "Book Review of *Cane.*" *BANC!* 2 (May–June 1972): 11–14.

Rubin, Louis D., Jr., and C. Hugh Holman, eds. *Southern Literary Study: Problems and Possibilities.* Chapel Hill: University of North Carolina Press, 1975.

Rusch, Frederik L. Review of *The Wayward and the Seeking: A Collection of Writings by Jean Toomer.* Intro. and ed. Darwin T. Turner. *Melus* 8 (Spring 1981): 83–85.

_____. "A Tale of the Country Round: Jean Toomer's Legend 'Monrovia.'" *Melus* 7 (Summer 1980): 37–46.

_____. "The Blue Man: Jean Toomer's Solution to His Problems of Identity." *Obsidian* 6 (Spring–Summer 1980): 38–54.

Rush, Theressa Gunnels, Carol Fairbanks Myers, and Esther Spring Arata. *Black American Writers Past and Present: A Biographical and Bibliographical Dictionary.* 2 vols. Metuchen, N.J.: Scarecrow Press, 1975.

Schraufnagel, Noel. *From Apology to Protest: The Black American Novel.* Deland, Fla.: Everett/Edwards, 1973. 13.

Schultz, Elizabeth. "Jean Toomer's 'Box Seat': The Possibility for 'Constructive Crisises'." *Black American Literature Forum* 13 (Spring 1979): 7–12.

Scruggs, Charles W. "The Mark of Cain and the Redemption of Art: A Study in Theme and Structure of Jean Toomer's *Cane.*" *American Literature* 44 (May 1972): 276–91.

_____. "Jean Toomer: Fugitive." *American Literature* 47 (March 1975): 84–96.

Sergeant, Elizabeth. "The New Negro." *New Republic* 46 (12 May 1926): 371–72.

Shockley, Ann Ellen. "Dedicated to Jean Toomer." *BANC!* 2 (May–June 1972): i–ii.

Simon, Myron, ed. *Ethnic Writers in America.* New York: Harcourt Brace Jovanovich, 1972.

Singh, Amritjit. *The Novels of the Harlem Renaissance: Twelve Black Writers, 1923–1933.* University Park: Pennsylvania State University Press, 1976. 64–69, *et passim.*

Singh, Raman K. "The Black Novel and Its Tradition." *Colorado Quarterly* 20 (Summer 1971): 23–29.

Smith, Jessie Carney. "Special Collections of Black Literature in the Traditionally Black College." *College & Research Libraries* 35 (September 1974): 322–35.

Solard, Alain. "Myth and Narrative Fiction in *Cane:* 'Blood-Burning Moon.'" *Callaloo* 8 (Fall 1985): 551–60.

_____. "The Impossible Unity: Jean Toomer's 'Kabnis.'" In *Myth and Ideology in American Culture,* ed. Regis Durand. Villeneuve d'Ascq: U de Lille III, 1976. 175–94.

Sollors, Werner, ed. *A Bibliographic Guide to Afro-American Studies* (based on the holdings of the John F. Kennedy-Institüt Library). With introductory essays by Ernest Kaiser and the compiler. Berlin, 1972. 159, 186.

Spofford, William K. "The Unity of Part One of Jean Toomer's *Cane*." *Markham Review* 3 (May 1972): 58–60.

Starke, Catherine Juanita. *Black Portraiture in American Fiction: Stock Characters, Archetypes, and Individuals*. New York: Basic Books, 1971. 101–2.

Stein, Marian L. "The Poet-Observer and 'Fern' in Jean Toomer's *Cane*." *Markham Review* 2 (October 1970): 64–65.

Stepto, Robert B. *From Behind the Veil: A Study in Afro-American Narrative*. Urbana: University of Illinois Press, 1979.

Tausseg, Charlotte E. "The New Negro as Revealed in His Poetry." *Opportunity* 5 (April 1927): 108–11.

Taylor, Clyde. "The Second Coming of Jean Toomer." *Obsidian* 1 (Winter 1975): 37–57.

Thompson, Larry E. "Jean Toomer: As Modern Man." In *The Harlem Renaissance Remembered*, ed. Arna Bontemps. New York: Dodd, Mead, 1972. 51–62.

Thurman, Wallace. "Negro Artists and the Negro." *New Republic* 52 (31 August 1927): 37–39.

_____. "Nephews of Uncle Remus." *The Independent* 119 (24 September 1927): 296–98.

_____. *Infants of the Spring*. New York: Macaulay, 1932. 221.

Titus, William A. *Wisconsin Writers: Sketches and Studies*. Chicago: Privately Printed, 1930. 87.

Trachtenberg, Alan, ed. *Memoirs of Waldo Frank*. Amherst: University of Massachusetts Press, 1973. 102–8.

Turner, Darwin T. "*The Negro Novel in America*: In Rebuttal." *CLA Journal* 10 (December 1966): 122–34.

_____. "The Failure of a Playwright." *CLA Journal* 10 (June 1967): 308–18.

_____. "And Another Passing." *Negro American Literature Forum* 1 (Fall 1967): 3–4.

_____. "Jean Toomer's *Cane*." *Negro Digest* 18 (January 1969): 54–61.

_____. "Jean Toomer (1894–1967)." In *A Bibliographical Guide to the Study of Southern Literature*, ed. Louis D. Rubin, Jr. Baton Rouge: Louisiana State University Press, 1969. 311–12.

_____, ed. *Black American Literature: Poetry*. Columbus, Ohio: Charles E. Merrill, 1969. 53–59.

_____, ed. *Black American Literature: Fiction*. Columbus, Ohio: Charles E. Merrill, 1969. 4, 37–42.

_____, ed. *Black American Literature: Essays, Poetry, Fiction, Drama*. Columbus, Ohio: Charles E. Merrill, 1970. 5, 161, 209–15, 327–32.

_____. *Afro-American Writers.* New York: Appleton-Century-Crofts, 1970. 73–74, 116.
_____. *In a Minor Chord: Three Afro-American Writers and Their Search for Identity.* Carbondale: Southern Illinois University Press, 1971. xix, xxi–xxii, 1–59, 121–31, 140–43.
_____, comp. *Voices from the Black Experience: African and Afro-American Literature.* Lexington, Mass.: Ginn, 1972.
_____. "An Intersection of Paths: Correspondence Between Jean Toomer and Sherwood Anderson." *CLA Journal* 17 (June 1974): 455–67.
_____, ed. *The Wayward and the Seeking: A Collection of Writings by Jean Toomer.* Washington, D.C.: Howard University Press, 1980.
Turpin, Waters E. "Four Short Fiction Writers of the Harlem Renaissance—Their Legacy of Achievement." *CLA Journal* 11 (September 1967): 59–72.
Twombly, Robert C. "A Disciple's Odyssey: Jean Toomer's Gurdjieffian Career." *Prospects: Annual of American Cultural Studies*, 2:437–62.
Unterecker, John. *Voyager: A Life of Hart Crane.* New York: Farrar, Straus and Giroux, 1969. 203, 249, 289–91, 314–15, 325–29, 361–63, *et passim.*
Van Doren, Carl. "Negro Renaissance." *Century Magazine* 111 (March 1926): 635–37.
Van Mol, Kay R. "Primitivism and Intellect in Toomer's *Cane* and McKay's *Banana Bottom*: The Need for an Integrated Black Consciousness." *Negro American Literature Forum* 10 (Summer 1976): 48–52.
Wagner, Jean. *Les poètes nègres des États-Unis, le sentiment racial et religieux dans la poésie de P. L. Dunbar a L. Hughes.* Paris: Librairie Istra, 1963. Trans. Kenneth Douglas as *Black Poets of the United States: From Paul Laurence Dunbar to Langston Hughes.* Urbana: University of Illinois Press, 1973. xvi, 149, 173–74, 259–81, *et passim.*
Waldron, Edward E. "The Search for Identity in Jean Toomer's 'Esther'." *CLA Journal* 14 (March 1971): 277–80.
_____. *Walter White and the Harlem Renaissance.* Port Washington, New York: Kennikat Press, 1978. 28, 29, 31, 57, 75.
Walker, Alice. "In Search of Our Mothers' Gardens: The Creativity of Black Women in the South." *Ms* 2 (May 1974): 64–70, 105.
Watkins, Patricia. "Is There a Unifying Theme in *Cane*?" *CLA Journal* 15 (March 1972): 303–5.
Weber, Brom. *Hart Crane: A Biographical and Critical Study.* New York: Bodley Press, 1948. 223.
_____, ed. *The Letters of Hart Crane, 1916–1932.* Berkeley and Los Angeles: University of California Press, 1965. 149, 155, 162, 166–67, 185, 195.
Welch, William. "The Gurdjieff Period." *BANC!* 2 (May–June 1972) 4–5.
Westerfield, Hargis. "Jean Toomer's 'Fern': A Mythical Dimension." *CLA Journal* 14 (March 1971): 274–76.

Whiteman, Maxwell. *A Century of Fiction by American Negroes: 1853–1952: A Descriptive Bibliography*. Philadelphia: Maurice Jacobs, 1955. 45, 54.

Whitlow, Roger. "The Harlem Renaissance and After: A Checklist of Black Literature of the Twenties and Thirties." *Negro American Literature Forum* 7 (Winter 1973): 143–46.

———. *Black American Literature: A Critical History*. Chicago: Nelson Hall, 1975. 80–83.

Williams, Kenny J. *They Also Spoke: An Essay on Negro Literature in America, 1787–1930*. Nashville: Townsend Press, 1970. 265, 273.

Withrow, Dolly. "Cutting Through Shade" [Jean Toomer's "Reapers"]. *CLA Journal* 21 (September 1977): 98–99.

Yellin, Jean Fagan. "An Index of Literary Materials in *The Crisis*, 1910–1934: Articles, Belles Lettres, and Book Reviews." *CLA Journal* 14 (June 1971): 452–65; *CLA Journal* 15 (December 1971): 197–234.

Notes on Contributors

BERNARD W. BELL is professor of American and Afro-American literature, Department of English, at the University of Massachusetts. He is the author of *The Afro-American Novel and Its Tradition* and *The Folk Roots of Contemporary Afro-American Poetry* and the editor of *Modern and Contemporary Afro-American Poetry, An Anthology*. He holds the B.A. and M.A. degrees from Howard University and the Ph.D. degree from the University of Massachusetts. His articles and reviews have appeared in *Phylon*, *The Massachusetts Review*, *Michigan Quarterly Review*, *American Dialog*, *Black World*, *Black American Literature Forum*, and the *CLA Journal*. He has been a visiting professor at the University of Freiburg in Germany, 1974–75, and a Senior Fulbright-Hays Scholar at the University of Coimbra in Portugal, 1982–83.

LOUISE BLACKWELL is associate professor of English at Florida A. & M. University. She and Professor Frances Clay are coauthors of *Lillian Smith* in Twayne's United States Authors Series and of the article, "Lillian Smith, Novelist," which appeared in the June 1972 issue of the *CLA Journal*. Professor Blackwell is also the author of articles on Tennessee Williams, William Faulkner, Flannery O'Connor, and Eudora Welty.

SUSAN L. BLAKE is a Phi Beta Kappa graduate of Brown University, where she received both the B.A. and M.A. degrees, and holds the Ph.D. degree from the University of Connecticut. An assistant professor of English at Lafayette College, she has contributed articles and reviews to the *CLA Journal*, *Black American Literature Forum*, *Modern Fiction Studies*, *Melus*, and *Callaloo*, as well as a selection on Toni Morrison in *The Dictionary of Literary Biography, 33: Afro-American Fiction Writers After 1955*. She has held a National Endowment for the Humanities Fellowship-in-Resident at Brown University, 1977–78, a Fulbright Senior Lectureship at the University of Benin in Lome, Togo, 1983–84, and a National Endowment Fellowship for College Teachers, 1987–88.

RAFAEL A. CANCEL is a professor in the English Department at the University of Puerto Rico at Mayaguez, Puerto Rico. He received the M.A. degree from the University of Puerto Rico and the Ph.D. degree from the University of Southwestern Louisiana. His studies of Bernard Malamud, Sean O'Casey, Albert Camus, and Samuel Beckett have appeared in *Revista de Letras*, *Atenea*, and *The D. H. Lawrence Review*. His current works in progress include "Slapstick: The Literary Technique of Samuel Beckett and Kurt Vonnegut, Jr."

PATRICIA CHASE holds the B.A. and M.A. degrees from Ohio University, where she was a graduate assistant and where she studied English, English education, and ethnic literature. Her poetry has appeared in various little magazines, including *Sphere* and the *University of Kentucky Literary Journal*, and she has published articles in the *Now 68 Magazine*.

JACK M. CHRIST is director of the Leadership Studies Program, an interdisciplinary liberal arts program he founded in 1979 at Ripon College. He is a Phi Beta Kappa graduate of Dartmouth College and holds the Ph.D. degree in British and American literature from the University of Pennsylvania. He is formerly an assistant professor of English at Ripon College, where he taught Black American Literature.

J. MICHAEL CLARK is an alumnus of Emory University, where he received the B.A. degree in Religion and Philosophy, the M. Div. degree in Theological Studies, and the Ph.D. degree in literature and theology. He currently teaches in the Freshman English Program at Georgia State University. His articles have appeared in the *CLA Journal*, *Iron Mountain Review*, *R.F.D.*, *Ganymede* (London), and the *Journal of Pastoral Counseling*.

MABEL M. DILLARD is a retired professor of English from the North Carolina Agricultural and Technical State University in Greensboro, North Carolina. She holds the B.A., M.A., and Ph.D. degrees in English from Ohio University, where, in 1967, she wrote her dissertation on Jean Toomer. This work was expanded and published as *Jean Toomer: Herald of the Negro Renaissance* and is part of the Twayne United States Authors Series.

BOWIE DUNCAN holds the Ph.D. degree from the University of Maryland, where he was a University Fellow. He is the author of *The Critical Reception of Howard Nemerov* and *Stuart Davis, Abstractionist and Activist*.

WILLIAM L. DUTCH is a retired professor of English at Morgan State University. A graduate of Howard University, he holds the M.A. degree from New York University and the Ph.D. degree from Indiana University of Pennsylvania. In addition, he has studied at Harvard and Indiana universities, Oxford University, and the University of London. An active member of several professional organizations in his field, he is a former officer of the College Language Association and a book reviewer for the CLA *Journal*.

RICHARD ELDRIDGE is associate professor of English at the Community College of Baltimore. He holds the B.A. degree from Oberlin College, the M.Ed. from Cornell University, and the Ph.D. degree from the University of Maryland. He is coauthor of *The Lives of Jean Toomer: A Hunger for Wholeness.*

WILLIAM EDWARD FARRISON was the author of the definitive biography *William Wells Brown: Author and Reformer*, and was editor of the Citadel Press editions of Brown's *Clotel or, The President's Daughter* and Brown's *The Negro in the American Rebellion.* A *magna cum laude* graduate of Lincoln University in Pennsylvania, he held the M.A. degree from the University of Pennsylvania and a Ph.D. degree from Ohio State University. He was a frequent contributor of articles and book reviews to scholarly publications, and was also coeditor, with Hugh M. Gloster and the late Nathaniel P. Tillman, of *My Life, My Country, My World: College Readings for Modern Living.*

ALICE POINDEXTER FISHER earned her B.A. and M.A. degrees in English literature at California State University, San Diego, where she subsequently taught for two years. She earned her Ph.D. degree at the Graduate School and University Center of the City University of New York. Currently, she is an assistant professor of English at Hostos Community College of the City University of New York, where she has developed a women's studies department for Third World women.

ROBERT E. FLEMING is professor of English at the University of New Mexico. He holds the B.A. and M.A. degrees from Northern Illinois University and the Ph.D. degree from the University of Illinois. His articles have appeared in *American Literature*, the CLA *Journal*, *Negro Contemporary Literature*, and *Phylon*. He is the author of two books in the Twayne United States Authors Series: *Willard Motley* and *James Weldon Johnson.* He is also the author of *James Weldon Johnson and Arna Wendell Bontemps: A Reference Guide.*

S. P. FULLINWIDER is associate professor of history at Arizona State University in Tempe, Arizona. A graduate of the United States Naval Academy with a B.S. degree, he holds the M.S. and Ph.D. degrees from the University of Wisconson. He is the author of *The Mind and Mood of Black*

America and of "H. L. Mencken and the American Language," which appeared in *Menckeniana* in 1971.

William J. Goede is professor of English at the University of Victoria in Victoria, British Columbia. His dissertation at the University of California, Riverside, is entitled "Tradition in the American Negro Novel," and his articles have appeared in *Phylon* and other journals.

Sue R. Goodwin is a *cum laude* graduate of Meredith College in Raleigh, North Carolina, and holds the M.A. degree in English from the University of North Carolina at Charlotte. Currently, she teaches English and world cultures at Forest Hills High School in Union County, North Carolina.

Sister Mary Kathryn Grant, formerly of Mercy College of Detroit, is now a member of the faculty at Mount Saint Mary's College in Los Angeles, California. She is the author of *The Tragic Vision of Joyce Carol Oates*, published by Duke University Press, and of articles in the *Arizona Quarterly, Negro American Literature Forum*, and other journals.

Mark Helbling is associate professor of American studies at the University of Hawaii at Manoa. He received his Ph.D. in American studies from the University of Minnesota in 1972. His articles have appeared in *Phylon, Black American Literature Forum, Research Studies*, and *Polish Review*. He received Fulbright Grants for work and study at the University of Tunis, Tunis, Tunisia, 1974–75, and at the National University of Abidjan, Ivory Coast, 1984–85.

Cason L. Hill is chairperson of the Department of English at Morehouse College. A graduate of Morehouse, he earned the M.A. degree from Atlanta University and the Ph.D. degree from the University of Georgia. He is the author of "A Bibliographical Study of George Washington Cable and A Checklist of Criticism, 1870–1970," and of two Mellon Project Studies—"Twentieth-Century Thought and Culture: Studies in the Intellectual and Cultural History of Mankind," and "Modern World Political Geography: Studies in the Intellectual and Cultural History of Mankind." Since 1979 he has been the assistant editor of the *Journal of Negro History* and editor of the *CLA Journal*. He has also been named editor of CLA special publications. It is in this capacity that he contributed his editorial expertise to the completion of this volume, which was begun by the late Therman B. O'Daniel.

Burney J. Hollis, dean of the College of Arts and Sciences at Morgan State University, holds the B.A. degree summa cum laude from Morgan and the M.A. and Ph.D. degrees from the University of Pennsylvania, where he wrote his dissertation on black novelist and playwright Waters E. Turpin. A former Fulbright Scholar (1968), Woodrow Wilson Fellow (1968), and Ford Foundation Fellow (1978–79), he has taught in India and has served as scholar-in-residence at the University of Pennsylvania.

He is chairman of the Board of Directors of the Middle-Atlantic Writers Association and the founding editor of that organization's publications, the *Middle-Atlantic Writers Review* and the *Middle-Atlantic Writers Newsletter*.

CATHERINE L. INNES earned a First Class Honors B.A. degree from Sydney University, the M.A. degree from the University of Oregon, and the Ph.D. degree from Cornell University. She has taught in universities in Australia, the United States, and England, and she is currently a lecturer in English and African Caribbean literatures at the University of Kent, Canterbury, England. She is the author of *The Devil's Own Mirror*, a comparative study of Irish and black nationalism in literature, and she has published articles on African, Afro-American, Irish, and Australian writers.

HARRY L. JONES, former chairman of the English department at Morgan State University, is a retired professor of English there and a former lecturer at the University of Pennsylvania. He holds the B.A. and M.A. degrees from Howard University and the Ph.D. degree from The Catholic University of America, where he wrote his dissertation on Jones Very. He is a former lecturer in world literature at the International Peoples' College in Elsinore, Denmark. A frequent contributor to the *CLA Journal*, his articles have appeared in *Satire Newsletter* and other periodicals, as well as in collections of critical research.

UDO O. H. JUNG was educated at the universities of Freiburg, Edinburgh, and Kiel. He holds the Ph.D. degree from Kiel and was the former director of the language laboratory there. Currently, he is a member of the staff of the University of Marburg, Federal Republic of Germany, where his main research interests are in applied linguistics and educational technology. He is the review editor of *System*, an international journal of applied linguistics and educational technology.

GEORGE KOPF, a creative writer, is a contributor of poems and stories to little magazines, including *Sou'wester*, Southern Illinois University's quarterly. He has served as a graduate assistant at the University of Toledo.

JAMES KRAFT, a graduate of Princeton University, holds the M.A. and Ph.D. degrees from Fordham University. A former teacher of English at Phillips Academy, the University of Virginia, and Wesleyan University, he has been a member of the staff of the National Endowment for the Humanities since 1972.

VICTOR A. KRAMER is associate professor of English at Georgia State University in Atlanta, Georgia. A graduate of St. Edward's University in Austin, Texas, he holds the M.A. and Ph.D. degrees from the University of Texas. His articles have appeared in *Papers of the Bibliographic Society of America*, *Proof*, *Mississippi Quarterly*, *Journal of Popular Culture*, *Modern*

Poetry Studies, and the *CLA Journal*. In addition, he is the James Agee biographer for the Twayne's United States Authors Series.

MICHAEL J. KRASNY, associate professor of English at San Francisco State University, received his Ph.D. from the University of Wisconsin, with a dissertation entitled "Jean Toomer and the Quest for Consciousness." His articles in the field of Black American literature have appeared in *Negro American Literature Forum*, *Margins*, and *The Black Scholar*. He is a member of the National Committee on Third World Literature and participates in Modern Language Association seminars in that area of study.

JAMES E. LEWIS, artist and sculptor, did the pen-and-ink drawing of Jean Toomer for this volume. He is Henry O. Tanner professor of art and director of the art gallery at Morgan State University. A graduate of Philadelphia College of Art with the B.F.A. degree and of Temple University with the M.F.A. degree, he has also studied at Yale University and has been recipient of honors, awards, and fellowships, including a Carnegie Grant in art, various medals and awards for high achievement, and a Ford Foundation Fellowship for art study. His works have been exhibited in Philadelphia, Baltimore, Washington, and Atlanta, and many of his pieces are in the collections of the museums of these cities. His eight-foot, bronze sculpture of Frederick Douglass graces the campus of Morgan State University, and his eight-and-one-half-foot sculpture of a Negro soldier occupies a central place in downtown Baltimore. He has lectured widely in this country and at universities throughout East, West, and South Africa.

TODD LIEBER is professor of English and director of the College Poets and Writers Series at Simpson College in Indianola, Iowa. A Phi Beta Kappa graduate of Duke University, he holds the M.A. and Ph.D. degrees from Case Western Reserve University. His articles have appeared in the *CLA Journal*, *Black American Literature Forum*, *American Quarterly*, and *Western Humanities Review*, and his fiction has been published in the *Missouri Review*, the *Yale Review*, and *Sun Dog*. He also received a National Endowment for the Arts Fellowship Grant in 1987.

GEORGE C. MATTHEWS earned a Ph.D. degree at the University of Iowa in 1977 and wrote a dissertation entitled "Subjects and Shadows: Images of Black Primitives in Fiction of the 1920's." Jean Toomer is one of the authors treated in this study.

DANIEL P. MCCARTHY received his B.A. degree from Loyola College in Baltimore and has done graduate work at the University of Delaware, where he served as a teaching assistant. He has also taught on the secondary level in Wilmington, Delaware, and in Towson and Baltimore, Maryland.

NELLIE YVONNE MCKAY is a *cum laude* graduate of Queens College with departmental honors in English and holds the M.A. and Ph.D. degrees in English and American literature from Harvard University, where she won English department awards. She has been a Woodrow Wilson Fellow, a Marion and Jasper Whiting Fellow, and W. E. B. Du Bois Institute Dissertation Fellow. She has taught at Simmons College, has been a visiting professor at Boston University and the Massachusetts Institute of Technology, and currently is associate professor of American and Afro-American literature at the University of Wisconsin at Madison. She is the author of *Jean Toomer, the Artist: A Study of His Literary Life,* the editor of *Critical Essays on Toni Morrison,* and coeditor, with William Andrews, of the forthcoming "Twentieth Century Afro-American Autobiography."

BENJAMIN F. MCKEEVER, formerly a teacher of English at Denison University in Granville, Ohio, now teaches in the English Department of Sinclair Community College, Dayton, Ohio. His articles have appeared in *Black American Literature Forum* and other publications.

THERMAN B. O'DANIEL, editor of this volume, died in 1986. He was a professor of English from Morgan State University for several years. One of the founders of the *CLA Journal* in 1957, he was its only editor for twenty-one years. After graduating from Lincoln University in Pennsylvania, he earned the M.A. degree from the University of Pennsylvania and the Ph.D. degree from the University of Ottawa. He also studied at Harvard University and Pennsylvania State University and was a General Education Board Fellow at the University of Chicago and a Ford Foundation Fellow at the University of Ottawa. His articles on Cooper, Melville, Emerson, Hughes, Baldwin, Ellison, and other writers have appeared in *Phylon*, the *CLA Journal*, and other publications. In 1970 he wrote the introduction to Collier Books' reprint of Wallace Thurman's *The Blacker the Berry*; in 1971, he edited for the College Language Association and for William Morrow and Company, *Langston Hughes, Black Genius: A Critical Evaluation*; and in 1977, he edited for the College Language Association and for Howard University Press, *James Baldwin: A Critical Evaluation.*

On June 26, 1981, Dr. O'Daniel and five other individuals founded the Langston Hughes Society; he also became the founding editor of the Society's official publication, *The Langston Hughes Review.*

THOMAS QUIRK, who holds the Ph.D. degree in English from the University of New Mexico, Albuquerque, is professor of English at the University of Missouri, Columbia. He is the author of *Melville's Confidence Man: From Knave to Knight* and has just completed a new volume "A New Reality: Bergsonian Vitalism in American Life and Letters." In addition to essays on Mark Twain, Nathaniel Hawthorne, Joyce Carol Oates, Herman Melville, F. Scott Fitzgerald, and Willa Cather, he contributed to *Black Journals of the United States.*

MERLE A. RICHMOND is the author of *Bid the Vassal Soar: Interpretive Essays on the Life and Poetry of Phillis Wheatley and Goerge Moses Horton*, published by the Howard University Press. She is a retired lecturer in English from the University of California.

ELIZABETH AVERY SCHULTZ is associate professor of English at the University of Kansas, where she has been teaching courses in Afro-American literature since 1971. A graduate of Wellesley College, she holds the M.A. and Ph.D. degree in English from the University of Michigan.

LEONARD A. SLADE, JR., earned the Ph.D. degree in English at the University of Illinois and is currently chairperson of the Department of African and Afro-American Studies at the State University of New York, Albany. He was formerly professor of English and Dean of the College of Arts and Sciences at Kentucky State University, where he taught for twenty-two years. He is the author of *Critical Essays on Language and Literature: A Selected Working Bibliography of Twenty-four American Authors*; and of a book of poetry, *Another Black Voice: A Different Drummer*. His poems have also appeared in several journals, including the *Zora Neale Hurston Forum*, *The Griot: The Journal of Afro-American Studies*, *The Kentucky Poetry Review*, *Prophetic Voices: An International Literary Journal*, *Testimony: Journal of African-American Studies*, *River City Review*, and *The Black Scholar*. His "Elegy for Therman B. O'Daniel," which appears in this volume, has been set to music by Grace Yin, professor of music at the Peabody Conservatory of Music, Baltimore.

DARWIN T. TURNER, a University of Iowa Foundation Distinguished Professor of English and Chair of African-American World Studies, has published critical studies of Afro-American literature, American literature, drama and literary criticism in the *CLA Journal*, *Southern Humanities Review*, *Massachusetts Review*, *Mississippi Quarterly*, *Black World*, and other publications. A Phi Beta Kappa graduate of the University of Cincinnati, he received his M.A. degree there and the Ph.D. degree from the University of Chicago. He is coeditor, with Jean M. Bright, of *Images of the Negro*; compiler of *Afro-American Writers*, a bibliography; and author of study guides to *The Scarlet Letter* and *Huckleberry Finn*, of *Katharsis*, a volume of verse, and of *In a Minor Chord: Three Afro-American Writers and Their Search for Identity*. In addition, he is the editor of three companion volumes for black studies (*Black American Literature: Essay*; *Black American Literature: Fiction*; and *Black American Literature: Poetry*) and the editor of *Black Drama in America: An Anthology*. Among his edited books are *The Wayward and the Seeking: A Collection of the Writings of Jean Toomer*, published in 1980 by Howard University Press, and *The Art of Slave Narrative: Original Essays in Criticism and Theory*, coedited, with John Sekora, and published in 1982 by the Western Illinois University Press.

EDWARD E. WALDRON is assistant professor of English at Yankton College, Yankton, South Dakota. He holds the Ph.D. degree in English from Arizona State University and has taught at all three state universities in Arizona and at Howard University. His articles have appeared in the *CLA Journal*, the *Arizona English Bulletin*, *Negro American Literature Forum*, and *Phylon*. A National Endowment for the Humanities Fellowship in 1970 enabled him to study Afro-American literature under Arthur P. Davis at Howard University, and out of this study and research came his book, *Walter White and the Harlem Renaissance.*

HARGIS WESTERFIELD is a retired professor of English from Kearney State College, Kearney, Nebraska. A graduate of the University of Cincinnati, he holds the M.A. degree from the University of Kentucky and the Ph.D. degree from the University of Indiana. His articles have appeared in *Negro Digest*, *Education Digest*, *Review of English Studies*, *College English*, *College Composition* and *Communication*, *Quarterly Journal of Speech*, *Ball State University Forum*, *American Book Collector*, and the *CLA Journal*. He has published some thirty poems on religion, nature, and other subjects and is the author of two books of Army combat poetry, *The Fighting Jungleers* and *Death Valley at Zamboanga*. He is currently working on the study "History of the 41st Infantry Division in World War II."

ANN VENTURE YOUNG is associate professor of foreign languages at Morgan State University. A graduate of Morgan, she holds the M.A. degree from the University of Puerto Rico and the Ph.D. from Union Graduate School. Her articles and reviews have appeared in several collections and journals, including the *Dictionary of Afro-Latin American Civilization*, *Blacks in Hispanic Literature: Critical Essays*, *Latin American Literature in English Translation: An Annotated Bibliography*, the *CLA Journal*, the *Morgan Journal for Educational Research*, and the *Afro-Hispanic Review*, of which she is founder and associate editor. She is also the editor of *The Image of Black Women in Twentieth Century South American Poetry: A Bilingual Anthology*. In addition to being a past vice president and a past president of the College Language Association, she is currently that organization's special publications director. It is in this capacity that she contributed her administrative and editorial expertise to the completion of this volume, which was begun by the late Therman B. O'Daniel.

Index